WILFRED A. FERRELL
NICHOLAS A. SALERNO
Arizona State University

Strategies in Prose
Fourth Edition

HOLT, RINEHART AND WINSTON
New York   Chicago   San Francisco   Atlanta   Dallas   Montreal   Toronto

Library of Congress Cataloging in Publication Data

Ferrell, Wilfred A comp.
  Strategies in prose.

1. College readers.   I. Salerno, Nicholas A., joint
author.   II. Title.
PE1122.F38 1978   808'.04275   77-20119
ISBN 0-03-089961-3

PREFACE

In preparing the fourth edition of *Strategies in Prose* we followed the same guidelines we had adopted for the earlier editions. These derive from the long-established fact that people best learn to write by writing. But the writing experience serves this purpose only when the writer has something to say and has a reason for saying it. Students in freshman composition courses may discover the substance for their writing by reading and discussing essays that lie within the range of their interests and experiences, engage their intellectual capabilities, and cause them to respond. By analyzing and studying *how* the authors present their ideas, students may develop a sense of style and rhetorical strategy.

The major changes in this edition are in the total number of essays, the number of new essays, and the addition of two new sections. In the last edition we had 74 essays; in this edition we have 85. And 63 of these are new. The last edition had six topical sections; this edition has eight. One of the new sections is on violence, and the other is on writing about literature. We created the latter section by taking the Hawthorne material out of *The Arch of Experience* and setting up a separate section for it.

As in the earlier editions we have included in each section either a pro and con review of a book, with a chapter of the book included as one of the essays in the section, or we have two opposing essays on a controversial topic. In addition we have included at least one short story in each section. Related to their section by subject or theme, these may be used for individual study and analysis or for composition and contrast with the other rhetorical types in the section.

The authors of the selections are, for the most part, all recognized authorities, either as writers or as experts in their field of specialization. Several authors are represented twice. Our purpose here is to give students an opportunity to see how writers may adjust their styles and rhetorical approaches to serve different subjects, purposes, and audiences.

In addition to the obvious reasons for selecting known writers, we chose them to emphasize the importance of authority in the prose voice. Students must recognize that a basic requirement for effective prose is the authority of a voice that has something to say and a compelling reason for saying it. We want to stress the students' need to prepare before they write, not necessarily so that they may speak as experts but so that they will have given genuine thought to a topic before attempting to write about it.

Although most of our selections come from twentieth-century writers, we do include a few from writers of earlier periods. These older selections have gained acceptance as classics. Their place in the collection is to demonstrate that many current issues and ideas were the concerns of writers in other eras. These old chestnuts also provide a means for students to compare and contrast the styles and rhetorical methods of different periods.

The study questions at the end of each section are intended to help students read the selection critically and to assist them in analyzing the writer's method and techniques. The questions are not intended to be exhaustive for these purposes, but merely to suggest ways in which students may start to study and analyze the essays. For further exploration an Instructor's Manual is available from the English Editor, Holt, Rinehart and Winston, 383 Madison Avenue, New York, N.Y. 10017.

In the Rhetorical Contents the type of each selection is indicated. We have used the rhetorical categories—exposition, argument, description, narration, persuasion—that Cleanth Brooks and Robert Penn Warren used in *Modern Rhetoric.* These labels are not to be considered exclusive, since any given essay may incorporate forms of several different rhetorical methods and modes, as we have indicated in the Rhetorical Contents. Some of the essays are listed under more than one rhetorical type. For those listed under Exposition, we have indicated Brooks and Warren's breakdown of expositional processes. Our designations are intended to serve as a ready reference for those who wish to examine a particular rhetorical type.

We are deeply grateful to friends and colleagues who kindly made suggestions and recommendations for *Strategies in Prose.* In particular we wish to acknowledge the generous assistance of Albert Adams, William Agopsowicz, Tom Allender, Richard S. Beal, Barbara Bixby, Lynne Brewster, Betty Brugh, William C. Creasy, Frank D'Angelo, Susan Ferrell, Nicholas D. Fratt, Leon Gatlin, George Haich, Nancy J. Hawkey, Bruce Hollingsworth, Leonard Kulseth, Charles R. Lefcourt, Thom Martin, Rebecca Martino, R. Paul Murphy, Marjorie Neumann, John Noll, Dixie Lee Powell, Peggy Pryzant, Daniel Quirk, Betty Renshaw, Clifford Roth, Richard Schroeder, Shelby Stephenson, James Van Pernis, Roger Widmeyer, and William H. Young.

Tempe, Arizona   *W.A.F.*
December 1977   *N.A.S.*

CONTENTS

3   Modern Social Problems

4   Violent America

5 The Natural and the Supernatural

"Brave New World" 268

6 Language

"The Soul of Wit" 339

7   Media and the Arts

"The Winter of Our Discontent"   396

8   Writing About Literature

"Imagination All Compact"   469

RHETORICAL CONTENTS

(Many selections are cross-listed because they illustrate more than one rhetorical type.)

Exposition

Argument

Persuasion

Description

Narration

1 The Arch of Experience
"This Above All"

Contemporary human problems and concerns seem ever more complex. Indeed, common goals now make cooperation so important that a section on the individual seems almost immoral. Yet, some of the greatest human joys are strictly personal, and the dark night of the soul is essentially a private affair. Thus, the necessity both to acknowledge our ever-expanding search for self-awareness and to provide a variety of rhetorical types has resulted in The Arch of Experience.

The essays by Joan Didion, Barbara Tuchman, and Mark Twain form the nucleus of this section. Twain demolishes the human claims to being the highest animal with satiric, bitter thrusts. He examines the claims to being *patriotic, religious,* and *reasonable* and finds humanity deficient, insofar as he finds those terms pejorative. Didion and Tuchman, on the other hand, are more exploratory and optimistic. Both their essays are calls to action; the tone, form, and style are sufficiently different to make the essays extremely useful for comparison and contrast.

The subsection on Bruno Bettelheim's study of myth and fairy tales concerns itself with the psychological appeal of those forms. Bettelheim himself is here presented in an analysis of "The Three Little Pigs." The reviews that follow are extremely complex and detailed. Although Lurie generally approves of Bettelheim's study, her praise is highly qualified; yet Bloom feels it is a splendid achievement. These two lengthy reviews demonstrate that while reviewers may differ in their conclusions, their approach is basically the same: they first summarize Bettelheim's major concepts and then critically analyze and comment on them. Neither settles for generalities.

The style of D. Keith Mano's essay on "Cruel Lib" reflects

its source: *Newsweek* is a periodical with broad appeal to large numbers of people. Mano's tone, style, and structure are therefore colloquial and simple. Hoffer, on the other hand, provides us with a more studied, literary style in his examination of the undesirables in society. Then, Max Shulman's "logical" analysis of love demonstrates how humor and dialogue can be used in developing an argument. The three pieces together offer vivid proof that an argument can be made more effective by suiting the style and method not only to the material but also to the audience for whom one writes.

The selections by Woody Allen, Martin E. Marty, and E. M. Forster use three very different forms to probe man's search for God and a reason for existence. Woody Allen writes what is almost a parody of the detective story, as his narrator tries to learn who killed God. Marty imitates the style and methodology of news analysts and gives us Jesus as a candidate for President. With Forster, allegory is the vehicle to carry the message.

A careful analysis of the selections included in this section reminds us forcefully and effectively that "experience is an arch wherethro' / Gleams that untrav'd world whose margin fades / For ever and for ever" when we move. Our hope is that both the subjects and the strategies will help students bring the meaning of their own experiences into clearer focus.

Joan Didion
ON SELF-RESPECT

Joan Didion (1934–   ) was born in Sacramento, California. She received a B.A. from the University of California in 1956. Her published books include *Run River* (1963), *Slouching Towards Bethelehem* (1968), *Play It as It Lays* (1970), and *A Book of Common Prayer* (1976). *Play It as It Lays* was filmed with Tony Perkins and Tuesday Weld starring. Didion has coauthored a number of screenplays, among them the Streisand version of *A Star Is Born.* Her work has appeared regularly in periodicals, among them *Vogue, Saturday Evening Post, National Review, Holiday, Harper's Bazaar,* and *Esquire.* Honors and awards include *Vogue*'s Prix de Paris (1956) and the Bread Loaf Fellowship in Fiction (1965).

Once, in a dry season, I wrote in large letters across two 1 pages of a notebook that innocence ends when one is stripped of the delusion that one likes oneself. Although now, some years later, I marvel that a mind on the outs with itself should have nonetheless made painstaking record of its every tremor, I recall with embarrassing clarity the flavor of those particular ashes. It was a matter of misplaced self-respect.

I had not been elected to Phi Beta Kappa. This failure could scarcely 2 have been more predictable or less ambiguous (I simply did not have the grades), but I was unnerved by it; I had somehow thought myself a kind of academic Raskolnikov, curiously exempt from the cause-effect relationships which hampered others. Although even the humorless nineteen-year-old that I was must have recognized that the situation lacked real tragic stature, the day that I did not make Phi Beta Kappa nonetheless marked the end of something, and innocence may well be the word for it. I lost the conviction that lights would always turn green for me, the pleasant certainty that those rather passive virtues which had won me approval as a child automatically guaranteed me not only Phi Beta Kappa keys but happiness, honor, and the love of a good man; lost a certain touching faith in the totem power of good manners, clean hair, and proven competence on the Stanford-Binet scale. To such doubtful amulets had my self-respect been pinned, and I faced myself that day with the nonplused apprehension of someone who has come across a vampire and has no crucifix at hand.

Although to be driven back upon oneself is an uneasy affair at best, 3 rather like trying to cross a border with borrowed credentials, it seems to me now the one condition necessary to the beginnings of real self-respect. Most of our platitudes notwithstanding, self-deception remains the most difficult deception. The tricks that work on others count for nothing in that very well-lit back alley where one keeps assignations with oneself: no winning smiles will do here, no prettily drawn lists of good intentions. One shuffles flashily but in vain through one's marked cards — the kindness done for the wrong reason, the apparent triumph which involved no real effort, the seemingly heroic act into which one had been shamed. The dismal fact is that self-respect has nothing to do with the approval of others — who are, after all, deceived easily enough; has nothing to do with reputation, which, as Rhett Butler told Scarlett O'Hara, is something people with courage can do without.

To do without self-respect, on the other hand, is to be an unwilling 4 audience of one to an interminable documentary that details one's failings, both real and imagined, with fresh footage spliced in for every screening. *There's the glass you broke in anger, there's the hurt on X's face; watch now, this next scene, the night Y came back from Houston, see how you muff this one.* To live without self-respect is to lie awake some night, beyond the reach of warm milk, phenobarbital, and the sleeping hand on the coverlet, counting up the sins of commission and omission, the trusts betrayed, the promises subtly broken, the gifts irrevocably wasted through sloth or cowardice or carelessness. However long we postpone it, we eventually lie down alone in that notoriously uncomfortable bed, the one we make ourselves. Whether or not we sleep in it depends, of course, on whether or not we respect ourselves.

To protest that some fairly improbable people, some people who 5 *could not possibly respect themselves,* seem to sleep easily enough is to miss the point entirely, as surely as those people miss it who think that self-respect has necessarily to do with not having safety pins in one's underwear. There is a common superstition that "self-respect" is a kind of charm against snakes, something that keeps those who have it locked in some unblighted Eden, out of strange beds, ambivalent conversations, and trouble in general. It does not at all. It has nothing to do with the face of things, but concerns instead a separate peace, a private reconciliation. Although the careless, suicidal Julian English in *Appointment in Samarra* and the careless, incurably dishonest Jordan Baker in *The Great Gatsby* seem equally improbable candidates for self-respect, Jordan Baker had it, Julian English did not. With that genius for accommodation more often seen in women than in men, Jordan took her own measure, made her own peace, avoided threats to that peace: "I hate careless people," she told Nick Carraway. "It takes two to make an accident."

Like Jordan Baker, people with self-respect have the courage of their 6 mistakes. They know the price of things. If they choose to commit adultery, they do not then go running, in an excess of bad conscience, to receive absolution from the wronged parties; nor do they complain unduly of the unfairness, the undeserved embarrassment, of being named co-respondent. In brief, people with self-respect exhibit a certain toughness, a kind of moral nerve; they display what was once called *character,* a quality which, although approved in the abstract, sometimes loses ground to other, more instantly negotiable virtues. The measure of its slipping prestige is that one tends to think of it only in connection with homely children and United States senators who have been defeated, preferably in the primary, for re-election. Nonetheless, character—the willingness to accept responsibility for one's own life—is the source from which self-respect springs.

Self-respect is something that our grandparents, whether or not they 7 had it, knew all about. They had instilled in them, young, a certain discipline, the sense that one lives by doing things one does not particularly want to do, but putting fears and doubts to one side, by weighing immediate comforts against the possibility of larger, even intangible, comforts. It seemed to the nineteenth century admirable, but not remarkable, that Chinese Gordon put on a clean white suit and held Khartoum against the Mahdi; it did not seem unjust that the way to free land in California involved death and difficulty and dirt. In a diary kept during the winter of 1846, an emigrating twelve-year-old named Narcissa Cornwall noted coolly: "Father was busy reading and did not notice that the house was being filled with strange Indians until Mother spoke about it." Even lacking any clue as to what Mother said, one can scarcely fail to be impressed by the entire incident: the father reading, the Indians filing in, the mother choosing the words that would not alarm, the child duly recording the event and noting further that those particular Indians were not, "fortunately for us," hostile. Indians were simply part of the *donnée.*

In one guise or another, Indians always are. Again, it is a question of 8 recognizing that anything worth having has its price. People who respect themselves are willing to accept the risk that the Indians will be hostile, that the venture will go bankrupt, that the liaison may not turn out to be one in which *every day is a holiday because you're married to me.* They are willing to invest something of themselves; they may not play at all, but when they do play, they know the odds.

That kind of self-respect is a discipline, a habit of mind that can 9 never be faked but can be developed, trained, coaxed forth. It was once suggested to me that, as an antidote to crying, I put my head in a paper bag. As it happens, there is a sound physiological reason, something to do with oxygen, for doing exactly that, but the psychological effect alone is incalculable: it is difficult in the extreme to continue fancying oneself Cathy in *Wuthering Heights* with one's head in a Food Fair bag. There is a similar case for all the small disciplines, unimportant in themselves; imagine maintaining any kind of swoon, commiserative or carnal, in a cold shower.

But those small disciplines are valuable only insofar as they represent 10 larger ones. To say that Waterloo was won on the playing fields of Eton is not to say that Napoleon might have been saved by a crash program in cricket; to give formal dinners in the rain forest would be pointless did not the candlelight flickering on the liana call forth deeper, stronger disciplines, values instilled long before. It is a kind of ritual, helping us to remember who and what we are. In order to remember it, one must have known it.

To have that sense of one's intrinsic worth which constitutes self- 11
respect is potentially to have everything: the ability to discriminate, to
love and to remain indifferent. To lack it is to be locked within oneself,
paradoxically incapable of either love or indifference. If we do not respect ourselves, we are on the one hand forced to despise those who
have so few resources as to consort with us, so little perception as to remain blind to our fatal weaknesses. On the other, we are peculiarly in
thrall to everyone we see, curiously determined to live out — since our
self-image is untenable — their false notions of us. We flatter ourselves by
thinking this compulsion to please others an attractive trait: a gist for
imaginative empathy, evidence of our willingness to give. *Of course* I will
play Francesca to your Paolo, Helen Keller to anyone's Annie Sullivan:
no expectation is too misplaced, no role too ludicrous. At the mercy of
those we cannot but hold in contempt, we play roles doomed to failure
before they are begun, each defeat generating fresh despair at the urgency of divining and meeting the next demand made upon us.

It is the phenomenon sometimes called "alienation from self." In its 12
advanced stages, we no longer answer the telephone, because someone
might want something; that we could say *no* without drowning in self-
reproach is an idea alien to this game. Every encounter demands too
much, tears the nerves, drains the will, and the specter of something as
small as an unanswered letter arouses such disproportionate guilt that answering it becomes out of the question. To assign unanswered letters
their proper weight, to free us from the expectations of others, to give us
back to ourselves — there lies the great, the singular power of self-respect.
Without it, one eventually discovers the final turn of the screw: one runs
away to find oneself, and finds no one at home.

Study Questions

1. How does the author make her idea on self-respect very
   specific?
2. Didion's allusions are many and frequent. From what disciplines do they derive? What is their effect on the reader?
3. This essay is also replete with metaphors and metaphorical
   language. Cite examples, and comment on their originality
   and appropriateness.
4. Note the construction of the sentences in a typical paragraph — the third, for instance. What variations are
   achieved?
5. If *you* were rewriting this essay on self-respect, what basic
   changes would you make in it to accommodate your personal style and to reflect your own interests and knowledge?

Barbara Tuchman
THE MISSING ELEMENT: MORAL COURAGE

Barbara Tuchman (1912–   ) was born in New York City. She received a B.A. from Radcliffe College in 1933, and has been awarded
honorary degrees from, among others, Yale and Columbia. As a staff
writer for the *Nation* she reported on the Spanish Civil War from
Madrid; later she served as United States correspondent for the *New
Statesman and Nation*. Her contributions to *Foreign Affairs, Atlantic
Monthly, American Heritage, Harper's, The New York Times,* and the
Christian Science Monitor are highly respected. Two of Tuchman's
books—*The Guns of August* (1962) and *Stilwell and the American Experience in China 1911–1945* (1971)—earned Pulitzer Prizes; her
other books include *The Lost British Policy* (1958), *The Zimmerman
Telegram* (1958), *The Proud Tower* (1966), and *Notes from China*
(1972).

What I want to say is concerned less with leadership than 1
with its absence, that is, with the evasion of leadership. Not in the physical sense, for we have, if anything, a superabundance of leaders—hundreds of Pied Pipers, or would-be Pied Pipers, running about, ready and
anxious to lead the population. They are scurrying around, collecting consensus, gathering as wide an acceptance as possible. But what they are *not*
doing, very notably, is standing still and saying, *"This is* what I believe.
This I will do and that I will not do. This is my code of behavior and that
is outside it. This is excellent and that is trash."* There is an abdication of
moral leadership in the sense of a general unwillingness to state standards.

Of all the ills that our poor criticized, analyzed, sociologized society 2
is heir to, the focal one, it seems to me, from which so much of our
uneasiness and confusion derive is the absence of standards. We are too
unsure of ourselves to assert them, to stick by them, or if necessary, in
the case of persons who occupy positions of authority, to impose them.
We seem to be afflicted by a widespread and eroding reluctance to take
any stand on any values, moral, behavioral, or aesthetic.

Everyone is afraid to call anything wrong, or vulgar, or fraudulent, or 3
just bad taste or bad manners. Congress, for example, pussyfooted for

Reprinted by permission of the author.

months (following years of apathy) before taking action on a member convicted by the courts of illegalities; and when they finally got around to unseating him, one suspects they did it for the wrong motives. In 1922, in England, a man called Horatio Bottomley, a rather flamboyant character and popular demagogue — very similar in type, by the way, to Adam Clayton Powell, with similarly elastic financial ethics — who founded a paper called *John Bull* and got himself elected to Parliament, was found guilty of misappropriating the funds which his readers subscribed to victory bonds and other causes promoted by his paper. The day after the verdict, he was expelled from the House of Commons, with no fuss and very little debate, except for a few friendly farewells, as he was rather an engaging fellow. But no member thought the House had any other course to consider: out he went. I do not suggest that this represents a difference between British and American morality; the difference is in the *times.*

Our time is one of disillusion in our species and a resulting lack of self-confidence — for good historical reasons. Man's recent record has not been reassuring. After engaging in the Great War with all its mud and blood and ravaged ground, its disease, destruction, and death, we allowed ourselves a bare twenty years before going at it all over again. And the second time was accompanied by an episode of man's inhumanity to man of such enormity that its implications for all of us have not yet, I think, been fully measured. A historian has recently stated that for such a phenomenon as the planned and nearly accomplished extermination of a people to take place, one of three preconditions necessary was public indifference.   4

Since then the human species has been busy overbreeding, polluting the air, destroying the balance of nature, and bungling in a variety of directions so that is is no wonder we have begun to doubt man's capacity for good judgment. It is hardly surprising that the self-confidence of the nineteenth century and its belief in human progress has been dissipated. "Every great civilization," said Secretary Gardner last year, "has been characterized by confidence in itself." At mid-twentieth century, the supply is low. As a result, we tend to shy away from all judgments. We hesitate to label anything wrong, and therefore hesitate to require the individual to bear moral responsibility for his acts.   5

We have become afraid to fix blame. Murderers and rapists and muggers and persons who beat up old men and engage in other forms of assault are not guilty; society is guilty; society has wronged them; society beats its breast and says *mea culpa* — it is our fault, not the wrongdoer's. The wrongdoer, poor fellow, could not help himself.   6

I find this very puzzling because I always ask myself, in these cases, what about the many neighbors of the wrongdoer, equally poor, equally disadvantaged, equally sufferers from society's neglect, who nevertheless maintain certain standards of social behavior, who do *not* commit crimes, who do not murder for money or rape for kicks. How does it happen that they know the difference between right and wrong, and how long will they abide by the difference if the leaders and opinion-makers and pacesetters continue to shy away from bringing home responsibility to the delinquent?   7

Admittedly, the reluctance to condemn stems partly from a worthy 8
instinct — *tout comprendre, c'est tout pardonner* — and from a rejection of
what was often the hypocrisy of Victorian moral standards. True, there
was a large component of hypocrisy in nineteenth-century morality. Since
the advent of Freud, we know more, we understand more about human
behavior, we are more reluctant to cast the first stone — to condemn —
which is a good thing; but the pendulum has swung to the point where
we are now afraid to place moral responsibility at all. Society, that large
amorphous, nonspecific scapegoat, must carry the burden for each of us,
relieving us of guilt. We have become so indoctrinated by the terrors
lurking in the dark corridors of the guilt complex that guilt has acquired
a very bad name. Yet a little guilt is not a dangerous thing; it has a certain social utility.

When it comes to guilt, a respected writer — respected in some cir- 9
cles — has told us, as her considered verdict on the Nazi program, that
evil is banal — a word that means something so ordinary that you are not
bothered by it; the dictionary definition is "commonplace and hackneyed." Somehow that conclusion does not seem adequate or even apt.
Of course, evil is commonplace; *of course* we all partake of it. Does that
mean that we must withhold disapproval, and that when evil appears in
dangerous degree or vicious form we must not condemn but only understand? That may be very Christian in intent, but in reality it is an escape
from the necessity of exercising judgment — which exercise, I believe, is a
prime function of leadership.

What it requires is courage — just a little, not very much — the cour- 10
age to be independent and stand up for the standard values one believes
in. That kind of courage is the quality most conspicuously missing, I
think, in current life. I don't mean the courage to protest and walk
around with picket signs or boo Secretary McNamara which, though it
may stem from the right instinct, is a group thing that does not require
any very stout spirit. I did it myself for Sacco and Vanzetti when I was
about twelve and picketed in some now forgotten labor dispute when I
was a freshman and even got arrested. There is nothing to that; if you
don't do that sort of thing when you are eighteen, then there is something wrong with you. I mean, rather, a kind of lonely moral courage, the
quality that attracted me to that odd character, Czar Reed, and to Lord
Salisbury, neither of whom cared a rap for the opinion of the public or
would have altered his conduct a hair to adapt to it. It is the quality
someone said of Lord Palmerston was his "you-be-damnedness." That is
the mood we need a little more of.

Standards of taste, as well as morality, need continued reaffirmation 11
to stay alive, as liberty needs eternal vigilance. To recognize and to pro-
claim the difference between the good and the shoddy, the true and the
fake, as well as between right and wrong, or what we believe at a given
time to be right and wrong, is the obligation, I think, of persons who presume to lead, or are thrust into leadership, or hold positions of authority.
That includes — whether they asked for it or not — all educators and even,
I regret to say, writers.

For educators it has become increasingly the habit in the difficult cir- 12 cumstances of college administration today to find out what the students want in the matter of curriculum and deportment and then give it to them. This seems to me another form of abdication, another example of the prevailing reluctance to state a standard and expect, not to say require, performance in accord with it. The permissiveness, the yielding of decision to the student, does not—from what I can tell—promote responsibility in the young so much as uneasiness and a kind of anger at *not* being told what is expected of them, a resentment of their elders' unwillingness to take a position. Recently a student psychiatric patient of the Harvard Health Services was quoted by the director, Dr. Dana Farnsworth, as complaining, "My parents never tell me what to do. They never stop me from doing anything." That is the unheard wail, I think, extended beyond parents to the general absence of a guiding, reassuring pattern, which is behind much of society's current uneasiness.

It is human nature to want patterns and standards and a structure of behavior. A pattern to conform to is a kind of shelter. You see it in kindergarten and primary school, at least in those schools where the children when leaving the classroom are required to fall into line. When the teacher gives the signal, they fall in with alacrity; they know where they belong and they instinctively like to *be* where they belong. They like the feeling of being in line.   13

Most people need a structure, not only to fall into but to fall out of. The rebel with a cause is better off than the one without. At least he knows what he is "agin." He is not lost. He does not suffer from an identity crisis. It occurs to me that much of the student protest now may be a testing of authority, a search for that line to fall out of, and when it isn't there students become angrier because they feel more lost, more abandoned than ever. In the late turmoil at Berkeley, at least as regards the filthy speech demonstration, there was a missed opportunity, I think (however great my respect for Clark Kerr) for a hearty, emphatic, and unmistakable "No!" backed up by sanctions. Why? Because the act, even if intended as a demonstration of principle, was in this case, like any indecent exposure, simply offensive, and what is offensive to the greater part of society is anti-social, and what is anti-social, so long as we live in social groups and not each of us on his own island, must be curtailed, like Peeping Toms or obscene telephone calls, as a public nuisance. The issue is really not complicated or difficult but, if we would only look at it with more self-confidence, quite simple.   14

So, it seems to me, is the problem of the CIA.[1] You will say that in this case people have taken a stand, opinion-makers have worked themselves into a moral frenzy. Indeed they have, but over a false issue. The CIA is not, after all, the Viet Cong or the Schutzstaffel in blackshirts. Its initials do not stand for Criminal Indiscretions of America. It is an arm of the American government, our elected, representative government (whatever may be one's feelings toward that body at the moment). Virtually

[1] The Central Intelligence Agency was discovered to be giving secret financial support to the National Student Association—eds.

every government in the world subsidizes youth groups, especially in the international relations, not to mention in athletic competitions. (I do not know if the CIA is subsidizing our Equestrian Team, but I know personally a number of people who would be only too delighted if it were.) The difficulty here is simply that the support was clandestine in the first place and not the proper job of the CIA in the second. An intelligence agency should be restricted to the gathering of intelligence and not extend itself into operations. In armies the two functions are distinct: intelligence is G2 and operations is G3. If our government could manage its functions with a little more precision and perform openly those functions that are perfectly respectable, there would be no issue. The recent excitement only shows how easily we succumb when reliable patterns or codes of conduct are absent, to a confusion of values.

A similar confusion exists, I think, with regard to the omnipresent 16 pornography that surrounds us like smog. A year ago the organization of my own profession, the Authors League, filed a brief *amicus curiae* in the appeal of Ralph Ginzburg, the publisher of a periodical called *Eros* and other items, who had been convicted of disseminating obscenity through the mails. The League's action was taken on the issue of censorship to which all good liberals automatically respond like Pavlov's dogs. Since at this stage in our culture pornography has so far gotten the upper hand that to do battle in its behalf against the dragon Censorship is rather like doing battle today against the bustle in behalf of short skirts, and since I believe that the proliferation of pornography in its sadistic forms is a greater social danger at the moment than censorship, and since Mr. Ginzburg was not an author anyway but a commercial promoter, I raised an objection, as a member of the Council, to the Authors League's spending its funds in the Ginzburg case. I was, of course, outvoted; in fact, there was no vote. Everyone around the table just sat and looked at me in cold disapproval. Later, after my objection was printed in the *Bulletin,* at my request, two distinguished authors wrote privately to me to express their agreement but did not go so far as to say so publicly.

Thereafter, when the Supreme Court upheld Mr. Ginzburg's con- 17 viction, everyone in the intellectual community raised a hullaballoo about censorship advancing upon us like some sort of Frankenstein's monster. This seems to me another case of getting excited about the wrong thing. The cause of pornography is *not* the same as the cause of free speech. There *is* a difference. Ralph Ginzburg is *not* Theodore Dreiser and this is not the 1920's. If one looks around at the movies, especially the movie advertisements, and the novels and the pulp magazines glorifying perversion and the paperbacks that make de Sade available to school children, one does not get the impression that in the 1960's we are being stifled in the Puritan grip of Anthony Comstock. Here again, leaders—in this case authors and critics—seem too unsure of values or too afraid of being unpopular to stand up and assert the perfectly obvious difference between smut and free speech, or to say "Such and such is offensive and can be harmful." Happily, there are signs of awakening. In a *Times* review of a book called *On Iniquity* by Pamela Hansford Johnson, which related pornography to the Moors murders in England, the reviewer concluded that "this may be the opening of a discussion that must come, the opening shot."

In the realm of art, no less important than morals, the abdication of judgment is almost a disease. Last fall when the Lincoln Center opened its glittering new opera house with a glittering new opera on the tragedy of Anthony and Cleopatra, the curtain rose on a gaudy crowd engaged in energetic revels around a gold box in the shape of a pyramid, up whose sides (conveniently fitted with toe-holds, I suppose) several sinuous and reasonably nude slave girls were chased by lecherous guards left over from "Aida." When these preliminaries quieted down, the front of the gold box suddenly dropped open, and guess who was inside? No, it was not Cleopatra, it was Antony, looking, I thought, rather bewildered. What he was doing inside the box was never made clear. Thereafter everything happened—and in crescendos of gold and spangles and sequins, silks and gauzes, feathers, fans, jewels, brocades, and such a quantity of glitter that one began to laugh, thinking that the spectacle was intended as a parody of the old Shubert revue. But no, this was the Metropolitan Opera in the vaunted splendor of its most publicized opening since the Hippodrome. I gather it was Mr. Bing's idea of giving the first night customers a fine splash. What he achieved was simply vulgarity, as at least some reviewers had the courage to say next day. Now, I cannot believe that Mr. Bing and his colleagues do not know the difference between honest artistry in stage design and pretentious ostentation. If they know better, why do they allow themselves to do worse? As leaders in their field of endeavor, they should have been setting standards of beauty and creative design, not debasing them.

One finds the same peculiarities in the visual arts. Non-art, as its practitioners describe it—the blob school, the all-black canvasses, the paper cutouts and Campbell soup tins and plastic hamburgers and pieces of old carpet—is treated as art, not only by dealers whose motive is understandable (they have discovered that shock value sells); not only by a gullible pseudocultural section of the public who are not interested in art but in being "in" and wouldn't, to quote an old joke, know a Renoir from a Jaguar; but also, which I find mystifying, by the museums and the critics. I am sure they know the difference between the genuine and the hoax. But not trusting their own judgment, they seem afraid to say not to anything, for fear, I suppose, of making a mistake and turning down what may be next decade's Matisse.

For the museums to exhibit the plastic hamburgers and twists of scrap iron is one thing, but for them to *buy* them for their permanent collection puts an imprimatur on what is fraudulent. Museum curators, too, are leaders who have an obligation to distinguish—I will not say the good from the bad in art because that is an elusive and subjective matter dependent on the eye of the time—but at least honest expression from phony. Most of what fills the galleries on Madison Avenue is simply stuff designed to take advantage of current fads and does not come from an artist's vision or an honest creative impulse. The dealers know it; the critics know it; the purveyors themselves know it; the public suspects it;

but no one dares say it because that would be committing oneself to a standard of values and even, heaven forbid, exposing oneself to being called square.

In the fairy story, it required a child to cry out that the Emperor was 21 naked. Let us not leave that task to the children. It should be the task of leaders to recognize and state the truth as they see it. It is their task not to be afraid of absolutes.

If the educated man is not willing to express standards, if he cannot 22 show that he has them and applies them, what then is education for? Its purpose, I take it, is to form the civilized man, whom I would define as the person capable of the informed exercise of judgment, taste and values. If at maturity he is not willing to express judgment on matters of policy or taste or morals, if at fifty he does not believe that he has acquired more wisdom and informed experience than is possessed by the student at twenty, then he is saying in effect that education has been a failure.

Study Questions

1. It is clear from the first sentence that this essay was presented orally. How might the manner of its presentation have influenced its construction?
2. Discuss the transitions between paragraphs.
3. Tuchman begins the third paragraph by talking of "everyone." How does she proceed from there to make her generalization more specific? Does it work?
4. The author finds "a similar confusion" in the CIA case and the Ginzburg case. She says Ginzburg is not Drieser. What is the basis or the explanation she provides for the similarity, the difference?
5. What are the connotations of *disease* in paragraph 18? How appropriate is the metaphor? How would the meaning be changed if we altered the sentence to read "almost like a disease"? Can you cite other examples of this sort of statement in this essay?

Mark Twain
THE LOWEST ANIMAL

Mark Twain, pen name for Samuel Langhorne Clemens (1835–1910), internationally known humorist and satirist, was born in Florida, Missouri, and spent his boyhood in Hannibal, Missouri. In his youth and early manhood he worked at a variety of occupations — journeyman printer, steamboat pilot, newspaper reporter, prospector, free-lance writer, and lecturer. His experiences gave him a lifetime of material for his writings. In his own time he enjoyed an international reputation as a wit and social commentator. In his later years he became bitterly cynical, but he is remembered by most Americans as the author of *Tom Sawyer* (1876) and *The Adventures of Huckleberry Finn* (1884).

In August, 1572, similar things were occurring in Paris and 1 elsewhere in France. In this case it was Christian against Christian. The Roman Catholics, by previous concert, sprang a surprise upon the unprepared and unsuspecting Protestants, and butchered them by thousands — both sexes and all ages. This was the memorable St. Bartholomew's Day. At Rome the Pope and the Church gave public thanks to God when the happy news came.

During several centuries hundreds of heretics were burned at the 2 stake every year because their religious opinions were not satisfactory to the Roman Church.

In all ages the savages of all lands have made the slaughtering of 3 their neighboring brothers and the enslaving of their women and children the common business of their lives.

Hypocrisy, envy, malice, cruelty, vengefulness, seduction, rape, rob- 4 bery, swindling, arson, bigamy, adultery, and the oppression and humiliation of the poor and the helpless in all ways have been and still are more or less common among both the civilized and uncivilized peoples of the earth.

For many centuries "the common brotherhood of man" has been 5 urged — on Sundays — and "patriotism" on Sundays and weekdays both. Yet patriotism *contemplates the opposite of a common brotherhood.*

Reprinted from *Mark Twain, Letters From Earth,* edited by Bernard DeVoto. Copyright © 1962, by The Mark Twain Company. Reprinted by permission of Harper & Row, Publishers, Inc.
* This was to have been prefaced by newspaper clippings which, apparently, dealt with religious persecutions in Crete. The clippings have been lost.

Women's equality with man has never been conceded by any people, 6
ancient or modern, civilized or savage.

I have been studying the traits and dispositions of the "lower ani- 7
mals" (so-called), and contrasting them with the traits and dispositions of
man. I find the result humiliating to me. For it obliges me to renounce
my allegiance to the Darwinian theory of the Ascent of Man from the
Lower Animals; since it now seems plain to me that that theory ought to
be vacated in favor of a new and truer one, this new and truer one to be
named the *Des*cent of Man from the Higher Animals.

In proceeding toward this unpleasant conclusion I have not guessed 8
or speculated or conjectured, but have used what is commonly called the
scientific method. That is to say, I have subjected every postulate that
presented itself to the crucial test of actual experiment, and have adopted
it or rejected it according to the result. Thus I verified and established
each step of my course in its turn before advancing to the next. These
experiments were made in the London Zoological Gardens, and covered
many months of painstaking and fatiguing work.

Before particularizing any of the experiments, I wish to state one or 9
two things which seem to more properly belong in this place than further
along. This in the interest of clearness. The massed experiments established to my satisfaction certain generalizations, to wit:

1. That the human race is of one distinct species. It exhibits slight 10
   variations — in color, stature, mental caliber, and so on — due to climate, environment, and so forth; but it is a species by itself, and
   not to be confounded with any other.
2. That the quadrupeds are a distinct family, also. This family ex- 11
   hibits variations — in color, size, food preferences, and so on; but
   it is a family by itself.
3. That the other families — the birds, the fishes, the insects, the 12
   reptiles, etc. — are more or less distinct, also. They are in the procession. They are links in the chain which stretches down from
   the higher animals to man at the bottom.

Some of my experiments were quite curious. In the course of my 13
reading I had come across a case where, many years ago, some hunters
on our Great Plains organized a buffalo hunt for the entertainment of an
English earl — that, and to provide some fresh meat for his larder. They
had charming sport. They killed seventy-two of those great animals; and
ate part of one of them and left the seventy-one to rot. In order to determine the difference between an anaconda and an earl — if any — I caused
seven young calves to be turned into the anaconda's cage. The grateful
reptile immediately crushed one of them and swallowed it, then lay back
satisfied. It showed no further interest in the calves, and no disposition to
harm them. I tried this experiment with other anacondas; always with the
same result. The fact stood proven that the difference between an earl
and an anaconda is that the earl is cruel and the anaconda isn't; and that
the earl wantonly destroys what he has no use for, but the anaconda
doesn't. This seemed to suggest that the anaconda was not descended

from the earl. It also seemed to suggest that the earl was descended from the anaconda, and had lost a good deal in the transition.

I was aware that many men who have accumulated more millions of money than they can ever use have shown a rabid hunger for more, and have not scrupled to cheat the ignorant and the helpless out of their poor servings in order to partially appease that appetite. I furnished a hundred different kinds of wild and tame animals the opportunity to accumulate vast stores of food, but none of them would do it. The squirrels and bees and certain birds made accumulations, but stopped when they had gathered a winter's supply and could not be persuaded to add to it either honestly or by chicane. In order to bolster up a tottering reputation the ant pretended to store up supplies, but I was not deceived. I know the ant. These experiments convinced me that there is this difference between man and the higher animals: he is avaricious and miserly, they are not. 14

In the course of my experiments I convinced myself that among the animals man is the only one that harbors insults and injuries, broods over them, waits till a chance offers, then takes revenge. The passion of revenge is unknown to the higher animals. 15

Roosters keep harems, but it is by consent of their concubines; therefore no wrong is done. Men keep harems, but it is by brute force, privileged by atrocious laws which the other sex were allowed no hand in making. In this matter man occupies a far lower place than the rooster. 16

Cats are loose in their morals, but not consciously so. Man, in his descent from the cat, has brought the cat's looseness with him but has left the unconsciousness behind — the saving grace which excuses the cat. The cat is innocent, man is not. 17

Indecency, vulgarity, obscenity — these are strictly confined to man; he invented them. Among the higher animals there is no trace of them. They hide nothing; they are not ashamed. Man, with his soiled mind, covers himself. He will not even enter a drawing room with his breast and back naked, so alive are he and his mates to indecent suggestion. Man is "The Animal that Laughs." But so does the monkey, as Mr. Darwin pointed out; and so does the Australian bird that is called the laughing jackass. No — Man is the Animal that Blushes. He is the only one that does it — or has occasion to. 18

At the head of this article we see how "three monks were burnt to death" a few days ago, and a prior "put to death with atrocious cruelty." Do we inquire into the details? No; or we should find out that the prior was subjected to unprintable mutilations. Man — when he is a North American Indian — gouges out his prisoner's eyes; when he is King John, with a nephew to render untroublesome, he uses a red-hot iron; when he is a religious zealot dealing with heretics in the Middle Ages, he skins his captive alive and scatters salt on his back; in the first Richard's time he shuts up a multitude of Jew families in a tower and sets fire to it; in Columbus's time he captures a family of Spanish Jews and — but *that* is not printable; in our day in England a man is fined ten shillings for beating his mother nearly to death with a chair, and another man is fined forty shillings for having four pheasant eggs in his possession without being 19 able to satisfactorily explain how he got them. Of all the animals, man is the only one that is cruel. He is the only one that inflicts pain for the pleasure of doing it. It is a trait that is not known to the higher animals. The cat plays with the frightened mouse; but she has this excuse, that she does not know that the mouse is suffering. The cat is moderate—unhumanly moderate: she only scares the mouse, she does not hurt it; she doesn't dig out its eyes, or tear off its skin, or drive splinters under its nails—man-fashion; when she is done playing with it she makes a sudden meal of it and puts it out of its trouble. Man is the Cruel Animal. He is alone in that distinction.

The higher animals engage in individual fights, but never in orga- 20 nized masses. Man is the only animal that deals in that atrocity of atrocities, War. He is the only one that gathers his brethren about him and goes forth in cold blood and with calm pulse to exterminate his kind. He is the only animal that for sordid wages will march out, as the Hessians did in our Revolution, and as the boyish Prince Napoleon did in the Zulu war, and help to slaughter strangers of his own species who have done him no harm and with whom he has no quarrel.

Man is the only animal that robs his helpless fellow of his country— 21 takes possession of it and drives him out of it or destroys him. Man has done this in all ages. There is not an acre of ground on the globe that is in possession of its rightful owner, or that has not been taken away from owner after owner, cycle after cycle, by force and bloodshed.

Man is the only Slave. And he is the only animal who enslaves. He 22 has always been a slave in one form or another, and has always held other slaves in bondage under him in one way or another. In our day he is always some man's slave for wages, and does that man's work; and this slave has other slaves under him for minor wages, and they do *his* work. The higher animals are the only ones who exclusively do their own work and provide their own living.

Man is the only Patriot. He sets himself apart in his own country, un- 23 der his own flag, and sneers at the other nations, and keeps multitudinous uniformed assassins on hand at heavy expense to grab slices of other people's countries, and keep *them* from grabbing slices of *his*. And in the intervals between campaigns he washes the blood off his hands and works for "the universal brotherhood of man"—with his mouth.

Man is the Religious Animal. He is the only Religious Animal. He is 24 the only animal that has the True Religion—several of them. He is the only animal that loves his neighbor as himself, and cuts his throat if his theology isn't straight. He has made a graveyard of the globe in trying his honest best to smooth his brother's path to happiness and heaven. He was at it in the time of the Caesars, he was at it in Mahomet's time, he was at it in the time of the Inquisition, he was at it in France a couple of centuries, he was at it in England in Mary's day, he has been at it ever since he first saw the light, he is at it today in Crete—as per the telegrams quoted above—he will be at it somewhere else tomorrow. The higher animals have no religion. And we are told that they are going to be left out, in the Hereafter. I wonder why? It seems questionable taste.

Man is the Reasoning Animal. Such is the claim. I think it is open to 25 dispute. Indeed, my experiments have proven to me that he is the Unreasoning Animal. Note his history, as sketched above. It seems plain to me that whatever he is, he is *not* a reasoning animal. His record is the fantastic record of a maniac. I consider that the strongest count against his intelligence is the fact that with that record back of him he blandly sets himself up as the head animal of the lot: whereas by his own standards he is the bottom one.

In truth, man is incurably foolish. Simple things which the other ani- 26 mals easily learn, he is incapable of learning. Among my experiments was this. In an hour I taught a cat and a dog to be friends. I put them in a cage. In another hour I taught them to be friends with a rabbit. In the course of two days I was able to add a fox, a goose, a squirrel and some doves. Finally a monkey. They lived together in peace; even affectionately.

Next, in another cage I confined an Irish Catholic from Tipperary, 27 and as soon as he seemed tame I added a Scotch Presbyterian from Aberdeen. Next a Turk from Constantinople; a Greek Christian from Crete; an Armenian; a Methodist from the wilds of Arkansas; a Buddhist from China; a Brahman from Benares. Finally, a Salvation Army Colonel from Wapping. Then I stayed away two whole days. When I came back to note results, the cage of Higher Animals was all right, but in the other there was but a chaos of gory odds and ends of turbans and fezzes and plaids and bones and flesh — not a specimen left alive. These Reasoning Animals had disagreed on a theological detail and carried the matter to a Higher Court.

One is obliged to concede that in true loftiness of character, Man 28 cannot claim to approach even the meanest of the Higher Animals. It is plain that he is constitutionally incapable of approaching that altitude; that he is constitutionally afflicted with a Defect which must make such approach forever impossible, for it is manifest that this defect is permanent in him, indestructible, ineradicable.

I find this Defect to be the *Moral Sense.* He is the only animal that 29 has it. It is the secret of his degradation. It is the quality *which enables him to do wrong.* It has no other office. It is incapable of performing any other function. It could never have been intended to perform any other. Without it, man could do no wrong. He would rise at once to the level of the Higher Animals.

Since the Moral Sense has but the one office, the one capacity — to 30 enable man to do wrong — it is plainly without value to him. It is as valueless to him as is disease. In fact, it manifestly *is* a disease. *Rabies* is bad, but it is not so bad as this disease. Rabies enables a man to do a thing which he could not do when in a healthy state: kill his neighbor with a poisonous bite. No one is the better man for having rabies. The Moral Sense enables a man to do wrong. It enables him to do wrong in a thousand ways. Rabies is an innocent disease, compared to the Moral Sense. No one, then, can be the better man for having the Moral Sense. What, now, do we find the Primal Curse to have been? Plainly what it was in the beginning: the infliction upon man of the Moral Sense; the ability to distinguish good from evil; and with it, necessarily, the ability to *do* evil; for there can be no evil act without the presence of consciousness of it in the doer of it.

And so I find that we have descended and degenerated, from some far ancestor—some microscopic atom wandering at its pleasure between the mighty horizons of a drop of water perchance —insect by insect, animal by animal, reptile by reptile, down the long highway of smirchless innocence, till we have reached the bottom stage of development—namable as the Human Being. Below us—nothing. Nothing but the Frenchman. 31

There is only one possible stage below the Moral Sense; that is the Immoral Sense. The Frenchman has it. Man is but little lower than the angels. This definitely locates him. He is between the angels and the French. 32

Man seems to be a rickety poor sort of thing, any way you take him; a kind of British Museum of infirmities and inferiorities. He is always undergoing repairs. A machine that was as unreliable as he is would have no market. On top of his specialty—the Moral Sense—are piled a multitude of minor infirmities; such a multitude, indeed, that one may broadly call them countless. The Higher Animals get their teeth without pain or inconvenience. Man gets his through months and months of cruel torture; and at a time of life when he is but ill able to bear it. As soon as he has got them they must all be pulled out again, for they were of no value in the first place, not worth the loss of a night's rest. The second set will answer for a while, by being reinforced occasionally with rubber or plugged up with gold; but he will never get a set which can really be depended on till a dentist makes him one. This set will be called "false" teeth—as if he had ever worn any other kind.

In a wild state—a natural state—the Higher Animals have a few diseases; diseases of little consequence; the main one is old age. But man starts in as a child and lives on diseases till the end, as a regular diet. He has mumps, measles, whooping cough, croup, tonsillitis, diphtheria, scarlet fever, almost as a matter of course. Afterward, as he goes along, his life continues to be threatened at every turn: by colds, coughs, asthma, bronchitis, itch, cholera, cancer, consumption, yellow fever, bilious fever, typhus fevers, hay fever, ague, chilblains, piles, inflammation of the entrails, indigestion, toothache, earache, deafness, dumbness, blindness, influenza, chicken pox, cowpox, smallpox, liver complaint, constipation, bloody flux, warts, pimples, boils, carbuncles, abscesses, bunions, corns, tumors, fistulas, pneumonia, softening of the brain, melancholia and fifteen other kinds of insanity; dysentery, jaundice, diseases of the heart, the bones, the skin, the scalp, the spleen, the kidneys, the nerves, the brain, the blood; scrofula, paralysis, leprosy, neuralgia, palsy, fits, headache, thirteen kinds of rheumatism, forty-six of gout, and a formidable supply of gross and unprintable disorders of one sort and another. Also—but why continue the list? The mere names of the agents appointed to keep this shackly machine out of repair would hide him from sight if printed on his body in the smallest type known to the founder's art. He is but a basket of pestilent corruption provided for the support 34 and entertainment of swarming armies of bacilli—armies commissioned to rot him and destroy him, and each army equipped with a special detail of the work. The process of waylaying him, persecuting him, rotting him, killing him, begins with his first breath, and there is no mercy, no pity, no truce till he draws his last one.

Look at the workmanship of him, in certain of its particulars. What **35** are his tonsils for? They perform no useful function; they have no value. They have no business there. They are but a trap. They have but the one office, the one industry: to provide tonsillitis and quinsy and such things for the possessor of them. And what is the vermiform appendix for? It has no value; it cannot perform any useful service. It is but an ambuscaded enemy whose sole interest in life is to lie in wait for stray grape-seeds and employ them to breed strangulated hernia. And what are the male's mammals for? For business, they are out of the question; as an ornament, they are a mistake. What is his beard for? It performs no useful function; it is a nuisance and a discomfort; all nations hate it; all nations persecute it with the razor. And because it is a nuisance and a discomfort, Nature never allows the supply of it to fall short, in any man's case, between puberty and the grave. You never see a man bald-headed on his chin. But his hair! It is a graceful ornament, it is a comfort, it is the best of all protections against certain perilous ailments, man prizes it above emeralds and rubies. And because of these things Nature puts it on, half the time, so that it won't stay. Man's sight, smell, hearing, sense of locality—how inferior they are. The condor sees a corpse at five miles; man has no telescope that can do it. The bloodhound follows a scent that is two days old. The robin hears the earthworm burrowing his course under the ground. The cat, deported in a closed basket, finds its way home again through twenty miles of country which it has never seen.

Certain functions lodged in the other sex perform in a lamentably in- **36** ferior way as compared with the performance of the same functions in the Higher Animals. In the human being, menstruation, gestation and parturition are terms which stand for horrors. In the Higher Animals these things are hardly even inconveniences.

For style, look at the Bengal tiger—that ideal of grace, beauty, physi- **37** cal perfection, majesty. And then look at Man—that poor thing. He is the Animal of the Wig, the Trepanned Skull, the Ear Trumpet, the Glass Eye, the Pasteboard Nose, the Porcelain Teeth, the Silver Windpipe, the Wooden Leg—a creature that is mended and patched all over, from top to bottom. If he can't get renewals of his bric-a-brac in the next world, what will he look like?

He has just one stupendous superiority. In his intellect he is su- **38** preme. The Higher Animals cannot touch him there. It is curious, it is noteworthy, that no heaven has ever been offered him wherein his one sole superiority was provided with a chance to enjoy itself. Even when he himself has imagined a heaven, he has never made provision in it for intellectual joys. It is a striking omission. It seems a tacit confession that heavens are provided for the Higher Animals alone. This is a matter for thought; and for serious thought. And it is full of a grim suggestion: that we are not as important, perhaps, as we had all along supposed we were.

Study Questions

1. What is the thesis of this essay, and why does it occur where it does?
2. In paragraph 9 Twain presents you with the generalizations which he says his experiments established to his satisfaction. Why does he put the results before the experiments themselves?
3. What is a *syllogism?* Where and why does the author use them?
4. What use does Twain make of capitalization?
5. Paragraphs 13–14 and 18–22 form groups based on parallel opening sentences. What is achieved by these groupings?
6. If this essay is humorous, from what does the humor derive?
7. Comment on the tone of this essay. Is it bitter? Satirical? Sarcastic? Ironic? What?

D. Keith Mano
CRUEL LIB

D. Keith Mano (1942–   ) was born in New York City. He graduated *summa cum laude* from Columbia University (1963) and did postgraduate work at Cambridge (England) University. He has served as the vice president of a building-materials firm since 1964, while also acting as columnist and contributing editor to *National Review* and film critic for *Oui.* His books include *Bishop's Progress* (1968), *Horn* (1969), *War Is Heaven!* (1970), *The Death and Life of Harry Goth* (1971), *The Proselytizer* (1972), and *The Bridge* (1973).

Let's call him Fred. I met Fred during his junior year in college. All Fred wanted was love and a rewarding sexual relationship—is that not an inalienable right by now? Fred was purposelessly big, overweight. His arm flesh hung down, white as a brandy Alexander, full of stretch marks. His face, in contrast, was bluish: acne scars that might have been haphazard tattooing. A nice guy, intelligent enough, but the coeds were put off. Fred wooed them at mixers with his face half-averted, as if it were an illicit act.

Fred was without sexual prejudice: as they say, he could go both 2 ways. There was a militant gay-lib branch on campus. For months, struck out at mixers, he had considered joining. It was a painful decision: if he came out of the closet, Fred knew, his mother and father would probably go in—hidden there for shame. Yet mimeo sheets from gay lib offered a tacit, thrilling promise: new life, freedom. I remember the day Fred told me he had come out: he was relieved, optimistic. But being gay and free didn't cosmetize his face. When Fred let it all hang out, it just dangled there. After a while he noticed the good-looking gays dated the good-looking gays, as a first-string quarterback goes out with a homecoming queen. Fred had caused his family anguish for small compensation: he was now a wallflower in both sexes. Liberation. The tacit promise had been empty, and it had cracked his fragile spirit. Three months later Fred commited suicide.

Uncreative

Let's call her Gwen. The usual: $40,000 bilevel house, three kids, mar- 3 ried to a good provider. Her unwed sister-in-law, however, ran the local women's-lib cell. Gwen's sister-in-law made fun of the drudgery: dishes; that unending double-play combo, hamper to washer to dryer; the vacuum she used and the one she lived in. It seemed so *uncreative.* Creativity, you know, it another inalienable American right. Gwen was 34 and, good grief, only a housewife. There were wonderful, though unspecified, resources inside her. After some time marriage, in Gwen's mind, became a kind of moth closet.

Ms. Gwen is divorced now. Mr. Gwen still loves her; he has taken 4 the children. Gwen enrolled in a community college, but she didn't do well. Term papers were drudgery. For some time she made lopsided ashtrays at the Wednesday-night ceramics class. She was free and bored to death with herself. Now Gwen drinks a lot; she has some talent in that direction. Her children, well ... all three understand, of course, that they were exploiting Gwen for twelve and nine and seven years respectively.

Nothing There

It's an unattractive human truth, but every now and then someone should 5 put it on record: most people—Christians used to acknowledge this fact without embarrassment—most people are not particularly talented or beautiful or charismatic. Set free to discover "the true self," very often they find nothing there at all. Men and women who determine "to do their own thing" commonly learn that they have little of note to do. Yet these people are harassed, shamed by the Zeitgeist and its glib armies into disparaging their conventional roles. The bubble-gum tune goes like this: American civilization, through some spiteful, stupid conspiracy, means to thwart self-expression. We are all frustrated painters, explorers, starlets, senators. But there are times when it's more healthful to be frustrated than to have one's mediocrity confirmed in the light of common day.

Roles don't limit people; roles protect them. And, yes, most people 6 need protection: deserve it. Not so long ago our society honored the husband and the wife, the mother and the father. These were titles that carried merit enough to justify a full human life. Remember the phrase? "It's like attacking motherhood." Times have changed. On the lecture circuit today, you can pull down a nice income plus expenses attacking motherhood.

Yet probably the cruelest of libs is educational lib. Ed lib hasn't been 7 formally incorporated, but it's very well sustained by an immense bureaucracy of teachers, professors, administrators, foundations, Federal agencies. Strike a match and you learn inside the pad how John earned respect from his bowling team as a correspondence-school computer executive. And on the crosstown bus they tell you DON'T PREPARE FOR TOMORROW WITH YESTERDAY'S SKILLS (picture of a wheelbarrow). Or, A MIND IS A TERRIBLE THING TO WASTE. Sure. But what about a pair of hands, damn it? Even at fifteen bucks per hour, we humiliate our labor force in a programmatic way. The elitism of it all is pernicious and disgusting.

Some few centuries ago another kind of lib prevailed. Christianity, 8 they called it. Christian lib isn't a "now" item; it comes due in another life. Prerequisites are faith, works, humility: children are raised, things are made, to God's glory. Christians know personal gratification for what it is: a brummagem trinket. And this has been the shrewd beauty of Communism. Lenin cribbed his tactics from the New Testament. Liberation is promised through an arduous class struggle — but not in anyone's lifetime. This lib movement, moreover, functions within a powerfully structured, oppressive social system. Not only do totalitarian governments curtail personal liberty, but they are downright prissy when it comes to permissive sex. Yet people, in general, accept. Their roles are clear, and those roles are esteemed.

Unruly Beast

In this country, circa 1975, lib has become a growth industry. Many who 9 are otherwise talentless have made it their profession. But what Ralph Nader will hold them accountable for the Freds and the Gwens, for those who have been dispirited by a society that no longer prizes sexual restraint or menial labor or the nuclear family? We have, I hold it self-evident, an inalienable right to be unliberated. This nation — another unattractive truth — doesn't need more personal freedom. The human spirit can be an unruly beast; a little restraint is wholesome. Let people be cherished for what they are, not for ambiguous thwarted gifts, or for the social responsibilities they default on. The men and women of Middle America have earned that small consideration. Really "creative" people will surface anyway. They usually do. And they will have their great rewards.

Study Questions

1. What is Mano's attitude toward Fred and Gwen? How can you tell?
2. What makes the style of the essay colloquial rather than formal? Be specific.
3. To what extent could the author's remarks be documented? For instance, what about the "unattractive human truth" in paragraph 5?
4. Linguists commonly observe that language changes with the times. Sometimes old words are used in new ways. Sometimes two words are joined to make a single word. Sometimes new words must be invented to fit specific needs. Sometimes the original becomes a cliche. Find specific examples of each of these in Mano's diction.
5. How can you tell that this essay was not meant to be pored over?

Bruno Bettelheim
"THE THREE LITTLE PIGS"

Bruno Bettelheim (1903–   ) was born in Vienna and became a naturalized U. S. citizen in 1944. He received his doctorate from the University of Vienna in 1938. His distinguished career as a professor of psychology at the University of Chicago began in 1944. Bettelheim's articles are welcomed by readers of both popular and professional journals. Among his books are *The Dynamics of Prejudice* (with Morris Janowitz) and *Love Is Not Enough* (1950), *Truants from Life* (1955), *The Informed Heart* (1960), *The Empty Fortress* (1967), *The Children of the Dream* (1969), and the highly praised *The Uses of Enchantment: The Meaning and Importance of Fairy Tales* (1976).

The myth of Hercules deals with the choice between follow- 1
ing the pleasure principle or the reality principle in life. So, likewise, does the fairy story of "The Three Little Pigs."

Stories like "The Three Little Pigs" are much favored by children 2
over all "realistic" tales, particularly if they are presented with feeling by the storyteller. Children are enraptured when the huffing and puffing of

the wolf at the pig's door is acted out for them. "The Three Little Pigs" teaches the nursery-age child in a most enjoyable and dramatic form that we must not be lazy and take things easy, for if we do, we may perish. Intelligent planning and foresight combined with hard labor will make us victorious over even our most ferocious enemy—the wolf! The story also shows the advantages of growing up, since the third and wisest pig is usually depicted as the biggest and oldest.

The houses the three pigs build are symbolic of man's progress in 3 history: from a lean-to shack to a wooden house, finally to a house of solid brick. Internally, the pigs' actions show progress from the id-dominated personality to the superego-influenced but essentially ego-controlled personality.

The littlest pig builds his house with the least care out of straw; the 4 second uses sticks; both throw their shelters together as quickly and effortlessly as they can, so they can play for the rest of the day. Living in accordance with the pleasure principle, the younger pigs seek immediate gratification, without a thought for the future and the dangers of reality, although the middle pig shows some growth in trying to build a somewhat more substantial house than the youngest.

Only the third and oldest pig has learned to behave in accordance 5 with the reality principle: he is able to postpone his desire to play, and instead acts in line with his ability to foresee what may happen in the future. He is even able to predict correctly the behavior of the wolf—the enemy, or stranger within, which tries to seduce and trap us; and therefore the third pig is able to defeat powers both stronger and more ferocious than he is. The wild and destructive wolf stands for all asocial, unconscious, devouring powers against which one must learn to protect oneself, and which one can defeat through the strength of one's ego.

"The Three Little Pigs" makes a much greater impression on chil- 6 dren than Aesop's parallel but overtly moralistic fable of "The Ant and the Grasshopper." In this fable a grasshopper, starving in winter, begs an ant to give it some of the food which the ant had busily collected all summer. The ant asks what the grasshopper was doing during the summer. Learning that the grasshopper sang and did not work, the ant rejects his plea by saying, "Since you could sing all summer, you may dance all winter."

This ending is typical for fables, which are also folk tales handed 7 down from generation to generation. "A fable seems to be, in its genuine state, a narrative in which beings irrational, and sometimes inanimate, are, for the purpose of moral instruction, feigned to act and speak with human interests and passions" (Samuel Johnson). Often sanctimonious, sometimes amusing, the fable always explicitly states a moral truth; there is no hidden meaning, nothing is left to our imagination.

The fairy tale, in contrast, leaves all decisions up to us, including 8 whether we wish to make any at all. It is up to us whether we wish to make any application to our life from a fairy tale, or simply enjoy the fantastic events it tells about. Our enjoyment is what induces us to respond in our own good time to the hidden meanings, as they may relate to our life experience and present state of personal development.

A comparison of "The Three Little Pigs" with "The Ant and the   9
Grasshopper" accentuates the difference between a fairy tale and a fable.
The grasshopper, much like the little pigs and the child himself, is bent
on playing with little concern for the future. In both stories the child
identifies with the animals (although only a hypocritical prig can identify
with the nasty ant, and only a mentally sick child with the wolf); but after
having identified with the grasshopper, there is no hope left for the child,
according to the fable. For the grasshopper beholden to the pleasure
principle, nothing but doom awaits; it is an "either/or" situation, where
having made a choice once settles things forever.

But identification with the little pigs of the fairy tale teaches that there   10
are developments — possibilities of progress from the pleasure principle to
the reality principle, which, after all, is nothing but a modification of the
former. The story of the three pigs suggests a transformation in which much
pleasure is retained, because now satisfaction is sought with true respect for
the demands of reality. The clever and playful third pig outwits the wolf
several times: first, when the wolf tries three times to lure the pig away from
the safety of home by appealing to his oral greed, proposing expeditions to
where the two would get delicious food. The wolf tries to tempt the pig with
turnips which may be stolen, then with apples, and finally with a visit to a
fair.

Only after these efforts have come to naught does the wolf move in for   11
the kill. But he has to enter the pig's house to get him, and once more the
pig wins out, for the wolf falls down the chimney into the boiling water and
ends up as cooked meat for the pig. Retributive justice is done: the wolf,
which has devoured the other two pigs and wished to devour the third, ends
up as food for the pig.

The child, who throughout the story has been invited to identify   12
with one of its protagonists, is not only given hope, but is told that
through developing his intelligence he can be victorious over even a
much stronger opponent.

Since according to the primitive (and a child's) sense of justice only   13
those who have done something really bad get destroyed, the fable seems
to teach that it is wrong to enjoy life when it is good, as in summer.
Even worse, the ant in this fable is a nasty animal, without any compassion for the suffering of the grasshopper — and this is the figure the
child is asked to take for his example.

The wolf, on the contrary, is obviously a bad animal, because it wants   14
to destroy. The wolf's badness is something the young child recognizes
within himself: his wish to devour, and its consequence — the anxiety
about possibly suffering such a fate himself. So the wolf is an ex-
ternalization, a projection of the child's badness — and the story tells how
this can be dealt with constructively.

The various excursions in which the oldest pig gets food in good   15
ways are an easily neglected but significant part of the story, because they
show that there is a world of difference between eating and devouring.
The child subconsciously understands it as the difference between the
pleasure principle uncontrolled, when one wants to devour all at once, ignoring the consequences, and the reality principle, in line with which one

goes about intelligently foraging for food. The mature pig gets up in good time to bring the goodies home before the wolf appears on the scene. What better demonstration of the value of acting on the basis of the reality principle, and what it consists of, than the pig's rising very early in the morning to secure the delicious food and, in so doing, foiling the wolf's designs?

In fairy tales it is typically the youngest child who, although at first 16 thought little of or scorned, turns out to be victorious in the end. "The Three Little Pigs" deviates from this pattern, since it is the oldest pig who is superior to the two little pigs all along. An explanation can be found in the fact that all three pigs are "little," thus immature, as is the child himself. The child identifies with each of them in turn and recognizes the progression of identity. "The Three Little Pigs" is a fairy tale because of its happy ending, and because the wolf gets what he deserves.

While the child's sense of justice is offended by the poor grasshopper 17 having to starve although it did nothing bad, his feeling of fairness is satisfied by the punishment of the wolf. Since the three little pigs represent stages in the development of man, the disappearance of the first two little pigs is not traumatic; the child understands subconsciously that we have to shed earlier forms of existence if we wish to move on to higher ones. In talking to young children about "The Three Little Pigs," one encounters only rejoicing about the deserved punishment of the wolf and the clever victory of the oldest pig — not grief over the fate of the two little ones. Even a young child seems to understand that all three are really one and the same in different stages — which is suggested by their answering the wolf in exactly the same words: "No, no, not by the hair of my chinni-chin-chin!" If we survive in only the higher form of our identity, this is as it should be.

"The Three Little Pigs" directs the child's thinking about his own de- 18 velopment without ever telling what it ought to be, permitting the child to draw his own conclusions. This process alone makes for true maturing, while telling the child what to do just replaces the bondage of his own immaturity with a bondage of servitude to the dicta of adults.

Study Questions

1. How are the introduction and conclusion related?
2. How much knowledge on the reader's part does the author take for granted?
3. What judicious use of quotation do you find in this essay? Why does Bettelheim feel it sufficient to name the author of the quotation but not the source?
4. How does the comparison of "The Three Little Pigs" and "The Ant and the Grasshopper" advance Bettelheim's argument?
5. To what extent does he rely on psychological jargon?

Alison Lurie
THE HAUNTED WOOD

Alison Lurie (1926–   ) was born in Chicago and earned an A.B. at Radcliffe (1947). Since 1973 she has been Adjunct Professor of English at Cornell University; she held a Guggenheim fellowship in 1965–1966. One of the most widely respected contemporary novelists, her books include *Love and Friendship* (1962), *The Nowhere City* (1965), *Imaginary Friends* (1967), *Real People* (1969), and *The War Between the Tates* (1974). Recently she has been writing scripts for television.

One mark of a literary classic is that nobody can definitely say 1
what it means. Every age, even every reader, reinterprets the story to suit the situation. In London recently I saw a production of *Henry IV: Part I* of which the point seemed to be that when the leaders of a country are divided and failing it is better to transfer power to ex-hippies than to ex-rockers. Prince Hal, dressed in an elegant period costume of denim patches, was the complete disaffected student, waking slowly from his experience with the counterculture (Falstaff and company). At first he looked limp, freaky, and disoriented, but he turned out to be basically intelligent and courageous. Hotspur, in a sixteenth-century version of studded black-leather motorcycle jacket and jeans, seemed far more attractive at the start, full of energy and wit and passion, but later scenes brought out fatal flaws of character. You could see that he was a violent, impatient egotist, and a male chauvinist pig besides.

If this can happen to Shakespeare, no wonder that anonymous works 2
should go through cycles of reinterpretation. Bruno Bettelheim is only the latest, though one of the most distinguished, in a parade of experts determined to explain for once and all what folk tales, and especially fairy stories, mean.

The news that such a famous child psychologist—author of *Love is* 3
Not Enough, The Empty Fortress, and *Children of the Dream*—has turned his attention to fairy tales is bound to arouse high expectations. I am sorry to report that they are only partly fulfilled. *The Uses of Enchantment* is extremely interesting; it is also uneven and at times infuriating.

Bettelheim does not appear to realize how large and how long a pa- 4
rade of experts and would-be experts he has joined. Much of what has been written about fairy tales over the past hundred years, by psychologists as well as by folklorists, anthropologists, sociologists, and literary

critics, seems to be unknown to him. For instance, he describes, with considerable indulgence, the so-called solar theory put forth in the late nineteeth century by Max Muller and other German writers. According to them, every folk tale was really just a silly poetic myth about the movements of sun, moon, weather, and seasons. (Red Riding Hood, the red setting sun, and her grandmother, the elderly day, were devoured by the wolf, night, and rescued by the huntsman of the dawn, et cetera.) Bettelheim does not seem to have heard that this theory was laughed out of court more than seventy-five years ago by the English folklorist Andrew Lang, whom he mentions only as the compiler of collections of tales for children.

There are many other important studies which Bettelheim is unfamil- 5 iar with, or fails to mention — to the detriment of his own. He puzzles over the fact that most fathers in fairy tales are weak or ineffectual, without considering the belief of some anthropologists that these stories date from an early matriarchal culture, or the fact that they were handed on principally by women. There is no reference to the writings of the structuralists, including Vladimir Propp's central work on Russian fairy stories. The popular modern cautionary tale *Tootle,* by Gertrude Crampton, is discussed at length without any mention of David Riesman's famous and very similar analysis of it in *The Lonely Crowd;* and Erich Fromm's equally well-known *The Forgotten Language* is dismissed at the end of a long footnote with the slighting remark that it "makes some references to fairy tales, particularly to 'Little Red Riding Hood,' " although Bettelheim has repeated most of Fromm's points in his discussion of the story.

Even more surprisingly, there is no reference (even in the notes) to 6 the extensive work on fairy tales done by transactional analysts such as Eric Berne, who see children's favorite tales as "scripts" for a future life story. (Jack the Giant-Killer, for instance, grows up to be Ralph Nader.) This last omission is especially irritating, since a combination of Berne's insights with Bettelheim's could have been tremendously productive.

The folk tale, of course, was one of the first subjects of applied psy- 7 choanalysis. Most of the early studies now seem rather simple-minded and reductive: eager Freudians saw every magic staff or sword as a penis, every castle or gingerbread house as a womb: Jungians found anima figures and alchemical symbols everywhere.

Though Bettelheim's style is often as clumsy and heavy with jargon 8 as theirs, his own approach to the fairy tale is far more thoughtful, humane, and sensitive. The reader who perseveres past sentences like "As these stories unfold, they give credence and body to id pressures and show ways to satisfy these which are in line with ego and superego requirements" will be well rewarded. For instance, Bettelheim remarks that the various protagonists of a story often represent conflicting motives or emotions within a single individual. The ambitious, single-minded brother who has no time to waste on old beggar-woman or wounded animals, and the good-natured simpleton who shares his last piece of bread are the same fellow on different days. The stepmothers and witches who appear in so many tales are really our mothers seen by black light after the blissful years of babyhood are over.

Bettelheim, however, is not only the analyst of fairy tales, but their 9 champion, as one can see from the title of the book; he has set out to defend this literature against what he sees as a horde of hostile and disapproving colleagues. I have never met a psychologist who hated fairy stories, but perhaps they do exist. Certainly the complaint that such tales are bad for children — unrealistic, immoral, violent — has a long history. According to Bettelheim, this prejudice can have serious and destructive social effects: "I have known many examples where, particularly in late adolescence, years of belief in magic are called upon to compensate for the person's having been deprived of it prematurely in childhood.... Many young people who today suddenly seek escape in drug-induced dreams, apprentice themselves to some guru, believe in astrology, engage in practicing 'black magic,' or who in some other fashion escape from reality into daydreams about magic experiences which are to change their life for the better, were prematurely pressed to view reality in an adult way."

In my experience, it is not only adolescents deprived of fairy tales   10
who take up with drugs and gurus. Still, if Bettelheim's long and well-argued defense convinces one parent to start telling his children bedtime stories, or persuades a single nervous teacher not to ban "Jack and the Beanstalk" and "Snow White," we should be grateful. Yet to any reader who loves fairy tales for themselves, the idea that enchantment must be useful causes a small unpleasant shiver.

As we read further, this shiver develops into a severe chill. The princi-   11
pal use of fairy tales, according to Bettelheim, is to symbolize a child's unconscious psychological problems and suggest their solution. In his introductory chapters he tells us that a story may have different meanings (or "uses") depending on the emphasis given to it by both teller and hearer. Yet later on, when he analyzes individual tales, each one tends to have a single meaning which more often than not illustrates some aspect of the "oedipus conflict." In "Cinderella," for instance, "sibling rivalry takes the place of an oedipal involvement that has been repressed." If we protest that we never saw it that way, we are told that because of our own repressions it is impossible for us "to recognize consciously that [Cinderella's] unhappy state is due to oedipal involvements." Catch-222.

One of the greatest shortcomings of psychoanalytic theory, it has   12
been said, is that it is culture-bound, and the culture it is bound to is that of middle-class late-Victorian Europe. Though Bettelheim sometimes breaks away from orthodox Freudianism, all too often he slips back, telling us, for example, that we consider the passive and sexually ignorant Sleeping Beauty "the incarnation of perfect femininity," or that "in the typical nuclear family setting, it is the father's duty to protect the child against the dangers of the outside world, and also those that originate in the child's own social tendencies. The mother is to provide nurturing care and the general satisfaction of immediate bodily needs."

The European fairy tales that we know best today, and which Bettel-   13
heim analyzes here, are only a score or so of the literally thousands recorded by collectors all over the world. We know this handful of stories because they are the ones chosen from among those thousands by Victorian editors to suit a rigid, paternalistic, bourgeois society not unlike that of Freud's Vienna.

Yet we live in a changing world where passivity and ignorance are 14
not the mark of a perfect woman, and where it is not necessarily only the
father who protects and disciplines children and not only the mother
who cares for their physical needs. Today the "nuclear family setting" itself is being destroyed, or, if you prefer, transformed. Perhaps for this
world we need new fairy tales — or at least a new understanding of the
old ones.

Study Questions

1. What is the purpose of the introductory paragraph?
2. What specific word or words are used to praise Bettelheim's book?
3. Which paragraphs are clearly organized around a stated and
   then supported topic sentence?
4. How objective is Lurie is paragraphs 4 and 5 in contrast
   with paragraph 10?
5. What are the implications of the concluding sentence?

Harold Bloom
DRIVING OUT DEMONS

Harold Bloom (1930–   ) was born in New York City. He re-
ceived his B.A. from Cornell (1951) and his Ph.D. from Yale (1955).
On the faculty of Yale since 1955, he was named Professor of
English in 1965. Among the numerous prizes and awards heaped on
Bloom have been Fulbright (1955) and Guggenheim (1962) fellow-
ships. Among his critical works are *Shelley's Mythmaking* (1959), *The
Visionary Company* (1961), *Wallace Stevens: The Poems of Our Climate*
(1974), and *Poetry and Repression* (1975).

Freud's essay on "The Uncanny" (1919) can be said to have 1
defined, for our century, what criticism once called the Sublime. An apprehension of a beyond or of the daemonic — a sense of transcendence —
appears in literature or life, according to Freud, when we feel that something uncanny (*unheimlich*) is being represented, or conjured up, or at
least intimated. Freud locates the source of the uncanny in our narcissis-
tic and atavistic tendency to believe in "the omnipotence of thought,"

that is, in the power of our own or of others' minds over the natural world. The uncanny is thus a return to animistic conceptions of the universe, and is produced by the psychic defense Freud called repression, an unconsciously purposeful forgetting of drives that might menace our socially conditioned "ego-ideals," that is, the models we attempt to imitate.

It would have seemed likely for Freud to find his literary instances of the uncanny, or at least some of them, in fairy tales, since as much as any other fictions they seem to be connected with repressed desires and archaic forms of thought. But Freud specifically excluded fairy tales from the realm of the uncanny. "Who would be so bold," Freud asks, "as to call it an uncanny moment, for instance, when Snow-White opens her eyes once more?" Why not? Because, he goes on to say, in those stories everything is possible and so nothing is incredible, and therefore no conflicts in the reader's judgment are provoked. Freud concludes his essay, "The Uncanny," by an even more arbitrary judgment: "In fairy-stories feelings of fear—including uncanny sensations—are ruled out altogether." 2

Why Freud takes this attitude toward fairy tales is something of a mystery, at least to me, though two surmises immediately suggest themselves: there may be a hidden polemic here, against Jung and his excursions into daemonic romance, and there always is an ambivalence on Freud's part toward literary romance, so that the forms of what Northrop Frye, adapting Schiller, calls "naive romance" are not tempting to Freud's interpretive skills. Essentially, Freud chose dreams and mistakes and neurotic symptoms in preference to stories, and his keen sense of texts did not betray him in such choosing; for even the simplest fairy tale tends to be a palimpsest, a textual jungle in which one interpretation has grown itself upon another, until by now the interpretations have become the story. 3

Where Freud would not venture, few orthodox Freudians have trespassed, though Karl Abraham and Otto Rank (in his earlier work) in different ways verged upon the area of the folk tale. Now Bruno Bettelheim, with a kind of wise innocence, has subjected fairy tales, in general and in particular, to very close, generally orthodox, and wholly reductive Freudian interpretations. Bettelheim's book, written in apparent ignorance of the vast critical traditions of interpreting literary romance, is nevertheless a splendid achievement, brimming with useful ideas, with insights into how young children read and understand, and most of all overflowing with a realistic optimism and with an experienced and therapeutic good will. What Freud might have thought of it hardly can be conjectured, and many readers may find themselves somewhat baffled by its perpetual vigor in reductiveness, in discovering the same common denominators in what plainly are very varied stories. I myself am bothered by Bettelheim's need to see nearly all his stories as being equally coherent and consistent, but that is only a secondary reaction. Primarily, I am moved, charmed, and frequently persuaded by this humane effort to clarify the daemonic ground of romance and so to substitute the uses of enchantment for the uncanny actualities of the enchantment. 4

Bruno Bettelheim's major concern has been with autistic children, and inevitably his interpretative activity is directed against any child's tendency 5

to defensive withdrawal, to submit to the temptations of an abnormal sub-
jectivity or virtual solipsism. Throughout this book, Bettelheim argues for
the child's legitimate needs, and against the parent's self-centeredness. The
child's desperate isolation and loneliness, his inarticulate anxieties, are addressed directly by fairy tales, according to Bettelheim, and the parents'
function is to mediate by telling the child the story, thus strengthening the
therapeutic effect by the authority of their approval. But why should fairy
tales, *in themselves,* be therapeutic? Bettelheim's answer depends upon the
child being his own interpreter:

> The fairy tale is therapeutic because the patient finds his *own* solutions, 6
> through contemplating what the story seems to imply about him and his in-
> ner conflicts at this moment in his life.

Bettelheim proceeds on the basis of two complementary assump- 7
tions: that the child *will* interpret a story benignly, for his own good; and
that the Freudian interpretations will yield an accurate account of the
child's interpretations. The child, questing for help, and the analyst, attempting to find helpful patterns in the stories, thus read alike, though in
different vocabularies. A layman, reading Bettelheim's interpretation of a
fairy tale, will come into possession of a key to what the child finds. That
both of his assumptions might be questioned does not occur to Bettelheim. Perhaps this is all to the good, since it leaves unimpaired his confidence as an interpreter; and a child analyst, like any analyst, would be
destroyed without such confidence.

The first half of Bettelheim's book, in which he explains and justifies 8
his approach to fairy tales, is almost wholly a success. Fairy tale is compared to fable and to myth, and preferred to either because of its realistic
optimism. A gentle, persuasive reading of "The Three Little Pigs" becomes a masterly demonstration of the opposition between Pleasure
Principle and Reality Principle, and Bettelheim develops a considerable
defense of fantasy as a mode of overcoming the vestiges of infancy and
bringing the young self to an early sense of autonomy.

Perhaps the best pages in this fine Part One: A Pocketful of Magic" 9
concern "The Goose Girl," a superb Grimm Brothers story, in which a
princess is displaced by her wicked maid, whose crime of usurpation is
augmented when she has the head of Falada, the faithful talking horse of
the princess, chopped off. Reduced for a time to herding geese, the princess nevertheless ends happily, her true identity disclosed, while the unfaithful maid is stripped naked, placed inside a barrel with pointed nails,
and dragged by horses up street and down until she is dead, a punishment she has unwittingly suggested as appropriate for someone with her
guilt.

Bettelheim reads this as an Oedipal pattern, with the story warning 10
the child against the desire to usurp the place of the parent of the same
sex, just as the maid took the place of the princess. This displacement occurred after the princess lost a white handkerchief given to her by her
mother, a handkerchief stained deliberately by three drops of the
mother's blood. Noting that the Queen gave this handkerchief to her
daughter as she was leaving home to be married, Bettelheim interprets

the blood as symbolic of potential sexual maturity, and the loss of the handkerchief as indicating the princess was not ready for such maturity.

To have lost the handkerchief, Bettelheim writes, is a " 'Freudian' 11 slip, by means of which she avoided what she did not wish to be reminded of: the impending loss of her maidenhood." It allowed her to revert to childhood as a goose girl. This regression brings about tragedy for poor Falada, whose head is nailed to a gateway. Each morning, the goose girl laments to the horse's head: "Falada, thou who hangest there," to which the head replies: "If this your mother knew, / Her heart would break in two." Bettelheim translates this as expressing the mother's helpless grief, and so as admonishing the goose girl to cease being passive, at least for her poor mother's sake. "All the bad things that happen are the girl's own fault because she fails to assert herself."

When the maid eventually is punished, Bettelheim urges us not to 12 believe that children will be repelled by so ghastly an execution. Instead, they will say she chose it for herself, deserved it anyway, and fittingly is destroyed by horses in retribution for having killed the noble Falada. The Oedipal situation has been redressed, with the usurper serving as a scapegoat for the princess herself, who will believe no longer that her own mother was a usurper threatening the princess's true place, and whose story serves to warn other children against prolonging dependence with its attendant passivities. Here Bettelheim has been shrewd and observant, and his interpretation has a curious rightness.

Part Two: In Fairy Land" is a descent, and I suspect that it will please 13 fewer readers who have some care for romance and its interpretation. Bettelheim takes a series of the most famous tales — "Hansel and Gretel," "Little Red Riding Hood," "Jack and the Beanstalk," "Snow White," "Cinderella" among them — and tries to give rather straightforward Freudian readings that become less analyses of the texts, and rather more explanations of how and why young children *should* emerge with particular meanings to each story. Freud's belief that fairy tales lack a repressed element, a daemonic or uncanny aspect, is developed implicitly by Bettelheim's well-intentioned pleasure in uncovering only beneficent meanings, except in the instance of "Goldilocks and the Three Bears," which frustrates the analyst's best efforts, until he ends by condemning it as a story:

> Parents would like their daughters to remain eternally their little girls, 14
> and the child would like to believe that it is possible to evade the struggle of
> growing up. That is why the spontaneous reaction to "Goldilocks" is: "What
> a lovely story." But it is also why this story does not help the child to gain
> emotional maturity.

Why does "Goldilocks" fail Bettelheim? Because, as he says, it raises 15 questions which it does not answer, "while the greatest merit of a fairy story is that it gives answers, fantastic though these may overtly be, even to questions of which we are unaware because they perturb us only in our unconscious." The more unresolved a text, the less therapeutic, thus threatens to become a Bettelheimian formula. But "Goldilocks" presents problems for Bettelheim precisely because "the three bears form a happy family, where things proceed in such unison that no sexual or oedipal problems exist for them." Unable to break into the happily balanced world of Father Bear, Mother Bear, and Baby Bear, Goldilocks achieves "no resolution of the identity problem ..., no self-discovery, no becoming a new and independent person."

Bettelheim greatly prefers "Snow White" (which he recognizes as a precursor-text to "Goldilocks"), and his full, approving commentary upon "Snow White" ought therefore to be useful for assessing his interpretative method. I think that, as a reading, it fails, but the failure stems from the Freudian view of fairy tales as not belonging to the uncanny, to the sometimes Sublime world of romance. **16**

Before giving the gist of Bettelheim on "Snow White," let me venture a brief sketch of a different reading, one that would assume a repressed or daemonic component in the story. Ruskin, writing on "Fairy Stories" (1868), warned that their "fair deceit and innocent error ... cannot be interpreted nor restrained by a wilful purpose," including surely a therapeutic one. Fairy stories, as Ruskin observed, cannot be "removed altogether from their sphere of religious faith," since in them: "the good spirit descends gradually from an angel into a fairy, and the demon shrinks into a playful grotesque of diminutive malevolence." For Ruskin what is repressed most strongly in fairy tales is a world of angels and demons, a world of energies that transcend familial conflicts, and that offer irrational solutions to the sorrows of "growing up." Those energies inform "Snow White" as a fiction, but are either unseen or evaded by Bettelheim. **17**

What kind of a story is "Snow White," when an adult encounters it again in a good translation of the Grimms? It is about as uncanny as Coleridge's "Christabel," would be an accurate answer, and it is hardly a paradigm for the process of maturing beyond Oedipal conflicts as Bettelheim wants it to be. Snow White's mother, like Christabel's, dies in childbirth. The relations between her wicked and disguised stepmother and Snow White, during the three attempts to murder the girl, are about as equivocal as the Sapphic encounters between Geraldine and Christabel. Trying to kill a girl by successively tight-lacing her, combing her hair with a poisoned comb, and sharing a partly poisoned apple with her — all these testify to a mutual sexual attraction between Snow White and her stepmother. The stepmother's desire to devour the liver and lungs of Snow White is demonic in itself, but takes on a particularly uncanny luster in the primal narcissim of a tale dominated by mirrors. When the tale ends, the wicked stepmother, dressed in her most beautiful clothes, has danced herself to death in red-hot slippers at the wedding feast of Snow White, a horror that is an expressive emblem of her frustrated desires. **18**

Bettelheim seems on the verge of taking these hints as when, in one instance, he says: "That which is symbolized by the apple in 'Snow White' is something mother and daughter have in common which runs even deeper than their jealousy of each other — their mature sexual desires," to which I would add: "for each other," but that is to see a repressed element in a text where Bettelheim, faithful to Freud, cannot bear to see it. Where there is romance, I would argue, there *must* be re- **19** pression, because enchantment is necessarily founded upon partial or misleading knowledge. Whatever the uses of enchantment may or may not be, the continuity of enchantment depends upon the ability of the enchanted reader or lover to sustain repression.

Bettelheim says of the stepmother's terrible end that: "Untrammeled 20 sexual jealousy, which tries to ruin others, destroys itself," by which he means the stepmother's supposed jealousy of a love between Snow White and the father, but the father is nowhere involved in the story. All the text tells us is that the stepmother envies a beauty that is greater than her own, in the opinion of her mirror, which after all must represent her own repressed opinion. Rather desperately, Bettelheim tries to import the father into the text in the figure of the hunter assigned to kill Snow White No moment in his book is lamer than Bettelheim's explanation for his naming the hunter as the royal father:

> At that time princes and princesses were as rare as they are today, and 21
> fairy tales simply abound with them. But when and where these stories origi-
> nated, hunting was an aristocratic privilege, which supplies a good reason to
> see the hunter as an exalted figure like a father.

What can we do with this mode of interpretation, except to see it as con- 22 firming Ruskin's admonition against substituting the moral will for the spirit of the text?

Yet Bettelheim's moral will is so admirable that we are (and ought to 23 be) uneasy at seeing him interpret so weakly. "Who is the interpreter and what power does he seek to gain over the text?" is the question that Nietzsche taught us to ask of every interpretation. Here the answer is: a benign healer of children is the interpreter, and his will-to-power is a will-to-health for young children who so badly require it. In the presence of motives so authentic and admirable as Bettelheim's, I feel a sense of shame in yet urging interpretation that would be closer, and better suited, to the daemonic text itself.

Bettelheim's polemic, as he keeps saying, is against a modern tradi- 24 tion in which parents have deprived their children of fairy tales, because they supposedly wished to protect the children from the pervasive violence of so many of the tales. I suspect that the true motive of many parents was founded rather upon a troubled apprehension, one that Freud, in his ambivalence toward romance, could not allow himself. "Snow White" is as Gnostic in its sexual and spiritual overtones as "Christabel" is; both are romances that set themselves *contra naturam.*

Bettelheim's book is pragmatically right, but for the wrong reasons. 25 Yes, fairy tales are good for young children, and for all the rest of us, but not because they are paradigms or parables that teach us how to adjust to an adult reality. They are good for us because their uncanny energies liberate our potential for the Sublime, for that little beyond ourselves that reason, nature, and society together cannot satisfy. As told by Bettelheim, a fairy tale may help a particular child, but the larger teaching of the tale, rather than the teller, is that the instinct for Sublime experience can never be satisfied, except perhaps by romance, human and literary.

Study Question

1. Why is Bloom's introduction more appropriate than Lurie's?
2. How does Bloom help us to understand the points he raises even if we haven't read Bettelheim's book?
3. To what extent do the last two paragraphs change the effect of that which precedes them?
4. Which of the two reviewers seems the more reasonable? Why?

Eric Hoffer
THE ROLE OF THE UNDESIRABLES

Eric Hoffer (1902–   ) was born in New York City. A philosophical writer who has had a lifelong passion for books, he has been compared to such diverse personalities as Machiavelli and the Duc de La Rochefoucauld. Hoffer early felt the stifling complexities of the big city and moved to California at the first opportunity. There he worked in a box factory, as a migrant field hand, in the gold mines and in construction, finally coming to rest in San Francisco, where he was a longshoreman for some twenty years. At present he holds weekly seminars at the University of California at Berkeley, where he has refused a full-time professorship. A logical, somewhat cold, and pessimistic writer, Hoffer nonetheless sees great potential for human growth. His first book, *The True Believer* (1951), won for him the Commonwealth Club of California Gold Medal in 1952. Other publications include *The Passionate State of Mind* (1955), *First Things, Last Things* (1971), *Reflections on the Human Condition* (1973), and a Journal of his waterfront days, which was published in 1969.

In the winter of 1934, I spent several weeks in a federal transient camp in California. These camps were originally established by Governor Rolph in the early days of the Depression to care for the single homeless unemployed of the state. In 1934 the federal government took charge of the camps for a time, and it was then that I first heard of them.

How I happened to get into one of the camps is soon told. Like 2 thousands of migrant agricultural workers in California I then followed the crops from one part of the state to the other. Early in 1934 I arrived in the town of El Centro, in the Imperial Valley. I had been given a free ride on a truck from San Diego, and it was midnight when the truck driver dropped me on the outskirts of El Centro. I spread my bedroll by the side of the road and went to sleep. I had hardly dozed off when the rattle of a motorcycle drilled itself into my head and a policeman was bending over me saying, "Roll up, Mister." It looked as though I was in for something; it happened now and then that the police got overzealous and rounded up the freight trains. But this time the cop had no such thought. He said, "Better go over to the federal shelter and get yourself a bed and maybe some breakfast." He directed me to the place.

I found a large hall, obviously a former garage, dimly lit, and packed 3 with cots. A concert of heavy breathing shook the thick air. In a small office near the door, I was registered by a middle-aged clerk. He informed me that this was the "receiving shelter" where I would get one night's lodging and breakfast. The meal was served in the camp nearby. Those who wished to stay on, he said, had to enroll in the camp. He then gave me three blankets and excused himself for not having a vacant cot. I spread the blankets on the cement floor and went to sleep.

I awoke with dawn amid a chorus of coughing, throat-clearing, the 4 sound of running water, and the intermittent flushing of toilets in the back of the hall. There were about fifty of us, of all colors and ages, all of us more or less ragged and soiled. The clerk handed out tickets for breakfast, and we filed out to the camp located several blocks away, near the railroad tracks.

From the outside the camp looked like a cross between a factory and 5 a prison. A high fence of wire enclosed it, and inside were three large sheds and a huge boiler topped by a pillar of black smoke. Men in blue shirts and dungarees were strolling across the sandy yard. A ship's bell in front of one of the buildings announced breakfast. The regular camp members — there was a long line of them — ate first. Then we filed in through the gate, handing our tickets to the guard.

It was a good, plentiful meal. After breakfast our crowd dispersed. I 6 heard some say that the camps in the northern part of the state were better, that they were going to catch a northbound freight. I decided to try this camp in El Centro.

My motives in enrolling were not crystal clear. I wanted to clean up. 7 There were shower baths in the camp and wash tubs and plenty of soap. Of course I could have bathed and washed my clothes in one of the irrigation ditches, but here in the camp I had a chance to rest, get the wrinkles out of my belly, and clean up at leisure. In short, it was the easiest way out.

A brief interview at the camp office and a physical examination were 8 all the formalities for enrollment.

There were some two hundred men in the camp. They were the kind 9

I had worked and traveled with for years. I even saw familiar faces — men I had worked with in orchards and fields. Yet my predominant feeling was one of strangeness. It was my first experience of life in intimate contact with a crowd. For it is one thing to work and travel with a gang, and quite another thing to eat, sleep, and spend the greater part of the day cheek by jowl with two hundred men.

I found myself speculating on a variety of subjects: the reasons for 10 their chronic bellyaching and beefing — it was more a ritual than the expression of a grievance; the amazing orderliness of the men; the comic seriousness with which they took their games of cards, checkers, and dominoes; the weird manner of reasoning one overheard now and then. Why, I kept wondering were these men within the enclosure of a federal transient camp? Were they people temporarily hard up? Would jobs solve all their difficulties? Were we indeed like the people outside?

Up to then I was not aware of being one of a specific species of hu- 11 manity. I had considered myself simply a human being — not particularly good or bad, and on the whole harmless. The people I worked and traveled with I knew as Americans and Mexicans, whites and Negroes, Northerners and Southerners, etc. It did not occur to me that we were a group possessed of peculiar traits, and that there was something — innate or acquired — in our make-up which made us adopt a particular mode of existence.

It was a slight thing that started me on a new track. 12

I got to talking to a mild-looking, elderly fellow. I liked his soft 13 speech and pleasant manner. We swapped trivial experiences. Then he suggested a game of checkers. As we started to arrange the pieces on the board, I was startled by the sight of his crippled right hand. I had not noticed it before. Half of it was chopped off lengthwise, so that the horny stump with its three fingers looked like a hen's leg. I was mortified that I had not noticed the hand until he dangled it, so to speak, before my eyes. It was, perhaps, to bolster my shaken confidence in my powers of observation that I now began paying close attention to the hands of the people around me. The result was astounding. It seemed that every other man had had his hand mangled. There was a man with one arm. Some men limped. One young, good-looking fellow had a wooden leg. It was as though the majority of the men had escaped the snapping teeth of a machine and left part of themselves behind.

It was, I knew, an exaggerated impression. But I began counting the 14 cripples as the men lined up in the yard at mealtime. I found thirty (out of two hundred) crippled either in arms or legs. I immediately sensed where the counting would land me. The simile preceded the statistical deduction: we in the camp were a human junk pile.

I began evaluating my fellow tramps as human material, and for the 15 first time in my life I became face-conscious. There were some good faces, particularly among the young. Several of the middle-aged and the old looked healthy and well preserved. But the damaged and decayed faces were in the majority. I saw faces that were wrinkled, or bloated, or raw as the surface of a peeled plum. Some of the noses were purple and swollen, some broken, some pitted with enlarged pores. There were many toothless mouths (I counted seventy-eight). I noticed eyes that were blurred, faded, opaque, or bloodshot. I was struck by the fact that the old men, even the very old, showed their age mainly in the face. Their bodies were still slender and erect. One little man over sixty years of age looked a mere boy when seen from behind. The shriveled face joined to a boyish body made a startling sight.

My diffidence had now vanished. I was getting to know everybody in the camp. They were a friendly and talkative lot. Before many weeks I knew some essential fact about practically everyone. 16

And I was continually counting. Of the two hundred men in the camp there were approximately as follows: 17

Cripples	30
Confirmed drunkards	60
Old men (55 and over)	50
Youths under twenty	10
Men with chronic diseases, heart, asthma, TB	12
Mildly insane	4
Constitutionally lazy	6
Fugitives from justice	4
Apparently normal	70

(The numbers do not tally up to two hundred since some of the men were counted twice or even thrice—as cripples and old, or as old and confirmed drunks, etc.)

In other words: less than half the camp inmates (seventy normal, plus ten youths) were unemployed workers whose difficulties would be at an end once jobs were available. The rest (60 per cent) had handicaps in addition to unemployment. 18

I also counted fifty war veterans, and eighty skilled workers representing sixteen trades. All the men (including those with chronic diseases) were able to work. The one-armed man was a wizard with the shovel. 19

I did not attempt any definite measurement of character and intelligence. But it seemed to me that the intelligence of the men in the camp was certainly not below the average. And as to character, I found much forbearance and genuine good humor. I never came across one instance of real viciousness. Yet, on the whole, one would hardly say that these men were possessed of strong characters. Resistance, whether to one's appetites or to the ways of the world, is a chief factor in the shaping of character; and the average tramp is, more or less, a slave of his few appetites. He generally takes the easiest way out. 20

The connection between our make-up and our mode of existence as migrant workers presented itself now with some clarity. 21

The majority of us were incapable of holding onto a steady job. We lacked self-discipline and the ability to endure monotonous, leaden hours. We were probably misfits from the very beginning. Our contact with a steady job was not unlike a collision. Some of us were maimed, some got frightened and ran away, and some took to drink. We inevitably drifted 22 in the direction of least resistance – the open road. The life of a migrant worker is varied and demands only a minimum of self-discipline. We were now in one of the drainage ditches of ordered society. We could not keep a footing in the ranks of respectability and were washed into the slough of our present existence.

Yet, I mused, there must be in this world a task with an appeal so 23 strong that were we to have a taste of it we would hold on and be rid for good of our restlessness.

My stay in the camp lasted about four weeks. Then I found a haying 24 job not far from town, and finally, in April, when the hot winds began blowing, I shouldered my bedroll and took the highway to San Bernardino.

It was the next morning, after I had got a lift to Indio by truck, that 25 a new idea began to take hold of me. The highway out of Indio leads through waving date groves, fragrant grapefruit orchards, and lush alfalfa fields; then, abruptly, passes into a desert of white sand. The sharp line between garden and desert is very striking. The turning of white sand into garden seemed to me an act of magic. This, I thought, was a job one would jump at – even the men in the transient camps. They had the skill and ability of the average American. But their energies, I felt, could be quickened only by a task that was spectacular, that had in it something of the miraculous. The pioneer task of making the desert flower would certainly fill the bill.

Tramps as pioneers? It seemed absurd. Every man and child in California knows that the pioneers had been giants, men of boundless courage and indomitable spirit. However, as I strode on across the white sand, I kept mulling the idea over.

Who were the pioneers? Who were the men who left their homes 27 and went into the wilderness? A man rarely leaves a soft spot and goes deliberately in search of hardship and privation. People become attached to the places they live in; they drive roots. A change of habitat is a painful act of uprooting. A man who has made good and has a standing in his community stays put. The successful businessmen, farmers, and workers usually stayed where they were. Who then left for the wilderness and the unknown? Obviously those who had not made good: men who went broke or never amounted to much; men who though possessed of abilities were too impulsive to stand the daily grind; men who were slaves of their appetites – drunkards, gamblers, and woman-chasers; outcasts – fugitives from justice and ex-jailbirds. There were no doubt some who went in search of health – men suffering with TB, asthma, heart trouble. Finally there was a sprinkling of young and middle-aged in search of adventure.

All these people craved change, some probably actuated by the naive 28 belief that a change in place brings with it a change in luck. Many wanted to go to a place where they were not known and there make a new beginning. Certainly they did not go out deliberately in search of hard work and suffering. If in the end they shouldered enormous tasks, endured unspeakable hardships, and accomplished the impossible, it was because they had to. They became men of action on the run. They acquired strength and skill in the inescapable struggle for existence. It was a question of do or die. And once they tasted the joy of achievement, they craved for more.

Clearly the same types of people which now swelled the ranks of migratory workers and tramps had probably in former times made up the bulk of the pioneers. As a group the pioneers were probably as unlike the present-day "native sons"—their descendants—as one could well imagine. Indeed, were there to be today a new influx of typical pioneers, twin brothers of the forty-niners only in a modern garb, the citizens of California would consider it a menace to health, wealth, and morals. 29

With few exceptions, this seems to be the case in the settlement of all new countries. Ex-convicts were the vanguard in the settling of Australia. Exiles and convicts settled Siberia. In this country, a large portion of our earlier and later settlers were failures, fugitives, and felons. The exceptions seemed to be those who were motivated by religious fervor, such as the Pilgrim Fathers and the Mormons. 30

Although quite logical, this train of thought seemed to me then a wonderful joke. In my exhilaration I was eating up the road in long strides, and I reached the oasis of Elim in what seemed almost no time. A passing empty truck picked me up just then and we thundered through Banning and Beaumont, all the way to Riverside. From there I walked the seven miles to San Bernardino 31

Somehow, this discovery of a family likeness between tramps and pioneers took a firm hold on my mind. For years afterward it kept intertwining itself with a mass of observations which on the face of them had no relation to either tramps or pioneers. And it moved me to speculate on subjects in which, up to then, I had no real interest, and of which I knew very little. 32

I talked with several old-timers—one of them over eighty and a native son—in Sacramento, Placerville, Auburn, and Fresno. It was not easy, at first, to obtain the information I was after. I could not make my questions specific enough. "What kind of people were the early settlers and miners?" I asked. They were a hard-working, tough lot, I was told. They drank, fought, gambled, and wenched. They were big-hearted, grasping, profane, and God-fearing. They wallowed in luxury, or lived on next to nothing with equal ease. They were the salt of the earth. 33

Still it was not clear what manner of people they were. 34

If I asked what they looked like, I was told of whiskers, broadbrimmed hats, high boots, shirts of many colors, sun-tanned faces, horny hands. Finally I asked: "What group of people in present-day California most closely resembles the pioneers?" The answer, usually after some hesitation, was invariably the same: "The Okies and the fruit tramps." 35

I tried also to evaluate the tramps as potential pioneers by watching them in action. I saw them fell timber, clear firebreaks, build rock walls, put up barracks, build dams and roads, handle steam shovels, bulldozers, tractors, and concrete mixers. I saw them put in a hard day's work after a night of steady drinking. They sweated and growled, but they did the work. I saw tramps elevated to positions of authority as foremen and superintendents. Then I could notice a remarkable physical transformation: a seamed face gradually smoothed out and the skin showed a healthy 36 hue; an indifferent mouth became firm and expressive; dull eyes cleared and brightened; voices actually changed; there was even an apparent increase in stature. In almost no time these promoted tramps looked as if they had been on top all of their lives. Yet sooner or later I would meet up with them again in a railroad yard, on some skid row, or in the fields—tramps again. It was usually the same story: they got drunk or lost their temper and were fired, or they got fed up with the steady job and quit. Usually, when a tramp becomes a foreman, he is careful in his treatment of the tramps under him; he knows the day of reckoning is never far off.

In short, it was not difficult to visualize the tramps as pioneers. I re- 37
flected that if they were to find themselves in a singlehanded life-and-death struggle with nature, they would undoubtedly display persistence. For the pressure of responsibility and the heat of battle steel a character. The inadaptable would perish, and those who survived would be the equal of the successful pioneers.

I also considered the few instances of pioneering engineered from 38 above—that is to say, by settlers possessed of lavish means, who were classed with the best where they came from. In these instances, it seemed to me, the resulting social structure was inevitably precarious. For pioneering deluxe usually results in a plantation society, made up of large landowners and peon labor, either native or imported. Very often there is a racial cleavage between the two. The colonizing activities of the Teutonic barons in the Baltic, the Hungarian nobles in Transylvania, the English in Ireland, the planters in our South, and present-day plantation societies in Kenya and other British and Dutch colonies are cases in point. Whatever their merits, they are characterized by poor adaptability. They are likely eventually to be broken up either by a peon revolution or by an influx of typical pioneers—who are usually of the same race or nation as the landowners. The adjustment is not necessarily implemented by war. Even our old South, had it not been for the complication of secession, might eventually have attained stability without war: namely, by the activity of its own poor whites or by influx of the indigent from other states.

There is in us a tendency to judge a race, a nation, or an organization 39 by its least worthy members. The tendency is manifestly perverse and unfair; yet it has some justification. For the quality and destiny of a nation is determined to a considerable extent by the nature and potentialities of its inferior elements. The inert mass of a nation is in its middle section. The industrious, decent, well-to-do, and satisfied middle classes—whether in cities or on the land—are worked upon and shaped by minorities at both extremes: the best and the worst.

The superior individual, whether in politics, business, industry, 40 science, literature, or religion, undoubtedly plays a major role in the shaping of a nation. But so do the individuals at the other extreme: the poor, the outcasts, the misfits, and those who are in the grip of some overpowering passion. The importance of these inferior elements as formative factors lies in the readiness with which they are swayed in any direction. This peculiarity is due to their inclination to take risks ("not giving a damn") and their propensity for united action. They crave to merge their drab, wasted lives into something grand and complete. Thus they are the first and most fervent adherents of new religions, political upheavals, patriotic hysteria, gangs, and mass rushes to new lands.

And the quality of a nation — its innermost worth — is made manifest 41 by its dregs as they rise to the top: by how brave they are, how humane, how orderly, how skilled, how generous, how independent or servile; by the bounds they will not transgress in their dealings with man's soul, with truth, and with honor.

The average American of today bristles with indignation when he is 42 told that this country was built, largely, by hordes of undesirables from Europe. Yet, far from being derogatory, this statement, if true, should be a cause for rejoicing, should fortify our pride in the stock from which we have sprung.

This vast continent with its towns, farms, factories, dams, aqueducts, 43 docks, railroads, highways, powerhouses, schools, and parks is the handiwork of common folk from the Old World, where for centuries men of their kind had been as beasts of burden, the property of the masters — kings, nobles, and priests — and with no will and no aspirations of their own. When on rare occasions one of the lowly had reached the top in Europe he had kept the pattern intact and, if anything, tightened the screws. The stuffy little corporal from Corsica harnessed the lusty forces released by the French Revolution to a gilded state coach, and could think of nothing grander than mixing his blood with that of the Hapsburg masters and establishing a new dynasty. In our day a bricklayer in Italy, a house painter in Germany, and a shoemaker's son in Russia have made themselves masters of their nations; what they did was to re-establish and reinforce the old pattern.

Only here, in America, were the common folk of the Old World 44 given a chance to show what they could do on their own, without a master to push and order them about. History contrived an earth-shaking joke when it lifted by the nape of the neck lowly peasants, shopkeepers, laborers, paupers, jailbirds, and drunks from the midst of Europe, dumped them on a vast, virgin continent and said: "Go to it, it is yours!"

And the lowly were not awed by the magnitude of the task. A hun- 45 ger for action, pent up for centuries, found an outlet. They went to it with ax, pick, shovel, plow, and rifle; on foot, on horse, in wagons, and on flatboats. They went to it praying, howling, singing, brawling, drinking, and fighting. Make way for the people! This is how I read the statement that this country was built by hordes of undesirables from the Old World.

Small wonder that we in this country have a deeply ingrained faith in 46 human regeneration. We believe that, given a chance, even the degraded and the apparently worthless are capable of constructive work and great deeds. It is a faith founded on experience, not on some idealistic theory. And no matter what some anthropologists, sociologists, and geneticists may tell us, we shall go on believing that man, unlike other forms of life, is not a captive of his past — of his heredity and habits — but is possessed of infinite plasticity, and his potentialities for good and for evil are never wholly exhausted.

Study Questions

1. Hoffer's point is long in coming, in being expressed. Why? How does he achieve immediacy in coming to that point?
2. Are the categories presented in paragraph 17 mutually exclusive? How important to the argument is your answer?
3. What function is served by the garden-desert images in paragraph 25?
4. Suggest any two paragraphs that could be effectively combined.
5. What does first-person point contribute to the argument?
6. The sentences frequently contain series or lists. What rhetorical purpose do such lists serve?

Max Shulman
LOVE IS A FALLACY

Max Shulman (1919–   ) was born in St. Paul and received his A.B. from the University of Minnesota (1942). He served with the Army Air Force from 1942 to 1946. Later his short stories began appearing in such periodicals as *Saturday Evening Post, Good Housekeeping, Esquire,* and *Mademoiselle.* His writing credits include fiction — *Barefoot Boy With Cheek* (1943), *The Feather Merchants* (1944), and *Rally Round the Flag, Boys!* (1957; movie scripts — *Confidentially Connie, The Affairs of Dobie Gillis, Half a Hero* and *The Tender Trap;* Broadway musical comedies — *How Now Dow Jones* (1967) and *Potatoes Are Cheaper* (1971); and authorship of the television series, "Dobie Gillis."

Charles Lamb, as merry and enterprising a fellow as you will meet in a month of Sundays, unfettered the informal essay with his memorable *Old China* and *Dream Children.* There follows an informal essay that ventures even beyond Lamb's frontier. Indeed, "informal" may not be quite the right word to describe this essay; "limp" or "flaccid" or possibly "spongy" are perhaps more appropriate.

Vague though its category, it is without doubt an essay. It develops an argument; it cites instances; it reaches a conclusion. Could Carlyle do more? Could Ruskin?

Read, then, the following essay which undertakes to demonstrate that logic, far from being a dry, pedantic discipline, is a living, breathing thing, full of beauty, passion, and trauma.

— AUTHOR'S NOTE

Cool was I and logical. Keen, calculating, perspicacious, acute 1 and astute — I was all of these. My brain was as powerful as a dynamo, as precise as a chemist's scales, as penetrating as a scalpel. And — think of it! — I was only eighteen.

It is not often that one so young has such a giant intellect. Take, for 2 example, Petey Burch, my roommate at the University of Minnesota. Same age, same background, but dumb as an ox. A nice enough fellow, you understand, but nothing upstairs. Emotional type, unstable. Impressionable. Worst of all, a faddist. Fads, I submit are the very negation of reason. To be swept up in every new craze that comes along, to surrender yourself to idiocy just because everybody else is doing it — this, to me, is the acme of mindlessness. Not, however, to Petey.

One afternoon I found Petey lying on his bed with an expression of 3 such distress on his face that I immediately diagnosed appendicitis. "Don't move," I said. "Don't take a laxative. I'll get a doctor."

"Raccoon," he mumbled thickly.   4

"Raccoon?" I said, pausing in my flight.   5

"I want a raccoon coat," he wailed.   6

I perceived that his trouble was not physical, but mental. "Why do 7 you want a raccoon coat?"

"I should have known it," he cried, pounding his temples. "I should 8 have known they'd come back when the Charleston came back. Like a fool I spent all my money for textbooks, and now I can't get a raccoon coat."

"Can you mean," I said incredulously, "that people are actually wear- 9 ing raccoon coats again?"

"All the Big Men on Campus are wearing them. Where've you 10 been?"

"In the library," I said, naming a place not frequented by Big Men 11 on Campus.

He leaped from the bed and paced the room. "I've got to have a rac- 12 coon coat," he said passionately. "I've got to!"

"Petey, why? Look at it rationally. Raccoon coats are unsanitary. 13 They shed. They smell bad. They weigh too much. They're unsightly. They —"

"You don't understand," he interrupted impatiently. "It's the thing to 14 do. Don't you want to be in the swim?"

"No," I said truthfully.   15

"Well, I do," he declared. "I'd give anything for a raccoon coat. Any- 16
thing!"

My brain, that precision instrument, slipped into high gear. "Any- 17
thing?" I asked, looking at him narrowly.

"Anything," he affirmed in ringing tones.   18

I stroked my chin thoughtfully. It so happened that I knew where to 19
get my hands on a raccoon coat. My father had had one in his under-
graduate days; it lay now in a trunk in the attic back home. It also happened that Petey had something I wanted. He didn't *have* it exactly, but
at least he had first rights on it. I refer to his girl, Polly Espy.

I had long coveted Polly Espy. Let me emphasize that my desire for 20
this young woman was not emotional in nature. She was, to be sure, a
girl who excited the emotions, but I was not one to let my heart rule my
head. I wanted Polly for a shrewdly calculated, entirely cerebral reason.

I was a freshman in law school. In a few years I would be out in 21
practice. I was well aware of the importance of the right kind of wife in
furthering a lawyer's career. The successful lawyers I had observed were,
almost without exception, married to beautiful, gracious, intelligent
women. With one omission, Polly fitted these specifications perfectly.

Beautiful she was. She was not yet of pin-up proportions, but I felt 22
sure that time would supply the lack. She already had the makings.

Gracious she was. By gracious I mean full of graces. She had an 23
erectness of carriage, an easè of bearing, a poise that clearly indicated the
best of breeding. At table her manners were exquisite. I had seen her at
the Kozy Kampus Korner eating the speciality of the house—a sandwich
that contained scraps of pot roast, gravy, chopped nuts, and a dipper of
sauerkraut—without even getting her fingers moist.

Intelligent she was not. In fact, she veered in the opposite direction. 24
But I believed that under my guidance she would smarten up. At any
rate, it was worth a try. It is, after all, easier to make a beautiful dumb
girl smart than to make an ugly smart girl beautiful.

"Petey," I said, "are you in love with Polly Espy?"   25

"I think she's a keen kid," he replied, "but I don't know if you'd call 26
it love. Why?"

"Do you," I asked, "have any kind of formal arrangement with her? I 27
mean are you going steady or anything like that?"

"No. We see each other quite a bit, but we both have other dates. 28
Why?"

"Is there," I asked, "any other man for whom she has a particular 29
fondness?"

"Not that I know of. Why?"   30

I nodded with satisfaction. "In other words, if you were out of the 31
picture, the field would be open. Is that right?"

"I guess so. What are you getting at?"   32

"Nothing, nothing," I said innocently, and took my suitcase out of 33
the closet.

"Where are you going?" asked Petey.   34

"Home for the weekend." I threw a few things into the bag.   35

"Listen," he said, clutching my arm eagerly, "while you're home, you 36
couldn't get some money from your old man, could you, and lend it to
me so I can buy a raccoon coat?"

"I may do better than that," I said with a mysterious wink and closed 37
my bag and left.

"Look," I said to Petey when I got back Monday morning. I threw 38
open the suitcase and revealed the huge, hairy, gamy object that my father had worn in his Stutz Bearcat in 1925.

"Holy Toledo!" said Petey reverently. He plunged his hands into the 39
raccoon coat and then his face. "Holy Toledo!" he repeated fifteen or
twenty times.

"Would you like it?" I asked.   40

"Oh yes!" he cried, clutching the greasy pelt to him. Then a canny 41
look came into his eyes. "What do you want for it?"

"Your girl," I said, mincing no words.   42

"Polly?" he said in a horrified whisper. "You want Polly?"   43

"That's right."   44

He flung the coat from him. "Never," he said stoutly.   45

I shrugged. "Okay. If you don't want to be in the swim, I guess it's 46
your business."

I sat down in a chair and pretended to read a book, but out of the 47
corner of my eye I kept watching Petey. He was a torn man. First he
looked at the coat with the expression of a waif at a bakery window.
Then he turned away and set his jaw resolutely. Then he looked back at
the coat, with even more longing in his face. Then he turned away, but
with not so much resolution this time. Back and forth his head swiveled,
desire waxing, resolution waning. Finally he didn't turn away at all; he
just stood and stared with mad lust at the coat.

"It isn't as though I was in love with Polly," he said thickly. "Or go- 48
ing steady or anything like that."

"That's right," I murmured.   49

"What's Polly to me, or me to Polly?"   50

"Not a thing," said I.   51

"It's just been a casual kick — just a few laughs, that's all."   52

"Try on the coat," said I.   53

He complied. The coat bunched high over his ears and dropped all 54
the way down to his shoe tops. He looked like a mound of dead rac-
coons. "Fits fine," he said happily.

I rose from my chair. "Is it a deal?" I asked, extending my hand.   55

He swallowed. "It's a deal," he said and shook my hand.   56

I had my first date with Polly the following evening. This was in the 57
nature of a survey; I wanted to find out just how much work I had to do
to get her mind up to the standard I required. I took her first to dinner.
"Gee, that was a delish dinner," she said as we left the restaurant. Then I
took her to a movie. "Gee, that was a marvy movie," she said as we left
the theater. And then I took her home. "Gee, I had a sensaysh time," she
said as she bade me good night.

I went back to my room with a heavy heart. I had gravely under- 58 estimated the size of my task. This girl's lack of information was terrifying. Nor would it be enough merely to supply her with information. First she had to be taught to *think*. This loomed as a project of no small dimensions, and at first I was tempted to give her back to Petey. But then I got to thinking about her abundant physical charms and about the way she entered the room and the way she handled a knife and fork, and I decided to make an effort.

I went about it, as in all things, systematically. I gave her a course in 59 logic. It happened that I, as a law student, was taking a course in logic myself, so I had all the facts at my finger tips. "Polly," I said to her when I picked her up on our next date, "tonight we are going over to the Knoll and talk."

"Oo, terrif," she replied. One thing I will say for this girl: you would 60 go far to find another so agreeable.

We went to the Knoll, the campus trysting place, and we sat down 61 under an old oak, and she looked at me expectantly. "What are we going to talk about?" she asked.

"Logic."
                                                                                  62
She thought this over for a minute and decided she liked it. "Magnif," 63 she said.

"Logic," I said, clearing my throat, "is the science of thinking. Before 64 we can think correctly, we must first learn to recognize the common fallacies of logic. These we will take up tonight."

"Wow-dow!" she cried, clapping her hands delightedly.   65

I winced, but went bravely on. "First let us examine the fallacy called 66 Dicto Simpliciter."

"By all means," she urged, batting her lashes eagerly.   67

"Dicto Simpliciter means an argument based on a unqualified gen- 68 eralization. For example: Exercise is good. Therefore everybody should exercise."

"I agree," said Polly earnestly. "I mean exercise is wonderful. I mean 69 it builds the body and everything."

"Polly," I said gently, "the argument is a fallacy. *Exercise is good* is an 70 unqualified generalization. For instance, if you have heart disease, exercise is bad, not good. Many people are ordered by their doctors *not* to exercise. You must *qualify* the generalization. You must say exercise is *usually* good, or exercise is good *for most people*. Otherwise you have committed a Dicto Simpliciter. Do you see?"

"No," she confessed. "But this is marvy. Do more! Do more!"   71

"It will be better if you stop tugging at my sleeve," I told her, and 72 when she desisted, I continued. "Next we take up a fallacy called Hasty Generalization. Listen carefully: You can't speak French. I can't speak French. Petey Burch can't speak French. I must therefore conclude that nobody at the University of Minnesota can speak French."

"Really?" said Polly, amazed. *"Nobody?"*   73

I hid my exasperation. "Polly, it's a fallacy. The generalization is 74 reached too hastily. There are too few instances to support such a conclusion."

"Know any more fallacies?" she asked breathlessly. "This is more fun 75 than dancing even."

I fought off a wave of despair. I was getting nowhere with this girl, 76 absolutely nowhere. Still, I am nothing if not persistent. I continued. "Next comes Post Hoc. Listen to this: Let's not take Bill on our picnic. Every time we take him out with us, it rains."

"I know somebody just like that," she exclaimed. "A girl back 77 home — Eula Becker, her name is. It never fails. Every single time we take her on a picnic — "

"Polly," I said sharply, "it's a fallacy. Eula Becker doesn't *cause* the 78 rain. She has no connection with the rain. You are guilty of Post Hoc if you blame Eula Becker."

"I'll never do it again," she promised contritely. "Are you mad at 79 me?"

I sighed deeply. "No, Polly, I'm not mad."   80

"Then tell me some more fallacies."   81

"All right. Let's try Contradictory Premises."   82

"Yes, let's," she chirped, blinking her eyes happily.   83

I frowned, but plunged ahead. "Here's an example of Contradictory 84 Premises: If God can do anything, can He make a stone so heavy that He won't be able to lift it?"

"Of course," she replied promptly.   85

"But if He can do anything, He can lift the stone," I pointed out.   86

"Yeah," she said thoughtfully. "Well, then I guess He can't make the 87 stone."

"But He can do anything," I reminded her.   88

She scratched her pretty, empty head. "I'm all confused," she admit- 89 ted.

"Of course you are. Because when the premises of an argument con- 90 tradict each other, there can be no argument. If there is an irresistible force, there can be no immovable object. If there is an immovable object, there can be no irrisistible force. Get it?"

"Tell me some more of this keen stuff," she said eagerly.   91

I consulted my watch. "I think we'd better call it a night. I'll take you 92 home now, and you go over all the things you've learned. We'll have another session tomorrow night."

I deposited her at the girl's dormitory, where she assured me that 93 she had had a perfectly terrif evening, and I went glumly home to my room. Petey lay snoring in his bed, the raccoon coat huddled like a great hairy beast at his feet. For a moment I considered waking him and telling him that he could have his girl back. It seemed clear that my project was doomed to failure. The girl simply had a logic-proof head.

But then I reconsidered. I had wasted one evening; I might as well 94 waste another. Who knew? Maybe somewhere in the extinct crater of her mind, a few embers still smoldered. Maybe somehow I could fan them into flame. Admittedly it was not a prospect fraught with hope, but I decided to give it one more try.

Seated under the oak the next evening I said, "Our first fallacy 95
tonight is called Ad Misericordiam."

She quivered with delight.   96

"Listen closely," I said. "A man applies for a job. When the boss asks 97
him what his qualifications are, he replies that he has a wife and six children at home, the wife is a helpless cripple, the children have nothing to
eat, no clothes to wear, no shoes on their feet, there are no beds in the
house, no coal in the cellar, and winter is coming."

A tear rolled down each of Polly's pink cheeks. "Oh, this is awful, 98
awful," she sobbed.

"Yes, it's awful," I agreed, "but it's no argument. The man never an- 99
swered the boss's question about his qualifications. Instead he appealed
to the boss's sympathy. He committed the fallacy of Ad Misericordiam.
Do you understand?"

"Have you got a hankerchief?" she blubbered.   100

I handed her a hankerchief and tried to keep from screaming while 101
she wiped her eyes. "Next," I said in a carefully controlled tone, "we will
discuss False Analogy. Here is an example: Students should be allowed
to look at their textbooks during examinations. After all, surgeons have
X-rays to guide them during an operation, lawyers have briefs to guide
them during a trial, carpenters have blueprints to guide them when they
are building a house. Why, then, shouldn't students be allowed to look at
their textbooks during an examination?"

"There now," she said enthusiastically, "is the most marvy idea I've 102
heard in years."

"Polly," I said testily, "the argument is all wrong. Doctors, lawyers, 103
and carpenters aren't taking a test to see how much they have learned,
but students are. The situations are altogether different, and you can't
make an analogy between them."

"I still think it's a good idea," said Polly.   104

"Nuts," I muttered. Doggedly I pressed on. "Next we'll try Hypothe- 105
sis Contrary to Fact."

"Sounds yummy," was Polly's reaction.   106

"Listen: If Madame Curie had not happened to leave a photographic 107
plate in a drawer with a chunk of pitchblende, the world today would not
know about radium."

"True, true," said Polly, nodding her head. "Did you see the movie? 108
Oh, it just knocked me out. That Walter Pidgeon is so dreamy. I mean
he fractures me."

"If you can forget Mr. Pidgeon for a moment," I said coldly, "I 109
would like to point out that the statement is a fallacy. Maybe Madame
Curie would have discovered radium at some later date. Maybe somebody else would have discovered it. Maybe any number of things would
have happened. You can't start with a hypothesis that is not true and
then draw any supportable conclusions from it."

"They ought to put Walter Pidgeon in more pictures," said Polly. "I 110
hardly ever see him any more."

One more chance, I decided. But just one more. There is a limit to   111
what flesh and blood can bear. "The next fallacy is called Poisoning the
Well."

"How cute!" she gurgled.   112

"Two men are having a debate. The first one gets up and says, 'My   113
opponent is a notorious liar. You can't believe a word that he is going to
say.' Now, Polly, think. Think hard. What's wrong?"

I watched her closely as she knit her creamy brow in concentration.   114
Suddenly a glimmer of intelligence — the first I had seen — came into her
eyes. "It's not fair," she said with indignation. "It's not a bit fair. What
chance has the second man got if the first man calls him a liar before he
even begins talking?"

"Right!" I cried exultantly. "One hundred per cent right. It's not fair.
The first man has *poisoned the well* before anybody could drink from it.
He has hamstrung his opponent before he could even start. ... Polly, I'm
proud of you."

"Pshaw," she murmured, blushing with pleasure.   116

"You see, my dear, these things aren't so hard. All you have to do is   117
concentrate. Think — examine — evaluate. Come now, let's review everything we have learned."

"Fire away," she said with an airy wave of her hand.   118

Heartened by the knowledge that Polly was not altogether a cretin, I   119
began a long, patient review of all I had told her. Over and over and
over again I cited instances, pointed out flaws, kept hammering away
without let up. It was like digging a tunnel. At first everything was work,
sweat, and darkness. I had no idea when I would reach the light, or even
if I would. But I persisted. I pounded and clawed and scraped, and finally
I was rewarded. I saw a chink of light. And then the chink got bigger and
the sun came pouring in and all was bright.

Five grueling nights this took, but it was worth it. I had made a logi-   120
cian out of Polly; I had taught her to think. My job was done. She was
worthy of me at last. She was a fit wife for me, a proper hostess for my
many mansions, a suitable mother for my well-heeled children.

It must not be thought that I was without love for this girl. Quite the   121
contrary. Just as Pygmalion loved the perfect woman he had fashioned,
so I loved mine. I determined to acquaint her with my feelings at our
very next meeting. The time had come to change our relationship from
academic to romantic.

"Polly," I said when next we sat beneath our oak, "tonight we will   122
not discuss fallacies."

"Aw, gee," she said, disappointed.   123

"My dear," I said, favoring her with a smile, "we have now spent five   124
evenings together. We have gotten along splendidly. It is clear that we
are well matched."

"Hasty Generalization," said Polly brightly.   125

"I beg your pardon," said I.   126

"Hasty Generalization," she repeated. "How can you say that we are   127
well matched on the basis of only five dates?"

I chuckled with amusement. The dear child had learned her lessons 128
well. "My dear," I said, patting her hand in a tolerant manner, "five dates
is plenty. After all, you don't have to eat a whole cake to know that it's
good."

"False Analogy," said Polly promptly. "I'm not a cake. I'm a girl." 129

I chuckled with somewhat less amusement. The dear child had 130
learned her lessons perhaps too well. I decided to change tactics. Obviously the best approach was a simple, strong, direct declaration of love. I
paused for a moment while my massive brain chose the proper words.
Then I began:

"Polly, I love you. You are the whole world to me, and the moon 131
and the stars and the constellations of outer space. Please, my darling, say
that you will go steady with me, for if you will not, life will be meaningless. I will languish. I will refuse my meals. I will wander the face of
the earth, a shambling, hollow-eyed hulk."

There, I thought, folding my arms, that ought to do it.   132

"Ad Misericordiam," said Polly.   133

I ground my teeth. I was not Pygmalion; I was Frankenstein, and my 134
monster had me by the throat. Frantically I fought back the tide of panic
surging through me. At all costs I had to keep cool.

"Well, Polly," I said, forcing a smile, "you certainly have learned your 135
fallacies."

"You're darn right," she said with a vigorous nod.   136

"And who taught them to you, Polly?"   137

"You did."   138

"That's right. So you do owe me something, don't you, my dear? If I 139
hadn't come along you never would have learned about fallacies."

"Hypothesis Contrary to Fact," she said instantly.   140

I dashed perspiration from my brow. "Polly," I croaked, "you mustn't 141
take all these things so literally. I mean this is just classroom stuff. You
know that the things you learn in school don't have anything to do with
life."

"Dicto Simpliciter," she said, wagging her finger at me playfully. 142

That did it. I leaped to my feet, bellowing like a bull. "Will you or 143
will you not go steady with me?"

"I will not," she replied.   144

"Why not?" I demanded.   145

"Because this afternoon I promised Petey Burch that I would go 146
steady with him."

I reeled back, overcome with the infamy of it. After he promised, af- 147
ter he made a deal, after he shook my hand! "The rat!" I shrieked, kicking up great chunks of turf. "You can't go with him, Polly. He's a liar.
He's a cheat. He's a rat."

"Poisoning the Well," said Polly, "and stop shouting. I think shouting 148
must be a fallacy too."

With an immense effort of will, I modulated my voice. "All right," I 149
said. "You're a logician. Let's look at this thing logically. How could you
choose Petey Burch over me? Look at me — a brilliant student, a tremen-

dous intellectual, a man with an assured future. Look at Petey—a knot-head, a jitterbug, a guy who'll never know where his next meal is coming from. Can you give me one logical reason why you should go steady with Petey Burch?"

"I certainly can," declared Polly. "He's got a raccoon coat." 150

Study Questions

1. Is this an essay or a short story? How do you know?
2. Shulman repeatedly inverts normal subject-verb order. What does he accomplish by doing this?
3. This selection is entitled "Love Is a Fallacy." The narrator tells Polly that her "argument is a fallacy." The statements are similar in form. Are their meanings similar? Why?
4. By what means does Shulman characterize Polly?
5. Analyze in detail any one of the narrator's "logical" statements.

Woody Allen
MR. BIG

Woody Allen, or Allen Stewart Konigsberg (1935–   ) was born in Brooklyn. Although he has described himself as a student at both the Neighborhood School for Bit Players and the House of Vocal Cords, Allen actually attended New York University and City College of New York. Best known as the writer and star of such films as *Play It Again, Sam* (1972), *Everything You Always Wanted to Know About Sex But Were Afraid to Ask* (1972), *Sleeper* (1973), *Love and Death* (1975), and *Annie Hall* (1977), Allen also writes for television and stage. He is in addition a contributor to magazines, notably the *New Yorker* and *Playboy.* Two collections of his magazine pieces have been published; *Getting Even* (1971) and *Without Feathers* (1975). In the program for the stage production of *Play It Again, Sam,* Allen claims to have played the title role in *Lady Windermere's Fan,* Porgy in *Porgy and Bess,* and Willy Loman in *Mr. Roberts.*

I was sitting in my office, cleaning the debris out of my thirty- 1
eight and wondering where my next case was coming from. I like being a

private eye, and even though once in a while I've had my gums massaged with an automobile jack, the sweet smell of greenbacks makes it all worth it. Not to mention the dames, which are a minor preoccupation of mine that I rank just ahead of breathing. That's why, when the door to my office swung open and a long-haired blonde named Heather Butkiss came striding in and told me she was a nudie model and needed my help, my salivary glands shifted into third. She wore a short skirt and a tight sweater and her figure described a set of parabolas that could cause cardiac arrest in a yak.

"What can I do for you, sugar?"   2
"I want you to find someone for me."   3
"Missing person? Have you tried the police?"   4
"Not exactly, Mr. Lupowitz."   5
"Call me Kaiser, sugar. All right, so what's the scam?"   6
"God."   7
"God?"   8
"That's right, God. The Creator, the Underlying Principle, the First   9
Cause of Things, the All Encompassing. I want you to find Him for me."

I've had some fruit cakes up in the office before, but when they're   10
built like she was, you listened.

"Why?"   11
"That's my business, Kaiser. You just find Him."   12
"I'm sorry, sugar. You got the wrong boy."   13
"But why?"   14
"Unless I know all the facts," I said, rising.   15
"O.K., O.K.," she said, biting her lower lip. She straightened the   16
seam of her stocking, which was strictly for my benefit, but I wasn't buying any at the moment.

"Let's have it on the line, sugar."   17
"Well, the truth is—I'm not really a nudie model."   18
"No?"   19
"No. My name is not Heather Butkiss, either. It's Claire Rosensweig   20
and I'm a student at Vassar. Philosophy major. History of Western Thought and all that. I have a paper due January. On Western religion. All the other kids in the course will hand in speculative papers. But I want to *know*. Professor Grebanier said if anyone finds out for sure, they're a cinch to pass the course. And my dad's promised me a Mercedes if I get straight A's."

I opened a deck of Luckies and a pack of gum and had one of each.   21
Her story was beginning to interest me. Spoiled coed. High IQ and a body I wanted to know better.

"What does God look like?"   22
"I've never seen him."   23
"Well, how do you know He exists?"   24
"That's for you to find out."   25
"Oh, great. Then you don't know what he looks like? Or where to   26
begin looking?"

"No. Not really. Although I suspect he's everywhere. In the air, in   27
every flower, in you and I—and in this chair."

"Uh huh." So she was a pantheist. I made a mental note of it and   28
said I'd give her case a try—for a hundred bucks a day, expenses, and a
dinner date. She smiled and okayed the deal. We rode down in the eleva-
tor together. Outside it was getting dark. Maybe God did exist and
maybe He didn't, but somewhere in that city there were sure a lot of
guys who were going to try and keep me from finding out.

My first lead was Rabbi Itzhak Wiseman, a local cleric who owed me   29
a favor for finding out who was rubbing pork on his hat. I knew something was wrong when I spoke to him because he was scared. Real
scared.

"Of course there's a you-know-what, but I'm not even allowed to say   30
His name or He'll strike me dead, which I could never understand why
someone is so touchy about having his name said."

"You ever see Him?"   31

"Me? Are you kidding? I'm lucky I get to see my grandchildren."   32

"Then how do you know He exists?"   33

"How do I know? What kind of question is that? Could I get a suit   34
like this for fourteen dollars if there was no one up there? Here, feel a
gabardine—how can you doubt?"

"You got nothing more to go on?"   35

"Hey—what's the Old Testament? Chopped liver? How do you   36
think Moses got the Israelites out of Egypt? With a smile and a tap
dance? Believe me, you don't part the Red Sea with some gismo from
Korvette's. It takes power."

"So he's tough, eh?"   37

"Yes. Very tough. You'd think with all that success he'd be a lot   38
sweeter."

"How come you know so much?"   39

"Because we're the chosen people. He takes best care of us of all   40
His children, which I'd also like to someday discuss with Him."

"What do you pay Him for being chosen?"   41

"Don't ask."   42

So that's how it was. The Jews were into God for a lot. It was the   43
old protection racket. Take care of them in return for a price. And from
the way Rabbi Wiseman was talking, He soaked them plenty. I got into a
cab and made it over to Danny's Billiards on Tenth Avenue. The manager was a slimy little guy I didn't like.

"Chicago Phil here?"   44

"Who wants to know?"   45

I grabbed him by the lapels and took some skin at the same time.   46

"What, punk?"   47

"In the back," he said, with a change of attitude.   48

Chicago Phil. Forger, bank robber, strong-arm man, and avowed athe-   49
ist.

"The guy never existed, Kaiser. This is the straight dope. It's a big   50
hype. There's no Mr. Big. It's a syndicate. Mostly Sicilian. It's international. But there is no actual head. Except maybe the Pope."

"I want to meet the Pope."   51

"It can be arranged," he said, winking.   52

"Does the name Claire Rosensweig mean anything to you?"   53
"No."   54
"Heather Butkiss?"   55
"Oh, wait a minute. Sure. She's that peroxide job with the bazooms   56
from Radcliffe."
"Radcliffe? She told me Vassar."   57
"Well, she's lying. She's a teacher at Radcliffe. She was mixed up   58
with a philosopher for a while."
"Pantheist?"   59
"No. Empiricist, as I remember. Bad guy. Completely rejected Hegel   60
or any dialectical methodology."
"One of those."   61
"Yeah. He used to be a drummer with a jazz trio. Then he got   62
hooked on Logical Positivism. When that didn't work, he tried Pragma-
tism. Last I heard he stole a lot of money to take a course in Schopen-
hauer at Columbia. The mob would like to find him—or get their hands
on his textbooks so they can resell them."
"Thanks, Phil."   63
"Take it from me, Kaiser. There's no one out there. It's a void. I   64
couldn't pass all those bad checks or screw society the way I do if for
one second I was able to recognize any authentic sense of Being. The
universe is strictly phenomenological. Nothing's eternal. It's all meaningless."
"Who won the fifth at Aqueduct?"   65
"Santa Baby."   66
I had a beer at O'Rourke's and tried to add it all up, but it made no 67
sense at all. Socrates was a suicide—or so they said. Christ was murdered.
Nietzsche went nuts. If there was someone out there, He sure as hell
didn't want anybody to know it. And why was Claire Rosensweig lying
about Vassar? Could Descartes have been right? Was the universe dualis-
tic? Or did Kant hit it on the head when he postulated the existence of
God on moral grounds?
That night I had dinner with Claire. Ten minutes after the check   68
came, we were in the sack and, brother, you can have your Western
thought. She went through the kind of gymnastics that would have won
first prize in the Tia Juana Olympics. After, she lay on the pillow next to
me, her long blond hair sprawling. Our naked bodies still intertwined. I
was smoking and staring at the ceiling.
"Claire, what if Kierkegaard's right?"   69
"You mean?"   70
"If you can never really *know*. Only have faith."   71
"That's absurd."   72
"Don't be so rational."   73
"Nobody's being rational, Kaiser." She lit a cigarette. "Just don't get 74
ontological. Not now. I couldn't bear it if you were ontological with me."
She was upset. I leaned over and kissed her, and the phone rang. She   75
got it.
"It's for you."   76
The voice on the other end was Sergeant Reed of Homicide.   77

"You still looking for God?"   78
"Yeah."   79
"An all-powerful Being? Great Oneness, Creator of the Universe? 80
First Cause of All Things?"
"That's right."   81
"Somebody with that description just showed up at the morgue. You 82
better get down here right away."
"It was Him all right, and from the looks of Him it was a profes- 83
sional job.
"He was dead when they brought Him in."   84
"Where'd you find Him?"   85
"A warehouse on Delancey Street."   86
"Any clues?"   87
"It's the work of an existentialist. We're sure of that."   88
"How can you tell?"   89
"Haphazard way how it was done. Doesn't seem to be any system 90
followed. Impulse."
"A crime of passion?"   91
"You got it. Which means you're a suspect, Kaiser."   92
"Why me?"   93
"Everybody down at headquarters knows how you feel about Jas- 94
pers."
"That doesn't make me a killer."   95
"Not yet, but you're a suspect."   96
Outside on the street I sucked air into my lungs and tried to clear 97
my head. I took a cab over to Newark and got out and walked a block to
Giordino's Italian Restaurant. There, at a back table, was His Holiness. It
was the Pope, all right. Sitting with two guys I had seen in half a dozen
police line-ups.
"Sit down," he said, looking up from his fettucine. He held out a 98
ring. I gave him my toothiest smile, but didn't kiss it. It bothered him
and I was glad. Point for me.
"Would you like some fettucine?"   99
"No thanks, Holiness. But you go ahead."   100
"Nothing? Not even a salad?"   101
"I just ate."   102
"Suit yourself, but they make a great Rocquefort dressing here. Not 103
like at the Vatican, where you can't get a decent meal."
"I'll come right to the point, Pontiff. I'm looking for God."   104
"You came to the right person."   105
"Then He does exist?" They all found this very amusing and 106
laughed. The hood next to me said, "Oh, that's funny. Bright boy wants
to know if He exists."
I shifted my chair to get comfortable and brought the leg down on 107
his little toe. "Sorry." But he was steaming.
"Sure He exists, Lupowitz, but I'm the only one that communicates 108
with him. He speaks only through me."
"Why you, pal?"   109

"Because I got the red suit." 110

"This get-up?" 111

"Don't knock it. Every morning I rise, put on this red suit, and sud- 112 denly I'm a big cheese. It's all in the suit. I mean, face it, if I went around in slacks and a sports jacket, I couldn't get arrested religion-wise."

"Then it's a hype. There's no God." 113

"I don't know. But what's the difference? The money's good." 114

"You ever worry the laundry won't get your red suit back on time 115 and you'll be like the rest of us?"

"I use the special one-day service. I figure it's worth the extra few 116 cents to be safe."

"Name Claire Rosensweig mean anything to you?" 117

"Sure. She's in the science department at Bryn Mawr." 118

"Science, you say? Thanks." 119

"For what?" 120

"The answer, Pontiff." I grabbed a cab and shot over the George 121 Washington Bridge. On the way I stopped at my office and did some fast checking. Driving to Claire's apartment, I put the pieces together, and for the first time they fit. When I got there she was in a diaphanous peignoir and something seemed to be troubling her.

"God is dead. The police were here. They're looking for you. They 122 think an existentialist did it."

"No, sugar. It was you." 123

"What? Don't make jokes, Kaiser." 124

"It was you that did it." 125

"What are you saying?" 126

"You, baby. Not Heather Butkiss or Claire Rosensweig, but Doctor 127 Ellen Shepherd."

"How did you know my name?" 128

"Professor of physics at Bryn Mawr. The youngest one ever to head 129 a department there. At the midwinter Hop you get stuck on a jazz musi- cian who's heavily into philosophy. He's married, but that doesn't stop you. A couple of nights in the hay and it feels like love. But it doesn't work out because something comes between you. God. Y'see, sugar, he believed, or wanted to, but you, with your pretty little scientific mind, had to have absolute certainty."

"No, Kaiser, I swear." 130

"So you pretend to study philosophy because that gives you a chance 131 to eliminate certain obstacles. You get rid of Socrates easy enough, but Descartes takes over, so you use Spinoza to get rid of Descartes, but when Kant doesn't come through you have to get rid of him too."

"You don't know what you're saying." 132

"You made mincemeat out of Leibnitz, but that wasn't good enough 133 for you because you knew if anybody believed Pascal you were dead, so he had to be gotten rid of too, but that's where you made your mistake because you trusted Martin Buber. Except, sugar, he was soft. He belived in God, so you had to get rid of God yourself."

"Kaiser, you're mad!" 134

"No, baby, You posed as a pantheist and that gave you access to 135
Him — *if* He existed, which he did. He went with you to Shelby's party
and when Jason wasn't looking, you killed Him."

"Who the hell are Shelby and Jason?"   136

"What's the difference? Life's absurd now anyway."   137

"Kaiser," she said, suddenly trembling. "You wouldn't turn me in?"   138

"Oh yes, baby. When the Supreme Being gets knocked off, *somebody's* 139
got to take the rap."

"Oh, Kaiser, we could go away together. Just the two of us. We 140
could forget about philosophy. Settle down and maybe get into semantics."

"Sorry, sugar. It's no dice."   141

She was all tears now as she started lowering the shoulder straps of 142
her peignoir and I was standing there suddenly with a naked Venus
whose whole body seemed to be saying, Take me — I'm yours. A Venus
whose right hand tousled my hair while her left hand had picked up a
forty-five and was holding it behind my back. I let go with a slug from
my thirty-eight before she could pull the trigger, and she dropped the
gun and doubled over in disbelief.

"How could you, Kaiser?"   143

She was fading fast, but I managed to get it in, in time.   144

"The manifestation of the universe as a complex idea unto itself as 145
opposed to being in or outside the true Being of itself is inherently a
conceptual nothingness or Nothingness in relation to any abstract form
of existing or to exist or having existed in perpetuity and not subject to
laws of physicality or motion or ideas relating to non-matter or the lack
of objective Being or subjective otherness."

It was a subtle concept but I think she understood before she died.   146

Study Questions

1. Is "Mr. Big" a satire or a parody? Of what? Is it form or
   plot that makes it so? Is "Mr. Big" irreverent?
2. List some of the objects and institutions that Allen makes
   us laugh at.
3. Comment on the names of the characters in this piece.
4. What is funny about the progression from *absurd* to *rational* to *ontological* (paragraphs 72–74)?
5. Is the dialogue realistic? Why is it couched in the form it
   is?

Martin E. Marty
THE BEST MAN

Martin E. Marty (1928–   ) was born in West Point, Nebraska. He is now Professor of the History of Modern Christianity at the University of Chicago and associate editor of the *Christian Century*. After receiving B.A. and B.D. degrees from Concordia Seminary (1949, 1952), he attended the Lutheran School of Theology (S.T.M., 1954), and received a Ph.D. from the University of Chicago (1956). A regular contributor to numerous religious periodicals, he has published *The Improper Opinion* (1961), *Varieties of Unbelief* (1964), *The Modern Schism* (1969), *You Are Promise* (1973), and *The Pro and Con Book of Religious America* (1975), among others. For *Righteous Empire* (1970) he received the National Book Award.

    At 7:00 A.M. the networks broke the news simultaneously: 1

    "What had been mere rumors when America retired last night became confirmed as fact moments ago. 2

    "The long convention deadlock was finally broken at dawn and the veil of secrecy was lifted at the convention hall. The new candidate, identified first only as The Favorite Son, met with all delegations and caucuses, none of whom opposed him. He was nominated by all the deadlocked candidates and became the party's choice by acclamation. Party officials expressed delight that he had chosen their party. 3

    "The candidate told network representatives, however, that he was not showing favoritism. In fact, he reminded them, 'My kingdom is not of this world.' Why had he made an appearance in America's Bicentennial Year, and why had he agreed to run for office? 'Oh, because this time I thought I should "work within the system." ' Was he surprised when the bandwagon rolled for him? 'It's happened before.' Was he worried about possible voter rejection? 'It's happened before.' 4

    "Legal experts advised that a constitutional amendment may be necessary because the candidate, Jesus of Nazareth, was born in Israel...." 5

    The event brought disarray in the ranks of the other party. Late-morning special editions of the newspapers, however, carried a statement signed by all members of the national committee saying that their campaign plans would go ahead. "We remain in the race out of a deep sense of responsibility to our wonderful American two-party system. But we will not vote for our candidate, and ask the American people not to. No 6 one votes against Jesus." The public-relations people picked up that last sentence. It became the slogan. In the course of the day buttons and posters were ready: "NO ONE VOTES AGAINST JESUS."

By noon it dawned on the party chairman that he had a religious is- 7 sue on his hands. "We forgot to check this all out with the religious leaders!" But the leaders, it turns out, had taken care of the issue on their own. The Catholic bishops announced their delight that for a third time there was a Catholic candidate. Meanwhile the Houston Protestant clergy bulletined their approval. Since the candidate was a Protestant, they were sure he would veto any proposed support for parochial schools. The Central Conference of American Rabbis promised not to oppose a candidate who, after all, "was a Jew, a rabbi, a friend of Israel," and added: "We do not hold against him the almost unbroken bad record of his followers against his own people, the Jews." In response to a phone call, Mrs. Madlyn Murray O'Hair, who had been uncharacteristically silent all day, announced that she was coming out of her recent self-imposed retirement in order to organize Atheists for Jesus: "When religious people hear his positions they'll be embarrassed. But now that he has reappeared I cannot find anyone who admits to being atheist. No one votes against Jesus."

The last skeptic, an unnamed member of the liberal Eastern Estab- 8 lishment in the media, checked out the candidate's identity with Billy Graham: "Is this really Jesus?" Billy: "Oh, yes, I'd know him anywhere." The computers at the National Opinion Research Center gave instant scientific support for these claims. The C.I.A. clearly agreed that this was Jesus and that he needed special protection. A Defense Department representative who had been contacted by the Secret Service and the C.I.A. announced: "Despite the candidate's well-known nonviolent position and over his protests, we want to make it clear that if Cuba tries any assassination activity, the full force of our nuclear capabilities will be unleashed on that hostile island."

The candidate rested the first day but began his campaign by show- 9 ing up late at the next morning's Congressional Prayer Breakfast. Reporters were barred, but they had no difficulty picking up leaks after a while. Jesus had begun: "My Father and I have little stomach for these events. Early in the morning we hear your prayers. They inform us of your desire to please us. Then you climb the Hill and vote against our poor." A Senator broke the ensuing silence. "If elected — I mean, when elected — will you re-establish worship in the White House East Room?" The response: "Beware of practicing your piety before men in order to be seen by them. I said that long ago. Matthew 6:1. You could look it up."

The postbreakfast exchanges were revealing. Since the candidate, 10 who had no problem with the recognition factor, had skipped the primaries, his positions were not well known. What was his own platform? "Oh, you've had my platform for almost 2,000 years. It's set forth in a well-enough-known set of writings. The Gospels."

Q: Why are you here now?" 11

A: "Simple. The Bicentennial. While America does not have 'most fa- 12 vored-nation' status, my Father and I have always looked kindly on it. Never much impressed by the 'In God We Trust' on your money, we have been attracted by some lines in your founding creed. My Father, for example, has always liked that line about all people being 'endowed by their Creator with certain unalienable rights.' For 200 years your politicians and preachers have been reminding us that you are a nation 'under God.' We cannot even escape such prayers when we look in on a televised professional football game. I knew, however, that you were in trouble. True, as recently as 1970, I heard your former President say, 'I know America, and the American heart is good.' But I thought you should have a chance to show it."

The breakfast chaplain asked the candidate whether he thought im- 13 moral America would respond to the principles of his ethical system. Jesus answered: "Here the nonbelievers and the scholars have it more correct than you do. I don't have a system of ethical principles. I left you with a set of active verbs: 'repent,' 'believe,' 'heal,' 'love.' I announced a coming Kingdom. The Gospels do not provide general principles for everyone. True, I have always asked people to love everyone, including their enemies. That ought to keep this nation busy for a while. But if you'll reread them, you'll see that the Gospels are full of my announcement of the coming Kingdom. They are full of urgency and calls to change your ways. At such a time we don't set forth mild guidelines for living. I am aware that in these latter days there have been many bizarre best sellers that tell exactly what I would do if I returned to earth. Well, you can imagine: Each author has me saying exactly what he or she wants me to say. I rather think of myself as a misfit in any circumstance. It is your idea that your nation should be measured by my teachings. You say that often enough. So, for a few months or years, I'll play the game your way. How are you doing at feeding the hungry, peacemaking, loving your enemies?" The chaplain immediately pronounced the benediction.

One late afternoon, framed against the 10-story library mosaic — a 14 "poor likeness," everyone said — at Notre Dame stadium, the candidate appeared at the largest press conference in history. He was asked whether this was the Second Coming.

"No. The Second Coming is still waiting for some first-class repent- 15 ances. You'll recognize it when it occurs. The Gospels tell about angels and trumpets and clouds of power and glory and thrones. (We have a little taste for the theatrical at big occasions like Second Comings. This is only a dry run, a sort of trial balloon.)"

Patrick Buchanan spoke up. "Three urgent questions are left over 16 from the McGovern campaign. Alphabetically, how are you on abortion, acid and amnesty?"

"On abortion, I am, of course, prolife. I wish the prolife people were 17 prolife. We are pleased to see how solicitous many of them are about the life of fetuses. How many of them spoke up for life when you were bombing real, live, innocent babies back in Cambodia? We seldom heard a peep then. [A headline after that exchange was: "CANDIDATE DUCKS ABORTION ISSUE."] Acid? I have a great concern for health and wholeness. Amnesty? My platform is quite clear. On almost every page there is something about being reconciled to your brother."

Sensing that the Buchanan alphabet was getting close to "busing," 18 party officials decided not to test their "No One Votes Against Jesus" slogan, and adjourned the conference. As the 55,000 reporters hurried out, party leaders assessed the damage. Asked one: "Did you hear him sneak in that new line for a benediction? What's this 'Blessed are the peacemakers, for they shall be called sons of God' stuff? The peace issue is controversial enough, but this business about 'sons' will alienate the E.R.A. people."

The image experts tried a rescue job, and whisked the candidate 19 back to New York. Taken to the top of the World Trade Center, he looked down on all the kingdoms of the world. What he saw was New York. He wept. A press agent said, "Don't let that get out. You know what a good cry did to Ed Muskie four years ago. The people don't want a human candidate. We certainly don't dare let them think Jesus is one!" At a midnight reception, the candidate was asked by New York leaders what he would do about their debts. "Remember my counsel in Luke? 'For which of you, intending to build a tower, sitteth not down first, and counteth the cost, whether he hath sufficient to finish it?'" The guests dispersed into the night.

In the midst of the night, there came to him a religious delegation. 20 "Aren't you at least pleased with our religious revival? Everyone is talking about you." Jesus answered them saying, "Not everyone that saith unto me, 'Lord Lord,' shall enter into the Kingdom of heaven, but he that doeth the will of my Father which is in heaven." Did he not like anything he'd seen in America? "Oh, yes, I am not hard to please, except when I use the drastic standards of the Kingdom for measurement. I enjoy the faith of children. Some people are not grim and despairing. I've looked in on a couple of good parties. I've seen some acts of grace in homes for the aged and heard a good choir or two. Some simple people say wonderful prayers and then share their bread. I even heard of an offended woman who forgave her husband."

Any complaints about organized religion and its role in the cam- 21 paign? "I am not enthusiastic about the 'Bingo for Jesus' support. I'd like redistribution of church wealth. Your churches own $80 billion in property. Couldn't a bit more of your income go for bread for the hungry?"

That $80 billion figure leaked out, and someone brought it up on 22 "Meet the Press" the next day. "Yes," the candidate agreed, "$80 billion is a lot for 300 years' worth of church building. It is almost as much as one year's defense budget and would more than pay for your next single weapon, the B-1 bomber. Buy my enemy—not the candidate of the other party, but The Enemy—need have no fear about your getting priorities confused. He and I both know that most of your funds will go into killing. Where your treasure is, there is your heart also."

That exchange inspired a question about defense and then about de- 23 tente. "We don't use that word. We speak of 'reconciliation.'" When he went on about "turning the other cheek" to the attacker, the party chairman, watching at home, turned off his television. "That crack will produce a million goddamn letters from the National Rifle Association."

No letters came in. No one was against Jesus. He could say anything 24 without provoking a negative response. The common people heard him

gladly. Columnists Evans and Novak were puzzled: "He sounds conservative half the time and super-liberal the rest of the time, but Gallup
and Harris polls find no one ready to vote against him. To date he has
said things that ought to have provoked the opposition of prayer break-
fasters, the clergy, pro- and antiabortionists, acid droppers, enemies of
amnesty, New Yorkers, the military and defense establishments, socialists
and capitalists." At a party in his home William F. Buckley whispered, "If
you keep taking these positions, my God, they'll *crucify* you!" He
blanched as he heard himself and gasped, "Oh, I'm sorry." His guest
smiled. A knowing, forgiving smile.

The months passed. It was a good year. People had been looking for 25
a candidate who favored small government and this one seemed to favor
no government at all. Voters wanted a candidate who was compassionate,
decent, trustworthy. He was all of these.

September and October produced two delicate moments. First, the 26
males in the antipornography movement brought their huge collections
of hardcore materials to the candidate, asking him to condemn those who
produced them. But he, knowing their own hearts, said to them that "everyone who looks at a woman lustfully has committed adultery with her
in his heart." He went on, "If your right eye causes you to sin, pluck it
out and throw it away." The National Conference of Ophthalmologists
announced that while they would still vote for Jesus, they opposed this
specific policy because of malpractice hazards. In any case, after having
confronted the candidate, the antipornography forces themselves dispersed and the issue was dropped. In October the Foundation for Christian Economic Freedom brought economic issues to a head. The F.C.E.F.
wanted the candidate to promise that he would name Prof. Milton Fried-
man to be his chief economic adviser, since it was clear that *this* candidate at last was one who would favor an absolutely free market and permit unlimited accumulation of private property, untrammeled by
regulation or other concerns. The candidate's press aide put them off
with a release that said simply: "If you would be perfect, go, sell what
you possess and give to the poor ... and come, follow me. Matthew
19:21."

Election Day came. How many would vote against Jesus? Now the 27
answer would be clear. The usual number of people went to cast ballots.
They voted for road commissioners and recorders of deeds and Senators.
When the first returns—from Dixville Notch, N.H.—came in at 12:01
A.M. on Election Day, everyone got a hint of what was going on. By
6:45 that evening, with the first projections in Kentucky and Indiana, everyone was sure.

There was no winner of the Presidency. No one had voted against 28
Jesus. No one had voted *for* him, either.

Next morning, the cleaning woman began to work in the now-vacant 29
hotel room of the former candidate. He had left her a nice tip in the ash
tray. On the night stand she saw two scribbled notes. Both had references to Bible verses. One said "Matt. 15:8." The other: "Luke 23:34."
The Gideon Bible was at hand, and she opened it. The first verse read,
"This people draweth nigh unto me with their mouth, and honoureth me

with their lips; but their heart is far from me." The one from Luke began, "Father, forgive...." She crumpled the first, and pushed the second one, along with the tip, into her apron pocket. She wondered whether America would go four years without any President. If so, would anyone notice?

Two months later, Vogue's column began: "PEOPLE are talking 30 about ... the impact left by America's first Presidential candidate who did not receive a single negative vote. Everyone liked him. He was loving. We remember a look of almost infinite tenderness in his eyes. We will never forget him.... THE NEW KICK: Bisexual parties for the Bicentennial...."

Study Questions

1. Although this essay is written in the past tense, there is a real sense of immediacy, of the present, about it. Why?
2. What is the style an imitation of?
3. How does Marty manage to avoid writing in a strict Q. and A. format?
4. Many of the allusions are distinctly contemporary. Does that date the essay?
5. What is the effect of 'He wept' in paragraph 19?
6. What is "The Best Man"? Satire? Allegory? Parody? Parable?

E. M. Forster
THE OTHER SIDE OF THE HEDGE

E. M. Forster (1879–1970) was born in London and educated at the Tonbridge School in Kent and at King's College, Cambridge. His first published works were short stories, many of them later collected into *The Celestial Omnibus* (1911) and *The Eternal Moment* (1928). He is best known as a novelist; among his fiction are *Where Angels Fear to Tread* (1905), *A Room With a View* (1908), *Howards End* (1910), and *A Passage to India* (1924). *Maurice,* a novel with a homosexual theme, was published posthumously in 1971. Forster's critical work, *Aspects of the Novel* (1927), is required reading in many litera-

Reprinted from *The Collected Tales of E. M. Forster.* Published 1947 by Alfred A. Knopf, Inc.

ture courses. A prolific writer, he has reviewed for numerous journals; coauthored the libretto for Benjamin Britten's opera, *Billy Budd;* delivered radio talks over the BBC; and written film scripts. A bequest made it unnecessary for Forster to earn a living. When his house at Abinger was destroyed during World War II, he took up residence at King's College, as an honorary Fellow.

My pedometer told me that I was twenty-five; and, though it 1 is a shocking thing to stop walking, I was so tired that I sat down on a milestone to rest. People outstripped me, jeering as they did so, but I was too apathetic to feel resentful, and even when Miss Eliza Dimbleby, the great educationist, swept past, exhorting me to persevere, I only smiled and raised my hat.

At first I thought I was going to be like my brother, whom I had had 2 to leave by the roadside a year or two around the corner. He had wasted his breath on singing, and his strength on helping others. But I had travelled more wisely, and now it was only the monotony of the highway that oppressed me—dust under foot and brown crackling hedges on either side, ever since I could remember.

And I had already dropped several things—indeed, the road behind 3 was strewn with all the things we all had dropped; and the white dust was settling down on them, so that already they looked no better than stones. My muscles were so weary that I could not even bear the weight of those things I still carried. I slid off the milestone into the road, and lay there prostrate, with my face to the great parched hedge, praying that I might give up.

A little puff of air revived me. It seemed to come from the hedge; 4 and, when I opened my eyes, there was a glint of light through the tangle of boughs and dead leaves. The hedge could not be as thick as usual. In my weak, morbid state, I longed to force my way in, and see what was on the other side. No one was in sight, or I should not have dared to try. For we of the road do not admit in conversation that there is another side at all.

I yielded to the temptation, saying to myself that I would come back 5 in a minute. The thorns scratched my face, and I had to use my arms as a shield, depending on my feet alone to push me forward. Halfway through I would have gone back, for in the passage all the things I was carrying were scraped off me, and my clothes were torn. But I was so wedged that return was impossible, and I had to wriggle blindly forward, expecting every moment that my strength would fail me, and that I should perish in the undergrowth.

Suddenly cold water closed round my head, and I seemed sinking 6 down for ever. I had fallen out of the hedge into a deep pool. I rose to the surface at last, crying for help, and I heard someone on the opposite bank laugh and say: "Another!" And then I was twitched out and laid panting on the dry ground.

Even when the water was out of my eyes, I was still dazed, for I had 7 never been in so large a space, nor seen such grass and sunshine. The blue sky was no longer a strip, and beneath it the earth had risen gradually into hills—clean, bare buttresses, with beech trees in their folds, and meadows and clear pools at their feet. But the hills were not high, and there was in the landscape a sense of human occupation—so that one might have called it a park, or garden, if the words did not imply a certain triviality and constraint.

As soon as I got my breath, I turned to my rescuer and said: 8

"Where does this place lead to?"   9

"Nowhere, thank the Lord!" said he, and laughed. He was a man of 10 fifty or sixty—just the kind of age we mistrust on the road—but there was no anxiety in his manner, and his voice was that of a boy of eighteen.

"But it must lead somewhere!" I cried, too much surprised at his an- 11 swer to thank him for saving my life.

"He wants to know where it leads!" he shouted to some men on the 12 hillside, and they laughed back, and waved their caps.

I noticed then that the pool into which I had fallen was really a moat 13 which bent round to the left and to the right, and that the hedge followed it continually. The hedge was green on this side—its roots showed through the clear water, and fish swam about in them—and it was wreathed over with dog-roses and Traveller's Joy. But it was a barrier, and in a moment I lost all pleasure in the grass, the sky, the trees, the happy men and women, and realized that the place was but a prison, for all its beauty and extent.

We moved away from the boundary, and then followed a path almost 14 parallel to it, across the meadows. I found it difficult walking, for I was always trying to out-distance my companion, and there was no advantage in doing this if the place led nowhere. I had never kept step with anyone since I left my brother.

I amused him by stopping suddenly and saying disconsolately, "This 15 is perfectly terrible. One cannot advance: one cannot progress. Now we of the road—"

"Yes, I know."   16

"I was going to say, we advance continually."   17

"I know."   18

"We are always learning, expanding, developing. Why, even in my 19 short life I have seen a great deal of advance—the Transvaal War, the Fiscal Question, Christian Science, Radium. Here for example—"

I took out my pedometer, but it still marked twenty-five, not a de- 20 gree more.

"Oh, it's stopped! I meant to show you. It should have registered all 21 the time I was walking with you. But it makes me only twenty-five."

"Many things don't work in here," he said. "One day a man brought 22 in a Lee-Metford, and that wouldn't work."

"The laws of science are universal in their application. It must be the 23 water in the moat that has injured the machinery. In normal conditions everything works. Science and the spirit of emulation—those are the forces that have made us what we are."

I had to break off and acknowledge the pleasant greeting of people 24 whom we passed. Some of them were singing, some talking, some engaged in gardening, hay-making, or other rudimentary industries. They all seemed happy; and I might have been happy too, if I could have forgotten that the place led nowhere.

I was startled by a young man who came sprinting across our path, 25 took a little fence in the fine style, and went tearing over a ploughed field till he plunged into a lake, across which he began to swim. Here was true energy, and I exclaimed: "A cross-country race! Where are the others?"

"There are no others," my companion replied; and, later on, when 26 we passed some long grass from which came the voice of a girl singing exquisitely to herself, he said again: "There are no others." I was bewildered at the waste in production, and murmured to myself, "What does it all mean?"

He said: "It means nothing but itself"—and he repeated the words 27 slowly, as if I were a child.

"I understand," I said quietly, "but I do not agree. Every achieve- 28 ment is worthless unless it is a link in the chain of development. And I must not trespass on your kindness any longer. I must get back somehow to the road, and have my pedometer mended."

"First, you must see the gates," he replied, "for we have gates, 29 though we never use them."

I yielded politely, and before long we reached the moat again, at a 30 point where it was spanned by a bridge. Over the bridge was a big gate, as white as ivory, which was fitted into a gap in the boundary hedge. The gate opened outwards, and I exclaimed in amazement, for from it ran a road—just such a road as I had left—dusty under foot, with brown crackling hedges on either side as far as the eye could reach.

"That's my road!" I cried. 31

He shut the gate and said: "But not your part of the road. It is 32 through this gate that humanity went out countless ages ago, when it was first seized with the desire to walk."

I denied this, observing that the part of the road I myself had left 33 was not more than two miles off. But with the obstinacy of his years he repeated: "It is the same road. This is the beginning, and though it seems to run straight away from us, it doubles so often, that it is never far from our boundary and sometimes touches it." He stooped down by the moat, and traced on its moist margin an absurd figure like a maze. As we walked back through the meadows, I tried to convince him of his mistake.

"The road sometimes doubles, to be sure, but that is part of our dis- 34 cipline. Who can doubt that its general tendency is onward? To what goal we know not—it may be to some mountain where we shall touch the sky, it may be over precipices into the sea. But that it goes forward—who can doubt that? It is the thought of that that makes us strive to excel, each in his own way, and gives us an impetus which is lacking with you. Now that man who passes us—it's true that he ran well, and jumped well, and swam well; but we have men who can run better, and men who can jump better, and who can swim better. Specialization has produced results which would surprise you. Similarly, that girl—"

Here I interrupted myself to exclaim: "Good gracious me! I could 35
have sworn it was Miss Eliza Dimbleby over there, with her feet in the
fountain!"

He believed that it was.   36

"Impossible! I left her on the road, and she is due to lecture this 37
evening at Tunbridge Wells. Why, her train leaves Cannon Street in — of
course my watch has stopped like everything else. She is the last person
to be here."

"People always are astonished at meeting each other. All kinds come 38
through the hedge, and come at all times — when they are drawing ahead
in the race, when they are lagging behind, when they are left for dead. I
often stand near the boundary listening to the sounds of the road — you
know what they are — and wonder if anyone will turn aside. It is my great
happiness to help someone out of the moat, as I helped you. For our
country fills up slowly, though it was meant for all mankind."

"Mankind have other aims," I said gently, for I thought him well- 39
meaning; "and I must join them." I bade him good evening, for the sun
was declining, and I wished to be on the road by nightfall. To my alarm,
he caught hold of me, crying: "You are not to go yet!" I tried to shake
him off, for we had no interests in common, and his civility was becoming irksome to me. But for all my struggles the tiresome old man would
not let go; and, as wrestling is not my speciality, I was obliged to follow
him.

It was true that I could never have found alone the place where I 40
came in, and I hoped that, when I had seen the other sights about which
he was worrying, he would take me back to it. But I was determined not
to sleep in the country, for I mistrusted it, and the people too, for all
their friendliness. Hungry though I was, I would not join them in their
evening meals of milk and fruit, and, when they gave me flowers, I flung
them away as soon as I could do so unobserved. Already they were lying
down for the night like cattle — some out on the bare hillside, others in
groups under the beeches. In the light of an orange sunset I hurried on
with my unwelcome guide, dead tired, faint for want of food, but mur-
muring indomitably: "Give me life, with its struggles and victories, with
its failures and hatreds, with its deep moral meaning and its unknown
goal!"

At last we came to a place where the encircling moat was spanned by 41
another bridge, and where another gate interrupted the line of the
boundary hedge. It was different from the first gate; for it was half transparent like horn, and opened inwards. But through it, in the waning light,
I saw again just such a road as I had left — monotonous, dusty, with
brown crackling hedges on either side, as far as the eye could reach.

I was strangely disquieted at the sight, which seemed to deprive me 42
of all self-control. A man was passing us, returning for the night to the
hills, with a scythe over his shoulder and a can of some liquid in his
hand. I forgot the destiny of our race. I forgot the road that lay before
my eyes, and I sprang at him, wrenched the can out of his hand, and began to drink.

It was nothing stronger than beer, but in my exhausted state it over- 43 came me in a moment. As in a dream, I saw the old man shut the gate, and heard him say: "This is where your road ends, and through this gate humanity—all that is left of it—will come in to us."

Though my senses were sinking into oblivion, they seemed to ex- 44 pand ere they reached it. They perceived the magic song of nightingales, and the odour of invisible hay, and stars piercing the fading sky. The man whose beer I had stolen lowered me down gently to sleep off its effects, and, as he did so, I saw that he was my brother.

Study Questions

1. Clearly, this is an *allegory*. What values would you assign to specifics in the story, i.e., the road, the thorns in the hedge?
2. How does Forster create and maintain a sense of movement?
3. Despite the fact that this story begins with so mundane an object as a pedometer, rarely does the reader feel that the story is set in the real world. How does the author achieve a feeling of otherworldliness?
4. Explain the last line.

2 Education

"Unwillingly to School"

In updating this section for the fourth edition of *Strategies in Prose* we have retained not a single one of the essays from the third edition. Only the short story "Archways," by Joyce Carol Oats, has been carried over from the earlier edition. This is not to suggest that the issues and problems that characterized education in the early 1970s are no longer contemporary. Quite the contrary, for these issues have remained little changed. Writers are still addressing themselves to such questions as: What is the nature of education? Who should be educated? What should be taught? How should it be taught? These issues and questions may be regarded as universal, or the nearest thing to it. Our intention in completely overhauling this section was to present newer and fresher writings about these issues, as well as to include some different and more appealing topics related to these issues.

Isaac Asimov's "His Own Particular Drummer" deals with the controversial issue of methods of education. He argues for more reliance on technology, particularly on the use of machines to make education more effective and more fun. Students will be more likely to favor Asimov's position, while many teachers trained in older methods of education will have reservations about the author's claims for machines. But few can object to his premise that "education cannot exist apart from the world. Its nature must be affected by the state of society."

Among the essays dealing with what should be taught in our schools, Derek Bok's "Can Ethics Be Taught?" is perhaps the most provocative. Noting society's loss of faith in national leaders, politics, and institutions as an aftermath of Watergate, Bok argues that colleges and universities have a role to play in restoring moral values. His approach would be the case-study method of teaching applied ethics in various academic disciplines. This essay can be useful to stimulate thought about theme topics and to serve as a model of how to advance a proposal to correct a situation or condition.

Sloan Wilson's "Why Jessie Hates English" is a contrast to the tone and manner of the Bok essay. Wilson's concern is what should be taught in English courses, but he takes an indirect approach by objecting to what is taught — grammar — at the expense of composition and literature.

The pro and con essays for this section are short and bare of most rhetorical trimmings. Students should have little difficulty in analyzing the arguments in Shirley Chisholm's "Needed: Equal Educational Opportunity for All" and Norman Hackerman's "Higher Education: Who Needs It?" Chisholm's position is that higher education is a constitutional right in a democratic society, while Hackerman argues that higher education should be for the elite.

The essay by Judith Plotz, "Is a Crime Against the Mind No Crime at All?" deals with a subject that practically guarantees student interest and will stimulate students' thinking and writing. In dealing with the topic of plagiarism and its almost epidemic development in colleges and universities, she presents an excellent example of composition about a situation that needs to be corrected.

Teachers of composition who used the third edition of *Strategies in Prose* strongly recommended that Joyce Carol Oates' short story "Archways" be retained in the new edition. This is a poignant story of a graduate teaching assistant in English and his affair with one of his students. Analysis and discussion of the story will raise many theme topic possibilities dealing with the two characters, their motives, basic needs, and value systems. And, of course, a close study of the story will prove useful in treating such rhetorical concerns as style, tone, and point of view.

Isaac Asimov
HIS OWN
PARTICULAR DRUMMER

Isaac Asimov (1920–   ) was born in Petrovich, Russia, and became a United States citizen in 1928. A biochemist, he received his B.S. (1939), M.A. (1941), and Ph.D. (1948) from Columbia University. His verbal skill earned him the American Chemical Society's James T. Grady Award for scientific writing. Asimov's books include *Pebble in the Sky* and *I, Robot* (1950), *The Intelligent Man's Guide to Science* (1960), *Of Time and Space and Other Things* (1965), *Earth: Our Crowded Spaceship* (1974), and *Buy Jupiter and Other Stories* (1975). So far he has written an astonishing 164 books.

Back in 1951, I wrote a story called "The Fun They Had." It 1 was only a thousand words long and its plot was a simple one:

Two children of the twenty-second century find an old book that, 2 among other things, reveals the nature of the educational system of the twentieth century. To their astonishment, they discover that large groups of children once went to special buildings to be subjected to community education by human teachers.

As the younger child, Margie, returns to her own home where her 3 own teaching machine is waiting to continue working with her on proper fractions, the story concludes:

She was thinking about the old schools they had when her grandfather's 4 grandfather was a little boy. All the kids from the whole neighborhood came, laughing and shouting in the schoolyard, sitting together in the schoolroom, going home together at the end of the day. They learned the same things so they could help one another on the homework, and talk about it.

And the teachers were people.... 5

The mechanical teacher was flashing on the screen: "When we add the 6 fractions ½ and ¼...."

Margie was thinking about how the kids must have loved it in the old 7 days. She was thinking about the fun they had.

The circumstances surrounding the writing of the story were these: 8 An old friend of mine was editing a syndicated children's newspaper page, and he asked me for a little science fiction story. I was in the mood to try irony and I was certain that children have as keen a sense of irony

Reprinted from *Phi Delta Kappan,* September, 1976, by permission of the author.

as adults do. Of course, children fall short through lack of experience, so I thought I would hit them right where they *did* have experience, and wrote "The Fun They Had."

Is there any youngster, I thought, who would not instantly be aware 9 that school was *not* fun? Wouldn't he see that it was ridiculous for the child who had all the advantages of a personally oriented private education to long for the barbarism of an earlier day?

After all, I myself had gone to school once and had done very well, 10 too. I had managed to finish high school at 15, and I hovered near the top of the class, if not at the actual top, at all times. School was about as good for me as it could be for anyone. Yet I remember

—The bullies who made life a misery in the halls and yards.   11
—The slow students along with whom you had to crawl in weary 12 boredom (or the fast students, to look at the other side, along with whom you had to race in anxious frustration).
—The inept teachers who could make any subject dull.   13
—The cruel teachers who sharpened their claws of sarcasm on the 14 backs of suffering children who were not allowed to talk back.
—The strict teachers who, dissatisfied with the innate deficiencies of 15 a school, made it a prison as well.
—The relentless competition for marks that taught every kid he was 16 nothing, unless he could grind his fellow kid's face into the dirt.

Do you expect children to have fun under those circumstances? Is 17 there a child who wouldn't rather have a television set of his own, interested only in him, infinitely patient, and adjusted to the beat of his own particular drummer?

Since "The Fun they Had" first appeared, it has been in constant de- 9 mand for anthologies, and has appeared more than 30 times that I know of. I would think, then, that I had accomplished my purpose effectively were it not for the fact that, among adults at least, a sense of irony seems notably absent in many cases. The comments that some of the anthologists print in connection with the story, together with certain letters I get, often make it clear that the story is interpreted nonironically as a boost for contemporary education and as an author's expression of horror at the thought of education by machine.

Apparently there is a strong trend of thought among educators that 19 there is something dehumanizing about machine education.

Why, I wonder?   20

Is there a feeling that a machine is cold and hard and cannot possibly 21 understand the needs of children?

Yet if every human teacher who was cold and hard and could not 22 possibly understand the needs of children were removed from his or her position, I suspect our educational system would dissolve.

Is there a feeling that a child would not relate to a machine?   23

I suppose that in the early days of the automobile there were those 24 who felt that no one could possibly relate to a cold, hard, dead machine as they could to a beautiful, sensitive, living horse. Yet though there may be faults in our automobile culture, those do not arise out of any shortage of affection of human beings for the cars they drive.

Is there a feeling that a machine-educated child would not have contact with other human beings and would therefore be seriously lacking in many values? 25

Yet who would suggest a total substitution? There would be many fields of study that would require the mass experience — sports, for instance, nature study field trips, drama, public speaking, and so on. On the other hand, there would be academic subjects that do not require companionship. In fact, one could study mathematics, or history, to begin with, all the better if the artificial and unnecessary open competition of the classroom were removed. Then, at appropriate times, seminars could be arranged in which students could listen to each other, comment, and profit. 26

In short, machine education is not a substitute for human interaction, but a supplement. In fact, human interaction could proceed all the better were it not oppressed by the negative conditioning of an association with a dull and uninspired mass-education procedure involving subject matter that has nothing to do with the interaction. 27

Suppose, now, that our civilization endures into the twenty-first century (a supposition that can by no means be taken for granted) and that technology continues to advance. 28

Suppose that communications satellites are numerous, and are far more versatile and sophisticated than they are today. Suppose that in place of rather limited radio wave carriers, the incredibly capacious laser beam of visible light is used to carry messages from earth to satellite and back again. 29

Under these circumstances, there would be room for many millions of separate channels for voice and picture, and it can be easily imagined that every human being on earth might have a particular wavelength assigned to him, as now he might be assigned a particular telephone number. 30

We can then imagine, as in "The Fun They Had," that each child might have his own private outlet to which could be attached, at certain desirable periods of time, his personal teaching machine. 31

It would be a far more versatile and interactive teaching machine than anything we could put together now, for computer technology will also have advanced in the interval. 32

We can reasonably hope that the teaching machine will be flexible, versatile and capable of modifying its own program (that is, "learning") as a result of the student's input. In other words, the student can ask questions which the machine can answer, and he can make statements and answer tests which the machine can evaluate. As a result of what the machine gets back, the machine can adjust the speed and intensity of its course of instruction, and can shift it in whatever direction student interest leads. 33

Nor need we suppose that the teaching machine is self-contained and is as finite as an object the size of a television set might be. We can imagine that the machine will have at its disposal any book, periodical, or 34 document in the vast, central, thoroughly encoded planetary library. And if the machine has it, the student has it, either placed directly on a viewing screen, or reproduced in print-on-paper for more leisurely study.

Naturally, education cannot exist apart from the world. Its nature 35 must be affected by the state of society.

If civilization is to survive into the age of the communications satel- 36 lite, laser-beam transmission of information, computerized central libraries, and teaching machines, we can be reasonably sure that the world will, by then, be far more closely knit than it is now.

Living, as we do now, in an age of life-and-death problems, we can 37 see that without adequate solution of such problems as population, pollution, scarcity, alienation, and violence, civilization will not survive. Every one of these problems affects the entire globe and cannot be solved by any one nation within its own territory.

If, for instance, the United States were to stabilize its population at a 38 reasonable level, while the rest of the world continued to expand in numbers, then the chaos, anarchy, and starvation beyond our borders would upset the smooth functioning of world trade on which our own exalted standard of living depends. The economic strains upon us would topple us into chaos as well.

Similarly, pollution of the air and ocean at any one point on earth 39 contributes to that pollution everywhere. We can in no way isolate our air and water from that of the rest of the world. We cannot isolate our section of the ozone layer. We cannot be sure epidemics elsewhere will not spread to us, or radioactive contamination either.

Our problems are global in nature, and they can only be dealt with 40 globally.

Consequently, in a process that has already begun, international orga- 41 nizations will multiply and grow more powerful as they face those various problems. However much the world may continue to give lip service to an outmoded, unworkable, deadly nationalism, the twenty-first century may see us effectively, if unacknowledgedly, under a world government, and local differences in culture, society, or economy won't alter that fact.

Education will have to adjust to such a world. History, for instance, 42 will have to be *human* history, with the accent on social, cultural, and economic trends, while much of the hero/villain business of war and politics will be deemphasized. It would, after all, be ridiculous to perpetuate hatred in a world in which there is no alternative to cooperation.

Then, too, while the local languages will be used in teaching stu- 43 dents, it would be only reasonable to suppose that some lingua franca will have developed for a world grown small and interconnected. There need be no reason to try to suppress language—for cultural variety is a great good and contributes to the sparkle and excitement of the species—but to be multilingual is not so unusual. Why, then, should not everyone speak at least two languages, his or her own, and "Planetary."

Would it not be safer to have machine education in so global a 44 society? Could we expect human beings to be entirely free of the prejudices of an earlier and nonglobal day? And even if machines were programmed by human beings not devoid of prejudice, the mere fact that machines could modify their programs in accordance with the needs and abilities of students might mean that they would drift toward globality.

For instance, it seems to me very likely (though my own chauvinistic 45 wish may be father to the thought) that Planetary would be closer to English than to any other language, since English is already the first or second language of more people on earth than any other, with the possible exception of the multidialect, and geographically isolated, Chinese language.

Even if this is so, however, Planetary will undoubtedly absorb 46 enough of other-language vocabulary and grammar to become a foreign language to those who speak English as a native tongue. Teaching machines may be so programmed, and so self-modified, as to encourage the drift of Planetary away from English, in order that it be, as much as possible, a new language without too-obvious antecedents. On the other hand, they may be programmed to resist the too-extreme breakup of Planetary into mutually incomprehensible dialects (as once happened to Latin in Western Europe).

Another important revolution that education may undergo in the 47 twenty-first century is simply this: It will no longer be child oriented.

It is natural to suppose that it is children only who must be edu- 48 cated. They are born with no more than a handful of biological instincts and must learn everything that makes them culturally and socially human.

Once they have learned a certain minimum of what is required — to 49 speak, to read, to earn a living — their education is considered complete. Of course, certain aspects of education continue, for an adult is bound to learn new matters in fields of interest, or to become more proficient in the social graces, or to adapt to new cities, new conditions, new situations. Such adult continuation, however, is left to itself — a matter for each individual to take care of. *Institutionalized* education is left to the young.

As a result, we think of education as closed-ended. One *has* an edu- 50 cation; one *is* educated; one is *done* with education and enters the "real world."

This view damages both young and old. Children quickly learn that 51 grown-ups don't have to go to school. If there is any inconvenience to school, it is attributed by children to their crime of being young. They come to realize that one great reward of growing up is to become free of the school-prison. Their goal becomes not that of being educated, but that of getting out.

Similarly, adults are sure to associate education with childhood, 52 something they have fortunately survived and escaped from. The freedom of adulthood would be sullied if they were to go back to the life-habits associated with the education of children. As a result, many adults, whether consciously or unconsciously, find it beneath their adult dignity to do anything as childish as read a book, think a thought, or get an idea. Adults are rarely embarrassed at having forgotten what little algebra or geography they once learned, just as they are rarely embarrassed at no longer wearing diapers.

People, as they grow old under such circumstances, generally cannot 53 change views or attitudes to conform with changing conditions and environments. They have forgotten how to learn and must rely entirely on what scraps of dimly remembered catchphrases they picked up as teenagers. There is, in consequence, a hardening conservatism, a growing intolerance of whatever is new, and a certain mindless refusal to adjust even where that would be to their benefit. (There are, of course, individual exceptions to this.)

The relatively young, who have just escaped from school, or who are 54 in the process of escaping, tend to despise the previous generation for its conservatism and obscurantism, and even a very few years is enough to produce a noticeable difference. That is why we had the catchphrase of the 1960s: "Don't trust anyone over 30."

The distrust of the young for the old and their acceptance of the 55 stereotype of age as inseparable from dullness, backwardness, stodginess, and noncreativity helps produce and confirm the truth of that very stereotype. To the degree that the young accept that stereotype, they shrink into it as they age and the whole becomes a vicious cycle of self-fulfillment.

This stereotype of age as an unprofitable excrescence on the body 56 social is not exactly new, but, as it continues, it is becoming more dangerous and, by the twenty-first century, it may be deadly.

The reason for this is that the age profile of our society is changing. 57 Through most of humankind's stay on the planet, a high birthrate and a high death rate have sufficed to keep the average age of human beings low. (The average age would have been lower still were it not that infant mortality contributed a disproportionate share to the death rate.)

Since the mid-nineteenth century, however, the death rate has been 58 dropping, thanks to the advance of modern medicine. The drop in infant mortality and the slower sag in birthrate have not been able to offset the effect on the age profile of an extended life span. In nations where the effects have been most marked, the average age of the population has been increasing relentlessly.

In the United States, the steadily increasing percentage of the popu- 59 lation made up by those over 65 has now made the oldsters a formidable voting power. What's more, we are becoming, increasingly, a nation with its finances organized about pensions, Medicaid, and social security benefits, which are enjoyed by so many and looked forward to by so many more. As some have pointed out, there are ever more and more unproductive oldsters being supported by the labors of a smaller and smaller reservoir of productive youngsters.

And what if this tendency continues? Consider: 60

The total population of the world stands now at four billion and it is 61 increasing at the rate of 2% a year. By 2010, if this growth continues unchecked, the world population will be eight billion; by 2045 it will be 16 billion, and so on.

No one really expects the population rise to continue unchecked for 62 very many decades, however. The only question is, What will check it?

It could be a rise in the death rate through starvation, disease, social 63 strife, and the like. Checking the population rise in this fashion would, of course, produce enough misery and anarchy to shake the lofty and formidable—but rickety—underpinnings of our complex industrial society. It would shatter the technological structure that alone keeps the earth's population fed, clothed, and secure (however inadequately). With that structure destroyed, there will be no twenty-first century worth discussing.

The alternative is to lower the birthrate the world over. There are 64 formidable obstacles to this, but as catastrophe comes closer, and as a lowered birthrate is more and more clearly seen as the only route to survival, a panicky humankind will take more and more drastic measures to insure it, and then, perhaps, we will win through with only a minor catastrophe—that is, one from which civilization can recover.

In that case, though, a drastically lowered birthrate the world over 65 will insure the continued increase of the average age of humankind. There will be a steady increase in the proportion of oldsters who will have to be supported by a steadily decreasing number of youngsters. This change will be further exacerbated by the fact that a continuing civilization will insure further advances in medicine, so that there will be an increasingly successful treatment of the degenerative diseases that now strike the aging with such dreadful consistency—and a further drop in death rate that the falling birthrate will have to match.

To be sure, the aged will be healthier and stronger as medicine 66· learns to inhibit and/or ameliorate arthritis, cancer, circulatory disorders, kidney disease, and others. To that extent, the oldsters will be less of a physical drain on society than they would be under present conditions. On the other hand, if the stereotype of the aging as mentally rigid and creatively incompetent continues to be converted into actuality, all of society will calcify. Humankind will avoid the death-by-bang of the population explosion to suffer the death-by-whimper of massive old age.

Unless education does something to destroy the stereotype. . . .   67

Education must not any longer be confined to the young. The young 68 must not look forward to its completion; the old must not look back on it as an accompaniment of immaturity. For all people, education must be made to seem a requirement of human life as long as that endures.

Why not? That for which a living and healthy organism is adapted is 69 easy to do, and there is no reluctance attached to it. It is no pain for a cell to divide, for a tree to put forth leaves, for a horse to run, a seal to swim, a hawk to fly. Where an animal is sufficiently advanced to follow an apparent display of emotion, it is almost inevitable to interpret its behavior as indicating outright pleasure in the utilization of its body for the purposes to which it is adapted.

For what, then, is the human body adapted? Consider the colossal 70 human brain, making up 2% of the human body and weighing three pounds altogether. No other organism, with the exception of the dolphin, has a brain that is at once so large and is combined with so comparatively small a body. For what is this brain adapted but for all the processes we call thought, reason, insight, intuition, creativity?

Would it not seem natural to suppose that there must be pleasure 71 for the human being in the very act of thinking, since the brain is so well adapted for it, and since its underutilization gives rise to that very painful condition we call boredom?

When a child learns to talk, he talks constantly, he asks questions, he 72 pries and probes, and is endlessly curious. He clearly loves the thinking ability he develops—and then he goes to school and has curiosity shot out from under him.

School *isn't* fun, but might not education by machine—personalized, 73 adaptable, versatile—prove to be fun? If it were, might it not be the kind of fun that people would hate to give up? If so, then education could continue into advanced age. Oldsters aren't likely to give up golf or tennis (or sex, for that matter) just because they were better at it when they were younger. Why, then, should they give up education, if *that* proves to be a continuing pleasure?

In fact, given a long vigorous, and healthy life, and one in which it is 74 no disgrace for a mature person to "go to school," why should there not be regular switches in fields of endeavor? At age 60, why might not someone suddenly decide to study Russian, or take up mathematics or physics, or venture into chess or archaeology or bricklaying? What could better serve to keep a person's mind active and happy and alive and creative than to send it surging in new directions?

Computers, programmed with ever-greater versatility and themselves 75 increasingly capable of learning by interaction with human beings, could be ready to help further those new interests, and in this way, too, teaching machines could help save our society.

The key to this vision of education is, of course, that people enjoy 76 learning *if* they learn what they want to learn. This is not a very profound observation, actually. A child who finds every school subject boring and incomprehensible, and who seems incapable of learning, may yet bend his every faculty to an understanding of the rules of baseball, and may succeed in memorizing, with fiendish intensity, unrelated statistics that a mathematics professor might have trouble with.

Then why not allow a child to learn what he wants to learn? If he 77 wants to learn baseball, let the machine teach him the academic aspects of baseball, which he can then apply in the field. He may, as a result, want of his own accord to learn to read better in order to read more about baseball, and want to learn arithmetic in order to calculate baseball averages. Eventually, he may find he likes mathematics more than baseball. Remove constraint and he may well move in a direction toward which force would never budge him.

But can the world continue if everyone has the option of choosing 78 what he is to learn? Can society survive with an educational system that consists entirely and solely of electives?

Why not, if we take into account the likely nature of technological 79 advance—assuming civilization survives? An increasing rate of computerization and automation of the industrial structure of society should diminish the kind of dull and mindless scut-work that now occupies so large a proportion of the efforts of humanity. One might imagine a world of robots and computers that farm and mine and tend machinery; leaving for human beings precisely the type of creative endeavor for which their brains are suited.

Every child not markedly brain-damaged shows the capacity of learn- 80 ing to walk, to speak, to adjust himself to life in a million ways even before he enters the first grade. It is clear, therefore, that the potential for creativity is present in everyone, provided only that we make learning pleasant, and stimulate (not penalize, as we usually do today) any demonstration of that creativity.

Let each follow his own particular drummer, and if some decide to 81 sink into what we would think of as ignoble sloth, or to indulge in what we would now consider trivia, they may later in life grow weary and try, instead, something that our present prejudices consider more worthy — scientific research, politics and command, literature, arts, entertainment, and, of course, education. And some may move in that direction from the start (and, perhaps, abandon it later). Might it not be likely that, on a strictly voluntary basis, enough people will opt for the socially important activities to keep the world going?

And perhaps it will turn out that the activity which is of greater im- 82 portance is education — the designing of computer programs in new and esoteric directions — and of greater subtlety in the older disciplines. There could be a steady, synergistic interaction of man and machine, each learning from the other, and each advancing with the help of the other. The distinction between the two varieties of intelligence may grow dimmer and the discovery and refinement of knowledge, and the beating back of the vast cloud of ignorance, may be carried on at a faster rate by both together than would be possible by either alone.

In such a utopian world as I describe (assuming it can be attained — 83 which is, of course, doubtful) there is the danger that everything will run so smoothly and safely and securely as to remove all interest, and produce a society that will slowly and somnolently sink into the slumber of desuetude.

Yet that need not be so, for out there in space we can find a new 84 and more distant horizon than any we have encountered before; a greater and more dangerous frontier; a larger and more unexpected habitat; an outspreading volume with more fearful unknowns and more exciting possibilities than anything we can now imagine.

But that is a subject for another article. . . .   85

Study Questions

1. A relatively long introduction leads into the main part of his essay. What might be gained and lost by a shorter introduction?
2. What effect is achieved by short paragraphs 19, 20, 21, 22, 23, 25?
3. How does the first-person voice in the early part of the essay set the tone of the essay?

4. Although this piece appears to be loosely organized, it follows a definite pattern of development. Trace this development and note the transitions.
5. Is the thesis stated or implied?
6. Asimov asks a number of questions. He answers some, but not others. What is the rhetorical function of these?
7. What effect is achieved by the concluding sentence?

Derek C. Bok
CAN ETHICS BE TAUGHT?

Derek C. Bok (1930–   ) was born in Ardmore, Pennsylvania. His earned degrees include a B.A. from Stanford (1951), an LL.B. from Harvard (1954), and an M.A. from George Washington (1958). He joined the faculty of Harvard Law School in 1958, became dean in 1968, and president of the university in 1971. His numerous publications include the coauthored books *Labor Law* (with Archibald Cox, 1962) and *Labor and the American Community* (with John T. Dunlop, 1970).

Americans have few rivals in their willingness to talk openly 1 about ethical standards. They are preached in our churches, proclaimed by public officials, debated in the press, and discussed by professional societies to a degree that arouses wonder abroad. Yet there has rarely been a time when we have been so dissatisfied with our moral behavior or so beset by ethical dilemmas of every kind. Some of these problems have arisen in the backwash of the scandals that have recently occurred in government, business, and other areas of national life. Others are the product of an age when many new groups are pressing claims of a distinctly moral nature — racial minorities, women, patients, consumers, environmentalists, and many more.

It will be difficult to make headway against these problems without a 2 determined effort by the leaders of our national institutions. But the public is scarcely optimistic over the prospects, for society's faith in its leaders has declined precipitously in recent years. From 1966 to 1975, the proportion of the public professing confidence in Congress dropped from 42 to 13 percent; in major corporate presidents from 55 to 19 percent; in doctors from 72 to 43 percent; and in leaders of the bar from 46 to

Reprinted from *Change*, October 1976, by permission.

16 percent. Worse yet, 69 percent of the public agreed in 1975 that "over the past 10 years, this country's leaders have consistently lied to the people."

It is also widely believed that most of the sources that transmit moral 3 standards have declined in importance. Churches, families, and local communities no longer seem to have the influence they once enjoyed in a simpler, more rural society. While no one can be certain that ethical standards have declined as a result, most people seem to think that they have, and this belief in itself can erode trust and spread suspicion in ways that sap the willingness to behave morally toward others.

In struggling to overcome these problems, we will surely need help 4 from many quarters. Business organizations and professional associations will have to take more initiative in establishing stricter codes of ethics and providing for their enforcement. Public officials will need to use imagination in seeking ways of altering incentives in our legal and regulatory structure to encourage moral behavior.

But it is also important to look to our colleges and universities and 5 consider what role they can play. Professors are often reluctant even to talk about this subject because it is so easy to seem censorious or banal. Nevertheless, the issue should not be ignored if only because higher education occupies such strategic ground from which to make a contribution. Every businessman and lawyer, every public servant and doctor will pass through our colleges, and most will attend our professional schools as well. If other sources of ethical values have declined in influence, educators have a responsibility to contribute in any way they can to the moral development of their students.

Unfortunately, most colleges and universities are doing very little to 6 meet this challenge. In several respects, they have done even less in recent decades than they did a hundred years ago. In the nineteenth century, it was commonplace for college presidents to present a series of lectures to the senior class expounding the accepted moral principles of the time. This practice may seem quaint today, but in its time it served reasonably well as a method of moral education. In 1850, it was easier to discern a common moral code that could be passed along from one generation to the next. Partly because of their positions of authority, and partly because of the force of their personalities, many presidents seem to have left a deep impression on the minds and characters of their students.

In the intervening years, society changed in ways that eventually dis- 7 credited these lectures. Students became less inclined to fear authority or to be greatly impressed by those who held it. More serious still, the sense of a prevailing moral code broke down. As early as the 1850s, the president of Oberlin College could declare with certitude that slavery was immoral, even as his counterpart at Mercer College was vigorously upholding the practice on biblical and pragmatic grounds. As social change led to new sources of conflict, college presidents seemed increasingly arbitrary and doctrinaire when they attempted to convey a set of proper ethical precepts. And since their lectures were didactic in style, they failed to prepare students to think for themselves in applying their moral principles to the new controversies and new ethical issues that an industrializing society seemed constantly to create. By World War I, the tradition had all but ended.

In its place, many colleges introduced survey courses on moral phi- 8 losophy. These offerings have acquainted students with a great intellectual tradition in a manner that could scarcely be called doctrinaire. But they have rarely attempted to make more than a limited contribution to moral education. Since the classes usually consist of lectures, they do not develop the power of moral reasoning. To the extent that these courses are simply surveys of ethical theory, they likewise do little to help the student cope with the practical moral dilemmas he may encounter in his own life.

Professional schools have never shown much interest in providing 9 lectures on moral conduct or surveys of ethical theory. Many of them have simply ignored moral education altogether. But others have tried to approach the subject in another way by attempting to weave moral issues throughout a variety of courses and problems in the regular curriculum. This method has the advantage of suggesting to students that ethical questions are not isolated problems but an integral part of the daily life and experience of the profession. As such, the efforts are valuable and should be encouraged. But it is doubtful whether this approach by itself can have more than limited success in bringing students to reason more carefully about moral issues. Most professors have so much ground to cover that they will rarely take the time to acquaint their students with the writings of moral philosophers on the ethical issues under discussion.

Still more important, if a professional school divides the responsi- 10 bility for moral education among a large number of faculty members, most instructors will not have a knowledge of ethics that is equal to the task. Many of them will give short shrift to the moral problems and concentrate on other aspects of the course materials that they feel more equipped to teach. The difficulties are clearly illustrated by the findings of a recent report from a prominent business school. After listing a wide variety of moral issues distributed throughout the curriculum, the report described the reactions of a sample of students and faculty: "Almost without exception, the faculty members indicated that they touch on one or more of these issues frequently ... but while they were certain they covered the issues, they often had second thoughts about how explicit they had been. Almost equally without exception, students felt the issues are seldom touched on, and when they are, are treated as afterthoughts or digressions."

In view of the disadvantages of the traditional approaches, more at- 11 tention is being given today to developing problem-oriented courses in ethics. These classes are built around a series of contemporary moral dilemmas. In colleges, the courses tend to emphasize issues of deception, breach of promise, and other moral dilemmas that commonly arise in everyday life. In schools of law, public affairs, business, and medicine, the emphasis is on professional ethics. Medical students will grapple with abortion, euthanasia, and human experimentation, while students of public administration will discuss whether government officials are ever justified in lying to the public, or leaking confidential information, or refusing to carry out the orders of their superiors. In schools of business, such courses may take up any number of problems — corporate bribes abroad, deceptive advertising, use of potentially hazardous products and methods of production, or employment practices in South Africa.

Whatever the problem may be, the classes generally proceed by dis- 12 cussion rather than lecturing. Instructors may present their own views, if only to demonstrate that it is possible to make carefully reasoned choices about ethical dilemmas. But they will be less concerned with presenting solutions than with carrying on an active discussion in an effort to encourage students to perceive ethical issues, wrestle with the competing arguments, discover the weaknesses in their own position, and ultimately reach thoughtfully reasoned conclusions.

What can these courses accomplish? One objective is to help stu- 13 dents become more alert in discovering the moral issues that arise in their own lives. Formal education will rarely improve the character of a scoundrel. But many individuals who are disposed to act morally will often fail to do so because they are simply unaware of the ethical problems that lie hidden in the situations they confront. Others will not discover a moral problem until they have gotten too deeply enmeshed to extricate themselves. By repeatedly asking students to identify moral problems and define the issues at stake, courses in applied ethics can sharpen and refine the moral perception of students so that they can avoid these pitfalls.

Another major objective is to teach students to reason carefully 14 about ethical issues. Many people feel that moral problems are matters of personal opinion and that it is pointless even to argue about them since each person's views will turn on values that cannot be established or refuted on logical grounds. A well-taught course can demonstrate that this is simply not true, and that moral issues can be discussed as rigorously as many other problems considered in the classroom. With the help of carefully selected readings, students can then develop their capacity for moral reasoning by learning to sort out all of the arguments that bear upon moral problems and apply them to concrete situations.

A final objective of these courses is to help students clarify their 15 moral aspirations. Whether in college or professional school, many students will be trying to define their identity and to establish the level of integrity at which they will lead their professional lives. By considering a series of ethical problems, they can be encouraged to consider these questions more fully. In making this effort, students will benefit from the opportunity to grapple with moral issues in a setting where no serious personal consequences are at stake. Prospective lawyers, doctors, or businessmen may set higher ethical standards for themselves if they first encounter the moral problems of their calling in the classroom instead of waiting to confront them at a point in their careers when they are short of time and feel great pressure to act in morally questionable ways.

Despite these apparent virtues, the problem-oriented courses in eth- 16 ics have hardly taken the curriculum by storm. A few experimental offerings have been introduced, but they are still regarded with indifference or outright skepticism by many members of the faculty. What accounts for these attitudes? To begin with, many skeptics question the value of trying to teach students to reason about moral issues. According to these critics, such courses may bring students to perceive more of the arguments and complexities that arise in moral issues, but this newfound sophistication will simply leave them more confused than ever and quite unable to reach any satisfactory moral conclusions.

This attitude is puzzling. It may be impossible to arrive at answers to 17
certain ethical questions through analysis alone. Even so, it is surely better for students to be aware of the nuance and complexity of important human problems than to act on simplistic generalizations or unexamined premises. Moreover, many ethical problems are not all that complicated if students can only be taught to recognize them and reason about them carefully. However complex the issue, analysis does have important uses, as the following illustrations make clear:

> In one Harvard class, a majority of the students thought it proper for 18
> a government official to lie to a congressman in order to forestall a regressive piece of legislation. According to the instructor, "The students seem to see things essentially in cost-benefit terms. Will the lie serve a good policy? What are the chances of getting caught? If you get caught, how much will it hurt you?" This is a very narrow view of deception. Surely these students might revise their position if they were asked to consider seriously what would happen in a society that invited everyone to lie whenever they believed that it would help to avoid a result which they believed to be wrong.
>
> The *New York Times* reports that many young people consider it per- 19
> missible to steal merchandise because they feel that they are merely reducing the profits of large corporations. At the very least, analysis will be useful in pointing out that theft is not so likely to diminish profits as to increase the price to other consumers.
>
> Courses in moral reasoning can also help students to avoid moral dif- 20
> ficulties by devising alternate methods of achieving their ends. This is a simple point, but it is often overlooked. For example, many researchers commonly mislead their human subjects in order to conduct an important experiment. Careful study can often bring these investigators to understand the dangers of deception more fully and exert more imagination in devising ways of conducting their experiments which do not require such questionable methods.
>
> Even in the most difficult cases—such as deciding who will have ac- 21
> cess to some scarce, life-sustaining medical technique—progress can be made by learning to pay attention not only to the ultimate problem of who shall live, but to devising procedures for making such decisions in a manner that seems reasonable and fair to all concerned.

There are other skeptics who concede that courses can help students 22
reason more carefully about ethical problems. But these critics argue that

moral development has less to do with reasoning than with acquiring proper moral values and achieving the strength of character to put these values into practice. Since such matters are not easily taught in a classroom, they question whether a course on ethics can accomplish anything of real importance. It is this point of view that accounts for the statement of one business school spokesman in explaining why there were no courses on ethics in the curriculum: "On the subject of ethics, we feel that either you have them or you don't."

There is clearly some force to this argument. Professors who teach 23 the problem-oriented courses do not seek to persuade students to accept some preferred set of moral values. In fact, we would be uneasy if they did, since such an effort would have overtones of indoctrination that conflict with our notions of intellectual freedom. As for building character, universities can only make a limited contribution, and what they accomplish will probably depend more on what goes on outside the classroom than on the curriculum itself. For example, the moral aspirations of Harvard students undoubtedly profited more from the example of Archibald Cox than from any regular course in ethics. Moreover, if a university expects to overcome the sense of moral cynicism among its students, it must not merely offer courses; it will have to demonstrate its own commitment to principled behavior by making a serious effort to deal with the ethical aspects of its investment policies, its employment practices, and the other moral dilemmas that inevitably confront every educational institution.

But it is one thing to acknowledge the limitations of formal learning 24 and quite another to deny that reading and discussion can have any effect in developing ethical principles and moral character. As I have already pointed out, problem-oriented courses encourage students to define their moral values more carefully and to understand more fully the reasons that underlie and justify these precepts. Unless one is prepared to argue that ethical values have no intellectual basis whatsoever, it seems likely that this process of thought will play a useful role in helping students develop a clearer, more consistent set of ethical principles that takes more careful account of the needs and interests of others. And it is also probable that students who fully understand the reasons that support their ethical principles will be more inclined to put their principles into practice and more uncomfortable at the thought of sacrificing principle to serve their own private ends.

To be sure, no one would deny that ethical values and moral charac- 25 ter are profoundly dependent on many forces beyond the university—on family influences, religious experience, and the personal example of friends and public figures. But this is true of all of education. Everyone knows that outstanding lawyers, businessmen, and public servants succeed not only because of the instruction they received as students but because of qualities of leadership, integrity, judgment, and imagination that formal education cannot hope to supply. Nevertheless, we still have faith in the value of professional schools because we believe that most students possess these personal qualities in sufficient measure to benefit from professional training and thereby become more effective practitioners. In the same way, we should be willing to assume that most students have sufficient desire to live a moral life that they will profit from instruction that helps them to become more alert to ethical issues, and to apply their moral values more carefully and rigorously to the ethical dilemmas they encounter in their professional lives.

Even if we are prepared to agree that these problem-oriented courses 26 on ethics have a valuable contribution to make, there is a final, practical objection to consider. To put it bluntly, much of the skepticism about these courses probably arises not from doubts about their potential value but from deeper reservations as to whether those who teach the courses are really qualified to do so. Unfortunately, it is simply a fact that many courses in applied ethics have been taught by persons with little qualification beyond a strongly developed social conscience. Of all the problems that have been considered, this is the most substantial. Poor instruction can harm any class. But it is devastating to a course on ethics, for it confirms the prejudices of those students and faculty who suspect that moral reasoning is inherently inconclusive and that courses on moral issues will soon become vehicles for transmitting the private prejudices of the instructor.

What does a competent professor need to know to offer a course of 27 this type? To begin with, instructors must have an adequate knowledge of moral philosophy so that they can select the most useful readings for their students and bring forth the most illuminating theories and arguments that have been devised to deal with recurrent ethical dilemmas. In addition, teachers must have an adequate knowledge of the field of human affairs to which their course is addressed. Otherwise, they will neither be credible to students nor succeed in bringing students to understand all of the practical implications and consequences of choosing one course of action over another. Finally, instructors must know how to conduct a rigorous class discussion that will elicit a full consideration of the issues without degenerating into a windy exchange of student opinion.

These requirements are not insuperable, but they present real diffi- 28 culties because in most universities there is no single department or program that is equipped to train a fully qualified instructor. Professors of law or business may understand judicial procedures and corporate finance—they may even be masters of the Socratic method—but they will rarely have much background in moral philosophy. Philosophers in turn will usually know virtually nothing about any of the professions and may even lack experience in teaching problem-oriented classes. If moral education is ever to prosper, we will have to find ways of overcoming these deficiencies by creating serious interdisciplinary programs for students seeking careers of teaching and scholarship in this field. Fortunately, the time is ripe for developing such programs, since professional schools are beginning to recognize the moral demands being made on their professions while philosophy departments are finding it more and more difficult to place their PhDs in traditional teaching posts.

But is the effort worth making? I firmly believe that it is. Even if 29 courses in applied ethics turned out to have no effect whatsoever on the moral development of our students, they would still make a contribution. There is value to be gained from any course that forces students to think carefully and rigorously about complex human problems. The growth of such courses will also encourage professors to give more systematic study and thought to a wide range of contemporary moral issues. Now that society is expressing greater concern about ethics in the professions and in public life, work of this kind is badly needed, for it is surprising how little serious, informed writing has been devoted even to such pervasive moral issues as lying and deception. But beyond these advantages, one must certainly hope that courses on ethical problems will affect the lives and thought of students. We cannot be certain of the impact these courses will have. But certainty has never been the criterion for educational decisions. Every professor knows that much of the information conveyed in the classroom will soon be forgotten. The willingness to continue teaching rests on an act of faith that students will retain a useful conceptual framework, a helpful approach to the subject, a valuable method of analysis, or some other intangible residue of intellectual value. Much the same is true of courses on ethical problems. Although the point is still unproved, it does seem plausible to suppose that the students in these courses will become more alert in perceiving ethical issues, more aware of the reasons underlying moral principles, and more equipped to reason carefully in applying these principles to concrete cases. Will they behave more ethically? We may never know. But surely the experiment is worth trying, for the goal has never been more important to the quality of the society in which we live.

Study Questions

1. What is the general organization of Bok's arguments?
2. In addition to serving as the introduction, what is the function of paragraphs 1–4?
3. Identify the topic sentence of paragraph 29. What type of development is used in this paragraph?
4. What words and phrases link paragraphs 1–10?
5. Paragraphs 13, 27, and 29 begin with questions. What is the purpose of the questions?
6. What types of arguments does the author use to support his position?

Sloan Wilson
WHY JESSIE HATES ENGLISH

Sloan Wilson (1920–   ) was born in Norwalk, Connecticut, and received an A.B. from Harvard University (1946). During World War II he was an officer in the Coast Guard. Then he wrote for the Providence *Journal* and later Time, Inc. In 1953 he taught English at Buffalo University. He was assistant director for the White House Conference on Education (1955) and a member of the National Citizens Committee for Public Schools (1949–1953). His books include *Voyage to Somewhere* (1946), *The Man in the Gray Flannel Suit* (1955), *A Summer Place* (1958), *Away from It All* (1969), and *All the Best People* (1970). Moviegoers will remember the film versions of *The Man in the Gray Flannel Suit* and *Summer Place.*

Not long ago, my youngest daughter, Jessica, who is twelve 1 years old, came home from school, dropped her book bag in the middle of our living room, and yelled, "I hate English!"

In some families this might not cause much of a stir, but I am an old 2 English teacher, as well as a writer. My father was an English teacher and so was *his* father. As a matter of fact, my father, who enjoyed exaggeration, used to claim that all his progenitors had been English teachers, going clear back to a lone Wilson aboard the *Santa Maria,* who died horribly while attempting to give a lesson in English grammar to the Indians. They skinned him alive, Dad said, and boiled him.

When Jessie came home with her shocking announcement, my first 3 impulse was to find the teacher who had made her hate English and give her the same treatment that the aborigines had given my ancestor. I should add here my objective, impartial view that my youngest daughter is extremely bright, especially gifted in English, and a surprisingly dedicated scholar. All right, the opinion of a father concerning his youngest daughter has to be discounted at least 50 percent. Even so, Jessie is a child who reads far more than most adults do at home, and she writes well enough to get the highest marks whenever she pens a report for a course other than English. In her English course she never has had to write much of anything. In many modern six-grade English courses, I had already discovered, writing does not occupy a large part of the curriculum, if any.

Reprinted from *Saturday Review,* September 18, 1976, by permission.

But what had the teacher been doing to make Jessie hate English? 4
She was not, Jessie hastened to tell me, the kind of classroom ogre who
can make a student hate anything.

"It's not the teacher, Daddy," she said with some exasperation, as 5
though I were a very slow pupil, "it's just *English.*"

"Don't you enjoy all the stories and poems you get in English?"   6

"We hardly ever get stories and poems. All we get, Daddy, is gram- 7
mar. That's all we're supposed to study, right through high school. I'll
show you my books."

That night I spent several hours poring over my daughter's textbooks 8
after she had finished her homework.

"What do you think?" my wife asked, poking her head into my study 9
when it was time for bed.

"I hate English!" I replied. "These books have converted me from a 10
lifelong lover of the language to a truant."

"What's the matter with them?"   11

I showed her two books. They were the official kind of modern text- 12
book that apparently is contrived to look as little like a textbook as possible. The layout looks as though it is the brainstorm of the art director
of a struggling new advertising agency after a three-martini lunch. Much
of the copy was apparently supplied by a deposed editor of the New
York *Daily News.* Headlines scream. There are eye-catching photographs
of football players and full-page reproductions of old advertisements for
expensive coats, cosmetics, and automobiles. In one book, my favorite
horror, there is an entire section on the grammar of Madison Avenue,
which the authors obviously admire.

For a long time I have been aware that we all live in a nightmare 13
world, but I had not realized that the schools have substituted advertising
copy for the prose and poetry of the masters, which students in my antique day used to study and occasionally enjoy. Why are they doing this
sort of thing?

To find out, I telephoned my *oldest* daughter, Lisa, who followed the 14
family trade and is or, rather, was an English teacher. Unlike me, she has
recent knowledge of what goes on in the public schools.

"A lot of advertising copy is used to teach English nowadays," she 15
said. "The words are short and the sentences simple —"

"I'm not talking about a class for retarded children," I objected.   16

"Neither am I. That's the depressing part of it. Even in classes for 17
the brightest children, the advertising copy is sometimes useful, just to
keep the kids awake."

"I hate the whole system!" I exploded. "Jessie spends hours at home 18
looking at television, and when she finally goes to school, they teach her
advertisements as though they were gems of English prose! Pretty soon
she's going to think and talk like a deodorant commercial!"

"Do I?" Lisa asked with a laugh. "What do you think I had to study? 19
The lucky thing is that most kids ignore school."

Perhaps in an effort to preserve some façade of respectability, Jessie's 20
English textbooks also included some brief snippets of good books by
recognizable authors. A few paragraphs by the masters, from Mark Twain

to Ray Bradbury, were sandwiched between the gaudy photographs and the advertising copy, free samples of a product that many of the students may never see in its entirety.

The jazzy layout, which made a textbook look like a sales brochure, 21 and the snippets of real writing were all sugarcoating for the main subject of Jessie's English books, which was, of course, grammar. Page after page was devoted to this dismal exercise, chapter after chapter. Many little tests in grammar were offered. Most of them I could not pass despite a lifetime of making a living by writing English.

What are "derivational suffixes"? How about a "subjective com- 22 pletion"? While I puzzled over "subjective completion," I thought it might be some sort of euphemism for "premature ejaculation," but the textbook tells me that it is "a word which completes the verb and refers back to the subject." Understand now?

I have here a whole bagful of nuggets of information mined from 23 Jessie's textbook. Here is one sentence: "Just as there are determiners to signal the presence of nouns in a sentence, so too are there signal words which point to the presence of verbs—structure words called *auxiliaries.*"

That is the kind of sentence that I cannot understand and do not 24 want to understand. People who understand sentences like that are thrown out of the Authors League and the Roma Bar, my favorite hangout.

Do you have "terminal clusters"? They are not a form of cancer, but 25 something that adds to the descriptive power of prose, the book assures me. Are you a master of the "multi-level sentence"? Apparently it has nothing to do with the critics' favorite, the multi-level novel. Are you good at "parallel repetition" and "chain linking"? We are still talking about English prose, mind you, not wire fences. Are you a master of that new addition of marlinespike scholarship, the "comma splice"?

My twelve-year-old daughter has to be able to interpret all this non- 26 sense. If she can't, she will fail her examinations in English, no matter how much she reads at home, no matter how well she writes for other classes.

Who invented all this hideous jargon used by grammarians? I don't 27 know, but my quotations are from that favorite horror book of Jessie's, *Grammar Lives.* The title becomes more nonsensical the more one thinks about it. This mercifully slender volume, which presumably has been sold to many school systems, was published in 1975 by McDougal, Littell & Company. The names of the people responsible for this reverse masterpiece go on like the "crawl" preceding a pornographic movie, constituting a list of individuals eagerly seeking credit for the discreditable. The "consultant" is Karen J. Kuehner. The "authors" are Ronald T. Shephard and John MacDonald. The "editorial direction," which must have been remarkable, was supplied by Claudia Norlin. These people presumably all got together, invented or borrowed phrases like "terminal clusters," reprinted some old advertisements and snippets of legitimate prose, and then really demonstrated their talents by finding a way to make this stuff compulsory reading for hundreds of thousands, if not millions, of innocent children. They should not, however, feel alone in their guilt.

Plenty of other "educators" are helping them to make children hate English and to be illiterate.

I could quote many more examples of the grammarian's art, but I 28 have to take it easy on my blood pressure.

"Why does grammar make you so angry?" my wife asked. "Doesn't 29 everybody have to study it?"

The answer, of course, is that for the last few thousand years nobody 30 was asked to study grammar anywhere near as much as the pupils in most American public schools, where it often occupies most of the English curriculum. In my own youth I studied formal grammar briefly in the fifth grade. I remember it because it seemed so silly. Who but a schoolteacher would diagram sentences and make simple prose so complex? Fortunately my teacher hated grammar as much as I did. Soon she returned to assigning us themes and correcting them in detail, a much better way to teach the mechanics of the language. She also asked us to read good books—*whole books,* not snippets. When we wrote book reports, the teacher got another shot at correcting our English. I often wonder what she would have said if someone had asked her to give us advertisements for study.

I have heard it said that the students of my generation and of prior 31 ones did not need to learn grammar because we studied so much Latin. I believe that this contradicts everything that has been learned about learning, part of which can be summed up with the astonishing news that when a boy studies Latin, he just learns Latin. My own case provides only one correction to that. For eight years I studied Latin, but I didn't acquire any lasting knowledge of Latin. I just learned to hate school, except for English, which made sense. I do not owe my knowledge of English to Latin, except for the fact that Latin made everything else appear easy.

Those who are in charge of planning English courses in the public 32 schools do not seem to be aware of the fact that those who study grammar do not learn English—they just learn the crazy jargon of the grammarians and all their rules and regulations for English when studied as a dead language. Grammar is an attempt to codify the English language, reduce it to abstractions devoid of meaning or beauty, break it into "rules," "laws," and pseudomathematical "rights" and "wrongs." The fact that it is necessary to learn to speak and write grammatically does not mean that one must devote much time to the abstract study of grammar. One should, instead, study, of all things, speaking and writing.

Some youngsters can find real joy in writing a good theme and wel- 33 come a teacher's attempts to show them how to improve it, even if the corrections involve the use of a few basic rules of grammar. In a properly run English composition class, grammar has specific applications and is not taught as an abstract "science." As it should be, it is always subordinate to the basic urge to communicate, not an end in itself.

I think I know how the public schools came to rely more and more 34 heavily on the teaching of grammar as an abstract science. As the children of parents who themselves spoke broken English flooded the public schools, something had to be done to help countless students learn whole new speech patterns. The study of grammar is not good remedial English, as the performance of so many high school graduates sadly proves, but it must have seemed a good solution at first and a much cheaper one than the complex programs necessary for helping a person change speech patterns acquired in infancy.

Although classes in grammar didn't teach children anything but how 35 to pass examinations devised by the grammarians, they offered certain practical advantages. Tests in grammar can be graded by machines. A teacher who asks his class to write themes every day may be deluged with papers that have to be corrected line after line by the human hand. It is also true that almost any adult, after a few months of specialized instruction, can teach grammar. To be a good teacher of English composition, one has to be able to write good English oneself. As has been often remarked, English has rarely been a strong point of the teachers colleges and departments of education, which have produced most of our public school teachers. The jargon of the educator is not conducive to teaching good, clear English.

The current discovery that high school graduates on the whole read 36 and write with more difficulty than even their recent predecessors hits educators hard. The public schools have been supported and defended as an act of faith by most Americans all during their periods of rapid growth, especially since World War II. Criticisms have been shrugged off as the work of crackpots or intellectual snobs. When the book *Why Johnny Can't Read* came out, more than twenty years ago, it sold a lot of copies, but it was never quite respectable among people who were seriously concerned with the schools. If the schools were not teaching reading well at the moment, the feeling was, the difficulties would soon be overcome.

Now decades have passed, and there is evidence that the schools are 37 teaching reading worse than they have in the past and that writing among recent high school graduates is almost a lost art. There have been loud cries for "a return to the fundamentals." And what are the fundamentals? Reading? Writing? Of course not! In the minds of the educators, *grammar* is the real fundamental. If the proliferation of courses in grammar has resulted in the graduation of countless youngsters who can hardly read or write, the obvious answer is to give the youngsters even more grammar. If one aspirin doesn't stop your headache, take two.

Apparently no one puts himself in the position of the student who 38 sits squirming while the teacher drills him in grammar day after day, year after year. It's easy to see why such a student doesn't want to read anything—he is taught to regard the text as a boneyard of grammar problems on which he will probably be quizzed. Writing, too, becomes a test of fitting together words and phrases in a way that is *grammatical,* not interesting, funny, or meaningful. My youngest daughter is not the only pupil in her school who hates English, and as a result, she gives it as little time as possible.

Like many other parents, I have tried to do something about this sit- 39 uation for my child. I wrote a long letter to my old friend David S. Siegel, the superintendent of schools in Ticonderoga, N.Y., the upstate village where we live. Dave really wanted to help. He referred the matter to the "language arts coordinator," a title that apparently means "head English teacher" in the language of contemporary public schools. He turned out to be a pleasant, intelligent young chap who is alarmingly well versed in the theories of modern public schools, but ambitious and idealistic concerning the English courses nonetheless. He organized a class for students from three grades who are especially gifted in English and invited my youngest daughter to join it. The class is known as a speed group, and now, poor Jessie reports, she is being fed about three times as much grammar as before. Her new ambition is to be a veterinarian. With animals, after all, she will be asked neither to write, to read, nor even to talk.

Study Questions

1. What is the effect of the narrative method the author uses to develop this essay?
2. Describe the author's attitude. What words and expressions establish the tone?
3. What are the advantages of the author's use of the first-person point-of-view?
4. In paragraphs 11, and 19–26 what method does the author use to make his point?
5. In dealing with a situation he feels needs to be corrected, what is the author's strategy?

Sheridan Baker
WRITING AS DISCOVERY

Sheridan Baker (1918–   ) was born in Santa Rosa, California. He received an A.B. (1939), M.A. (1946), and Ph.D. (1950) from the University of California at Berkeley. He has taught at Berkeley and the University of Michigan, and was a Fulbright lecturer in Japan in 1961–1962. He has contributed poems and critical articles, many of them on eighteenth-century English literature, to numerous periodicals. His influential books include *The Practical Stylist* (1962) and *Ernest Hemingway: An Introduction and Interpretation* (1967).

Reprinted from *AVE Bulletin,* November, 1974 by permission of the author.
    An address delivered before the Wyoming Conference on Freshman and Sophomore English at the University of Wyoming, Laramie, 25 July 1974, here revised and amplified slightly.

My idea here is simple, even self-evident: that the process of writing is a process of discovery. Everyone who writes has experienced this process, has discovered, through writing it out, what he has in mind. Yet this simple fact is one not frequently propounded in our textbooks, and it seems utterly alien to the students who come to us from high-school courses in English, some of which may have included almost no writing at all. Even the growing emphasis on creative writing seems to cut against such a concept, which is one I urge upon my students, and would like to urge upon you as an almost desperate necessity if we are to make our courses in composition truly valuable and lead our students — and their teachers — to see the full value of writing in intellectual education and the intellectual life.

I believe, quite simply, that writing is our chief means, as individuals, of discovering knowledge, and eventually of discovering values and what is valid. Reading, of course, takes us well into that territory, as do lectures and TV and films and talk and all the rest of our experience, raw and otherwise. But only by *realizing* — making real — our new ideas by writing them out do we really discover them fully and as our own. We discover what we know by writing it out, bringing up from our tumbling mists of thought and intuition, our perpetual daydreams, those concepts we hardly knew we had. On blank paper we shape thoughts from what we thought were our blank minds. We discover that we know something after all. Only on paper can we hold those thoughts still, straighten them out, test them out. Like our inner dialogues, speech helps, of course, so we warm up our ideas with discussion. But only writing makes the full discovery of thought.

"How can I know what I think till I see what I say?" writes W. H. Auden in explaining how poetry is a "game of knowledge, a bringing to consciousness, by naming them, of emotions and their hidden relationships."[1] *Seeing* thought, *seeing* meaning: "Oh, I see," we say when we understand, and writing makes this literally true, makes our thoughts visible to the eye. All writing bears out Auden's observations, bringing to consciousness, by naming them, not only our emotions and their hidden relationships but all our wordless visual pictures and all our pictureless ideas as well. Writing is seeing, or seeing anew and in a more enduring way. In a sense, we do not see the woods and the trees, nor the valid and the invalid, until we conceptualize them in words and sentences and paragraphs on paper, telling one from the other, discovering them.

Dis-cover means to uncover. We uncover to ourselves what we had somewhere in mind, and we then uncover it further, *discovering* it to the reader, as the eighteenth-century writers would say. I have, in the past, suggested that language *is* thought.[2] I think this is only partially true,

[1] "Squares and Oblongs," *Poets at Work,* Rudolf Arnheim, et al. (New York: Harcourt, Brace and Co., 1948), pp. 174, 173. This quotation, and the rest of this paragraph, I have borrowed and adapted slightly from preface to *The Crowell College Reader,* with David B. Hamilton (New York: Thomas Y. Crowell Co., 1974), p. vii.

[2] *The Written Word,* with Jacques Barzun and I. A. Richards (Rowley, Mass.: Newbury House Publishers, Inc., 1971), p. 5.

however, and only of what we might call rational thought, or rationalized thought (to borrow a seminal idea from James Harvey Robinson's book of some years ago, *The Mind in the Making*). We need words to get hold of, to grasp, in a rational, conceptual way, ideas provided by our minds below the level of language. Language comes from that left lobe of the brain that controls our right thinking, from the hemisphere able to achieve analytic thought, but it also comprehends, as best it can, the clouds and lightning in the darks of the right-lobed intuitions formed in the part of the brain controlling holistic and nonverbal activity. Language thus gets things together—reason and instinct, left and right—and writing our language out is like spinning a straight thread from the woolly heaps of whatever we have in our minds. Ideas and language are not identical, as any effort to express our ideas in writing soon illustrates. As the transformational grammarians have reminded us, we can express the same idea in a number of different ways. We have something to say, even though we don't quite know what it is or how to say it. Then we find the words that lift the thought up into the light, that fit it, like the shell of a snail, embodying it, giving it form and being. Again, only on paper, by writing and rewriting, can we get the fit, make the thought visible, bring it into some kind of nonsubjective being where it will bear inspection from both ourselves and others. In short, we discover it fully for the first time.

I am really talking about two things, both of which are discoveries. 5 The first is having a conviction: for instance, that writing is somehow vitally important to our conceptual and rational thinking, our most distinctive characteristic as humans in this animated kingdom. All right, we have an idea, a conviction. Then we must find the language to express it, to make it clear both to others and ourselves. This process is a discovery, because in writing it out, in expressing it, we discover not only its conceptual being but its depths and ramifications. We have discovered, through writing, our idea's meaning and force. We have made it tangible. We have established it as something either to embrace or challenge, or to qualify and deepen for new discoveries. This is the first discovery of ideas in language, possible only through the process of writing which gives fibre to the process of thought.

The second process of discovery is akin to the first, part of the inevi- 6 table process set in motion by the first, in fact—the actual creating of thought in our minds as we work thought into some graspable statement on paper. The blank paper and the blank mind seem to conspire, like white clouds, to generate the flash of an idea and all its zigzags of implication—light out of chaos, just as the Biblical writers pictured being and light as forming simultaneously in the initial act of creation, the discovery of order and clarity and harmony. The words draw forth the idea, separate the mud from the water, populate teeming emptiness with categories of being, and with a measure of beauty and order in the process.

Now this idea that language brings thought into being, and that writ- 7 ing brings this being into something like palpable permanence, clarifying it further as it holds it still for consideration—this idea is quite contrary to what I find my students assuming about freshman composition. Their first assumption is that everyone knows how to write, at least after twelve years of schooling, just as everyone knows how to talk. Their second is that writing is something specialized, something for the specialist or the classroom, not really related to life as they live it. Composition is thus something dry and schoolmarmish, a kind of superficial fussing with inessential details like commas, something utterly elementary, something to be excused from.

A couple of years ago, I came back to the freshman program at 8 Michigan after about a decade away from it. The freshmen seemed as bright as ever, and much the same as ever (and mercifully more docile than students in some of those intervening years). But they could not write even as well as their peers of a decade earlier, which was indeed not well. Many simply could not see, and never learned with any certainty that a phrase is not a sentence, that they had not completed the idea they had in mind. They could not distinguish the meaning of a comma from the meaning of a period. Some had never written an essay.

One was a young man named Rand. He stood out that first hour— 9 alert, interested, keen of question—and I remember his name, as frequently I do not, because of the Rand Corporation's famous think-tank. "Wow," I thought, "maybe I have the Son of Rand in hand." Then I read his first paper, a simple fifteen-minute impromptu deriving from that opening discussion. He had written two or three painful and garbled sentences, and, judging from his smile as he handed them in, had thought he had written well.

"What did you do in high-school English?" I asked him later.   10

"Well, we had some great discussions about how we see things, about 11 perception. You know, when you see green and I see green do we see the same green, and how do we know we do if we do."

"It's a fascinating question," I said. "It really is. But didn't you write 12 about it? Didn't you look up some articles and maybe write something about what you thought as to whether green was green?"

"No, not really. We really didn't write anything. The teacher brought 13 in some stuff, some pictures and slides and stuff, and we had some great discussions."

Well, my class was reading other things than the physiology and psy- 14 chology of perception, and I didn't follow it up. But I know now I should have prompted the student to write an essay on the subject. It interested him, even though he could say, at the time, very little about it. I should have encouraged him to write his ideas and knowledge into being, to discover the idea he must have had somewhere in mind from all that interest, to assert that green was or was not green and to find the evidence and the reasons to prove it, discovering the idea that he seemed to have but not to know, to test its validity, to argue it into being, discovering and creating thought from all that interesting vagueness he was content to let drift off into thin air. Writing in an atmosphere already mildly charged would have discovered thought, would have created it.

Writing is essentially creative. And here I want to make a further dis- 15 tinction that many of our students and many of our teachers do not see or do not believe in. Creative writing is all the rage these days. Students and teachers—all of us, I suppose—give it a higher value than poor old plodding freshman composition. When I rose to the call to take on our freshman program, I discovered to my dismay that we had been exempting a number of freshmen, in addition to those exempted by examination in participating high schools, on individual pleas to the director, that is, to me. Some came armed with sheafs of essays, others with a short story or poem or two, others with nothing but perfect confidence in their case and their charm. What surprised me most was the number of high schools that seemed to have converted composition into creative writing, and the almost universal assumption that anyone who has written a poem or story has already passed to a sphere far beyond the dusty pedestrian world of composition.

Now, I am an old creative writer myself, and a teacher of creative   16 writing too. I got deeply hooked on the writing of poetry in my early years of teaching, when I inherited a creative writing class at the same time I was really getting excited about poetry for the first time by teaching it in another course. I know the intensities of trying to create a poem, and I know I learned in that cauldron something about verbal economies and the meanings of words and the potencies of metaphor that I would not have learned otherwise. But I also know that settling for self-expression as the whole of writing will leave in darkness another whole continent that writing can and should discover for each and every one of our students — the realm of rational thinking, the realm of reason.

I believe that education should be primarily intellectual, since the in-   17 tuitional, passional, sensational side of our existence is where we start — in sin, as St. Augustine would put it, the sin of the self-centered ego. We need to stretch upward and away from our sole selves toward the enlightened intellect, which is also part of ourselves, the fullest potential of every person. Creative writing at the elementary level — beyond which it rarely goes in elementary courses — usually leaves us trapped in self expression. Even worse, it leaves us with the illusion that we know all we need to know about writing. We are doubly trapped in ourselves because pleased with ourselves, and thus incapable of getting beyond ourselves into rational thought, into ideas, into the truths and truth about this mysterious and wonderful and perhaps frightening life and universe of which we are a part.

I am quite content to start with self-expression, with automatic   18 stream-of-consciousness writing, with anything to get the pencils and thoughts in motion, but only as a pump-primer, as something other than, or auxiliary to, the real business of the course — certainly not as something to exclude the rational discovery and validification of ideas through writing, which is the primary contribution of writing to one's education and intellectual life. I also frequently try an excursion into self-expression later in the term to help the students infuse the power of personality into their reasoning.

One of the results of emphasizing creative writing at the expense of   19 expository writing is to separate the two and to encourage the assumption that expository prose should be bloodless and dry as dust, with no personality whatsoever. Perhaps the most valuable discovery through writing one's ideas into being is that good ideas are both personal (meaningful in here) and impersonal (meaningful out there, generally valid out there), and that the satisfaction of writing them out well, of bringing others to see the validity one has discovered, comes also in finding a language, an expression, alive with one's own personality and conviction. Good writing contains that personal joy in having hit the right words, the right rhythms, and the right figures of speech to catch the ideas that are being discovered fully in the process of attempting to make them as persuasive and attractive to others as to oneself. From the first, I urge each student to find his own written voice, to give his writing personality (his own), to write as he speaks, but with everything tightened up a notch, all the hems and haws chipped out, all uncertainties and repetitions cleaned up, everything smoother, clearer, more sure, more attractive, more fully stated, more completely expressed in words everyone will understand and respect. Perhaps the final discovery in writing is precisely this pleasure in discovering that private convictions can be affirmed as public validities in a language that carries the fullest possible force—the force of human personality, one's own personality.

Ideas are valuable only insofar as they are humanly valuable, of course. And self-expression is valuable—aside from the psychic therapy of letting off steam, or soothing or bolstering the needy ego—only when it discovers validities beyond the self. To expand one's grasp of these validities is education. And in this educational process the very process of writing is of the highest value as it helps us discover those validities and to realize them, to make them realities for us and for others. **20**

The process of writing, in fact, expands our capacity to think as nothing else can. Aside from trying to solve mathematical problems and puzzles and playing tough intellectual games like chess, our intellectual beings—our physical brains, in fact—are never so intensely engaged as in the process of writing an essay. Writing is hard, and we shy away from it precisely because it demands such intense engagement. It is solving continuous sets of complex problems, finding the idea, from among myriad choices, by fitting the word to it. Writing is so highly valuable because it exercises our highest capacity so fully. And it increases the capacity. The old-fashioned notion that thinking makes our brains grow seems indeed to be true. Professor Mark Rosenzweig and his associates at the University of California have for some time been demonstrating by scalpel, calipers, and scales that the brains of thinking rats grow as compared to those of rats who don't have to think to eat.[3] The problem-solvers developed bumps on their cerebral cortexes, enlarging that cortex far beyond those of the nonthinkers, to whom everything was given but the necessity to think. The brain is muscular after all. Problems develop its brawny powers. And writing is a kind of moment-by-moment problem-solving that exercises us along the very frontiers of thought itself, developing our most valuable capacities. **21**

Thus writing does physically develop our ability to think, as it also **22**

[3] From here on, I borrow from my portion of *The Written Word,* rephrasing slightly and clearing up typographical errors, some serious, in a book that got into print without at least this author's seeing galley proof, through an unfortunate editorial oversight.

helps us in each instance to discover and clarify our thoughts. I suppose we all know this from our own experience of writing and rewriting, but most of us somehow fail to get this simple truth across to our students, perhaps because we ourselves do not write persistently enough. Like any others, Charles Darwin discovered this obvious but neglected truth:

> I have as much difficulty as ever in expressing myself clearly and concisely; 23
> ... but it has had the compensating advantage of forcing me to think long
> and intently about every sentence, and thus I have been led to see errors in
> reasoning and in my own observations or those of others.[4]

In an era that prizes the irrational and praises blowing the mind, we 24 have an immense task to convince our students, all over again, of what Charles Darwin discovered: writing can bring one to think rationally, to uncover errors not only in reasoning but in what seems to be factual, empirical observation, until the struggle with words and thought reveals those observations to have been misinterpretations of what we thought we saw.

So, to conclude, writing will discover ideas for us, will bring them to 25 realization, and with them will increase our capacity to realize. To bring every student to fulfill his capacities is the teacher's aim, and the process of writing is our most immediate and important way to that fulfillment. We need to remember that, to convince our students of it, and to keep the process of writing prominently in the forefront of what we require to be educated. Otherwise we may discover we have frittered away and abandoned our very best means of intellectual discovery.

Study Questions

1. What is Baker's thesis? Is it stated or implied?
2. Baker wastes no words getting into his subject. Compare his opening with those of other essays. What is the advantage and disadvantage of each?
3. In paragraph 2 and 4 what is the relationship of the first and last sentence in each paragraph?
4. What is the purpose of the type of development used in paragraphs 10–13?
5. In paragraphs 1–4 what type of sentence occurs most frequently? What type least frequently?
6. Describe the author's attitude toward his subject and his audience. What specific words and expressions reflect his attitude?

[4] *Autobiography,* The Life of Science Library, ed. George Gaylord Simpson (New York: Schuman Publishers, 1950), p. 65.

Shirley Chisholm

NEEDED: EQUAL EDUCATIONAL OPPORTUNITY FOR ALL

Shirley Chisholm (1924–   ) was born in Brooklyn. She graduated *cum laude* from Brooklyn College, later received an M.A. from Columbia, and has been the recent recipient of numerous honorary degrees. She has served in both the New York State Assembly and in the 91st–94th Congresses, representing New York. Her books include *Unbought and Unbossed* (1970) and *The Good Fight* (1973).

A democratic society depends upon the intelligence and wisdom of the mass of people to keep the country moving. A government of the people, by the people, and for the people necessarily depends upon the people's judgment to make decisions that affect the growth of the country. In America, we have delegated to institutions of higher education the responsibility to train the minds of those who will make scientific and medical discoveries; who will give us an intellectual basis for law, order, and justice; and who will propagate an appreciation for the arts — thus, supplying us with cultural training. 1

While the fulfillment of these responsibilities remain the central purpose of institutions of higher education, American society casts another, less theoretical responsibility upon institutions of higher learning — that of granting "union cards" for upward social mobility. The slogan, "education is the key to success," is interpreted, in the United States, to mean that graduation from college opens up job possibilities at a salary range which is above that of the average American. Indeed, this very practical consideration of what one can do with a college degree — usually referred to as a college education — too often interferes with the more esoteric concern of how one's mind is strengthened by studying a particular curriculum at school. 2

It is the mundane and practical consideration of acquiring a college degree for the purpose of upward mobility which is inescapably on the minds of minority groups in their demand for equal participation in the mainstream of American society. Higher education is the key to this 3

Reprinted from *School and Society*, April 1972, by permission.

goal; and institutions of higher learning must address themselves to a relatively new constituency.

Toward this end, there must be universal acceptance of the premise 4 that higher education is the right of every American who has demonstrated the ability of potential for doing academic work at the college level. Many Americans have come to accept this in theory, but few have become directly involved in seeking ways of implementation. The municipal government of New York City, in conjunction with the Board of Education, has taken a bold step in practically applying the theory. New York City now has a policy of open admissions, where high school graduates who are residents of the city are guaranteed admission to one of the colleges in the city's college system upon application. The program was devised after the demands of the blacks from Bedford-Stuyvesant and Harlem and of Puerto Ricans from the Bronx, but it has proved to be as valuable to the white residents of Queens and Staten Island as it has to minorities from ghettoes.

Neither the quality of education offered nor respect for the integrity 5 of a college diploma has been impaired by the institution of open enrollment. It is certainly a program worthy of implementation throughout the country, and one which is absolutely necessary for allowing the economically disadvantaged to assume their right of education. But, at this point, our nation lacks the commitment to invest the proper resources in higher education.

Resources from the government and private sources are mandatory, 6 for open enrollment as well as any other program designed to open college doors to minorities places an extra financial burden upon the institutions. Thus, institutions of higher education must be given plenty of financial assistance if they are to fulfill the new obligations of allowing minorities and the poor access to higher education—toward the ultimate end of entrance into the mainstream of American society.

Will we have the courage and commitment to stop utilizing our re- 7 sources on warfare and to work on the intellectual and economic development of the American people? Will we desist from practices that deprive minorities and women of the opportunity to participate fully in our society? These are questions which the great majority of Americans will have to answer; and higher education must do the same.

There must be a willingness on the part of college administrators to 8 propose policies on admission that will take into consideration the obligation of higher education to address itself to the needs of minorities, women, and the poor. There also must be steps taken to make sure that the course of study effectively treats the contributions of minorities to the growth and development of American society and that courses are offered which will educate college students to the abuses and inequalities in our system and which will urge their involvement in activities designed to promote equality of rights for all Americans.

Such education should be part of the curriculum in any democratic 9 society; and it does not involve, in my view, the institutions, themselves, in social activity. Rather, it presents the students with the opportunity to apply certain theories to practical situations, which is in keeping with the notion that the only valuable education is one which promotes an understanding of what is necessary in order for human beings to make a contribution to the growth, prosperity, and durability of an orderly society.

Study Questions

1. Compare and contrast the types of arguments used by Hackerman and Chisholm.
2. Which paragraph contains the conclusions of Chisholm's argument?
3. Identify the topic sentence of paragraph 4. What type of development is used in this paragraph?
4. Paragraph 8 is composed of two long sentences. Would the effect be different if there were three or four shorter sentences?
5. What is the function of paragraph 7? Why are questions used in this paragraph?

Norman Hackerman
HIGHER EDUCATION: WHO NEEDS IT?

Norman Hackerman (1912–   ) was born in Baltimore and received both an A.B. (1932) and Ph.D. (1935) from Johns Hopkins. He has taught chemistry at Loyola College (Baltimore), the University of Texas, and Rice University. In his distinguished career he has been president of both Texas and Rice, chairman of the National Science Board, the editor of the *Journal of the Electrochemical Society.* Throughout that career he has regularly contributed articles to learned journals.

In the general run of human activity currently there seems to   1
be a pervasive idea, adhered to by many but perhaps not really accepted, that given time and effort anyone can master anything of an intellectual nature. Thus, the concept of elitism in education has become almost ob-

Reprinted from *Science,* Vol. 190, p. 513, 7 November 1975 by permission of the author.

solete. It has come to be associated with a high position in society, being better born, rich, and so on. The idea that one individual may be better endowed than another for a particular function or pursuit has remained respectable only in some less essential, although not less interesting, areas such as sports and entertainment.

Few would disagree that, for some, no amount of training would en- 2 able them to perform some physical feat such as lifting a 500-pound weight off the floor. Why then is there a general belief that equal mastery of educational course material by all is possible? This is not to say that there are not differences in learning rates. Such differences are certainly the basis for the self-paced method of instruction, which has proved reasonably successful in some areas. Nevertheless, it is recognizing the obvious to say that we do not all develop the same capacity in all endeavors, even though we may be given the opportunity to do so.

Given that there is a natural range of intellectual as well as physical 3 abilities, why do we persist in trying to diminish or even eliminate elitism in education? Why persist in the fiction that exposure to certain types of developed understanding beneficial to a few is of more than passing interest to most? Indeed in some areas like quantum electrodynamics we do not subscribe to this idea, but in many more common ones we do and insist that all of us can attain uniform intellectual skills.

Perhaps this current obsession, the taint of elitism, stems from two 4 attitudes based on experiences of the past. One of these is that the mere acquisition of a certificate of exposure to education has made some feel superior, wrongly of course. The other is generated by the previously demonstrable fact that white collar skills were more highly paid than blue-collar skills, which is no longer true.

If the experiences of the past no longer hold true, why do we cling 5 to beliefs which sprang from them? It does not follow that making maximum use of those most talented in intellectual pursuits demeans the rest of us. If we applaud the identification and careful nurturing of the talented performer, why not that of the talented mind? The difficulty may be that our dissonant musical notes are readily recognized and accepted, but our inability to master mathematics is not. It is easy to ascribe limited intellectual ability in one or another area to lack of interest.

This position does not lead to a negative attitude toward equal edu- 6 cational opportunity nor to the attitude that the intellectually able in one field are socially better or generally wiser. It does say that talented individuals are not too plentiful and that talent should be nourished where it appears. In other words, it is unwise to disregard the real differences in intellectual capabilities, both for the individual and for society.

This argument leads inevitably to the conclusion that not all are 7 equally educable. But it also leads to the proposition that that form of training does not necessarily produce wiser or nobler individuals.

So recognize elitism in education for what it is: the opportunity for 8 creative individuals to pursue intellectual goals and ideals somewhat beyond the boundaries confining many of us. If we destroy this environment of creative endeavor, whether it be scientific, artistic, or literary, we will have lost a great gift for humanity.

Study Questions

1. What is basic structure of Hackerman's arguments? How does he develop his arguments?
2. What is the purpose of questions in paragraphs 2, 3, and 5?
3. Identify specific words and phrases that link the paragraphs of this essay.
4. What are the sentence patterns in paragraph 5? What effect is achieved by these patterns?
5. Compare and contrast the tone of this essay with Chisholm's.

Samuel Johnson
THE STUDY OF LIFE

To many scholars of English literature Samuel Johnson *is* the eighteenth century. Johnson (1709–1784) was a student at Pembroke College, Oxford, for one year but was later awarded both an M.A. and LL.D. by the university. His literary career is almost unparalleled. He wrote a novel, *Rasselas: Prince of Abyssinia;* some fine poems, among them "London"; periodical essays now known as the *Rambler* and *Idler* papers; *Dictionary of the English Language,* in 1755; numerous biographies of English poets; a play, *Irene;* and even edited Shakespeare's works. He was gloomy and irritable, kind and generous—a strange compound of disparate traits, according to an almost equally famous writer, Thomas B. Macaulay. Johnson was the subject of one of the English language's most famous biographies, that by James Boswell.

Ταῦτ' εἰδὼς σοφὸς ἴσθι. μάτην δ'' Επίκουρον ἔασον
ποῦ τὸ κενὸν ιητεῖν, καὶ τίνες αἱ μονάδες — Automedon

On life, on morals, be thy thoughts employ'd;
Leave to the schools their atoms and their void.

It is somewhere related by Le Clerc that a wealthy trader of 1 good understanding, having the common ambition to breed his son a scholar, carried him to a university, resolving to use his own judgment in

First published in *The Rambler,* December 7, 1751.

the choice of a tutor. He had been taught, by whatever intelligence, the nearest way to the heart of an academic, and at his arrival entertained all who came about him with such profusion, that the professors were lured by the smell of his table from their books, and flocked round him with all the cringes of awkward complaisance. This eagerness answered the merchant's purpose. He glutted them with delicacies, and softened them with caresses till he prevailed upon one after another to open his bosom and make a discovery of his competitions, jealousies, and resentments. Having thus learned each man's character, partly from himself and partly from his acquaintances, he resolved to find some other education for his son, and went away convinced that a scholastic life has no other tendency than to vitiate the morals and contract the understanding. Nor would he afterwards hear with patience the praises of the ancient authors, being persuaded that scholars of all ages must have been the same, and that Xenophon and Cicero were professors of some former university, and therefore mean and selfish, ignorant and servile, like those whom he had lately visited and forsaken.

Envy, curiosity, and a sense of imperfection of our present state incline us to estimate the advantages which are in the possession of others above their real value. Everyone must have remarked what powers and prerogatives the vulgar imagine to be conferred by learning. A man of science is expected to excel the unlettered and unenlightened even on occasions where literature is of no use; and among weak minds loses part of his reverence by discovering no superiority in those parts of life in which all are unavoidably equal, as when a monarch makes a progress to the remoter provinces the rustics are said sometimes to wonder that they find him of the same size with themselves. 2

These demands of prejudice and folly can never be satisfied; and therefore many of the imputations which learning suffers from disappointed ignorance are without reproach. But there are some failures to which men of study are peculiarly exposed. Every condition has its disadvantages. The circle of knowledge is too wide for the most active and diligent intellect, and while science is pursued other accomplishments are neglected, as a small garrison must leave one part of an extensive fortress naked when an alarm calls them to another. 3

The learned, however, might generally support their dignity with more success if they suffered not themselves to be misled by the desire of superfluous attainments. Raphael, in return to Adam's inquiries to the courses of the stars and the revolutions of heaven, counsels him to withdraw his mind from idle speculations and employ his faculties upon nearer and more interesting objects, the survey of his own life, the subjection of his passions, the knowledge of duties which must daily be performed, and the detection of dangers which must daily be incurred. 4

This angelic counsel every man of letters should always have before him. He that devotes himself to retired study naturally sinks from omission to forgetfulness of social duties. He must be therefore sometimes awakened and recalled to the general condition of mankind. 5

I am far from any intention to limit curiosity or confine the labours of learning to arts of immediate and necessary use. It is only from the 6 various essays of experimental industry and the vague excursions of minds sent out upon discovery that any advancement of knowledge can be expected. And though many must be disappointed in their labours, yet they are not to be charged with having spent their time in vain. Their example contributed to inspire emulation, and their miscarriages taught others the way to success.

But the distant hope of being one day useful or eminent ought not 7 to mislead us too far from that study which is equally requisite to the great and mean, to the celebrated and obscure — the art of moderating the desires, of repressing the appetites, and of conciliating or retaining the favour of mankind.

No man can imagine the course of his own life or the conduct of the 8 world around him unworthy his attention. Yet among the sons of learning many seem to have thought of everything rather than of themselves, and to have observed everything but what passes before their eyes. Many who toil through the intricacy of complicated systems are insuperably embarrassed with the least perplexity in common affairs. Many who compare the actions and ascertain the characters of ancient heroes let their own days glide away without examination, and suffer vicious habits to encroach upon their minds without resistance or detection.

The most frequent reproach of the scholastic race is the want of for- 9 titude, not martial but philosophic. Men bred in shades and silence, taught to immure themselves at sunset, and accustomed to no other weapon than syllogism, may be allowed to feel terror at personal danger and to be disconcerted by tumult and alarm. But why should he whose life is spent in contemplation, and whose business is only to discover truth, be unable to rectify the fallacies of imagination or contend successfully against prejudice and passion? To what end has he read and meditated if he gives up his understanding to false appearances and suffers himself to be enslaved by fear of evils to which only folly or vanity can expose him, or elated by advantages to which, as they are equally conferred upon the good and bad, no real dignity is annexed?

Such, however, is the state of the world, that the most obsequious of 10 the slaves of pride, the most rapturous of the gazers upon wealth, the most officious of the whisperers of greatness are collected from seminaries appropriated to the study of wisdom and of virtue, where it was intended that appetite should learn to be content with little, and that hope should aspire only to honours which no human power can give or take away.

The student, when he comes forth into the world, instead of con- 11 gratulating himself upon his exemption from the errors of those whose opinions have been formed by accident or custom and who live without any certain principles of conduct is commonly in haste to mingle with the multitude and show his sprightliness and ductility by an expeditious compliance with fashions or vices. The first smile of a man whose fortune gives him power to reward his dependants commonly enchants him beyond resistance. The glare of equipage, the sweets of luxury, the liberality of general promises, the softness of habitual affability fill his imagination: and he soon ceases to have any other wish than to be well received, or any measure of right and wrong but the opinion of his patron.

A man flattered and obeyed learns to exact grosser adulation and enjoin lower submission. Neither our virtues nor vices are all our own. If there were no cowardice there would be little insolence. Pride cannot rise to any great degree but by the concurrence of blandishment or the sufferance of tameness. The wretch who would shrink and crouch before one that should dart his eyes upon him with the spirit of natural equality becomes capricious and tyrannical when he sees himself approached with a downcast look and hears the soft address of awe and servility. To those who are willing to purchase favour by cringes and compliance is to be imputed the haughtiness that leaves nothing to be hoped by firmness and integrity.

If, instead of wandering after the meteors of philosophy which fill the world with splendour for a while and then sink and are forgotten, the candidates of learning fixed their eyes upon the permanent lustre of moral and religious truth, they would find a more certain direction to happiness. A little plausibility of discourse and acquaintance with unnecessary speculations is dearly purchased when it excludes those instructions which fortify the heart with resolution and exalt the spirit to independence.

Study Questions

1. What words, expressions, and constructions date this essay earlier than the twentieth century?
2. Identify the topic sentence of the opening paragraph.
3. Which paragraph contains a statement of the central idea?
4. What type of development is used in paragraphs 2, 8, 12?
5. Which paragraphs contain series of parallel structures? What is the effect of parallel structure in either sentences or parts of sentences?

Judith Plotz

IS A CRIME AGAINST THE MIND NO CRIME AT ALL?

Judith Plotz (1938–   ) was born in Brooklyn. She received an A.B. from Radcliffe College in 1960 and a Ph.D. from Harvard in 1965. In 1968–1969 an American Association of University Women Fellowship sent her to England, after which she returned to teaching English at George Washington University. Her *Ideas of the Decline of Poetry* was published in 1965.

Twenty research papers are submitted in one freshman com- 1 position section; nine are plagiarized. A sharp-eyed history professor, disheartened by yearly bumper crops of plagiarists, gives up on the term paper: "I even have graduate students do annotated bibliographies now." Another professor in the social sciences retains papers, but with cynical fatalism: "Plagiarism? Sure, there's lots of it, but I'm busy and try not to look too closely." An allegedly original English paper is submitted bearing a fresh top-sheet over the unaltered text of a roommate's year-old paper, unaltered even to the roommate's name and the original instructor's comments and grade.

These are representative examples of university life in the '70's, 2 where plagiarism is epidemic. The academic community has proffered a number of explanations for the plague, each more dismal than the last. The general decline in moral standards is a recurrent theme: something is rotten—the students, the country, even the university. The students, one argument goes, are intellectually corrupt; growing up in unearned ease, they have never learned to respect the hard-earned achievements of intellect. Or, more vastly, the nation, as the Watergate affair illustrates, is corrupt and has taught its children to seek success at any price. Alternatively, or additionally, the university is corrupt in employing a judgmental grading system that encourages students to jockey for grades rather than to seek truth. Less moralistically, others trace the problem to a presumed drop in standards of admissions. Traditional university programs demand too much of poorly prepared students, who plagiarize out of panic.

These explanations may account for some cases, but not all. Actually, 3

Reprinted from *The Chronicle of Higher Education*, February 2, 1976, by permission of the author.

the very concept of plagiarism, a relatively new phenomenon, has grown up with modern ideas of individuality.

In the medieval and Renaissance periods, the concept of plagiarism— 4 the *illegitimate* borrowing from another author—was virtually unknown. With the exception of direct comma-for-comma copying of another writer's work, most sorts of borrowing were legitimate, even laudable. An authoritarian social system nurtured literary authoritarianism. To model one's style, one's plots, one's ideas on a literary master was the time-honored way of learning to write well. One rather boasted of than tried to hide one's appropriations from the masters. Medieval poets, recognizing Virgil as a supreme craftsman, believing that one could not have too much of a good thing, translated and versified great swatches of the *Aeneid;* rather than condemning such poets for theft, their audiences praised them for pleasing versions of an honored favorite.

The classical masters were regarded, as nature itself was regarded, as 5 a writer's resource. The writer foolish enough to aim at total individuality was not admirable, but an eccentric deliberately impoverishing himself.

Plagiarism first came into existence as a significant literary problem 6 only toward the end of the 17th century. Like Renaissance writers, critics of this period were predominantly authoritarian and held that all the major subjects for literature had already been pre-empted, seized upon by writers of genius when the world was young, when "nature," as Samuel Johnson said of Shakespeare, "was still open" to them. But a favorite Latin tag of the age, *"Pereant qui ante nos nostra dixerunt"* (Damn those who had all our best ideas before we did), captures the increasing discontent with this situation. Eighteenth-century writers, despite their traditionalism, also felt an envious esteem for originality, the power to look at something in a new way, and for invention, the power to discover a new subject. Originality, now held to be a prime literary virtue, was despairingly deemed typical only of young civilizations and virtually unattainable in a modern age. Despite their desire for originality, modern writers could never be much more than copyists of the past, or so the prevailing theory went.

It was during this period of reluctant traditionalism and longing for 7 originality that critics began fervidly to hunt down plagiarists. Whether out of a thirst for originality or out of an aggrieved desire to show originality impossible to anyone, critics began to make accusations of plagiarism against writers who did no more than echo a word or phrase from an earlier writer. The presence of plagiarism was held to be an inevitability in a period which was a reluctant heir to the treasures of the ages. Nevertheless, it was fiercely derided as an enemy of originality. The failure to be original became culpable only when originality became desirable.

By the Romantic age plagiarism should have become unnecessary. 8 The early 19th-century Romantics took a high view of the potential creativity of every human soul. Originality, they argued, is the birthright of every individual. So liberating, so antiauthoritarian a theory of creativity should have set a writer free from the necessity of literary theft. Yet the greatest plagiarist in literary history—great in the number of his depredations, great in his genius—Samuel Taylor Coleridge, is a product of the age of originality. As Norman Fruman's recent book, *Coleridge, the Damaged Archangel,* makes plain, Coleridge compulsively appropriated the materials of other writers, notably German critics and philosophers, and equally compulsively protested his absolute originality.

Like Coleridge, contemporary undergraduates labor under a double 9 burden: the burden of originality imposed by the age and the burden of intellectual coherence imposed by the university. That the burdens often prove intolerable, the present state of academic morality attests.

American undergraduates of the '70's are heirs to the by-now sleazy 10 and dilapidated Romantic ideal of creativity. I call the ideal sleazy because it was degenerated from its original heroic summons to immense productive and synthetic efforts into a slack and sentimental invitation to self-complacent ease. It is one thing to hold that every child is innately imaginative and another to argue that all self-expression, no matter how feeble, is artistic creation. To believe that the inner spirit, the childlike soul in and of itself, untouched by any particular knowledge, is alone creative, has led in much contemporary secondary education to a loss of confidence in forms and in substantive knowledge. Since creativity comes from the naked self, it is no longer necessary to furnish that self with facilitating knowledges (grammar, German, Latin, calculus, physics) and forms (syntax, the sonnet, the book report). With "writing" in secondary schools largely confined to English class (though extracts copied from encyclopedias and other unimpeachable sources frequently surface as "research" papers in various other subject areas) and with English dedicated to evoking individual creativity, students are losing the habit of unselfconscious writing as a means of communication, as a mechanical knack in which the deepest self is not necessarily involved.

Habitually to write free verse, impressionistic responses to literature, 11 and ruminative short stories without any compensatory training in the mere prose of communication is to hole up the self in a very narrow cell. Originality has been confounded with the spontaneous, unmediated productions of the sole self and the real experience of the sole self has been identified with pre-verbal incommunicable states which are impossible to express discursively. To be true to one's self, therefore, to be appropriately original, is to draw back from the world of facts and forms, the world of science and high culture. Authenticity lies in expressing the self rather than in expressing the world.

Parallel with the development of this solipsistic idea of originality has 12 been the knowledge explosion. The first-hand knowledge of any individual, even if he has the curiosity of a Leonardo and the stamina of a Casanova, is puny beside the vast stores of genuine scholarship that are piling up with unprecedented speed and to an unprecedented density in our libraries. The act of synthesizing preceding knowledge requires humility, ardor, and dedication to the life of the mind. Even a seasoned scholar feels intimidated by the mass of materials he must master and comprehend.

When a student is asked to write an essay synthesizing or assessing 13 literary or historical or political data, he finds himself facing materials on which considerable authoritative commentary may already exist. To write a good essay, the student must digest the data and commentary, synthesize them, and then go beyond them. The process, once second nature to well-trained college students, has by now become remarkably difficult for them. My guess is that the act of writing is increasingly tied up with the idea of self-expression and has little connection with the comprehension of any external aspect of the world. Because the presumably true, the creative self, exists most fully in isolation from the multiple intellectual constructions and historical accumulations with which liberal education is concerned, many students find all questions involving comment on a body of knowledge artificial, mechanical, and alien. When a student regards a paper assignment as merely mechanical, he quite consistently feels something of a hypocrite in devoting his full strength to so empty a pursuit. To many students it seems no greater a self-violation to commit fraud and plagiarize their papers than to push themselves through an exercise personally meaningless.

If my hypothesis is correct, if plagiarism does derive from a perverted ideal of creativity, is there anything at all the university can do? Clearly, the plagiarist's contempt for earned intellectual distinction, his assumption that a crime against the mind is no crime, his theft from his sources and his fraud against his professors destroy any possible value from his education. 14

The quick way to abolish the problem, of course, is to abolish term papers; but this is decapitation for a headache. The problem goes so deep that individual actions may be only palliative, but some new approaches to writing might help. Three kinds of papers might be useful. In order to combat the association between the act of writing and self-expression, I suggest that numerous small exercises be demanded — quizzes, summaries, paraphrases — all cast in consecutive prose. I also suggest the revival of the deliberate Imitation, an educational device so old, so aboriginal, as to be new. Students might be asked to write about English history in the manner of Macaulay, about the Vietnam war as Karl Marx. This would give the aid an established form always provides while still demanding the expression of individual judgment. 15

With exercises and imitations encouraging impersonal prose, major paper assignments might be made more personal. The rote assignment, the question unreal both to instructor and student, might be replaced by assignments that deliberately cross the subjective self with the objective world, assignments that demand a reaching out into the world from a frankly acknowledged personal center. One might even try tapping the tremendous energy of animus, of anger, and ask students to write on those aspects of subjects they find most objectionable. 16

One might, one might ... In any case, one must. The epidemic of plagiarism is sad testimony to student estrangement from the goals of education. The increasing inability of students to leap the gap between their sole selves and the realm of knowledge means that it is vital to build more bridges, more crossings, to ease the passage. 17

Study Questions

1. In which paragraph does the thesis of this essay appear?
2. Does the first paragraph set the overall tone? If so, how?
3. What is the function of paragraphs 4–8?
4. Identify the topic sentence in paragraph 2. What type of development is used in this paragraph?
5. What type of structure is the first sentence of paragraph 17? What effect is achieved by this structure?

Joyce Carol Oates
ARCHWAYS

Joyce Carol Oates (1938–   ) was born in Lockport, New York. She received a B.A. degree from Syracuse University and an M.A. from the University of Wisconsin. She has taught at the University of Detroit and at present teaches English at the University of Windsor in Ontario. She has received many awards and honors for her fiction. In 1967 she was awarded a Guggenheim fellowship. Her fiction has been selected to appear in the *O. Henry Award Anthologies* and in *Best American Short Stories.* In 1970 Oates's novel *Them* won the National Book Award. Her fiction has appeared in *Southwest Review, Colorado Quarterly, Prairie Schooner,* and *Cosmopolitan.* She has had articles and essays in *Dalhousie Review, Bucknell Review, Renascense,* and *Texas Studies.* Her books are *By the North Gate* (1963), *With Shuddering Fall* (1965), *Upon the Sweeping Flood* (1966), *A Garden of Earthly Delights* (1967), *Expensive People* (1968), *Them* (1969), *Anonymous Sins* (1969), *Dreaming America* (1973), *Where Are You Going, Where Have You Been?* (1974), *The Seduction and Other Stories* (1975), and *The Assassins* (1975).

Klein, a nervous young man whose overcoat in winter hung 1 down far below his knees, felt shame that he was several years older than his fellow students, felt shame that he was seized often by an inexplicable panic, alone or with others, felt shame that he was poor. He was a graduate student in a state university that serviced thirty thousand students, having come to his life's work (he realized with shame) after having been frightened out of other, lesser tasks: clerking, work in the Railway Express, work at his father's filling station. He had slid from one job to another, one segment of his life to another, as if he had been loosed at the top of a great jagged hill and could not control his destiny. Once come to the university, he had known that this was the fate he desired, but he did not feel strong enough to attain it. He imitated others: he bought, he read books (his room was filled with books), he wrote papers for his courses, he studied French and German, he lived alone, lost weight (his mother's mechanical accusation), had few friends, acquaintances rather, he made his own meals up in the room or had them in drugstores, he took notes hour after hour in the library, he appeared, a gentle weary apparition, on the sidewalk before his apartment house with books in his arms. With shame he was familiar: he had grown up with it. Before his father he had had to be ashamed of his mother, who cried endlessly, was endlessly sick, was insulted by his father's mother, a stout woman with a coat that had a meager fur collar he had always been fascinated by as a child; before his mother he had had to be ashamed of his father, who begged for work around the neighborhood, offering estimates no one wanted, reading up on modern mechanics so he could compete with other service stations—a desperate attempt that Klein, when no more than a child of eight, knew to be hopeless. At the garage his father scurried about in all weather, checking air in tires, checking oil, his face reddened and forlorn. Of his bony wrists Klein had had to be ashamed, taking the bus downtown to the library: they had stuck out of his shirt sleeves for all to see. Of his sister's ruthless blond hair, and of her language to their mother he had had to be ashamed. Of their house (they lived over the garage), the stairs on the outside of the building and enclosed by a feeble tarpapered canopy: of his thin arms and legs, in gym class at school: of his shame itself. Now, at twenty-nine, he took assessment of himself in his room five blocks from the great university library, sitting on the edge of his bed, doing nothing, having done nothing all day (it was Sunday), and understood that his shame for his life had grown so great that he must die: but he had ten weeks to go before the semester was over, and he did not like to betray the people who had hired him, trusted him, given him fifteen hundred dollars for the year and the title "emergency help."

He attended classes during the day and taught two classes of his 2 own, remedial composition, in the late afternoon and evening, three days a week. Before each class he was visited with panic, terror that he would break down before the hour ended. This never happened, but his panic did not end. He was perhaps ashamed of the old building to which his classes had been assigned, and he understood that the dank, dusty air of the basement room had come to suffuse him, had been breathed into him, had come to define him. His students were desperate, doomed young people, many of them from the country, remote incidental rural sections of the state, bewildered at their failure (they were assigned to this course because they were far below average in English), unable to comprehend his teaching, his encouragement, his love. Their failure had widened their eyes, giving them the alert, electric look of animals to whom all movements signal danger. Like animals, they appeared mild and obedient until, knowing themselves trapped, they slashed out at him as if he were the crystallization of the forces that had maimed them — the obscure, mysterious spirit of the famous university itself, so available to them (they, with their high-school diplomas) and yet, as it turned out, so forbidden to them, its great machinery even now working, perhaps, to process cards, grades, symbols that would send them back to their families and the lives they supposed they had escaped.

Standing before his classes, eraser and chalk in hand, Klein sometimes deluded himself into thinking that his students' grave, attentive expressions were related to his presence; that they were actually learning, changing before his eyes. He wrote sentences on the board in his nervous handwriting: they watched. There in the first row, in the four-thirty class, the usual girls, crowded in close, staring and sightless — the lank handsome girl with the blond braids coiled ascetically about her head, chill and feigning attention, absolutely illiterate; the plump, smiling, perpetually astonished little girl in the pink sweater, also illiterate, with a baby's tiny handwriting and circled dots over her i's; the thin bespeckled girl who mentioned often in her compositions that she had been a JV cheerleader back in high school, back in Oriole, whether he, Klein, would believe it or not — he could not take that away from her. Behind them, the three other girls in the class, pens poised, and when he asked who could improve this sentence, at once the older girl with the dark, dissatisfied face would shoot her hand up. He thought her part Negro; she was almost pretty, attractive in a hard, frowning way. Beside her one of his troublemakers, a wise guy not from the country but from the city, illiterate despite his handsome sweaters and bored, bland expression; and behind him adolescents with blemished faces, huge hands and feet, educated now into knowing their unworth, torn between despising him (their "Mr. Klein") or falling before him to embrace his knees, begging aid, magic. The pipes in this basement room groaned with effort; it was too hot; yet the students went on, drugged and brave, improving sentences by hit or miss, staring at compositions shot into vicious clarity by the opaque projector for their criticism (all were interested in this: charmed and hypnotized by the procedure's resemblance to the form of the movie, which they knew they liked), accepting red-inked papers back, ceremoniously, at the end of each Monday's class, walking out alone, quickly, or dawdling behind to speak with him, sad-eyed or coquettish or swollen with gratitude depending on their grades. When Klein thought of his life, his essential life, nothing came to him except an image of this class. The classes he himself took, sat in wearily and hopefully, faded away as if they were no more than dreams. He pitied his students and feared them. Of course they hated him, they had no one else, and yet he would have expressed his sorrow for them had he not known they would have rejected it angrily — for he was to them a transparent obstacle, a blemish, something between them and their "careers" (in conferences they talked familiarly of their "future careers" as if these ghosts were real, actually existed somewhere and had only to be located), and he did not possess any meaning in himself. He yawned at the thought of his stu-

3

dents, they at the thought of him. If he died they would not mourn him, would not miss him, in a month would be unable to recall his name. And he accepted their justified indifference, and the probable indifference of his professors, as two more reasons why he should die—if no one cared, why keep on?

His room was dirty. He cleaned it but it was dirty just the same. It 4 looked as if no one lived in it, as if the clutter had accumulated noiselessly over the years, knocked about by anonymous intruders. His books, which he loved, the seven-dollar Van Gogh print above the desk, the little braided rug he had bought at a sale, these things should have made his room his own, but they did not. The worn, shredding paperback books were not related to the print; the arty print not related to the modest rug; the rug not related to the paint-splashed floor; none of them related to him. The curtains at the window, feebly imprinted with green geometrical designs, could not have been purchased by Klein, who had better taste. A mistake. The wastebasket beside the desk was a glaring blue metal, stamped with the university's official animal (a kind of rodent he did not recognize): another mistake. His bedspread, costing eleven dollars, had been put away in the closet because it was too much trouble to make the bed. The thought of his room exhausted him, as did the thought of his classes (he met them again tomorrow, the weekends flew by); in fact, the only thought that nourished him was the thought of his death. This he felt to be truly his, as nothing else was. This alone was personal, private. It would perhaps not be magnificent, but no one would laugh. He need not be ashamed of it at least. To insure this he must choose a proper means of suicide: nothing violent, nothing theatrical. He had narrowed his choices down to two, either sleeping pills or hanging. For a while he had considered slashing his wrists (he lingered over the word "slashing"), but it would have to be done in the bathroom and there was no dignity there. Or if he did it in bed, in the landlord's bed, the blood might seep through the floor and drip from the ceiling below, an ambulance would arrive, and he would wake in a hospital thwarted and under arrest. . . . He got up and put on his overcoat and went out for a walk.

The sidewalks were deserted. Sundays were tedious, deadly, one had 5 too much time to think on Sundays. He would do it on a Sunday, then, after his final examinations were graded and the grades turned in. Years ago he had supposed Sundays sacred, his family had gone to church, but what happened there seemed to him never related to anything else: a game, a bore. Then his family had stopped going and he had stopped. He had not been told why. Perhaps there had been no reason. . . . Yet that was what terrified him, he thought angrily, stopping on the sidewalk with his hands clenched into fists: no reason, nothing explained. His childhood was without explanation. Why this particular failure (his father's poverty), why his mother crying at the kitchen table, why that particular argument, why footsteps up and down the stairs that night? What were these mysteries? Why could he understand nothing? Why was he always the victim, always the silent one, absorbing all blows, all pain, all indifference? Why could he control nothing? And why, now, was he here—standing before a slummy shoe repair shop — what had brought him here? Had he willed it, had he anything to do with it? He was furious at himself. Only his death would be meaningful, yet was he not fearful of this? His most shameful knowledge was that, ugly as his life was, part of him did not want to leave it.

He went back to his apartment house at that moment and his life 6 was changed.

On the stairs going up he met the dark girl from his afternoon class. 7 She was alone; she wore a red coat that looked new. Seeing him, she stiffened and her hand rose from the railing, hesitantly, as if the gesture were rehearsed. "Hello, Mr. Klein," she said in her student's voice. He greeted her irritably. He had tried to look past her, around her, but had not been able to avoid her gaze. She stepped aside to let him pass and he went by. But, inside his room, he felt oddly agitated and did not want to take off his coat. Something was wrong, something would happen. He went to the window and looked out: below, on the walk, strangers passed by in their gloomy winter coats. In a minute someone knocked at his door.

Klein turned, arguing with himself. His lips framed words but he 8 went to the door and opened it: the girl. "Yes?" he said coldly. He had been too kind to them in class. He had failed to suggest the distance between them. The girl touched her nose with a tissue, a nervous gesture she might have been hiding behind. "It's a coincidence meeting you like this," she said, "but a friend of mine lives upstairs." She waited; Klein looked behind her, did not help her. "I wanted to see you anyway to explain something."

He sighed. He surrendered, stepping back. "Come in."   9

She looked everywhere and nowhere, the tissue prominent in her 10 hand. "Do you have a roommate?"

"No, none."   11

"That's nice — there," she said, pointing at the print. She stared at it. 12 Then she turned. "No, my coat's all right, I'm only going to stay a minute. I'm sorry to barge in like this, I didn't mean to —" She ran out of breath suddenly.

"Sit over there, the desk chair," Klein said.   13

She pulled the chair out and sat as if participating in a ritual. "It's 14 about the theme I handed in on Friday, Mr. Klein. I thought I better explain it a little, so you don't get the wrong idea."

"I haven't read them yet," Klein said.   15

"Haven't?"   16

She watched him awkwardly. A peculiar girl, he thought, older than 17 the other students, carrying about with her like a disfigurement the weight of obscure, remote disappointments: she could have been one of the girls he often saw waiting at bus stops, working girls, cheaply glamorous and forlorn. She had a full face, eyebrows too thick, eyes worked over with black pencil, not exactly beautiful but stern and bright enough to attract the approval of random city boys — not college boys. Despite her open, generous face she had a habit of squinting (he recalled from class) that emphasized her deep-socketed eyes and gave her a look of doubt, disbelief. Her hair was black and thick and heavy, not lustrous. From under the cheap red coat her legs emerged muscular and stubborn, crossed primly at the ankles. She came to him in fragments: nervous as he was, and hungry (he had forgotten to eat), Klein fumbled with the buttons of his coat as if she had asked him to stay.

"May I ask if you're Jewish?" she said.   18

"I am not."   19

Was she disappointed? Her face shifted to show emotion, but Klein   20
wondered if it was not planned. Then she went on, as he had somehow expected, "Some of the kids wondered." Vaguely she called up the magical, censorious presence of the classroom; Klein was disarmed. He remained where he was, standing, with his coat in his arms.

"Are you from around here?" the girl went on.   21

"What?"   22

"Are you from around here? The city?"   23

"No," he said. His words were straining up to the surface, pulling   24
themselves up from a great obstinate distance. "Are you?"

She smiled slightly at his question. She had relaxed a little; her legs   25
were now crossed at the knee. "I have a sister that lives here but I don't see her much. My folks are moved away—I don't see them much either. I get kind of lonely sometimes."

"Yes, well." Klein's face had grown warm. Despite his irritation, he   26
felt a tenderness for the girl: for this clumsy loneliness, for the clenched tissue that was probably to her a vague, desperate attempt at feminine ornament. On campus, on the sidewalks between buildings, she would walk solidly on her heels, unaccustomed to the aloof competitive grace of the college girls; she would walk with her strong shoulders thrust slightly forward, as if to show her courage. Klein's voice was abrupt when he spoke. "Did you want to see me about something?"

"Look, I'm sorry to take up your time, I know you're busy. I just   27
wanted to explain something about the paper, so you won't think it's—"

"Yes, what?" He glanced over at the untidy pile of themes on the   28
floor beside his bed. Saddened by the stupidity of the first theme he had looked at, Klein had let them all fall to the floor. "What about it?"

"I guess I'm taking up your time. I'd better leave."   29

"No, it's all right. As long as you're here—"   30

"I wouldn't want to take up any of your valuable time."   31

Klein's heart had begun to pound at the change in the girl's tone.   32

"I mean, you're a teacher and all, you're pretty important. I wouldn't   33
want to take up any of your precious time that you don't get paid for by the school."

"Look—"   34

"Look, I'm tired of being treated like dirt by everybody around   35
here," she said quietly. "Nobody here is better than me. I know that. I've been told that enough times. Is it true or not?"

Klein sighed. "True."   36

"Yes, like hell it's true."   37

He lay his overcoat on the bed and sat beside it. "Do you want a   38
cigarette?" he said.

"Sure, thanks."   39

They lit cigarettes. "What's your problem?" said Klein.   40

She was staring at the floor and he feared she would begin to cry. 41
"Well, it's hard to begin, I—I don't know. Or which one is the worst one,
but anyway that's not why I'm here—like I said, I happened to be visiting
this friend of mine—"

"Should I read your theme now?"   42

"No, please, that's all right," she said shakily. She looked away. 43
"Maybe I better leave. I made a mess of this."

"A mess of what?" Klein laughed. "What's wrong? I've got time."   44

"And I'm grateful for it, I mean I really know you are busy, I didn't 45
mean what I said before—I'm sort of confused. I never was at college until now." She looked at him, squinting against the smoke from her cigarette. "This is all pretty new to me. I didn't finish school when I was supposed to, but had to quit for a reason, and I just got my diploma last
year. Went at night."

"Your writing isn't bad," Klein offered.   46

"Yeah, that's a surprise. I'm doing better than I hoped," she said, and 47
Klein felt another absurd rush of tenderness. "I work forty hours, you
know, at a store, and I don't get enough time. You know, it's pretty hard
to come back like this—nobody here cares if you make it or not. Nobody cares."

"Yes, that's life." But the banality of his remark startled Klein, for he 48
had meant to be sincere. "That's the way life is," he said, clearing his
throat.

"I'm going into psychology."   49

"That's nice—"   50

"You're thinking how stupid that is, how I'll never make it," she said. 51
"Okay. Maybe I know it myself. But I'm going to try just the same."

"I don't think—"   52

"It's all right, it doesn't matter. Maybe I should act like I'm in class 53
and pretend something, I don't know. I'm too dumb to know what to do.
And I guess I better go now, to hell with the theme." She was dabbing at
her eyes with the delicate shredded tissue. "If you think it's worth talking
about later, okay, but otherwise I'm just wasting your time, right?"

He was helpless before her heavy, obstinate passivity. She seemed 54
older than he, and stronger; he could not compete with her. All he could
do was wave her remarks aside weakly. "Of course not. It's what I'm here
for."

"Here? Up here in your room?" She stood. The tissue had dis- 55
appeared; her coat protected her. "I guess I'll see you tomorrow."

"Yes, tomorrow," he said. He went to open the door for her. Her 56
slowness, which was not graceful, and her calculating averted gaze made
him awkward; he was relieved when she left. Yet he stood, his hand on
the doorknob, as if listening for her footsteps to return. Perhaps he
should open the door, call her back? But he had nothing to say to her.
He stood, he listened. She had left.

He read her theme at once. It was a description, in small slanted 57
proper handwriting, of childbirth. Klein became weakened at her words,

his stomach cringed at her dramatic underlined conclusion: "That was how I knew that I was really alone."

Monday he returned the papers. She was there, waiting, and he tried 58 not to watch her. Like the others, she opened the paper to the back, read the grade, and without expression folded it again and left. He was disappointed, though he had not really wanted her to talk to him again; talking with students exhausted him, made him nervous. The prospect of teaching that day for some reason had been terrifying—more than ever his panic had come upon him, for had he not perhaps given some of himself to that girl, however unwillingly? He had been unable to eat, and now the girl's behavior disappointed him (he could not deny this), he would take refuge in thoughts of his death: he had decided upon sleeping pills the night before. He would go to a doctor and complain of sleeplessness....

Someone awaited him in the hall. Late afternoon, and stuffy and dark 59 in the basement, the corridor with its cracked plaster and dirty floor—he looked around to see the girl approaching, shy and pleased. His heartbeat startled him. "Well, I guess you didn't think too bad of it," the girl said.

She and Klein both looked at the paper she held. "Your writing isn't 60 bad," Klein said after a moment.

"Well," said the girl. Her coquetry was clumsy yet touching: she 61 seemed to release herself to a gesture, a rehearsed mannerism, yet draw back at the last moment as if frightened at her daring. Now she had been about to raise her eyes from the paper to Klein's face, but she froze with her gaze in mid-air, fixed and surprised. She said, "Are you going out that way?"

"Out that door? Yes," Klein said abruptly, as if surrendering himself 62 to something grim. They walked down the corridor together, acutely conscious of each other. "I'm going over to the clinic," Klein heard himself say.

He had not been prepared for this remark, nor had the girl. She 63 frowned as he opened the door for her, leaning against the tarnished brass bar so that the door swung open with a mechanical violence. They ascended the stone steps into a gray afternoon. Limply the girl caught up his words, as if they had been precious: "Going over to the clinic? Is there something wrong?"

"Nothing much," Klein said.   64

They walked slowly. Klein did not know where he was going. The 65 girl walked with her gaze downcast, watching her feet perhaps, as if she did not know either and were waiting to be told. "Look," Klein said, his eyes half shut, "if you want to explain this paper to me, all right. I would like to hear about it."

She looked up. "What about the clinic?"   66

"It can wait," said Klein.   67

They had coffee together and were still in the restaurant, a dingy 68 campus place, at six. Klein offered, as if spontaneously, to buy her dinner. The sudden intimacy of their sitting together, coats off, books aside, had made him a little giddy. While they talked, the girl's abrasive coarseness ebbed; he felt in her hesitant speech and her occasional abrupt vulgarity something that seemed familiar. Did she remind him perhaps of his sister? But his sister's grittiness had no humor, no fragility, no hint of being vulnerable. In the presence of his occasional smile, her flirtation lapsed and she looked at him frankly. "Sure, I was married when the baby was born and that made a big difference to my mother," she told him, a dreary predictable story that seemed to him also familiar, as if it were a memory of his as well as of hers. "I didn't have any illusions about it and I turned out to be right. I thought maybe it would be a change — not so lonely as before. But it wasn't, but I wasn't surprised. I had the baby put out for adoption and we got divorced; he used to bother me for a while, then he quit — went out of town or something. If anything like that happens to me again. . . ." He was sympathetic but not surprised. Nothing about her could surprise him. Her failure made him angry, not at her but at the closed, paneled world that excluded her as it excluded him.

They returned to the same restaurant the next evening, some change 69 in their relations having occurred (she smoking airily; he patient with the clumsy waitress), and he understood that the other people in the restaurant and those who had passed them languidly out on the street constituted for her, as they did for him, one aspect of the enemy, that great impersonal block of humanity whose surfaces were slick and impenetrable. The multiplicity of planes these surfaces suggested did not fool him: he longed to rescue her. "We all feel that way," he said quietly. Their glances, their kindnesses, their words were unmistakable; Klein felt himself drifting. "We all feel lonely. There are some people . . ." But he did not want to talk about other people. He veered back to the girl at once, who sat across the table from him listening to him with her deep-set eyes, the flesh slightly shadowed beneath them, perhaps pleased with her hair, which had been recently washed. "You must understand that it's nothing to be ashamed of," he said. "I've got to understand it myself. Some people get loneliness as if it were a disease. It makes them sick. I suppose I'm one of them." She nodded. They looked not at each other but toward each other, their gazes offset, sightless, pretending distraction: someone was arguing at the counter. Suddenly Klein thought of the sleeping pills he had yet to acquire and his heart pounded. He could not eat. "This place is a dump, isn't it?" he said.

They went to his apartment. He had to teach the next day, he had 70 reading to do, but he did not care. Opening the door, he became dizzy. He had not wanted any of this to happen, yet it had happened; they were mute and warmed before it. The girl was a little nervous and sat at his desk, smoking, with the ash tray on her lap. They talked for hours: Klein could see his raw young voice prod at her eyes, her mouth. "I try not to show it in class," he said. She was deeply moved, he could see. He sensed in her silence and in the affected mannerisms of her smoking a generosity he was not accustomed to, which alarmed him because he was not certain he could meet it. "No, you don't show it, it's a surprise to me," she said slowly. He had been telling her of his nausea before classes. "Nobody thinks of teachers like that. Though I had a teacher in high school once, a woman . . . Most of the teachers here, you know, they separate themselves from you, they take care of your work for the course but outside of that they don't give a damn. You could be lying on the sidewalk and they'd go around you. They don't want to waste their time. What they're afraid of is getting mixed up with you. I suppose I don't blame them, because somebody like me, somebody that's out of place here ..." "Why do you feel out of place?" Klein said. "I don't know, I was born that way," she said. "I was born out of place." He did not know whether the mirroring of his plight in her evoked in him contempt or love.

They awoke at three-thirty. Klein had left the meek desk lamp on, 71 channeling its light into a halo on the wall. His room looked different, ghostly and rich: why not? The girl was shy, softened, younger; he believed he loved her. Words suggested themselves to him, but he rejected them, they were not adequate, they would be embarrassing. He wanted to feel that she shared this magical intimacy—that was why she said little, hushed as if at church—yet, walking her to her apartment (in a darkened building on a side street), he was jealous of her distraction when she glanced up at an automobile passing, jealous of her failure to hint to him, however insincerely, that she was at all surprised at what they had done: that they had even done anything extraordinary. Klein felt like a person in a dream. "Good night," he said, not going up the stairs with her, and was overcome by an impulse to laugh. The girl herself smiled suddenly. Yet he became immediately dissatisfied, for he thought ahead to the next day, the next morning, the girl alone in her room (he imagined it a room exactly like his own, just as anonymous), having forgotten him.

Back home he had time now to feel shame for the soiled sheets he 72 had had for her. Dreamily, his hands trembling as he remade the bed, he recalled that he had planned that morning to do something profound; but he could not remember what it was.

In class she was no different, though quieter. He could not always 73 count on her to answer the questions he sent out to the class, hopeful and indefatigable. She did not wait for him afterward, but they had dinner together, at his place or at hers: a room smaller than he had imagined, decorated with travel posters. "They're just junk," she said of the posters, "but they look like windows or something. It isn't just the wall there but openings looking out—that's how I think of pictures." They were able to work together, as if relieved of the necessity of thinking about each other; Klein did not have to imagine her, and so he was freed. She did not let him read her work for his class until she handed it in, and he read her compositions eagerly, before leaving the classroom, his eyes racing along the neat handwritten lines as if looking for something he could not identify. She wrote of her family, their poverty, and he muttered, "Yes, yes," to each cliché, each undignified detail of the uninteresting truths by which both their lives had been shaped.

This was November: the last week of the month, one weekday morn- 74 ing, he saw her in a drugstore buying something. She wore the red coat, though it did not look so new any more, was wrinkled slightly behind, and she stood fingering her hair nervously while the clerk reached down to get something beneath the counter. Klein was about to go to her when he stopped. He waited for her to turn around and see him, but she did not; then he stepped aside, out of the way, until she turned to leave. What had she been buying? She had been at the cosmetics counter. Klein strolled by, his eyes dazzled by the gold and silver displays: the tubes of lipstick, studded with rhinestones, the little dressing table mirrors, the pencils, brushes, mysterious tubes. These things were fictions, he thought, they were not real. They were fictions, but his own world — he thought of his room, of the girl and her bowed, attentive head — was real and would not betray him.

That night they admitted to loving each other. Klein had been drink- 75 ing wine, was extremely agitated, not quite himself. The girl looked different: different lipstick? They ate spaghetti she had made. "I was never taught anything, how to cook," she said. "I learned it all by myself. So don't be surprised what it tastes like." Yes, she did love him: he knew now that she had loved him for some time. Why else those frightened glances, that uncomfortably comfortable domesticity here in this room? Her staying with him that first night, far from being casual, had been to her a tremendous event; he saw that now and the knowledge urged him to tell her again that he loved her. He loved her. Suffused with her love for him, he towered above her, protective and kind, his gaze distracted toward the shaded window as if lured to contemplate the future: no sleeping pills, no death after all, only a new life.

The first week of December, bitter cold. Klein returned from the li- 76 brary with an armload of books. Excited, he ran up the stairs as if he believed something awaited him in his room, some adventure. He let the books fall on his bed. Lately he had been reading a great deal, sometimes at the girl's room, sometimes here. His hair had been cut the day before, he had bought new shoes. He and the girl saw each other every evening; but already his interest in her had begun to wane, he wanted to read while she talked, telling him in detail of her life (her trouble with neighbors in the apartment house, with teachers). He was patient with her. That afternoon, after his composition class, he had known that he did not love her and that he had never loved her; that he did not especially want to see her again; that perhaps she had freed him, giving herself and thereby freeing him to himself — he did not quite understand. He was in a hurry. She was to come that evening for dinner, and he sat down to write out the note she would find taped on the door: the problem was how to be kind, considerate, to take it seriously (for already his thoughts were running wild, seizing upon the scattered lines of the medieval poetry he was to write an essay on, upon the respectful answer of one of his professors when he had asked a question in class that day). There was too much to think of. He could not concentrate.

She did not come to the next class meeting. Klein, nervously antici- 77 pating her gaze, was relieved; his gratitude made him eloquent and he believed he could see some of the students reappraising him. He understood that matters like that between the girl and himself happened often, perhaps daily, at this great university. Pity he felt for her, but not love, not even interest any more (she with her dreary half-smiling recollections of past insults, past pain, which impressed upon him too persistently the shabby detours and stumblings of his own life). If their relationship had begun in a dream, its termination woke Klein into something further: complexity, excitement, a new anxiety about his life, his future, even his personal appearance. He had bought the shoes with money saved week by week; he looked forward to buying something else—a suit, an overcoat. He spoke to his colleagues and appreciated their response to his humor, forced though it sometimes was. The secretaries in the English department knew him; he was able to be heard joking with them carelessly, like anyone else. The girl did not come to class. He did not see her. He contemplated writing another note, a letter this time, but he did not get around to doing it. Too much had happened between them, or perhaps too little had happened. He did not know. Between his classes he joked with the secretaries or dawdled with his colleagues or talked with his professors about things he had just discovered in his reading: ideas he hoped were his own, original ideas that excited him immensely. In his composition class he thought himself eloquent, and the desk at which the girl had once sat became for him not a depressing sight but (though he disliked himself for this) a symbol of something he possessed—perhaps power, the power of his new freedom. He had been loved. He had been worthy of love. The semester ended, the girl did not appear, he was forced to fail her in the course, though he talked the problem over seriously with another teaching assistant, a young married man given to a rather pleasing, keen, intellectual recklessness, popular in the department, talked it over discreetly and without embarrassment of humor, simply as a problem. The young man saw no choice, she would have to be failed, and he reminded Klein that maneuvering for grades was common at the university and that he himself suspected the girl's motives, really, though perhaps she liked Klein well enough. He said he would have supposed Klein wiser than to have been involved in such a dangerous situation; Klein, chagrined, in a way disappointed to know it was probably true she had only wanted a good grade from him, had to agree. The semester ended and she did not appear, he put an F beside her name (which did not look familiar), and supposed he would forget her, which he did.

That spring two students committed suicide; one, a girl but not the girl he had known, someone else, the other an Indian student, and Klein was reminded of the peculiar state of his own feelings months before: he recalled them in alarm, as if they had been the insane impulses of a stranger, someone in a novel. The girl had not appeared, he had not met her on the street or anywhere, and he never met her again. Perhaps she left school. In any case he never met her again and went on with his work, doing well, as well as any of the second-best students (for he recognized his limitations honestly), committing much to memory, grateful for and humble to the great academic tradition in which he would live out his life. With his degree he left for a comfortable though not well-known little college, married, had children, achieved happiness, did not seriously join in with his colleagues' criticisms of their lives, did not call attention to himself, bought a brick home, was proud of his wife for her chic competent womanly look, was proud of his children (two boys), took up sailing as a hobby since there was a fair-sized lake near the college. What possibility of happiness without some random, incidental death?

Study Questions

1. The author uses the third-person point of view in this story. Why is this point of view more appropriate for this story than, say, the first-person point of view?

2. In paragraph 1 what types of details are used to characterize Klein? What does the description in paragraph 4 of his room tell us about him?

3. Is there any significance to the fact that the name of the girl is never revealed to us? Any significance in the mention of the two suicides in the concluding paragraphs of the story?

4. What does the final sentence of the story contribute? Is this from Klein or the author?

5. What is the basic conflict in the story?

3 Modern Social Problems

"Some Must Watch"

It was difficult to decide which subjects and issues included in the general category of modern social problems could have the most appeal to students. Once these were determined, it was even more difficult to find essays that met the rhetorical standards we had set for all the essays selected for this text. We believe that the ten essays and the short story in this section have a wide range of appeal, in both form and substance.

The feminist movement is still a very important area of modern social concerns, so it is more than fitting that we include an essay dealing with it. Gloria Steinem's "Wonder Woman" is an account of her early introduction to feminism and all it implies. Surprisingly, she found it in the comic book *Wonder Woman,* created by psychologist William Moulton Marston. This is a provocative essay that should appeal to students who have found serious social implications in comic books and comic strips.

Robert Christgau's "Beth Ann and Macrobioticism," deals with dieting fads, particularly those that appeal to the young. Christgau uses a reportorial narrative form in a remarkable manner, and he creates very credible characters, dramatic development, and suspense, all handled from an objective point of view.

Crime as a major social concern is treated by Gresham M. Sykes in his essay, "New Crime for Old." He explores various explanations put forth by sociologists for the increase in crime. After dismissing most of these as inconclusive or invalid, he presents his own explanation. He sees the rise of a new crime, committed for one of three possible reasons: as a sport, as a political act, or as an act of alienation. This essay can serve as a useful model of organization for themes that deal with a situation or condition of such consequence that it justifies an explanation or reason for being.

In contrast to the sober tones and the length of the first two essays, the ones by Buchwald and Bombeck are humorous short pieces that can prove useful in stimulating theme topics to be developed in playful and satirical styles and forms.

For an example of irony at its classic best we have retained Swift's "A Modest Proposal" from the earlier editions of *Strategies in Prose.* It may be used to suggest ways students can handle similar topics. As a companion selection to this essay on population control, we have also retained Vonnegut's "Welcome to the Monkey House." In his satirical treatment of population control, Vonnegut will outrage some students, but more likely will delight most of them.

Alex Haley's "My Furthest-Back Person—The African" was included for fairly obvious reasons. But its real appeal is not through the popularity of the book *Roots* and its television version, but to the deeper significance of modern man's search for identity and origins. For the pro and con essays for this section we have used two reviews of Haley's book, *Roots.* In Larry King's "From the Seed of Kunta Kinte" Haley's book is highly praised as a "remarkable tour de force." And while Jason Berry commends it in "The Search for Roots," he expresses some concern about the obvious fictional nature of some of this historical account.

Gloria Steinem
WONDER WOMAN

Gloria Steinem (1936–   ) was born in Ohio. After graduating
from Smith College *magna cum laude,* she became a Chester Bowles
Asian Fellow at the Universities of Delhi and Calcutta A free-lance
writer, Steinem founded *Ms.* magazine in 1972. One of the foremost
proponents of the women's liberation movements, she was a founding member of the National Women's Political Caucus and has been
chairperson and member of the board of the Women's Action Alliance. Her awards include the Penney-Missouri journalism award for
1970 and a Doctor of Human Justice from Simmons College in
1973. A contributor to many magazines, including *Esquire, Ms.,
Vogue, Cosmopolitan,* and *Time,* Steinem's writings include *The Thousand Indias* (1957) and *The Beach Book* (1963). She also has written
for television, including parts of the series "That Was the Week That
Was."

Comic books were not quite respectable, which was a large 1
part of the reason I read them: under the covers with a flashlight, in the
car while my parents told me I was ruining my eyes, in a tree or some
other inaccessible spot; any place that provided sweet privacy and independence. Along with cereal boxes and ketchup labels, they were the pri-
mers that taught me how to read. They were even cheap enough to be
the first items I could buy on my own; a customer whose head didn't
quite reach the counter but whose dignity was greatly enhanced by making a selection (usually after much agonizing) and offering up money of
her own.

If as I have always suspected children are simply short people— 2
ancient spirits who happen to be locked up in bodies that aren't big
enough or skillful enough to cope with the world—then the superhuman
feats in comic books and fairy tales become logical and necessary. It's satisfying for anyone to have heroes who can see through walls or leap over
skyscrapers in a single bound. But it's especially satisfying if our world-
view consists mostly of knees, and tying our shoes is still an exercise in
frustration.

The touble is that the comic book performers of such superhuman 3
feats—and even of only dimly competent ones—are almost always
heroes, literally. The female child is left to believe that, even when her
body is as grown-up as her spirit, she will still be in the childlike role of

helping with minor tasks, appreciating men's accomplishments, and being so incompetent and passive that she can only hope some man can come to her rescue. Of course, rescue and protection are comforting, even exhilarating experiences that should be and often are shared by men and boys. Even in comic books, the hero is frequently called on to protect his own kind in addition to helpless women. But dependency and zero accomplishments get very dull as a steady diet. The only option for a girl reader is to identify with the male characters—pretty difficult, even in the androgynous years of childhood. If she can't do that, she faces limited prospects: an "ideal" life of sitting around like a technicolor clothes horse, getting into jams with villains, and saying things like "Oh, Superman! I'll always be grateful to you," even as her hero goes off to bigger and better adventures. It hardly seems worth learning to tie our shoes.

I'm happy to say that I was rescued from this plight at about the age 4 of seven or eight; rescued (Great Hera!) by a woman. Not only was she as wise as Athena and as lovely as Aphrodite, she had the speed of Mercury and the strength of Hercules. Of course, being an Amazon, she had a head start on such accomplishments, but she had earned them in a human way by training in Greek-style contests of dexterity and speed with her Amazon sisters. (Somehow it always seemed boring to me that Superman was a creature from another planet, and therefore had bullet-proof skin, X-ray vision, and the power to fly. Where was the contest?) This beautiful Amazon did have some fantastic gadgets to help her: an invisible plane that carried her through dimensions of time and space, a golden magic lasso, and bullet-proof bracelets. But she still had to get to the plane, throw the lasso with accuracy, and be agile enough to catch bullets on the steel-enclosed wrists.

Her creator had also seen straight into my heart and understood the 5 secret fears of violence hidden there. No longer did I have to pretend to like the "pow!" and "crunch!" style of Captain Marvel or the Green Hornet. No longer did I have nightmares after reading ghoulish comics filled with torture and mayhem, comics made all the more horrifying by their real-life setting in World War II. (It was a time when leather-clad Nazis were marching in the newsreels *and* in the comics, and the blood on the pages seemed frighteningly real.) Here was a heroic person who might conquer with force, but only a force that was tempered by love and justice. She converted her enemies more often than not, and if they were destroyed, they did it to themselves, usually in some unbloody accident.

She was beautiful, brave, and explicitly out to change "a world torn 6 by the hatreds and wars of men."

She was Wonder Woman. 7

Looking back now at these Wonder Woman stories from the '40's, I 8 am amazed by the strength of their feminist message. One typical story centers on Prudence, a young pioneer in the days of the American frontier. (Wonder Woman is transported there by her invisible plane, of course, which also served as a time machine.) Rescued by Wonder Woman, Prudence realizes her own worth and the worth of all women: "I've learned my lesson," she says proudly in the final scene. "From now on, I'll rely on myself, not on a man." In yet another episode, Wonder Woman herself says, "I can never love a dominant man who is stronger than I am." And throughout the strips, it is only the destructive, criminal woman—the woman who has brought the whole idea that male means aggression and female means submitting—who says "Girls want superior men to boss them around."

Many of the plots revolve around evil men who treat women as infe- 9 rior beings. In the end, all are brought to their knees and made to recognize women's strength and value. Some of the stories focus on weak women who are destructive and confused. These misled females are converted to self-reliance and self-respect through the example of Wonder Woman. The message of the strips is sometimes inconsistent and always oversimplified (these are, after all, comics), but it is still a passable version of the truisms that women are rediscovering today: that women are full human beings; that we cannot love others until we love ourselves; that love and respect can only exist between equals.

Wonder Woman's family of Amazons on Paradise Island, her band of 10 college girls in America, and her efforts to save individual women are all welcome examples of women working together and caring about each other's welfare. The idea of such cooperation may not seem particularly revolutionary to the male reader: men are routinely depicted as working well together. But women know how rare and therefore exhilarating the idea of sisterhood really is.

Wonder Woman's mother, Queen Hippolyte, offers yet another wel- 11 come example to young girls in search of strong identity. Queen Hippolyte founds nations, wages war to protect Paradise Island, and sends her daughter off to fight the forces of evil in the world. Perhaps most impressive in an age fraught with Freudian shibboleths, she also marshals her queenly strength to protect her daughter in bad times. How many girl children grew to adulthood with no experience of a courageous and worldly mother, except in these slender stories? How many adult women disdain the birth of a female child, believe it is "better" to bear male children, and fear the competition and jealousy they have been conditioned to believe is "natural" to a mother and daughter? Feminism is just beginning to uncover the sense of anger and loss in girls whose mothers had no power to protect them in the world, and so trained them to be victims, or left them to identify with their fathers if they had any ambitions outside the traditional female role.

Wonder Woman symbolizes many of the values of the women's cul- 12 ture that feminists are now trying to introduce into the mainstream: strength and self-reliance for women; sisterhood and mutual support among women; peacefulness and esteem for human life; a diminishment both of "masculine" aggression and of the belief that violence is the only way of solving conflicts.

Of course, the Wonder Woman stories are not admirable in all ways. 13 Many feminist principles are distorted or ignored. Thus, women are converted and saved. Mad scientists, foreign spies, criminals, and other male villains are regularly brought to the point of renouncing violence and, more often, of saying, "You're right, Wonder Woman. I'll never make

the mistake of thinking women are inferior again." Is the reader supposed to conclude women are superior? The Wonder Woman stories not
only depict women as culturally different (in ways that are sometimes
constructive and sometimes not), they also hint that women are biologically, and therefore immutably, superior to men.

Few modern feminists would agree. There are as yet no perfectly cul- 14
ture-free tests to prove to us which traits come from conditioning and
which do not, but the consensus seems to be that society, not biology, assigns some human traits to males and others to females. Women have
suffered from being taught to develop what society considers the less-val-
ued traits of humanity, but this doesn't mean we want to switch to a sole
claim on the "more valuable" ones either. That might accomplish nothing
more than changing places with men in the hierarchy. Most feminist philosophy supposes that the hierarchy itself must be eliminated; that individuals who are free of roles assigned because of sex or race will also be
free to develop the full range of human qualities. It's the multitudinous
differences in individuals that count, not the localized differences of sex
or race.

For psychologist William Moulton Marston—who, under the pen 15
name of "Charles Moulton," created Wonder Woman—females were
sometimes romanticized as biologically and unchangeably superior.
"Women," he wrote, "represent love; men represent force. Man's use of
force without love brings evil and unhappiness. Wonder Woman proves
that women are superior to men because they have love in addition to
force." If that's the case, then we're stuck with yet another social order
based on birth.

For the purposes of most Wonder Woman stories, however, the clas- 16
sic argument of nature versus nurture is a mere intellectual quibble. Just
helping women to respect themselves, to use their strength and refuse
domination by men is time-consuming enough: Wonder Woman rarely
has the leisure to hint at what the future social order ought to be. As for
men, we do get the idea that they have some hope—even if vague—of
collective redemption. "This man's world of yours," explains Wonder
Woman, "will never be without pain and suffering until it learns respect
for human rights." Put in more positive terms, this does seem to indicate
that humanized men will have full membership in the new society.

Some of the Wonder Woman stories preach patriotism in a false way, 17
but much of the blame rests with history. Wonder Woman was born in
1941, just about the time that World War II became a reality for most
Americans, and she therefore had to spend much of her time protecting
this country from foreign threats. Usually, that task boiled down to proving that women could be just as brave and loyal as men in the service of
their country. Even when her adventures took place in other countries or
at other times, they still invariably ended with simplistic commercials
about democracy. Although Wonder Woman was shocked by America's
unjust patriarchial system—a shock she recorded on her arrival here
from Paradise Island—she never had much opportunity to follow up on
it; a nation mobilized for war is not a nation prepared to accept criticism.
In fact, her costume was patterned after the American flag, and her war-

time adventures sometimes had highly jingoistic and even racist overtones, especially when she was dealing with Japanese and Germans.

Compared to the other comic book characters of the period, however, Wonder Woman is still a relief. Marston invented her as a counter to the violence and "bloodcurdling masculinity" that pervaded most comic books, and he remained true to his purpose. Wonder Woman and her sisters were allowed to use violence, but only in self-defense and only if it stopped short of actually killing someone. Most group conflicts between men and women were set not in America, but in a mythological past. Thus Mars, the God of War, periodically endangered the Amazon community and sometimes tried to disarm Queen Hippolyte through the ruses of love. Mars, of course, was the "heavy." He preached that women "are the natural spoils of war" and must remain at home, the helpless slaves of the male victors. Marston used Mars as the symbol of everything Wonder Woman must fight against, but he also gave the God of War a rationale for his beliefs that was really the female superiority argument all over again: If women were allowed to become warriors like the Amazons, they would grow stronger than men, and put an end to war. What future for an unemployed god?

The inconsistencies in Wonder Woman's philosophy are especially apparent in her love life. It is confused, to say the least. Sometimes her adventures with Steve, the pilot she is supposedly "in love" with, bear a feminist message. And sometimes they simper and go conventional in a way that contradicts everything that has gone before. In her American disguise as mild-mannered Diana Prince (a clear steal from Superman), she plays the classic feminine role: secretary, nurse, and worshipful, unrequited sidekick to Steve. The implicit moral is that, at least as Wonder Woman, she can love only an equal. But an equal never turns up, and sometimes she loses her grip on herself and falls for the masculine notion that there must be a permanent winner and a permanent loser, a conqueror and a conquered. "Some girls love to have a man stronger than they are to make them do things," she muses aloud. "Do I like it? I don't know, it's sort of thrilling. But isn't it more fun to make a man obey?"

I remember being worried by these contradictions. How could Wonder Woman be interested in Steve, who seemed so weak and so boring? Did women really have to live in a community by themselves—a separate country like Paradise Island—in order to be both happy and courageous? The very fact that the ideal was an island—insular, isolated, self-contained, cut-off—both pleased and bothered me. And why, when she chose an earthly disguise, did Wonder Woman have to pick such a loser? How could she bear to be like Diana Prince? Did that mean that all women really had to disguise their true selves in weak feminine stereotypes in order to survive?

But all these doubts paled beside the relief, the sweet vengeance, the toe-wriggling pleasure of reading about a woman who was strong, beautiful, courageous, and a fighter for social justice. A woman who strode forth, stopping wars and killing with one hand, distributing largesse and compassionate aid with the other. A Wonder Woman.

In 1947, William Marston died, leaving his heroine in the hands of 22
writers who didn't really understand her spirit. Gradually, her feminist ori-
entation began to wane. She became simultaneously more submissive to
men. I don't remember the transition very well, possibly because I myself
was on the verge of adolescence and was therefore putting comic books behind me. Or possibly because the comparatively free years of my childhood
were at an end. Like Wonder Woman, the full impact of the feminine role
was beginning to close around me. Now I was thirteen and made to see that
the idea of accomplishing anything on my own was at best eccentric and at
worst impossible. Recognition and status through men was the best possibility; it was also socially rewarded and socially enforced. Both Wonder
Woman and I fell into some very hard times in the '50's.

Looking at her most recent adventures is even more discouraging. By 23
1968, she had given up her magic lasso, her bracelets, her invisible plane,
and all her superhuman Amazonian powers. She had become Diana
Prince, a mere mortal who walked about in boutique clothes and took
the advice of a male mastermind named "I Ching." She still had adventures and she had learned something about karate, but any attractive man
could disarm her. She was a female James Bond — but far more boring
since she was denied his sexual freedom. She had become a sim-
pleminded "good girl."

In 1973, Wonder Woman comics will be born again; I hope with the 24
feminism and strength of the original Wonder Woman — my Wonder
Woman — restored. But regardless of her future, these selections from the
original adventures of the golden forties will remain classics for children,
boys as well as girls. And perhaps for many heroine-starved and nostalgic
grownups as well. If we had all read more about Wonder Woman and
less about Dick and Jane, the new wave of the feminist revolution might
have happened less painfully and sooner.

Wonder Woman is a comic book character. She and her Amazon sis- 25
ters are fictional creations. Indeed, Amazons have generally been considered figments of the imagination, perhaps the mythological evidence of
man's fear of woman. Yet there is a tentative but growing body of anthropological and archeological evidence to support the theory that Amazon societies were real; they did exist. German and Brazilian scientists
exploring the jungles of Brazil, for instance, recently came upon the
caves of what appears to have been an all-female society. The caves are
strikingly devoid of the usual phallic design and theme; they feature, instead, the triangular female symbol. (The only cave that does bear male
designs is believed to have been the copulatorium.)

Though the Brazilian research is still too indefinite for conclusions, 26
there are many evidences of the existence of Amazon societies in all
parts of the world. Dr. Phyllis Chesler details them in book to mind-
blowing effect and with great scholarship. Being a writer, not a scientist
tied to proven fact, I have fused the sometimes contradictory versions of
Amazonia into one amalgam; into a story that sounds right to me in the
way that a dream interpretation or a race-memory seems suddenly,
thuddingly right as it strikes off our subconscious. Much of it has been
proved, but I tell it as a story.

Once upon a time, the many cultures of this world were all part of   27
the Gynocratic Age. Paternity had not yet been discovered, and it was
thought (as it still is in some tribal cultures) that women bore fruit like
trees—when they were ripe. Childbirth was mysterious. It was vital. And
it was envied. Women were worshipped because of it, were considered
superior because of it. Men prayed to female gods and, in their religious
ceremonies, imitated the act of birth (as many tribesmen still do). In such
a world, the only clear grouping was that of 'mothers and children. Men
were on the periphery—an interchangeable body of workers for, and
worshippers of, the female center, the principle of life.

The discovery of paternity, of sexual cause and childbirth effect, was   28
as cataclysmic for society as, say, the discovery of fire or the shattering of
the atom. Gradually, the idea of male ownership of children took hold;
with it came the idea of private property that could be passed down to
children. If paternity was to be unquestioned, then women had to be sexually restricted. That was the origin of marriage.

Gynocracy also suffered from the periodic invasions of nomadic   29
tribes. Gynocracies were probably stable and peaceful agricultural societies since agriculture was somewhat more—though not totally—a female occupation. Nomadic tribes survived by hunting, which was somewhat more—though not totally—a male occupation. The conflict between
the hunters and the growers was really the conflict between male-domi-
nated and female-dominated cultures.

Restricted by new systems of marriage as well as by occasional preg-   30
nancies, women gradually lost their freedom, mystery, and superior position. For five thousand years or more, the Gynocratic Age had flowered
in peace and productivity. Slowly, in varying stages and in different parts
of the world, the social order was painfully reversed. Women became the
underclass, marked by their visible differences regardless of whether they
had children. Often, the patriarchal take-over of female-dominated societies was accomplished violently. Everywhere, fear of goddesses, of
women's magical procreative powers, and of the old religions caused men
to suppress the old social order very cruelly indeed.

Some women resisted the patriarchal age. They banded together to   31
protect their female-centered culture and religions from a more violent,
transient, and male-centered way of life. Men were dangerous, to be tol-
erated only during periodic mating ceremonies. The women themselves
became adept at self-defense.

These were backlash cultures, doomed by their own imbalance. But   32
they did survive in various groupings on every continent for many thousands of years. Why don't they turn up in history? For one reason, most
of their existence was lived in those thousands of years dismissed as *pre-*
history—that is, preliterate. The few records that are available to us were
written under the patriarchal assumptions of a much later age. Even arch-
eology and anthropology have suffered from the fundamental, almost
subconscious assumption that male and female roles as we see them in
the patriarchal age are "natural"; therefore, they must have been the
same in the prehistoric past. Only lately have we begun to question and
check out those assumptions. Large, strong, and presumably male skele-

tons from prehistoric sites, for instance, have turned out on closer examination to be female after all.

Perhaps the mystery story Dr. Chesler traces through history and 33 mythology is soon to be solved. After all, mythology is a collective human memory that has, on other occasions, turned out to be accurate about invasions, great floods, the collision of stars. The Amazon cultures may also one day be proven as fact. Meanwhile, the fascination that brings them up as fantasy again and again may itself be some psychic evidence of their existence.

If so, Wonder Woman becomes just one small, isolated outcropping 34 of a larger human memory. And the girl children who love her are responding to one small echo of dreams and capabilities in their own forgotten past.

Study Questions

1. The punctuation of the first sentence is unconventional. How might it be punctuated under the guidelines from a standard rhetoric?
2. Why does Steinem postpone naming the woman who rescued her at seven or eight? At what point would a reader of "Wonder Woman" know about whom Steinem is talking?
3. How literally are we to take *looking back* in paragraph 8? How is *looking back* usually used?
4. Does Steinem find any acceptable explanation for those elements of "Wonder Woman" that she finds inadmirable or false?
5. What are the implications of the concluding paragraph?

Robert Christgau
BETH ANN AND
MACROBIOTICISM

Robert Christgau (1942 –   ) was born in New York City. Although
his sixth-grade teacher called him "the sloppiest boy I have ever
taught," he still managed to graduate Phi Beta Kappa from Dartmouth
College. After hitchhiking across the country, he became a police
reporter in New Jersey and then a free-lance writer. He has taught
at the California Institute of the Arts and Richmond College, and
is currently the Senior Editor for the *Village Voice,* where his Consumer
Guide to current records appear monthly. He has published in *Esquire*
and *Newsday,* among others. *Any Way You Choose It: Rock and Other
Pop Music 1967–1973,* a collection of his articles, was published by
Penguin in 1973.

One afternoon last February, Charlie Simon and his wife, 1
Beth Ann, were walking in Washington Square Park. The Simons did not
get out often, but when they did, people noticed them. Charlie, lean and
dark, wore a bushy beard and shoulder-length hair, striking even in the
Village. Beth Ann, small in the bust and full in the hip, with shimmering
black hair and a wide-eyed olive-skinned face, was more than striking —
she was beautiful.

Beth Ann and Charlie were feeling high. They were high on the 2
weather, which was clear and mild. They were also high on marijuana,
which was nothing new. They had been high on marijuana very often
ever since returning from Mexico at the end of 1963. During that time
they had also been high on hashish, cocaine, heroine, amphetamine, LSD
and DMT (Di-Methyl-Tryptamine) not to mention sex, food, art and the
infinite reaches of the human spirit.

Unfortunately, they had also been wretched on precisely the same 3
things, and the wretchedness seemed to be taking over. The sexual freedom of their marriage was turning a little scary. They were thinking of
becoming vegetarians without knowing exactly why. They produced art
objects in a compulsive stream, though they suspected that art was only
an ego defense, a fortification erected by the self against the self's larger
possibilities. And yet it was these larger possibilities, illuminated by
drugs, which made them most wretched of all, for they had discovered
that the religious experience induced by hallucinogens had its diabolic

Reprinted from *The New Journalism,* edited by Tom Wolfe, with permission of the
author.

side, and the Devil had been taking them on trips they didn't really want
to make.

The Simons were in deep, and they knew it could get deeper. Physi- 4
cal addiction was not the problem; the addiction was psychological and
social. Kicking drugs would mean kicking a whole way of life. Yet,
though it seemed impossible, they were trying. They managed to give up
coffee and cigarettes and dreamed of moving to the country and having
the baby they had almost had two years before, when Beth Ann mis-
carried. It is likely that as they tasted a bit of Nature in the park, with
the sun beaming down among the bare trees, they were dreaming just
that dream—the two of them off on a farm, away from all the ugliness
and complexity of the urban drug scene, with time to meditate, to work,
to grow. The dream must have seemed almost palpable in the freshening
air. Then Nature turned around and kicked Charlie in the head.

For the wretchedness wasn't just spiritual—it manifested itself physi- 5
cally. Beth Ann suffered from intermittent leg pains, Charlie from migraine headaches. The migraines had struck almost daily for years, as often as four or five times a day. A two-hour headache was not uncommon,
and one siege had lasted two days. Doctors could do nothing; psycho-
analysts were helpless. Once in a while there was a respite—LSD had
provided relief for almost a month—but they always came back. And so,
inevitably, on that lovely day in Washington Square, a bolt of pain seared
through Charlie Simon's head.

The Simons lived at 246 Grand Street, between Chrystie and the 6
Bowery, where they rented the two floors over a luncheonette for $100.
But Charlie, Fiorinal and Cafergot pills in his pocket, decided to seek relief at the home of a friend on Bedford Street in the West Village, and
when he got there, the friend had something new for him to try.

His wife had been fooling around with the macrobiotic diet, a largely 7
vegetarian regime based on organically grown whole grain and the avoidance of sugar, which is expounded in a book called *Zen Macrobiotics* by
self-described philosopher-scientist Georges Ohsawa. The book contains
a lengthy section in which cures for virtually every human ailment from
dandruff to leprosy are prescribed, as: "MIGRAINE: Diet No. 7 with a
little gomasio. You will be cured in a few days."

Charlie was skeptical. He had eaten at the macrobiotic restaurant, the 8
Paradox, about six months before, and had not been impressed with food
or clientele. But he consented to a spoonful of gomasio, a mixture of sea
salt and sesame seeds, which is the staple condiment of the macrobiotic
diet. He swallowed. The headache vanished. It was the end of the old life
for Charlie. For Beth Ann, it was the end of a lot more.

Charlie and Beth Ann—friends invariably speak of them as a unit— 9
were something special on the scene. Both 23, they lived largely on the
weekly check from Charlie's father, a prosperous but by no means opulent Clifton, N.J., dentist. Although the run-of-the-mill coffee-house gab-
bler might pine for such an arrangement, it is rarely considered cool
among working artists to live off your parents. Yet the working artists in
the Simons' circle never asked questions. The mystical tenor of the Sim-

ons' involvement with drugs was also unusual. For most of their older friends, marijuana was a giggle, not a way of life, and the other stuff was to be handled with extreme caution.

But Charlie and Beth Ann were not cautious people, and it was that, 10 more than their considerable artistic and intellectual gifts, which made them charismatically attractive to a good number of serious and moderately successful young artists. Charlie and Beth Ann were the enthusiasts, the extremists, the evangelists. If there was something to be tried—be it jazz or Morgan automobiles or psychedelics (consciousness-expanding drugs) or a new recipe for meat loaf—they would try it to the limit. Their involvement was always complete. And they always came back to spread the word.

Suddenly, macrobiotics was the new gospel, as the Simons com- 11 pletely transformed their lives in a few weeks. They cut off drugs, and politely but firmly informed the itinerant hopheads who were in the habit of dropping around that they would have to turn on somewhere else. They gave up sex, not permanently, they told themselves, but until they could readjust to the new life. Beth Ann stopped taking birth-control pills. Charlie shaved his beard and cut his hair. They sold books, records and hi-fi equipment to make a little extra money and they stopped painting. Their new-found time was spent studying, discussing and contemplating the philosophy of macrobiotics.

Macrobiotics has almost nothing to do with Zen. Its central concept, 12 yin and yang, is borrowed from Taoism. Ohsawa contends that all of the physical and spiritual diseases of modern man result from his consuming too much yin (basically, potassium, although there are dozens of parallels) or too much yang (sodium)—usually too much yin. Grain is the basic food because it contains the same five-to-one potassium-sodium balance which is found in healthy blood. Dieters increase their intake of (yang) salt and drink as little (yin) liquid as possible.

Most fruits (too yin) and all red meat (too yang) are shunned, as are 13 chemicals (additives and drugs, almost all yin, as well as "unnatural") and Western medicine. According to Ohsawa, the diet is not merely a sure means to perfect physical health. Adhered to in religious faith and humility, it is also the path to spiritual health and enlightenment. And significantly for the Simons, whose psychedelic journeys had turned into nightmares, the source of health is placed not in the depths of the self, but in "the absolute justice and infinite wisdom of the Order of the Universe."

Most nutritionists regard the diet as dangerously unsound. Even in 14 its most liberal form it provides virtually no calcium or Vitamin C, and the version which the Simons followed, Diet No. 7, was anything but liberal, consisting entirely of grain and tea. The reason they chose No. 7, of course, was that it *wasn't* liberal; Ohsawa proclaims it as the most extreme, most direct way to health. As usual, Charlie jumped on first, but Beth Ann, after some initial skepticism, soon overtook him in enthusiasm.

Enthusiasm was necessary, for Diet No. 7 was difficult. The worst 15 trial was Charlie's third day, when he went through a period of "sugar withdrawal," which he claims was every bit as violent as a previous withdrawal from heroin. After that it was just a little rigorous for a while, and then it became a way of life. Although Ohsawa places no limit on quantity, the Simons ate relatively little—it's hard to gorge yourself when you're required to chew every mouthful 50 times—and each lost 20 pounds in a month, with Beth Ann's weight settling at about 110 and Charlie's at 120. But the loss didn't bother them; in fact, they took it as a sign of health.

And why not? They felt better than they ever had in their lives. Not 16 only were the migraines and leg pains gone, but all of the minor fatigues and aches, the physical annoyances that everyone lives with, seemed to have disappeared. They slept less than six hours a night. They even felt high on the diet, with spontaneous flashes that seemed purer and more enlightening than anything they had felt on drugs. Always domestic, Beth Ann became an excellent macrobiotic cook. She and Charlie spent most of their time outdoors, together, although they were seeing their old friends occasionally and converting many of them to modified versions of the diet. One joyous day, they threw out every useless palliative in the medicine cabinet and then transformed their empty refrigerator—a beautiful $250 Gibson Double-Door Deluxe—into a piece of pop sculpture, with sea shells in the egg compartments and art supplies and various pieces of whimsy lining the shelves.

But at least one person was totally unimpressed—Sess Wiener, Beth 17 Ann's father. A vigorous pragmatist who had fought off both poverty and tuberculosis in his youth to become a prominent Paterson lawyer, all Sess knew was that his beautiful daughter was much too skinny. Unlike the drugs, which had been more or less out of his ken, the diet ran directly contrary to his own experience, and he opposed it vehemently. It was one more false step on the road to nowhere which his daughter had been traveling ever since she had insisted on marrying one of the most conspicuous young bums in the state of New Jersey four years before. The salubrious effects of the diet he regarded as a combination of self-hypnosis and folk medicine. He certainly didn't think they had anything to do with the absolute justice and infinite wisdom of the Order of the Universe.

Charlie himself experienced similar suspicions occasionally, but Beth 18 Ann's faith in the diet was always strong. Her only doubts were about herself. She felt she was dangerously *sanpaku,* which is to say (in Japanese) that the whites of her eyes showed underneath the iris, which is to say (in Macrobiotic) that she was gravely ill and destined for a tragic end. She was ashamed of the yang-ness of her upper legs, which were still muscular (strength is male, yang) and covered with downy hair. ("If a Japanese man discovers hair on the legs of a woman," Ohsawa writes, "it makes his flesh crawl.") The yang troubles in her legs she attributed to meat, a food she had always eaten but never relished, and she assumed the complete cure for both herself and her husband would be a long, long process because of the poisonous drugs their systems had accumulated. Their sin had been deep. She did not feel ready to start sex again.

But after a few months, the Simons did feel ready for art. Before the 19 diet, they had balanced their pastoral impulse with a pop sensibility which delighted in the trivia of an affluent culture. That sensibility slowly atrophied. Beth Ann's work, in which the romantic mood had always been tempered by a hard-edge quality, became softer and vaguer. But she was happy with it — all of its "diabolic aspects," she said, had disappeared.

In the ensuing months, the Simons studied Oriental philosophy, theories of reincarnation, hara, breathing exercises, astrology, alchemy, spiritualism and hermeticism, and became more and more impatient with Western thought. They went for rides in the country, or swimming with Irma Paule, head of the Ohsawa Foundation on Second Avenue, where most macrobiotic people in New York buy their food. At Irma's request they provided lodging for a Zen monk named Oki. Beth Ann suspected he was a fraud — in a month they saw him consume nothing but tea and beer, and he laughed at macrobiotics. Early in August, they took Oki to visit Paradox Lost, a macrobiotic camp in New Jersey. The Wiener summer home was near by, so the Simons decided to drop in. It was a mistake. 20

Sess Wiener had not seen his daughter in three weeks, and what he saw now appalled him. She had begun to lose weight again. There were red spots on her skin. She was complaining of pains in her hips and back and having some difficulty walking. Charlie was troubled with what he said were kidney stones, and sometimes his kidney attacks were accompanied by migraine. The Simons took a quick swim, then looked at each other. The vibrations from Sess were very bad. They left. 21

But Beth Ann was sick, and she kept on getting sicker. Her legs began to swell, and when she took the macrobiotic specific for swelling, a third of a pint of radish drink for three successive days, nothing happened. (Later, when Charlie's legs began to swell, he followed his instincts instead of the book and took a full pint of the drink every day, a most unmacrobiotic quantity. He got better.) Irma Paule, who claims to have been cured of paralytic arthritis on macrobiotics five years ago, told Beth Ann she had been through a similar period. She could have told Beth Ann some other things. She could have told her about Monty Scheier, who had died at her side in Union City on April 18, 1961. Or she could have told the story of Rose Cohen, who died in Knickerbocker hospital early in October, 1961, of salt poisoning and malnutrition, after having gone on macrobiotics a few months before. Or she might have told Beth Ann she was showing all the symptoms of scurvy. Instead, she told Beth Ann to vary Diet No. 7 with some raw vegetables. 22

As far as it went, this was good advice. In his books in English, Ohsawa's endorsement of No. 7 is somewhat ambiguous — while he prescribes it for almost every ill, he also implies that it is not a lifetime regimen. Beth Ann's sister Wendy and her brother-in-law Paul Klein, both on a more liberal macrobiotic diet, tried to tell her this, and so did Charlie. But Beth Ann was unmoved.* Irma, she said, a little self-righteously, was a coward — afraid to "encounter the deep change" which con- 23

*She may very well have been suffering from *anorexia neurose,* a compulsive inability to eat.

tinued adherence to Diet No. 7 entailed. Instead of widening her diet, she fasted altogether—four times for a total of about fourteen days in September. During each fast she would seem to improve, then tail off when it was over. The same thing would happen in the aftermath of any especially painful period of suffering. By the end of September she was bedridden, and Charlie was doing all the cooking and housework. He never really tried to convince Beth Ann that she should get off the diet, or even that she should see a doctor, although he did broach the subject a few times. Sometimes his will to stick with it was even stronger than hers. He was not feeling too well either. Sex had ceased to be a possibility.

On the evening of October 13, Sess and Min Wiener came to visit 24 their daughter in New York. When Sess glimpsed her lying on a mattress in a corner, he gasped and visibly turned color. Beth Ann was a living skeleton. Her legs were no longer yang, they were skin and bones. Her eyes, still *sanpaku,* were sunken in their sockets. She could barely sit up. She could not have weighed more than 80 pounds.

"Beth Ann," Sess said, "You are going to die. Do you want to die?" 25

Slowly, Beth Ann explained it once again. "Daddy, I am not going to 26 die. I am going to get well, and when I get rid of all these poisons in my body I will be well for the rest of my life."

For the next two hours, Sess Wiener used every iota of his hortatory 27 power to get Beth Ann to see a doctor, but it was useless. For Beth Ann, this was just another version of the argument she and her father had been having ever since her marriage, and before. Now she could show him once and for all that it was possible to do things differently and still be right. She had never understood her father's values, grounded in the everyday world he had overcome with such difficulty. The everyday world had never been a problem for her, and now she felt herself on the verge of conquering a much greater world, the world within. She had arrived at the perfect antithesis. What better way to set yourself against materialism than to destroy the very substance of your own body? As her father's vehemence grew, she became more and more immovable. It was very bad, and before it was over Min Wiener had threatened to kill Charlie if he let her daughter die, and Charlie had threatened to call the police because Min threatened to kill him, and Sess had dared Charlie to do just that, and Beth Ann had decided she never wanted to see her parents again. The vibrations were just too much.

But Sess Wiener could not desert his daughter. The next day he en- 28 listed the aid of Paul Klein, who together with Charlie, convinced Beth Ann to move in with Charlie's parents in Clifton. She had two conditions: that under no circumstances would a doctor be summoned, and that under no circumstances would her parents be permitted to see her.

Charlie was relieved. He had felt for a long time that it would do 29 Beth Ann good to get away from the city, and especially Grand Street, which had so many bad connotations for both of them. And although Beth Ann carped and complained for the entire ambulance ride to Clifton, she cheered up when she got there, and did some watercolors—from a prone position, for she could no longer sit up — of the garden outside her window. Her parents tried to see her after she arrived, but the Simons stuck to their promise.

Beth Ann was still on Diet No. 7, with extra salt to counteract what 30 she now believed was an excess of yin. She had written to Ohsawa describing her case and asking his advice. A few days after she got to Clifton she got her reply: You are a brave girl; stay on No. 7. Charlie, meanwhile, made an alarming discovery: in one of Ohsawa's innumerable books in French, he warns specifically that no one is to stay on Diet No. 7 for more than two months except under his personal care.

But Beth Ann stayed on No. 7. She got no better. She spoke to one 31 of her parents on the phone almost every day, but she claimed their negative waves were making it harder for her to get well. And she could feel negative waves from Dorothy Simon all the way across the house. She wrote Ohsawa again.

About two weeks after the move to Clifton, Charlie got a telegram 32 from Oki asking for a lift from Kennedy Airport. As he drove out, Charlie had a sudden premonition that Beth Ann wasn't going to make it. He had never felt that way before, but at the airport he asked Oki, who was famous as a healer, to come and take a look at Beth Ann. Oki said he'd try to find the time. He didn't.

Two days later, Beth Ann sat up — not by herself, but with the aid of 33 Dorothy Simon. Charlie, too weak to assist, watched as she agonized. It was awful. There had always been something people couldn't quite get hold of in Beth Ann, and as she had advanced on the diet this ethereal side had become more prominent. Even Charlie no longer felt in complete touch. But now he looked into his wife's face and was sure of what he saw: horror, horror at the extent of her own weakness and at the outpouring of will it would take to overcome it. Then the horror changed to resignation, and Charlie's premonition returned. For the next five days his temperature ranged between 102 and 104 degrees.

On the morning of November 9, he woke at six in a high fever. 34 Across the room, Dr. and Mrs. Simon were sitting with Beth Ann. He could not understand what was wrong and drifted off. When he got up again, his parents were gone, but Beth Ann told him what she believed was wrong — she had poisoned herself with too much salt.

Despite Irma Paule's reluctance to discuss such matters, almost every 35 macrobiotic person has heard the story of the 24-year-old macrobiotic in Boston who died with carrot juice being poured down his throat after an overdose of salt. Charlie called Paul Klein, then set about fixing his wife some carrots. Paul arrived. They decided Irma must be summoned. Paul went back to New York for Irma.

Charlie sat at the head of his wife's bed. In the mail that morning 36 there had been another letter from Ohsawa, telling Beth Ann she had misunderstood the diet completely and advising her to start all over again. He advised her especially to avoid salt. But all Charlie could do now was give her carrots. He lifted her head and fed her a spoonful. An orange dribble remained on her mouth.

"That's good," she said. Then her head rolled back in his hands, her 37
eyes became very *sanpaku,* and she died. Charlie was still giving mouth-
to-mouth resuscitation when the police arrived half an hour later.

Study Questions

1. What is the central idea of this narration?
2. How does the author maintain his objectivity? Does he
   ever make judgments?
3. What is the advantage of narration over exposition in presenting such material as this?
4. How does the author develop suspense in his development
   of the narration?
5. Although the author uses narration, he restricts dialogue to
   paragraphs 25 and 26. Why is dialogue more appropriate
   here than elsewhere in the narration?
6. For what purpose does the author use description?

Gresham M. Sykes
NEW CRIMES FOR OLD

Gresham M. Sykes (1922–   ) was born in Plainfield, New Jersey.
He attended Hofstra College and Mexico City College before earning an A.B. from Princeton (1950) and a Ph.D. from Northwestern
(1953). He taught at the University of Denver and Dartmouth before becoming Professor of Sociology at the University of Virginia.
Sykes was advisor to the New Jersey Governor's Committee on Prisons and is editor of the Scott Foresman Series on Institutions and
Modern Social Problems. His books include *Crime and Society* (1967),
Law and the Lawless (1969), and *Social Problems in America* (1971).

At first glance, the intense public concern with crime in the 1
United States today seems understandable enough. Even though the suffering and distress that flow from assaults, thefts, burglaries, and other illegal acts are not easily calculated, we are constantly reminded of the

Reprinted from *The American Scholar,* Volume 40, Number 4, Autumn, 1971. Copyright
© 1971 by the United Chapters of Phi Beta Kappa. By permission of the publishers.

high and rising cost of crime. And if a member of the public has not yet been victimized, his anxiety about the prospect—at a time when there is one major crime committed per year for every twenty persons—is hardly surprising.

The concern about crime is so pervasive, however, so emotionally 2 laden, that we must suspect that somewhat deeper causes may be involved. Psychiatry, quick to turn the tables on us in such matters, tells us that a good share of our concern may be due to our own unconscious impulses that we cannot bear to face. And, in recent years, a number of social critics have claimed that "crime in the streets" and similar slogans are no more than code words for bigotry; the public clamor about lawbreakers, it is said, is simply a disguise for widespread racial fear and hatred.

There is undoubtedly some truth to these ideas, but I think that it 3 would be a serious mistake to reduce the present unease about the problem of crime to a Freudian projection or a political artifact; and, in fact, there remains another possible basis for today's concern about crime that may be more significant.

Despite a good deal of skepticism on the part of many liberals about 4 talk of crime waves and the problems of law enforcement, it was clear by the end of the sixties that crime rates had increased sharply. Much of this growth in criminal behavior was of a familiar sort, but no less a serious source of worry for all that. In addition, however, it appeared to many that new kinds of crimes were coming into existence—or at least new kinds of motivations for crime that were mysterious and disturbing. More and more, lawbreakers failed to fit the poverty syndrome of crime where the offender uses illegal behavior as a deliberate means of breaking free of material deprivation. Inexplicable goals and values seemed to be involved and this, at root, was the thing that made the surge of crime so disquieting. Crime—or at least a significant portion of it in the mind of the public—had become a moral challenge, an alternative view of the social order. In an era when there are many people ready to believe that all things are falling apart and "mere anarchy is loosed upon the world," a concern with crime has become an anxiety about the continuity of American society.

When we examine past theories about the motivation of those who 5 break the law, the persistent image of the criminal as somehow tainted or alien stands out sharply beneath the scrim of changing ideas. In an age of belief, it was the Devil that had crept into his soul and steered him into evil actions. In the nineteenth century, a biological interpretation had captured people's imagination and the criminal was likely to be viewed as a throwback to a more primitive form, with the cause of bad-doing lodged somewhere in the soma. By the beginning of the twentieth century, Freud dominated our demonology and we looked to the psyche for the origins of crime. Now, to a large extent, it is the turn of sociology. It is the deviant social groups to which the individual belongs and the patterns of his socialization that becomes the villain.

At the present time, there are actually three major strands in the so- 6 ciological explanation of criminal behavior. There is, first, the idea that people learn to be criminal in a perfectly ordinary learning process, but it happens to take place in association with criminal or delinquent groups. In this model—which could be called the Fagin style of criminalization—the picture is one of a normal boy growing up in an abnormal atmosphere and taking on the values, attitudes and norms of his peers, who unfortunately are lawbreakers.

Second, there is the idea that most people, to some degree or an- 7 other, have impulses to seize on illegal means as the shortest and most effective path to their goals. The likelihood of these impulses finding expression, however, is a product of a breakdown of social controls. And such a breakdown is to be found in the form of disorganized families, ineffective school authorities, and the close example of adult criminals, a set of conditions encountered all too often in the slum.

A third view of criminal and delinquent behavior, stemming from the 8 work of sociologists such as Durkheim and Merton, has argued that in a number of societies a great emphasis is placed on achievement and success, particularly in monetary terms. In the United States especially, it is said, these are goals implanted in almost everyone; we are all strivers, not because of some acquisitive instinct but because our culture tells us to be so. At the same time, our society fails to provide equal opportunities for reaching these goals, and places little moral weight behind the regulation of the means used. The resulting frustration, surrounded by ethical ambiguities, means that there is a constant pressure toward deviant or illegitimate behavior with few normative restraints—a state of so-called anomie. Crime becomes prevalent, not because people are brought up in deviant subgroups or because of "abnormal" socialization, but because the society itself suffers from a general discontinuity between ends and means.

These generalizations about crime might seem too embracing, and it 9 is true that for the sociologist a broad generalization is like catnip for a cat. Some critics might fault these ideas for being too simple, and it must be admitted that these explanations of crime boil down the wild diversity of human behavior to a few variables, although for this brief discussion I have simplified them even further. Nonetheless, these theories have helped enlarge our understanding of crime and delinquency in the past, and they are in fact being used as the intellectual underpinning for many programs of treatment.

The trouble with these sociological explanations of criminal behavior 10 is due, I believe, not so much to their inadequacy in dealing with the more or less conventional crime for which they were designed, but to the fact that they have been overtaken by the rush of history and are being used to interpret behavior patterns that are a new element on the scene. The position of the social scientist, like that of many others, is undermined by social change.

When we look at the sociological theories of crime causation, they 11 evidently share something of a common viewpoint. They are all inclined to assume that the criminal or the delinquent wants very much the same thing everyone wants—and what everyone wants is said to be money, prestige and personal aggrandizement. The goals of the lawbreaker are commonly held to be legitimate or "normal," but the means used to reach them are deviant. If the behavior of the criminal has appeared too irrational or bizarre to be encompassed by this picture, the problem of finding an explanation has been handed back to the psychiatrist. But since the great bulk of criminal behavior has seemed to have an economic objective, the emphasis on deviant means has laid a comfortable claim on a large share of the field.

Now, however, there appears to be a growing number of criminals 12 and delinquents who cannot be stuffed into this particular theoretical box. Perhaps one of the more easily seen forms of this emerging illegal behavior is crime as a form of sport or play. It is true, of course, that Frederic Thrasher, who wrote the classical account of boys' gangs in the 1920s, put a good deal of emphasis on the playfulness that he saw running through much delinquent behavior. And Albert Cohen, who made a study of delinquent boys in the fifties, stressed the nonutilitarian character of much of their activity, for example, stealing from one store, taking the things that were stolen to another store, leaving them there, and stealing again. A few other criminologists have pointed to the thrill-seeking that may be involved in breaking the law, both for adults and juveniles, and crime as a form of sport has not gone unrecognized; but in general it has tended to be discounted.

At the present time, however, there is a strong possibility that crime 13 and delinquency as sport may be on the increase. Auto theft, for example, is often a kind of game, a white-collar form of juvenile daring; and in the last ten years, according to the Uniform Crime Reports of the F.B.I., the rate has gone up 138 percent. There are also many reports that shop-lifting is showing a marked growth, not simply among the poor, but among those well up the socioeconomic scale and often by people who are stealing neither from need nor compulsion, but from a search for excitement. Secretaries in New York, for example, are reported sometimes to find stealing from Macy's far more appealing than a luncheon at Schrafft's.

We are looking, I think, at a new kind of crime, in the sense that it 14 doesn't fit much of the theorizing of criminology in the past. And, in fact, there are some writers who see in the future the possibility of a large increase in crime as sport, with relatively well-educated people using sophisticated techniques to create havoc in parts of the social system. We are already familiar with the students at M.I.T. and Harvard University who recorded the sound of different amounts of money being deposited in a pay phone—and then beat the telephone company out of a sizable sum on long distance calls. But Alvin Toffler, in *Future Shock*, suggests that this sort of thing could be just the beginning. Tampering with the survey samples of national opinion polls, rerouting mail, modifying computer programs—all could become forms of "fun," of illegal excitement.

Another kind of "new" crime that appears to be emerging from the 15 wings is political crime. Such crimes are hard to define precisely, and we do not have any good measure of them at the present time—although Governor Reagan early in 1971 was reported as saying that there had been more than five thousand bombings in the United States in the past eighteen months. He clearly views these as political acts, and he may be right. Perhaps more telling is the fact that of the sixteen persons on the F.B.I.'s most wanted list, ten could be placed in the category of politically motivated offenders. In any event, the kinds of acts that frequently involve political goals, such as violent antiwar demonstrations, the seizing of property, the destruction of records, and so on, have reached a new high and may very well increase, despite the supposed cooling-off of the American scene at the beginning of the seventies. These forms of breaking the law pose difficult questions of causation and rehabilitation, for they fall quite outside the view of crime and the criminal that has come to dominate our thinking. Unable to rely on some notion of personality defect or the pathologies of ghetto life as a way of explaining—and thus morally neutralizing—the behavior, we are forced to confront the illegality as a denial of the validity of the political and social order. The offender becomes not a mere deviant from accepted rules (a view of the matter that leaves us with the relatively reassuring problem of finding the abnormality that drives him), but a symbol for a competing system of power.

Another type of "new" criminal behavior centers on the theme of 16 alienation. A number of social scientists have accorded some role to alienation in the causation of criminal behavior in the past, but what I have in mind differs from this thinking in a number of ways. First, I am not talking about the alienation that springs from socioeconomic frustration in which the individual is unable to achieve the goals of society that he has accepted. Instead, the alienation I have in mind involves a rejection of the goals themselves. Second, this alienation is much more widespread than the alienation that social scientists have talked about in the past, and is found shot through much of the social structure. And third, it is much more thoroughgoing, in the sense that it involves more than a sense of social estrangement from material aspirations or selected political symbols. Instead, it embraces the entire range of social institutions, including the family, work, social stratification, conventional religion, and so on. If we took *The Greening of America* as a simple description of how some people think rather than as a tested theory of social change (which I think is the more reasonable view), the alienation I am talking about is somewhat like a "Consciousness III" turned very sour indeed and revolving around a bitter rejection of America and everything it stands for. And when this kind of alienation appears in society, we are likely to get a new kind of crime, or, perhaps more accurately, we should speak of new or additional motives for many old kinds of crime. Trashing the Establishment, or vandalism, acts of rage so diffuse in their targets that they appear virtually inexplicable—these become important symbolic gestures, not deliberate means to limited ends but affronts to society as a whole.

There is one more type of "new" crime that is worth considering— 17 namely, behavior that runs counter to the criminal law but about which the individual feels no sense of right or wrong. The law is not so much violated as ignored. When an individual fails to make moral judgments about his illegal behavior, he is sometimes labeled a psychopath, although psychiatry has long been suspicious of that term: the personality defect, it is said, is a lack of conscience, superego, or internalized values. But what

I am referring to here is not an individual failure or a form of psychological illness. Instead, I am pointing to a sociological phenomenon in which large areas of behavior become divested of any ethical or normative imperatives for large numbers of people over a prolonged period of time.

An example of this we are all familiar with can be found in the case 18 of divorce. One hundred years ago, the act of divorce was widely viewed as something wrong or shameful. Through the years, however, the stigma attached to divorce has faded; and just as the concept of fault in the legal sense is fast disappearing from the breaking of the marriage contract, so too is the concept of the wrongfulness of divorce being eroded in the public consciousness. The argument here is that there are a number of areas of behavior, labeled criminal by the law, for which this same sort of "slipping out from morality" may be occurring for a number of people. The use of drugs, for example, particularly in the case of marihuana, may often be of this order; similarly, certain kinds of sexual behavior, such as premarital sexual relations, seem to be losing a great deal of their moral resonance. The question of whether to engage in such behavior becomes very pragmatic; the question is whether one will be caught.

It would be an error to exaggerate the number of these "new" 19 crimes, and what I have discussed here must be counted as tentative. Nevertheless, it would seem worthwhile to reexamine the explanatory schemes we bring to the crime problem to see if, as I have suggested, shifts in social reality have made our existing theories miss their mark. The true nature of crime in society has always been difficult to grasp and the intellectual orientations that illuminate one part of the problem may black out other, more significant portions. Ideology can distort our perspective, as can a passion for scientific understanding that steers clear of questions of justice or morality because they cannot be measured. But if we fail to gauge accurately what is happening to crime in the United States today, at the very least we will be ineffective in dealing with a serious dilemma. At worst, we could feed the ignorance and fear that flare up in the struggle between the law-abiding and the lawbreaker, and lead to brutal repression.

Study Questions

1. What is Sykes' overall strategy in presenting his arguments?
2. What is the function of paragraph 11?
3. Identify words and phrases that link paragraphs 14–19.
4. What method of development is used in paragraph 16?
5. How does Sykes use examples in the development of his arguments?

Art Buchwald
ACID INDIGESTION

Art Buchwald (1925–   ) was born in Mt. Vernon, New York, and attended the University of Southern California for three years. His syndicated column appears daily in hundreds of newspapers and has made him one of the most popular American humorists. His recent books include *And Then I Told the President* (1965), *The Establishment Is Alive and Well in Washington* (1969), *I Never Danced at the White House* (1973), and *I Am Not a Crook* (1974).

America is an abundant land that seems to have more of everything than anybody else. And if one were to ask what we have the most of the answer would be acid indigestion. 1

No country can touch us when it comes to heartburn and upset stomachs. This nation, under God, with liberty and justice for all, neutralizes more stomach acid in one day than the Soviet Union does in a year. We give more relief from discomfort of the intestinal tract than China and Japan combined. 2

They can say what they will about us, but we Americans know what to do with our excess gas. 3

It is no accident that the United States became the largest producer of acid indigestion in the world. When the first settlers came to the New World they found their lives fraught with danger. First they had to worry about Indians, then they had to worry about their crops. Afterward they had to worry about witches. This played hell with everyone's stomach and the early settlers realized if they ever hoped to survive they would have to come up with a cure for acid indigestion. 4

Providence was on their side, because amongst the early settlers were two brothers, Alka and Bromo Seltzer. They were both chemists who had experimented with various potions that had been given to them by the Indians. 5

One potion was a white powder than the Indians used for athlete's foot. Why, asked the Seltzer brothers, couldn't the same powder be used for upset stomachs. Al was neater than Bromo and rolled his powder into a tablet which he then dropped into a mug of water where it immediately fizzed. Bromo said it was too expensive to make tablets, and it was much easier just to dump the powder into the water, which would produce the same effect. 6

Reprinted from *Esquire*, December 1975, with permission.

The brothers split in anger, and Al put out his product under the name 7
Alka-Seltzer, while Bromo put his out as Bromo-Seltzer. Fortunately for the
country, both methods worked, and as soon as the cure for acid indigestion
had been concocted the New World could be settled once and for all.

You would think that after we killed all the Indians and won the 8
West and became a large industrial nation Americans would have
stopped having queasy stomachs. But the truth is we suffer more from
the blaahhs now than we ever did before. Some of it still comes from
fear, some of it comes from ambition, and some of it comes from eating
the whole thing.

As a people who strive for the best we must accept the fact that it 9
takes a cup of acid for every step we take up the ladder of success. It is
no accident that the men and women who run our corporations and our
advertising agencies and our networks and our government are the same
people who keep the Maalox, Pepto-Bismol, Bisodol tum and Rolaid
companies alive.

Show me a man who has to drink milk instead of wine with his 10
meals and I'll show you a titan of American industry.

For years other nations have tried to catch up with us when it came 11
to sour stomachs and heartburn. But they never had the drive to produce
a good case of acid indigestion. They never understood what it takes to
keep up with the Joneses or outdo the Smiths. They don't realize that in
order to live in the best of all possible worlds you have to have a certain
amount of stomach discomfort to go with it.

If there is anything that shows up our system to that of the Commu- 12
nist nations, it is that we Americans can not only live with acid indigestion but we have three thousand different remedies to give us relief. In a
Communist society the state decides what you should coat your digestive
tract with, and if it doesn't soothe you, the state couldn't care less if you
burp all night long.

Acid indigestion is as American as Mom's apple pie (which is one of 13
the reasons we get it) and as long as there is enough heartburn to go
around, we, as a great nation, will survive.

Study Questions

1. What is the type and source of humor in this essay?
2. Although he has obviously written this article primarily to
   entertain, does the author have a serious intent? If so, summarize it in a thesis sentence.
3. What is the author's strategy in using one-sentence paragraphs 3 and 10?
4. What purpose is served by the account about the Seltzer
   brothers?
5. Study the types of sentences Buchwald uses. Which type
   appears most frequently? Which least frequently?

Francis Bacon
OF MARRIAGE AND SINGLE LIFE

Francis Bacon (1561–1629), English statesman, scholar, and writer, is best known today for his pithy essays, that are models for their concise expression and symmetry. Among his many works are *Advancement of Learning* (1605), and *Essays on Counsels, Civil and Moral* (1597). In 1618 he became Lord High Chancellor of England, under James I.

HE THAT hath wife and children hath given hostages to fortune; for they are impediments to great enterprises, either of virtue or mischief. Certainly the best works, and of greatest merit for the public, have proceeded from the unmarried or childless men; which both in affection and means, have married and endowed the public. Yet it were great reason that those that have children, should have greatest care of future times; unto which they know they must transmit their dearest pledges. Some there are, who though they lead a single life, yet their thoughts do end with themselves, and account future times impertinences.[1] Nay, there are some other, that account wife and children, but as bills of charges. Nay more, there are some foolish rich covetous men, that take a pride, in having no children, because they may be thought so much the richer. For perhaps they have heard some talk, *Such an one is a great rich man*, and another except to it, *Yea, but he hath a great charge of children;* as if it were an abatement to his riches. But the most ordinary cause of a single life, is liberty, especially in certain self-pleasing and humorous[2] minds, which are so sensible of every restraint, as they will go near to think their girdles and garters, to be bonds and shackles. Unmarried men are best friends, best masters, best servants; but not always best subjects; for they are light to run away; and almost all fugitives, are of that condition. A single life doth well with churchmen; for charity will hardly water the ground, where it must first fill a pool. It is indifferent for judges and magistrates; for if they be facile and corrupt, you shall have a servant, five times worse than a wife. For soldiers, I find the generals commonly in their hortatives, put men in mind of their wives and children; and I think the despising of marriage amongst the Turks, maketh the vulgar soldier more base. Certainly wife and children are a kind of discipline of humanity; and single men, though they may be

[1] Trifles
[2] Odd

many times more charitable, because their means are less exhaust,[3] yet, on the other side, they are more cruel and hardhearted (good to make severe inquisitors), because their tenderness is not so oft called upon. Grave natures, led by custom, and therefore constant, are commonly loving husbands, as was said of Ulysses, *vetulam suam prætulit immortalitati.*[4] Chaste women are often proud and forward, as presuming upon the merit of their chastity. It is one of the best bonds, both of chasity and obedience, in the wife, if she think her husband wise; which she will never do, if she find him jealous. Wives are young men's mistresses; companions for middle age; and old men's nurses. So as a man may have a quarrel[5] to marry, when he will. But yet he was reputed one of the wise men, that made answer to the question, when a man should marry,—*A young man not yet, an elder man not at all.*[6] It is often seen that bad husbands, have very good wives; whether it be, that it raiseth the price of their husband's kindness, when it comes; or that the wives take a pride in their patience. But this never fails, if the bad husbands were of their own choosing, against their friends' consent; for then they will be sure to make good their own folly.

Study Questions

1. How valid are Bacon's observations on marriage? On single life?
2. What is Bacon's conclusion in the last two sentences?
3. What figure of speech does Bacon use in the sentence dealing with churchmen?
4. How does the punctuation differ from the standard practices of today?
5. Note the parallel structure of the sentences. What does this type of structure contribute to Bacon's style?
6. Although this is presented as one paragraph it could be broken down to several paragraphs. Indicate them.

---

[3] Exhausted

[4] He preferred his aged wife Penelope to immortality.

[5] Pretext

[6] Thales, when urged by his mother to marry, said he was too young; later, when pressed, he replied that he was too old. Plutarch, *Symposiaca* III, 6. Also quoted by Montaigne, *Essays*, II, 8.

Erma Bombeck
SUPER MOM IN THE SUBURBS
A cautionary tale about how to be neat, clean, cheerful, organized — and friendless

Erma Bombeck (1927–   ) was born in Dayton, Ohio, and received a B.A. from the University of Dayton. She is a contributing editor to *Good Housekeeping,* and her syndicated column appears in newspapers across the nation. Her wit has endeared her to both the general public and the intellectual. Among her books are *At Wit's End* (1967), *"Just Wait Till You Have Children of Your Own!"* (1971), and *I Lost Everything in the Post-Natal Depression* (1973).

Suburban mothers are divided into two distinct groups: The 1 Super Moms and the Interim Mothers.

The Super Moms are faster than a speeding bullet, more powerful 2 than a harsh laxative, and able to leap six shopping carts on double-stamp day. They are a drag for all seasons.

Super Moms are the product of isolation, a husband who is rarely 3 home and a clean-oven wish. There is a waiting list for canonization.

The Interim Mothers are just biding their time until the children are 4 grown. They never give their right name at PTA meetings, hide candy under the dish towels so the kids will never find it, have newspapers lining the cupboard shelves that read MALARIA STOPS WORK ON THE CANAL, and secretly believe that someday they will be kissed by an ugly meter reader and turned into Joey Heatherton.

There are no restrictions in our suburb. Super Moms are free to in- 5 tegrate at any time they wish, and when one moved in across the street, I felt the only decent thing to do was welcome her to the neighborhood.

The moving van hadn't been gone a minute when we saw her in the 6 yard waxing her garden hose. I walked over with my nine-bean salad and knocked on the door. Her name was Estelle. I could not believe the inside of her house. The furniture was shining and in place, the mirrors and pictures were hung, there was not a cardboard box in sight, the books were on the shelves, there were fresh flowers on the kitchen table and she had an iron tablet in her hand, ready to pop into her mouth.

"I know things are an absolute mess on moving day," I fumbled.   7

"Are people ever settled?" she asked, picking a piece of lint off the 8
refrigerator.

Then she waltzed in the children and, seeing one lock of hair in her 9
son's eyes, grimaced and said, "Boys will be boys!"

If my kids looked that good, I'd have sold them.   10

"Hey, if you need anything from the store, I go every three hours," I 11
offered.

"I shop once a month," she said. "I find I save money that way by buying 12
in quantity and by planning my meals. Besides, I'm a miser with my time. I
read voraciously — right now I'm into Cather — and try to go three or four
places a week with the children. They're very aware of contemporary art.
Now they're starting the romantics. Could I get you something?" she asked
softly. "I just baked a chiffon cake."

I felt my face break out.   13

"The doctor said I have to put on some weight," she went on, "and I 14
try desperately ... I really do."

I wanted to smack her right across the mouth.   15

Frankly, what it boiled down to was this: Could a woman who dyed 16
all her household linens black to save time find happiness with a woman
who actually had a baby picture of her last child?

The Interim Mothers tried to get along with Estelle, but it wasn't 17
easy. There was just no getting ahead of her.

She cut the grass, baked her own bread, shoveled the driveway, grew 18
her own herbs, made the children's clothes, altered her husband's suits,
played the organ at church, planned the vacation, paid the bills, was on
three telephone committees, five car pools, two boards, took her garden
hose in during the winter, took her ironing board down every week,
stocked the freezer with sides of beef, made her own Christmas cards,
voted in every election, saw her dentist twice a year, assisted in the delivery of her dog's puppies, melted down old candles, saved the antifreeze
and had a pencil by her telephone.

"Where is Estelle?" asked my friend Helen when she dropped by 19
one day.

"Who knows? Probably painting her varicose veins to make them 20
look like textured stockings. I tell you that woman gets on my nerves."

"She is a bit much," said Helen.   21

"A bit much! Would you trust a woman who always knows where 22
her car keys are?"

"I think she'd like to be your friend."   23

"It wouldn't work."   24

"You could try."   25

"You don't know what you are saying. She's so ... so organized. 26
Hers is the only house on the block that has fire drills. Take the other
day — the school called to tell her Kevin had been hurt. Do you remember what happened when the school called me when my son flunked his
eye test?"

"You became hysterical and had to be put under sedation."   27

"Right. Not Estelle. She calmly got her car keys off the hook, threw 28
a coordinated sweater over her coordinated slacks, put the dinner in the

oven on 'warm,' picked up that pencil by the phone, wrote a note, went
to school to pick up Kevin and drove him to the emergency ward."

"So. You could have done that."   29

"I'm not finished. In the emergency ward, she deposited Kevin, re-   30
membered his birth date, his father's name, and recited their hospital-
ization number from *memory*."

"I remember when you took Andy to the hospital."   31

"I don't want to talk about it."   32

"You had to write a check for a dime to make a phone call."   33

"Okay. I remember."   34

Actually, Estelle didn't bother anyone. She wasn't much more than a   35
blur, whipping in and out of the driveway each day. I was surprised when
she appeared at my mailbox. "Erma," she said, "what's wrong with me?"

"Nothing," I hedged. "Why?"   36

"Be honest with me. I don't fit into the neighborhood. Why?"   37

"I don't know how to explain it," I faltered. "It's just that ... you're 38
the type of woman you'd call from the drugstore and ask what you use
for your irregularities."

"All I want is to be someone's friend."   39

"I know you do, Estelle, and I'd like to help you, but first you have   40
to understand what a friend is."

"Tell me."   41

"It's sorta hard to understand. But a friend doesn't go on a diet when   42
you are fat. A friend never defends a husband who gets his wife an electric skillet for her birthday by saying, 'At least, he's not one to carouse
around at night.'

"A friend will tell you she saw your old boyfriend ... and he's a   43
priest.

"A friend will baby-sit your children when they are contagious.   44

"A friend when asked what she thinks of a home permanent will lie.   45
A friend will threaten to kill anyone who tries to come into the fitting
room when you are trying on bathing suits. But, most of all, a friend will
not make each minute of every day count and screw it up for the rest of
us."

From then on, Estelle, neighborhood Super Mom, began to change.   46
Not all at once. But week by week we saw her learning how to compromise with herself. At first, she did little things like buying a deodorant that wasn't on sale and scraping the list of emergency numbers off
the phone with her fingernail.

One morning one of her children knocked on my door and asked to   47
use our bathroom. He said his mommy had locked him out.

The next week Estelle ran out of gas while making the Girl Scout   48
run. A few days later she forgot to tie her garbage cans together, and the
dogs dragged TV-dinner boxes all over her lawn for the world to see.

You could almost see her image beginning to crumble. She dropped   49
in unexpectedly one afternoon and leaned over the divider to confide, "I
have come to the conclusion there is an afterlife."

"An afterlife?"   50

"Right. I think life goes on after the children are grown."   51

"Who told you that?"   52

"I read it on a vitamin label."   53

"What are you trying to say, Estelle?"   54

"I am trying to tell you that I am going to run away from home. 55
Back to the city. There's a life for me back there."

"Don't talk crazy," I said.   56

"I've tried to be so perfect," she sobbed.   57

"I know. I know."   58

At that moment one of Estelle's children ran excitedly into the room. 59
"Mommy! Mommy!" she said wildly. "I was on the team that used a
toothpaste with fluoride and I only have one cavity."

Estelle looked at her silently for a full minute, then said, "Who 60
cares?"

She was one of us.   61

Study Questions

1. What is the central idea of this short humorous essay?
2. What is gained by the narrative method in this type of essay?
3. How does the author use comparison and contrast? What is the purpose of this type of development?
4. What method of identification is used to define "a friend" in paragraphs 43–45?
5. Identify at least three sources of humor in this essay.
6. What are the implied topic sentences in paragraphs 6 and 18? How are they developed?

Simone de Beauvoir
ON AGING

Translated by Judy Oringer and David Kolooney

Simone de Beauvoir (1908–   ) was born in Paris. After graduating
from the Sorbonne in 1929, she taught school for several years and
then devoted full time to writing. She enjoys an international reputation as a writer of fiction and nonfiction, and most of her works have

been translated into English. Along with her lifelong friend Jean-Paul Sartre, she became a leading exponent of Existentialism, a literary and philosophical movement that dominated French intellectual circles for many years. The novels include *She Came to Stay, The Blood of Others, The Mandarins,* and *All Men Are Mortal.* Her works of non-fiction include *The Ethics of Ambiguity, America Day by Day, The Second Sex, Must We Burn Sade?, The Long March, Brigitte Bardot,* and *The Prime of Life.*

O̲ld age is not the necessary conclusion of human existence. 1 Unlike the human body, old age does not even represent what Sartre has called "the necessity of our contingency." Many animals die after reproducing themselves, without going through a degenerative stage. However, it is an empirical, universal truth that after a certain number of years the human organism submits to degeneration. The process is inexorable. After a time the individual's activities are reduced; very often his mental faculties diminish and his attitude toward the world is altered.

Sometimes old age has been valued for political or social reasons. 2 Certain individuals—for example the women in Old China—could find refuge in it from the harshness of the adult condition. Others accept old age with deep pessimism: when the will to live seems a source of unhappiness, it is logical to prefer a half-death. But the vast majority approach old age either with sorrow or rebellion. It inspires more repugnance than death itself.

In fact it is old age, more than death, that is the negation of life. It 3 parodies life. Death transforms life with destiny; in a way, it saves life by conferring on it an absolute dimension, "so that finally eternity itself changes it." It abolishes time. The man who is buried—his last days on earth have no more validity than the rest; his existence has become a totality, all of whose parts are equally present in the grasp of nothingness. Victor Hugo is at the same time and never both 30 and 80 years old. But when he was 80 his present life obliterated his past. This supersedence is saddening when, as is almost always the case, the present is a degradation or even a denial of what was. Past events, acquired knowledge, retain their place when life is extinguished: they have been. But when memory crumbles they are engulfed in a mocking darkness: life is unraveled thread by thread like a tattered sweater, leaving nothing in the hands of the aged but the formless shreds. Even worse, the indifference which has overcome him challenges his own passions, his convictions and his activities. That was the case when de Charlus ruined the aristocratic pride which had been his raison d'être with a gesture of his hat. Or when Arina Pavlovki reconciled herself with a son she had always hated. What good is it to have worked so hard—"wasting your trouble," as Rousseau put it—if you no longer value the results you have achieved? Michelangelo's disdain for his "puppets" is heartbreaking—if we consider with him his old age we also feel sadly the vanity of his efforts. But with death these moments of discouragement can do nothing against the grandeur of his work.

Not all old people are resigned. On the contrary, many are distin- 4
guished by their stubbornness. Often, however, they become caricatures
of themselves. Their will power perseveres out of a kind of inertia, without reason or even against all reason. At the beginning they were strong-
willed because they had a certain goal in view. Now they remain strong-
willed because they were strong-willed before. What happens on the
whole with old people is that they substitute habits, reflexes, rigidity, for
innovation. There is truth in an angry essay written by Faguet called
"The Ten Commandments of Old Age" when he says: Old age is a continual comedy that people act out to create an illusion for themselves and
others, and it is comical above all when it is badly acted.

Morality preaches the serene acceptance of those evils which science 5
and technology are powerless to eliminate: pain, sickness, age. To bear
bravely the very state which diminishes us will, it is claimed, help us
grow. For lack of anything else to do, an aging person might become involved in this project. But here we are just playing with words. Projects
only concern our activities. Growing old isn't an activity. Growing up,
maturing, aging, dying: the passage of time is a fatality.

If old age is not to be a derisive parody of our past existence there is 6
only one solution: to continue to pursue the goals which give meaning to
our lives—devotion to individuals, to collectivities, to causes, to social or
political work which is intellectual and creative. Contrary to what the
moralists advise, we should wish to retain in our old age passions which
are strong enough to prevent us from withdrawing into ourselves. Life
keeps its rewards as long as people give of it to others, through love,
friendship, indignation, compassion. Then there are still reasons to act or
to speak. People are often advised to "prepare" for their old age. But if
that simply means putting money aside, choosing a place for retirement
or planning hobbies, one won't be any more ready when the day arrives.
Instead of thinking about it too much, people would be better off if they
lived lives of involvement and purpose to sustain them after all illusions
have been lost and passions cooled.

However, these options are only granted to a handful of the privi- 7
leged: it is during old age that the gap between the privileged and the
vast majority of men is widest. In comparing the two groups we can answer the question: what is there that is inevitable in the decline of the individual? To what extent is it society that is responsible?

It is clear that the age at which decline begins has always depended 8
on the class one belongs to. Today a miner is finished at 50, whereas
among the privileged, many carry their 80 years with ease. Drained of his
forces sooner, the worker also suffers a much more rapid decline. His exhausted body is prey to injuries and sickness even in his prime, whereas
an old person who has been able to take care of his body can keep it
more or less intact until the day he dies.

The exploited are condemned in old age to squalor or, at the very 9
least, to severe poverty, oppressive living conditions and solitude, which
lead to a sense of failing and a generalized anxiety. They sink into a
stunned numbness which is reflected in their bodies: even the diseases
which affect them are to a large extent the product of the system.

Even if a person in retirement preserves his health and his mental 10
faculties he is still prey to the terrible blight of boredom. Deprived of his
grip on the world, he is unable to regain it because apart from his work
his leisure was alienated. The manual laborer isn't even able to kill time.
His morose idleness turns into apathy which compromises what remains
to him of his physical and moral balance.

But the injury that is done to him in the course of his existence is 11
even more basic. If a retired person feels desperate about the mean-
inglessness of his present life it is because his life has been robbed of
meaning throughout. A law implacable as the "Iron Law" has permitted
him only to reproduce his life, denying him the opportunity of creating
justifications for it. Outside the limits of his profession, he sees around
him nothing but a wasteland: he was never given the chance to involve
himself in projects which would have contributed to world aims, values,
raisons d'être.

This is the crime of our society. Its "politics of old age" is scan- 12
dalous. But even more scandalous is the treatment the society inflicts on
the majority of people during their youth and their maturity. Society
"prefabricates" the mutilated, miserable condition which is their lot in
old age. It is the fault of society that the decline of age begins prematurely and is precipitous, physically painful and morally terrifying—because people come to it with empty hands. When their strength deserts
them, the exploited and alienated are fatally transformed into discarded
rubbish.

That is why all the remedies that are proposed to alleviate the dis- 13
tress of old people are so ludicrous: none is capable of repairing the systematic destruction that has victimized them throughout their entire existence. Even if they are cared for, no one can give them back their health.
Even if one builds for them decent places to live, one will not have
created the culture, interests and responsibilities which would give meaning to their lives. I am not saying that it is entirely vain to try to improve
their condition at this time. But that won't offer any solution to the real
problem of old age, which is: What should a society be like so that in his
old age a man can remain a man?

The answer is simple: he must always have been treated like a man. 14
Society reveals itself in the fate it assigns to its inactive members: society
has always considered them merely idle equipment. Society admits that
only profit counts, that its "humanism" is purely facade. In the 19th century the ruling classes explicitly categorized the proletariat as barbarians.
Workers' struggles have succeeded in integrating the proletariat into humanity, but only insofar as they are productive. The old workers' society
turns its back on them as if they were a strange species.

This is precisely why the question has been buried in concerted silence. 15
Old age denounces the failure of our whole civilization. It is the whole man
that must be remade, and all relations among people recreated, if we want
the condition of the old to be acceptable. A man shouldn't come to the end
of his life alone and empty-handed. If culture were life and practice—and
not inert knowledge, acquired once and then ignored—if the individual had,
through culture, a grasp on his environment which fulfilled and renewed it-

self over the years, he would be an active, useful citizen at any age. If the individual from childhood on were not atomized, shut off and isolated among other atoms, if he participated in life, he would never know exile. Nowhere have such conditions ever been achieved. The socialist countries, if they approach this condition a little more closely than the capitalist countries, remain very distant from it.

In the ideal society I am picturing we could dream that old age, so to   16 speak, would not exist. Just as with certain privileged cases now, the individual, privately weakened by age but not visibly diminished, would one day fall victim to a fatal illness; he would die without suffering degradation. Old age would conform in reality to the definition that certain bourgeois theories give to it: that is, a moment in existence which is different from youth and maturity, but possessing its own balance, and leaving open to the individual a wide range of possibilities.

We are far from that. Society concerns itself with the individual only   17 insofar as he is productive. Young people know all about this. Their anxiety on entering social life is the counterpart of the agony of old people on being excluded from it. In the intervening time, daily routine masks these problems. A young person fears this machine which will use him up; sometimes he tries to fight back by throwing paving stones; the old man, rejected by it, used up, exposed, has nothing left but his eyes to cry with. Between the two the machine turns, crusher of men who let themselves be crushed because they cannot even imagine escaping from it. Once one has understood what the condition of old people is, one cannot be content to demand more generous "politics of old age," higher pensions, decent housing, organized leisure activities. It is the whole system which is at stake, and the demand can only be radical: to change life.

Study Questions

1. What types of argument does the author use to support her thesis?
2. How does the author establish her authority within the essay?
3. What is the rhetorical effect of sentence variety and length in paragraph 3?
4. What is the basic organization of this essay?
5. What is the function of paragraph 11 in the total structure of the essay?

Jonathan Swift
A MODEST PROPOSAL

Jonathan Swift (1667–1745) is recognized as one of England's greatest prose writers. He was born in Dublin, Ireland, and was educated there at Trinity College. The fact that he was a priest in the Church of England did not prevent him from becoming involved in politics, first as a Whig, then a Tory. However, Queen Anne disapproved of *A Tale of a Tub* (1704), and Swift was given the deanery of St. Patrick's, Dublin, instead of the English preferment he wanted. Among his now-classic works are *The Battle of the Books* (1970), *Gulliver's Travels* (1726), *A Modest Proposal* (1729), and *Journal to Stella* (1766).

It is a melancholly Object to those, who walk through this great Town or travel in the Country, when they see the Streets, the Roads and Cabbin-doors crowded with Beggars of the Female Sex, followed by three, four, or six Children, all in Rags, and importuning every Passenger for an Alms. These Mothers instead of being able to work for their honest livelyhood, are forced to employ all their time in Stroling to beg Sustenance for their helpless Infants, who, as they grow up, either turn Thieves for want of Work, or leave their dear Native Country, to fight for the Pretender in Spain, or sell themselves to the Barbadoes. 1

I think it is agreed by all Parties, that this prodigious number of Children in the Arms, or on the Backs, or at the Heels of their Mothers, and frequently of their Fathers, is in the present deplorable state of the Kingdom, a very great additional grievance; and therefore whoever could find out a fair, cheap and easy method of making these Children sound and useful Members of the Common-wealth, would deserve so well of the publick, as to have his Statue set up for a Preserver of the Nation. 2

But my Intention is very far from being confined to provide only for the Children of professed Beggers, it is of a much greater Extent, and shall take in the whole Number of Infants at a certain Age, who are born of Parents in effect as little able to support them, as those who demand our Charity in the Streets. 3

As to my own part, having turned my Thoughts, for many Years, upon this important Subject, and maturely weighed the several Schemes of other Projectors, I have always found them grossly mistaken in their computation. It is true, a Child just dropt from its Dam, may be supported by her Milk, for a Solar Year with little other Nourishment, at most not above the Value of two Shillings, which the Mother may cer- 4

First published in 1729.

tainly get, or the Value in Scraps, by her lawful Occupation of Begging; and it is exactly at one Year Old that I propose to provide for them in such a manner, as, instead of being a Charge upon their Parents, or the Parish, or wanting Food and Raiment for the rest of their Lives, they shall, on the Contrary, contribute to the Feeding and partly to the Cloathing of many Thousands.

There is likewise another great Advantage in my Scheme, that it will 5 prevent those voluntary Abortions, and that horrid practice of Women murdering their Bastard Children, alas! too frequent among us, Sacrificing the poor innocent Babes, I doubt, more to avoid the Expense than the Shame, which would move Tears and Pity in the most Savage and inhuman breast.

The number of Souls in this Kingdom being usually reckoned one 6 Million and a half, Of these I calculate there may be about two hundred thousand Couples whose Wives are Breeders; from which number I subtract thirty Thousand Couples, who are able to maintain their own Children, although I apprehend there cannot be so many, under the present Distresses of the Kingdom; but this being granted, there will remain an hundred and seventy thousand Breeders. I again Substract fifty Thousand, for those Women who miscarry, or whose Children die by accident, or disease within the Year. There only remain an hundred and twenty thousand Children of poor Parents annually born: The question therefore is, How this number shall be reared, and provided for? which, as I have already said, under the present Situation of Affairs, is utterly impossible by all the Methods hitherto proposed; for we can neither employ them in Handicraft or Agriculture; we neither build Houses, (I mean in the Country) nor cultivate Land: They can very seldom pick up a Livelihood by Stealing till they arrive at six years Old; except where they are of towardly parts; although, I confess, they learn the Rudiments much earlier; during which time they can however be properly looked upon only as Probationers; as I have been informed by a principal Gentleman in the County of Cavan, who protested to me, that he never knew above one or two Instances under the Age of six, even in a part of the Kingdom so renowned for the quickest proficiency in that Art.

I am assured by our Merchants, that a Boy or Girl before twelve 7 years Old, is no saleable Commodity, and even when they come to this Age, they will not yield above three Pounds, or three Pounds and half a Crown at most, on the Exchange; which cannot turn to Account either to the Parents or Kingdom, the Charge of Nutriment and Rags having been at least four times that Value.

I shall now therefore humbly propose my own Thoughts, which I 8 hope will not be liable to the least Objection.

I have been assured by a very knowing American of my acquaintance 9 in London, that a young healthy Child well Nursed is at a year Old a most delicious nourishing and wholesome Food, whether Stewed, Roasted, Baked, or Boiled; and I make no doubt that it will equally serve in a Fricasie, or a Ragout.

I do therefore humbly offer it to publick consideration, that of the 10 Hundred and twenty thousand Children, already computed, twenty thousand may be reserved for Breed, whereof only one fourth part to be Males; which is more than we allow to Sheep, black Cattle, or Swine, and my Reason is, that these Children are seldom the Fruits of Marriage, a Circumstance not much regarded by our Savages, therefore, one Male will be sufficient to serve four Females. That the remaining Hundred thousand may at a year Old be offered in Sale to the Persons of Quality and Fortune, through the Kingdom, always advising the Mother to let them Suck plentifully in the last Month, so as to render them Plump, and Fat for a good Table. A Child will make two Dishes at an Entertainment for Friends, and when the Family dines alone, the fore or hind Quarter will make a reasonable Dish, and seasoned with a little Pepper or Salt will be very good Boiled on the fourth Day, especially in Winter.

I have reckoned upon a Medium, that a Child just born will weigh 11 12 pounds, and in a solar Year, if tolerably nursed, encreaseth to 28 Pounds.

I grant this food will be somewhat dear, and therefore very proper 12 for Landlords, who, as they have already devoured most of the Parents seem to have the best Title of the Children.

Infant's flesh will be in Season throughout the Year, but more plenti- 13 ful in March, and a little before and after; for we are told by a grave Author an eminent French Physician, that Fish being a prolifick Dyet, there are more Children born in Roman Catholic Countries about nine Months after Lent, than at any other Season; therefore reckoning a Year after Lent, the Markets will be more glutted than usual, because the Number of Popish Infants, is at least three to one in this Kingdom, and therefore it will have one other Collateral advantage, by lessening the Number of Papists among us.

I have already computed the Charge of nursing a Begger's Child (in 14 which List I reckon all Cottagers, Labourers, and four fifths of the Farmers) to be about two Shillings per Annum, Rags included; and I believe no Gentleman would repine to give Ten Shillings for the Carcass of a good fat Child, which, as I have said will make four Dishes of excellent Nutritive Meat, when he hath only some particular Friend, or his own family to dine with him. Thus the Squire will learn to be a good Landlord, and grow popular among his Tenants, the Mother will have Eight Shillings neat Profit, and be fit for Work till she produces another Child.

Those who are more thrifty (as I must confess the Times require) 15 may flay the Carcass; the Skin of which, Artificially dressed, will make admirable Gloves for Ladies, and Summer Boots for fine Gentlemen.

As to our City of Dublin, Shambles may be appointed for this pur- 16 pose, in the most convenient parts of it, and Butchers we may be assured will not be wanting; although I rather recommend buying the Children alive, and dressing them hot from the Knife, as we do roasting Pigs.

A very worthy Person, a true Lover of his Country, and whose Vir- 17 tues I highly esteem, was lately pleased, in discoursing on this matter, to offer a refinement upon my Scheme. He said, that many Gentlemen of this Kingdom, having of late destroyed their Deer, he conceived that the Want of Venison might be well supply'd by the Bodies of young Lads and Maidens, not exceeding fourteen Years of Age, nor under twelve; so great a Number of both Sexes in every Country being now ready to Starve, for want of Work and Service: And these to be disposed of by their Parents if alive, or otherwise by their nearest Relations. But with due deference to so excellent a Friend, and so deserving a Patriot, I cannot be altogether in his Sentiments; for as to the Males, my American acquaintance assured me from frequent Experience, that their Flesh was generally Tough and Lean, like that of our Schoolboys, by continual exercise, and their Taste disagreeable, and to fatten them would not answer the Charge. Then as to the Females, it would, I think with humble Submission, be a Loss to the Publick, because they soon would become Breeders themselves: And besides it is not improbable that some scrupulous People might be apt to Censure such a Practice, (although indeed very unjustly) as a little bordering upon Cruelty, which I confess, hath always been with me the strongest Objection against any Project, how well soever intended.

But in order to justify my Friend, he confessed, that this expedient 18 was put into his Head by the famous Sallmanaazor, a Native of the Island Formosa, who came from thence to London, above twenty Years ago, and in Conversation told my Friend, that in his Country when any young Person happened to be put to Death, the Executioner sold the Carcass to Persons of Quality, as a prime Dainty, and that, in his Time, the Body of a plump Girl of fifteen, who was crucified for an attempt to poison the Emperor, was sold to his Imperial Majesty's prime Minister of State, and other great Mandarins of the Court, in Joints from the Gibbet, at four hundred Crowns. Neither indeed can I deny, that if the same Use were made of several plump young Girls in this Town, who, without single Groat to their Fortunes, cannot stir abroad without a Chair, and appear at a Play-house, and Assemblies in Foreign fineries, which they never will pay for; the Kingdom would not be the worse.

Some Persons of a desponding Spirit are in great concern about that 19 vast Number of poor People, who are Aged, Diseased, or Maimed, and I have been desired to imploy my Thoughts what Course may be taken, to ease the Nation of so grevious an Incumbrance. But I am not in the least Pain upon that matter, because it is very well known, that they are every Day dying, and rotting, by cold and famine, and filth, and vermin, as fast as can be reasonably expected. And as to the younger Labourers, they are now in almost as hopeful a Condition. They cannot get Work, and consequently pine away for want of Nourishment, to a degree, that if at any Time they are accidentally hired to common Labour, they have not Strength to perform it, and thus the Country and themselves are happily delivered from the Evils to come.

I have too long digressed, and therefore shall return to my Subject. I 20 think the Advantages by the Proposal which I have made are obvious and many, as well as of the highest Importance.

For *First,* as I have already observed, it would greatly lessen the Number of Papists, with whom we are Yearly over-run, being the principal Breeders of the Nation, as well as our most dangerous Enemies, and who stay at home on purpose with a Design to deliver the Kingdom to the Pretender, hoping to take their Advantage by the Absence of so many good Protestants, who have chosen rather to leave their Country, than stay at home, and pay Tithes against their conscience, to an Episcopal Curate.

Secondly, The poorer Tenants will have something valuable of their 22 own which by Law may be made lyable to Distress, and help to pay their Landlord's Rent, their Corn and Cattle being already seized, and Money a Thing unknown.

Thirdly, Whereas the Maintenance of a hundred thousand Children, 23 from two Years old, and upwards, cannot be computed at less than Ten Shillings a Piece per Annum, the Nation's Stock will be thereby increased fifty thousand Pounds per Annum, beside the Profit of a new Dish, introduced to the Tables of all Gentlemen of Fortune in the Kingdom, who have any Refinement in Taste, and the Money will circulate among our Selves, the Goods being entirely of our own Growth and Manufacture.

Fourthly, The constant Breeders besides the gain of eight Shillings 24 Sterling per Annum, by the Sale of their Children, will be rid of the Charge of maintaining them after the first Year.

Fifthly, This Food would likewise bring great Custom to Taverns, 25 where the Vintners will certainly be so prudent as to procure the best Receipts for dressing it to Perfection; and consequently have their Houses frequented by all the fine Gentlemen, who justly value themselves upon their Knowledge in good Eating; and a skillful Cook, who understands how to oblige his Guests, will contrive to make it as expensive as they please.

Sixthly, This would be a great Inducement to Marriage, which all 26 wise Nations have either encouraged by Rewards, or enforced by Laws and Penalties. It would encrease the Care and Tenderness of Mothers towards their Children, when they were sure of a Settlement for Life, to the poor Babes, provided in some Sort by the Publick, to their annual Profit instead of Expence; we should soon see an honest Emulation among the married Women, which of them could bring the fattest Child to the Market. Men would become as fond of their Wives, during the Time of their Pregnancy, as they are now of their Mares in Foal, their Cows in Calf, or Sows when they are ready to farrow, nor offer to beat or kick them (as is too frequent a Practice) for fear of a Miscarriage.

Many other Advantages might be enumerated. For Instance, the Ad- 27 dition of some thousand Carcasses in our Exportation of Barrel'd Beef: The Propagation of Swine's Flesh, and Improvement in the Art of making good Bacon, so much wanted among us by the great Destruction of Pigs, too frequent at our Tables, which are no way comparable in Taste, or Magnificence to a well grown, fat yearling Child, which roasted whole will make a considerable Figure at a Lord Mayor's Feast, or any other Publik Entertainment. But this, and many others, I omit, being studious of Brevity.

Supposing that one thousand Families in this City, would be constant 28 Customers for Infant's Flesh, besides others who might have it at merry Meetings, particularly at Weddings and Christenings. I compute that Dublin would take off Annually about twenty thousand Carcasses, and the rest of the Kingdom (where probably they will be sold somewhat cheaper) the remaining eighty Thousand.

I can think of no one Objection, that will possibly be raised against 29 this Proposal, unless it should be urged, that the Number of People will be thereby much lessened in the Kingdom. This I freely own, and 'twas indeed one principal Design in offering it to the World. I desire the Reader will observe, that I calculate my Remedy for this one individual Kingdom of Ireland, and for no Other that ever was, is, or I think, ever can be upon Earth. Therefore let no man talk to me of other Expedients: Of taxing our Absentees at five Shillings a Pound: Of using neither Cloaths, nor Household Furniture, except what is of our own Growth and Manufacture: Of utterly rejecting the Materials and Instruments that promote Foreign Luxury: Of curing the Expensiveness of Pride, Vanity, Idleness, and Gaming in our Women: Of introducing a Vein of Parcimony, Prudence and Temperance: Of learning to love our Country, wherein we differ even from Laplanders, and the Inhabitants of Topinamboo: Of quitting our Animosities, and Factions, nor act any longer like the Jews, who were murdering one another at the very Moment their City was taken: Of being a little cautious not to sell our Country and Consciences for nothing: Of teaching Landlords to have at least one Degree of Mercy towards their Tenants. Lastly, Of putting a Spirit of Honesty, Industry, and Skill into our Shop-keepers, who, if a Resolution could now be taken to buy only our Native Goods, would immediately unite to cheat and exact upon us in the Price, the Measure, and the Goodness, nor could ever yet be brought to make one fair Proposal of just Dealing, though often and earnestly invited to it.

Therefore I repeat, let no Man talk to me of these and the like Ex- 30 pedients, till he hath at least some Glimpse of Hope, that there will ever be some hearty and sincere Attempt to put them in Practice.

But as to my self, having been wearied out for many Years with of- 31 fering vain, idle, visionary Thoughts, and at length utterly despairing of Success, I fortunately fell upon this Proposal, which as it is wholly new, so it hath something Solid and Real, of no Expence and little Trouble, full in our own Power, and whereby we can incur no Danger in disobliging England. For this kind of Commodity will not bear Exportation, the Flesh being of too tender a Consistence, to admit a long Continuance in Salt, although perhaps I cou'd name a Country, which wou'd be glad to eat up our whole Nation without it.

After all, I am not so violently bent upon my own Opinion, as to re- 32 ject any Offer, proposed by wise Men, which shall be found equally Innocent, Cheap, Easy, and Effectual. But before something of that Kind shall be advanced in Contradiction to my Scheme, and offering a better, I desire the Author or Authors, will be pleased maturely to consider two Points. *First,* As Things now stand, how they will be able to find Food and Raiment for a hundred Thousand useless Mouths and Backs. And *Secondly,* There being a round Million of Creatures in Human Figure, throughout this Kingdom, whose whole Subsistence put into a common Stock, would leave them in Debt two Millions of Pounds Sterling, adding those, who are Beggers by Profession, to the Bulk of Farmers, Cottagers, and Labourers, with their Wives and Children, who are Beggers in Effect; I desire those Politicians, who dislike my Overture, and may perhaps be so bold to attempt an Answer, that they will first ask the Parents of these Mortals, Whether they would not at this Day think it a great Happiness to have been sold for Food at a Year Old, in the manner I prescribe, and thereby have avoided such a perpetual Scene of Misfortunes, as they have since gone through, by the Oppression of Landlords, the Impossibility of paying Rent without Money or Trade, the Want of common Sustenance, with neither House nor Cloaths to cover them from the Inclemencies of the Weather, and the most inevitable Prospect of intailing the like, or greater Miseries, upon their Breed for ever.

I profess in the Sincerity of my Heart, that I have not the least Personal Interest in endeavoring to promote this Necessary Work, having no 33 other Motive than the Publick Good of my Country, by advancing our Trade, providing for infants, relieving the Poor, and giving some Pleasure to the Rich. I have no Children, by which I can propose to get a single Penny; the youngest being nine Years Old, and my Wife past Childbearing.

Study Questions

1. What is the strategy in describing the advantages of the proposal in paragraphs 1–8?
2. At what point in the essay is it evident that Swift is not to be taken literally in his proposal?
3. What do the statistics in paragraphs 6 and 10 and in other paragraphs contribute to the tone of the essay?
4. What is Swift's strategy in citing a number of authorities and sources?
5. What types of arguments does Swift use to advance his position?

Alex Haley

MY FURTHEST-BACK PERSON—"THE AFRICAN"

Alex Haley (1921–   ) was born in Ithaca, New York. He attended
Elizabeth City (N.C.) Teachers College and received a Litt.D. from
Simpson College in 1970. He retired from the U.S. Coast Guard in
1959, after twenty years of service. Although he was largely responsible for the writing of *The Autobiography of Malcolm X* (1965), he
became a national celebrity with the publication of *Roots* (1976) and
the successful television presentation of that book. He is founder
and president of the Kinte Foundation in Washington.

My Grandma Cynthia Murray Palmer lived in Henning, Tenn. 1
(pop. 500), about 50 miles north of Memphis. Each summer as I grew up
there, we would be visited by several women relatives who were mostly
around Grandma's age, such as my Great Aunt Liz Murray who taught in
Oklahoma, and Great Aunt Till Merriwether from Jackson, Tenn., or
their considerably younger niece, Cousin Georgia Anderson from Kansas
City, Kan., and some others. Always after the supper dishes had been
washed, they would go out to take seats and talk in the rocking chairs on
the front porch, and I would scrunch down, listening, behind Grandma's
squeaky chair, with the dusk deepening into night and the lightning bugs
flickering on and off above the now shadowy honeysuckles. Most often
they talked about our family—the story had been passed down for generations—until the whistling blur of lights of the southbound Panama Limited train *whooshing* through Henning at 9:05 P.M. signaled our bedtime.

So much of their talking of people, places and events I didn't under- 2
stand: For instance, what was an "Ol' Massa," an "Ol' Missus" or a "plantation"? But early I gathered that white folks had done lots of bad things
to our folks, though I couldn't figure out why. I guessed that all they
talked about had happened a long time ago, as now or then Grandma or
another, speaking of someone in the past, would excitedly thrust a finger
toward me, exclaiming, "Wasn't big as *this* young'un!" And it would as-
tound me that anyone as old and grey-haired as they could relate to my
age. But in time my head began both a recording and picturing of the
more graphic scenes they would describe, just as I also visualized David
killing Goliath with his slingshot, Old Pharaoh's army drowning, Noah

and his Ark, Jesus feeding that big multitude with nothing but five loaves and two fishes, and other wonders that I heard in my Sunday school lessons at our New Hope Methodist Church.

The furthest-back person Grandma and the others talked of—always 3 in tones of awe, I noticed—they would call "The African." They said that some ship brought him to a place that they pronounced "'Naplis." They said that then some "Mas' John Waller" bought him for his plantation in "Spotsylvania County, Va." This African kept on escaping, the fourth time trying to kill the "hateful po' cracker" slave-catcher, who gave him the punishment choice of castration or of losing one foot. This African took a foot being chopped off with an ax against a tree stump, they said, and he was about to die. But his life was saved by "Mas' John's" brother—"Mas' William Waller," a doctor, who was so furious about what had happened that he bought the African for himself and gave him the name "Toby."

Crippling about, working in "Mas' William's" house and yard, the Af- 4 rican in time met and mated with "the big house cook named Bell," and there was born a girl named Kizzy. As she grew up her African daddy often showed her different kinds of things, telling her what they were in his native tongue. Pointing at a banjo, for example, the African uttered, *"ko";* or pointing at a river near the plantation, he would say, *"Kamby Bolong."* Many of his strange words started with a *"k"* sound, and the little, growing Kizzy learned gradually that they identified different things.

When addressed by other slaves as "Toby," the master's name for 5 him, the African said angrily that his name was *"Kin-tay."* And as he gradually learned English, he told young Kizzy some things about himself—for instance, that he was not far from his village, chopping wood to make himself a drum, when four men had surprised, overwhelmed, and kidnaped him.

So Kizzy's head held much about her African daddy when at age 16 6 she was sold away onto a much smaller plantation in North Carolina. Her new "Mas' Tom Lea" fathered her first child, a boy she named George. And Kizzy told her boy all about his African grandfather. George grew up to be such a gamecock fighter that he was called "Chicken George," and people would come from all over and "bet big money" on his cockfights. He mated with Matilda, another of Lea's slaves; they had seven children, and he told them the stories and strange sounds of their African great-grandfather. And one of those children, Tom, became a blacksmith who was bought away by a "Mas' Murray" for his tobacco plantation in Alamance County, N.C.

Tom mated there with Irene, a weaver on the plantation. She also 7 bore seven children, and Tom now told them all about their African great-great-grandfather, the faithfully passed-down knowledge of his sounds and stories having become by now the family's prideful treasure.

The youngest of that second set of seven children was a girl, Cynthia, 8 who become my maternal Grandma (which today I can only see as fated). Anyway, all of this is how I was growing up in Henning at Grandma's, listening from behind her rocking chair as she and the other visiting old women talked of that African (never then comprehended as *my* great-

great-great-great-grandfather) who said his name was *"Kin-tay,"* and said *"ko"* for banjo, *"Kamby Bolong"* for river, and a jumble of other *"k"*-beginning sounds that Grandma privately muttered, most often while making beds or cooking, and who also said that near his village he was kidnapped while chopping wood to make himself a drum.

The story had become nearly as fixed in my head as in Grandma's by 9 the time Dad and Mama moved me and my two younger brothers, George and Julius, away from Henning to be with them at the small black agricultural and mechanical college in Normal, Ala., where Dad taught.

To compress my next 25 years: When I was 17 Dad let me enlist as 10 a mess boy in the U.S. Coast Guard. I became a ship's cook out in the South Pacific during World War II, and at night down by my bunk I began trying to write sea adventure stories, mailing them off to magazines and collecting rejection slips for eight years before some editors began purchasing and publishing occasional stories. By 1949 the Coast Guard had made me its first "journalist"; finally with 20 years' service, I retired at the age of 37, determined to make a full time career of writing. I wrote mostly magazine articles; my first book was "The Autobiography of Malcolm X."

Then one Saturday in 1965 I happened to be walking past the Na- 11 tional Archives building in Washington. Across the interim years I had thought of Grandma's old stories — otherwise I can't think what diverted me up the Archive's steps. And when a main reading room desk attendant asked if he could help me, I wouldn't have dreamed of admitting to him some curiosity hanging on from boyhood about my slave forebears. I kind of bumbled that I was interested in census records of Alamance County, North Carolina, just after the Civil War.

The microfilm rolls were delivered, and I turned them through the 12 machine with a building sense of intrigue, viewing in different census takers' penmanship an endless parade of names. After about a dozen microfilmed rolls, I was beginning to tire, when in utter astonishment I looked upon the names of Grandma's parents: Tom Murray, Irene Murray ... older sisters of Grandma's as well — every one of them a name that I'd heard countless times on her front porch.

It wasn't that I hadn't believed Grandma. You just *didn't* not believe 13 my Grandma. It was simply so uncanny actually seeing those names in print and in official U.S. Government records.

During the next several months I was back in Washington whenever 14 possible, in the Archives, the Library of Congress, the Daughters of the American Revolution Library. (Whenever black attendants understood the idea of my search, documents I requested reached me with miraculous speed.) In one source or another during 1966 I was able to document at least the highlights of the cherished family story. I would have given anything to have told Grandma, but, sadly, in 1949 she had gone. So I went and told the only survivor of those Henning front-porch storytellers: Cousin Georgia Anderson, now in her 80's in Kansas City, Kan. Wrinkled, bent, not well herself, she was so overjoyed, repeating to me the old stories and sounds; they were like Henning echoes: "Yeah, boy, that African say his name was '*Kin-tay*'; he say the banjo was '*ko,*' and river '*Kamby-Bolong,*' an' he was off choppin some wood to make his drum when they grabbed 'im?" Cousin Georgia grew so excited we had to stop her, calm her down, "You go' head, boy! Your grandma an' all of 'em—they up there watching what you do!"

That week I flew to London on a magazine assignment. Since by now 15 I was steeped in the old, in the past, scarcely a tour guide missed me—I was awed at so many historical places and treasures I'd heard of and read of. I came upon the Rosetta stone in the British Museum, marveling anew at how Jean Champollion, the French archeologist, had miraculously deciphered its ancient demotic and hieroglyphic texts . . .

The thrill of that just kept hanging around in my head. I was on a jet 16 returning to New York when a thought hit me. Those strange, unknown-tongue sounds, always part of our family's old story . . . they were obviously bits or our original African "*Kin-tay's*" native tongue. What specific tongue? Could I somewhere find out?

Back in New York, I began making visits to the United Nations 17 Headquarters lobby; it wasn't hard to spot Africans. I'd stop any I could, asking if my bits of phonetic sounds held any meaning for them. A couple of dozen Africans quickly looked at me, listened, and took off—understandably dubious about some Tennesseean's accent alleging "African" sounds.

My research assistant, George Sims (we grew up together in Hen- 18 ning), brought me some names of ranking scholars of African linguistics. One was particularly intriguing: a Belgian- and English-educated Dr. Jan Vansina; he had spent his early career living in West African villages, studying and tape-recording countless oral histories that were narrated by certain very old African men; he had written a standard textbook, "The Oral Tradition."

So I flew to the University of Wisconsin to see Dr. Vansina. In his 19 living room I told him every bit of the family story in the fullest detail that I could remember it. Then, intensely, he queried me about the story's relay across the generations, about the gibberish of "*K*" sounds Grandma had fiercely muttered to herself while doing her housework, with my brothers and me giggling beyond her hearing at what we had dubbed "Grandma's noises."

Dr. Vansina, his manner very serious, finally said, "These sounds 20 your family has kept sound very probably of the tongue called 'Mandinka.' "

I'd never heard of any "Mandinka." Grandma just told of the African 21 saying "*ko*" for banjo, or "*Kamby Bolong*" for a Virginia river.

Among Mandinka stringed instruments, Dr. Vansina said, one of the 22 oldest was the "*kora.*"

"*Bolong,*" he said was clearly Mandinka for "river." Preceded by 23 "*Kamby,*" it very likely meant "Gambia River."

Dr. Vansina telephoned an eminent Africanist colleague, Dr. Philip 24 Curtin. He said that the phonetic "*Kin-tay*" was correctly spelled "*Kinte,*" a very old clan that had originated in Old Mali. The Kinte men traditionally were blacksmiths, and the women were potters and weavers.

I knew I must get to the Gambia River.   25

The first native Gambian I could locate in the U.S. was named Ebou   26
Manga, then a junior attending Hamilton College in upstate Clinton,
N.Y. He and I flew to Dakar, Senegal, then took a smaller plane to Yun-
dum Airport, and rode a van to Gambia's capital, Bathurst. Ebou and his
father assembled eight Gambia government officials. I told them
Grandma's stories, every detail I could remember, as they listened intently, then reacted. " 'Kamby Bolong' of course is Gambia River!" I heard.
"But more clue is your forefather's saying his name was 'Kinte.' " " Then
they told me something I would never even have fantasized—that in
places in the back country lived very old men, commonly called griots,
who could tell centuries of the histories of certain very old family clans.
As for Kintes, they pointed out to me on a map some family villages,
Kinte-Kundah, and Kinte-Kundah Janneh-Ya, for instance.

The Gambian officials said they would try to help me. I returned to   27
New York dazed. It is embarrassing to me now, but despite Grandma's
stories, I'd never been concerned much with Africa, and I had the routine images of African people living mostly in exotic jungles. But a compulsion now laid hold of me to learn all I could, and I began devouring
books about Africa, especially about the slave trade. Then one Thursday's
mail contained a letter from one of the Gambian officials, inviting me to
return there.

Monday I was back in Bathurst. It galvanized me when the officials   28
said that a griot had been located who told the Kinte clan history—his
name was Kebba Kanga Fofana. To reach him, I discovered, required a
modified safari: renting a launch to get upriver, two land vehicles to carry
supplies by a roundabout land route, and employing finally 14 people, including three interpreters and four musicians, since a griot would not
speak the revered clan histories without background music.

The boat Baddibu vibrated upriver, with me acutely tense: Were   29
these Africans maybe viewing me as but another of the pith-helmets? After about two hours, we put in at James Island, for me to see the ruins of
the once British-operated James Fort. Here two centuries of slave ships
had loaded thousands of cargoes of Gambian tribespeople. The crum-
bling stones, the deeply oxidized swivel cannon, even some remnant links
of chain seemed all but impossible to believe. Then we continued upriver
to the leftbank village of Albreda, and there put ashore to continue on
foot to Juffure, village of the griot. Once more we stopped, for me to see
toubob kolong, "the white man's well," now almost filled in, in a swampy
area with abundant, tall, saw-toothed grass. It was dug two centuries ago
to "17 men's height deep" to insure survival drinking water for long-
driven, famishing coffles of slaves.

Walking on, I kept wishing that Grandma could hear how her stories   30
had led me to the "Kamby Bolong." (Our surviving storyteller Cousin
Georgia died in a Kansas City hospital during this same morning, I would
learn later.) Finally, Juffure village's playing children, sighting us, flashed
an alert. The 70-odd people came rushing from their circular, thatch-
roofed, mud-walled huts, with goats bounding up and about, and parrots

squawking from up in the palms. I sensed him in advance somehow, the small man amid them, wearing a pillbox cap and an off-white robe — the *griot*. Then the interpreters went to him, as the villagers thronged around me.

And it hit me like a gale wind: every one of them, the whole crowd, 31 was *jet black*. An enormous sense of guilt swept me — a sense of being some kind of hybrid ... a sense of being impure among the pure. It was an awful sensation.

The old *griot* stepped away from my interpreters and the crowd 32 quickly swarmed around him — all of them buzzing. An interpreter named A. B. C. Salla came to me; he whispered: "Why they stare at you so, they have never seen here a black American." And that hit me: I was symbolizing for them twenty-five millions of us they had never seen. What did they think of me — of us?

Then abruptly the old *griot* was briskly walking toward me. His eyes 33 boring into mine, he spoke in Mandinka, as if instinctively I should understand — and A. B. C. Salla translated:

"Yes ... we have been told by the forefathers ... that many of us 34 from this place are in exile ... in that place called America ... and in other places."

I suppose I physically wavered, and they thought it was the heat; 35 rustling whispers went through the crowd, and a man brought me a low stool. Now the whispering hushed — the musicians had softly begun playing *kora* and *balafon*, and a canvas sling lawn seat was taken by the *griot*, Kebba Kanga Fofane, aged 75 "rains" (one rainy season each year). He seemed to gather himself into a physical rigidity, and he began speaking the *Kinte* clan's ancestral oral history; it came rolling from his mouth across the next hours ... 17th- and 18th-century *Kinte* lineage details, predominantly what men took wives; the children they "begot," in the order of their births; those children's mates and children.

Events frequently were dated by some proximate singular physical 36 occurrence. It was as if some ancient scroll were printed indelibly within the *griot's* brain. Each few sentences or so, he would pause for an interpreter's translation to me. I distill here the essence:

The *Kinte* clan began in Old Mali, the men generally blacksmiths "... 37 who conquered fire," and the women potters and weavers. One large branch of the clan moved to Mauretania from where one son of the clan, Kairaba Kunta Kinte, a Moslem Marabout holy man, entered Gambia. He lived first in the village of Pakali N'Ding; he moved next to Jiffarong village; "... and then he came here, into our own village of Juffure."

In Juffure, Kairaba Kunta Kinte took his first wife, "... a Mandinka 38 maiden, whose name was Sireng. By her, he begot two sons, whose names were Janneh and Saloum. Then he got a second wife, Yaisa. By her, he begot a son, Omoro."

The three sons became men in Juffure. Janneh and Saloum went off 39 and founded a new village, Kinte-Kundah Janneh-Ya. "And then Omoro, the youngest son, when he had 30 rains, took as a wife a maiden, Binta Kebba.

"And by her, he begot four sons — Kunta, Lamin, Suwadu, and Madi   40
. . ."

Sometimes, a "begotten," after his naming, would be accompanied by   41
some later-occurring detail, perhaps as ". . . in time of big water (flood),
he slew a water buffalo." Having named those four sons, now the *griot*
stated such a detail.

"About the time the king's soldiers came, the eldest of these four   42
sons, Kunta, when he had about 16 rains, went away from this village, to
chop wood to make a drum . . . and he was never seen again . . ."

Goose-pimples the size of lemons seemed to pop all over me. In my   43
knapsack were my cumulative notebooks, the first of them including how
in my boyhood, my Grandma, Cousin Georgia and the others told of the
African *"Kin-tay"* who always said he was kidnapped near his village —
while chopping wood to make a drum . . .

I showed the interpreter, he showed and told the *griot,* who excitedly   44
told the people; they grew very agitated. Abruptly then they formed a
human ring, encircling me, dancing and chanting. Perhaps a dozen of the
women carrying their infant babies rushed in toward me, thrusting the infants into my arms — conveying, I would later learn, "the laying on of
hands . . . through this flesh which is us, we are you, and you are us." The
men hurried me into their mosque, their Arabic praying later being translated outside: "Thanks be to Allah for returning the long lost from
among us." Direct descendants of Kunta Kinte's blood brothers were hastened, some of them from nearby villages, for a family portrait to be
taken with me, surrounded by actual ancestral sixth cousins. More symbolic acts filled the remaining day.

When they would let me leave, for some reason I wanted to go away   45
over the African land. Dazed, silent in the bumping Land Rover, I heard
the cutting staccato of talking drums. Then when we sighted the next village, its people came thronging to meet us. They were all — little naked
ones to wizened elders — waving, beaming, amid a cacophony of crying
out; and then my ears identified their words: *"Meester Kinte! Meester
Kinte!*

Let me tell you something: I am a man. But I remember the sob   46
surging up from my feet, flinging up my hands before my face and bawling as I had not done since I was a baby . . . the jet-black Africans were
jostling, staring . . . I didn't care, with the feelings surging. If you really
knew the odyssey of us millions of black Americans, if you really knew
how we came in the seeds of our forefathers, captured, driven, beaten, in-
spected, bought, branded, chained in foul ships, if you really knew, you
needed weeping . . .

Back home, I knew that what I must write, really, was our black saga,   47
where any individual's past is the essence of the millions'. Now flat
broke, I went to some editors I knew, describing the Gambian miracle,
and my desire to pursue the research; Doubleday contracted to publish,
and Reader's Digest to condense the projected book; then I had advances to travel further.

What ship brought Kinte to Grandma's " 'Naplis" (Annapolis, Md.,   48
obviously)? The old *griot's* time reference to "king's soldiers" sent me fly-

ing to London. Feverish searching at last identified, in British Parliament records, "Colonel O'Hare's Forces," dispatched in mid-1767 to protect the then British-held James Fort whose ruins I'd visited. So Kunta Kinte was down in some ship probably sailing later that summer from the Gambia River to Annapolis.

Now I feel it was fated that I had taught myself to write in the U.S. 49 Coast Guard. For the sea dramas I had concentrated on had given me years of experience searching among yellowing old U.S. maritime records. So now in English 18th Century marine records I finally tracked ships reporting themselves in and out to the Commandant of the Gambia River's James Fort. And then early one afternoon I found that a Lord Ligonier under a Captain Thomas Davies had sailed on the Sabbath of July 5, 1767. Her cargo: 3,265 elephants' teeth, 3,700 pounds of beeswax, 800 pounds of cotton, 32 ounces of Gambian gold, and 140 slaves; her destination: "Annapolis."

That night I recrossed the Atlantic. In the Library of Congress the 50 Lord Ligonier's arrival was one brief line in "Shipping In The Port Of Annapolis — 1748–1775." I located the author, Vaughan W. Brown, in his Baltimore brokerage office. He drove to Historic Annapolis, the city's historical society, and found me further documentation of her arrival on Sept. 29, 1767. (Exactly two centuries later, Sept. 29, 1967, standing, staring seaward from an Annapolis pier, again I knew tears.) More help came in the Maryland Hall of Records. Archivist Phebe Jacobsen found the Lord Ligonier's arriving customs declaration listing, "98 Negroes" — so in her 86-day crossing, 42 Gambians had died, one among the survivors being 16-year-old Kunta Kinte. Then the microfilmed Oct. 1, 1767, Maryland Gazette contained, on page two, an announcement to prospective buyers from the ship's agents, Daniel of St. Thos. Jenifer and John Ridout (the Governor's secretary): "from the River GAMBIA, in AFRICA . . . a cargo of choice, healthy SLAVES . . ."

Study Questions

1. What is the basic structure of this essay?
2. How does the author maintain suspense?
3. Which paragraph marks the climax?
4. What types of details are used to describe people? What do these contribute to the narration?
5. At certain points the author uses dialogue. What does dialogue contribute that summary exposition may not?
6. What is the dramatic effect of the concluding paragraph?

Larry L. King

FROM THE SEED OF
KUNTA KINTE

Larry L. King (1929–   ) was born in Putnam, Texas, and attended
Texas Technological College. His journalistic endeavors have included writing for newspapers in Texas and New Mexico; news director for Radio KCRS in Midland, Texas; Washington correspondent for the *Texas Observer;* and editor of *Capitol Hill* magazine. He
has also served as administrative assistant to two U. S. congressmen.
He contributes to *New Times, Harper's, Progressive, Nation, True,
Sports Illustrated,* and *Esquire.* King has written television scripts for
the National Educational Television Network, and published *The
One-Eyed Man* (1966), a novel that achieved wide popularity, and
Confessions of a White Racist (1971).

Five years ago, at a writers' convocation in Chicago, I chanced 1
to sit for dinner near a loquacious black man, who almost immediately
launched into a non-stop two-hour narrative of his astonishing and painstaking search to trace his family back to its African origins. I was
spellbound by Alex Haley's story (which he has told more than 1,000
times from public platforms, to say nothing of how many other unsuspecting diners he may have ambushed), and, at its conclusion, I naively
hoped aloud that the author would let me know when his book would be
published. It proved entirely unnecessary for Mr. Haley to send me a
postcard.

Alex Haley's *Roots,* indeed, is being touted as the Big Book of this 2
bicentennial year. Some 200,000 hardback copies are in print; the film is
in the can for a multi-part network-television special, and one can only
imagine how many millions of copies *Roots* may sell in paperback. It is
nice to see Haley rewarded for his twelve years of labor on a work that
has obsessed him since he conceived of it.

We owe this remarkable tour de force not only to Haley's persistent 3
detective work but to his proud African ancestor Kunta Kinte, who, in
the summer of 1767, was out cutting wood near the Gambia River to
make himself a drum when slavers set upon him. Though he had no way
of knowing the place or the time, the seventeen-year-old Kunta Kinte arrived in chains at the port of Annapolis, Md., in September of that year
(as his descendant would later determine) and was sold into slavery in

Reprinted from the *Saturday Review,* September 18, 1976, with permission.

Spotsylvania County, Va., to John Waller. After attempting to run away four times and after suffering punishments, including the brutal amputation of half his right foot, the troublesome slave was deeded to another (Dr. William) Waller.

In time Kunta Kinte resigned himself to a weary accommodation of 4 the realities—though never to a spiritual acceptance of slavery—and became the buggy driver for Dr. Waller on his house calls to the plantations. In middle age, he married the cook of the master's big house, a woman known only as Bell, and produced a daughter, Kizzy. Kunta Kinte was careful to teach a smattering of African words and something of his heritage to Kizzy, who, in turn, passed the information along to her own children. Each succeeding generation kept the remarkable oral tradition alive, handing down all they'd retained about their ancestor Kunta Kinte and adding the basics of their own narrative. Almost 150 years later, the precious few original facts had filtered down to Alex Haley, then a child in Tennessee; his was the seventh generation to receive them. They would serve as the inspiration for this book.

Haley's story of how he came to write the book and of the demand- 5 ing research he undertook is more beguiling to this writer than is the story of his family, even though his family symbolizes all American blacks who came from slavery's bitter roots. The saga of Kunta Kinte, from a small boy in his African village to the midyears of his life, is absolutely first-rate and fascinating. Thereafter the story, with a few notable exceptions, seems overly familiar and without suspense. Perhaps after one has read a number of slave narratives and historical works, such as those by Lerone Bennett, and plantation potboilers, typified by Kyle Onstott's *Mandingo,* the stories of slave cruelties lose their punch and are no longer impressive. The whippings, the splitting up of families, and the maddening accumulation of "little" humiliations suffered by blacks remain no less terrible than before, but only rarely does Haley invoke them in a special way to bring fresh anger and compassion surging to the heart. Perhaps this is not Haley's fault so much as it is the heart's fault for growing tired and jaded.

Haley faced problems, to be sure. Except for such basic information 6 as he found documented and for interviews with the older members of his family in their declining years, he discovered many gaps and mysteries. He was thus forced to do a lot of conjecturing in his non-fiction work, improvising numerous scenes and numberless private conversations. Apparently he read everything on slavery he could get his hands on, and although his diligence helps the authenticity, it sometimes has the negative effect of making the experienced reader feel he has read the story before. *Roots,* unhappily, is not the masterwork one has hoped for, yet the flaws pale when compared with the enormity of Haley's task.

Alex Haley was a messman in the U.S. Coast Guard when World 7 War II broke out; he retired, in 1959, at age thirty-seven, with the unique designation of "journalist." He subsequently worked for *Playboy, Reader's Digest,* and other magazines. (His interview with Malxolm X led to his writing the book *The Autobiography of Malcolm X;* shortly after Haley completed the manuscript, Malcolm X was assassinated.)

While on assignment for a magazine, Haley visited the British Mu- 8 seum and found himself enthralled by the Rosetta stone. It started him thinking: could he, with the limited knowledge in his possession, learn the location in Africa from which his ancestor Kunta Kinte had come?

I had an unknown quotient in those strange words or sounds passed on 9 by the African. I got to thinking about them: "Kin-tay," he had said, was his name. "Ko" he had called a guitar. "Kamby Bolongo" he had called a river in Virginia. They were mostly sharp, angular sounds, with *k* predominating. These sounds probably had undergone some changes across the generations of being passed down, yet unquestionably they represented phonetic snatches of whatever was the specific tongue spoken by my African ancestor who was a family legend. My plane from London was circling to land at New York with me wondering: What specific African tongue was it? Was there any way in the world that maybe I could find out?

Haley went to the United Nations, in New York, "to tell my sounds 10 to African diplomats." And "within a couple of weeks, I guess I had stopped about two dozen Africans, each of whom had given me a quick look, a quick listen, and then took off. I can't say I blame them — me trying to communicate some African sounds in a Tennessee accent."

Haley next badgered friends and acquaintances for a list of people 11 "academically renowned for their knowledge of African linguistics." He found his man, a Belgian, Dr. Jan Varsina, then teaching at the University of Wisconsin. After hearing Haley's "African sounds," he consulted with colleagues and concluded the words came from the Mandinka tongue, the language spoken by Mandingo people. He guessed that perhaps Kunta Kinte might have been captured near the Gambia River. Haley never had heard of it.

At Hamilton College, he located a student, Ebou Manga, from the 12 region near the Gambia. The two men flew there and met with a small group of men familiar with their country's history. These natives told them that villages usually were named for families that had settled them centuries before and that "Kinte" was included in the names of numerous small villages.

With the help of his African friends, Haley set off for an older back- 13 country village to find the old men, called *griots,* who had been trained to be "living, walking archives of oral history; some could relate their villages' histories for three days without repeating themselves." He found a *griot* who specialized in the Kinte band and sat through a two-hour recitation of "begats" before the old man said, "About the time the King's soldiers came [1767], the eldest of these four sons, Kunta, went away from his village to chop wood ... and he was never seen again."

Writes Haley: "I sat as if I were carved of stone. My blood seemed 14 to have congealed. This man, whose lifetime had been in this backcountry African village, had no way in the world to know that he had just echoed what I had heard all through my boyhood years on my grandma's front porch, in Henning, Tennessee ... of an African who always had insisted that his name was 'Kin-tay'; who had called a guitar a 'ko' and a river within the state of Virginia, 'Kamby Bolongo'; and who had been kidnapped into slavery while not far from his village, chopping wood to make himself a drum."

Haley then trekked to the village of his ancestor. "I guess we had 15 moved a third of the way through the village when it suddenly registered in my brain what they were all crying out ... the wizened, robed elders and younger men, the mothers and the naked tar-black children, they were all waving up at me; their expressions buoyant, beaming, all were crying out together, *'Meester Kinte! Meester Kinte!'*

"Let me tell you something: I am a man. A sob hit me somewhere 16 around my ankles; it came surging upward, and flinging my hands over my face, I was just bawling as I hadn't since I was a baby. *'Meester Kinte!'* I just felt like I was weeping for all of history's incredible atrocities against fellowmen, which seems to be mankind's greatest flaw...."

Modernist that he is, Haley set about to reconcile available docu- 17 ments with the old *griot's* (and his African ancestor's) oral history. From English maritime records, he found that on July 5, 1767 ("The year the King's soldiers came"), a ship named *Lord Ligonier,* captained by Thomas E. Davies, had sailed from the Gambia River. Haley's heart must have leaped as he saw her destination: Annapolis, Md. (The family tale had it that Kunta Kinte had landed at a place in America he called "Napplis.")

Back in America, Haley learned that the ship had cleared the Port of 18 Annapolis on September 29, 1767. What had its cargo been? If slaves, Haley would be certain he had found the ship on which his ancestor had been shanghaied. In Annapolis, at the Hall of Records, he found a copy of the Maryland *Gazette* of October 1, 1767, and discovered there an advertisement in antique typeface: "JUST IMPORTED, in the ship *Lord Ligonier,* Capt. Davies, from the River Gambia, in Africa, and to be sold by the subscribers, in Annapolis, for cash, or good bills of exchange on Wednesday the 7th of October next, A Cargo of CHOICE HEALTHY SLAVES...."

Haley writes, "On September 29, 1967, I felt I should be nowhere 19 else in the world except standing on a pier at Annapolis—and I was; it was 200 years, to the day, after the *Lord Ligonier* had landed. Staring out to seaward across those waters over which my great-great-great-great-grandfather had been brought, again I found myself weeping."

Haley would go on to learn much more: the entire cargo of the *Lord* 20 *Ligonier* (ivory tusks, beeswax, raw cotton, two pounds of Gambian gold, and ninety-eight Negroes). He also would learn the ship had sailed with 140 slaves in her hold: "Her loss of forty-two Africans en route, or around one third, was average for slaving voyages." He searched census records, newspapers, and history books to add to his knowledge of what had happened to the descendants of Kunta Kinte and, of course, he learned much about the times in the process.

Kunta Kinte was a proud and stubborn man. Had Alex Haley not in- 21 herited those characteristics, then probably he would have been unable to sustain his prodigious effort or to endure the pain he suffered to produce this fine book.

Study Questions

1. How does the introduction of this review differ from the one in Berry's review?
2. In using narration in his presentation, what is King's rhetorical strategy?
3. Study the sentence structures and types in paragraphs 1–4. How do they differ, and what effect is achieved by these differences?
4. Identify the topic sentence in paragraph 6. What is the relation of the first and last sentences in this paragraph?
5. How does the author maintain reader interest in his review?

Jason Berry
THE SEARCH FOR ROOTS

Jason Berry (1949–   ) was born in New Orleans and graduated cum laude from Georgetown University in 1971. His articles have appeared in *New South* and newspapers in Louisiana, Virginia, and Mississippi. In 1971 he served as press secretary to Charles Evers, then candidate for Governor of Mississippi. Out of those experiences came *Amazing Grace: With Charles Evers in Mississippi* (1973).

$\mathbf{A}$merican history has been cursed by the long cherished im- 1
age of a nation whose origins reflect Jeffersonian ideals, a place where a man might forge reality out of the idealist's dreams. For white men, it has been a legitimate image. In 1965, Imamu Baraka (LeRoi Jones) cut through the image to expose historical truth: "The denial of reality has been institutionalized in America, and any honest man, especially an artist, suffers from it." The irony of his comment is that white intellectuals had by then placed faith in the struggles of the 1960s. Today, a handful of white social critics have discovered the shallowness of America's self-image, how the political lies and distorted values sink deeper into daily life causing a steady decay of the national character. Robert Brustein recently bemoaned what he called our "remake culture," our propensity to recycle old images, many of them soiled to begin with and better discarded.

Reprinted from *Nation,* Oct. 2, 1976 with permission.

A more meaningful irony of our sad time is that a decade after the 2 struggle for civil rights, some remarkable books have finally appeared tracing the lines of Afro-American culture and history from slavery down to the present. Seminally important work is being done by such historians as Eugene Genovese *(Roll, Jordan, Roll: The World the Slaveholders Made)* and Theodore Rosengarten *(All God's Dangers: The Life of Nate Shaw)*, to name but two. Novelists Berry Morgan *(The Mystic Adventures of Roxie Stoner)* and Al Murray *(Trainwhistle Guitar)* have drawn on the religious and musical strains of black Southern culture to render stories charged in language superior to that of much modern fiction. And finally, after more than a decade of research, Alex Haley has finished *Roots*.

Haley was Malcolm X's collaborator in the autobiography that is now 3 a classic. Shortly after they finished it Malcolm X was assassinated. Haley then began a personal odyssey, tracing the line of his genealogy back to the African forefather first sold into slavery. It's questionable how many black writers could have done this, since few written records were kept, families divided at the auction block lost touch, and normal generational ties were severed by the tragic movement of Southern history.

To maintain a semblance of racial identity in the plantation culture a 4 profound oral tradition arose among the slaves, an extension of the tradition maintained by the highly specialized African *griots,* who are literally oral historians, traveling from village to village. As *Roots* demonstrates, many uprooted slaves were unaware of their ancestry, and the oral tradition which developed was the sole fortress against the repressive measures of the planters who beat those who tried visibly to preserve their roots.

As a boy in Tennessee, Haley sat at the feet of his grandmother and 5 aunts, who told of

> ... the long cumulative family narrative that had been passed down across the generations ... slowly, from hearing the stories each passing summer, I began to recognize frequently repeated names among the people they talked about and to remember things they told about those people. The farthest-back person they ever talked about was a man they called "the African," whom they said had been brought to this country on a ship to some place that they pronounced "'Naplis." They said he was bought off this ship by a "Massa John Waller," who had a plantation in a place called "Spotsylvania County, Virginia." They would tell how the African kept trying to escape, and how on the fourth effort he had the misfortune to be captured by two white professional slave catchers, who apparently decided to make an example of him. This African was given the choice either of being castrated or having a foot cut off, and—"thanks to Jesus, or we wouldn't be here tellin' it"—the African chose his foot. I couldn't figure out why white folks would do anything as mean and lowdown as that.

More than half of this 587-page narrative chronicles the life of "that 6 African," Kunta Kinte, whose identity Haley verified on an investigative trip to the Gambia region. Like *Roots*, Kunta Kinte will become one of the great creations of American literature, a character endowed, through Haley's moving prose, with the thoughts, actions and strength of many millions of American slaves. It is no understatement to call him an Every-man but one who is unlike any allegorical figure in our written culture.

The advance publicity and sale of *Roots* for an autumn television se- 7
rial assure that the book will be widely read and discussed. No other
novelist or historian has provided such a shattering, human view of slavery. This said, and my admiration for the work on record, it is possible to
turn to some questions raised by Haley's book.

It seems to me that some sort of sequel to it is necessary, particularly 8
for scholars, since so much of the seminal research is rendered in a nov-
elistic manner. I do not doubt for a moment Haley's literary honesty. But
the following statement sent me back to many underlined passages:

> "How much of *Roots* is fact and how much is fiction?" To the best of 9
> my knowledge and of my effort, every lineage statement within *Roots* is from
> either my African or American families' carefully preserved oral history,
> much of which I have been able to conventionally corroborate with docu-
> ments. Those documents, along with the myriad textural details of what were
> contemporary indigenous life-styles, cultural history, and such that give *Roots*
> flesh have come from years of intensive research in fifty-odd libraries, ar-
> chives, and other repositories on three continents.
>
> Since I wasn't around when most of the story occurred, by far most of
> the dialogue and most of the incidents are of necessity a novelized amalgam
> of what I *know* took place together with what my researching led me to
> plausibly feel took place.

There are many historians who will wish to know where fictional line 10
diverged from factual basis. There is, for example, a powerful scene when
a fellow slave on Kinte's plantation, a fiddler who has just been denied
freedom by the *massa*, breaks his instrument and weeps: he had earned
the $700 necessary to buy his way out, only to have the planter up the
price when the money was produced. I don't doubt the human validity of
the event, but was the fiddler real? How many of the minor slave characters in the narrative were real? What more can Haley tell us about them?

Kinte's lone daughter, 14-year-old Kizzy, is sold to another slave 11
owner for helping a young boy forge a traveling pass for his escape. At
this point, Kinte and his wife Bell abruptly leave the narrative and do not
reappear. I have been thinking about Kunta Kinte, who struggled so
valiantly to pass on his real name and a few African facts to his sole
child. When did he die? Was Haley able to discern any other facts about
his life beyond those which Kizzy passed down?

Kizzy becomes the sexual slave of her new master, a North Carolina 12
redneck. Her illegitimate son, Kinte's grandson, then occupies a series of
fascinating chapters in which he travels around with his slave-owner father. The boy breeds the master's champion fighting cocks. How much of
the relationship did Haley base on fact? This is a question of particular
importance because in these passages we see a somewhat more positive
side of the white world through the grandson. In fact, the farther away
from Kinte the narrative moves, the less reprehensible the slavers become. The progression requires some explanation; Haley undoubtedly
did voluminous research into the background of the white men who

owned his early ancestors. It would be a great loss if he didn't assemble his factual data into some sort of formal statement. (Faulkner, for instance, provided a valuable guide to *The Sound and the Fury* in the appendix to a later pocket edition.)

A well-publicized, often bitter debate surrounded the 1968 publica- 13 tion of William Styron's *Confessions of Nat Turner*. Many of the black critics hostile to that novel now have in *Roots* a work which deserves their professional scrutiny. It is difficult to judge what influence this work will have on American history until scholars address themselves to the questions posed by *Roots* and set themselves to the task of unraveling answers. As it stands, *Roots* illustrates in deep human detail the historical patterns of slave life proposed by Genovese and other revisionist scholars. Alex Haley is in a unique position to generate important historical, cultural, perhaps even linguistic, research, offshoots of his own sweeping narrative, by serving as a reference guide to other scholars. In a larger way, to the vast popular audience *Roots* will reach, Haley has uncovered beneath the chronicles of white America the raging heart and tenacious history of a people in captivity.

Study Questions

1. How does the author handle the transition between the two major parts of his review?
2. Compare the structure and organization of this review with those of King's review.
3. Contrast the points of view used by Berry and King.
4. What is the purpose of quotations in paragraphs 5 and 10?
5. Identify the topic sentence of paragraph 13. What is the effect achieved by its position in the paragraph?

Kurt Vonnegut, Jr.
WELCOME TO THE MONKEY HOUSE

Kurt Vonnegut, Jr. (1922–   ) was born in Indianapolis, Indiana. After attending Cornell University and the University of Chicago, he worked as a reporter and was a public-relations representative. He was awarded a Guggenheim fellowship in 1967 for his fiction. Vonnegut enjoys an established reputation as a writer of short stories and novels. His publications include *Player Piano* (1952), *Sirens of Titan* (1959), *Mother Night* (1966), *Cat's Cradle* (1963), *God Bless You, Mr. Rosewater* (1965), *Welcome to the Monkey House* (1968), *Slaughterhouse-Five* (1969), *Happy Birthday, Wanda June* (a play, 1971), *Breakfast of Champions* (1973), and *Slapstick* (1976).

So Pete Crocker, the sheriff of Barnstable County, which was 1 the whole of Cape Cod, came into the Federal Ethical Suicide Parlor in Hyannis one May afternoon—and he told the two six-foot Hostesses there that they weren't to be alarmed, but that a notorious nothinghead named Billy the Poet was believed headed for the Cape.

A nothinghead was a person who refused to take his ethical birth- 2 control pills three times a day. The penalty for that was $10,000 and ten years in jail.

This was at a time when the population of Earth was 17 billion hu- 3 man beings. That was far too many mammals that big for a planet that small. The people were virtually packed together like drupelets.

Drupelets are the pulpy little knobs that compose the outside of a 4 raspberry.

So the World Government was making a two-pronged attack on 5 overpopulation. One pronging was the encouragement of ethical suicide, which consisted of going to the nearest Suicide Parlor and asking a Hostess to kill you painlessly while you lay on a Barcalounger. The other pronging was compulsory ethical birth control.

The sheriff told the Hostesses, who were pretty, tough-minded, 6 highly intelligent girls, that roadblocks were being set up and house-to-house searches were being conducted to catch Billy the Poet. The main difficulty was that the police didn't know what he looked like. The few people who had seen him and known him for what he was were women—and they disagreed fantastically as to his height, his hair color, his voice, he weight, the color of his skin.

"I don't need to remind you girls," the sheriff went on, "that a noth- 7 inghead is very sensitive from the waist down. If Billy the Poet somehow slips in here and starts making trouble, one good kick in the right place will do wonders."

He was referring to the fact that ethical birth-control pills, the only 8 legal form of birth control, made people numb from the waist down.

Most men said their bottom halves felt like cold iron or balsa wood. 9 Most women said their bottom halves felt like wet cotton or stale ginger-ale. The pills were so effective that you could blindfold a man who had taken one, tell him to recite the Gettysburg Address, kick him in the balls while he was doing it, and he wouldn't miss a syllable.

The pills were ethical because they didn't interfere with a person's 10 ability to reproduce, which would have been unnatural and immoral. All the pills did was take every bit of pleasure out of sex.

Thus did science and morals go hand in hand.   11

The two Hostesses there in Hyannis were Nancy McLuhan and Mary 12
Kraft. Nancy was a strawberry blonde. Mary was a glossy brunette. Their
uniforms were white lipstick, heavy eye make-up, purple body stockings
with nothing underneath and black-leather boots. They ran a small operation — with only six suicide booths. In a really good week, say the
one before Christmas, they might put 60 people to sleep. It was done
with a hypodermic syringe.

"My main message to you girls," said Sheriff Crocker, "is that every- 13
thing's well under control. You can just go about your business here."

"Didn't you leave out part of your main message?" Nancy asked him. 14
"I don't get you."   15
"I didn't hear you say he was probably headed straight for us."   16
He shrugged in clumsy innocence. "We don't know that for sure."   17
"I thought that was all anybody *did* know about Billy the Poet: that 18
he specializes in deflowering Hostesses in Ethical Suicide Parlors." Nancy
was a virgin. All Hostesses were virgins. They also had to hold advanced
degrees in psychology and nursing. They also had to be plump and rosy,
and at least six feet tall.

America had changed in many ways, but it had yet to adopt the met- 19
ric system.

Nancy McLuhan was burned up that the sheriff would try to protect 20
her and Mary from the full truth about Billy the Poet — as though they
might panic if they heard it. She told the sheriffs.

"How long do you think a girl would last in the E.S.S.," she said, 21
meaning the Ethical Suicide Service, "if she scared *that* easy?"

The sheriff took a step backward, pulled in his chin. "Not very long, 22
I guess."

"That's very true," said Nancy, closing the distance between them 23
and offering him a sniff of the edge of her hand, which was poised for a
karate chop. All Hostesses were experts at judo and karate. "If you'd like
to find out how helpless we are, just come toward me, pretending you're
Billy the Poet."

The sheriff shook his head, gave her a glassy smile. "I'd rather not." 24
"That's the smartest thing you've said today," said Nancy, turning her 25
back on him while Mary laughed. "We're not scared — we're *angry*. Or
we're not even *that*. He isn't *worth* that. We're *bored*. How boring that he
should come a great distance, should cause all this fuss, in order to —"
She let the sentence die there. "It's just too absurd."

"I'm not as mad at *him* as I am at the women who let him do it to 26
them without a struggle" — said Mary — "who let him do it and then
couldn't tell the police what he looked like. Suicide Hostesses at that!"

"Somebody hasn't been keeping up with her karate," said Nancy. 27
It wasn't just Billy the Poet who was attracted to Hostesses in Eth- 28
ical Suicide Parlors. All nothingheads were. Bombed out of their skulls
with the sex madness that came from taking nothing, they thought the
white lips and big eyes and body stocking and boots of a Hostess spelled
sex, sex, sex.

The truth was, of course, that sex was the last thing any Hostess ever 29
had in mind.

"If Billy follows his usual M.O.," said the sheriff, "he'll study your 30 habits and the neighborhood. And then he'll pick one or the other of you and he'll send her a dirty poem in the mail."

"Charming," said Nancy.   31

"He has also been known to use the telephone."   32

"How brave," said Nancy. Over the sheriff's shoulder, she could see 33 the mailman coming.

A blue light went on over the door of a booth for which Nancy was 34 responsible. The person in there wanted something. It was the only booth in use at the time.

The sheriff asked her if there was a possibility that the person in 35 there was Billy the Poet, and Nancy said, "Well, if it is, I can break his neck with my thumb and forefinger."

"Foxy Grandpa," said Mary, who'd seen him, too. A Foxy Grandpa 36 was any old man, cute and senile, who quibbled and joked and reminisced for hours before he let a Hostess put him to sleep.

Nancy rolled her eyes. "We've spent the past two hours trying to de- 37 cide on a last meal."

And then the mailman came in with just one letter. It was addressed 38 to Nancy in smeary pencil. She was splendid with anger and disgust as she opened it, knowing it would be a piece of filth from Billy.

She was right. Inside the envelope was a poem. It wasn't an original 39 poem. It was a song from the olden days that had taken on new meanings since the numbness of ethical birth control had become universal. It went like this, in smeary pencil again:

> We were walking through the park,
> A-goosing statues in the dark.
> If Sherman's horse can take it,
> So can you.

When Nancy came into the suicide booth to see what he wanted, the 40 Foxy Grandpa was lying on the mint-green Barcalounger, where hundreds had died so peacefully over the years. He was studying the menu from the Howard Johnson's next door and beating time to the Muzak coming from the loud-speaker on the lemon-yellow wall. The room was painted cinder block. There was one barred window with a Venetian blind.

There was a Howard Johnson's next door to every Ethical Suicide 41 Parlor, and vice versa. The Howard Johnson's had an orange roof and the Suicide Parlor had a purple roof, but they were both the Government. Practically everything was the Government.

Practically everything was automated, too. Nancy and Mary and the 42 sheriff were lucky to have jobs. Most people didn't. The average citizen moped around home and watched television, which was the Government. Every 15 minutes his television would urge him to vote intelligently or consume intelligently, or worship in the church of his choice, or love his fellow men, or obey the laws—or pay a call to the nearest Ethical Suicide Parlor and find out how friendly and understanding a Hostess could be.

The Foxy Grandpa was something of a rarity, since he was marked 43 by old age, was bald, was shaky, had spots on his hands. Most people looked 22, thanks to antiaging shots they took twice a year. That the old man looked old was proof that the shots had been discovered after his sweet bird of youth had flown.

"Have we decided on a last supper yet?" Nancy asked him. She 44 heard peevishness in her own voice, heard herself betray her exasperation with Billy the Poet, her boredom with the old man. She was ashamed, for this was unprofessional of her. "The breaded veal cutlet is very good."

The old man cocked his head. With the greedy cunning of second 45 childhood, he had caught her being unprofessional, unkind, and he was going to punish her for it. "You don't sound very friendly. I thought you were all supposed to be friendly. I thought this was supposed to be a pleasant place to come."

"I beg your pardon," she said. "If I seem unfriendly, it has nothing to 46 do with you."

"I thought maybe I bored you." 47

"No, no," she said gamely, "not at all. You certainly know some very 48 interesting history." Among other things, the Foxy Grandpa claimed to have known J. Edgar Nation, the Grand Rapids druggist who was the father of ethical birth control.

"Then *look* like you're interested," he told her. He could get away 49 with that sort of impudence. The thing was, he could leave any time he wanted to, right up to the moment he asked for the needle—and he had to *ask* for the needle. That was the law.

Nancy's art, and the art of every Hostess, was to see that volunteers 50 didn't leave, to coax and wheedle and flatter them patiently, every step of the way.

So Nancy had to sit down there in the booth, to pretend to marvel 51 at the freshness of the yarn the old man told, a story everybody knew, about how J. Edgar Nation happened to experiment with ethical birth control.

"He didn't have the slightest idea his pills would be taken by human 52 beings someday," said the Foxy Grandpa. "His dream was to introduce morality into the monkey house at the Grand Rapids Zoo. Did you realize that?" he inquired severely.

"No. No. I didn't. That's very interesting." 53

"He and his eleven kids went to church one Easter. And the day was 54 so nice and the Easter had been so beautiful and pure that they decided to take a walk through the zoo, and they were just walking on clouds."

"Um." The scene described was lifted from a play that was per- 55 formed on television every Easter.

The Foxy Grandpa shoehorned himself into the scene, had himself 56 chat with the Nations just before they got to the monkey house. " 'Good morning, Mr. Nation,' I said to him. 'It certainly is a nice morning.' 'And a good morning to *you*, Mr. Howard,' he said to me. 'There is nothing like an Easter morning to make a man feel clean and reborn and at one with God's intentions.' "

"Um." Nancy could hear the telephone ringing faintly, naggingly, 57 through the nearly soundproof door.

"So we went on to the monkey house together, and what do you 58
think we saw?"

"I can't imagine." Somebody had answered the phone.   59

"We saw a monkey playing with his private parts?"   60

"No!"   61

"Yes! And J. Edgar Nation was so upset he went straight home and 62
he started developing a pill that would make monkeys in the springtime
fit things for a Christian family to see."

There was a knock on the door.   63

"Yes?" said Nancy.   64

"Nancy," said Mary, "telephone for you."   65

When Nancy came out of the booth, she found the sheriff choking 66
on little squeals of law-enforcement delight. The telephone was tapped
by agents hidden in the Howard Johnson's. Billy the Poet was believed
to be on the line. His call had been traced. Police were already on their
way to grab him.

"Keep him on, keep him on," the sheriff whispered to Nancy, and he 67
gave her the telephone as though it were solid gold.

"Yes?" said Nancy.   68

"Nancy McLuhan?" said a man. His voice was disguised. He might 69
have been speaking through a kazoo. "I'm calling for a mutual friend."

"Oh?"   70

"He asked me to deliver a message."   71

"I see."   72

"It's a poem."   73

"All right."   74

"Ready?"   75

"Ready," Nancy could hear sirens screaming in the background of 76
the call.

The caller must have heard the sirens, too, but he recited the poem 77
without any emotion. It went like this:

> "Soak yourself in Jergen's Lotion.
> Here comes the one-man population explosion."

They got him. Nancy heard it all—the thumping and clumping, the 78
argle-bargle and cries.

The depression she felt as she hung up was glandular. Her brave 79
body had prepared for a fight that was not to be.

The sheriff bounded out of the Suicide Parlor in such a hurry to see 80
the famous criminal he'd helped catch that a sheaf of papers fell from the
pocket of his trench coat.

Mary picked them up, called after the sheriff. He halted for a mo- 81
ment, said the papers didn't matter anymore, asked her if maybe she
wouldn't like to come along. There was a flurry between the two girls,
with Nancy persuading Mary to go, declaring that she had no curiosity
about Billy. So Mary left, irrelevantly handing the sheaf to Nancy.

The sheaf proved to be photocopies of poems Billy had sent to 82
Hostesses in other places. Nancy read the top one. It made much of a
peculiar side effect of ethical birth-control pills: They not only made

people numb—they also made people piss blue. The poem was called
What the Somethinghead Said to the Suicide Hostess, and it went like this:

> I did not sow, I did not spin,
> And thanks to pills, I did not sin.
> I loved the crowds, the stink, the noise.
> And when I peed, I peed turquoise.
>
> I ate beneath a roof of orange;
> Swung with progress like a door hinge.
> 'Neath purple roof I've come today
> To piss my azure life away.
>
> Virgin Hostess, death's recruiter,
> Life is cute, but you are cuter.
> Mourn my pecker, purple daughter—
> All it passed was sky-blue water.

"You never heard that story before—about how J. Edgar Nation 83
came to invent ethical birth control?" the Foxy Grandpa wanted to know.
His voice cracked.

"Never did," lied Nancy.   84

"I thought everybody knew that."   85

"It was news to me."   86

"When he got through with the monkey house, you couldn't tell it 87
from the Michigan Supreme Court. Meanwhile, there was this crisis going on in the United Nations. The people who understood science said
people had to quit reproducing so much, and the people who understood
morals said society would collapse if people used sex for nothing but
pleasure."

The Foxy Grandpa got off his Barcalounger, went over to the win- 88
dow, pried two slats of the blind apart. There wasn't much to see out
there. The view was blocked by the backside of a mocked-up thermometer 20 feet high, which faced the street. It was calibrated in billions of
people on Earth from 0 to 20. The make-believe column of liquid was a
strip of translucent red plastic. It showed how many people there were
on Earth. Very close to the bottom was a black arrow that showed what
the scientists throught the population ought to be.

The Foxy Grandpa was looking at the setting sun through that red 89
plastic, and through the blind too, so that his face was banded with shadows and red.

"Tell me," he said, "when I die, how much will that thermometer go 90
down? A foot?"

"No."   91

"An inch?"   92

"Not quite."   93

"You know what the answer is, don't you?" he said, and he faced 94
her. The senility had vanished from his voice and eyes. "One inch on that
thing equals 83,333,333 people. You knew that, didn't you?"

"That—that might be true," said Nancy, "but that isn't the right way 95
to look at it, in my opinion."

He didn't ask her what the right way was, in her opinion. He com- 96
pleted a thought of his own, instead. "I'll tell you something else that's
true: I'm Billy the Poet, and you're a very good-looking woman."

With one hand, he drew a snub-nosed revolver from his belt. With 97
the other he peeled off his bald dome and wrinkled forehead, which
proved to be rubber. Now he looked 22.

"The police will want to know exactly what I look like when this is 98
all over," he told Nancy with a malicious grin. "In case you're not good
at describing people, and it's surprising how many women aren't:

> I'm five foot, two,
> With eyes of blue,
> With brown hair to my shoulders —
> A manly elf
> So full of self
> The ladies say he smoulders."

Billy was ten inches shorter than Nancy was. She had about 40 99
pounds on him. She told him he didn't have a chance, but Nancy was
much mistaken. He had unbolted the bars on the windows the night before and he made her go out the window and then down a manhole that
was hidden from the street by the big thermometer.

He took her down into the sewers of Hyannis. He knew where he 100
was going. He had a flashlight and a map. Nancy had to go before him
along the narrow catwalk, her own shadow dancing mockingly in the
lead. She tried to guess where they were, relative to the real world
above. She guessed correctly when they passed under the Howard Johnson's, guessed from the noises she heard. The machinery that processed
and served the food there was silent. But, so people wouldn't feel too
lonesome when eating there, the designers had provided sound effects
for the kitchen. It was these Nancy heard — a tape recording of the clash-
ing of silverware and the laughter of Negroes and Puerto Ricans.

After that she was lost. Billy had very little to say to her other than 101
"Right," or, "Left," or "Don't try anything funny, Juno, or I'll blow your
great big fucking head off."

Only once did they have anything resembling a conversation. Billy 102
began it, and ended it, too. "What in hell is a girl with hips like yours
doing selling death?" he asked her from behind.

She dared to stop. "I can answer that," she told him. She was con- 103
fident that she could give him an answer that would shrivel him like na-
palm.

But he gave her a shove, offered to blow her head off again.   104
"You don't even want to hear my answer," she taunted him. "You're 105
afraid to hear it."

"I never listen to a women till the pills wear off," sneered Billy. That 106
was his plan, then — to keep her a prisoner for at least eight hours. That
was how long it took for the pills to wear off.

"That's a silly rule."   107
"A woman's not a woman till the pills wear off."   108
"You certainly manage to make a women feel like an object rather 109

than a person."

"Thank the pills for that," said Billy.   110

There were 80 miles of sewers under Greater Hyannis, which had a   111
population of 400,000 drupelets, 400,000 souls. Nancy lost track of the
time down there. When Billy announced that they had at last reached
their destination, it was possible for Nancy to imagine that a year had
passed.

She tested this spooky impression by pinching her own thigh, by   112
feeling what the chemical clock of her body said. Her thigh was still
numb.

Billy ordered her to climb iron rungs that were set in wet masonry.   113
There was a circle of sickly light above. It proved to be moonlight fil-
tered through the plastic polygons of an enormous geodesic dome.
Nancy didn't have to ask the traditional victim's question, "Where am I?"
There was only one dome like that on Cape Cod. It was in Hyannis Port
and it sheltered the ancient Kennedy Compound.

It was a museum of how life had been lived in more expansive times.   114
The museum was closed. It was open in the summertime.

The manhole from which Nancy and then Billy emerged was set in   115
an expanse of green cement, which showed where the Kennedy lawn had
been. On the green cement, in front of the ancient frame houses, were
statues representing the 14 Kennedys who had been Presidents of the
United States or the World. They were playing touch football.

The President of the World at the time of Nancy's abduction, in-   116
cidentally was an ex-Suicide Hostess named "Ma" Kennedy. Her statue
would never join this particular touch-football game. Her name was Kennedy, all right, but she wasn't the real thing. People complained of her
lack of style, found her vulgar. On the wall of her office was a sign that
said, YOU DON'T HAVE TO BE CRAZY TO WORK HERE, BUT IT SURE HELPS, and another one that said, THINK!, and another one that said, SOMEDAY WE'RE GO-
ING TO HAVE TO GET ORGANIZED AROUND HERE.

Her office was in the Taj Mahal.   117

Until she arrived in the Kennedy Museum, Nancy McLuhan was con-   118
fident that she would sooner or later get a chance to break every bone in
Billy's little body, maybe even shoot him with his own gun. She wouldn't
have minded doing those things. She thought he was more disgusting
than a blood-filled tick.

It wasn't compassion that changed her mind. It was the discovery   119
that Billy had a gang. There were at least eight people around the manhole, men and women in equal number, with stockings pulled over their
heads. It was the women who laid firm hands on Nancy, told her to keep
calm. They were all at least as tall as Nancy and they held her in places
where they could hurt her like hell if they had to.

Nancy closed her eyes, but this didn't protect her from the obvious   120
conclusion: These perverted women were sisters from the Ethical Suicide
Service. This upset her so much that she asked loudly and bitterly, "How
can you violate your oaths like this?"

She was promptly hurt so badly that she doubled up and burst into   121
tears.

When she straightened up again, there was plenty more she wanted 122
to say, but she kept her mouth shut. She speculated silently as to what
on Earth could make Suicide Hostesses turn against every concept of human decency. Nothingheadedness alone couldn't being to explain it.
They had to be drugged besides.

Nancy went over in her mind all the terrible drugs she'd learned 123
about in school, persuaded herself that the women had taken the worst
one of all. That drug was so powerful, Nancy's teacher had told her, that
even a person numb from the waist down would copulate repeatedly and
enthusiastically after just one glass. That had to be the answer: The
women, and probably the men, too, had been drinking gin.

They hastened Nancy into the middle frame house, which was dark 124
like all the rest, and Nancy heard the men giving Billy the news. It was
in this news that Nancy perceived a glint of hope. Help might be on its
way.

The gang member who had phoned Nancy obscenely had fooled the 125
police into believing that they had captured Billy the Poet, which was
bad for Nancy. The police didn't know yet that Nancy was missing, two
men told Billy, and a telegram had been sent to Mary Kraft in Nancy's
name, declaring that Nancy had been called to New York City on urgent
family business.

That was where Nancy saw the glint of hope: Mary wouldn't believe 126
that telegram. Mary knew Nancy had no family in New York. Not one
of the 63,000,000 people living there was a relative of Nancy's.

The gang had deactivated the burglar-alarm of the museum. They 127
had also cut through a lot of the chains and ropes that were meant to
keep visitors from touching anything of value. There was no mystery as
to who and what had done the cutting. One of the men was armed with
brutal lopping shears.

They marched Nancy into a servant's bedroom upstairs. The man 128
with the shears cut the ropes that fenced off the narrow bed. They put
Nancy into the bed and two men held Nancy while a woman gave her a
knockout shot.

Billy the Poet had disappeared.   129

As Nancy was going under, the woman who had given her the shot 130
asked her how old she was.

Nancy was determined not to answer, but discovered that the drug 131
had made her powerless not to answer. "Sixty-three," she murmured.

"How does it feel to be a virgin at sixty-three?"   132

Nancy heard her own voice answer through a velvet fog. She was 133
amazed by the answer, wanted to protest that it couldn't possibly be hers.
"Pointless," she'd said.

Moments later, she asked the woman thickly, "What was in that 134
needle?"

"What was in the needle, honey bunch? Why honey bunch, they call 135
that 'truth serum.'"

The moon was down when Nancy woke up—but the night was still 136
out there. The shades were drawn and there was candlelight. Nancy had
never seen a lit candle before.

What awakened Nancy was a dream of mosquitoes and bees. Mos- 137
quitoes and bees were extinct. So were birds. But Nancy dreamed that
millions of insects were swarming about her from the waist down. They
didn't sting. They fanned her. Nancy was a nothinghead.

She went to sleep again. When she awoke next time, she was being 138
led into a bathroom by three women, still with stockings over their
heads. The bathroom was already filled with the steam from somebody
else's bath. There were somebody else's wet footprints criss-crossing the
floor and the air reeked of pine-needle perfume.

Her will and intelligence returned as she was bathed and perfumed 139
and dressed in a white nightgown. When the women stepped back to admire her, she said to them quietly. "I may be a nothinghead now. But
that doesn't mean I have to think like one or act like one."

Nobody argued with her.   140

Nancy was taken downstairs and out of the house. She fully expected 141
to be sent down a manhole again. It would be the perfect setting for her
violation by Billy, she was thinking—down in a sewer.

But they took her across the green cement, where the grass used to 142
be, and then across the yellow cement, where the beach used to be, and
then out onto the blue cement, where the harbor used to be. There were
26 yachts that had belonged to various Kennedys sunk up to their water
lines in blue cement. It was to the most ancient of these yachts, the Marlin, once the property of Joseph P. Kennedy, that they delivered Nancy.

It was dawn. Because of the high-rise apartments all around the Ken- 143
nedy Museum, it would be an hour before any direct sunlight would
reach the microcosm under the geodesic dome.

Nancy was escorted as far as the companionway to the forward cabin 144
of the Marlin. The women pantomimed that she was expected to go down
the five steps alone.

Nancy froze for the moment and so did the women. And there were 145
two actual statues in the tableau on the bridge. Standing at the wheel was
a statue of Frank Wirtanen, once skipper of the Marlin. And next to him
was his son and first mate, Carly. They weren't paying any attention to
poor Nancy. They were staring out through the windshield at the blue
cement.

Nancy, barefoot and wearing a thin white nightgown, descended 146
bravely into the forward cabin, which was a pool of candlelight and pine-
needle perfume. The companionway hatch was closed and locked behind
her.

Nancy's emotions and the antique furnishings of the cabin were so 147
complex that Nancy could not at first separate Billy the Poet from his
surroundings, from all the mahogany and leaded glass. And then she saw
him at the far end of the cabin, with his back against the door to the forward cockpit. He was wearing purple silk pajamas with a Russian collar.
They were piped in red, and writhing across Billy's silken breast was a
golden dragon. It was belching fire.

Anticlimactically, Billy was wearing glasses. He was holding a book. 148

Nancy poised herself on the next-to-the-bottom step, took a firm grip 149 on the handholds in the companionway. She bared her teeth, calculated, that it would take ten men Billy's size to dislodge her.

Between them was a great table. Nancy had expected the cabin to be 150 dominated by a bed, possibly in the shape of a swan, but the Marlin was a day boat. The cabin was anything but a seraglio. It was about as voluptuous as a lower-middle-class dining room in Akron, Ohio, around 1910.

A candle was on the table. So were an ice bucket and two glasses 151 and a quart of champagne. Champagne was as illegal as heroin.

Billy took off his glasses, gave her a shy, embarrassed smile, said, 152 "Welcome."

"This is as far as I come." 153

He accepted that. "You're very beautiful there." 154

"And what am I supposed to say—that you're stunningly handsome? 155 That I feel an overwhelming desire to throw myself into you manly arms?"

"If you wanted to make me happy, that would certainly be the way 156 to do it." He said that humbly.

"And what about *my* happiness?" 157

The question seemed to puzzle him. "Nancy—that's what this is all 158 about."

"What if my idea of happiness doesn't coincide with yours?" 159

"And what do you think my idea of happiness is?" 160

"I'm not going to throw myself into your arms, and I'm not going to 161 drink that poison, and I'm not going to budge from here unless somebody makes me," said Nancy. "So I think your idea of happiness is going to turn out to be eight people holding me down on that table, while you bravely hold a cocked pistol to my head—and do what you want. That's the way it's going to have to be, so call your friends and get it over with!"

Which he did. 162

He didn't hurt her. He deflowered her with a clinical skill she found 163 ghastly. When it was all over, he didn't seem cocky or proud. On the contrary, he was terribly depressed, and he said to Nancy, "Believe me, if there'd been any other way—"

Her reply to this was a face like stone—and silent tears of humili- 164 ation.

His helpers let down a folding bunk from the wall. It was scarcely 165 wider than a bookshelf and hung on chains. Nancy allowed herself to be put to bed in it, and she was left alone with Billy the Poet again. Big as she was, like a double bass wedged onto that narrow shelf, she felt like a pitiful little thing. A scratchy, war-surplus blanket had been tucked in around her. It was her own idea to pull up a corner of the blanket to hide her face.

Nancy sensed from sounds what Billy was doing, which wasn't much. 166 He was sitting at the table, sighing occasionally, sniffling occasionally, turning the pages of a book. He lit a cigar and the stink of it seeped under her blanket. Billy inhaled the cigar, then coughed and coughed and coughed.

When the coughing died down, Nancy said loathingly through the 167 blanket, "You're so strong, so masterful, so healthy. It must be wonderful to be so manly."

Billy only sighed at this.   168

"I'm not a very typical nothinghead," she said. "I hated it — hated ev- 169 erything about it."

Billy sniffed, turned a page.   170

"I suppose all the other women just loved it — couldn't get enough 171 of it."

"Nope."   172

She uncovered her face. "What do you mean, 'Nope'?"   173

"They've all been like you."   174

This was enough to make Nancy sit up and stare at him. "The 175 women who helped you tonight —"

"What about them?"   176

"You've done to them what you did to me?"   177

He didn't look up from his book. "That's right."   178

"Then why don't they kill you instead of helping you?"   179

"Because they understand." And then he added mildly. "They're 180 *grateful.*"

Nancy got out of bed, came to the table, gripped the edge of the 181 table, leaned close to him. And she said to him tautly, "I am not grateful."

"You will be."   182

"And what could possibly bring about that miracle?"   183

"Time," said Billy.   184

Billy closed his book, stood up. Nancy was confused by his magne- 185 tism. Somehow he was very much in charge again.

"What you've been through, Nancy," he said, "is a typical wedding 186 night for a straight-laced girl of a hundred years ago, when everybody was a nothinghead. The groom did without helpers, because the bride wasn't customarily ready to kill him. Otherwise, the spirit of the occasion was much the same. These are the pajamas my great-great-grandfather wore on his wedding night in Niagara Falls.

"According to his diary, his bride cried all that night, and threw up 187 twice. But, with the passage of time, she became a sexual enthusiast."

It was Nancy's turn to reply by not replying. She understood the 188 tale. It frightened her to understand so easily that, from gruesome beginnings, sexual enthusiasm could grow and grow.

"You're a very typical nothinghead," said Billy. "If you dare to think 189 about it now, you'll realize that you're angry because I'm such a bad lover, and a funny-looking shrimp besides. And what you can't help dreaming about from now on is a really suitable mate for a Juno like yourself.

"You'll find him, too — tall and strong and gentle. The nothinghead 190 movement is growing by leaps and bounds."

"But —" said Nancy, and she stopped there. She looked out a port- 191 hole at the rising sun.

"But what?"   192

"The world is in the mess it is today because of the nothing- 193 headedness of olden times. Don't you see?" She was pleading weakly. "The world can't afford sex anymore."

"Of course it can afford sex," said Billy. "All it can't afford anymore 194 is reproduction."

"Then why the laws?" 195

"They're bad laws," said Billy. "If you go back through history, you'll 196 find that the people who have been most eager to rule, to make the laws, to enforce the laws and to tell everybody exactly how God Almighty wants things here on Earth—those people have forgiven themselves and their friends for anything and everything. But they have been absolutely disgusted and terrified by the natural sexuality of common men and women.

"Why this is, I do not know. That is one of the many questions I 197 wish somebody would ask the machines. I do know this: The triumph of that sort of disgust and terror is now complete. Almost every man and woman looks and feels like something the cat dragged in. The only sexual beauty that an ordinary human being can see today is in the woman who will kill him. Sex is death. There's a short and nasty equation for you: 'Sex is death. Q.E.D.'

"So you see, Nancy," said Billy. "I have spent this night, and many 198 others like it, attempting to restore a certain amount of innocent pleasure to the world, which is poorer in pleasure than it needs to be."

Nancy sat down quietly and bowed her head. 199

"I'll tell you what my grandfather did on the dawn of his wedding 200 night," said Billy.

"I don't think I want to hear it." 201

"It isn't violent. It's—meant to be tender." 202

"Maybe that's why I don't want to hear it." 203

"He read his bride a poem." Billy took the book from the table, 204 opened it. "His diary tells which poem it was. While we aren't bride and groom, and while we may not meet again for many years, I'd like to read this poem to you, to have you know I've loved you."

"Please—no. I couldn't stand it." 205

"All right. I'll leave the book here, with the place marked, in case 206 you want to read it later. It's the poem beginning:

> 'How do I love thee? Let me count the ways.
> I love thee to the depth and breadth and height
> My soul can reach, when feeling out of sight
> For the ends of Being and ideal Grace.' "

Billy put a small bottle on top of the book. "I am also leaving you 207 these pills. If you take one a month, you will never have children. And still you'll be a nothinghead."

And he left. And they all left but Nancy. 208

When Nancy raised her eyes at last to the book and bottle, she saw 209 that there was a label on the bottle. What the label said was this: WELCOME TO THE MONKEY HOUSE.

Study Questions

1. How does Vonnegut attempt to create the illusion of reality, of authenticity, in his story?
2. What is the tone of this story, and how does the author establish and maintain it?
3. Compare and contrast this story with Swift's essay. What do they have in common?
4. Is satire presented in this form more effective or less effective than satire presented in a personal essay?
5. What is the thesis, or central idea, of this story?

4 Violent America
"Restless Violence Round About"

Violent America is new to *Strategies in Prose*. No other issue has become more prominent since the earlier editions of this text saw print. Hardly a day passes without some headline screaming the details of the latest violent crime. The media are constantly under study and under fire from critics, sociologists, and psychologists trying to determine the role of the media in breeding violence. We even hear of the violence of noise and the violence of language.

Albert Schweitzer opens this section with a finely modulated plea for reverence for life. Although Schweitzer is discussing an abstract idea, his particularity brings that idea within grasp. Martin Luther King, Jr., then approaches the issue head-on as he tells us of his own increasing involvement in a nonviolence movement. The scientist's approach to violence is represented by Karl A. Menninger's discussion of possible causes of ever-more conspicuous violence. He does not stop there; however, but follows up with some possible ways of diminishing the problem.

Larry Woiwode and "Saki" provide useful material for comparison and contrast. Although the forms are different — Woiwode uses the informal essay and "Saki" the short story — both are concerned with the effect of guns and violence-inducing toys on children and the adults those children grow to be. "Saki" also shows us how humor can be utilized in the treatment of a nonhumorous subject.

Still another writing style is introduced with Martin J. Gansberg's now famous *New York Times* article on the murder of Kitty Genovese. Especially worthy of note is Gansberg's choice of diction, which helps form the reader's opinion. If Gansberg does not use a traditional journalistic or news style, it is nevertheless a style seen more and more in contemporary reporting. Jacques Barzun and Abe Fortas provide the pro and con in this section. The issue is capital punishment; the discussants are educated and articulate. This grouping of essays concludes with George Orwell's moving narrative about a hanging. When Orwell's essay is played against Barzun's and Fortas', the dimensions of the issue are increased.

The last three essays deal with violence in some aspects of pop culture. Harry F. Waters uses the format and style of a popular news magazine to explore the effects of television violence on children. Robert Warshow writes convincingly of the screen's treatment of the gangster as another success (or failure) story. Finally, Tom Wolfe puts his acid pen to work on what he calls the Violence Press. Why violence sells and why it is replacing pornography are two of the issues he discusses. The effect of these three essays is to show three different styles — each of them in itself representative of a form of popular culture — aimed at different audiences, all trying to achieve the same goal.

Perhaps this section on violence will not be of great import in a fifth edition of *Strategies in Prose*. If that should indeed be true, surely part of the credit will be due to articulate writers, like those represented here, who put the issues clearly before us.

Albert Schweitzer
REVERENCE FOR LIFE

Albert Schweitzer (1875–1965) remains one of the most universally respected men of the century. Born in Kaysensberg, Upper Alsace, his university education prepared him in literature, medicine, and theology. Schweitzer has been awarded almost numberless honorary degrees and in 1952, the Nobel Peace Prize. His books include *Kulturphilosophie* (1923), *Memoirs of Childhood and Youth* (1924), *Out of My Life and Thought* (1931), *The Problem of Peace in the World Today* (1954), *A Declaration of Conscience* (1957), and *Peace or Atomic War?* (1958). He founded the hospital at Lambaréné, French Equatorial Africa, and was an expert on the construction of pipe organs.

Explore around you, penetrate to the furthest limits of human 1 knowledge, and always you will come up against something inexplicable in the end. It is called life. It is a mystery so inexplicable that the knowledge of the educated and the ignorant is purely relative when contemplating it.

But what is the difference between the scientist who observes in his 2 microscope the most minute and unexpected signs of life; and the old farmer who by contrast can barely read or write, who stands in springtime in his garden and contemplates the buds opening on the branches of his trees? Both are confronted with the riddle of life. One may be able to describe life in greater detail, but for both it remains equally inscrutable. All knowledge is, in the final analysis, the knowledge of life. All realization is amazement at this riddle of life—a reverence for life in its infinite and yet ever-fresh manifestations. How amazing this coming into being, living, and dying! How fantastic that in other existences something comes into being, passes away again, comes into being once more, and so forth from eternity to eternity! How can it be? We can do all things, and we can do nothing. For in' all our wisdom we cannot create life. What we create is dead.

Life means strength, will, arising from the abyss, dissolving into the 3 abyss again. Life is feeling, experience, suffering. If you study life deeply, looking with perceptive eyes into the vast animated chaos of this creation, its profundity will seize you suddenly with dizziness. In everything you recognize yourself. The tiny beetle that lies dead in your path—it was a living creature, struggling for existence like yourself, rejoicing in the sun like you, knowing fear and pain like you. And now it is no more than decaying matter — which is what you will be sooner or later, too. . . .

What is this recognition, this knowledge within the reach of the most 4 scientific and the most childlike? It is reverence for life, reverence for the unfathomable mystery we confront in our universe, an existence different in its outward appearance and yet inwardly of the same character as our own, terribly similar, awesomely related. The strangeness between us and other creatures is here removed.

Reverence for the infinity of life means removal of the alienation, 5 restoration of empathy, compassion, sympathy. And so by the final result of knowledge is the same as that required of us by the commandment of love. Heart and reason agree together when we desire and dare to be men who seek to fathom the depths of the universe.

Reason discovers the bridge between love for God and love for 6 men — love for all creatures, reverence for all being, compassion with all life, however dissimilar to our own.

I cannot but have reverence for all that is called life. I cannot avoid 7 compassion for everything that is called life. That is the beginning and foundation of morality. Once a man has experienced it and continues to do so — and he who has once experienced it will continue to do so — he is ethical. He carries his morality within him and can never lose it, for it continues to develop within him. He who has never experienced this has only a set of superficial principles. These theories have no root in him, they do not belong to him, and they fall off him. The worst is that the whole of our generation had only such a set of superficial principles. Then the time came to put the ethical code to the test, and it evaporated. For centuries the human race had been educated with only a set of superficial principles. We were brutal, ignorant, and heartless without being aware of it. We had no scale of values, for we had no reverence for life.

It is our duty to share and maintain life. Reverence concerning all 8 life is the greatest commandment in its most elementary form. Or expressed in negative terms: "Thou shalt not kill." We take this prohibition so lightly, thoughtlessly plucking a flower, thoughtlessly stepping on a poor insect, thoughtlessly, in terrible blindness because everything takes its revenge, disregarding the suffering and lives of our fellow men, sacrificing them to trivial earthly goals.

Much talk is heard in our times about building a new human race. 9 How are we to build a new humanity? Only by leading men toward a true, inalienable ethic of our own, which is capable of further development. But this goal cannot be reached unless countless individuals will transform themselves from blind men into seeing ones and begin to spell out the great commandment which is: Reverence for Life. Existence depends more on reverence for life than the law and the prophets. Reverence for life comprises the whole ethic of love in its deepest and highest sense. It is the source of constant renewal for the individual and for mankind.

Study Questions

1. By what means does Schweitzer make something concrete out of abstract concepts?
2. Why are particular examples of details used in this essay, i.e., the insect, the flower, the beetle?
3. Where and why is parallelism used?
4. What is the difference between *sentiment* and *sentimental?* Would either word be appropriate in discussing this essay?
5. We know Schweitzer was a Christian. Can you find internal evidence in "Reverence for Life" to prove or disprove this?
6. Schweitzer says that reverence for the infinity of life will bring the "restoration of empathy, compassion, sympathy." How do empathy, compassion, and sympathy differ?

Martin Luther King, Jr.
PILGRIMAGE TO NONVIOLENCE

Born in Atlanta, Georgia, the son of a Baptist minister, Martin Luther King, Jr. (1929–1968) received his B.A. from Morehouse College, his B.D. from Crozier Theological Seminary, and his Ph.D. in systematic theology from Boston University. President of the Southern Christian Leadership Conference from its formation in 1957, Dr. King received the Nobel Peace Prize in 1964. The quest for justice and equality for his people that began with the Montgomery bus boycott in 1955 ended for Martin Luther King, Jr. when he was assassinated in Nashville, Tennessee, 13 years later. He reached his summit as a charismatic figure in 1963, when he delivered his address—"I Have a Dream"—to 250,000 persons assembled at the Lincoln Memorial during the mammoth March on Washington. His writings include *Stride Toward Freedom* (1958) and *Why We Can't Wait* (1964), accounts of the civil-rights movement, and *Strength to Love* (1963), a collection of sermons.

When I went to Montgomery as a pastor, I had not the slightest idea that I would later become involved in a crisis in which nonviolent resistance would be applicable. I neither started the protest nor sug-   1

"Pilgrimage to Nonviolence" (pp. 90–107) from *Stride Toward Freedom* by Martin Luther King, Jr. Copyright © 1958 by Martin Luther King, Jr.

gested it. I simply responded to the call of the people for a spokesman. When the protest began, my mind, consciously or unconsciously, was driven back to the Sermon on the Mount, with its sublime teachings on love, and the Gandhian method of nonviolent resistance. As the days unfolded, I came to see the power of nonviolence more and more. Living through the actual experience of the protest, nonviolence became more than a method to which I gave intellectual assent; it became a commitment to a way of life. Many of the things that I had not cleared up intellectually concerning nonviolence were now solved in the sphere of practical action.

Since the philosophy of nonviolence played such a positive role in the Montgomery Movement, it may be wise to turn to a brief discussion of some basic aspects of this philosophy. 2

First, it must be emphasized that nonviolent resistance is not a method for cowards; it does resist. If one uses this method because he is afraid or merely because he lacks the instruments of violence, he is not truly nonviolent. This is why Gandhi often said that if cowardice is the only alternative to violence, it is better to fight. He made this statement conscious of the fact that there is always another alternative: no individual or group need submit to any wrong, nor need they use violence to right the wrong; there is the way of nonviolent resistance. This is ultimately the way of the strong man. It is not a method of stagnant passivity. The phrase "passive resistance" often gives the false impression that this is a sort of "do-nothing method" in which the resister quietly and passively accepts evil. But nothing is further from the truth. For while the nonviolent resister is passive in the sense that he is not physically aggressive toward his opponent, his mind and emotions are always active, constantly seeking to persuade his opponent that he is wrong. The method is passive physically, but strongly active spiritually. It is not passive nonresistance to evil, it is active nonviolent resistance to evil. 3

A second basic fact that characterizes nonviolence is that it does not seek to defeat or humiliate the opponent, but to win his friendship and understanding. The nonviolent resister must often express his protest through noncooperation or boycotts, but he realizes that these are not ends themselves; they are merely means to awaken a sense of moral shame in the opponent. The end is redemption and reconciliation. The aftermath of nonviolence is the creation of the beloved community, while the aftermath of violence is tragic bitterness. 4

A third characteristic of this method is that the attack is directed against forces of evil rather than against persons who happen to be doing the evil. It is evil that the nonviolent resister seeks to defeat, not the persons victimized by evil. If he is opposing racial injustice, the nonviolent resister has the vision to say that the basic tension is not between races. As I like to say to the people in Montgomery: "The tension in this city is not between white people and Negro people. The tension is, at bottom, between justice and injustice, between the forces of light and the forces of darkness. And if there is a victory, it will be a victory not merely for fifty thousand Negroes, but a victory for justice and the forces of light. We are out to defeat injustice and not white persons who may be unjust." 5

A fourth point that characterizes nonviolent resistance is a willing- 6
ness to accept suffering without retaliation, to accept blows from the opponent without striking back. "Rivers of blood may have to flow before
we gain our freedom, but it must be our blood," Gandhi said to his coun-
trymen. The nonviolent resister is willing to accept violence if necessary,
but never to inflict it. He does not seek to dodge jail. If going to jail is
necessary, he enters it "as a bridegroom enters the bride's chamber."

One may well ask: "What is the nonviolent resister's justification for 7
this ordeal to which he invites men, for this mass political application of
the ancient doctrine of turning the other cheek?" The answer is found in
the realization that unearned suffering is redemptive. Suffering, the nonviolent resister realizes, has tremendous educational and transforming
possibilities. "Things of fundamental importance to people are not se-
cured by reason alone, but have to be purchased with their suffering,"
said Gandhi. He continues: "Suffering is infinitely more powerful than
the law of the jungle for converting the opponent and opening his ears
which are otherwise shut to the voice of reason."

A fifth point concerning nonviolent resistance is that it avoids not 8
only external physical violence but also internal violence of spirit. The
nonviolent resister not only refuses to shoot his opponent but he also
refuses to hate him. At the center of nonviolence stands the principle of
love. The nonviolent resister would contend that in the struggle for human dignity, the oppressed people of the world must not succumb to the
temptation of becoming bitter or indulging in hate campaigns. To retaliate in kind would do nothing but intensify the existence of hate in the
universe. Along the way of life, someone must have sense enough and
morality enough to cut off the chain of hate. This can only be done by
projecting the ethic of love to the center of our lives.

In speaking of love at this point, we are not referring to some senti- 9
mental or affectionate emotion. It would be nonsense to urge men to
love their oppressors in an affectionate sense. Love in this connection
means understanding, redemptive good will. Here the Greek language
comes to our aid. There are three words for love in the Greek New Testament. First, there is *eros.* In Platonic philosophy *eros* meant the yearning
of the soul for the realm of the divine. It has come now to mean a sort
of aesthetic or romantic love. Second, there is *philia,* which means intimate affection between personal friends. *Philia* denotes a sort of reciprocal love; the person loves because he is loved. When we speak of loving those who oppose us, we refer to neither *eros* nor *philia;* we speak of
a love which is expressed in the Greek word *agape. Agape* means understanding, redeeming good will for all men. It is an overflowing love
which is purely spontaneous, unmotivated, groundless, and creative. It is
not set in motion by any quality or function of its object. It is the love of
God operating in the human heart.

Agape is disinterested love. It is a love in which the individual seeks 10
not his own good, but the good of his neighbor (I Cor. 10:24). *Agape*
does not begin by discriminating between worthy and unworthy people,
or any qualities people possess. It begins by loving others *for their sakes.*
It is entirely "neighbor-regarding concern for others," which discovers

the neighbor in every man it meets. There, *agape* makes no distinction between friend and enemy; it is directed toward both. If one loves an individual merely on account of friendliness, he loves him for the sake of the benefits to be gained from the friendship, rather than for the friend's own sake. Consequently, the best way to assure oneself that Love is disinterested is to have love for the enemy-neighbor from whom you can expect no good in return, but only hostility and persecution.

Another basic point about *agape* is that it springs from the *need* of 11 the other person — his need for belonging to the best in the human family. The Samaritan who helped the Jew on the Jericho Road was "good" because he responded to the human need that he was presented with. God's love is eternal and fails not because man needs his love. St. Paul assures us that the loving act of redemption was done "while we were yet sinners" — that is, at the point of our greatest need for love. Since the white man's personality is greatly distorted by segregation, and his soul is greatly scarred, he needs the love of the Negro. The Negro must love the white man, because the white man needs his love to remove his tensions, insecurities, and fears.

Agape is not a weak, passive love. It is love in action. *Agape* is love 12 seeking to preserve and create community. It is insistence on community even when one seeks to break it. *Agape* is a willingness to sacrifice in the interest of mutuality. *Agape* is a willingness to go to any length to restore community. It doesn't stop at the first mile, but it goes the second mile to restore community. It is a willingness to forgive, not seven times, but seventy times seven to restore community. The cross is the eternal expression of the length to which God will go in order to restore broken community. The resurrection is a symbol of God's triumph over all the forces that seek to block community. The Holy Spirit is the continuing community creating reality that moves through history. He who works against community is working against the whole of creation. Therefore, if I respond to hate with a reciprocal hate I do nothing but intensify cleavage in broken community. I can only close the gap in broken community by meeting hate with love. If I meet hate with hate, I become depersonalized, because creation is so designed that my personality can only be fulfilled in the context of community. Booker T. Washington was right: "Let no man pull you so low as to make you hate him." When he pulls you that low he brings you to the point of working against community; he drags you to the point of defying creation, and thereby becoming depersonalized.

In the final analysis, *agape* means a recognition of the fact that all life 13 is interrelated. All humanity is involved in a single process, and all men are brothers. To the degree that I harm my brother, no matter what he is doing to me, to that extent I am harming myself. For example, white men often refuse federal aid to education in order to avoid giving the Negro his rights; but because all men are brothers they cannot deny Negro children without harming their own. They end, all efforts to the contrary, by hurting themselves. Why is this? Because men are brothers. If you harm me, you harm yourself.

Love, *agape,* is the only cement that can hold this broken community 14 together. When I am commanded to love, I am commanded to restore community, to resist injustice, and to meet the needs of my brothers.

A sixth basic fact about nonviolent resistance is that it is based on   15
the conviction that the universe is on the side of justice. Consequently, the believer in nonviolence has deep faith in the future. This faith is another reason why the nonviolent resister can accept suffering without retaliation. For he knows that in his struggle for justice he has cosmic companionship. It is true that there are devout believers in nonviolence who find it difficult to believe in a personal God. But even these persons believe in the existence of some creative force that works for universal wholeness. Whether we call it an unconscious process, an impersonal Brahman, or a Personal Being of matchless power and infinite love, there is a creative force in this universe that works to bring the disconnected aspects of reality into a harmonious whole.

Study Questions

1. What is the thesis of this essay? Is it explicit or implicit?
2. How many "basic facts" about nonviolence are presented? Are they presented as being of equal importance?
3. Comment on the relevance, in terms of the structuring of this essay, of the disquisition on love.
4. Who or what are the sources of King's quotations. Are these sources appropriate to the topic? How do you feel about King's quoting himself (paragraph 5)?
5. Do you find the last paragraph serviceable as a conclusion? If not, supply an alternative of your own, drawn from the content of this essay.

Karl A. Menninger
A PSYCHIATRIST LOOKS AT VIOLENCE

Karl A. Menninger (1893–   ) was born in Topeka, Kansas. He attended Washburn College before earning an A.B. from the University of Wisconsin (1914) and an M.D. from Harvard (1917). He founded the Menninger School of Psychiatry in 1946. By then he had already received the national acclaim, which has since continued

Reprinted from *Catholic World*, ccix (September, 1969), with permission.

to grow. He received the first Distinguished Service Award of the American Psychiatric Association in 1965; in 1969 he served on the President's Task Force for Prison Reform. His first book, *The Human Mind,* was published in 1930. More recent titles include *A Psychiatrist's World* (1959), *The Vital Balance* (1963), *The Crime of Punishment* (1968), and *Whatever Became of Sin?* (1973).

Violence is in the news, now. The word "violence" has the 1 sound "vile" in it: the word itself is a little violent. It is an arresting word. It means something is being broken and crashed. Modern technology has speeded up the rate of living, the rate of moving about.

The acceleration that has been achieved implies a corresponding rate 2 of deceleration, in the process of which oftentimes we get jolted. Many people mistake "jolting" and other aspects of change for violence.

Sometimes people use the word "violent" as if it meant crime. Most 3 crime is not violent. Most crime is very quiet, just snitchy, sneaky quiet, nonviolent. Murder is not a typical crime. Murder constitutes a very small fraction of all crimes, numerically. Most crime isn't violent and most violence isn't crime.

I don't really think violence is increasing. I think people are increas- 4 ingly aware of violence. But if you mean by violence civic disturbances, you need only to read the reproductions of *Harper's* weekly magazine of 100 years ago, or look in any history book. Look at the description of the way people lived 100 years ago and see how much more violent it was then.

You say it isn't safe to walk down the street? Well, it never was safe 5 to walk down some streets. It wasn't safe then to walk down some country roads even. I'm convinced that the world is getting better, and we are getting better control of our own behavior, better control of our public behavior.

Why is violence getting more conspicuous? Let me suggest that there 6 are four or five reasons. First, there are more of us—a lot more of us. There are several times more of us than there were a century ago. Secondly, we have caught the great yen for all living as close together as possible. We all rush into the Boston-New York- Philadelphia-Baltimore-Washington axis or into the Chicago-Milwaukee-Toledo-Detroit-Cleveland axis, and try to find a place to light. Here are two great blobs of intense, crowded civilization. These people are living very close together.

But everywhere there are more people on the earth, and all these 7 people live closer to each other. They crowd each other and they watch each other. They want to learn about each other and there is more discussion about each other's behavior, proprieties, character, etc. Formerly it was bad manners to want to know about other people.

Most behavioral science was in the dark for a long time because it 8 was regarded as really a little rude, a little not-quite-proper, to be prying into the way other people think, the way they feel, the way they live. Today we watch what other people order and how they eat, and we listen to what they say. In all sorts of ways now this tendency to push together is evident. And when people push together, somebody's elbow nudges you, intentionally or unintentionally but a little violently, and it may provoke a little violence.

When seventeen people are living in two rooms in an apartment 9 house that has only two bathrooms for nine floors and one of them is stopped up, there's a good deal of contact with one another, and it isn't good-natured. Such situations make people ill-humored, frustrated and angry. They may not be in actual pain because they have to climb seven flights of steps to go to the toilet, but it's not very comfortable, and it is highly aggravating.

Crowding people as they are now crowded is in itself one of the 10 great aggravations of tension and irritation and proneness to violence. If you have a corn or a toothache or a stomach ulcer—if you have something that hurts you all the time—you are far more susceptible to having your tension raised by actions of somebody around you which may not of themselves be so violent.

Things like this happen to people, to everybody. Everybody gets 11 pains and aches and frustrations and irritations. The inner tension of maintaining self-control continues to mount and permit the escape of the ugly side of the personality which we ordinarily hide.

Not only are there more of us living closer together, but there's an- 12 other thing about violence awareness. We all know how some people have it a lot easier than others. Some feel a great sense of injustice about certain things. It isn't that we're just full of envy—we may be full of that, too—but our sense of great inequality and injustice that some people have so different a way of living—this gives us a "slow burn." Furthermore, we find that some of the people who are depressed and harrassed rebel about it; they do something, and so we have an example set for us and we imitate it. Then finally, I think that the communication media themselves contribute to our awareness of violence. They give information to the public that it is most curious and most eager to get. This is not necessarily what it should know, but what it wants to know, and the public likes violence.

By looking at violence, perhaps some of our own violence is dimin- 13 ished; by looking at violence, also, we have a pattern for more violence. Some of us didn't know until recently that you could fill a sack with bad tomatoes and throw it at people, but we see on television that you can, and it is soon done in some quarters.

I don't mean to condemn the news media for this because at least 14 they are telling us as it is, and we're prepared. We know now there are some people who fill sacks full of rotten tomatoes and throw them at policemen, and we know there are some policemen that get so mad at this they can't control themselves and retaliate furiously.

We must distinguish between public violence, of course, which we 15 sometimes see, and private violence which we rarely see. About 90 per cent of all violent crimes are committed in the home—usually toward the wife or the husband or the children or friends. Child-beating, which is very widespread, in the name of punishment or just from hate, takes place quietly. It doesn't take place where the neighbors can see it, or it wouldn't happen so often. The same is true of wife-beating and many of the inter-family quarrels and fights between brothers, cousins, relatives, and the like.

One must distinguish between noisy violence, and silent violence. 16 There is a great deal of silent violence. Like trapping or poisoning wild animals or stealing. The most widespread quiet violence is the dumping of filth of all kinds into the air and into the water. Then there's the violence of the good guy versus the violence of the bad guy—cops and robbers fantasies. Just label somebody a dragon and we'll go out and kill him and we'll be famous like St. George. Killing dragons is more fun than hunting the Grail.

Aggressive violence comes usually because somebody wants to know 17 how manly he is, or how angry, or how scared. Sometimes it's because people are doing it and we feel we have to belong, and even excel. It may be one has been gypped and cheated by the secondhand car dealer until he's just madder than the devil, and feels completely helpless in the matter. What do you do about it? Of course, first of all, you quit it. Just swear off of violence. (I mean your own.)

There isn't any question that we must cultivate more ways to take 18 care of the violence that we used to spend in perfectly well-approved ways. All behavioral scientists are talking about what are the substitute forms of violent expression. What do you do when you get so mad you don't know what to do about it? Do you play the piano? Do you paint? Do you cry? Do you swear? Do you go out and bat a tennis ball around?

Games, in a way, are symbolic ways of being violent, symbolic ways 19 of expressing superiority, or greater masculinity, or greater encouragement of all kinds of play—physical games, mental games, psychological games, games in which aggressiveness can be symbolically released—games are one answer to the problem of pent-up or roused-up aggression.

The course of civilization has been to substitute more and more sym- 20 bols for reality. Words are symbols. Gestures are symbols. Signs and smiles and conventions and names. All the letters on this page are symbols. Back a few centuries there weren't so many symbols—more action, more aggression, more violence. The whole course of civilization consists of increasing symbolization to assist in self-control.

I mention the self-control, rather than the control of others, and you 21 are going to ask, am I (also) my brother's keeper? Do I have to help control him, also? The answer is, yes, of course. We've all got to be policemen, to some extent. We can't stalk calmly down the street with our hands over our stomachs and our eyes on the ground, looking pious and self-controlled.

It's a good thing to have a cause or two to fight for. I have a dozen 22 causes. I'm always tilting at windmills of various kinds. Fighting against the trapping of wild animals is one. Guns are another. Guns are killing machines, and I see no point in people packing around killing machines.

Yes, I recommend getting a cause of some kind. Not a violent one. 23 Violence cannot be stopped by violence. That idea of violence being controlled by counterviolence is primitive thinking, 10-year-old boy thinking. That's what children think. But adults know better. Violence opposed to violence only makes for more violence. And that includes punishment.

In a recent article of mine, I said that there ought to be an end to 24 such silly things as punishment for offenders, not an end to penalty. I think penalties ought to be increased and speeded up. But non vindictiveness. I think that, if a man drives when he is drunk, he ought to be hit with a terrific penalty. I don't want to punish him, I don't want to beat him, I don't want to stick pins in him. I don't want to put him in the penitentiary to rot (while I pay his board bill). I don't think such things will do any good. The only way to control crime is to eliminate this yen to punish and impose penalties so every offender is justly and usefully treated.

Teaching, in a sense, consists of an attack upon ignorance. The right 25 kind of a teacher has a "thing" he wants to make clear to you. He says to you, "don't be ignorant on this point any longer, don't be stupid on this anymore; don't be uninformed or misinformed. This is the way it is; you can do it with this. You have the potentiality; you can make something. Go on. Try."

Ignorance resists, because when it yields you have to change. You 26 can't ever be the same after you find out what you didn't know before. That's the whole point of new information, new insights, new ideas, new ways of looking at things. Look at yourself—how violent are you? And how are you violent? How can you be less violent? How can you be more constructively violent?

Do people really believe what Jesus said about the other cheek? 27 "Don't pay your enemies back," He said. "Don't do what they do, then you become like them." But some people think we must wait till the world is better before we can begin taking Jesus' advice seriously.

I think that violence can be controlled. Not all at once, and not by 28 counterviolence. I'm not sure yet, but I think maybe the Czechs have something to teach us about dealing with violence: we'll watch and see— I hope so.

There is an antidote to violence. We have these aggressive tenden- 29 cies within us, true; but we also have positive, creative, loving tendencies within us, and they tend to get the upper hand if we give them a chance.

Study Questions

1. What is the effect of the comma in the first sentence?
2. Which paragraphs have explicitly stated topic sentences?
3. Menninger suggests "four or five reasons" for "violence getting more conspicuous." Why isn't he more specific?
4. How successful is Menninger's attempt to distinguish *kinds* of violence?
5. Is there any internal evidence to suggest that this paper might have been composed for oral presentation?

6. What is a *rhetorical question?* Are the author's questions real or rhetorical?
7. Menninger often uses sentence fragments to good effect. Where? What does he accomplish in each instance?

Larry Woiwode
GUNS

Larry Woiwode (1941–   ) was born in Carrington, North Dakota. His first novel, *What I'm Going to Do, I Think* (1969), resulted in national recognition. In 1971 he held a Guggenheim fellowship, and in 1972 he served on the executive board of P.E.N. He has been a judge in the National Book Awards and Writer in Residence at the University of Wisconsin. His essays and stories may be found in the *New Yorker, The New York Times, Audience, Atlantic Monthly, Esquire, Mademoiselle,* the *New American Review,* and the *Partisan Review,* among others. His most recent book was *Beyond the Bedroom Wall* (1975).

Once in the middle of a Wisconsin winter I shot a deer, my 1 only one, while my wife and daughter watched. It had been hit by a delivery truck along a country road a few miles from where we lived and one of its rear legs was torn off at the hock; a shattered shin and hoof lay steaming in the red-beaded snow. The driver of the truck and I stood and watched as it tried to leap a fence, kicked a while at the top wire it was entangled in, flailing the area with fresh ropes of blood, and then went hobbling across a pasture toward a wooded hill. Placid cows followed it with a curious awe. "Do you have a rifle with you?" the driver asked. "No, not with me. At home." He looked once more at the deer, then got in his truck and drove off.

I went back to our Jeep where my wife and daughter were waiting, 2 pale and withdrawn, and told them what I was about to do, and suggested that they'd better stay at home. No, they wanted to be with me, they said; they wanted to watch. My daughter was three and a half at the time. I got my rifle, a .22, a foolishly puny weapon to use on a deer but the only one I had, and we came back and saw that the deer was lying in some low brush near the base of the hill; no need to trail its blatant spoor. When I got about a hundred yards off, marveling at how it could have made it so far in its condition through snow that came over my

Reprinted from *Esquire,* December 1975, with permission.

boot tops, the deer tried to push itself up with its front legs, then collapsed. I aimed at the center of its skull, thinking, *This will be the quickest*, and heard the bullet ricochet off and go singing through the woods.

The deer was on its feet, shaking its head as though stung, and I 3 fired again at the same spot, quickly, and apparently missed. It was now moving at its fastest hobble up the hill, broadside to me, and I took my time to sight a heart shot. Before the report even registered in my mind, the deer went down in an explosion of snow and lay struggling there, spouting blood from its stump and a chest wound. I was shaking by now. Deer are color-blind as far as science can say, and as I went toward its quieting body to deliver the coup de grace, I realized I was being seen in black and white, and then the deer's eye seemed to home in on me, and I was struck with the understanding that I was its vision of approaching death. And then I seemed to enter its realm through its eye and saw the countryside and myself in shades of white and grey. *But I see the deer in color,* I thought.

A few yards away, I aimed at its head once more, and there was the 4 crack of a shot, the next-to-last round left in the magazine. The deer's head came up, and I could see its eye clearly now, dark, placid, filled with an appeal, it seemed, and then felt the surge of black and white surround and subsume me again. The second shot, or one of them, had pierced its neck; a grey-blue tongue hung out over its jaw; urine was trickling from below its tail; a doe. I held the rifle barrel inches from its forehead, conscious of my wife's and daughter's eyes on me from behind, and as I fired off the final and fatal shot, felt myself drawn by them back into my multicolored, many-faceted world again.

I don't remember my first gun, the heritage is so ingrained in me, 5 but know I've used a variety of them to kill birds, reptiles, mammals, amphibians, plant life, insects (bees and butterflies with a shotgun), fish that came too close to shore—never a human being, I'm quick to interject, although the accumulated carnage I've put away with bullets since boyhood is probably enough to add up to a couple of cows, not counting the deer; and have fired, at other targets living and fairly inert, an old ten gauge with double hammers that left a welt on my shoulder that lasted a week, a Mauser, a twelve-gauge sawed-off shotgun, an M-16, at least a dozen variations on the .22—pump, bolt action, lever action, target pistols, special scopes and sights and stocks—a .410 over-and-under, a zip gun that blew up and scattered shrapnel that's still imbedded in my arm, an Italian carbine, a Luger, and, among others, a fancily engraved, single-trigger, double-barreled twenty gauge at snowballs thrown from behind my shoulder out over a bluff; and on that same bluff on the first day of this year, after some wine and prodding, I found myself at the jittering rim of stutters from a paratrooper's lightweight machine gun with a collapsible, geometrically reinforced metal stock, watched the spout of its trajectory of tangible tracers go off across the night toward the already-set sun, and realized that this was perhaps the hundredth weapon I'd had performing in my hands.

I was raised in North Dakota, near the edge of the West, during the 6 turbulence and then the aftermath of the Second World War, which our country ended in such an unequivocal way there was a sense of vindication about our long-standing fetish for guns, not to say pride in it, too. "Bang! Bang! You're dead" returns to me from that time without the least speck of friction or reflection. When we weren't playing War, or Cowboys and Indians, or Cops and Robbers, we were reading War Comics (from which you could order for less than a dollar little cardboard chests of plastic weaponry and soldiers to stage your own debacles), or Westerns, or listening to *The Lone Ranger* and *Richard Diamond, Private Detective* and other radio shows — all of which openly glorified guns, and the more powerful the better.

My fantasies, when I was frustrated, angry, or depressed, were rife 7 with firearms of the most lethal sort, flying shot, endless rounds of shattering ammunition; the enemy bodies blown away and left in bloody tableaux. And any gun was an engineered instrument — much more far-ranging and accurate than bows and arrows or slingshots — that detached you from your destructiveness or crime or sometimes even from being a source of death.

I've only owned three firearms in my life as an adult. Two I brought 8 back to the shops within a week after I'd bought them, realizing I was trying to reach out in some archaic way, and the limits to my maturity and imagination that that implied, plus the bother to my daughter of their powing sounds; and the third, the .22, after trembling over it a few years and using it to shoot holes in the floor to enact a between-the-legs suicide, I gave away. To my younger brother. Who was initiated into the buck-fever fraternity in the forests of northern Wisconsin when he was an adolescent by a seasoned local who said to him, "If you see anything moving out there tomorrow, boy, *shoot* it. You can check out later what it is. Nobody gives a shit up here." And on a hunting trip years later, an acquaintance from the village my brother lived in then, a lawyer, was shot in the head with a deer rifle, but somehow survived. And even went back to practicing law. It was thought to be an accident at first, what with all the bullets embroidering the air that day, and then rumor had it that another member of the party hunting on adjoining land, an old friend of the lawyer's had found out a week before the season that the lawyer had been having his wife for a while. The two men were polite enough to one another in the village after that, my brother said, but not such good friends, of course. Just balanced, justice-balanced males.

For months and seasons after I'd shot the crippled doe, every time 9 we passed the field in our Jeep, my daughter would say, "Here's where Daddy shooted the deer." In exactly that manner, using the tone and detachment of a storyteller or tourist guide. And I'd glance into the rearview mirror and see her in her car seat, studying the hill with troubled and sympathetic eyes. One day I stopped. "Does it bother you so much that I shot it?" I asked. There was no answer, and then I saw that she was nodding her head, her gaze still fixed on the hill.

"Well, if I wouldn't have, it could have suffered a long time. You saw 10 how badly hurt it was. It couldn't have lived that way. I didn't like doing it, either, but it was best for the deer. When I told the game warden about it, he even thanked me and said, 'Leave it for the foxes and crows.'

They have to eat, too, you know, and maybe the deer made the winter easier for them." And I thought, Oh, what a self-justifying fool and ass and pig you are. Why didn't you leave her at home? Why didn't you go to the farmer whose land the deer was on, which would have been as quick or quicker than going back for the .22—a man who would have had a deer rifle, or at least a shotgun with rifled slugs, and would have put the deer away with dispatch in one shot and might have even salvaged the hide and venison? And who could say it wouldn't have lived, the way some animals do after tearing or chewing off a limb caught in a trap? Who was to presume it wouldn't have preferred to die a slow death in the brush, looking out over the pasture, as the crimson stain widening in the snow drew away and dimmed its colorless world until all went black? Why not admit that I was a common backcountry American and, like most men of my mold, had used an arsenal of firearms to kill and was as excited about putting away a deer as moved by compassion for its suffering? Then again, given my daughter's understanding and the person I am, perhaps she sensed this, and more.

I once choked a chicken to death. It was my only barefaced, not to   11 say barehanded, confrontation with death and the killer in me and happened on my grandparents' farm. I couldn't have been more than nine or ten and no firearms were included or necessary. I was on my knees and the chicken fluttered its outstretched wings with the last of the outraged protest. I gripped, beyond release, above its swollen crop, its beak gaping, translucent eyelids sliding up and down. An old molting specimen. A hen, most likely; a worse loss, because of eggs, than a capon or cock. My grandfather, who was widely traveled and world-wise, in his eighties then, and had just started using a cane from earlier times, came tapping at that moment around the corner of the chicken coop and saw what I was doing and started gagging at the hideousness of it, did a quick assisted spin away and never again, hours later nor for the rest of his life, for that matter, ever mentioned the homicidal incident to me. Keeping his silence, he seemed to understand; and yet whenever I'm invaded by the incident, the point of it seems to be his turning away from me.

My wife once said she felt I wanted to kill her. A common enough   12 feeling among long-married couples, I'm sure, and not restricted to either sex (I know, for instance, that there were times when she wanted to kill me), but perhaps with firsthand experience infusing the feeling, it became too much to endure. I now live in New York City, where the clock keeps moving toward my suitcase, alone, and she and my daughter in the Midwest. The city has changed in the seven years since the three of us lived here together. There are more frivolous and not-so-frivolous wares—silk kerchiefs, necklaces and rings, roach clips, rolling papers, socks, a display of Florida coral across a convertible top, books of every kind—being sold in the streets than anybody can remember seeing in recent years. People openly saying that soon it will be like the Thirties once were, with us *all* in the streets selling our apples, or whatever, or engaged in a tacit and friendly sort of gangsterism to survive. Outside my window, a spindly deciduous species has a sign strung on supporting posts on either side of it, in careful hand-lettering, that reads, THIS TREE GIVES OXYGEN. GIVE IT LOVE. More dogs in the streets and parks than they'd remembered, and more canine offal sending up its open-ended odor; at least half the population giving up cigarette smoking, at last, for good, they say, and many actually are. The mazed feeling of most everywhere now of being in the midst of a slowly forging and forgiving reciprocity. An air of bravura about most everybody in maintaining one's best face, with a few changes of costumish clothing to reflect it, perhaps, no matter what might yet evolve. A unisex barbershop or boutique on nearly every other block, it seems.

Sometimes I think this is where I really belong. Then a man is   13
gunned down in a neighborhood bar I used to drop into and the next day a mob leader assassinated, supposedly by members of his own mob. *Perhaps this is where I'm most at home,* I equivocate again and have an image of myself in a Stetson traveling down a crosstown street at a fast-paced and pigeon-toed shamble toward the setting sun (setting this far east, but not over my wife and daughter yet), my eyes cast down and shoulders forward, hands deep in my empty Levi pockets, a suspect closet-faggot-cowboy occasionally whistled at by queens.

I won't (and can't) refute my heritage, but I doubt that I'll use a fire-   14
arm again, or, if I do, only in the direst sort of emergency. Which I say to protect my flanks. The bloody, gun-filled fantasies seldom return now, and when they do they're reversed: I'm the one being shot, or shot at, or think I am.

Study Questions

1. The description of the shooting of the deer in paragraphs 3–4 is terribly specific. Why?
2. Which uses of italics in this essay are traditional? Explain the other occasions when they occur.
3. Woiwode moves easily back and forth between the present and the past. How does he make the transition in each instance?
4. Are there any paragraphs that occur for strictly narrative purposes rather than, for instance, persuasion or exposition?
5. How does Woiwode use the presence of his daughter to advance his case?

"Saki" (H. H. Munro)
THE TOYS OF PEACE

Hector Hugh Munro (1870–1916) published his first collection of short stories, *Reginald,* in 1904 under the pseudonym "Saki." Earlier he had worked as a political satirist for the *Westminster Gazette;* later he served as correspondent in Russia and France for the *Morning Post.* Although Saki is best remembered for his short stories, he published one novel, *The Unbearable Bassington* (1912). His short story collections include *Reginald in Russia* (1910), *The Chronicles Clovis* (1911), and *Beasts and Superbeasts* (1914). At the beginning of World War I he enlisted as a private in the 22nd Royal Fusiliers. He died in France in November, 1916.

"Harvey," said Eleanor Bope, handing her brother a cutting 1 from a London morning paper[1] of the 19th of March, "just read this about children's toys, please; it exactly carries out some of our ideas about influence and upbringing."

"In the view of the National Peace Council," ran the extract, "there 2 are grave objections to presenting our boys with regiments of fighting men, batteries of guns, and squadrons of 'Dreadnoughts.' Boys, the Council admits, naturally love fighting and all the panoply of war ... but that is no reason for encouraging, and perhaps giving permanent form to, their primitive instincts. At the Children's Welfare Exhibition, which opens at Olympia in three weeks' time, the Peace Council will make an alternative suggestion to parents in the shape of an exhibition of 'peace toys.' In front of a specially painted representation of the Peace Palace at The Hague will be grouped, not miniature soldiers but miniature civilians, not guns but ploughs and the tools of industry.... It is hoped that manufacturers may take a hint from the exhibit, which will bear fruit in the toy shops."

"The idea is certainly an interesting and very well-meaning one," said 3 Harvey; "whether it would succeed well in practice—"

"We must try," interrupted his sister; "you are coming down to us at 4 Easter, and you always bring the boys some toys, so that will be an excellent opportunity for you to inaugurate the new experiment. Go about in the shops and buy any little toys and models that have special bearing on civilian life in its more peaceful aspects. Of course you must explain the toys to the children and interest them in the new idea. I regret to say

Reprinted with permission from *The Short Stories of "Saki"* (H. H. Munro). New York: Viking Press, 1930.

that the 'Siege of Adrianople' toy, that their Aunt Susan sent them, didn't need any explanation; they knew all the uniforms and flags, and even the names of the respective commanders, and when I heard them one day using what seemed to be the most objectionable language they said it was Bulgarian words of command; of course it *may* have been, but at any rate I took the toy away from them. Now I shall expect your Easter gifts to give quite a new impulse and direction to the children's minds; Eric is not eleven yet, and Bertie is only nine-and-a-half, so they are really at a most impressionable age."

"There is primitive instinct to be taken into consideration, you 5 know," said Harvey doubtfully, "and hereditary tendencies as well. One of their great-uncles fought in the most intolerant fashion at Inkerman — he was specially mentioned in dispatches, I believe — and their great-grandfather smashed all his Whig neighbours' hothouses when the great Reform Bill was passed. Still, as you say, they are at an impressionable age. I will do my best."

On Easter Saturday Harvey Bope unpacked a large, promising-look- 6 ing red cardboard box under the expectant eyes of his nephews. "Your uncle has brought you the newest thing in toys," Eleanor had said impressively, and youthful anticipation had been anxiously divided between Albanian soldiery and a Somali camel-corps. Eric was hotly in favour of the latter contingency. "There would be Arabs on horseback," he whispered; "the Albanians have got jolly uniforms, and they fight all day long, and all night too, when there's a moon, but the country's rocky, so they've got no cavalry."

A quantity of crinkly paper shavings was the first thing that met the 7 view when the lid was removed; the most exciting toys always began like that. Harvey pushed back at the top layer and drew forth a square, rather featureless building.

"It's a fort!" exclaimed Bertie.   8

"It isn't, it's the palace of the Mpret of Albania," said Eric, im- 9 mensely proud of his knowledge of the exotic title; "it's got no windows, you see, so that passers-by can't fire in at the Royal Family."

"It's a municipal dust-bin," said Harvey hurriedly; "you see all the 10 refuse and litter of a town is collected there, instead of lying about and injuring the health of the citizens."

In an awful silence he disinterred a little lead figure of a man in 11 black clothes.

"That," he said, "is a distinguished civilian, John Stuart Mill. He was 12 an authority on political economy."

"Why?" asked Bertie.   13

"Well, he wanted to be; he thought it was a useful thing to be."   14

Bertie gave an expressive grunt, which conveyed his opinion that 15 there was no accounting for tastes.

Another square building came out, this time with windows and chim- 16 neys.

"A model of the Manchester branch of the Young Women's Chris- 17 tian Association," said Harvey.

"Are there any lions?" asked Eric hopefully. He had been reading 18

Roman history and thought that where you found Christians you might reasonably expect to find a few lions.

"There are no lions," said Harvey. "Here is another civilian, Robert 19 Raikes, the founder of Sunday schools, and here is a model of a municipal wash-house. These little round things are loaves baked in a sanitary bakehouse. That lead figure is a sanitary inspector, this one is a district councillor, and this one is an official of the Local Government Board."

"What does he do?" asked Eric wearily.   20

"He sees to things connected with his Department," said Harvey. 21 "This box with a slit in it is a ballot-box. Votes are put into it at election times."

"What is put into it at other times?" asked Bertie.   22

"Nothing. And here are some tools of industry, a wheelbarrow and a 23 hoe, and I think these are meant for hoppoles. This is a model beehive, and that is a ventilator, for ventilating sewers. This seems to be another municipal dustbin—no, it is a model of a school of art and a public library. This little head figure is Mrs. Hemans, a poetess, and this is Rowland Hill, who introduced the system of penny postage. This is Sir John Herschel, the eminent astrologer."

"Are we to play with these civilian figures?" asked Eric.   24

"Of course," said Harvey, "these are toys; they are meant to be 25 played with."

"But how?"   26

It was rather a poser. "You might make two of them contest a seat in 27 Parliament," said Harvey, "and have an election—"

"With rotten eggs, and free fights, and ever so many broken heads!" 28 exclaimed Eric.

"And noses all bleeding and everybody drunk as can be," echoed 29 Bertie, who had carefully studied one of Hogarth's pictures.

"Nothing of the kind," said Harvey, "nothing in the least like that. 30 Votes will be put in the ballot-box, and the Mayor will count them—the district councillor will do for the Mayor—and he will say who has received the most votes, and then the two candidates will thank him for presiding, and each will say that the contest has been conducted throughout in the pleasantest and most straightforward fashion, and they part with expressions of mutual esteem. There's a jolly game for you boys to play. I never had such toys when I was young."

"I don't think we'll play with them just now," said Eric, with an en- 31 tire absence of the enthusiasm that his uncle had shown; "I think perhaps we ought to do a little of our holiday task. It's history this time; we've got to learn up something about the Bourbon period in France."

"The Bourbon period," said Harvey, with some disapproval in his 32 voice.

"We've got to know something about Louis the Fourteenth," contin- 33 ued Eric; "I've learnt the names of all the principal battles already."

This would never do. "There were, of course, some battles fought 34 during his reign," said Harvey, "but I fancy the accounts of them were much exaggerated; news was very unreliable in those days, and there were practically no war correspondents, so generals and commanders could magnify every little skirmish they engaged in till they reached the proportions of decisive battles. Louis was really famous, now, as a landscape gardener; the way he laid out Versailles was so much admired that it was copied all over Europe."

"Do you know anything about Madame Du Barry?" asked Eric; 35 "didn't she have her head chopped off?"

"She was another great lover of gardening," said Harvey evasively; 36 "in fact, I believe the well-known rose Du Barry was named after her, and now I think you had better play for a little and leave your lessons till later."

Harvey retreated to the library and spent some thirty or forty 37 minutes in wondering whether it would be possible to compile a history, for use in elementary schools, in which there should be no prominent mention of battles, massacres, murderous intrigues, and violent deaths. The York and Lancaster period and the Napoleonic era would, he admitted to himself, present considerable difficulties, and the Thirty Years' War would entail something of a gap if you left it out altogether. Still, it would be something gained if, at a highly impressionable age, children could be got to fix their attention on the invention of calico printing instead of the Spanish Armada or the Battle of Waterloo.

It was time, he thought, to go back to the boys' room, and see how 38 they were getting on with their peace toys. As he stood outside the door he could hear Eric's voice raised in command; Bertie chimed in now and again with a helpful suggestion.

"That is Louis the Fourteenth," Eric was saying, "that one in knee- 39 breeches, that Uncle said invented Sunday schools. It isn't a bit like him, but it'll have to do."

"We'll give him a purple coat from my paintbox by and by," said 40 Bertie.

"Yes, an' red heels. That is Madame de Maintenon, that one he 41 called Mrs. Hemans. She begs Louis not to go on this expedition, but he turns a deaf ear. He takes Marshal Saxe with him, and we must pretend that they have thousands of men with them. The watchword is *Qui vive?* and the answer is *L'état c'est moi*—that was one of his favourite remarks, you know. They land at Manchester in the dead of night, and a Jacobite conspirator gives them the keys of the fortress."

Peeping in through the doorway Harvey observed that the municipal 42 dust-bin had been pierced with holes to accommodate the muzzles of imaginary cannon, and now represented the principal fortified position in Manchester; John Stuart Mill had been dipped in red ink, and apparently stood for Marshal Saxe.

"Louis orders his troops to surround the Young Women's Christian 43 Association and seize the lot of them. 'Once back at the Louvre and the girls are mine,' he exclaims. We must use Mrs. Hemans again for one of the girls; she says 'Never,' and stabs Marshal Saxe to the heart."

"He bleeds dreadfully," exclaimed Bertie, splashing red ink liberally 44 over the facade of the Association building.

"The soldiers rush in and avenge his death with the utmost savagery. 45 A hundred girls are killed"—here Bertie emptied the remainder of the red ink over the devoted building—"and the surviving five hundred are dragged off to the French ships. 'I have lost a Marshal,' says Louis, 'but I do not go back empty-handed.'"

Harvey stole away from the room, and sought out his sister.	46
"Eleanor," he said, "the experiment—"	47
"Yes?"	48
"Has failed. We have begun too late."	49

Study Questions

1. Most of the paragraphs in "The Toys of Peace" consist of dialogue. Can you posit reasons for the author's use of those paragraphs *without* dialogue?
2. How old are the children? Do they seem precocious?
3. The appearance of John Stuart Mill is preceded by this sentence: "In an awful silence he disinterred a little lead figure of a man in black clothes." Comment on the connotative value of specific words in that sentence.
4. Can you find internal evidence—evidence of a linguistic nature—that suggests this story was not written by an American?
5. Why is the emphasis on gardening appropriate in a short story about war versus peace?
6. Why does "Saki" interrupt Harvey's statement—"Eleanor, the experiment has failed"—with Eleanor's question?

Martin Gansberg
38 WHO SAW MURDER DIDN'T CALL THE POLICE

Martin Gansberg (1920-   ) was born in Brooklyn. He received a Bachelor of Sciences degree from St. John's University. The article reprinted here is just one of many in a long, distinguished career as editor and reporter for *The New York Times;* he joined the *Times* staff in 1942, and for three years served as editor of the Paris international edition. Gansberg also taught for fifteen years at Fairleigh Dickinson University. His byline may be found in numerous periodicals besides the *Times.*

For more than half an hour 38 respectable, law-abiding citi- 1
zens in Queens watched a killer stalk and stab a woman in three separate
attacks in Kew Gardens.

Twice their chatter and the sudden glow of their bedroom lights in- 2
terrupted him and frightened him off. Each time he returned, sought her
out, and stabbed her again. Not one person telephoned the police during
the assault; one witness called after the woman was dead.

That was two weeks ago today.   3

Still shocked is Assistant Chief Inspector Frederick M. Lussen, in 4
charge of the borough's detectives and a veteran of 25 years of homicide
investigations. He can give a matter-of-fact recitation on many murders.
But the Kew Gardens slaying baffles him — not because it is a murder,
but because the "good people" failed to call the police.

"As we have reconstructed the crime," he said, "the assailant had 5
three chances to kill this woman during a 35-minute period. He returned
twice to complete the job. If we had been called when he first attacked,
the woman might not be dead now."

This is what the police say happened beginning at 3:20 A.M. in the 6
staid, middle-class, tree-lined Austin Street area:

Twenty-eight-year-old Catherine Genovese, who was called Kitty by 7
almost everyone in the neighborhood, was returning home from her job
as manager of a bar in Hollis. She parked her red Fiat in a lot adjacent to
the Kew Gardens Long Island Rail Road Station, facing Mowbray Place.
Like many residents of the neighborhood, she had parked there day after
day since her arrival from Connecticut a year ago, although the railroad
frowns on the practice.

She turned off the lights of her car, locked the door, and started to 8
walk the 100 feet to the entrance of her apartment at 82–70 Austin
Street, which is in a Tudor building, with stores in the first floor and
apartments on the second.

The entrance to the apartment is in the rear of the building because 9
the front is rented to retail stores. At night the quiet neighborhood is
shrouded in the slumbering darkness that marks most residential areas.

Miss Genovese noticed a man at the far end of the lot, near a seven- 10
story apartment house at 82–40 Austin Street. She halted. Then, nervously, she headed up Austin Street toward Lefferts Boulevard, where
there is a call box to the 102nd Police Precinct in nearby Richmond Hill.

She got as far as a street light in front of a bookstore before the man 11
grabbed her. She screamed. Lights went on in the 10-story apartment
house at 82–67 Austin Street, which faces the bookstore. Windows slid
open and voices punctuated the early-morning stillness.

Miss Genovese screamed: "Oh, my God, he stabbed me! Please help 12
me! Please help me!"

From one of the upper windows in the apartment house, a man 13
called down: "Let that girl alone!"

The assailant looked up at him, shrugged and walked down Austin 14
Street toward a white sedan parked a short distance away. Miss Genovese
struggled to her feet.

Lights went out. The killer returned to Miss Genovese, now trying to   15
make her way around the side of the building by the parking lot to get
to her apartment. The assailant stabbed her again.

"I'm dying!" she shrieked. "I'm dying!"   16

Windows were opened again, and lights went on in many apartments.   17
The assailant got into his car and drove away. Miss Genovese staggered
to her feet. A city bus, O-10, the Lefferts Boulevard line to Kennedy International Airport, passed. It was 3:35 A.M.

The assailant returned. By then, Miss Genovese had crawled to the   18
back of the building, where the freshly painted brown doors to the apartment house held out hope for safety. The killer tried the first door; she
wasn't there. At the second door, 82-62 Austin Street, he saw her
slumped on the floor at the foot of the stairs. He stabbed her a third
time — fatally.

It was 3:50 by the time the police received their first call, from a   19
man who was a neighbor of Miss Genovese. In two minutes they were at
the scene. The neighbor, a 70-year-old woman, and another woman were
the only persons on the street. Nobody else came forward.

The man explained that he had called the police after much deliber-   20
ation. He had phoned a friend in Nassau County for advice and then he
had crossed the roof of the building to the apartment of the elderly
woman to get her to make the call.

"I didn't want to get involved," he sheepishly told the police.   21

Six days later, the police arrested Winston Moseley, a 29-year-old   22
business-machine operator, and charged him with homicide. Moseley had
no previous record. He is married, has two children and owns a home at
133-19 Sutter Avenue, South Ozone Park, Queens. On Wednesday, a
court committed him to Kings County Hospital for psychiatric observation.

When questioned by the police, Moseley also said that he had slain   23
Mrs. Annie May Johnson, 24, of 146-12 133d Avenue, Jamaica, on Feb.
29 and Barbara Kralik, 15, of 174-17 140th Avenue, Springfield Gardens, last July. In the Kralik case, the police are holding Alvin L. Mitch-
ell, who is said to have confessed that slaying.

The police stressed how simple it would have been to have gotten in   24
touch with them. "A phone call," said one of the detectives, "would have
done it." The police may be reached by dialing "0" for operator or
SPring 7-3100.

Today witnesses from the neighborhood, which is made up of one-   25
family homes in the $35,000 to $60,000 range with the exception of the
two apartment houses near the railroad station, find it difficult to explain
why they didn't call the police.

A housewife, knowingly if quite casually, said, "We thought it was a   26
lover's quarrel." A husband and wife both said, "Frankly, we were afraid."
They seemed aware of the fact that events might have been different. A
distraught woman, wiping her hands in her apron, said, "I didn't want 'my
husband to get involved."

One couple, now willing to talk about that night, said they heard the   27 first screams. The husband looked thoughtfully at the bookstore where the killer first grabbed Miss Genovese.

"We went to the window to see what was happening," he said, "but the light from our bedroom made it difficult to see the street." The wife, still apprehensive, added: "I put out the light and we were able to see better." 28

Asked why they hadn't called the police, she shrugged and replied: "I don't know." 29

A man peeked out from a slight opening in the doorway to his apartment and rattled off an account of the killer's second attack. Why hadn't he called the police at the time? "I was tired," he said without emotion. "I went back to bed." 30

It was 4:25 A.M. when the ambulance arrived to take the body of Miss Genovese. It drove off. "Then," a solemn police detective said, "the people came out." 31

Study Questions

1. This article was written for *The New York Times*. How does the journalistic style differ from the styles of the more traditional essayists in this book?

2. The police account of what happened begins with the sixth paragraph. Where does the account end? What transition does the author make at that point?

3. What is the implication of the first sentence? In what sense are *respectable* and *law-abiding* redefined?

4. Cite specific words that indicate Gansberg has a definite attitude about his subject. What parts of speech are these words?

5. Gansberg undoubtedly choose certain quotations and eliminated others. Posit reasons for his selections.

6. Comment on the meaning and effectiveness of the concluding paragraph.

Jacques Barzun
IN FAVOR OF CAPITAL PUNISHMENT

Jacques Barzun (1907–   ) was born in France and became a United States citizen in 1933. At Columbia University he earned an A.B. (1927), M.A. (1928), and Ph.D. (1932). His career on the faculty at Columbia has included positions as Professor of History, Dean of the Faculties and Provost, and University Professor of History. He is a member of the editorial board of the *American Scholar,* and president of the Institute of Arts and Letters. Barzun's many books include *The House of Intellect* (1959), *Classic, Romantic, and Modern* (1961), *Berlioz and the Romantic Century* (1969), and *The Use and Abuse of Art* (1974).

A passing remark of mine in the *Mid-Century* magazine has 1 brought me a number of letters and a sheaf of pamphlets against capital punishment. The letters, sad and reproachful, offer me the choice of pleading ignorance or being proved insensitive. I am asked whether I know that there exists a worldwide movement for the abolition of capital punishment which has everywhere enlisted able men of every profession, including the law. I am told that the death penalty is not only inhuman but also unscientific, for rapists and murderers are really sick people who should be cured, not killed. I am invited to use my imagination and acknowledge the unbearable horror of every form of execution.

I am indeed aware that the movement for abolition is widespread 2 and articulate, especially in England. It is headed there by my old friend and publisher, Mr. Victor Gollancz, and it numbers such well-known writers as Arthur Koestler, C. H. Rolph, James Avery Joyce and Sir John Barry. Abroad as at home the profession of psychiatry tends to support the cure principle, and many liberal newspapers, such as the *Observer,* are committed to abolition. In the United States there are at least twenty-five state leagues working to the same end, plus a national league and several church councils, notably the Quaker and the Episcopal.

The assemblage of so much talent and enlightened goodwill behind a 3 single proposal must give pause to anyone who supports the other side, and in the attempt to make clear my views, which are now close to unpopular, I start out by granting that my conclusion is arguable; that is, I am still open to conviction, *provided* some fallacies and frivolities in the

Reprinted from *The American Scholar,* Volume 31, Number 2, Spring 1962. Copyright © 1962 by the United Chapters of Phi Beta Kappa. By permission of the publishers.

abolitionist argument are first disposed of and the difficulties not ignored but overcome. I should be glad to see this happen, not only because there is pleasure in the spectacle of an airtight case, but also because I am not more sanguinary than my neighbor and I should welcome the discovery of safeguards — for society *and* the criminal — other than killing. But I say it again, these safeguards must really meet, not evade or postpone, the difficulties I am about to describe. Let me add before I begin that I shall probably not answer any more letters on this arousing subject. If this printed exposition does not do justice to my cause, it is not likely that I can do better in the hurry of private correspondence.

I readily concede at the outset that present ways of dealing out capital punishment are as revolting as Mr. Koestler says in his harrowing volume, *Hanged by the Neck.* Like many of our prisons, our modes of execution should change. But this objection to barbarity does not mean that capital punishment — or rather, judicial homicide — should not go on. The illicit jump we find here, on the threshold of the inquiry, is characteristic of the abolitionist and must be disallowed at every point. Let us bear in mind the possibility of devising a painless, sudden and dignified death, and see whether its administration is justifiable. 4

The four main arguments advanced against the death penalty are: *1.* punishment for crime is a primitive idea rooted in revenge; *2.* capital punishment does not deter; *3.* judicial error being possible, taking life is an appalling risk; *4.* a civilized state, to deserve its name, must uphold, not violate, the sanctity of human life. 5

I entirely agree with the first pair of propositions, which is why, a moment ago, I replaced the term capital punishment with "judicial homicide." The uncontrollable brute whom I want put out of the way is not to be punished for his misdeeds, nor used as an example or a warning; he is to be killed for the protection of others, like the wolf that escaped not long ago in a Connecticut suburb. No anger, vindictiveness or moral conceit need preside over the removal of such dangers. But a man's inability to control his violent impulses or to imagine the fatal consequences of his acts should be a presumptive reason for his elimination from society. This generality covers drunken driving and teen-age racing on public highways, as well as incurable obsessive violence; it might be extended (as I shall suggest later) to other acts that destroy, precisely, the moral basis of civilization. 6

But why kill? I am ready to believe the statistics tending to show that the prospect of his own death does not stop the murderer. For one thing he is often a blind egotist, who cannot conceive the possibility of his own death. For another, detection would have to be infallible to deter the more imaginative who, although afraid, think they can escape discovery. Lastly, as Shaw long ago pointed out, hanging the wrong man will deter as effectively as hanging the right one. So, once again, why kill? If I agree that moral progress means an increasing respect for human life, how can I oppose abolition? 7

I do so because on this subject of human life, which is to me the heart of the controversy, I find the abolitionist inconsistent, narrow or blind. The propaganda for abolition speaks in hushed tones of the sanc- 8 tity of human life, as if the mere statement of it as an absolute should silence all opponents who have any moral sense. But most of the abolitionists belong to nations that spend half their annual income on weapons of war and that honor research to perfect means of killing. These good people vote without a qualm for the political parties that quite sensibly arm their country to the teeth. The West today does not seem to be the time or place to invoke the absolute sanctity of human life. As for the clergymen in the movement, we may be sure from the experience of two previous world wars that they will bless our arms and pray for victory when called upon, the sixth commandment notwithstanding.

"Oh, but we mean the sanctity of life *within* the nation!" Very well: 9 is the movement then campaigning also against the principle of self-defense? Absolute sanctity means letting the cutthroat have his sweet will of you, even if you have a poker handy to bash him with, for you might kill. And again, do we hear any protest against the police firing at criminals on the street—mere bank robbers usually—and doing this, often enough, with an excited marksmanship that misses the artist and hits the bystander? The absolute sanctity of human life is, for the abolitionist, a slogan rather than a considered proposition.

Yet it deserves examination, for upon our acceptance or rejection of 10 it depend such other highly civilized possibilities as euthanasia and seemly suicide. The inquiring mind also wants to know, why the sanctity of *human* life alone? My tastes do not run to household pets, but I find something less than admirable in the uses to which we put animals—in zoos, laboratories, and space machines—without the excuse of the ancient law, "Eat or be eaten."

It should moreover be borne in mind that this argument about sanc- 11 tity applies—or would apply—to about ten persons a year in Great Britain and to between fifty and seventy-five in the United States. These are the average numbers of those executed in recent years. The count by itself should not, of course, affect our judgment of the principle: one life spared or forfeited is as important, morally, as a hundred thousand. But it should inspire a comparative judgment: there are hundreds and indeed thousands whom, in our concern with the horrors of execution, we forget: on the one hand, the victims of violence; on the other, the prisoners in our jails.

The victims are easy to forget. Social science tends steadily to mark a 12 preference for the troubled, the abnormal, the problem case. Whether it is poverty, mental disorder, delinquency or crime, the "patient material" monopolizes the interest of increasing groups of people among the most generous and learned. Psychiatry and moral liberalism go together; the application of law as we have known it is thus coming to be regarded as an historic prelude to social work, which may replace it entirely. Modern literature makes the most of this same outlook, caring only for the disturbed spirit, scorning as bourgeois those who pay their way and do *not* stab their friends. All the while the determinism of natural science reinforces the assumption that society causes its own evils. A French jurist, for example, says that in order to understand crime we must first brush aside all ideas of Responsibility. He means the criminal's and takes for granted that of society. The murderer kills because reared in a broken home or, conversely, because at an early age he witnessed his parents making love. Out of such cases, which make pathetic reading in the literature of modern criminology, is born the abolitionist's state of mind: we dare not kill those we are beginning to understand so well.

If, moreover, we turn to the accounts of the crimes committed by 13 these unfortunates, who are the victims? Only dull ordinary people going about their business. We are sorry, of course, but they do not interest science on its march. Balancing, for example, the sixty to seventy criminals executed annually in the United States, there were the seventy to eighty housewives whom George Cvek robbed, raped and usually killed during the months of a career devoted to proving his virility. "It is too bad." Cvek alone seems instructive, even though one of the law officers who helped track him down quietly remarks: "As to the extent that his villainies disturbed family relationships, or how many women are still haunted by the specter of an experience they have never disclosed to another living soul, those questions can only lead themselves to sterile conjecture."

The remote results are beyond our ken, but it is not idle to speculate 14 about those whose death by violence fills the daily two inches at the back of respectable newspapers — the old man sunning himself on a park bench and beaten to death by four hoodlums, the small children abused and strangled, the middle-aged ladies on a hike assaulted and killed, the family terrorized by a released or escaped lunatic, the half-dozen working people massacred by the sudden maniac, the boatload of persons dispatched by the skipper, the mindless assaults upon schoolteachers and shopkeepers by the increasing horde of dedicated killers in our great cities. Where does the sanctity of life begin?

It is all very well to say that many of these killers are themselves 15 "children," that is, minors. Doubtless a nine-year-old mind is housed in that 150 pounds of unguided muscle. Grant, for argument's sake, that the misdeed is "the fault of society," trot out the broken home and the slum environment. The question then is, What shall we do, not in the Utopian city of tomorrow, but here and now? The "scientific" means of cure are more than uncertain. The apparatus of detention only increases the killer's antisocial animus. Reformatories and mental hospitals are full and have an understandable bias toward discharging their inmates. Some of these are indeed "cured" — so long as they stay under a rule. The stress of the social free-for-all throws them back on their violent modes of self-expression. At that point I agree that society has failed — twice: it has twice failed the victims, whatever may be its guilt toward the killer.

As in all great questions, the moralist must choose, and choosing has 16 a price. I happen to think that if a person of adult body has not been endowed with adequate controls against irrationally taking the life of another, that person must be judicially, painlessly, regretfully killed before that mindless body's horrible automation repeats.

I say "irrationally" taking life, because it is often possible to feel 17 great sympathy with a murderer. Certain *crimes passionnels* can be forgiven without being condoned. Blackmailers invite direct retribution. Long provocation can be an excuse, as in that engaging case of some years ago, in which a respectable carpenter of seventy found he could no longer stand the incessant nagging of his wife. While she excoriated him from her throne in the kitchen—a daily exercise for fifty years—the husband went to his bench and came back with a hammer in each hand to settle the score. The testimony to his character, coupled with the sincerity implied by the two hammers, was enough to have him sent into quiet and brief seclusion.

But what are we to say of the type of motive disclosed in a journal 18 published by the inmates of one of our Federal penitentiaries? The author is a bank robber who confesses that money is not his object:

> My mania for power, socially, sexually, and otherwise can feel no degree of satisfaction until I feel sure I have struck the ultimate of submission and terror in the minds and bodies of my victims.... It's very difficult to explain all the queer fascinating sensations pounding and surging through me while I'm holding a gun on a victim, watching his body tremble and sweat.... This is the moment when all the rationalized hypocrisies of civilization are suddenly swept away and two men stand there facing each other morally and ethically naked, and right and wrong are the absolute commands of the man behind the gun.

This confused echo of modern literature and modern science defines 19 the choice before us. Anything deserving the name of cure for such a man presupposes not only a laborious individual psychoanalysis, with the means to conduct and to sustain it, socially and economically, but also a re-education of the mind, so as to throw into correct perspective the garbled ideas of Freud and Nietzsche, Gide and Dostoevski, which this power-seeker and his fellows have derived from the culture and temper of our times. Ideas are tenacious and give continuity to emotion. Failing a second birth of heart and mind, we must ask: How soon will this sufferer sacrifice a bank clerk in the interests of making civilization less hypocritical? And we must certainly question the wisdom of affording him more than one chance. The abolitionists' advocacy of an unconditional "let live" is in truth part of the same cultural tendency that animates the killer. The Western peoples' revulsion from power in domestic and foreign policy has made of the state a sort of counterpart of the bank robber: both having power and neither knowing how to use it. Both waste lives because hypnotized by irrelevant ideas and crippled by contradictory emotions. If psychiatry were sure of its ground in diagnosing the individual case, a philosopher might consider whether such dangerous obsessions should not be guarded against by judicial homicide *before* the shooting starts.

I raise the question not indeed to recommend the prophylactic exe- 20 cution of potential murderers, but to introduce the last two perplexities that the abolitionists dwarf or obscure by their concentration on changing an isolated penalty. One of these is the scale by which to judge the offenses society wants to repress. I can for example imagine a truly democratic state in which it would be deemed a form of treason punishable by death to create a disturbance in any court or deliberative assembly. The aim would be to recognize the sanctity of orderly discourse in arriving at justice, assessing criticism and defining policy. Under such a law, a natural selection would operate to remove permanently from the scene persons who, let us say, neglect argument in favor of banging on the desk with their shoe. Similarly , a bullying minority in a diet, parliament or skupshtina would be prosecuted for treason to the most sacred institutions when fists or flying inkwells replace rhetoric. That the mere suggestion of such a law sounds ludicrous shows how remote we are from civilized institutions, and hence how gradual should be our departure from the severity of judicial homicide.

I say gradual and I do not mean standing still. For there is one form 21 of barbarity in our law that I want to see mitigated before any other. I mean imprisonment. The enemies of capital punishment—and liberals generally—seem to be satisfied with any legal outcome so long as they themselves avoid the vicarious guilt of shedding blood. They speak of the sanctity of life, but have no concern with its quality. They give no impression of ever having read what it is certain they have read, from Wilde's *De Profundis* to the latest account of prison life by a convicted homosexual. Despite the infamy of concentration camps, despite Mr. Charles Burney's remarkable work, *Solitary Confinement,* despite riots in prisons, despite the round of escape, recapture and return in chains, the abolitionists' imagination tells them nothing about the reality of being caged. They read without a qualm, indeed they read with rejoicing, the hideous irony of "Killer Gets Life"; they sigh with relief instead of horror. They do not see and suffer the cell, the drill, the clothes, the stench, the food; they do not feel the sexual racking of young and old bodies, the hateful promiscuity, the insane monotony, the mass degradation, the impotent hatred. They do not remember from Silvio Pellico that only a strong political faith, with a hope of final victory, can steel a man to endure long detention. They forget that Joan of Arc, when offered "life," preferred burning at the stake. Quite of another mind, the abolitionists point with pride to the "model prisoners" that murderers often turn out to be. As if a model prisoner were not, first, a contradiction in terms, and second, an exemplar of what a free society should not want.

I said a moment ago that the happy advocates of the life sentence ap- 22 pear not to have understood what we know they have read. No more do they appear to read what they themselves write. In the preface to his useful volume of cases, *Hanged in Error,* Mr. Leslie Hale, M.P., refers to the tardy recognition of a minor miscarriage of justice—one year in jail: "The prisoner emerged to find that his wife had died and that his children and his aged parents had been removed to the workhouse. By the time a small payment had been assessed as 'compensation' the victim was incurably insane." So far we are as indignant with the law as Mr. Hale. But what comes next? He cites the famous Evans case, in which it is very probable that the wrong man was hanged, and he exclaims: "While such mistakes are possible, should society impose an irrevocable sentence?"

Does Mr. Hale really ask us to believe that the sentence passed on the first man, whose wife died and who went insane, was in any sense *revocable*? Would not any man rather be Evans dead than that other wretch "emerging" with his small compensation and his reasons for living gone?

Nothing is revocable here below, imprisonment least of all. The 23 agony of a trial itself is punishment, and acquittal wipes out nothing. Read the heart-rending diary of William Wallace, accused quite implausibly of having murdered his wife and "saved" by the Court of Criminal Appeals — but saved for what? Brutish ostracism by everyone and a few years of solitary despair. The cases of Adolf Beck, of Oscar Slater, of the unhappy Brooklyn bank teller who vaguely resembled a forger and spent eight years in Sing Sing only to "emerge" a broken, friendless, useless, "compensated" man — all these, if the dignity of the individual has any meaning, had better have been dead before the prison door ever opened for them. This is what counsel always says to the jury in the course of a murder trial and counsel is right: far better hang this man than "give him life." For my part, I would choose death without hesitation. If that option is abolished, a demand will one day be heard to claim it as a privilege in the name of human dignity. I shall believe in the abolitionist's present views only after he has emerged from twelve months in a convict cell.

The detached observer may want to interrupt here and say that the 24 argument has now passed from reasoning to emotional preference. Whereas the objector to capital punishment *feels* that death is the greatest of evils, I *feel* that imprisonment is worse than death. A moment's thought will show that feeling is the appropriate arbiter. All reasoning about what is right, civilized and moral rests upon sentiment, like mathematics. Only, in trying to persuade others, it is important to single out the fundamental feeling, the prime intuition, and from it to reason justly. In my view, to profess respect for human life and be willing to see it spent in a penitentiary is to entertain liberal feelings frivolously. To oppose the death penalty because, unlike a prison term, it is irrevocable is to argue fallaciously.

In the propaganda for abolishing the death sentence the recital of nu- 25 merous miscarriages of justice commits the same error and implies the same callousness: what is at fault in our present system is not the sentence but the fallible procedure. Capital cases being one in a thousand or more, who can be cheerful at the thought of all the "revocable" errors? What the miscarriages point to is the need for reforming the jury system, the rules of evidence, the customs of prosecution, the machinery of appeal. The failure to see that this is the great task reflects the sentimentality I spoke of earlier, that which responds chiefly to the excitement of the unusual. A writer on Death and the Supreme Court is at pains to point out that when the tribunal reviews a capital case, the judges are particularly anxious and careful. What a left-handed compliment to the highest judicial conscience of the country! Fortunately, some of the champions of the misjudged see the issue more clearly. Many of those who are thought wrongly convicted now languish in jail because the jury was uncertain or because a doubting governor commuted the death sentence. Thus Dr. Samuel H. Sheppard, Jr., convicted of his wife's murder in the second degree is serving a sentence that is supposed to run for the term of his natural life. The story of his numerous trials, as told by Mr. Paul Holmes, suggests that police incompetence, newspaper demagogy, public envy of affluence and the mischances of legal procedure fashioned the result. But Dr. Sheppard's vindicator is under no illusion as to the conditions that this "lucky" evader of the electric chair will face if he is granted parole after ten years: "It will carry with it no right to resume his life as a physician. His privilege to practice medicine was blotted out with his conviction. He must all his life bear the stigma of a parolee, subject to unceremonious return to confinement for life for the slightest misstep. More than this, he must live out his life as a convicted murderer."

What does the moral conscience of today think it is doing? If such a 26 man is a dangerous repeater of violent acts, what right has the state to let him loose after ten years? What is, in fact, the meaning of a "life sentence" that peters out long before life? Paroling looks suspiciously like an expression of social remorse for the pain of incarceration, coupled with a wish to avoid "unfavorable publicity" by freeing a suspect. The man is let out when the fuss has died down; which would mean that he was not under lock and key for our protection at all. He *was* being punished, just a little—for so prison seems in the abolitionist's distorted view, and in the jury's and the prosecutor's, whose "second-degree" murder suggests killing someone "just a little."*

If, on the other hand, execution and life imprisonment are judged to 27 serve and the accused is expected to be harmless hereafter—punishment being ruled out as illiberal—what has society gained by wrecking his life and damaging that of his family?

What we accept, and what the abolitionist will clamp upon us all the 28 more firmly if he succeeds, is an incoherence which is not remedied by the belief that second-degree murder merits a kind of second-degree death; that a doubt as to the identity of a killer is resolved by commuting real death into intolerable life; and that our ignorance whether a maniac will strike again can be hedged against by measuring "good behavior" within the gates and then releasing the subject upon the public in the true spirit of experimentation.

These are some of the thoughts I find I cannot escape when I read 29 and reflect upon this grave subject. If, as I think, they are relevant to any discussion of change and reform, resting as they do on the direct and concrete perception of what happens, then the simple meliorists who expect to breathe a purer air by abolishing the death penalty are deceiving themselves and us. The issue is for the public to judge; but I for one shall not sleep easier for knowing that in England and America and the West generally a hundred more human beings are kept alive in degrading

*The British Homicide Act of 1957, Section 2, implies the same reasoning in its definition of "diminished responsibility" for certain forms of mental abnormality. The whole question of irrationality and crime is in utter confusion, on both sides of the Atlantic.

conditions to face a hopeless future; while others — possibly less conscious, certainly less controlled — benefit from a premature freedom dangerous alike to themselves and society. In short, I derive no comfort
from the illusion that in giving up one manifest protection of the law-
abiding, we who might well be in any of these three roles — victim, prisoner, licensed killer — have struck a blow for the sanctity of human life.

Study Questions

1. How are the introduction and conclusion related?
2. What specific purpose is served by the italics in this essay?
3. Analyze the argument in paragraph 15.
4. Where are the major turning points in Barzun's arguments?
5. To what extent do you feel the author's style and diction
   are literary rather than colloquial? Cite examples to show
   what you mean.

Abe Fortas
THE CASE AGAINST CAPITAL PUNISHMENT

Abe Fortas (1910–   ) was born in Memphis, Tennessee. He received an A.B. from Southwestern College in Memphis in 1930 and
an LL.B. from Yale in 1933. Throughout his distinguished legal and
public career Fortas has contributed regularly to legal periodicals and to
others of a more general nature. He has served the federal government as Under Secretary of Interior, acting general counsel to the
National Power Policy Commission, advisor to the U. S. delegation
to the United Nations, and Associate Justice of the Supreme Court,
among many such positions. He has also been Chairman of the
Board of the Kennedy Center for the Performing Arts.

I believe that most Americans, even those who feel it is nec-   1
essary, are repelled by capital punishment; the attitude is deeply rooted
in our moral reverence for life, the Judeo-Christian belief that man is
created in the image of God. Many Americans were pleased when on

June 29, 1972, the Supreme Court of the United States set aside death sentences for the first time in its history. On that day the Court handed down its decision in *Furman v. Georgia,* holding that the capital-punishment statutes of three states were unconstitutional because they gave the jury complete discretion to decide whether to impose the death penalty or a lesser punishment in capital cases. For this reason, a bare majority of five Justices agreed that the statutes violated the "cruel and unusual punishment" clause of the Eighth Amendment.

The result of this decision was paradoxical. Thirty-six states proceeded to adopt new death-penalty statutes designed to meet the Supreme Court's objection, and beginning in 1974, the number of persons sentenced to death soared. In 1975 alone, 285 defendants were condemned — more than double the number sentenced to death in any previously reported year. Of those condemned in 1975, 93 percent had been convicted of murder; the balance had been convicted of rape or kidnapping. 2

The constitutionality of these death sentences and of the new statutes, however, was quickly challenged, and on July 2, 1976, the Supreme Court announced its rulings in five test cases. It rejected "mandatory" statutes that automatically imposed death sentences for defined capital offenses, but it approved statutes that set out "standards" to guide the jury in deciding whether to impose the death penalty. These laws, the court ruled, struck a reasonable balance between giving the jury some guidance and allowing it to take into account the background and character of the defendant and the circumstances of the crime. 3

The decisions may settle the basic constitutional issue until there is a change in the composition of the Court, but many questions remain. Some of these are questions of considerable constitutional importance, such as those relating to appellate review. Others have to do with the sensational issues that accompany capital punishment in our society. Gary Gilmore generated an enormous national debate by insisting on an inalienable right to force the people of Utah to kill him. So did a district judge who ruled that television may present to the American people the spectacle of a man being electrocuted by the state of Texas. 4

The recent turns of the legislative and judicial process have done nothing to dispose of the matter of conscience and judgment for the individual citizen. The debate over it will not go away; indeed, it has gone on for centuries. 5

Through the years, the number of offenses for which the state can kill the offender has declined. Once, hundreds of capital crimes, including stealing more than a shilling from a person and such religious misdeeds as blasphemy and witchcraft, were punishable by death. But in the United States today, only two principal categories remain — major assaults upon persons, such as murder, kidnapping, rape, bombing and arson, and the major political crimes of espionage and treason. In addition, there are more than 20 special capital crimes in some of our jurisdictions, including train robbery and aircraft piracy. In fact, however, in recent years murder has accounted for about 90 percent of the death sentences and rape for most of the others, and the number of states prescribing the death penalty for rape is declining. 6

At least 45 nations, including most of the Western democracies, have 7
abolished or abandoned capital punishment. Ten U.S. states have no provision for the death penalty. In four, the statutes authorizing it have
recently been declared unconstitutional under state law. The Federal
Criminal Code authorizes capital punishment for various offenses, but
there have been no executions under Federal civil law (excluding military
jurisdiction) since the early 1960's.

Public-opinion polls in our nation have seesawed, with some in- 8
dication that they are affected by the relative stability or unrest in our
society at the time of polling. In 1966, a public-opinion poll reported
that 42 percent of the American public favored capital punishment, 47
percent opposed it and 11 percent were undecided. In 1972–1973, both
the Gallup and Harris polls showed that 57 percent to 59 percent of the
people favored capital punishment, and a recent Gallup poll asserts that
65 percent favor it.

Practically all scholars and experts agree that capital punishment can- 9
not be justified as a significantly useful instrument of law enforcement or
of penology. There is no evidence that it reduces the serious crimes to
which it is addressed. Professor William Bowers, for example, concludes
in his excellent study, "Executions in America" that statutory or judicial
developments that change the risk of execution are not paralleled by
variations in homicide rates. He points out that over the last 30 years,
homicide rates have remained relatively constant while the number of executions has steadily declined. He concludes that the "death penalty, as
we use it, exerts no influence on the extent or rate of capital offenses."

I doubt that fear of the possible penalty affects potential capital of- 10
fenders. The vast majority of capital offenses are murders committed in
the course of armed robbery that result from fear, tension or anger of
the moment, and murders that are the result of passion or mental disorder. The only deterrence derived from the criminal process probably
results from the fear of apprehension and arrest, and possibly from the
fear of significant punishment. There is little, if any, difference between
the possible deterrent effect of life imprisonment and that of the death
penalty.

In fact, the statistical possibility of execution for a capital offense is 11
extremely slight. We have not exceeded 100 executions a year since
1951, although the number of homicides in death-sentence jurisdictions
alone has ranged from 7,500 to 10,000. In 1960, there were only 56 executions in the United States, and the number declined each year thereafter. There have been no executions since 1967. In the peak years of
1933, there were only 199 executions in the United States, while the average number of homicides in all of the states authorizing capital punishment for 1932–33 was 11,579.

A potential murderer who rationally weighted the possibility of pun- 12
ishment by death (if there is such a person), would figure that he has
considerably better than a 98 percent chance of avoiding execution in the
average capital-punishment state. In the years from 1960 to 1967, his

chances of escaping execution were better than 99.5 percent. The professional or calculating murderer is not apt to be deterred by such odds.

An examination of the reason for the infrequency of execution is illuminating: 13

(1) Juries are reluctant to condemn a human being to death. The evidence is that they are often prone to bring in a verdict of a lesser offense, or even to acquit, if the alternative is to impose the death penalty. The reluctance is, of course, diminished when powerful emotions come into play — as in the case of a black defendant charged with the rape of a white woman. 14

(2) Prosecutors do not ask for the death penalty in the case of many, perhaps a majority, of those who are arrested for participation in murder or other capital offenses. In part, this is due to the difficulty of persuading juries to impose death sentences; in part, it is due to plea bargaining. In capital cases involving more than one participant, the prosecutor seldom asks for the death penalty for more than one of them. Frequently, in order to obtain the powerful evidence necessary to win a death sentence, he will make a deal with all participants except one. The defendants who successfully "plea bargain" testify against the defendant chosen for the gallows and in return receive sentences of imprisonment. 15

This system may be defensible in noncapital cases because of practical exigencies, but it is exceedingly disturbing where the result is to save the witness's life at the hazard of the life of another person. The possibility is obvious that the defendant chosen for death will be selected on a basis that has nothing to do with comparative guilt, and the danger is inescapable that the beneficiary of the plea-bargain, in order to save his life, will lie or give distorted testimony. To borrow a phrase from Justice Byron R. White: "This is a grisly trade. . . ." A civilized nation should not kill A on the basis of testimony obtained from B in exchange for B's life. 16

(3) As a result of our doubts about capital punishment, and our basic aversion to it, we have provided many escape hatches. Every latitude is allowed the defendant and his counsel in the trial; most lawyers representing a capital offender quite properly feel that they must exhaust every possible defense, however technical or unlikely; appeals are generally a matter of right; slight legal errors, which would be disregarded in other types of cases, are grounds for reversal; governors have, and liberally exercise, the power to commute death sentences. Only the rare, unlucky defendant is likely to be executed when the process is all over. 17

In 1975, 65 prisoners on death row had their death penalty status changed as a result of appeals, court actions, commutation, resentencing, etc. This was more than 20 percent of the new deathrow prisoners admitted during that peak year. 18

It is clear that American prosecutors, judges and juries are not likely to cause the execution of enough capital offenders to increase the claimed deterrent effect of capital-punishment laws or to reduce the "lottery" effect of freakish selection. People generally may favor capital punishment in the abstract but pronouncing that a living person shall be 19 killed is quite another matter. Experience shows that juries are reluctant to order that a person be killed. Where juries have been commanded by law to impose the death penalty, they have often chosen to acquit or, in modern times to convict of a lesser offense rather than to return a verdict that would result in execution.

The law is a human instrument administered by a vast number of different people in different circumstances, and we are inured to its many inequalities. Tweedledee may be imprisoned for five years for a given offense, while Tweedledum, convicted of a similar crime, may be back on the streets in a few months. We accept the inevitability of such discriminations although we don't approve of them, and we constantly seek to reduce their frequency and severity. But the taking of a life is different from any other punishment. It is final; it is ultimate; if it is erroneous, it is irreversible and beyond correction. It is an act in which the state is presuming to function so to speak, as the Lord's surrogate. 20

We have gone a long way toward recognition of the unique character of capital punishment. We insist that it be imposed for relatively few crimes of the most serious nature and that it be imposed only after elaborate precautions to reduce the possibility of error. We also inflict it in a fashion that avoids the extreme cruelty of such methods as drawing and quartering, though it still involves the barbaric rituals attendant upon electrocution, the gallows or the firing squad. 21

But fortunately, the death penalty is and will continue to be sought in only a handful of cases and rarely carried out. So long as the death penalty is a highly exceptional punishment, it will serve no deterrent or penological function; it will fulfill no pragmatic purpose of the state; and inevitably, its selective imposition will continue to be influenced by racial and class prejudice. 22

All of the standards that can be written, all of the word magic and the procedural safeguards that can be devised to compel juries to impose the death penalty on capital offenders without exception or discrimination will be of no avail. In 1971 capital-punishment case, Justice John Harlan wrote on the subject of standards. "They do no more," he said, "than suggest some subjects for the jury to consider during its deliberations, and [the criteria] bear witness to the intractable nature of the problem of 'standards' which the history of capital punishment has from the beginning reflected." 23

Form and substance are important to the life of the law, but when the law deals with a fundamental moral and constitutional issue — the disposition of human life — the use of such formulas is not an acceptable substitute for a correct decision on the substance of the matter. 24

The discrimination that is inescapable in the selection of the few to be killed under our capital-punishment laws is unfortunately of the most invidious and unacceptable sort. Most of those who are chosen for extinction are black (53.5 percent in the years 1930 to 1975). The wheels of chance and prejudice begin to spin in the police station; they continue through the prosecutor's choice of defendants for whom he will ask the 25 death penalty and those he will choose to spare; they continue through the trial and in the jury room, and finally they appear in the Governor's office. Solemn "presumptions of law" that the selection will be made rationally and uniformly violate human experience and the evidence of the facts. Efforts to bring about equality of sentence by writing "standards" or verbal formulas may comfort the heart of the legislator or jurist, but they can hardly satisfy his intelligence.

26 If deterrence is not a sufficient reason to justify capital punishment laws and if their selective application raises such disturbing questions, what possible reason is there for their retention? One other substantive reason, advanced by eminent authorities, is that the execution of criminals is justifiable as "retribution." This is the argument that society should have the right to vent its anger or abhorrence against the offender, that it may justifiably impose a punishment people believe the criminal "deserves." Albert Camus, in a famous essay, says of capital punishment:

27 "Let us call it by the name which, for lack of any other nobility, will at least give the nobility of truth, and let us recognize it for what it is essentially: a revenge."

28 We may realize that deep-seated emotions underlie our capital-punishment laws, but there is a difference between our understanding of the motivation for capital punishment and our acceptance of it as an instrument of our society. We may appreciate that the *lex talionis,* the law of revenge, has it roots in the deep recesses of the human spirit, but that awareness is not a permissible reason for retaining capital punishment.

29 It is also argued that capital punishment is an ancient sanction that has been adopted by most of our legislatures after prolonged consideration and reconsideration, and that we should not override this history.

30 But the argument is not persuasive. If we were to restrict the implementation of our Bill of Rights, by either constitutional decisions or legislative judgments, to those practices that its provisions contemplated in 1791, we would indeed be a retarded society. In 1816, Thomas Jefferson wrote a letter in which he spoke of the need for constitutions as well as other laws and institutions to move forward "hand in hand with the progress of the human mind." He said, "We might as well require a man to wear still the coat which fitted him when a boy, as civilized society to remain ever under the regimen of their barbarous ancestors."

31 As early as 1910, the Supreme Court, in the case of *Weems v. United States,* applied this principle to a case in which the defendant had been sentenced to 15 years in prison for the crime of falsifying a public document as part of an embezzlement scheme. The Court held that the sentence was excessive and constituted "cruel and unusual punishment" in violation of the Eighth Amendment. In a remarkable opinion, Justice Joseph McKenna eloquently rejected the idea that prohibitions of the Bill of Rights, including the Eighth Amendment, must be limited to the practices to which they were addressed in 1791, when the great amendments were ratified. He said, "Time works changes, brings into existence new conditions and purposes. Therefore a principle, to be vital, must be ca-

pable of wider application than the mischief which gave it birth. This is peculiarly true of constitutions. They are not ephemeral enactments, designed to meet passing occasions." As to the "cruel and unusual punishment" clause of the Constitution, he said that it "is not fastened to the obsolete, but may acquire meaning as public opinion becomes enlightened by a humane justice."

We have also long recognized that the progressive implementation of 32 the Bill of Rights does not depend upon first obtaining a majority vote or a favorable Gallup or Harris poll. As the Supreme Court stated in the famous 1943 flag-salute case, "The very purpose of a Bill of Rights was to place [certain subjects] beyond the reach of majorities and officials...."

Indeed, despite our polls, public opinion is unfathomable; in the 33 words of Judge Jerome Frank, it is a "slithery shadow"; and if known, no one can predict how profound or shallow it is as of the moment, and how long it will persist. Basically, however, the obligation of legislators and judges who question whether a law or practice is or is not consonant with our Constitution is inescapable; it cannot be delegated to the Gallup poll, or to the ephemeral evidence of public opinion.

We will not eliminate the objections to capital punishment by legal 34 legerdemain, by "standards," by procedures or by word formulas. The issue is fundamental. It is wrong for the state to kill offenders; it is a wrong far exceeding the numbers involved. In exchange for the pointless exercise of killing a few people each year, we expose our society to brutalization; lower the essential value that is the basis of our civilization; a pervasive, unqualified respect for life. And we subject ourselves and our legal institutions to the gross spectacle of a pageant in which death provides degrading, distorting excitement. Justice Felix Frankfurter once pointed out: "I am strongly against capital punishment.... When life is at hazard in a trial, it sensationalizes the whole thing almost unwittingly; the effect on juries, the bar, the public, the judiciary, I regard as very bad. I think scientifically the claim of deterrence is not worth much. Whatever proof there may be in my judgment does not outweigh the social loss due to the inherent sensationalism of a trial for life."

Beyond all of these factors is the fundamental consideration: In the name of all that we believe in and hope for, why must we reserve to ourselves the right to kill 100 or 200 people? Why, when we can point to no tangible benefit; why, when in all honesty we must admit that we are not certain that we are accomplishing anything except serving the cause of "revenge" or retribution? Why, when we have bravely and nobly progressed so far in the recent past to create a decent, humane society, must we perpetuate the senseless barbarism of offical murder?

In 1971, speaking of the death penalty, Justice William O. Douglas 36 wrote: "We need not read procedural due process as designed to satisfy man's deep-seated sadistic instincts. We need not in deference to those sadistic instincts say we are bound by history from defining procedural due process so as to deny men fair trials."

I hope to believe we will conclude that the time has come for us to 37 join the company of those nations that have repudiated killing as an instrument of criminal law enforcement.

Study Questions

1. To what extent is the paradox discussed in the second paragraph tied to the belief stated in the first?
2. What are the major points in Fortas' case?
3. Comment on the use of statistics in this essay.
4. Barzun and Fortas are not writing directly for one another, but does either of them clearly seem to have bettered the other at any point in his essay?
5. Whose essay — Fortas' or Barzun's — seems the more reasoned? Is one of them more logical than the other? Which uses emotionally charged language to a greater extent?

George Orwell
A HANGING

George Orwell (1903–1950) was the pen name of Eric Blair, who was born in Bengal, India. He graduated from Eton, served with the Indian Imperial Police in Burma from 1922 to 1927, and then returned to England to begin his (1938), as a writer. His works include *Burmese Days* (1934), *Homage to Catalonia* (1938). *Dickens, Dali, and Others* (1946), and *Shooting an Elephant* (1950). His fame, however, is primarily the result of *Animal Farm* (1945) and *1984* (1949), the former one of the most famous modern satires and the latter a classic novel of social protest. His *Collected Essays* were published in 1969.

It was in Burma, a sodden morning of the rains. A sickly light, 1
like yellow tinfoil, was slanting over the high walls into the jail yard. We were waiting outside the condemned cells, a row of sheds fronted with double bars, like small animal cages. Each cell measured about ten feet by ten and was quite bare within except for a plank bed and a pot for drinking water. In some of them brown, silent men, were squatting at the inner bars, with their blankets draped round them. These were the condemned men, due to be hanged within the next week or two.

One prisoner had been brought out of his cell. He was a Hindu, a 2
puny wisp of a man, with a shaven head and vague liquid eyes. He had a thick, sprouting moustache, absurdly too big for his body, rather like the

From *Shooting an Elephant and Other Essays* by George Orwell, copyright, 1945, 1946, 1949, 1950, by Sonia Brownell Orwell. Reprinted by permission of Harcourt Brace Jovanovich, Inc.

moustache of a comic man on the films. Six tall Indian warders were guarding him and getting him ready for the gallows. Two of them stood by with rifles and fixed bayonets, while the others handcuffed him, passed a chain through his handcuffs and fixed it to their belts, and lashed his arms tight to his sides. They crowded very close about him, with their hands always on him in a careful, caressing grip, as though all the while feeling him to make sure he was there. It was like men handling a fish which is still alive and may jump back into the water. But he stood quite unresisting, yielding his arms limply to the ropes, as though he hardly noticed what was happening.

Eight o'clock struck and a bugle call, desolately thin in the wet air, 3 floated from the distant barracks. The superintendent of the jail, who was standing apart from the rest of us, moodily prodding the gravel with his stick, raised his head at the sound. He was an army doctor, with a grey toothbrush moustache and a gruff voice. "For God's sake hurry up, Francis," he said irritably. "The man ought to have been dead by this time. Aren't you ready yet?"

Francis, the head jailer, a fat Dravidian in a white drill suit and gold 4 spectacles, waved his black hand. "Yes sir, yes sir," he bubbled. "All iss satisfactorily prepared. The hangman iss waiting. We shall proceed."

"Well, quick march, then. The prisoners can't get their breakfast till 5 this job's over."

We set out for the gallows. Two warders marched on either side of 6 the prisoner, with their rifles at the slope; two others marched close against him, gripping him by arm and shoulder, as though at once pushing and supporting him. The rest of us, magistrates and the like, followed behind. Suddenly, when we had gone ten yeards, the procession stopped short without any order or warning. A dreadful thing had happened—a dog, come goodness knows whence, had appeared in the yard. It came bounding among us with a loud volley of barks and leapt round us wagging its whole body, wild with glee at finding so many human beings together. It was a large woolly dog, half Airedale, half pariah. For a moment it pranced round us, and then, before anyone could stop it, it had made a dash for the prisoner, and jumping up tried to lick his face. Everybody stood aghast, too taken aback even to grab the dog.

"Who let that bloody brute in here?" said the superintendent angrily. 7 "Catch it, someone!"

A warder detached from the escort, charged clumsily after the dog, 8 but it danced and gambolled just out of his reach, taking everything as part of the game. A young Eurasian jailer picked up a handful of gravel and tried to stone the dog away, but it dodged the stones and came after us again. Its yaps echoed from the jail walls. The prisoner, in the grasp of the two wardens looked on incuriously, as though this was another formality of the hanging. It was several minutes before someone managed to catch the dog. Then we put my handkerchief through its collar and moved off once more, with the dog still straining and whimpering.

It was about forty yards to the gallows. I watched the bare brown 9 back of the prisoner marching in front of me. He walked clumsily with his bound arms, but quite steadily, with that bobbing gait of the Indian who never straightens his knees. At each step his muscles slid neatly into place, the lock of hair on his scalp danced up and down, his feet printed themselves on the wet gravel. And once, in spite of the men who gripped him by each shoulder, he stepped lightly aside to avoid a puddle on the path.

It is curious, but till that moment I had never realized what it means 10 to destroy a healthy, conscious man. When I saw the prisoner step aside to avoid the puddle I saw the mystery, the unspeakable wrongness, of cutting a life short when it is in full tide. This man was not dying, he was alive just as we are alive. All the organs of his body were working—bowels digesting food, skin renewing itself, nails growing, tissues forming—all toiling away in solemn foolery. His nails would still be growing when he stood on the drop, when he was falling through the air with a tenth-of-a-second to live. His eyes saw the yellow gravel and the grey walls, and his brain still remembered, foresaw, reasoned—even about puddles. He and we were a party of men walking together, seeing, hearing, feeling, understanding the same world; and in two minutes, with a sudden snap, one of us would be gone—one mind less, one world less.

The gallows stood in a small yard, separate from the main grounds of 11 the prison, and overgrown with tall prickly weeds. It was a brick erection like three sides of a shed, with planking on top, and above that two beams and a crossbar with the rope dangling. The hangman, a grey-haired convict in the white uniform of the prison, was waiting beside his machine. He greeted us with a servile crouch as we entered. At a word from Francis the two warders, gripping the prisoner more closely than ever, half led, half pushed him to the gallows and helped him clumsily up the ladder. Then the hangman climbed up and fixed the rope round the prisoner's neck.

We stood waiting, five yards away. The warders had formed in a 12 rough circle round the gallows. And then, when the noose was fixed, the prisoner began crying to his god. It was a high, reiterated cry of "Ram! Ram! Ram! Ram!" not urgent and fearful like a prayer or cry for help, but steady, rhythmical, almost like the tolling of a bell. The dog answered the sound with a whine. The hangman, still standing on the gallows, produced a small cotton bag like a flour bag and drew it down over the prisoner's face. But the sound, muffled by the cloth, still persisted, over and over again: "Ram! Ram! Ram! Ram! Ram!"

The hangman climbed down and stood ready, holding the lever. 13 Minutes seemed to pass. The steady, muffled crying from the prisoner went on and on, "Ram! Ram! Ram!" never faltering for an instant. The superintendent, his head on his chest, was slowly poking the ground with his stick; perhaps he was counting the cries, allowing the prisoner a fixed number—fifty, perhaps, or a hundred. Everyone had changed colour. The Indians had gone grey like bad coffee, and one or two of the bayonets were wavering. We looked at the lashed, hooded man on the drop, and listened to his cries—each cry another second of life; the same thought was in all our minds: oh, kill him quickly, get it over, stop that abominable noise!

Suddenly the superintendent made up his mind. Throwing up his 14

head he made a swift motion with his stick. "Chalo!" he shouted almost
fiercely.

There was a clanking noise, and then dead silence. The prisoner had   15
vanished, and the rope was twisting on itself. I let go of the dog, and it
galloped immediately to the back of the gallows; but when it got there it
stopped short, barked, and then retreated into a corner of the yard,
where it stood among the weeds, looking timorously out at us. We went
round the gallows to inspect the prisoner's body. He was dangling with
his toes pointed straight downwards, very slowly revolving, as dead as a
stone.

The superintendent reached out with his stick and poked the bare   16
brown body; it oscillated slightly. "*He's* all right," said the superintendent.
He backed out from under the gallows, and blew out a deep breath. The
moodly look had gone out of his face quite suddenly. He glanced at his
wrist-watch. "Eight minutes past eight. Well, that's all for this morning,
thank God."

The warders unfixed bayonets and marched away. The dog, sobered   17
and conscious of having misbehaved itself, slipped after them. We walked
out of the gallows yard, past the condemned cells with their waiting prisoners, into the big central yard of the prison. The convicts, under the
command of warders armed with lathis, were already receiving their
breakfast. They squatted in long rows, each man holding a tin pannikin,
while two warders with buckets marched round ladling out rice; it
seemed quite a homely, jolly scene, after the hanging. An enormous relief had come upon us now that the job was done. One felt an impulse to
sing, to break into a run, to snigger. All at once everyone began chattering gaily.

The Eurasian boy walking beside me nodded towards the way we   18
had come, with a knowing smile: "Do you know, sir, our friend (he
meant the dead man) when he heard his appeal had been dismissed, he
pissed on the floor of his cell. From fright. Kindly take one of my cigarettes, sir. Do you not admire my new silver case, sir? From the boxwal-
lah, two rupees eight annas. Classy European style."

Several people laughed — at what, nobody seemed certain.   19

Francis was walking by the superintendent talking garrulously: "Well,   20
sir, all hass passed off with the utmost satisfactoriness. It was all finished — flick! like that. It iss not always so — oah, no! I have known cases
where the doctor wass obliged to go beneath the gallows and pull the
prissoner's legs to ensure decease. Most disagreeable!"

"Wriggling about, eh? That's bad," said the superintendent.   21

"Ach, sir, it iss worse when they become refractory! One man, I re-   22
call, clung to the bars of hiss cage when we went to take him out. You
will scarcely credit, sir, that it took six warders to dislodge him, three
pulling at each leg. We reasoned with him. 'My dear fellow, we said,
'think of all the pain and trouble you are causing to us!' But no, he
would not listen! Ach, he wass very troublesome!"

I found that I was laughing quite loudly. Everyone was laughing.   23
Even the superintendent grinned in a tolerant way. "You'd better all

come out and have a drink," he said quite genially. "I've got a bottle of whisky in the car. We could do with it."

We went through the big double gates of the prison into the road. 24 "Pulling at his legs!" exclaimed a Burmese magistrate suddenly, and burst into a loud chuckling. We all began laughing again. At the moment Francis' anecdote seemed extraordinarily funny. We all had a drink together, native and European alike, quite amicably. The dead man was a hundred yards away.

Study Questions

1. What is the *tone* of the essay? How does the narrator's attitude toward the hanging help determine the response eli-
   cited from the reader?
2. Why is the superintendent irritated by the delay in the hanging?
3. How does the incident with the dog contribute to the effectiveness of "A Hanging"?
4. Why does the prisoner's stepping aside to avoid a puddle bring the narrator to a full realization of the scene before him?
5. Why do the men feel "an impulse to sing, to break into a run, to snigger" after the hanging? Why does Orwell end his essay with "The dead man was a hundred yards away"?

Harry F. Waters
WHAT TV DOES TO KIDS

His first polysyllabic utterance was "Bradybunch." He learned to spell Sugar Smacks before his own name. He has seen Monte Carlo, witnessed a cocaine bust in Harlem and already has full-color fantasies involving Farrah Fawcett-Majors. Recently, he tried to karate-chop his younger sister after she broke his Six Million Dollar Man bionic transport station. (She retaliated by bashing him with her Cher doll.) His nursery-school teacher reports that he is passive, noncreative, unresponsive to instruction, bored during play periods and possessed of an almost nonexistent attention span—in short, very much like his classmates. Next fall, he will officially reach the age of reason and begin his formal education: His parents are beginning to discuss their apprehensions—when they are not too busy watching television.

The wonder of it all is that the worry about television has so belatedly moved anyone to action. After all, the suspicion that TV is turning children's minds to mush and their psyches toward mayhem is almost as old as the medium itself. But it is only in recent years—with the first TV generation already well into its 20s—that social scientists, child psychologists, pediatricians and educators have begun serious study of the impact of television on the young. "The American public has been preoccupied with governing our children's schooling," says Stanford University psychologist Alberta Siegel. "We have been astonishingly unconcerned about the medium that reaches into our homes. Yet we may expect television to alter our social arrangements just as profoundly as printing has done over the past five centuries."

The statistics are at least alarming. Educators like Dr. Benjamin Bloom, of the University of Chicago, maintain that by the time a child reaches the age of 5, he has undergone as much intellectual growth as will occur over the next thirteen years. According to A. C. Nielsen, children under 5 watch an average of 23.5 hours of TV a week. That may be less than the weekly video diet of adults (about 44 hours), but its effects are potentially enormous. Multiplied out over seventeen years that rate of viewing means that by his high-school graduation today's typical teenager will have logged at least 15,000 hours before the small screen—more time than he will have spent on any other activity except sleep. And at present levels of advertising and mayhem, he will have been exposed to 350,000 commercials and vicariously participated in 18,000 murders.

The conclusion is inescapable: after parents, television has become perhaps the most potent influence on the beliefs, attitudes, values and behavior of those who are being raised in its all-pervasive glow. George Gerbner, dean of the University of Pennsylvania's Annenberg School of Communications, is almost understating it when he says: "Television has profoundly affected the way in which members of the human race learn to become human beings."

A Question of Air Pollution

Unquestionably, the plug-in picture window has transmitted some beneficial images. Last month's showing of "Roots," for example, may have done more to increase the understanding of American race relations than any event since the civil rights activities of the '60s. And the fact that 130 million Americans could share that experience through the small screen points up the powerful—and potentially positive—influence the industry can have on its audience. In general, the children of TV enjoy a more sophisticated knowledge of a far larger world at a much younger age. They are likely to possess richer vocabularies, albeit with only a superficial comprehension of what the words mean. Research on the impact of "Sesame Street' has established measurable gains in the cognitive skills of pre-schoolers. And many benefits cannot be statistically calibrated. A New York pre-schooler tries to match deductive wits with Columbo; a Los Angeles black girl, who has never seen a ballet, decides she wants to be a ballerina after watching Margot Fonteyn perform on TV.

Nonetheless, the overwhelming body of evidence—drawn from more 5 than 2,300 studies and reports—is decidedly negative. Most of the studies have dealt with the antisocial legacy of video violence. Michael Rothenberg, a child psychiatrist at the University of Washington, has reviewed 25 years of hard data on the subject—the 50 most comprehensive studies involving 10,000 children from every possible background. Most showed that viewing violence tends to produce aggressive behavior among the young. "The time is long past due for a major, organized cry of protest from the medical profession in relation to what, in political terms, is a national scandal," concludes Rothenberg.

An unexpected salvo was sounded last week when the normally cau- 6 tious American Medical Association announced that it had asked ten major corporations to review their policies about sponsoring excessively gory shows. "TV violence is both a mental-health problem and an environmental issue," explained Dr. Richard E. Palmer, president of the AMA. "TV has been quick to raise questions of social responsibility with industries which pollute the air. In my opinion, television ... may be creating a more serious problem of air pollution." Reaction was immediate: General Motors, Sears Roebuck and the Joseph Schlitz Brewing Co. quickly announced they would look more closely into the content of the shows they sponsor.

The AMA action comes in the wake of a grass-roots campaign mobi- 7 lized by the national Parent-Teacher Association. The 6.6 million-member PTA recently began a series of regional forums to arouse public indignation over TV carnage. If that crusade fails, the PTA is considering organizing station-license challenges and national boycotts of products advertised on offending programs.

'The Flickering Blue Parent'

In their defense, broadcasting officials maintain that the jury is still out 8 on whether video violence is guilty of producing aggressive behavior.

And they marshal their own studies to support that position. At the same time, the network schedulers say they are actively reducing the violence dosage. "People have said they want another direction and that's what we're going to give them," promises NBC-TV president Robert T. Howard. Finally, the broadcast industry insists that the responsibility for the impact of TV on children lies with parents rather than programmers. "Parents should pick and choose the shows their kids watch," says CBS vice president Gene Mater. "Should TV be programmed for the young through midnight? It's a real problem. TV is a mass medium and it must serve more than just children."

But the blight of televised mayhem is only part of TV's impact. Be- 9
yond lies a vast subliminal terrain that is only now being charted. The investigators are discovering that TV has affected its youthful addicts in a host of subtle ways, varying according to age and class. For deprived children, TV may, in some cases, provide more sustenance than their home — or street — life; for the more privileged, who enjoy other alternatives, it may not play such a dominating role.

Nonetheless, for the average kid TV has at the very least preempted 10
the traditional development of childhood itself. The time kids spend sitting catatonic before the set has been exacted from such salutary pursuits as reading, outdoor play, even simple, contemplative solitude. TV prematurely jades, rendering passe the normal experiences of growing up. And few parents can cope with its tyrannical allure. Recently, Dr. Benjamin Spock brought his stepdaughter and granddaughter to New York for a tour of the Bronx Zoo and the Museum of Modern Art. But the man who has the prescription for everything from diaper rash to bedwetting could not dislodge the kids from their hotel room. "I couldn't get them away from the goddamned TV set," recalls Spock. "It made me sick."

Small wonder that television has been called "the flickering blue par- 11
ent." The after-school and early-evening hours used to be a time for "what-did-you-do-today" dialogue. Now, the electronic box does most of the talking. Dr. David Pearl of the National Institute of Mental Health suspects that the tube "has displaced many of the normal interactional processes between parents and children ... Those kinds of interactions are essential for maximum development." One veteran elementary-school teacher in suburban Washington, D.C., has noticed that her students have grown inordinately talkative when they arrive for class. "At home, they can't talk when the TV is on," she says. "It's as if they are starved for conversation."

The Passive Generation

Even more worrisome is what television has done to, rather than denied, 12
the tube-weaned population. A series of studies has shown that addiction to TV stifles creative imagination. For example, a University of Southern California research team exposed 250 elementary students — who had been judged mentally gifted — to three weeks of intensive viewing. Tests

conducted before and after the experiment found a marked drop in all forms of creative abilities except verbal skill. Some teachers are encountering children who cannot understand a simple story without visual illustrations. "TV has taken away the child's ability to form pictures in his mind," says child-development expert Dorothy Cohen at New York City's Bank Street College of Education.

Parenthetically, nursery-school teachers who have observed the pre- 13 TV generation contend that juvenile play is far less imaginative and spontaneous than in the past. The vidkids' toys come with built-in fantasies while their playground games have been programed by last night's shows. "You don't see kids making their own toys out of crummy things like we used to," says University of Virginia psychology professor Stephen Worchel, who is the father of a 6-year-old. "You don't see them playing hopscotch, or making up their own games. Everything is suggested to them by television."

Too much TV too early also instills an attitude of spectatorship, a 14 withdrawal from direct involvement in real-life experiences. "What television basically teaches children is passivity," says Stanford University researcher Paul Kaufman. "It creates the illusion of having been somewhere and done something and seen something, when in fact you've been sitting at home," New York Times writer Joyce Maynard, 23, a perceptive member of the first TV generation, concludes: "We grew up to be observers, not participants, to respond to action, not initiate it."

Conditioned to see all problems resolved in 30 or 60 minutes, the 15 offspring of TV exhibit a low tolerance for the frustration of learning. Elementary-school educators complain that their charges are quickly turned off by any activity that promises less than instant gratification. "You introduce a new skill, and right away, if it looks hard, they dissolve into tears," laments Maryland first-grade teacher Eleanor Berman. "They want everything to be easy—like watching the tube." Even such acclaimed educational series as "Sesame Street," "The Electric Company" and "Zoom" have had some dubious effects. Because such shows sugarcoat their lessons with flashy showbiz techniques, they are forcing real-life instructors into the role of entertainers in order to hold their pupils' attention. "I can't turn my body into shapes or flashlights," sighs a Connecticut teacher. "Kids today are accustomed to learning through gimmicks."

For the majority of American children, television has become the 16 principal socializing agent. It shapes their view of what the world is like and what roles they should play in it. As the University of Pennsylvania's Gerbner puts it: "The socialization of children has largely been transferred from the home and school to TV programmers who are unelected, unnamed and unknown, and who are not subject to collective—not to mention democratic—review."

What does TV's most impressionable constituency learn from prime- 17 time entertainment? No one can really be sure, but psychologists like Robert Liebert of the State University of New York, one of the most respected observers of child behavior, don't hesitate to express sweeping indictments. "It teaches them that might makes right," Liebert says flatly.

"The lesson of most TV series is that the rich, the powerful and the conniving are the most successful."

The View from the Victims

Whatever the truth of that, the tube clearly tends to reinforce sex-role 18 stereotypes. In a Princeton, N.J., survey of sixteen programs and 216 commercials, it was found that men outnumbered women by three to one and that females were twice as likely to display imcompetence. By and large, men were portrayed as dominant, authoritative and the sole source of their family's economic support. "These roles are biased and distorted, and don't reflect the way a woman thinks or feels," complains Liebert. "And it's just as bad for blacks."

It may, in fact, be even worse for blacks. Not only do black children 19 watch more TV than whites, but they confront a far greater disparity between the illusions of videoland and the reality of their own lives. Two yet-to-be published studies conducted by University of South Carolina psychology professor Robert Heckel found that young black viewers regard whites as more competent than blacks, and model their conduct accordingly. In one study, black children were shown a TV film of an interracial group of peers choosing toys to play with — an then given the same toys to pick from themselves. All the blacks selected the toys chosen by whites in the film, even though many of those toys were smaller or inferior in quality. "On TV, the competent roles tend to go to whites, particularly young white males," explains Heckel. "Thus black children regard whites as someone to copy."

A classic example of such racial imprinting is Rowena Smith, a 14- 20 year-old old Los Angeles black who remains glued to the tube from school recess to 11 each night. Rowena's favorite TV characters are CBS's Phyllis and her teen-age daughter. "They get along so good," she sighs. "I wish me and Mom could talk that way." When Rowena was scolded for getting her clothes dirty, she indignantly told her mother that "the kid in the Tonka truck ad gets dirty all the time." Rowena's first awareness of the facts of non-TV life came after she ran away for two days — and her mother gave her a licking. "When TV shows runaways," she complains, "they don't show the part about being beaten." Nowadays, Rowena is more skeptical about television, but she has become increasingly concerned about her 8-year-old brother. He wistfully talks about getting seriously injured and then being reassembled like the Six Million Dollar Man. "This kid really *believes* TV," sighs his sister. I gotta keep an eye on him 24 hours a day."

Indeed, call on the children themselves to testify and the message 21 comes through clear — and sometimes poignantly. A vidkid sampler:

■ Fourteen-year-old, Los Angeles: "Television is perfect to tune 22 out the rest of the world. But I don't relate with my family much because we're all too busy watching TV."

■ **Eleven-year-old, Denver:** "You see so much violence that it's 23
meaningless. If I saw someone really get killed, it wouldn't be a big
deal. I guess I'm turning into a hard rock."

■ **Nine-year-old, San Francisco:** "I'd rather watch TV than play 24
outside because it's boring outside. They always have the same rides,
like swings and things."

■ **Fifteen-year-old, Lake Forest, Ill.:** "Sometimes when I watch an 25
exciting show, I don't blink my eyes once. When I close them after
the show, they hurt hard."

■ **Thirteen-year-old, Glastonbury, Conn.:** "When I see a beautiful 26
girl using a shampoo or a cosmetic on TV, I buy them because I'll
look like her. I have a ton of cosmetics. I play around with them and
save them for when I'm older."

■ **Ten-year-old, New York:** "It bugs me when someone is watching 27
with me. If your friend is bored, you have to go out or make conversation. That's hard."

It would be preposterous, of course, to suggest that television alone 28
is responsible for everything that is wrong with America's young. Permissiveness at home and in school, the dispersion of the extended family,
confusion over moral standards and the erosion of traditional institutions — all help explain why Dick and Jane behave as they do. Moreover, any aspect of child psychology is enormously complex, especially
when it comes to measuring cause and effect. There is always the temptation among social scientists to set up their experiments in a way guaranteed to reinforce their preconceptions. Nevertheless, there is one thrust
of reliable study — into video violence — that has produced an unmistakable pattern of clear and present danger.

Paranoia and Propaganda

The debate over the link between TV violence and aggressive behavior 29
in society has had a longer run than "Gunsmoke." Today, however, even
the most chauvinist network apologists concede that some children, under certain conditions, will imitate antisocial acts that they witness on the
tube. Indeed, a study of 100 juvenile offenders commissioned by ABC
found that no fewer than 22 confessed to having copied criminal techniques from TV. Last year, a Los Angeles judge sentenced two teen-age
boys to long jail terms after they held up a bank and kept 25 persons
hostage for seven hours. In pronouncing the sentence, the judge noted
disgustedly that the entire scheme had been patterned on an "Adam 12"
episode the boys had seen two weeks earlier.

Convinced that they have proved their basic case, the behavioral 30
sleuths on the violence beat have switched their focus to less obvious
signs of psychic dysfunction. They are now uncovering evidence that the
tide of TV carnage increases children's tolerance of violent behavior in
others. In one experiment, several hundred fifth-graders were asked to
act as baby-sitters for a group of younger kids — shown on a TV screen —

who were supposedly playing in the next room. The baby-sitters were instructed to go to a nearby adult for assistance if their charges began fighting. Those who had been shown a violent TV film just before taking up their duties were far slower to call for help than those who had watched a pro-baseball telecast. "Television desensitizes children to violence in real life," observes University of Mississippi psychology professor Ronald Drabman, who helped conduct the study. "They tolerate violence in others because they have been conditioned to think of it as an everyday thing."

Beyond that, some researchers are finding that TV may be instilling 31 paranoia in the young. Three years of tests directed by Gerbner, who is perhaps the nation's foremost authority on the subject, established that heavy TV watchers tend to exaggerate the danger of violence in their own lives — creating what Gerbner calls a "mean-world syndrome." As for children, he reports that "the pattern is exactly the same, only more so. The prevailing message of TV is to generate fear."

And now a word about the sponsors. The late Jack Benny once quip- 32 ped that television is called a medium because nothing it serves up is ever well-done. But as the child watchers see it, the not-so-funny problem with TV commercials is precisely that they are so well put together. "Everybody has had the experience of seeing a 2-year-old playing on the floor, and when the commercial comes on, he stops and watches it," notes F. Earle Barcus, professor of communications at Boston University. "TV ads probably have more effect on children than any other form of programming."

Junk Food for Thought

The hottest battle involves the impact of child-directed commercials on 33 their audience's eating habits. More than 70 per cent of the ads on Saturday and Sunday-morning "kidvid" peddle sugar-coated cereals, candy and chewing gum. Laced with action-packed attention grabbers and pitched by an ingratiating adult authority figure, such messages hook children on poor eating habits long before they develop the mental defenses to resist. "This is the most massive educational program to eat junk food in history," charges Sid Wolinsky, an attorney for a San Francisco public-interest group. "We are creating a nation of sugar junkies."

Research has also established that as kids grow older their attitudes 34 toward commercials move from innocent acceptance to outrage about those ads that mislead and finally to a cynical recognition of what they perceive as adult hypocrisy. According to a study by Columbia University psychology professor Thomas Bever, TV ads may be "permanently distorting children's views of morality, society and business." From in-depth interviews with 48 youngsters between the ages of 5 and 12, Bever concluded that by the time they reach 12, many find it easier to decide that all commercials lie than to try to determine which are telling the truth.

Concludes Bever: "They become ready to believe that, like advertising, business and other institutions are riddled with hypocrisy."

Who is to blame and what, if anything, can be done? The networks 35 argue that the number of violent incidents portrayed on TV has declined by 24 per cent since 1975. That figure has been challenged, but there is little question that the networks have instituted some reforms. The number of "action-adventure" series has decreased of late, and the weekend-morning kidvid scene is gradually being pacified. Such superhero cartoon characters as CBS's "Superman" and NBC's "Granite Man" have been replaced with gentler fare; ABC even canceled "Bugs Bunny" and "Road Runner" because of their zap-and-whap antics.

There is also considerable merit to the broadcasters' argument that 36 parents are to blame if they don't regulate their children's viewing habits. By the time the Family Hour experiment was struck down by the courts last year, it had already proved unworkable because so many parents refused to cooperate. Nielsen found that 10.5 million youngsters under the age of 12 were still hooked to the tube after 9 p.m., when the Family Hour ended. And a recent Roper study reported that only two-fifths of the parents polled enforced rules about what programs their children could watch. "Parents who take active charge of most of the elements of their children's upbringing allow a kind of anarchy to prevail where television viewing is concerned," says Elton Rule, president of ABC, Inc.

The Public Strikes Back

In rebuttal, public-interest groups point out that TV stations have been 37 granted Federal licenses to ride the public airwaves — a highly lucrative privilege that carries a unique responsibility. In addition to the nation-wide pressure being exerted by the AMA and the PTA, local organizations like the Lansing (Mich.) Committee for Children's Television have persuaded local stations to drop gory shows from their late-afternoon schedules. But no one has achieved more reform than the activist mothers of Action for Children's Television, based in Newtonville, Mass. ACT is largely credited with persuading the networks to reduce time for commercials on children's weekend shows from sixteen to nine and a half minutes an hour, to halt the huckstering of vitamins on kidvid and to end the practice of having the hosts deliver the pitches. ACT's ultimate — perhaps chimeric — goal is to rid kidvid of all advertising. "We feel it is wise to separate children from the marketplace until they are ready to deal with it," explains Peggy Charren, ACT's indefatigable president.

The shrewdest reform movement is aimed at persuading network 38 programmers and advertisers that violence really doesn't sell. J. Walter Thompson, the nation's largest advertising agency, has begun advising its clients to stop purchasing spots on violent series — pointing out that a sampling of adult viewers revealed that 8 per cent of the consumers surveyed had already boycotted products advertised on such shows, while 10 per cent more were considering doing so. To help viewers identify the worst offenders among the shows, the National Citizens Committee for Broadcasting now disseminates rankings of the most violent series. At last body count, the bloodiest were ABC's "Starsky & Hutch" and "Baretta," NBC's "Baa Baa Black Sheep" and CBS's "Hawaii Five-O."

On the brighter side, some educators have begun harnessing commercial TV's power in positive ways. The movement first took hold a few years ago in Philadelphia's school system, which started tying reading assignments to TV offerings. For example, scripts for such docu-dramas as "The Missiles of October" and "Eleanor and Franklin" were distributed to more than 100,000 Philadelphia students in advance of the TV dates. 39

From Violence to Social Values

The children watched the shows while following along in the scripts, and discussed them in class the next day. The program has worked so well— some pupils' reading skills advanced by three years—that 3,500 other U.S. school systems are imitating it. This week WBNS-TV, the CBS affiliate in Columbus, Ohio, is transmitting four hours of classroom programming each day aimed at 96,000 local students whose schools are closed due to the natural-gas shortage (page 39). 40

Prime Time School TV, a nonprofit Chicago organization, has come up with the most innovative approach: PTST uses some of TV's most violent fare to implant positive social values. In one seven-week course, pupils were given questionnaires and told to fill them out while watching "Kojak," "Baretta" and the like. The questions, which were subsequently kicked around in class, dealt with everything from illegal search and seizure to forced confessions. "One boy told us that we had ruined television for him," reports PTST official Linda Kahn. "He couldn't watch a police show any more without counting the number of killings." Says PTST president William Singer: "We are saying that there are alternatives to merely railing against television, and this is just one of them." 41

ALL ABOUT KIDVID

Harry F. Waters

In their less circumspect moments, the people who create, manufacture and market weekend-morning children's shows refer to their audience as "mice." Last year, advertisers laid out more than $400 million for commercials ingeniously designed to lure those mice to the corporate cheese. And in return for delivering its most captive audience, the television industry reaped no less than 25 per cent of its annual profit from children's video. Nowhere else on TV is the medium more the message, and the programing so much wrapping around the huckster's package. To watch kidvid is to be engulfed in a tide of sugary glop—Kit Kat chocolate bars, Starburst Fruit Chews, Charm's Blow Pops, Fruit Stripe gum, Moonstones and Honeycombs. The look of kidvid is that of a mouth doomed to dental catastrophe.

What about the shows that interrupt the sales spiels? Reform is fleetingly visible. Those mindless cartoons now make up less than half of the kidvid schedule. And some of the newer shows, such as CBS's "Ark II" and "Fat Albert," gently weave in benign messages: international brotherhood, the perils of smoking and drugs and the joys of facing up to bullies. Of late, the networks' news departments have classed up the act. ABC's "Animals Animals Animals" is a sort of peewee "60 Minutes" with a zoological theme. CBS's periodic "In the News" introduces its audience to such adult concerns as environmental pollution and bankrupt school systems.

Spunky: And then there is "Muggsy." This new NBC series about an orphaned teen-age white girl adrift in an inner-city slum realistically deals with growth pains that afflict all races. Recently, Muggsy straightened out a black youngster who was being mercilessly harassed by his super-cool friends for joining the Boy Scouts. "Why you jivin' around with those honkies?" demanded one tormentor. Sensitively played by 13-year-old Sarah MacDonnell, who has more freckles than Sissy Spacek, Muggsy is spunky, vulnerable and—unlike the polyethylene Disney clones who populate most of kidvid—altogether real.

Unfortunately, the rest of chil-dren's video has matured woefully little since the days when Howdy Doody flashed his bicuspids. NBC's "Big John, Little John" stereotypes parents as incorrigible klutzes, while the network's "Speed Buggy" is nothing but a weekly lesson in reckless driving. There are even kiddie game shows to instill avarice early. On Metromedia's "Guess Your Best," the audience of moppets screams in a "Let's Make a Deal" frenzy as its panelist peers compete for AMF sports equipment and Panasonic tape recorders. "Kids are people, too . . . wackadoo, wackadoo," warbles the show's unctuous emcee.

The schlock depths, however, are reached by "The Krofft Supershow." With a stupefyingly silly music group called Kaptain Kool and the Kongs acting as host, this one-hour ABC adventure series focuses on Dr. Shrinker, a mad scientist who reduces his victims to 6-inch miniatures. The quality of the special effects would draw boos at a student film festival. The series also features two female magazine reporters who, when evildoers appear, transform themselves into Electra Woman and Dynagirl outfitted in costumes apparently picked up at a Woolworth's post-Halloween sale. When last observed, the superheroines had been ensnared by Glitter Rock, an epicene Elton John type who sported a green Afro coiffure set off by a spangled body stocking. Perhaps this show's most heinous crime is that each episode costs nearly $200,000 to produce.

Lessons: Relief, of course, can still be found on the public-TV channels. Noncommercial television's best new offerings are "Rebop," which imparts lessons in interracial harmony, and "Infinity Factory," aimed at inner-city adolescents who have trouble fathoming math. "Infinity Factory" is after an older audience than "Sesame Street" and it understands the turf. A jive-spouting disk jockey announces: "Let me tell you all about this weird dude — the number 36." A man-in-the-street survey to introduce the concept of six-digit figures asks adults and children how much money the President of the U.S. makes. "I dunno," shrugs a Harlem housewife, "but we sure ain't making none of it here."

No one is proposing that kid-vid should be nothing but a sixth day of school. The 14 million youngsters who use it to unwind on weekends are just as entitled to their video Martinis as their elders. But they are also entitled to nourishment for their imaginations, even a brief massage of their thought glands, and on those counts commercial children's programing flunks the test. If there is such a thing as the evil of banality, then it is seeping through the looking glass with every Saturday's dawn. Even mice, after all, deserve an occasional change in diet. How about something truly wackadoo — or at least a spin-off of "Muggsy"?

Life Without the Tube

Unfortunately, the options available to the individual parent are considerably more limited. A few daring souls have simply pulled the plug. Charles Frye, a San Francisco nursery-school teacher and the father of five boys, decided he would not replace his set after it conked out in 1972. Frye's brood rebelled at first, but today none of them voices regret that theirs is a TV-less household. Fourteen-year-old Mark fills his afternoon hours with tap-dancing lessons, Sea Scout meetings and work in a gas station. Kirk, his 13-year-old brother, plays a lot of basketball and football and recently finished "Watership Down" and all four of the Tolkien hobbit books. "I know of no other children that age who have that range of interests," says their father. 42

Short of such a draconian measure, some parents are exercising a greater degree of home rule. Two years ago, the administrators of New York's Horace Mann nursery school became distressed over an upsurge of violence in their students' play. Deciding that television was to blame, they dispatched a letter to all parents urging them to curb their children's viewing. "After we sent the letter, we could see a change," recalls Horace Mann principal Eleanor Brussel. "The kids showed better concentration, better comprehension, an ability to think things through." Sheila Altschuler, one of the mothers who heeded the school's request, noticed that her 4-year-old son began making up his own playtime characters instead of imitating those on the tube. "If I didn't feel it was kind of freaky, I wouldn't own a set," allows Altschuler. "But these days it's a matter of conformity. Kids would be outcasts without TV." 43

Clearly, there is no single antidote for the vidkid virus. For the chil- 44
dren of the global village, and their progeny to come, TV watching will
continue to be their most shared—and shaping—experience. Virtually all
the experts, however, agree on one palliative for parents of all socioeconomic levels. Instead of using TV as an electronic baby-sitter, parents
must try to involve themselves directly in their youngsters' viewing. By
watching along with the kids at least occasionally, they can help them
evaluate what they see—pointing out the inflated claims of a commercial,
perhaps, or criticizing a gratuitously violent scene. "Parents don't have to
regard TV as a person who can't be interrupted," says behavioral scientist
Charles Corder-Bolz. "If they view one show a night with their kids, and
make just one or two comments about it, they can have more impact
than the whole program."

Reduced to the essentials, the question for parents no longer is: "Do 45
you know where your children are tonight?" The question has become:
What are they watching—and with whom?

Study Questions

1. If this article is not in newspaper style, neither is it in the
   style of a formal essay. If this article is typical of news
   magazine, how does it differ from newspaper writing and
   formal essays?
2. What is accomplished by the subtitles? The insert about
   kidvid? The sampler?
3. One of the ways a language extends its vocabulary is by
   coining new words. *Kidvid* is an example. What elements
   went into its construction? Cite and comment on other examples of *coinage*.
4. The major part of this article (that apart from "All About
   Kidvid") was written by "Harry F. Waters with bureau reports." What are the implications of "with bureau reports"?
5. News articles generally make much use of statistics in the
   supporting evidence. Why? Are statistics more conclusive
   than other sorts of evidence?

Robert Warshow

THE GANGSTER AS TRAGIC HERO

Robert Warshow (1917–1955) was born in New York City and educated at the University of Michigan. He was a translator and research analyst for the Army Security Agency during World War II, and then returned to civilian life and the editorship of *Commentary* magazine. He was still working for *Commentary* when he died of a heart attack at thirty-seven. In addition to his articles in *Commentary* Warshow often published in the *Partisan Review* and the *American Mercury. The Immediate Experience* (1962) is a collection of some of his more important essays.

America, as a social and political organization, is committed to 1 a cheerful view of life. It could not be otherwise. The sense of tragedy is a luxury of aristocratic societies, where the fate of the individual is not conceived of as having a direct and legitimate political importance, being determined by a fixed and supra-political — that is, non-controversial — moral order or fate. Modern equalitarian societies, however, whether democratic or authoritarian in their political forms, always base themselves on the claim that they are making life happier; the avowed function of the modern state, at least in its ultimate terms, is not only to regulate social relations, but also to determine the quality and the possibilities of human life in general. Happiness thus becomes the chief political issue — in a sense, the only political issue — and for that reason it can never be treated as an issue at all. If an American or a Russian is unhappy, it implies a certain reprobation of his society, and therefore, by a logic of which we can all recognize the necessity, it becomes an obligation of citizenship to be cheerful; if the authorities find it necessary, the citizen may even be compelled to make a public display of his cheerfulness on important occasions, just as he may be conscripted into the army in time of war.

Naturally, this civic responsibility rests most strongly upon the or- 2 gans of mass culture. The individual citizen may still be permitted his private unhappiness so long as it does not take on political significance, the extent of this tolerance being determined by how large an area of private life the society can accommodate. But every production of mass culture

From *The Immediate Experience*, published by Doubleday and Company, Inc. Reprinted with permission.

is a public act and must conform with accepted notions of the public good. Nobody seriously questions the principle that it is the function of mass culture to maintain public morale, and certainly nobody in the mass audience objects to having his morale maintained.* At a time when the normal condition of the citizen is a state of anxiety, euphoria spreads over our culture like the broad smile of an idiot. In terms of attitudes towards life, there is very little difference between a "happy" movie like *Good News,* which ignores death and suffering, and a "sad" movie like *A Tree Grows in Brooklyn,* which uses death and suffering as incidents in the service of a higher optimism.

But, whatever its effectiveness as a source of consolation and a 3 means of pressure for maintaining "positive" social attitudes, this optimism is fundamentally satisfying to no one, not even to those who would be most disoriented without its support. Even within the area of mass culture, there always exists a current of opposition, seeking to express by whatever means are available to it that sense of desperation and inevitable failure which optimism itself helps to create. Most often, this opposition is confined to rudimentary or semi-literate forms: in mob politics and journalism, for example, or in certain kinds of religious enthusiasm. When it does enter the field of art, it is likely to be disguised or attenuated: in an unspecific form of expression like jazz, in the basically harmless nihilism of the Marx Brothers, in the continually reasserted strain of hopelessness that often seems to be the real meaning of the soap opera. The gangster film is remarkable in that it fills the need for disguise (though not sufficiently to avoid arousing uneasiness) without requiring any serious distortion. From its beginning, it has been a consistent and astonishingly complete presentation of the modern sense of tragedy.*

In its initial character, the gangster film is simply one example of the 4 movies' constant tendency to create fixed dramatic patterns that can be repeated indefinitely with a reasonable expectation of profit. One gangster film follows another as one musical or one Western follows another. But this rigidity is not necessarily opposed to the requirements of art. There have been very successful types of art in the past which developed such specific and detailed conventions as almost to make individual examples of the type interchangeable. This is true, for example, of Elizabethan revenge tragedy and Restoration comedy.

For such a type to be successful means that its conventions have im- 5 posed themselves upon the general consciousness and become the accepted vehicles of a particular set of attitudes and a particular aesthetic

---

*In her testimony before the House Committee on Un-American Activities, Mrs. Leila Rogers said that the movie *None But the Lonely Heart* was un-American because it was gloomy. Like so much else that was said during the unhappy investigation of Hollywood, this statement was at once stupid and illuminating. One knew immediately what Mrs. Rogers was talking about; she had simply been insensitive enough to carry her philistinism to its conclusion.

*Efforts have been made from time to time to bring the gangster film into line with the prevailing optimism and social constructiveness of our culture; *Kiss of Death* is a recent example. These efforts are usually unsuccessful; the reasons for their lack of success are interesting in themselves, but I shall not be able to discuss them here.

effect. One goes to any individual example of the type with very definite expectations, and originality is to be welcomed only in the degree that it intensifies the expected experience without fundamentally altering it. Moreover, the relationship between the conventions which go to make up such a type and the real experience of its audience or the real facts of whatever situation it pretends to describe is of only secondary importance and does not determine its aesthetic force. It is only in an ultimate sense that the type appeals to its audience's experience of reality; much more immediately, it appeals to previous experience of the type itself: it creates it own field of reference.

Thus the importance of the gangster film, and the nature and intensity of its emotional and aesthetic impact, cannot be measured in terms of the place of the gangster himself or the importance of the problem of crime in American life. Those European movie-goers who think there is a gangster on every corner in New York are certainly deceived, but defenders of the "positive" side of American culture are equally deceived if they think it relevant to point out that most Americans have never seen a gangster. What matters is that the experience of the gangster *as an experience of art* is universal to Americans. There is almost nothing we understand better or react to more readily or with quicker intelligence. The Western film, though it seems never to diminish in popularity, is for most of us no more than the folklore of the past, familiar and understandable only because it has been repeated so often. The gangster film comes much closer. In ways that we do not easily or willingly define, the gangster speaks for us, expressing the part of the American psyche which rejects the qualities and the demands of modern life, which rejects "Americanism" itself. 6

The gangster is the man of the city, with the city's language and knowledge, with its queer and dishonest skills and its terrible daring, carrying his life in his hands like a placard, like a club. For everyone else, there is at least the theoretical possibility of another world—in that happier American culture which the gangster denies, the city does not really exist; it is only a more crowded and more brightly lit country—but for the gangster there is only the city; he must inhabit it in order to personify it: not the real city, but that dangerous and sad city of the imagination which is so much more important, which is the modern world. And the gangster—though there are real gangsters—is also, and primarily, a creature of the imagination. The real city, one might say, produces only criminals; the imaginary city produces the gangster: he is what we want to be and what we are afraid we may become. 7

Thrown into the crowd without background or advantages, with only those ambiguous skills which the rest of us—the real people of the real city—can only pretend to have, the gangster is required to make his way, to make his life and impose it on others. Usually, when we come upon him, he has already made his choice or the choice has already been made for him, it doesn't matter which: we are not permitted to ask whether at some point he could have chosen to be something else than what he is. 8

The gangster's activity is actually a form of rational enterprise, in- 9 volving fairly definite goals and various techniques for achieving them. But this rationality is usually no more than a vague background; we know, perhaps, that the gangster sells liquor or that he operates a numbers racket; often we are not given even that much information. So his activity becomes a kind of pure criminality; he hurts people. Certainly our response to the gangster film is most consistently and most universally a response to sadism; we gain the double satisfaction of participating vicariously in the gangster's sadism and then seeing it turned against the gangster himself.

But on another level the quality of irrational brutality and the quality   10
of rational enterprise become one. Since we do not see the rational and routine aspects of the gangster's behavior, the practice of brutality — the quality of unmixed criminality — becomes the totality of his career. At the same time, we are always conscious that the whole meaning of this career is a drive for success: the typical gangster film presents a steady upward progress followed by a very precipitate fall. Thus brutality itself becomes at once the means to success and the content of success — a success that is defined in its most general terms, not as accomplishment or specific gain, but simply as the unlimited possibility of aggression. (In the same way, film presentations of businessmen tend to make it appear that they achieve their success by talking on the telephone and holding conferences and that success *is* talking on the telephone and holding conferences.)

From this point of view, the initial contact between the film and its   11
audience is an agreed conception of human life: that man is a being with the possibilities of success or failure. This principle, too, belongs to the city; one must emerge from the crowd or else one is nothing. On that basis the necessity of the action is established, and it progresses by inalterable paths to the point where the gangster lies dead and the principle has been modified: there is really only one possibility — failure. The final meaning of the city is anonymity and death.

In the opening scene of *Scarface,* we are shown a successful man; we   12
know he is successful because he has just given a party of opulent proportions and because he is called Big Louie. Through some monstrous lack of caution, he permits himself to be alone for a few moments. We understand from this immediately that he is about to be killed. No convention of the gangster film is more strongly established than this: it is dangerous to be alone. And yet alone, for success is always the establishment of an *individual* pre-eminence that must be imposed on others, in whom it automatically arouses hatred; the successful man is an outlaw. The gangster's whole life is an effort to assert himself as an individual, to draw himself out of the crowd, and he always dies *because* he is an individual; the final bullet thrusts him back, makes him, after all, a failure. "Mother of God," says the dying Little Caesar, "is this the end of Rico?" — speaking of himself thus in the third person because what has been brought low is not the undifferentiated *man,* but the individual with a name, the gangster, the success; even to himself he is a creature of the imagination. (T. S. Eliot has pointed out that a number of Shakespeare's

tragic heroes have this trick of looking at themselves dramatically; their true identity, the thing that is destroyed when they die, is something outside themselves — not a man, but a style of life, a kind of meaning.)

At bottom, the gangster is doomed because he is under the obligation to succeed, not because the means he employs are unlawful. In the deeper layers of the modern consciousness, *all* means are unlawful, every attempt to succeed is an act of aggression, leaving one alone and guilty and defenseless among enemies: one is *punished* for success. This is our intolerable dilemma: that failure is a kind of death and success is evil and dangerous, is — ultimately — impossible. The effect of the gangster film is to embody this dilemma in the person of the gangster and resolve it by his death. The dilemma is resolved because it *is his* death, not ours. We are safe; for the moment, we can acquiesce in our failure, we can choose to fail. 13

Study Questions

1. Are gangsters the subject of this essay, or is it something else?
2. It is not necessary to have seen the movies cited in order to understand the points he makes about them. Why not?
3. How often does Warshow use a simple sentence? How does this help establish the tone of his essay?
4. Comment on the words that begin the sentences in paragraphs 9 and 10.
5. How does *dilemma* serve to organize the concluding paragraph?

Tom Wolfe
PORNOVIOLENCE

Tom Wolfe (1931–   ) was born in Richmond, Virginia. He received his A.B. from Washington and Lee (1951) and his Ph.D. from Yale (1957). He has been a reporter for the Springfield (Mass.) *Union*, the Washington *Post*, and the New York *Herald-Tribune*. His essays were published in 1965 under the wildly improbable but singularly appropriate title of *The Kandy-Kolored Tangerine-Flake Stream-*

line Baby. His most recent books include *The Electric Kool-Aid Acid Test* and *The Pump House Gang* (1968), and *Radical Chic & Mau-Mauing the Flak Catchers* (1970), *The Painted Word* and *The Right Stuff,* both 1975, and *Mauve Gloves & Madmen, Clutter & Vine* (1976).

"**K**eeps *His Mom-in-law in Chains,* meet *Kills Son and Feeds 1 Corpse to Pigs.*"

"Pleased to meet you."   2

"*Teenager Twists Off Corpse's Head . . . to Get Gold Teeth,* meet *Stran- 3 gles Girl Friend, Then Chops Her to Pieces.*"

"How you doing?"   4

"*Nurse's Aide Sees Fingers Chopped Off in Meat Grinder,* meet *I Left 5 My Babies in the Deep Freeze.*"

"It's a pleasure."   6

It's a pleasure! No doubt about that! In all these years of journalism 7 I have covered more conventions than I care to remember. Podiatrists, theosophists, Professional Budget Finance dentists, oyster farmers, mathematicians, truckers, dry cleaners, stamp collectors, Esperantists, nudists, and newspaper editors — I have seen them all, together, in vast assemblies, sloughing through the wall-to-wall of a thousand hotel lobbies (the nudists excepted) in their shimmering gray-metal suits and pajama-stripe shirts with white Plasti-Coat name cards on their chests, and I have sat through their speeches and seminars (the nudists included) and attentively endured ear baths such as you wouldn't believe. And yet none has ever been quite like the convention of the stringers for *The National Enquirer.*

The Enquirer is a weekly newspaper that is probably known by sight 8 to millions more than know it by name. No one who ever came face-to-face with *The Enquirer* on a newsstand in its wildest days is likely to have forgotten the sight: a tabloid with great inky shocks of type all over the front page saying something on the order of *Gouges Out Wife's Eyes to Make Her Ugly, Dad Hurls Hot Grease in Daughter's Face, Wife Commits Suicide After 2 Years of Poisoning Fail to Kill Husband . . .*

The stories themselves were supplied largely by stringers, i.e., corre- 9 spondents, from all over the country, the world, for that matter, mostly copy editors and reporters on local newspapers. Every so often they would come upon a story, usually via the police beat, that was so grotesque the local sheet would discard it or run it in a highly glossed form rather than offend or perplex its readers. The stringers would preserve them for *The Enquirer,* which always rewarded them well and respectfully.

One year *The Enquirer* convened and feted them at a hotel in Man- 10 hattan. This convention was a success in every way. The only awkward moment was at the outset when the stringers all pulled in. None of them knew each other. Their hosts got around the problem by introducing them by the stories they had supplied. The introductions went like this:

"Harry, I want you to meet Frank here. Frank did that story, you re- 11
member that story, *Midget Murderer Throws Girl Off Cliff after She
Refuses to Dance with Him*"

"Pleased to meet you. That was some story." 12

"And Harry did the one about *I Spent Three Days Trapped at Bottom* 13
of Forty-Foot-Deep Mine Shaft and Was Saved by a Swarm of Flies."

"Likewise, I'm sure." 14

And *Midget Murderer Throws Girl Off Cliff* shakes hands with *I Spent* 15
Three Days Trapped at Bottom of Forty-Foot-Deep Mine Shaft, and *Buries
Her Baby Alive* shakes hands with *Boy, Twelve, Strangles Two-Year-Old
Girl,* and *Kills Son and Feeds Corpse to Pigs* shakes hands with *He Strangles
Old Woman and Smears Corpse with Syrup, Ketchup, and Oatmeal . . . and . . .*

. . . There was a great deal of esprit about the whole thing. These 16
men were, in fact, the avant-garde of a new genre that since then has become institutionalized throughout the nation without anyone knowing its
proper name. I speak of the new pornography, the pornography of violence.

Pornography comes from the Greek word *"porne,"* meaning harlot, 17
and pornography is literally the depiction of the acts of harlots. In the
new pornography, the theme is not sex. The new pornography depicts
practitioners acting out another, murkier drive: people staving teeth in,
ripping guts open, blowing brains out, and getting even with all those
bastards . . .

The success of *The Enquirer* prompted many imitators to enter the 18
field, *Midnight, The Star Chronicle, The National Insider, Inside News, The
National Close-up, The National Tattler, The National Examiner.* A truly
competitive free press evolved, and soon a reader could go to the newspaper of his choice for *Kill the Retarded! (Won't You Join My Movement?)*
and *Unfaithful Wife? Burn Her Bed!, Harem Master's Mistress Chops Him
with Machete, Babe Bites Off Boys's Tongue,* and *Cuts Buddy's Face to Pieces
for Stealing His Business and Fiancée.*

And yet the last time I surveyed the Violence press, I noticed a curi- 19
ous thing. These pioneering journals seem to have pulled back. They
seem to be regressing to what is by now the Redi-Mix staple of literate
Americans, mere sex. *Ecstasy and Me (by Hedy Lamarr),* says *The National
Enquirer. I Run a Sex Art Gallery,* says *The National Insider.* What has
happened, I think, is something that has happened to avant-gardes in
many fields, from William Morris and the Craftsmen to the Bauhaus
group. Namely, their discoveries have been preempted by the Establishment and so thoroughly dissolved into the mainstream they no longer
look original.

Robert Harrison, the former publisher of *Confidential,* and later pub- 20
lisher of the aforementioned *Inside News,* was perhaps the first person to
see it coming. I was interviewing Harrison early in January 1964 for a
story in *Esquire* about six weeks after the assassination of President Kennedy, and we were in a cab in the West Fifties in Manhattan, at a stop-
light, by a newsstand, and Harrison suddenly pointed at the newsstand
and said, "Look at that. They're doing the same thing *The Enquirer* does."

There on the stand was a row of slick-paper, magazine-size publica- 21 tions, known in the trade as one-shots, with titles like *Four Days That Shook the World, Death of a President, An American Tragedy,* or just *John Fitzgerald Kennedy* (1921–1963). "You want to know why people buy those things?" said Harrison. "People buy those things to see a man get his head blown off."

And, of course, he was right. Only now publishers were in many 22 cases the pillars of the American press. Invariably, these "special coverages" of the assassination bore introductions piously commemorating the fallen President, exhorting the American people to strength and unity in a time of crisis, urging greater vigilance and safeguards for the new President, and even raising the nice metaphysical question of collective guilt in "an age of violence."

In the years since then, of course, there has been an incessant replay, 23 with every recoverable clinical detail, of those less than five seconds in which a man got his head blown off. And throughout this deluge of words, pictures, and film frames, I have been intrigued with one thing: The point of view, the vantage point, is almost never that of the victim, riding in the Presidential Lincoln Continental. What you get is ... the view from Oswald's rifle. You can step right up here and look point-blank right through the very hairline cross in Lee Harvey Oswald's Optics Ordinance four-power Japanese telescopic sight and watch, frame by frame by frame by frame by frame, as that man there's head comes apart. Just a little History there before your very eyes.

The television networks have schooled us in the view from Oswald's 24 rifle and made it seem a normal pastime. The TV viewpoint is nearly always that of man who is going to strike. The last time I watched *Gunsmoke,* which was not known as a very violent Western in TV terms, the action went like this: The Wellington agents and the stagecoach driver pull guns on the badlands gang leader's daughter and Kitty, the heart-of-gold saloonkeeper, and kidnap them. Then the badlands gang shoots two Wellington agents. Then they tie up five more and talk about shooting them. Then they desist because they might not be able to get a hotel room in the next town if the word got around. Then one badlands gang gunslinger attempts to rape Kitty while the gang leader's younger daughter looks on. Then Kitty resists, so he slugs her one in the jaw. Then the gang leader slugs him. Then the gang leader slugs Kitty. Then Kitty throws hot stew in the gang member's face and hits him over the back of the head with a revolver. Then he knocks her down with a rock. Then the gang sticks up a bank. Here comes the marshal, Matt Dillon. He shoots a gang member and breaks it up. Then the gang leader shoots the guy who was guarding his daughter and the woman. Then the marshal shoots the gang leader. The final exploding bullet signals The End.

It is not the accumulated slayings and bone crushings that make this 25 pornoviolence, however. What makes it pornoviolence is that in almost every case the camera angle, therefore the viewer, is with the gun, the fist, the rock. The pornography of violence has no point of view in the old sense that novels do. You do not live the action through the hero's eyes. You live with the aggressor, whoever he may be. One moment you are the hero. The next you are the villain. No matter whose side you may be on consciously, you are in fact with the muscle, and it is you who disintegrate all comers, villains, lawmen, women, anybody. On the rare occasions in which the gun is emptied into the camera—i.e., into your face—the effect is so startling that the pornography of violence all but loses its fantasy charm. There are not nearly so many masochists as sadists among those little devils whispering into one's ears.

In fact, sex—"sadomasochism"—is only a part of the pornography of 26 violence. Violence is much more wrapped up, simply, with status. Violence is the simple, ultimate solution for problems of status competition, just as gambling is the simple, ultimate solution for economic competition. The old pornography was the fantasy of easy sexual delights in a world where sex was kept unavailable. The new pornography is the fantasy of easy triumph in a world where status competition has become so complicated and frustrating.

Already the old pornography is losing its kick because of over- 27 exposure. In the late thirties, Nathanael West published his last and best-regarded novel, *The Day of the Locust,* and it was a terrible flop commercially, and his publisher said if he ever published another book about Hollywood it would "have to be *My Thirty-nine Ways of Making Love by Hedy Lamarr.*" He thought he was saying something that was funny because it was beyond the realm of possibility. Less than thirty years later, however, Hedy Lamarr's *Ecstasy and Me* was published. Whether she mentions thirty-nine ways, I'm not sure, but she gets off to a flying start: "The men in my life have ranged from a classic case history of impotence, to a whip-brandishing sadist who enjoyed sex only after he tied my arms behind me with the sash of his robe. There was another man who took his pleasure with a girl in my own bed, while he thought I was asleep in it."

Yet she was too late. The book very nearly sank without a trace. The 28 sin itself is wearing out. Pornography cannot exist without certified taboo to violate. And today Lust, like the rest of the Seven Deadly Sins—Pride, Sloth, Envy, Greed, Anger, and Gluttony—is becoming a rather minor vice. The Seven Deadly Sins, after all, are only sins against the self. Theologically, the idea of Lust—well, the idea is that if you seduce some poor girl from Akron, it is not a sin because you are ruining her, but because you are wasting your time and your energies and damaging your own spirit. This goes back to the old work ethic, when the idea was to keep every able-bodied man's shoulder to the wheel. In an age of riches for all, the ethic becomes more nearly: Let him do anything he pleases, as long as he doesn't get in my way. And if he does get in my way, or even if he doesn't ... well ... we have *new* fantasies for that. *Put hair on the walls.*

"Hair on the walls" is the invisible subtitle of Truman Capote's book 29 *In Cold Blood.* The book is neither a who-done-it nor a will-they-be-caught, since the answers to both questions are known from the outset. It does ask why-did-they-do-it, but the answer is soon as clear as it is going to be. Instead, the book's suspense is based largely on a totally new idea in detective stories: the promise of gory details, and the withholding of them until the end. Early in the game one of the two murderers, Dick, starts promising to put "plenty of hair on them-those walls" with a shotgun. So read on, gentle readers, and on and on; you are led up to the moment before the crime on page 60 — yet the specifics, what happened, the gory details, are kept out of sight, in grisly dangle, until page 244.

But Dick and Perry, Capote's killers, are only a couple of Low Rent 30 bums. With James Bond the new pornography reached dead center, the bureaucratic middle class. The appeal of Bond has been explained as the appeal of the lone man who can solve enormously complicated, even world problems through his own bravery and initiative. But Bond is not a lone man at all, of course. He is not the Lone Ranger. He is much easier to identify than that. He is a salaried functionary in a bureaucracy. He is a sport, but a believable one; not a millionaire, but a bureaucrat on an expense account. He is not even a high-level bureaucrat. He is an operative. This point is carefully and repeatedly made by having his superiors dress him down for violations of standard operating procedure. Bond, like the Lone Ranger, solves problems with guns and fists. When it is over, however, the Lone Ranger leaves a silver bullet. Bond, like the rest of us, fills out a report in triplicate.

Marshall McLuhan says we are in a period in which it will become 31 harder and harder to stimulate lust through words and pictures — i.e., the old pornography. In the latest round of pornographic movies the producers have found it necessary to introduce violence, bondage, torture, and aggressive physical destruction to an extraordinary degree. The same sort of bloody escalation may very well happen in the pure pornography of violence. Even such able craftsmen as Truman Capote, Ian Fleming, NBC, and CBS may not suffice. Fortunately, there are historical models to rescue us from this frustration. In the latter days of the Roman Empire, the Emperor Commodus became jealous of the celebrity of the great gladiators. He took to the arena himself, with his sword, and began dispatching suitably screened cripples and hobbled fighters. Audience participation became so popular that soon various *illuminati* of the Commodus set, various boys and girls of the year, were out there, suited up, gaily cutting a sequence of dwarf and feebles down to short ribs. Ah, swinging generations, what new delights await?

Study Questions

1. How does Wolfe use definitions to advance his case?
2. How do ellipses, dashes, and parentheses help create the tone of this essay?
3. The style used in recounting the episode of *Gunsmoke* is notably different from the rest of the essay. How and why?
4. Comment on the humor in this essay.
5. To what uses does Wolfe put the episode of his cab ride with Robert Harrison?

5 The Natural and Supernatural

"Brave New World"

This section brings together a number of selections concerned with objectivity and truth in the scientific approach to life. Structurally, this section is probably the most tightly organized for student and instructor alike. Each of the essays and stories is part of a cluster in which the individual selections offer a variety of approaches.

The search for truth, stars, hawks, and ecology serve as the basis for the four clusters that follow.

The search for truth is not uniquely the province of scientists, as Marchette Chute demonstrates in her essay about the challenge facing biographers. Perhaps her style is less objective, her diction more connotative than we expect in scientific writing; her goal is nonetheless the same. Sir Edmund Hillary also leads the reader down the steps he followed in search of truth, the truth about the "abominable snowman"; particularly enlightening is his examination of the evidence. C. P. Snow calls himself an ex-scientist; now a novelist and professor, he here argues against the doctrine of the ethical neutrality of scientists. His thesis is more abstract than either Chute's or Hillary's, but his approach to it is through the particular.

Rhetorically, the selections on stars and hawks offer the widest opportunity for comparisons of types and styles. George Santayana's literary style provides a great contrast to Clarke's more matter-of-fact examination; the two men are not using the same lens in their scanning of the heavens. Then Loren C. Eiseley and Walter Van Tilburg Clark use entirely different forms in writing of hawks. Eiseley's prose is lyrical, almost poetic. Clark demonstrates his expert skill with point of view and paragraph structure. Richard Allen then presents us with the student's-eye view of Clark's mastery of style. The five essays in these two clusters vividly reveal the effectiveness of suiting style and form to content.

Finally, a selection from Rachel Carson's famous study of the harmful effects of pesticides, *Silent Spring,* unifies the final group in this section. "The Obligation to Endure" is a fine representative of Carson's thesis and her style. Her book was the center of a controversy that has not yet ended. Loren C. Eiseley defends and praises Carson and her book, while William J. Darby condemns her work and wants her silenced. That two scientists with equally unimpeachable credentials should sit on such radically opposed poles surely demonstrates the crucial need for a writer not only to gather the facts before putting pen to paper but also to interpret those facts as objectively as possible. Virginia Woolf's "The Death of the Moth" provides an antidote.

We hasten to add that our clusters need not be read as clusters. We have been careful to make selections that stand independently as models of basic rhetorical modes for the student writer to emulate.

Marchette Chute
GETTING AT THE TRUTH

Marchette Chute (1909-   ) was born in Wayzata, Minnesota. She earned an A.B. from the University of Minnesota (1930), and has been the recipient of many honorary degrees. A member of Phi Beta Kappa, she has won awards for her writing from the Poetry Society of America and the New York Shakespeare Club, among others. Her popular studies of Shakespeare, Ben Jonson, George Herbert and Robert Herrick, and Chaucer have brought her a large reading public. Among her other books are *Jesus of Israel* (1961), *The First Liberty* (1969), and *The Green Tree of Democracy* (1971).

This is a rather presumptuous title for a biographer to use, 1 since truth is a very large word. In the sense that it means the reality about a human being it is probably impossible for a biographer to achieve. In the sense that it means a reasonable presentation of all the available facts it is more nearly possible, but even this limited goal is harder to reach than it appears to be. A biographer needs to be both humble and cautious when he remembers the nature of the material he is working with, for a historical fact is rather like the flamingo that Alice in Wonderland tried to use as a croquet mallet. As soon as she got its neck nicely straightened out and was ready to hit the ball, it would turn and look at her with puzzled expression, and any biographer knows that what is called a "fact" has a way of doing the same.

Here is a small example. When I was writing my forthcoming biogra- 2 phy, "Ben Jonson of Westminster," I wanted to give a paragraph or two to Sir Philip Sidney, who had a great influence on Jonson. No one thinks of Sidney without thinking of chivalry, and to underline the point I intended to use a story that Sir Fulke Greville told of him. Sidney died of gangrene, from a musket shot that shattered his thigh, and Greville says that Sidney failed to put on his leg armor while preparing for battle because the marshal of the camp was not wearing leg armor and Sidney was unwilling to do anything that would give him a special advantage.

The story is so characteristic both of Sidney himself and of the mis- 3 placed high-mindedness of late Renaissance chivalry that I wanted to use it, and since Sir Fulke Greville was one of Sidney's closest friends the information seemed to be reliable enough. But it is always well to check each piece of information as thoroughly as possible and so I consulted

From *Saturday Review*, xxxvi (September 19, 1953). Copyright 1953 by the Saturday Review Associates, Inc. Reprinted by permission.

another account of Sidney written by a contemporary, this time a doctor who knew the family fairly well. The doctor, Thomas Moffet, mentioned the episode but he said that Sidney left off his leg armor because he was in a hurry.

The information was beginning to twist in my hand and could no 4 longer be trusted. So I consulted still another contemporary who had mentioned the episode, to see which of the two he agreed with. This was Sir John Smythe, a military expert who brought out his book a few years after Sidney's death. Sir John was an old-fashioned conservative who advocated the use of heavy armor even on horseback, and he deplored the current craze for leaving off leg protection, "the imitating of which ... cost that noble and worthy gentleman Sir Philip Sidney his life."

So here I was with three entirely different reasons why Sidney left 5 off his leg armor, all advanced by careful writers who were contemporaries of his. The flamingo had a legitimate reason for looking around with a puzzled expression.

The only thing to do in a case like this is to examine the point of 6 view of the three men who are supplying the conflicting evidence. Sir Fulke Greville was trying to prove a thesis: that his beloved friend had an extremely chivalric nature. Sir John Smythe also was trying to prove a thesis: that the advocates of light arming followed a theory that could lead to disaster. Only the doctor, Thomas Moffet, was not trying to prove a thesis. He was not using his own explanation to reinforce some point he wanted to make. He did not want anything except to set down on paper what he believed to be the facts; and since we do not have Sidney's own explanation of why he did not put on leg armor, the chances are that Dr. Moffet is the safest man to trust.

For Moffet was without desire. Nothing can so quickly blur and dis- 7 tort the facts as desire — the wish to use the facts for some purpose of your own — and nothing can so surely destroy the truth. As soon as the witness wants to prove something he is no longer impartial and his evidence is no longer to be trusted.

The only safe way to study contemporary testimony is to bear con- 8 stantly in mind this possibility of prejudice and to put almost as much attention on the writer himself as on what he has written. For instance, Sir Anthony Weldon's description of the Court of King James is lively enough and often used as source material; but a note from the publisher admits that the pamphlet was issued as a warning to anyone who wished to "side with this bloody house" of Stuart. The publisher, at any rate, did not consider Weldon an impartial witness. At about the same time Arthur Wilson published his history of Great Britain, which contained an irresistibly vivid account of the agonized death of the Countess of Somerset. Wilson sounds reasonably impartial; but his patron was the Earl of Essex, who had good reason to hate that particular countess, and there is evidence that he invented the whole scene to gratify his patron.

Sometimes a writer will contradict what he has already written, and 9 in that case the only thing to do is to investigate what has changed his point of view. For instance, in 1608 Captain John Smith issued a description of his capture by Powhatan, and he made it clear that the Indian chief had treated him with unwavering courtesy and hospitality. In 1624 the story was repeated in Smith's "General History of Virginia," but the writer's circumstances had changed. Smith needed money, "having a prince's mind imprisoned in a poor man's purse," and, he wanted the book to be profitable. Powhatan's daughter, the princess Pocahontas, had recently been in the news, for her visit to England had aroused a great deal of interest among the sort of people that Smith hoped would buy his book. So Smith supplied a new version of the story, in which the once-hospitable Powhatan would have permitted the hero's brains to be dashed out if Pocahontas had not saved his life. It was the second story that achieved fame, and of course it may have been true. But it is impossible to trust it because the desire of the writer is so obviously involved; as Smith said in his prospectus, he needed money and hoped that the book would give "satisfaction."

It might seem that there was an easy way for a biographer to avoid 10 the use of this kind of prejudiced testimony. All he has to do is to construct his biography from evidence that cannot be tampered with—from parish records, legal documents, bills, accounts, court records, and so on. Out of these solid gray blocks of impersonal evidence it should surely be possible to construct a road that will lead straight to the truth and that will never bend itself to the misleading curve of personal desire.

This might be so if the only problem involved were the reliability of 11 the material. But there is another kind of desire that is much more subtle, much more pervasive, and much more dangerous than the occasional distortions of fact that contemporary writers may have permitted themselves to make; and this kind of desire can destroy the truth of a biography even if every individual fact in it is as solid and as uncompromising as rock. Even if the road is built of the best and most reliable materials it can still curve away from the truth because of this other desire that threatens it: the desire of the biographer himself.

A biographer is not a court record or a legal document. He is a hu- 12 man being, writing about another human being, and his own temperament, his own point of view, and his own frame of reference are unconsciously imposed upon the man he is writing about. Even if the biographer is free from Captain Smith's temptation—the need for making money—and wants to write nothing but the literal truth, he is still handicapped by the fact that there is no such thing as a completely objective human being.

An illustration of what can happen if the point of view is sufficiently 13 strong is the curious conclusion that the nineteenth-century biographers reached about William Shakespeare. Shakespeare joined a company of London actors in 1594, was listed as an actor in 1598 and 1603, and was still listed as one of the "men actors" in the company in 1609. Shortly before he joined this company Shakespeare dedicated two narrative poems to the Earl of Southampton, and several years after Shakespeare died his collected plays were dedicated to the Earl of Pembroke. This was his only relationship with either of the two noblemen, and there is nothing to connect him with them during the fifteen years in which he belonged to the same acting company and during which he wrote nearly all his plays.

But here the desire of the biographers entered in. They had been 14 reared in the strict code of nineteenth-century gentility and they accepted two ideas without question. One was that there are few things more important than an English lord; the other was that there are few things less important than a mere actor. They already knew the undeniable fact that Shakespeare was one of the greatest men who ever lived; and while they could not go quite so far as to claim him as an actual member of the nobility, it was clear to them that he must have been the treasured friend of both the Earl of Southampton and the Earl of Pembroke and that he must have written his plays either while basking in their exalted company or while he was roaming the green countryside by the waters of the river Avon. (It is another basic conviction of the English gentleman that there is nothing so inspiring as nature.) The notion that Shakespeare had spent all these years as the working member of a company of London actors was so abhorrent that it was never seriously considered. It could not be so, therefore it was not.

These biographers did their work well. When New South Wales 15 built its beautiful memorial library to Shakespeare, it was the coat of arms of the Earl of Southampton that alternated with that of royalty in dignified splendor over the bookshelves. Shakespeare had been recreated in the image of desire, and desire will always ignore whatever is not relevant to its purpose. Because the English gentlemen did not like Shakespeare's background it was explained away as though it had never existed, and Shakespeare ceased to be an actor because so lowly a trade was not suited to so great a man.

All this is not to say that a biography should be lacking in a point of 16 view. If it does not have a point of view it will be nothing more than a kind of expanded article for an encyclopedia—a string of facts arranged in chronological order with no claim to being a real biography at all. A biography must have a point of view and it must have a frame of reference. But it should be a point of view and a frame of reference implicit in the material itself and not imposed upon it.

It might seem that the ideal biographical system, if it could be 17 achieved, would be to go through the years of research without feeling any kind of emotion. The biographer would be a kind of fact-finding machine and then suddenly, after his years of research, a kind of total vision would fall upon him and he would transcribe it in his best and most persuasive English for a waiting public. But research is fortunately not done by machinery, nor are visions likely to descend in that helpful manner. They are the product not only of many facts but also of much thinking, and it is only when the biographer begins to get emotional in his thinking that he ought to beware.

It is easy enough to make good resolutions in advance, but a biogra- 18 pher cannot altogether control his sense of excitement when the climax of his years of research draws near and he begins to see the pieces fall into place. Almost without his volition, A, B, and D fit together and start to form a pattern, and it is almost impossible for the biographer not to start searching for C. Something turns up that looks remarkably like C, and with a little trimming of the edges and the ignoring of one very slight discrepancy it will fill the place allotted for C magnificently.

It is at this point that the biographer ought to take a deep breath and 19 sit on his hands until he has had time to calm down. He has no real, fundamental reason to believe that his discovery is C, except for the fact that he wants it to be. He is like a man looking for a missing piece in a difficult jigsaw puzzle, who has found one so nearly the right shape that he cannot resist the desire to jam it into place.

If the biographer had refused to be tempted by his supposed discov- 20 ery of C and had gone on with his research, he might have found not only the connecting, illuminating fact he needed but much more besides. He is not going to look for it now. Desire has blocked the way. And by so much his biography will fall short of what might have been the truth.

It would not be accurate to say that a biographer should be wholly 21 lacking in desire. Curiosity is a form of desire. So is the final wish to get the material down on paper in a form that will be fair to the reader's interest and worthy of the subject. But a subconscious desire to push the facts around is one of the most dangerous things a biographer can encounter, and all the more dangerous because it is so difficult to know when he is encountering it.

The reason Alice had so much trouble with her flamingo is that the 22 average flamingo does not wish to be used as a croquet mallet. It has other purposes in view. The same thing is true of a fact, which can be just as self-willed as a flamingo and has its own kind of stubborn integrity. To try to force a series of facts into a previously desired arrangement is a form of misuse to which no self-respecting fact will willingly submit itself. The best and only way to treat it is to leave it alone and be willing to follow where it leads, rather than to press your own wishes upon it.

To put the whole thing into a single sentence: you will never suc- 23 ceed in getting at the truth if you think you know, ahead of time, what the truth ought to be.

Study Questions

1. How does Chute limit the challenge faced by biographers?
2. How many examples does the author use to explain the methodology of the biographer? How does she make the transitions between these examples?
3. What purpose is served by paragraphs 18–20?
4. How does the flamingo image help unify this essay?
5. How is the conclusion an extension of the introduction?

Sir Edmund Hillary

EPITAPH TO THE ELUSIVE ABOMINABLE SNOWMAN

Edmund Percival Hillary (1919–   ) was born in Auckland, New Zealand. Always the adventurer, he blazed trails across New Zealand and Antarctica. His most famous exploit occurred in 1953, when with the Sherpa Tenzing he reached the summit of Mt. Everest and thus presented Queen Elizabeth with a spectacular coronation present; he was knighted for his accomplishment. Among his books are *High Adventure* (1955), *No Latitude for Error* (1961), *Schoolhouse in the Clouds* (1964), and his autobiography, *Nothing Venture, Nothing Win* (1975).

Does the yeti, or "abominable snowman," really exist? Or is it 1 just a myth without practical foundation? For the last four months our Himalayan scientific and mountaineering expedition has been trying to find out—and now we think we know the answer.

There has been a growing pile of evidence in favor of the creature's 2 existence: the tracks seen by many explorers on Himalayan glaciers, the complete conviction of the local people that yetis roam the mountains, the yeti scalps and hands kept as relics in the high monasteries, the many stories about people who claimed to have seen them.

But despite the firm belief of many Himalayan explorers and of 3 some anthropologists, I began the search for the yeti with some skepticism. My own experience had been limited to two incidents. In 1951 a tough and experienced Sherpa (Sherpas are a mountain people of Tibetan stock) had told me with absolute conviction that he had seen a yeti and watched it for some time. In 1952 Explorer George Lowe and I had found a tuft of black hair at an altitude of 19,000 feet, a tuft that our Sherpas swore was yeti hair—and immediately threw away in obvious fear.

Last September we set off from Katmandu in Nepal and walked for a 4 hundred miles through rain and leeches to the 12,000-foot-high Sherpa village of Beding. For eight days we were immobilized by weather, but we made profitable use of our time by interrogating the villagers and the lamas in the local monastery. One of our expedition members, Desmond Doig, speaks the language of Nepal with great fluency and has the ability,

From *Life* (Jan. 13, 1961), pp. 72–73. Reprinted with permission.

quite unprecedented in my experience, to gain the confidence and liking of the local peoples.

We confirmed much that we already knew and learned more besides. 5 The Sherpas believe there are three types of yetis:

1. The chuteh: a vast, hairy, ginger-and-black creature, sometimes 6 eight feet tall, generally vegetarian and not harmful to man unless disturbed or annoyed.
2. The miteh: usually four to five feet tall with a high, pointed 7 skull. His feet are said to be placed back to front. He has a decidedly unpleasant temperament and delights in eating any humans who come his way.
3. The thelma: a small creature from 18 inches to two feet high 8 who lives down in the jungle, has human features and takes great pleasure in piling sticks and stones into little mounds.

We couldn't find any Sherpa who had actually seen a yeti, but several 9 had heard them — usually when the winter snowfalls lay deep on the ground and the villagers were confined to their houses. Then, one gathered, the sound of the yeti was frequently heard at night, and next morning tracks were seen by the frightened Sherpas.

One of our own Sherpas, Ang Temba, now proved to be a veritable 10 Sherlock Holmes. He scoured the village for information and brought us the exciting news that there was a yeti skin here, the prized possession of a lama and his wife. The lama was away, and at first the wife refused to show us the skin. But Ang Temba and Desmond Doig were a formidable combination, and after much persuasion and chinking of rupees the skin became ours. In our opinion it was a fine specimen of the very rare Tibetan blue bear, but all our Sherpas disagreed emphatically. It wasn't a bear at all, they said, but undoubtedly the chuteh, or biggest type of yeti. Nothing we said could sway this belief.

When the weather cleared, we moved up the Rolwaling valley and 11 began our search for signs of the yeti. Several weeks later our efforts were rewarded by the discovery of many tracks on the Ripimu glacier between 18,000 and 19,000 feet. These tracks were positively identified by our Sherpas as those of yetis, and they certainly fulfilled the required specifications: large broad feet with clear toe marks.

We devoted much care to the examination of these tracks and made 12 some interesting discoveries. When we followed a line of tracks to a place where the footprints were in the shade of rocks or on the cold north side of a snow slope, the yeti tracks suddenly ceased to exist. In their place we found the small footprints of a fox or wild dog, bunched closely together as the animal bounded over the snow. Again and again we saw precise evidence of the effect of the sun on those bunches of small tracks. The warmth melted them out, ran them together, completely altered their contours and made as fine a yeti track as one could wish.

Probably the best known photographs of yeti tracks are those taken 13 by Explorer Eric Shipton and Dr. Michael Ward on the Menlung glacier in 1951. The tracks that we discovered were less than two miles from the

Shipton tracks and at a similar height and time of the year. Dr. Ward, who came back to the Himalayas as a member of my physiological team, said that among the yeti tracks on the Menlung glacier he and Shipton had noticed a number of small animal tracks, but at the time they had not thought them significant.

In November we continued our investigations in the Khumbu region 14 at the foot of Mt. Everest. In the villages of Namche Bazar and Khumjung we obtained two more blue bear skins. Whenever we showed these skins to a Sherpa, we got the confident reply, "Chuteh."

Doig and Marlin Perkins, our zoologist, carried out a thorough en- 15 quiry among the Khumbu villages and monasteries. All the Sherpas believed in the yeti, but it was practically impossible to find anyone who, under careful questioning, claimed to have seen one. Even in the Thyangboche monastery, traditionally the source of much yeti lore and many yeti sightings, we were unable to find anyone who had seen a yeti. In fact, the two oldest lamas, who had lived in the monastery since its founding over 40 years ago, said they had neither seen a yeti nor knew of anyone who had.

Relics of the yeti in the monasteries of Khumjung, Pangboche and 16 Namche Bazar came in for special attention. The bones of a hand in the Pangboche monastery were thought by our medical men to be those of a man — possibly the delicate hand of a lama. The yeti scalps we were shown in these monasteries were more of a puzzle. They were in the shape of high, pointed caps covered with coarse reddish and black hair and seemed to be very old. If they were authentic scalps, their very form indicated that they belonged to no known animal. Although they had no seams or needle marks, there was the chance that they had been cleverly fabricated many years before out of the molded skin of some other creature.

Doig and Perkins worked hard on this second possibility. Ang 17 Temba produced two skins which had hair similar in texture to the scalps. We made high, pointed molds out of blocks of wood. The skins were softened, then stretched over the molds and left to dry. The resultant scalps were similar enough to the yeti scalps we saw in the monastery to indicate that we might be on the right track.

We realized that unless we could get an authoritative answer on the 18 scalps, they would remain a constant challenge to any theories about the yeti. But the village elders of Khumjung firmly believed that their community would suffer a plague, earthquake, flood or avalanche if their relic scalp ever was removed. They insisted that it was the remains of a famous yeti slaughter that took place 240 years ago, when there were so many man-eating yetis about that the Sherpas resorted to ruse to eliminate them. The Sherpas pretended to get drunk and to kill each other with wooden swords. At night the Sherpas substituted real swords, which they left lying about. The yetis, who had been watching them and were great imitators, proceeded to drink heavily also, slashed at each other with the real swords and killed each other off.

After much negotiation with the Khumjung elders, we persuaded 19 them to lend us the scalp for exactly six weeks. In exchange I promised I would try to raise money for a school which they will share with nearby

Sherpa villages. To guarantee that we would bring the scalp back, the elders said they would hold as hostages our expedition's three head Sherpas, as well as their property and possessions.

Our faithful Sherpas unhesitatingly agreed. Then the villagers chose 20 Kunjo Chumbi, the keeper of the village documents, to accompany us and bring the scalp back. For his first trip to the West, he wondered if he should take Sherpas traveling rations with him—a dried sheep carcass, wheat flour and some of the local brew. After talking it over with Doig, he settled instead on some cakes of Tibetan brick tea and his silver teacup.

He, Doig, Perkins and I covered 170 miles of steep country to Kat- 21 mandu in 9 1/2 days. From there we flew to Chicago, Paris and London and showed the scalp and the chuteh skins to zoologists, anthropologists and other scientists. Their decision was unanimous: the yeti scalp was not a scalp at all. It had been molded out of some other skin, and the scientists agreed that it was the skin and hair of the serow, a rather uncommon Himalayan member of the large goat-antelope family. Also our chuteh skins were confirmed to be Tibetan blue bear.

We now know that a yeti track can be made by the sun melting the 22 footprints of a small creature such as a fox or wild dog. The same effect could occur with the prints of snow leopards, bears and even humans. We know that the large furs so confidently described by our Sherpas as chutehs are in fact the Tibetan blue bear. There is the strong possibility that some of these big, unfamiliar creatures strayed down from their only known habitations in eastern Tibet and crossed the Himalayan range. The small thelma in its habits and description sounds very much like the rhesus monkey. And the pointed scalps of the miteh have proved to be made from the skin of the much less frightening serow.

There is still much to be explained. Our theory on the tracks does 23 not cover every case. We have not yet found a satisfactory explanation for the noise of the yeti which many Sherpas claim to have heard. But all in all we feel we have solved some of the major problems surrounding this elusive creature. Of course, the yeti still remains a very real part of the mythology and tradition of the Himalayan people—and it is undoubtedly in the field of mythology that the yeti rightly belongs.

Study Questions

1. How does the essay's title portend its conclusion?
2. Is Hillary's argument inductive or deductive? Explain.
3. The author proceeds in a relatively scientific fashion. Does he ever demonstrate scorn or sarcasm? Is he patronizing to those with whom he is forced to deal?
4. What kinds of evidence does Hillary examine? Can you tell how much credence he puts in the testimony of the local people?
5. Are scientists necessarily skeptics? What is implied about mythology in the last paragraph?

C. P. Snow

THE MORAL UN-NEUTRALITY OF SCIENCE

C. P. Snow (1905–   ) was born in Leicester, England. He received his B.Sc. in 1927 and M.Sc. in 1928, both from the University of Leicester, and a Ph.D. from Christ's College, Cambridge, in 1930. His honorary degrees come from universities on both sides of the Atlantic. Snow has been a commissioner for the British Civil Service, physicist-director for the English Electric Co. Ltd., and director of the Educational Film Centre Ltd., as well as a lecturer at the universities of Cambridge, Harvard, Yale, California, and St. Andrews's. Among his works are *New Lives for Old* (1933), *The Two Cultures and the Scientific Revolution* (1959, *Variety of Men* (1967), *The State of Siege* (1969), and *Public Affairs* (1971). His series of novels collectively known as "Strangers and Brothers" includes many of his most famous books: *The Masters* (1951), *The Conscience of the Rich* (1958), and *The Affair* (1960).

Scientists are the most important occupational group in the 1 world today. At this moment, what they do is of passionate concern to the whole of human society. At this moment, the scientists have little influence on the world effect of what they do. Yet, potentially, they can have great influence. The rest of the world is frightened both of what they do — that is, of the intellectual discoveries of science — and of its effect. The rest of the world transferring its fears, is frightened of the scientists themselves and tends to think of them as radically different from other men.

As an ex-scientist, if I may call myself so, I know that is nonsense. I 2 have even tried to express in fiction some kinds of scientific temperament and scientific experience. I know well enough that scientists are very much like other men. After all, we are all human, even if some of us don't give that appearance. I think I would be prepared to risk a generalization. The scientists I have known (and because of my official life I have known as many as anyone in the world) have been in certain respects just perceptibly more morally admirable than most other groups of intelligent men.

"The Moral Un-Neutrality of Science," Snow, C. P. *Science* vol. 133, pp. 255–262, 27 January 1961. Copyright 1961 by the American Association for the Advancement of Science.

That is a sweeping statement, and I mean it only in a statistical sense. 3
But I think there is just a little in it. The moral qualities I admire in scientists are quite simple ones, but I am very suspicious of attempts to oversubtilize moral qualities. It is nearly always a sign, not of true sophistication, but of a specific kind of triviality. So I admire in scientists very simple virtues — like courage, truth-telling, kindness — in which, judged by the low standards which the rest of us manage to achieve, the scientists are not deficient. I think on the whole the scientists make slightly better husbands and fathers than most of us, and I admire them for it. I don't know the figures, and I should be curious to have them sorted out, but I am prepared to bet that the proportion of divorces among scientists is slightly but significantly less than that among other groups of similar education and income. I do not apologize for considering that a good thing.

A close friend of mine is a very distinguished scientist. He is also 4
one of the few scientists I know who has lived what we used to call a Bohemian life. When we were both younger, he thought he would undertake historical research to see how many great scientists had been as fond of women as he was. I think he would have felt mildly supported if he could have found a precedent. I remember his reporting to me that his researchers hadn't had any luck. The really great scientists seemed to vary from a few neutral characters to a large number who were depressingly "normal." The only gleam of comfort was to be found in the life of Jerome Cardan; and Cardan wasn't anything like enough to outweigh all the others.

So scientists are not much different from other men. They are certainly no worse than other men. But they do differ from other men in 5
one thing. That is the point I started with. Whether they like it or not, what they do is of critical importance for the human race. Intellectually, it has transformed the climate of our time. Socially, it will decide whether we live or die, and how we live or die. It holds decisive powers for good and evil. That is the situation in which the scientists find themselves. They may not have asked for it, or may only have asked for it in part, but they cannot escape it. They think, many of the most sensitive of them, that they don't deserve to have this weight of responsibility heaved upon them. All they want to do is to get on with their work. I sympathize. But the scientists can't escape the responsibility — any more than they, or the rest of us, can escape the gravity of the moment in which we stand.

There is of course one way to contract out. It has been a favorite 6
way for intellectual persons caught in the midst of water too rough for them.

It consists of the invention of categories — or, if you like, of the divi- 7
sion of moral labor. That is, the scientists who want to contract out say, we produce the tools. We stop there. It is for you — the rest of the world, the politicians — to say how the tools are used. The tools may be used for purposes which most of us would regard as bad. If so, we are sorry. But as scientists, that is no concern of ours.

This is the doctrine of the ethical neutrality of science. I can't accept 8 it for an instant. I don't believe any scientist of serious feeling can accept it. It is hard, some think, to find the precise statements which will prove it wrong. Yet we nearly all feel intuitively that the invention of comfortable categories is a moral trap. It is one of the easier methods of letting the conscience rust. It is exactly what the early 19th century economists, such as Ricardo, did in the face of the facts of the first industrial revolution. We wonder now how men, intelligent men, can have been so morally blind. We realize how the exposure of that moral blindness gave Marxism its apocalyptic force. We are now, in the middle of the scientific or second industrial revolution, in something like the same position as Ricardo. Are we going to let our consciences rust? Can we ignore that intimation we nearly all have, that scientists have a unique responsibility? Can we believe it, that science is morally neutral?

To me — it would be dishonest to pretend otherwise — there is only 9 one answer to those questions. Yet I have been brought up in the presence of the same intellectual categories as most western scientists. It would also be dishonest to pretend that I find it easy to construct a rationale which expresses what I now believe. The best I can hope for is to fire a few sighting shots. Perhaps someone who sees more clearly than I can will come along and make a real job of it.

Let me begin with a remark which seems some way off the point. 10 Anyone who has ever worked in any science knows how much esthetic joy he has obtained. That is, in the actual *activity* of science, in the process of making a discovery, however humble it is, one can't help feeling an awareness of beauty. The subjective experience, the esthetic satisfaction, seems exactly the same as the satisfaction one gets from writing a poem or a novel, or composing a piece of music. I don't think anyone has succeeded in distinguishing between them. The literature of scientific discovery is full of this esthetic joy. The very best communication of it that I know comes in G. H. Hardy's book, *A Mathematician's Apology.* Graham Greene once said he thought that, along with Henry James's prefaces, this was the best account of the artistic experience ever written. But one meets the same thing throughout the history of science. Bolyai's great yell of triumph when he saw he could construct a self-consistent, non-Euclidean geometry; Rutherford's revelation to his colleagues that he knew what the atom was like; Darwin's slow, patient, timorous certainty that at last he had got there — all these are voices, different voices, of esthetic ecstasy.

That is not the end of it. The result of the activity of science, the ac- 11 tual finished piece of scientific work, has an esthetic value in itself. The judgments passed on it by other scientists will more often than not be expressed in esthetic terms: "That's beautiful!" or "That really is very pretty!" (as the understating English tend to say). The esthetics of scientific constructs, like the esthetics of works of art, are variegated. We think some of the great syntheses, like Newton's beautiful because of their classical simplicity, but we see a different kind of beauty in the relativistic extension of the wave equation or the interpretation of the structure of deoxyribonucleic acid, perhaps because of the touch of unexpectedness. Scientists know their kinds of beauty when they see them. They are suspicious, and scientific history shows they have always been right to have been so, when a subject is in an "ugly" state. For example, most physicists feel in their bones that the present bizarre assembly of nuclear particles, as grotesque as a stamp collection, can't possibly be, in the long run, the last word.

We should not restrict the esthetic values to what we call "pure" 12 science. Applied science has its beauties, which are, in my view, identical in nature. The magnetron has been a marvelously useful device, but it was a beautiful device, not exactly apart from its utility but because it did, with such supreme economy, precisely what it was designed to do. Right down in the field of development, the esthetic experience is as real to engineers. When they forget it, when they begin to design heavy-power equipment about twice as heavy as it needs to be, engineers are the first to know that they are lacking virtue.

There is no doubt, then, about the esthetic content of science, both 13 in the activity and the result. But esthetics has no connection with morals, say the categorizers. I don't want to waste time on peripheral issues — but are you quite sure of that? Or is it possible that these categories are inventions to make us evade the human and social conditions in which we now exist? But let us move straight on to something else, which is right in the grain of the activity of science and which is at the same time quintessentially moral. I mean, the desire to find the truth.

By *truth*, I don't intend anything complicated, once again. I am using 14 the word as a scientist uses it. We all know that the philosophical examination of the concept of empirical truth gets us into some curious complexities, but most scientists really don't care. They know that the truth, as they use the word and as the rest of us use it in the language of common speech, is what makes science work. That is good enough for them. On it rests the whole great edifice of modern science. They have a sneaking sympathy for Rutherford, who, when asked to examine the philosophical bases of science, was inclined to reply, as he did to the metaphysician Samuel Alexander: "Well, what have you been talking all your life, Alexander? Just hot air! Nothing but hot air!"

Anyway, truth in their own straightforward sense is what the scientists are trying to find. They want to find what is *there*. Without that desire, there is no science. It is the driving force of the whole activity. It compels the scientist to have an overriding respect for truth, every stretch of the way. That is, if you're going to find what is *there*, you mustn't deceive yourself or anyone else. You mustn't lie to yourself. At the crudest level, you mustn't fake your experiments.

Curiously enough, scientists do try to behave like that. A short time 16 ago, I wrote a novel in which the story hinged on a case of scientific fraud. But I made one of my characters, who was himself a very good scientist, say that, considering the opportunities and temptations, it is aston-ishing how few such cases there are. We have all heard of perhaps half a dozen open and notorious ones, which are on the record for anyone to read — ranging from the "discovery" of the L radiation to the singular epi-sode of the Piltdown man.

We have all, if we have lived any time in the scientific world, heard 17 private talk of something like another dozen cases which for various rea-sons are not yet public property. In some cases, we know the motives for the cheating — sometimes, but not always, sheer personal advantage, such as getting money or a job. But not always. A special kind of vanity had led more than one man into scientific faking. At a lower level of research there are presumably some more cases. There must have been occasional Ph.D. students who scraped by with the help of a bit of fraud.

But the total number of all these men is vanishingly small by the 18 side of the total number of scientists. Incidentally, the effect on science of such frauds is also vanishingly small. Science is a self-correcting sys-tem. That is, no fraud (or honest mistake) is going to stay undetected for long. There is no need for an extrinsic scientific criticism, because critic-ism is inherent in the process itself. So that all that a fraud can do is waste the time of the scientists who have to clear it up.

The remarkable thing is not the handful of scientists who deviate 19 from the search for truth but the overwhelming numbers who keep to it. That is a demonstration, absolutely clear for anyone to see, of moral be-havior on a very large scale.

We take it for granted. Yet it is very important. It differentiates 20 science in its widest sense (which includes scholarship) from all other in-tellectual activities. There is a built-in moral component right in the core of the scientific activity itself. The desire to find the truth is itself a moral impulse, or at least contains a moral impulse. The way in which a scien-tist tries to find the truth imposes on him a constant moral discipline. We say a scientific conclusion — such as the contradiction of parity by Lee and Yang — is "true" in the limited sense of scientific truth, just as we say that it is "beautiful" according to the criteria of scientific esthetics. We also know that to reach this conclusion took a set of actions which would have been useless without the moral nature. That is, all through the mar-velous experiments of Wu and her colleagues, there was the constant moral exercise of seeking and telling the truth. To scientists, who are brought up in this climate, this seems as natural as breathing. Yet it is a wonderful thing. Even if the scientific activity contained only this one moral component, that alone would be enough to let us say that it was morally un-neutral.

But is this the only moral component? All scientists would agree 21 about the beauty and the truth. In the western world, they wouldn't agree on much more. Some will feel with me in what I am going to say. Some will not. That doesn't affect me much, except that I am worried by the growth of an attitude I think very dangerous, a kind of technological conformity disguised as cynicism. I shall say a little more about that later. As for disagreement, G. H. Hardy used to comment that a serious man ought not to waste his time stating a majority opinion — there are plenty of others to do that. That was the voice of classical scientific nonconformity. I wish that we heard it more often.

Let met cite some grounds for hope. Any of us who were working in science before 1933 can remember what the atmosphere was like. It is a terrible bore when aging men in their fifties speak about the charms of their youth. Yet I am going to irritate you — just as Talleyrand irritated his juniors — by saying that unless one was on the scene before 1933, one hasn't known the sweetness of the scientific life. The scientific world of the twenties was as near to being a full-fledged international community as we are likely to get. Don't think I'm saying that the men involved were superhuman or free from the ordinary frailties. That wouldn't come well from me, who have spent a fraction of my writing life pointing out that scientists are, first and foremost, men. But the atmosphere of the twenties in science was filled with an air of benevolence and magnanimity which transcended the people who lived in it. 22

Anyone who ever spent a week in Cambridge or Gottingen or Copenhagen felt it all round him. Rutherford had very human faults, but he was a great man with abounding human generosity. For him the world of science was a world that lived on a plane above the nation-state, and lived there with joy. That was at least as true of those two other great men. Niels Bohr and Franck, and some of that spirit rubbed off on to the pupils round them. The same was true of the Roman school of physics. 23

The personal links within this international world were very close. It is worth remembering that Peter Kapitza, who was a loyal Soviet citizen, honored my country by working in Rutherford's laboratory for many years. He became a fellow of the Royal Society, a fellow of Trinity College, Cambridge, and the founder and kingpin of the best physics club Cambridge has known. He never gave up his Soviet citizenship and is now director of the Institute of Physical Problems in Moscow. Through him a generation of English scientists came to have personal knowledge of their Russian colleagues. These exchanges were then, and have remained, more valuable than all the diplomatic exchanges ever invented. 24

The Kapitza phenomenon couldn't take place now. I hope to live to see the day when a young Kapitza can once more work for 16 years in Berkeley or Cambridge and then go back to an eminent place in his own country. When that can happen, we are all right. But after the idyllic years of world science, we passed into a tempest of history, and, by an unfortunate coincidence, we passed into a technological tempest too. 25

The discovery of atomic fission science, we the world of international physics. "This has killed a beautiful subject," said Mark Oliphant, the father figure of Australian physics, in 1945, after the bombs had dropped. In intellectual terms, he has not turned out to be right. In spiritual and moral terms, I sometimes think he has. 26

A good deal of the international community of science remains in other fields — in great areas of biology, for example. Many biologists are 27 feeling the identical liberation, the identical joy at taking part in a magnanimous enterprise, that physicists felt in the twenties. It is more than likely that the moral and intellectual leadership of science will pass to biologists, and it is among them that we shall find the Rutherfords, Bohrs, and Francks of the next generation.

Physicists have had a bitterer task. With the discovery of fission, and 28 with some technical breakthroughs in electronics, physicists became, almost overnight, the most important military resource a nation-state could call on. A large number of physicists became soldiers not in uniform. So they have remained, in the advanced societies, ever since.

It is very difficult to see what else they could have done. All this be- 29 gan in the Hitler war. Most scientists thought then that Nazism was as near absolute evil as a human society can manage. I myself thought so. I still think so, without qualification. That being so, Nazism had to be fought, and since the Nazis might make fission bombs — which we thought possible until 1944, and which was a continual nightmare if one was remotely in the know — well, then, we had to make them too. Unless one was an unlimited pacifist, there was nothing else to do. And unlimited pacificism is a position which most of us cannot sustain.

Therefore I respect, and to a large extent share, the moral attitudes 30 of those scientists who devoted themselves to making the bomb. But the trouble is, when you get onto any kind of moral escalator, to know whether you're ever going to be able to get off. When scientists became soldiers they gave up something, so imperceptibly that they didn't realize it, of the full scientific life. Not intellectually. I see no evidence that scientific work on weapons of maximum destruction has been different from other scientific work. But there is a moral difference.

It may be — scientists who are better men than I am often take this 31 attitude, and I have tried to represent it faithfully in one of my books — that this is a moral price which, in certain circumstances, has to be paid. Nevertheless, it is no good pretending that there is not a moral price. Soldiers have to obey. That is the foundation of their morality. It is not the foundation of the scientific morality. Scientists have to question and if necessary rebel. I don't want to be misunderstood. I am no anarchist. I am not suggesting that loyalty is not a prime virtue. I am not saying that all rebellion is good. But I am saying that loyalty can easily turn into conformity, and that conformity can often be a cloak for the timid and self-seeking. So can obedience, carried to the limit. When you think of the long and gloomy history of man, you will find that far more, and far more hideous, crimes have been committed in the name of pretending than have ever been committed in the name of rebellion. If you doubt that, read William Shirer's *Rise and Fall of the Third Reich*. The German officer corps were brought up in the most rigorous code of obedience. To them, no more honorable and God-fearing body of men could conceivably exist. Yet in the name of obedience, they were party to, and assisted in, the most wicked large-scale actions in the history of the world.

Scientists must not go that way. Yet the duty to question is not 32 much of a support when you are living in the middle of an organized society. I speak with feeling here. I was an official for 20 years. I went into official life at the beginning of the war, for the reasons that prompted by scientific friends to begin to make weapons. I stayed in that life until a year ago, for the same reason that made my scientific friends turn into civilian soldiers. The official's life in England is not quite so disciplined as a soldier's, but it is very nearly so. I think I know the virtues, which are very great, of the men who live that disciplined life. I also know what for me was the moral trap. I, too, had got onto an escalator. I can put the result in a sentence: I was coming to hide behind the institution; I was losing the power to say no.

Only a very bold man, when he is a member of an organized society, 33 can keep the power to say no. I tell you that, not being a very bold man, or one who finds it congenial to stand alone, away from his colleagues. We can't expect many scientists to do it. Is there any tougher ground for them to stand on? I suggest to you that there is. I believe that there is a spring of moral action in the scientific activity which is at least as strong as the search for truth. The name of this spring is *knowledge*. Scientists *know* certain things in a fashion more immediate and more certain than those who don't comprehend what science is. Unless we are abnormally weak or abnormally wicked men, this knowledge is bound to shape our actions. Most of us are timid, but to an extent, knowledge gives us guts. Perhaps it can give us guts strong enough for the jobs in hand.

I had better take the most obvious example. All physical scientists 34 *know* that it is relatively easy to make plutonium. We know this, not as a journalistic fact at second hand, but as a fact in our own experience. We can work out the number of scientific and engineering personnel needed for a nation-state to equip itself with fission and fusion bombs. We *know* that, for a dozen or more states, it will only take perhaps six years, perhaps less. Even the best informed of us always exaggerate these periods.

This we know, with the certainty of—what shall I call it?—engineer- 35 ing truth. We also—most of us—are familiar with statistics and the nature of odds. We know, with the certainty of statistical truth, that if enough of these weapons are made, by enough different states, some of them are going to blow up, through accident, or folly, or madness—the motives don't matter. What does matter is the nature of the statistical fact.

All this we *know*. We know it in a more direct sense than any politi- 36 cian because it comes from our direct experience. It is part of our minds. Are we going to let it happen?

All this we *know*. It throws upon scientists a direct and personal re- 37 sponsibility. It is not enough to say that scientists have a responsibility as citizens. They have a much greater one than that, and one different in kind. For scientists have a moral imperative to say what they know. It is going to make them unpopular in their own nation-states. It may do worse than make them unpopular. That doesn't matter. Or at least, it does matter to you and me, but it must not count in the face of the risks.

For we genuinely know the risks. We are faced with an either-or, and 38
we haven't much time. The *either* is acceptance of a restriction of nuclear
armaments. This is going to begin, just as a token, with an agreement on
the stopping of nuclear tests. The United States is not going to get the
99.9-percent "security" that it has been asking for. This is unobtainable,
though there are other bargains that the United States could probably secure. I am not going to conceal from you that this course involves certain
risks. They are quite obvious, and no honest man is going to blink them.
That is the *either*. The *or* is not a risk but a certainty. It is this. There is
no agreement on tests. The nuclear arms race between the United States
and U.S.S.R. not only continues but accelerates. Other countries join in.
Within, at the most, six years, China and several other states have a stock
of nuclear bombs. Within, at the most, ten years, some of those bombs
are going off. I am saying this as responsibly as I can. *That* is the certainty. On the one side, therefore, we have a finite risk. On the other
side we have a certainty of disaster. Between a risk and a certainty, a
sane man does not hesitate.

It is the plain duty of scientists to explain this either-or. It is a duty 39
which seems to me to come from the moral nature of the scientific activity itself.

The same duty, though in a much more pleasant form, arises with re- 40
spect to the benevolent powers of science. For scientists know, and again
with the certainty of scientific knowledge, that we possess every scientific
fact we need to transform the physical life of half the world. And transform it within the span of people now living. I mean, we have all the resources to help half the world live as long as we do and eat enough. All
that is missing is the will. We *know* that. Just as we know that you in the
United States, and to a slightly lesser extent we in the United Kingdom,
have been almost unimaginably lucky. We are sitting like people in a
smart and cozy restaurant and we are eating comfortably, looking out of
the window into the streets. Down on the pavement are people who are
looking up at us, people who by chance have different colored skins from
ours, and are rather hungry. Do you wonder that they don't like us all
that much? Do you wonder that we sometimes feel ashamed of ourselves, as we look out through that plate glass?

Well, it is within our power to get started on that problem. We are 41
morally impelled to. We all know that, if the human species does solve
that one, there will be consequences which are themselves problems. For
instance, the population of the world will become embarrassingly large.
But that is another challenge. There are going to be challenges to our intelligence and to our moral nature as long as man remains man. After all,
a challenge is not, as the word is coming to be used, an excuse for slink-
ing off and doing nothing. A challenge is something to be picked up.

For all these reasons, I believe the world community of scientists has 42
a final responsibility upon it—a greater responsibility than is pressing on

any body of men. I do not pretend to know how they will bear this responsibility. These may be famous last words, but I have an inextinguishable hope. For, as I have said, there is no doubt that the scientific activity is both beautiful and truthful. I cannot prove it, but I believe that, simply because scientists cannot escape their own knowledge, they also won't be able to avoid showing themselves disposed to good.

Study Questions

1. Snow has broken his essay into sections clearly marked by the spacing. What distinguishes each essay, in terms of the development of the argument, from the other sections?
2. What is the thesis of this essay, and is it explicit or implicit?
3. Often a word is repeated as an aid in the transition from paragraph to paragraph. Cite examples.
4. Snow defines abstract terms, but not in a conventional, dictionary like way. How does he accomplish the definition of such a word as *truth*?
5. The author is himself a scientist, but he writes novels too. Does his style seem to you that of a scientist or a novelist? Why?

George Santayana
THE STARS

George Santayana (1863–1952) was born in Madrid, Spain, and moved with his family to Boston in 1872. Although he attended the University of Berlin, he earned his B.A. (1886), M.A., and Ph.D. (1889) all at Harvard. Santayana taught philosophy at Harvard from 1889 to 1912, and then left the United States to spend the rest of his life in Oxford and Rome. He is generally considered among the most eminent of modern philosophers. Among his numerous books are philosophical studies: *The Sense of Beauty* (1896), *Reason in Religion* (1905), and *Realms of Being* (1942); poetry: *Lucifer: A Theological Tragedy* (1898) and *The Hermit of Carmel and Other Poems* (1901); and a novel: *The Last Puritan* (1935). His autobiography was published in three volumes: *Persons and Places* (1944), *The Middle Span*

Reprinted from *Little Essays from the Writings of George Santayana* with permission of Charles Scribner's Sons.

(1945), and *My Host the World* (1953). In his classes at Harvard were many who later achieved eminence, including T. S. Eliot, Conrad Aiken, Walter Lippmann, Felix Frankfurter, and Robert Benchley.

To most people, I fancy, the stars are beautiful; but if you ask 1 why, they would be at a loss to reply, until they remembered what they had heard about astronomy, and the great size and distance and possible habitation of those orbs. The vague and illusive ideas thus aroused fall in so well with the dumb emotion we were already feeling, that we attribute this emotion to those ideas, and persuade ourselves that the power of the starry heavens lies in the suggestion of astronomical facts.

The idea of the insignificance of our earth and of the incomprehen- 2 sible multiplicity of worlds is indeed immensely impressive; it may even be intensely disagreeable. There is something baffling about infinity; in its presence the sense of finite humility can never wholly banish the rebellious suspicion that we are being deluded. Our mathematical imagination is put on the rack by our attempted conception that has all the anguish of a nightmare and probably, could we but awake, all its laughable absurdity. But the obsession of this dream is an intellectual puzzle, not an aesthetic delight. Before the days of Kepler the heavens declared the glory of the Lord; and we needed no calculation of stellar distances, no fancies about a plurality of worlds, no image of infinite spaces, to make the stars sublime.

Had we been taught to believe that the stars governed our fortunes, 3 and were we reminded of fate whenever we looked at them, we should similarly tend to imagine that this belief was the source of their sublimity; and if the superstition were dispelled, we should think the interest gone from the apparition. But experience would soon undeceive us, and prove that the sensuous character of the object was sublime in itself. For that reason the parable of the natal stars governing our lives is such a natural one to express our subjection to circumstances, and can be transformed by the stupidity of disciples into a literal tenet. In the same way, the kinship of the emotion produced by the stars with the emotion proper to certain religious moments makes the stars seem a religious object. They become, like impressive music, a stimulus to worship. But fortunately there are experiences which remain untouched by theory, and which maintain the mutual intelligence of men through the estrangements wrought by intellectual and religious systems. When the superstructures crumble, the common foundation of human sentience and imagination is exposed beneath. Did not the infinite, by this initial assault upon our senses, awe us, and overwhelm us, as solemn music might, the idea of it would be abstract and mental like that of the infinitesimal, and nothing but an amusing curiosity. The knowledge that the universe is a multitude of minute spheres circling, like specks of dust, in a dark and boundless void, might leave us cold and indifferent, if not bored and depressed, were it not that we identify this hypothetical scheme with the visible splendor, the poignant intensity, and the baffling number of the stars. So far is the object from giving value to the impression, that it is here, as it must always ultimately be, the impression that gives value to the object. For all worth leads us back to actual feeling somewhere, or else evaporates into nothing—into a word and a superstition.

Now, the starry heavens are very happily designed to intensify the sensations on which their fascination must rest. The continuum of space is broken into points, numerous enough to give the utmost idea of multiplicity, and yet so distinct and vivid that it is impossible not to remain aware of their individuality. The sensuous contrast of the dark background—blacker the clearer the night and the more stars we can see—with the palpitating fire of the stars themselves, could not be exceeded by any possible device. 4

Fancy a map of the heavens and every star plotted upon it, even those invisible to the naked eye: why would this object, as full of scientific suggestions surely as the reality, leave us so comparatively cold? The sense of multiplicity is naturally in no way diminished by the representation; but the poignancy of the sensation, the life of the light, are gone; and with the dulled impression the keenness of the emotion disappears. Or imagine the stars, undiminished in number, without losing any of their astronomical significance and divine immutability, marshalled in geometrical patterns; say in a Latin cross, with the words *In hoc signo vinces* in a scroll around them. The beauty of the illumination would be perhaps increased, and its import, practical, religious, and cosmic, would surely be a little plainer; but where would be the sublimity of the spectacle? Irretrievably lost; and lost because the form of the object would no longer tantalize us with its sheer multiplicity, and with the consequent overpowering sense of suspense and awe. Accordingly things which have enough multiplicity, as the lights of a city seen across water, have an effect similar to that of the stars, if less intense; whereas a star, if alone, because the multiplicity is lacking, makes a wholly different impression. The single star is tender, beautiful, and mild; we can compare it to the humblest and sweetest of things: 5

> A violet by a mossy stone
> Half hidden from the eye,
> Fair as *a star when only one*
> *Is shining in the sky.*

It is, not only in fact but in nature, an attendant on the moon, associated with the moon, if we may be so prosaic here, not only by contiguity but also by similarity. 6

> Fairer than Phoebe's sapphire-regioned star
> Or vesper, amorous glow-worm of the sky.

The same poet can say elsewhere of a passionate lover: 7

> He arose
> Ethereal, flushed, and like a throbbing star,
> Amid the sapphire heaven's deep repose.

How opposite is all this from the cold glitter, the cruel and mysterious sublimity of the stars when they are many! With these we have no tender associations; they make us think rather of Kant who could hit 8 on nothing else to compare with his categorical imperative, perhaps because he found in both the same baffling incomprehensibility and the same fierce actuality. Such ultimate feelings are sensations of physical tension.

Study Questions

1. Santayana's argument advances by *dismissing* reasons given for people believing that stars are beautiful. How many of these explanations does he discard? Where does he provide the answer to the "why" of the first paragraph?
2. What is the function of the fourth paragraph? Comment on the use of *now* followed by a comma.
3. Cite examples of *periodic sentences* in this essay.
4. Santayana uses similes and metaphors sparingly. How effective and appropriate are those that he does use?
5. Kepler, Kant, poets—what disciplines do these represent? How is Santayana's argument aided by the accretion?

Arthur C. Clarke
THE STAR OF THE MAGI

Arthur C. Clarke (1917–   ) is a native of Somersetshire, England. He was educated at King's College, University of London, and served in the British Civil Service and the Royal Air Force. At home in both space and undersea explorations, Clarke's writings encompass both areas; he suggested the use of space satellites for communications as early as 1945. His nonfiction works include *The Challenge of the Spaceship* (1959), *The Challenge of the Sea* (1960), *Man and Space* (1964), *Earthlight* (1972), and *Rendevous with Rama* (1973). He is perhaps best known to the public for his screenplay *2001: A Space Odyssey*, written with Stanley Kubrick. Clarke's honors include the International Fantasy Award (1952), the Kalinga Prize (1961), and the Franklin Institute Ballantine Medal (1963).

Go out of doors any morning this December and look up at   1
the eastern sky an hour or so before dawn. You will see there one of the most beautiful sights in all the heavens—a blazing, blue-white beacon, many times brighter than Sirius, the most brilliant of the stars. Apart

Reprinted by permission of the author and the author's agents, Scott Meredith Literary Agency, Inc. 845 Third Avenue, New York, New York 10022.

from the Moon itself, it will be the brightest object you will ever see in the night sky. It will still be visible even when the Sun rises; you will even be able to find it at midday if you know exactly where to look.

It is the planet Venus, our sister world, reflecting across the gulfs of 2 space the sunlight glancing from her unbroken cloud shield. Every nineteen months she appears in the morning sky, rising shortly before the Sun, and all who see this brilliant herald of the Christmas dawn will inevitably be reminded of the star that led the Magi to Bethlehem.

What was that star, assuming that it had some natural explanation? 3 Could it, in fact, have been Venus? At least one book has been written to prove this theory, but it will not stand up to serious examination. To all the people of the Eastern world, Venus was one of the most familiar objects in the sky. Even today, she serves as a kind of alarm clock to the Arab nomads. When she rises, it is time to start moving, to make as much progress as possible before the Sun begins to blast the desert with its heat. For thousands of years, shining more brilliantly than we ever see her in our cloudy northern skies, she has watched the camps struck and the caravans begin to move.

Even to the ordinary, uneducated Jews of Herod's kingdom, there 4 could have been nothing in the least remarkable about Venus. And the Magi were no ordinary men; they were certainly experts on astronomy, and must have known the movements of the planets better than do ninety-nine people out of a hundred today. To explain the Star of Bethlehem we must look elsewhere.

The Bible gives us very few clues; all that we can do is to consider 5 some possibilities which at this distance in time can be neither proved nor disproved. One of these possibilities — the most spectacular and awe-inspiring of all — has been discovered only in the last few years, but let us first look at some of the earlier theories.

In addition to Venus, there are four other planets visible to the 6 naked eye — Mercury, Mars, Jupiter, and Saturn. During their movements across the sky, two planets may sometimes appear to pass very close to one another — though in reality, of course, they are actually millions of miles apart.

Such occurrences are called "conjunctions"; on occasion they may be 7 so close that the planets cannot be separated by the naked eye. This happened for Mars and Venus on October 4, 1953, when for a short while the two planets appeared to be fused together to give a single star. Such a spectacle is rare enough to be very striking, and the great astronomer Johannes Kepler devoted much time to proving that the Star of Bethlehem was a special conjunction of Jupiter and Saturn. The planets passed very close together (once again, remember, this was purely from the Earth's point of view — in reality they were half a billion miles apart!) in May, 7 B.C. This is quite near the date of Christ's birth, which probably took place in the spring of 7 or 6 B.C. (This still surprises most people, but as Herod is known to have died early in 4 B.C., Christ must have been born before 5 B.C. We should add six years to the calendar for A.D. to mean what it says.)

Kepler's proposal, however, is as unconvincing as the Venus theory. 8

Better calculations than those he was able to make in the seventeenth century have shown that this particular conjunction was not a very close one, and the planets were always far enough apart to be easily separated by the eye. Moreover, there was a closer conjunction in 66 B.C., which on Kepler's theory should have brought a delegation of wise men to Bethlehem sixty years too soon!

In any case, the Magi could be expected to be as familiar with such 9 events as with all other planetary movements, and the Biblical account also indicates that the Star of Bethlehem was visible over a period of weeks (it must have taken the Magi a considerable time to reach Judea, have their interview with Herod, and then go on to Bethlehem). The conjunction of two planets lasts only a very few days, since they soon separate in the sky and go once more upon their individual ways.

We can get over the difficulty if we assume that the Magi were as- 10 trologers ("Magi" and "magician" have a common root) and had somehow deduced the birth of the Messiah from a particular configuration of the planets, which to them, if to no one else, had a unique significance. It is an interesting fact that the Jupiter-Saturn conjunction of 7 B.C. occurred in the constellation Pisces, the Fish. Now though the ancient Jews were too sensible to believe in astrology, the constellation Pisces was supposed to be connected with them. Anything peculiar happening in Pisces would, naturally, direct the attention of Oriental astrologers toward Jerusalem.

This theory is simple and plausible, but a little disappointing. One 11 would like to think that the Star of Bethlehem was something more dramatic and not anything to do with the familiar planets whose behavior had been perfectly well known for thousands of years before the birth of Christ. Of course, if one accepts as *literally* true the statement that "the star, which they saw in the east, *went before them, till it came and stood over where the young Child was*," no natural explanation is possible. Any heavenly body – star, planet, comet, or whatever – must share in the normal movement of the sky, rising in the east and setting some hours later in the west. Only the Pole Star, because it lies on the invisible axis of the turning Earth, appears unmoving in the sky and can act as a fixed and constant guide.

But the phrase, "went before them," like so much else in the Bible, 12 can be interpreted in many ways. It may be that the star – whatever it might have been – was so close to the Sun that it could be seen only for a short period near dawn, and so would never have been visible except in the eastern sky. Like Venus when she is a morning star, it might have risen shortly before the Sun, then been lost in the glare of the new day before it could climb very far up the sky. The wise men would thus have seen it ahead of them at the beginning of each day, and then lost it in the dawn before it had veered around to the south. Many other readings are also possible.

Very well, then, can we discover some astronomical phenomenon 13 sufficiently startling to surprise men completely familiar with the movements of the stars and planets and which fits the Biblical text?

Let's see if a comet would answer the specification. There have been 14 no really spectacular comets in this century – though there were several in the 1800s — and most people do not know what they look like or how they behave. They even confuse them with meteors, which any observer is bound to see if he goes out on a clear night and watches the sky for half an hour.

No two classes of object could be more different. A meteor is a 15 speck of matter, usually smaller than a grain of sand, which burns itself up by friction as it tears through the outer layers of Earth's atmosphere. But a comet may be millions of times larger than the entire Earth, and may dominate the night sky for weeks on end. A really great comet may look like a searchlight shining across the stars, and it is not surprising that such a portentous object always caused alarm when it appeared in the heavens. As Calpurnia said to Caesar:

> When beggars die, there are no comets seen;
> The heavens themselves blaze forth the death of princes.

Most comets have a bright, starlike core, or nucleus, which is com- 16 pletely dwarfed by their enormous tail — a luminous appendage which may be in the shape of a narrow beam or a broad, diffuse fan. At first sight it would seem very unlikely that anyone would call such an object a star, but as a matter of fact in old records comets are sometimes referred to, not inaptly, as "hairy stars."

Comets are unpredictable: the great ones appear without warning, 17 come racing in through the planets, bank sharply around the Sun, and then head out toward the stars, not to be seen again for hundreds or even millions of years. Only a few large comets — such as Halley's — have relatively short periods and have been observed on many occasions. Halley's comet, which takes seventy-five years to go around its orbit, has managed to put in an appearance at several historic events. It was visible just before the sack of Jerusalem in A.D. 66, and before the Norman invasion of England in A.D. 1066. Of course, in ancient times (or modern ones, for that matter) it was never very difficult to find a suitable disaster to attribute to any given comet. It is not surprising, therefore, that their reputation as portents of evil lasted for so long.

It is perfectly possible that a comet appeared just before the birth of 18 Christ. Attempts have been made, without success, to see if any of the known comets were visible around that date. (Halley's, as will be seen from the figures above, was just a few years too early on its last appearance before the fall of Jerusalem.) But the number of comets whose paths and periods we do know is very small compared with the colossal number that undoubtedly exists. If a comet did shine over Bethlehem, it may not be seen again from Earth for a hundred thousand years.

We can picture it in that Oriental dawn — a band of light streaming 19 up from the eastern horizon, perhaps stretching vertically toward the zenith. The tail of a comet always points away from the Sun; the comet would appear, therefore, like a great arrow, aimed at the east. As the Sun rose, it would fade into invisibility; but the next morning, it would be in almost the same place, still directing the travelers to their goal. It might be visible for weeks before it disappeared once more into the depths of space.

The picture is a dramatic and attractive one. It may even be the cor- 20
rect explanation; one day, perhaps, we shall know.

But there is yet another theory, and this is the one which most as- 21
tronomers would probably accept today. It makes the other explanations
look very trivial and commonplace indeed, for it leads us to contemplate
one of the most astonishing—and terrifying—events yet discovered in
the whole realm of nature.

We will forget now about planets and comets and the other denizens 22
of our own tight little Solar System. Let us go out across *real* space, right
out to the stars—those other suns, many far greater than our own, which
sheer distance has dwarfed to dimensionless points of light.

Most of the stars shine with unwavering brilliance, century after cen- 23
tury. Sirius appears now exactly as it did to Moses, as it did to Neander-
thal man, as it did to the dinosaurs—if they ever bothered to look at the
night sky. Its brilliance has changed little during the entire history of our
Earth and will be the same a billion years from now.

But there are some stars—the so-called "novae," or new stars—which 24
through internal causes suddenly become celestial atomic bombs. Such a
star may explode so violently that it leaps a hundred-thousand-fold in
brilliance within a few hours. One night it may be invisible to the naked
eye; on the next, it may dominate the sky. If our Sun became such a
nova, Earth would melt to slag and puff into vapor in a matter of
minutes, and only the outermost of the planets would survive.

Novae are not uncommon; many are observed every year, though 25
few are near enough to be visible except through telescopes. They are
the routine, everyday disasters of the Universe.

Two or three times in every thousand years, however, there occurs 26
something which makes a mere nova about as inconspicuous as a firefly
at noon. When a star becomes a *super*nova, its brilliance may increase not
by a hundred thousand but by a *billion* in the course of a few hours. The
last time such an event was witnessed by human eyes was in A.D. 1604;
there was another supernova in A.D. 1572 (so brilliant that it was visible
in broad daylight); and the Chinese astronomers recorded one in A.D.
1054. It is quite possible that the Bethlehem star was such a supernova,
and if so one can draw some very surprising conclusions.

We'll assume that Supernova Bethlehem was about as bright as the 27
supernova of A.D. 1572—often called "Tycho's star," after the great astronomer who observed it at the time. Since this star could been seen by
day, it must have been as brilliant as Venus. As we also know that a supernova is, in reality, at least a hundred million times more brilliant than
our own Sun, a very simple calculation tells us how far away it must have
been for its *apparent* brightness to equal that of Venus.

It turns out that Supernova Bethlehem was more than three thou- 28
sand light years—or, if you prefer, 18 quadrillion miles—away. That
means that its light had been traveling for at least three thousand years
before it reached Earth and Bethlehem, so that the awesome catastrophe
of which it was the symbol took place five thousand years ago, when the
Great Pyramid was still fresh from the builders.

Let us, in imagination, cross the gulfs of space and time and go back 29 to the moment of the catastrophe. We might find ourselves watching an ordinary star—a sun, perhaps, no different from our own. There may have been planets circling it; we do not know how common planets are in the scheme of the Universe, and how many suns have these small companions. But there is no reason to think that they are rare, and many novae must be the funeral pyres of worlds, and perhaps races, greater than ours.

There is no warning at all—only a steadily rising intensity of the 30 sun's light. Within minutes the change is noticeable; within an hour, the nearer worlds are burning. The star is expanding like a balloon, blasting off shells of gas at a million miles an hour as it blows its outer layers into space. Within a day, it is shining with such supernal brilliance that it gives off more light than *all the other suns in the Universe combined.* If it had planets, they are now no more than flecks of flame in the still-expanding shells of fire. The conflagration will burn for weeks before the dying star collapses back into quiescence.

But let us consider what happens to the light of the nova, which 31 moves a thousand times more swiftly than the blast wave of the explosion. It will spread out into space, and after four or five years it will reach the next star. If there are planets circling that star, they will suddenly be illuminated by a second sun. It will give them no appreciable heat, but will be bright enough to banish night completely, for it will be more than a thousand times more luminous than our full Moon. All that light will come from a single blazing point, since even from its nearest neighbor Supernova Bethlehem would appear too small to show a disk.

Century after century, the shell of light will continue to expand 32 around its source. It will flash past countless suns and flare briefly in the skies of their planets. Indeed, on the most conservative estimate, this great new star must have shone over thousands of worlds before its light reached Earth—and to all those worlds it appeared far, far brighter than it did to the men it led to Judea.

For as the shell of light expanded, if faded also. Remember, by the 33 time it reached Bethlehem it was spread over the surface of a sphere six thousand light-years across. A thousand years earlier, when Homer was singing the song of Troy, the nova would have appeared twice as brilliant to any watchers further upstream, as it were, to the time and place of the explosion.

That is a strange thought; there is a stranger one to come. For the 34 light of Supernova Bethlehem is still flooding out through space; it has left Earth far behind in the twenty centuries that have elapsed since men saw it for the first and last time. Now that light is spread over a sphere ten thousand light-years across and must be correspondingly fainter. It is simple to calculate how bright the supernova must be to any beings who may be seeing it now as a new star in *their* skies. To them, it will still be far more brilliant than any other star in the entire heavens, for its brightness will have fallen only by 50 per cent on its extra two thousand years of travel.

At this very moment, therefore, the Star of Bethlehem may still be 35 shining in the skies of countless worlds, circling far suns. Any watchers on those worlds will see its sudden appearance and its slow fading, just as the Magi did two thousand years ago when the expanding shell of light swept past the Earth. And for thousands of years to come, as its radiance ebbs out toward the frontiers of the Universe, Supernova Bethlehem will still have power to startle all who see it, wherever — and whatever — they may be.

Astronomy, as nothing else can do, teaches men humility. We know 36 now that our Sun is merely one undistinguished member of a vast family of stars, and no longer think of ourselves as being at the center of creation. Yet it is strange to think that before its light fades away below the limits of vision, we may have shared the Star of Bethlehem with the beings of perhaps a million worlds — and that to many of them, nearer to the source of the explosion, it must have been a far more wonderful sight than ever it was to any eyes on earth.

What did they make of it — and did it bring them good tidings, or ill? 37

Study Questions

1. How does Clarke help the layman to understand the scientific information presented here?
2. Cite specific examples of words and phrases that create the colloquial tone of this essay.
3. A number of the paragraphs in this essay are short. Why?
4. How does Clarke use questions in presenting his evidence? Comment on the concluding question. Does it introduce new material? Is the real point of this essay embedded in it?
5. Why does Clarke use personal pronouns, i.e., *you, us, we?*

Loren C. Eiseley
THE BIRD AND THE MACHINE

Loren C. Eiseley (1907–1977) was born in Lincoln, Nebraska. He received his B.A. (1933) from the University of Nebraska, and his M.A. (1935) and Ph.D. (1937) from the University of Pennsylvania. He taught at the University of Kansas and Oberlin College before returning, in 1947, to Pennsylvania, where he became University Professor in Anthropology and History of Science and head of the Department of the History and Philosophy of Science. A Guggenheim fellow, he published widely in both popular periodicals and learned journals. *Darwin's Century* received the Phi Beta Kapa science award in 1958, and *The Firmament of Time* (1960) received the John Burroughs medal and the Lecomte de Nouy award. His other books include *The Immense Journey* (1957), *Francis Bacon and the Modern Dilemma* (1962), *Galapagos: The Flow of Wilderness* (1968), *The Invisible Pyramid* (1970) and *All The Strange Hours* (1975).

I suppose their little bones have years ago been lost among 1
the stones and winds of those high glacial pastures. I suppose their feathers blew eventually into the piles of tumbleweed beneath the straggling cattle fences and rotted there in the mountain snows, along with dead steers and all the other things that drift to an end in the corners of the wire. I do not quite know why I should be thinking of birds over the *New York Times* at breakfast, particularly the birds of my youth half a continent away. It is a funny thing what the brain will do with memories and how it will treasure them and finally bring them into odd juxtapositions with other things, as though it wanted to make a design, or get some meaning out of them, whether you want it or not, or even see it.

It used to seem marvelous to me, but I read now that there are ma- 2
chines that can do these things in a small way, machines that can crawl about like animals, and that it may not be long now until they do more things — maybe even make themselves — I saw that piece in the *Times* just now. And then they will, maybe — well, who knows — but you read about it more and more with no one making any protest, and already they can add better than we and reach up and hear things through the dark and finger the guns over the night sky.

This is the new world that I read about at breakfast. This is the 3 world that confronts me in my biological books and journals, until there are times when I sit quietly in my chair and try to hear the little purr of the cogs in my head and the tubes flaring and dying as the messages go through them and the circuits snap shut or open. This is the great age, make no mistake about it; the robot has been born somewhat appropriately along with the atom bomb, and the brain they say now is just another type of more complicated feedback system. The engineers have its basic principles worked out; it's mechanical, you know; nothing to get superstitious about; and man can always improve on nature once he gets the idea. Well, he's got it all right and that's why, I guess, that I sit here in my chair, with the article crunched in my hand, remembering those two birds and that blue mountain sunlight. There is another magazine article on my desk that reads "Machines Are Getting Smarter Every Day." I don't deny it, but I'll still stick with the birds. It's life I believe in, not machines.

Maybe you don't believe there is any difference. A skeleton is all 4 joints and pulleys, I'll admit. And when man was in his simpler stages of machine building in the eighteenth century, he quickly saw the resemblances. "What," wrote Hobbes, "is the heart but a spring, and the nerves but so many strings, and the joints but so many wheels, giving motion to the whole body?" Tinkering about in their shops it was inevitable in the end that men would see the world as a huge machine "subdivided into an infinite number of lesser machines."

The idea took on with a vengeance. Little automatons toured the 5 country—dolls controlled by clockwork. Clocks described as little worlds were taken on tours by their designers. They were made up of moving figures, shifting scenes and other remarkable devices. The life of the cell was unknown. Man, whether he was conceived as possessing a soul or not, moved and jerked about like these tiny puppets. A human being thought of himself in terms of his own tools and implements. He had been fashioned like the puppets he produced and was only a more clever model made by a greater designer.

Then in the nineteenth century, the cell was discovered, and the 6 single machine in its turn was found to be the product of millions of infinitesimal machines—the cells. Now, finally, the cell itself dissolves away into an abstract chemical machine—and that into some intangible, inexpressible flow of energy. The secret seems to lurk all about, the wheels get smaller and smaller, and they turn more rapidly, but when you try to seize it the life is gone—and so, by popular definition, some would say that life was never there in the first place. The wheels and the cogs are the secret and we can make them better in time—machines that will run faster and more accurately than real mice to real cheese.

I have no doubt it can be done, though a mouse harvesting seeds on 7 an autumn thistle is to me a fine sight and more complicated, I think, in his multiform activity, than a machine "mouse" running a maze. Also, I like to think of the possible shape of the future brooding in mice, just as it brooded once in a rather ordinary mousy insectivore who became a man. It leaves a nice fine indeterminate sense of wonder that even an electronic brain hasn't got, because you know perfectly well that if the electronic brain changes, it will be because of something man has done to it. But what man will do to himself he doesn't really know. A certain scale of time and a ghostly intangible thing called change are ticking in him. Powers and potentialities like the oak in the seed, or a red and awful ruin. Either way, it's impressive; and the mouse has it, too. Or those birds, I'll never forget those birds — yet before I measured their significance, I learned the lesson of time first of all. I was young then and left alone in a great desert — part of an expedition that had scattered its men over several hundred miles in order to carry on research more effectively. I learned there that time is a series of planes existing superficially in the same universe. The tempo is a human illusion, a subjective clock ticking in our own kind of protoplasm.

As the long months passed, I began to live on the slower planes and 8 to observe more readily what passed for life there. I sauntered, I passed more and more slowly up and down the canyons in the dry baking heat of mid-summer. I slumbered for long hours in the shade of huge brown boulders that had gathered in tilted companies out on the flats. I had forgotten the world of men and the world had forgotten me. Now and then I found a skull in the canyons, and these justified my remaining there. I took a serene cold interest in these discoveries. I had come, like many a naturalist before me, to view life with a wary and subdued attention. I had grown to take pleasure in the divested bone.

I sat once on a high ridge that fell away before me into a waste of 9 sand dunes. I sat through hours of a long afternoon. Finally, as I glanced beside my boot an indistinct configuration caught my eye. It was a coiled rattlesnake, a big one. How long he had sat with me I do not know. I had not frightened him. We were both locked in the sleepwalking tempo of the earlier world, baking in the same high air and sunshine. Perhaps he had been there when I came. He slept on as I left, his coils, so ill discerned by me, dissolving once more among the stones and gravel from which I had barely made him out.

Another time I got on a higher ridge, among some tough little wind- 10 warped pines half covered over with sand in a basin-like depression that caught everything carried by the air up to those heights. There were a few thin bones of birds, some cracked shells of indeterminate age, and the knotty fingers of pine roots bulged out of shape from their long and agonizing grasp upon the crevices of the rock. I lay under the pines in the sparse shade and went to sleep once more.

It grew cold finally, for autumn was in the air by then, and the few 11 things that lived thereabouts were sinking down into an even chillier scale of time. In the moments between sleeping and waking I saw the roots about me and slowly, slowly, a foot in what seemed many centuries, I moved my sleep-stiffened hands over the scaling bark and lifted my numbed face after the vanishing sun. I was a great awkward thing of knots and aching limbs, trapped up there in some long, patient endurance that involved the necessity of putting living fingers into rock and by slow, aching expansion bursting those rocks asunder. I suppose, so thin and slow was the time of my pulse by then, that I might have stayed on to drift still deeper into the lower cadences of the frost, or the crystalline life that glistens pebbles, or shines in a snowflake, or dreams in the meteoric iron between the worlds.

It was a dim descent, but time was present in it. Somewhere far 12 down in that scale the notion struck me that one might come the other way. Not many months thereafter I joined some colleagues heading higher into a remote windy tableland where huge bones were reputed to protrude like boulders from the turf. I had drowsed with reptiles and moved with the century-long pulse of trees; now, lethargically, I was climbing back up some invisible ladder of quickening hours. There had been talk of birds in connection with my duties. Birds are intense, fast-living creatures—reptiles, I suppose one might say, that have escaped out of the heavy sleep of time, transformed fairy creatures dancing over sunlit meadows. It is a youthful fancy, no doubt, but because of something that happened up there among the escarpments of that range, it remains with me a lifelong impression. I can never bear to see a bird imprisoned.

We came into that valley through the trailing mists of a spring night. 13 It was a place that looked as though it might never have known the foot of man, but our scouts had been ahead of us and we knew all about the abandoned cabin of stone that lay far up on one hillside. It had been built in the land rush of the last century and then lost to the cattlemen again as the marginal soils failed to take to the plow.

There were spots like this all over the country. Lost graves marked 14 by unlettered stones and old corroding rim-fire cartridge cases lying where somebody had made a stand among the boulders that rimmed the valley. They are all that remain of the range wars; the men are under the stones now. I could see our cavalcade winding in and out through the mist below us: torches, the reflection of the truck lights on our collecting tins, and the far-off bumping of a loose dinosaur thigh bone in the bottom of a trailer. I stood on a rock a moment looking down and thinking what it cost in money and equipment to capture the past.

We had, in addition, instructions to lay hands on the present. The 15 word had come through to get them alive—birds, reptiles, anything. A zoo somewhere abroad needed restocking. It was one of those reciprocal matters in which science involves itself. Maybe our museum needed a stray ostrich egg and this was the payoff. Anyhow, my job was to help capture some birds and that was why I was there before the trucks.

The cabin had not been occupied for years. We intended to clean it 16 out and live in it, but there were holes in the roof and the birds had come in and were roosting in the rafters. You could depend on it in a place like this where everything blew away, and even a bird needed some place out of the weather and away from coyotes. A cabin going back to nature in a wild place draws them till they come in, listening at the eaves, I imagine, pecking softly among the shingles till they find a hole and then suddenly the place is theirs and man is forgotten.

Sometimes of late years I find myself thinking the most beautiful 17 sight in the world might be the birds taking over New York after the last man has run away to the hills. I will never live to see it, of course, but I know just how it will sound because I've lived up high and I know the sort of watch birds keep on us. I've listened to sparrows tapping tentatively on the outside of air conditioners when they thought no one was listening, and I know how other birds test the vibrations that come up to them through the television aerials.

"Is he gone?" they ask, and the vibrations come up from below, 18 "Not yet, not yet."

Well, to come back, I got the door open softly and I had the spot- 19 light all ready to turn on and blind whatever birds there were so they couldn't see to get out through the roof, I had a short piece of ladder to put against the far wall where there was a shelf on which I expected to make the biggest haul. I had all the information I needed just like any skilled assassin. I pushed the door open, the hinges squeaking only a little. A bird or two stirred—I could hear them—but nothing flew and there was a faint starlight through the holes in the roof.

I padded across the floor, got the ladder up and the light ready, and 20 slithered up the ladder till my head and arms were over the shelf. Everything was dark as pitch except for the starlight at the little place back of the shelf near the eaves. With the light to blind them, they'd never make it. I had them. I reached my arm carefully over in order to be ready to seize whatever was there and I put the flash on the edge of the shelf where it would stand by itself when I turned it on. That way I'd be able to use both hands.

Everything worked perfectly except for one detail—I didn't know 21 what kind of birds were there. I never thought about it at all, and it wouldn't have mattered if I had. My orders were to get something interesting. I snapped on the flash and sure enough there was a great beating and feathers flying, but instead of my having them, they, or rather he, had me. He had my hand, that is, and for a small hawk not much bigger than my fist he was doing all right. I heard him give one short metallic cry when the light went on and my hand descended on the bird beside him; after that he was busy with his claws and his beak was sunk in my thumb. In the struggle I knocked the lamp over on the shelf, and his mate got her sight back and whisked neatly through the hole in the roof and off among the stars outside. It all happened in fifteen seconds and you might think I would have fallen down the ladder, but no, I had a professional assassin's reputation to keep up, and the bird, of course, made the mistake of thinking the hand was the enemy and not the eyes behind it. He chewed my thumb up pretty effectively and lacerated my hand with his claws, but in the end I got him, having two hands to work with.

He was a sparrow hawk and a fine young male in the prime of life. I 22 was sorry not to catch the pair of them, but as I dripped blood and folded his wings carefully, holding him by the back so that he couldn't strike again, I had to admit the two of them might have been more than I could have handled under the circumstances. The little fellow had saved his mate by diverting me, and that was that. He was born to it, and made no outcry now, resting in my hand hopelessly, but peering toward me in the shadows behind the lamp with a fierce, almost indifferent glance. He neither gave nor expected mercy and something out of the high air passed from him to me, stirring a faint embarrassment.

I quit looking into that eye and managed to get my huge carcass with 23 its fist full of prey back down the ladder. I put the bird in a box too small to allow him to injure himself by struggle and walked out to welcome the arriving trucks. It had been a long day, and camp still to make in the darkness. In the morning that bird would be just another episode. He would go back with the bones in the truck to a small cage in a city where he would spend the rest of his life. And a good thing, too. I sucked my aching thumb and spat out some blood. An assassin has to get used to these things. I had a professional reputation to keep up.

In the morning, with the change that comes on suddenly in that high 24 country, the mist that had hovered below us in the valley was gone. The sky was a deep blue, and one could see for miles over the high outcroppings of stone. I was up early and brought the box in which the little hawk was imprisoned out onto the grass where I was building a cage. A wind as cool as a mounting spring ran over the grass and stirred my hair. It was a fine day to be alive. I looked up and all around and at the hole in the cabin roof out of which the other little hawk had fled. There was no sign of her anywhere that I could see.

"Probably in the next county by now," I thought cynically, but be- 25 fore beginning work I decided I'd have a look at my last night's capture.

Secretively, I looked again all around the camp and up and down and 26 opened the box. I got him right out in my hand with his wings folded properly and I was careful not to startle him. He lay limp in my grasp and I could feel his heart pound under the feathers but he only looked beyond me and up.

I saw him look that last look away beyond me into a sky so full of 27 light that I could not follow his gaze. The little breeze flowed over me again and nearby a mountain aspen shook all its tiny leaves. I suppose I must have had an idea then of what I was going to do, but I never let it come up into consciousness. I just reached over and laid the hawk on the grass.

He lay there a long minute without hope, unmoving, his eyes still 28 fixed on that blue vault above him. It must have been that he was already so far away in heart that he never felt the release from my hand. He never even stood. He just lay with his breast against the grass.

In the next second after that long minute he was gone. Like a flicker 29 of light, he had vanished with my eyes full on him, but without actually seeing even a premonitory wing beat. He was gone straight into that towering emptiness of light and crystal that my eyes could scarcely bear to penetrate. For another long moment there was silence. I could not see. The light was too intense. Then from far up somewhere a cry came ringing down.

I was young then and had seen little of the world, but when I heard 30 that cry my heart turned over. I was not the cry of the hawk I had captured; for, by shifting my position against the sun, I was now seeing further up. Straight out of the sun's eye, where she must have been soaring restlessly above us for untold hours, hurtled his mate. And from far up, ringing from peak to peak of the summits over us, came a cry of such unutterable and ecstatic joy that it sounds down across the years and tingles among the cups on my quiet breakfast table.

I saw them both now. He was rising fast to meet her. They met in a 31 great soaring gyre that turned to a whirling circle and a dance of wings. Once more, just once, their two voices, joined in a harsh wild medley of question and response, struck and echoed against the pinnacles of the valley. Then they were gone forever somewhere into those upper regions beyond the eyes of men.

I am older now, and sleep less, and I have seen most of what there is 32 to see and am not very much impressed any more, I suppose, by anything. "What Next in the Attributes of Machines?" my morning headline runs. "It Might Be the Power to Reproduce Themselves."

I lay the paper down and across my mind a phrase floats insinu- 33 atingly: "It does not seem that there is anything in the construction, constituents, or behavior of the human being which it is essentially impossible for science to duplicate and synthesize. On the other hand ..."

All over the city the cogs in the hard, bright mechanisms have begun 34 to turn. Figures move through computers, names are spelled out, a thoughtful machine selects the fingerprints of a wanted criminal from an array of thousands. In the laboratory an electronic mouse runs swiftly through a maze toward the cheese it can either taste nor enjoy. On the second run it does better than a living mouse.

"On the other hand ..." Ah, my mind takes up, on the other hand 35 the machine does not bleed, ache, hang for hours in the empty sky in a torment of hope to learn the fate of another machine, nor does it cry out with joy or dance in the air with the fierce passion of a bird. Far off, over a distance greater than space, that remote cry from the heart of heaven makes a faint buzzing among my breakfast dishes and passes on and away.

Study Questions

1. If one sentence can be called the *thesis sentence* of this essay, which sentence is it? How effective is the *transition* between this sentence and the paragraph following it?
2. The *introduction* to this essay is set off from the *body* of the essay by extra spacing. Why isn't the *conclusion* similarly set off?
3. The essay is entitled "The Bird and the Machine." Does the essay compare birds and machines? Contrast them? Both *compare and contrast* them?
4. What is the relationship of the episode of the bird to the thesis sentence?
5. What is your reaction to the conversation between the sparrows and the vibrations? Is it too "cute"?
6. Why is Eiseley slightly embarrassed by the bird's glance? Why does he say, "I quit looking into that eye ..." instead of "those eyes"?

Walter Van Tilburg Clark
HOOK

Walter Van Tilburg Clarke (1909–1971) was a highly regarded writer and teacher of creative writing whose stories and novels about the West helped rescue Western fiction from the popularizers of the Western "myth." His *The Ox-Bow Incident* (1940) is considered a classic Western novel. Among his other well-known works are *The City of Trembling Leaves* (1945), *The Track of the Cat* (1949), and *The Watchful Gods and Other Stories* (1950). He was in great demand as a teacher of writers. He was Writer in Residence at the University of Nevada, Visting Lecturer at the Universities of Iowa, Utah, Wyoming, California, Washington, Oregon, and Stanford University and Reed College and later Writer in Residence at San Francisco State College. In 1945 he won the O. Henry Memorial Award for "The Wind and the Snow of Winter."

Hook, the hawks' child, was hatched in a dry spring among 1 the oaks, beside the seasonal river, and was struck from the nest early. In the drouth his single-willed parents had to extend their hunting ground by more than twice, for the ground creatures upon which they fed died and dried by the hundreds. The range became too great for them to wish to return and feed Hook, and when they had lost interest in each other they drove Hook down into the sand and brush and went back to solitary courses over the bleaching hills.

Unable to fly yet, Hook crept over the ground, challenging all large 2 movements with recoiled head, erected, rudimentary wings, and the small rasp of his clattering beak. It was during this time of abysmal ignorance and continual fear that his eyes took on the first quality of a hawk, that of being wide, alert and challenging. He dwelt, because of his helplessness, among the rattling brush which grew between the oaks and the river. Even in his thickets and near the water, the white sun was the dominant presence. Except in the dawn, when the land wind stirred, or in the late afternoon, when the sea wind became strong enough to penetrate the half-mile inland to this turn in the river, the sun was the major force, and everything was dry and motionless under it. The brush, small plants and trees alike husbanded the little moisture at their hearts; the moving creatures waited for dark, when sometimes the sea fog came over and made a fine, soundless rain which relieved them.

The two spacious sounds of his life environed Hook at this time. 3
One was the great rustle of the slopes of yellowed wild wheat, with over
it the chattering rustle of the leaves of the California oaks, already as
harsh and individually tremulous as in autumn. The other was the distant
whisper of the foaming edge of the Pacific, punctuated by the hollow
shoring of the waves. But these Hook did not yet hear, for he was at-
tuned by fear and hunger to the small, spasmodic rustlings of live things.
Dry, shrunken, and nearly starved, and with his plumage delayed, he
snatched at beetles, dragging in the sand to catch them. When swifter and
stronger birds and animals did not reach them first, which was seldom, he
ate the small, silver fish left in the mud by the failing river. He watched,
with nearly chattering beak, the quick, thin lizards pause, very alert, and
raise and lower themselves, but could not catch them because he had to
raise his wings to move rapidly, which startled them.

Only one sight and sound not of his world of microscopic necessity 4
was forced upon Hook. That was the flight of the big gulls from the
beaches, which sometimes, in quealing play, came spinning back over the
foothills and the river bed. For some inherited reason, the big, ship-
bodied birds did not frighten Hook, but angered him. Small and chewed-
looking, with his wide, already yellowing eyes glaring up at them, he
would stand in an open place on the sand in the sun and spread his shaping wings and clatter his bill like shaken dice. Hook was furious about
the swift, easy passage of gulls.

His first opportunity to leave off living like a ground owl came acci- 5
dentally. He was standing in the late afternoon in the red light under the
thicket, his eyes half-filmed with drowse and the stupefaction of starvation, when suddenly something beside him moved, and he struck, and
killed a field mouse driven out of the wheat by thirst. It was a poor
mouse, shriveled and lice ridden, but in striking, Hook had tasted blood,
which raised nest memories and restored his nature. With started neck
plumage and shining eyes, he tore and fed. When the mouse was devoured, Hook had entered hoarse adolescence. He began to seek with a
conscious appetite, and to move more readily out of shelter. Impelled by
the blood appetite, so glorious after his long preservation upon the flaky
and bitter stuff of bugs, he ventured even into the wheat in the open sun
beyond the oaks, and discovered the small trails and holes among the
roots. With his belly often partially filled with flesh, he grew rapidly in
strength and will. His eyes were taking on their final change, their yellow
growing deeper and more opaque, their stare more constant, their challenge less desperate. Once during this transformation, he surprised a
ground squirrel, and although he was ripped and wingbitten and could
not hold his prey, he was not dismayed by the conflict, but exalted. Even
while the wing was still drooping and the pinions not grown back, he was
excited by other ground squirrels and pursued them futilely, and was
angered by their dusty escapes. He realized that his world was a great
arena for killing, and felt the magnificence of it.

The two major events of Hook's young life occurred in the same 6
day. A little after dawn he made the customary essay and succeeded in

flight. A little before sunset, he made his first sustained flight of over two hundred yards, and at its termination struck and slew a great buck squirrel whose thrashing and terrified gnawing and squealing gave him a wild delight. When he had gorged on the strong meat, Hook stood upright, and in his eyes was the stare of the hawk, never flagging in intensity but never swelling beyond containment. After that the stare had only to grow more deeply challenging and more sternly controlled as his range and deadliness increased. There was no change in kind. Hook had mastered the first of the three hungers which are fused into the single, flaming will of a hawk, and he had experienced the second.

The third and consummating hunger did not awaken in Hook until 7 the following spring, when the exultation of space had grown slow and steady in him, so that he swept freely with the wind over the miles of coastal foothills, circling, and ever in sight of the sea, and used without struggle the warm currents lifting from the slopes, and no longer desired to scream at the range of his vision, but intently sailed above his shadow swiftly climbing to meet him on the hillsides, sinking away and rippling across the brush-grown canyons.

That spring the rains were long, and Hook sat for hours, hunched 8 and angry under their pelting, glaring into the fogs of the river valley, and killed only small, drenched things flooded up from their tunnels. But when the rains had dissipated, and there were sun and sea wind again, the game ran plentiful, the hills were thick and shining green, and the new river flooded about the boulders where battered turtles climbed up to shrink and sleep. Hook then was scorched by the third hunger. Ranging farther, often forgetting to kill and eat, he sailed for days with growing rage, and woke at night clattering on his dead tree limb, and struck and struck and struck at the porous wood of the trunk, tearing it away. After days, in the draft of a coastal canyon miles below his own hills, he came upon the acrid taint he did not know but had expected, and sailing down it, felt his neck plumes rise and his wings quiver so that he swerved unsteadily. He saw the unmated female perched upon the tall and jagged stump of a tree that had been shorn by storm, and he stooped, as if upon game. But she was older than he, and wary of the gripe of his importunity, and banked off screaming, and he screamed also at the intolerable delay.

At the head of the canyon, the screaming pursuit was crossed by an- 9 other male with a great wing-spread, and the light golden in the fringe of his plumage. But his more skillful opening played him false against the ferocity of the twice-balked Hook. His rising maneuver for position was cut short by Hook's wild, upward swoop, and at the blow he raked desperately and tumbled off to the side. Dropping, Hook struck him again, struggled to clutch, but only raked and could not hold, and, diving, struck once more in passage, and then beat up, yelling triumph, and saw the crippled antagonist side-slip away, half-tumble once, as the ripped wing failed to balance, then steady and glide obliquely into the cover of brush on the canyon side. Beating hard and stationary in the wind above the bush that covered his competitor, Hook waited an instant, but when the bush was still, screamed again, and let himself go off with the current, re-seeking, infuriated by the burn of his own wounds, the thin choke-thread of the acrid taint.

On a hilltop projection of stone two miles inland, he struck her 10 down, gripping her rustling body with his talons, beating her wings down with his wings, belting her head when she whimpered or thrashed, and at last clutching her neck with his hook and, when her coy struggles had given way to stillness, succeeded.

In the early summer, Hook drove the three young ones from their 11 nest, and went back to lone circling above his own range. He was complete.

II

Throughout that summer and the cool, growthless weather of the winter, 12 when the gales blew in the river canyon and the ocean piled upon the shore, Hook was master of the sky and the hills of his range. His flight became a lovely and certain thing, so that he played with the treacherous currents of the air with a delicate ease of surpassing that of the gulls. He could sail for hours, searching the blanched grasses below him with tele-scopic eyes, gaining height against the wind, descending in mile-long, gently declining swoops when he curved and rode back, and never beat-ing either wing. At the swift passage of his shadow within their vision, gophers, ground squirrels and rabbits froze, or plunged gibbering into their tunnels beneath matted turf. Now, when he struck, he killed easily in one hard-knuckled blow. Occasionally, in sport, he soared up over the river and drove the heavy and weaponless gulls downstream again, until they would no longer venture inland.

There was nothing which Hook feared now, and his spirit was wholly 13 belligerent, swift and sharp, like his gaze. Only the mixed smells and in-comprehensible activities of the people at the Japanese farmer's home, inland of the coastwise highway and south of the bridge across Hook's river, troubled him. The smells were strong, unsatisfactory and never clear, and the people, though they behaved foolishly, constantly running in and out of their built-up holes, were large, and appeared capable, with fearless eyes looking up at him, so that he instinctively swerved aside from them. He cruised over their yard, their gardens, and their bean fields, but he would not alight close to their buildings.

But this one area of doubt did not interfere with his life. He ignored 14 it, save to look upon it curiously as he crossed, his afternoon shadow slid-ing in an instant over the chicken-and-crate-cluttered yard, up the side of the unpainted barn, and then out again smoothly, just faintly, liquidly rippling over the furrows and then over the stubble of the grazing slopes. When the season was dry, and the dead earth blew on the fields, he ex-tended his range to satisfy his great hunger, and again narrowed it when the fields were once more alive with the minute movements he could not only see but anticipate.

Four times that year he was challenged by other hawks blowing up 15 from behind the coastal hills to scud down his slopes, but two of these he slew in mid-air, and saw hurtle down to thump on the ground and lie still while he circled, and a third, whose wing he tore, he followed closely to earth and beat to death in the grass, making the crimson jet out from its breast and neck into the pale wheat. The fourth was a strong flier and experienced fighter, and theirs was a long, running battle, with brief, rising flurries of striking and screaming, from which down and plumage soared off.

Here, for the first time, Hook felt doubts, and at moments wanted to 16 drop away from the scoring, burning talons and the twisted hammer strokes of the strong beak, drop away shrieking, and take cover and be still. In the end, when Hook, having outmaneuvered his enemy and come above him, wholly in control, and going with the wind, tilted and plunged for the death rap, the other, in desperation, threw over on his back and struck up. Talons locked, beaks raking, they dived earthward. The earth grew and spread under them amazingly, and they were not fifty feet above it when Hook, feeling himself turning toward the underside, tore free and beat up again on heavy, wrenched wings. The other, stroking swiftly, and so close to down that he lost wing plumes to a bush, righted himself and planed up, but flew on lumberingly between the hills and did not return. Hook screamed the triumph, and made a brief pretense of pursuit, but was glad to return, slow and victorious, to his dead tree.

In all these encounters Hook was injured, but experienced only the 17 fighter's pride and exultation from the sting of wounds received in successful combat. And in each of them he learned new skill. Each time the wounds healed quickly, and left him a more dangerous bird.

In the next spring, when the rains and the night chants of the little 18 frogs were past, the third hunger returned upon Hook with a new violence. In this quest, he came into the taint of a young hen. Others too were drawn by the unnerving perfume, but only one of them, the same with which Hook had fought his great battle, was a worthy competitor. This hunter drove off two, while two others, game but neophytes, were glad enough that Hook's impatience would not permit him to follow and kill. Then the battle between the two champions fled inland, and was a tactical marvel, but Hook lodged the neck-breaking blow, and struck again as they dropped past the treetops. The blood had already begun to pool on the gray, fallen foliage as Hook flapped up between branches, too spent to cry his victory. Yet his hunger would not let him rest until, late in the second day, he drove the female to ground among the laurels of a strange river canyon.

When the two fledglings of this second brood had been driven from 19 the nest, and Hook had returned to his own range, he was not only complete, but supreme. He slept without concealment on his bare limb, and did not open his eyes when, in the night, the heavy-billed cranes coughed in the shallows below him.

III

The turning point of Hook's career came that autumn, when the brush in 20
the canyons rustled dryly and the hills, mowed close by the cattle,
smoked under the wind as if burning. One midafternoon, when the black
clouds were torn on the rim of the sea and the surf flowered white and
high on the rocks, raining in over the low cliffs, Hook rode the wind
diagonally across the river mouth. His great eyes, focused for small
things, stirring in the dust and leaves, overlooked so large and slow a
movement as that of the Japanese farmer rising from the brush and lifting the two black eyes of his shotgun. Too late Hook saw and, startled,
swerved, but wrongly. The surf muffled the reports, and nearly without
sound, Hook felt the minute whips of the first shot, and the astounding,
breath-taking blow of the second.

Beating his good wing, tasting the blood that quickly swelled into his 21
beak, he tumbled off with the wind and struck into the thickets on the
far side of the river mouth. The branches tore him. Wild with rage, he
thrust up and clattered his beak, challenging, but when he had fallen over
twice, he knew that the trailing wing would not carry, and then heard the
boots of the hunter among the stones in the river bed and, seeing him
loom at the edge of the bushes, crept back among the thickest brush and
was still. When he saw the boots stand before him, he reared back, lifting
his good wing and cocking his head for the serpent-like blow, his beak
open but soundless, his great eyes hard and very shining. The boots
passed on. The Japanese farmer, who believed that he had lost chickens,
and who had cunningly observed Hook's flight for many afternoons, until
he could plot it, did not greatly want a dead hawk.

When Hook could hear nothing but the surf and the wind in the 22
thicket, he let the sickness and shock overcome him. The fine film of the
inner lid dropped over his big eyes. His heart beat frantically, so that it
made the plumage of his shot-aching breast throb. His own blood
throttled his breathing. But these things were nothing compared to the
lightning of pain in his left shoulder, where the shot had bunched, shattering the airy bones so the pinions trailed on the ground and could not
be lifted. Yet, when a sparrow lit in the bush over him, Hook's eyes flew
open again, hard and challenging, his good wing was lifted and his beak
strained open. The startled sparrow darted piping out over the river.

Throughout that night, while the long clouds blew across the stars 23
and the wind shook the bushes about him, and throughout the next day,
while the clouds still blew and massed until there was no gleam of sunlight on the sand bar, Hook remained stationary, enduring his sickness.
In the second evening, the rains began. First there was a long, running
patter of drops upon the beach and over the dry trees and bushes. At
dusk there came a heavier squall, which did not die entirely, but slacked
off to a continual, spaced splashing of big drops, and then returned with
the front of the storm. In long, misty curtains, gust by gust, the rain
swept over the sea, beating down its heavy, and coursed up the beach.
The little jets of dust ceased to rise about the drops in the fields, and the

mud began to gleam. Among the boulders of the river bed, darkling pools grew slowly.

Still Hook stood behind his tree from the wind, only gentle drops 24 reaching him, falling from the upper branches and then again from the brush. His eyes remained closed, and he could still taste his own blood in his mouth, though it had ceased to come up freshly. Out beyond him, he heard the storm changing. As rain conquered the sea, the heave of the surf became a hushed sound, often lost in the crying of the wind. Then gradually, as the night turned toward morning, the wind also was broken by the rain. The crying became fainter, the rain settled toward steadiness, and the creep of the waves could be heard again, quiet and regular upon the beach.

At dawn there was no wind and no sun, but everywhere the roaring 25 of the vertical, relentless rain. Hook then crept among the rapid drippings of the bushes, dragging his torn sail, seeking better shelter. He stopped often and stood with the shutters of film drawn over his eyes. At midmorning he found a little cave under a ledge at the base of the sea cliff. Here, lost without branches and leaves about him, he settled to await improvement.

When, at midday of the third day, the rain stopped altogether, and 26 the sky opened before a small, fresh wind, letting light through to glitter upon a tremulous sea, Hook was so weak that his good wing trailed also to prop him upright, and his open eyes were lusterless. But his wounds were hardened, and he felt the return of hunger. Beyond his shelter, he heard the gulls flying in great numbers and crying their joy at the cleared air. He could even hear, from the fringe of the river, the ecstatic and unstinted bubblings and chirpings of the small birds. The grassland, he felt, would be full of the stirring anew of the close-bound life, the undrowned insects clicking as they dried out, the snakes slithering down, heads half erect, into the grasses where the mice, gophers and ground squirrels ran and stopped and chewed and licked themselves smoother and drier.

With the aid of his hunger, and on the crutches of his wings, Hook 27 came down to stand in the sun beside his cave, whence he could watch the beach. Before him, in ellipses on tilting planes, the gulls flew. The surf was rearing again, and beginning to shelve and hiss on the sand. Through the white foam-writing it left, the long-billed pipers twinkled in bevies, escaping each wave, then racing down after it to plunge their fine drills into the minute double holes there the sand crabs bubbled. In the third row of breakers two seals lifted sleek, streaming heads and barked, and over them, trailing his spider legs, a great crane flew south. Among the stones at the foot of the cliff, small red and green crabs made a little, continuous rattling and knocking. The cliff swallows glittered and twanged on aerial forays.

The afternoon began auspiciously for Hook also. One of the two 28 gulls which came squabbling above him dropped a freshly caught fish to the sand. Quickly Hook was upon it. Gripping it, he raised his good wing and cocked his head with open beak at the many gulls which had circled and come down at once toward the fall of the fish. The gulls sheered off, cursing raucously. Left alone on the sand, Hook devoured the fish and, after resting in the sun, withdrew again to his shelter.

IV

In the succeeding days, between rains, he foraged on the beach. He 29 learned to kill and crack the small green crabs. Along the edge of the river mouth, he found the drowned bodies of mice and squirrels and even sparrows. Twice he managed to drive feeding gulls from their catch, charging upon them with buffeting wing and clattering beak. He grew stronger slowly, but the shot sail continued to drag. Often, at the choking thought of soaring and striking and the good, hot-blood kill, he strove to take off, but only the one wing came up, winnowing with a hiss, and drove him over onto his side in the sand. After these futile trials, he would rage and clatter. But gradually he learned to believe that he could not fly, that his life must now be that of the discharged nestling again. Denied the joy of space, without which the joy of loneliness was lost, the joy of battle and killing, the blood lust, became his whole concentration. It was his hope, as he charged feeding gulls, that they would turn and offer battle, but they never did. The sandpipers, at his approach, fled peeping, or, like a quiver of arrows shot together, streamed out over the surf in a long curve. Once, pent beyond bearing, he disgraced himself by shrieking challenge at the businesslike heron which flew south every evening at the same time. The heron did not even turn his head, but flapped and glided on.

Hook's shame and anger became such that he stood awake at night. 30 Hunger kept him awake also, for these little leavings of the gulls could not sustain his great body in its renewed violence. He became aware that the gulls slept at night in flocks on the sand, each with one leg tucked under him. He discovered also that the curlews and the pipers, often mingling, likewise slept, on the higher remnant of the bar. A sensation of evil delight filled him in the consideration of protracted striking among them.

There was only half of a sick moon in a sky of running but far-sepa- 31 rated clouds on the night when he managed to stalk into the center of the sleeping gulls. This was light enough, but so great was his vengeful pleasure that there broke from him a shrill scream of challenge as he first struck. Without the power of flight behind it, the blow was not murderous, and this newly discovered impotence made Hook crazy, so that he screamed again and again as he struck and tore at the felled gull. He slew the one, but was twice knocked over by its heavy flounderings, and all the others rose above him, weaving and screaming, protesting in the thin moonlight. Wakened by their clamor, the wading birds also took wing, startled and plaintive. When the beach was quiet again, the flocks had settled elsewhere, beyond his pitiful range, and he was left alone beside the single kill. It was a disappointing victory. He fed with lowering spirit.

Thereafter, he stalked silently. At sunset he would watch where the 32 gulls settled along the miles of beach, and after dark he would come like a sharp shadow among them, and drive with his hook on all sides of him, till the beatings of a poorly struck victim sent the flock up. Then he would turn vindictively upon the fallen and finish them. In his best night, he killed five from one flock. But he ate only a little from one, for the vigor resulting from occasional repletion strengthened only his ire, which became so great at such a time that food revolted him. It was not the joyous, swift, controlled hunting anger of a sane hawk, but something quite different, which made him dizzy if it continued too long, and left him unsatisfied with any kill.

Then one day, when he had very nearly struck a gull while driving it 33 from a gasping yellowfin, the gull's wing rapped against him as it broke for its running start, and, the trailing wing failing to support him, he was knocked over. He flurried awkwardly in the sand to regain his feet, but his mastery of the beach was ended. Seeing him, in clear sunlight, struggling after the chance blow, the gulls returned about him in a flashing cloud, circling and pecking on the wing. Hook's plumage showed quick little jets of irregularity here and there. He reared back, clattering and erecting the good wing, spreading the great, rusty tail for balance. His eyes shone with a little of the old pleasure. But it died, for he could reach none of them. He was forced to turn and dance awkwardly on the sand, trying to clash bills with each tormentor. They banked up quealing and returned, weaving about him in concentric and overlapping circles. His scream was lost in their clamor, and he appeared merely to be hopping clumsily with his mouth open. Again he fell sideways. Before he could right himself, he was bowled over, and a second time, and lay on his side, twisting his neck to reach them and clappering in blind fury, and was struck three times by three successive gulls, shrieking their flock triumph.

Finally he managed to roll to his breast, and to crouch with his good 34 wing spread wide and the other stretched nearly as far, so that he extended like a gigantic moth, only his snake head, with its now silent scimitar, erect. One great eye blazed under its level brow, but where the other had been was a shallow hole from which thin blood trickled to his russet gap.

In this crouch, by short stages, stopping repeatedly to turn and drive 35 the gulls up, Hook dragged into the river canyon and under the stiff cover of the bitter-leafed laurel. There the gulls left him, soaring up with great clatter of their valor. Till nearly sunset Hook, broken spirited and enduring his hardening eye socket, heard them celebrating over the waves.

When his will was somewhat replenished, and his empty eye socket 36 had stopped the twitching and vague aching which had forced him often to roll ignominiously to rub it in the dust, Hook ventured from the protective lacings of his thicket. He knew fear again, and the challenge of his remaining eye was once more strident, as in adolescence. He dared not return to the beaches, and with a new, weak hunger, the home hunger, enticing him, made his way by short hunting journeys back to the wild wheat slopes and the crisp oaks. There was in Hook an unwonted sensation now, that of the ever-neighboring possibility of death. This sensation was beginning, after his period as a mad bird on the beach, to solidify him into his last stage of life. When, during his slow homeward passage, the gulls wafted inland over him, watching the earth with curious, miserish eyes, he did not cower, but neither did he challenge, either by opened beak or by raised shoulder. He merely watched carefully, learning his first lessons in observing the world with one eye.

At first the familiar surroundings of the bend in the river and the 37 tree with the dead limb to which he could not ascend, aggravated his humiliation, but in time, forced to live cunningly and half-starved, he lost much of his savage pride. At the first flight of a strange hawk over his realm, he was wild at his helplessness, and kept twisting his head like an owl, or spinning in the grass like a small and feathered dervish, to keep the hateful beauty of the windrider in sight. But in the succeeding weeks, as one after another coasted his beat, his resentment declined, and when one of the raiders, a haughty yearling, sighted his upstaring eye, and plunged and struck him dreadfully, and failed to kill him only because he dragged under a thicket in time, the second of his great hungers was gone. He had no longer the true lust to kill, no joy of battle, but only the poor desire to fill his belly.

Then truly he lived in the wheat and the brush like a ground owl, 38 ridden with ground lice, dusty or muddy, ever half-starved, forced to sit for hours by small holes for petty and unsatisfying kills. Only once during the final months before his end did he make a kill where the breath of danger recalled his valor, and then the danger was such as a hawk with wings and eyes would scorn. Waiting beside a gopher hole, surrounded by the high, yellow grass, he saw the head emerge, and struck, and was amazed that there writhed in his clutch the neck and dusty coffin-skull of a rattlesnake. Holding his grip, Hook saw the great, thick body slither up after, the tip an erect, strident blur, and writhe on the dirt of the gopher's mound. The weight of the snake pushed Hook about, and once threw him down, and the rising and falling whine of the rattles made the moment terrible, but the vaulted mouth, gaping from the closeness of Hook's grip, so that the pale, envenomed sabers stood out free, could not reach him. When Hook replaced the grip of his beak with the grip of the talons, and was free to strike again and again at the base of the head, the struggle was over. Hook tore and fed on the fine, watery flesh, and left the tattered armor and the long, jointed bone for the marching ants.

When the heavy rains returned, he ate well during the period of the 39 first escapes from flooded burrows, and then well enough, in a vulture's way, on the drowned creatures. But as the rains lingered, and the burrows hung full of water, and there were no insects in the grass and no small birds sleeping in the thickets, he was constantly hungry, and finally unbearably hungry. His sodden and ground-broken plumage stood out ragedly about him, so that he looked fat, even bloated, but underneath it his skin clung to his bones. Save for his great talons and clappers, and the rain in his down, he would have been like a handful of air. He often stood for a long time under some bush or ledge, heedless of the drip, his one eye filmed over, his mind neither asleep or awake, but between. The gurgle and swirl of the brimming river, and the sound of chunks of the bank cut away to splash and dissolve in the already muddy flood, became familiar to him, and yet a torment, as if that great, ceaselessly working power of water ridiculed his frailty, within which only the faintest spark of valor still glimmered. The last two nights before the rain ended, he huddled under the floor of the bridge on the coastal highway, and heard the palpitant thunder of motors swell and roar over him. The trucks shook the bridge so that Hook, even in his famished lassitude, would sometimes open his one great eye wide and startled.

V

After the rains, when things became full again, bursting with growth and 40 sound, the trees swelling, the thickets full of song and chatter, the fields, turning green in the sun, alive with rustling passages, and the moonlit nights strained with the song of the peepers all up and down the river and in the pools in the fields, Hook had to bear the return of the one hunger left him. At times this made him so wild that he forgot himself and screamed challenge from the open ground. The fretfulness of it spoiled his hunting, which was not entirely a matter of patience. Once he was in despair, and lashed himself through the grass and thickets, trying to rise when that virgin scent drifted for a few moments above the current of his own river. Then, breathless, his beak agape, he saw the strong suitor ride swiftly down on the wind over him, and heard afar the screaming fuss of the harsh wooing in the alders. For that moment even the battle heart beat in him again. The rim of his good eye was scarlet, and a little bead of new blood stood in the socket of the other. With beak and talon, he ripped at a fallen log, and made loam and leaves fly from about it.

But the season of love passed over to the nesting season, and Hook's 41 love hunger, unused, shriveled in him with the others, and there remained in him only one stern quality befitting a hawk, and that the negative one, the remnant, the will to endure. He resumed his patient, plotted hunting, now along a field of the Japanese farmer, but ever within reach of the river thickets.

Growing tough and dry again as the summer advanced, inured to the 42 family of the farmer, whom he saw daily, stooping and scraping with sticks in the ugly, open rows of their fields, where no lovely grass rustled and no life stirred save the shameless gulls, which walked at the heels of the workers, gobbling the worms and grubs they turned up, Hook became nearly content with his shard of life. The only longing or resentment to pierce him was that which he suffered occasionally when forced to hide at the edge of the mile-long bean field from the wafted cruising and the restive, down-bent gaze of one of his own kind. For the rest, he was without flame, a snappish, dust-colored creature, fading into the grasses he trailed through, and suited to his petty ways.

At the end of that summer, for the second time in his four years, 43 Hook underwent a drouth. The equinoctial period passed without a rain. The laurel and the rabbit-brush dropped dry leaves. The foliage of the oaks shriveled and curled. Even the night fogs in the river canyon failed. The farmer's red cattle on the hillside lowed constantly, and could not feed on the dusty stubble. Grass fires broke out along the highways, and ate fast in the wind, filling the hollows with the smell of smoke, and died in the dirt of the shorn hills. The river made no sound. Scum grew on its vestigial pools, and turtles died and stank among the rocks. The dust rode before the wind, and ascended and flowered to nothing between the hills, and every sunset was red with the dust in the air. The people in the farmer's house quarreled, and even struck one another. Birds were silent, and only the hawks flew much. The animals lay breathing hard for very long spells, and ran and crept jerkily. Their flanks were fallen in, and their eyes were red.

At first Hook gorged at the fringe of the grass fires on the multi- 44 tudes of tiny things that came running and squeaking. But thereafter there were the blackened strips on the hills, and little more in the thin, crackling grass. He found mice and rats, gophers and ground-squirrels, and even rabbits, dead in the stubble and under the thickets, but so dry and fleshless that only a faint smell rose from them, even on the sunny days. He starved on them. By early December he had wearily stalked the length of the eastern foothills, hunting at night to escape the voracity of his own kind, resting often upon his wings. The queer trail of his short steps and great horned toes zigzagged in the dust and was erased by the wind at dawn. He was nearly dead, and could make no sound through the horn funnels of his clappers.

Then one night the dry wind brought him, with the familiar, lifeless 45 dust, another familiar scent, troublesome, mingled and unclear. In his vision-dominated brain he remembered the swift circle of his flight a year past, crossing in one segment, his shadow beneath him, a yard cluttered with crates and chickens, a gray barn and then again the plowed land and the stubble. Traveling faster than he had for days, impatient of his shrunken sweep, Hook came down to the farm. In the dark wisps of cloud blown among the stars over him, but no moon, he stood outside the wire of the chicken run. The scent of fat and blooded birds reached him from the shelter, and also within the enclosure was water. At the breath of the water, Hook's gorge contracted, and his tongue quivered and clove in its groove of horn. But there was the wire. He stalked its perimeter and found no opening. He beat it with his good wing, and felt it cut but not give. He wrenched at it with his beak in many places, but could not tear it. Finally, in a fury which drove the thin blood through him, he leaped repeatedly against it, beating and clawing. He was thrown back from the last leap as from the first, but in it he had risen so high as to clutch with his beak at the top wire. While he lay on his breast on the ground, the significance of this came upon him.

Again he leapt, clawed up the wire, and, as he would have fallen, 46 made even the dead wing bear a little. He grasped the top and tumbled within. There again he rested flat, searching the dark with quick-turning head. There was no sound or motion but the throb of his own body. First he drank at the chill metal trough hung for the chickens. The water was cold, and loosened his tongue and his tight throat, but it also made him drunk and dizzy, so that he had to rest again, his claws spread wide to brace him. Then he walked stiffly, to stalk down the scent. He trailed it up the runway. Then there was the stuffy, body-warm air, acrid with droppings, full of soft rustlings as his talons clicked on the board floor. The thick, white shapes showed faintly in the darkness. Hook struck quickly, driving a hen to the floor with one blow, its neck broken and stretched out stringily. He leaped the still pulsing body, and tore it. The rich, streaming blood was overpowering to his dried senses, his starved, leathery body. After a few swallows, the flesh choked him. In his rage, he struck down another hen. The urge to kill took him again, as in those night on the beach. He could let nothing go. Balked of feeding, he was compelled to slaughter. Clattering, he struck again and again. The hen-house was suddenly filled with the squawking and helpless rushing and buffeting of the terrified, brainless fowls.

Hook reveled in mastery. Here was game big enough to offer weight 47 against a strike, and yet unable to soar away from his blows. Turning in the midst of the turmoil, cannily, his fury caught at the perfect pitch, he struck unceasingly. When the hens finally discovered the outlet, and streamed into the yard, to run around the fence, beating and squawking, Hook followed them, scraping down the incline, clumsy and joyous. In the yard, the cock, a bird as large as he, and much heavier, found him out and gave valiant battle. In the dark, and both earthbound, there was little skill, but blow upon blow, and only chance parry. The still squawking hens pressed into one corner of the yard. While the duel went on, a dog, excited by the sustained scuffling, began to bark. He continued to bark, running back and forth along the fence on one side. A light flashed on in an uncurtained window of the farmhouse, and streamed whitely over the crates littering the ground.

Enthralled by his old battle joy, Hook knew only the burly cock be- 48 fore him. Now, in the farthest reach of the window light, they could see each other dimly. The Japanese farmer, with his gun and lantern, was already at the gate when the finish came. The great cock leapt to jab with his spurs and, toppling forward with extended neck as he fell, was struck and extinguished. Blood had loosened Hook's throat. Shrilly he cried his triumph. It was a thin and exhausted cry, but within him as good as when he shrilled in mid-air over the plummeting descent of a fine foe in his best spring.

The light from the lantern partially blinded Hook. He first turned 49 and ran directly from it, into the corner where the hens were huddled. They fled apart before his charge. He essayed the fence, and on the second try, in his desperation, was out. But in the open dust, the dog was on him, circling, dashing in, snapping. The farmer, who at first had not fired because of the chickens, now did not fire because of the dog, and, when he saw that the hawk was unable to fly, relinquished the sport to the dog, holding the lantern up in order to see better. The light showed his own flat, broad, dark face as sunken also, the cheekbones very prominent, and showed the torn-off sleeves of his shirt and the holes in the knees of his overalls. His wife, in a stained wrapper, and barefooted, heavy black hair hanging around a young, passionless face, joined him hesitantly, but watched, fascinated and a little horrified. His son joined them too, encouraging the dog, but quickly grew silent. Courageous and cruel death, however it may afterward sicken the one who has watched it, is impossible to look away from.

In the circle of the light, Hook turned to keep the dog in front of 50 him. His one eye gleamed with malevolence. The dog was an Airedale, and large. Each time he pounced, Hook stood ground, raising his good wing, the pinions newly torn by the fence, opening his beak soundlessly, and, at the closest approach, hissed furiously, and at once struck. Hit and ripped twice by the whetted horn, the dog recoiled more quickly from several subsequent jumps and, infuriated by his own cowardice, began to bark wildly. Hook maneuvered to watch him, keeping his head turned to avoid losing the foe on the blind side. When the dog paused, safely away, Hook watched him quietly, wing partially lowered, beak closed, but at the first move again lifted the wing and gaped. The dog whined, and the man spoke to him encouragingly. The awful sound of his voice made Hook for an instant twist his head to stare up at the immense figures behind the light. The dog again sallied, barking, and Hook's head spun back. His wing was bitten this time, and with a furious sideblow, he caught the dog's nose. The dog dropped him with a yelp, and then, smarting, came on more warily, as Hook propped himself up from the ground again between his wings. Hook's artificial strength was waning, but his heart still stood to the battle, sustained by a fear of such dimension as he had never known before, but only anticipated when the arrogant young hawk had driven him to cover. The dog, unable to find any point at which the merciless, unwinking eye was not watching him, the parted beak waiting, paused and whimpered again.

"Oh, kill the poor thing," the woman begged.   51

The man, though, encouraged the dog again, saying, "Sick him; sick 52 him."

The dog rushed bodily. Unable to avoid him, Hook was bowled 53 down, snapping and raking. He left long slashes, as from the blade of a knife, on the dog's flank, but before he could right himself and assume guard again, was caught by the good wing and dragged, clattering, and seeking to make a good stroke from his back. The man followed them to keep the light on them, and the boy went with him, wetting his lips with his tongue and keeping his fists closed tightly. The woman remained behind, but could not help watching the diminished conclusion.

In the little, palely shining arena, the dog repeated his successful ma- 54 neuver three times, growling but not barking, and when Hook thrashed up from the third blow, both wings were trailing, and dark, shining streams crept on his black-fretted breast from the shoulders. The great eye flashed more furiously than it ever had in victorious battle, and the beak still gaped, but there was no more clatter. He faltered when turning to keep front; the broken wings played him false even as props. He could not rise to use his talons.

The man had tired of holding the lantern up, and put it down to rub 55 his arm. In the low, horizontal light, the dog charged again, this time throwing the weight of his forepaws against Hook's shoulder, so that

Hook was crushed as he struck. With his talons up, Hook raked at the dog's belly, but the dog conceived the finish, and furiously worried the feathered bulk. Hook's neck went limp, and between his gaping clappers came only a faint chittering, as from some small kill of his own in the grasses.

In this last conflict, however, there had been some minutes of the su- 56 preme fire of the hawk whose three hungers are perfectly fused in the one will; enough to burn off a year of shame.

Between the great sails the light body lay caved and perfectly still. 57 The dog, smarting from his cuts, came to the master and was praised. The woman, joining them slowly, looked at the great wingspread, her husband raising the lantern that she might see it better.

"Oh, the brave bird," she said.   58

Study Questions

1. How does Clark's treatment of Hook differ from what would be presented in an essay?
2. "Hook" is divided into five sections. What major development of plot occurs in each of these sections?
3. How are sections I and IV related?
4. When is the first suggestion of Hook's approaching confrontation with the gulls? With the Japanese farmer?
5. Is there any consistent way in which Clark constructs his expository paragraphs?

Richard Allen
RHETORIC JUSTIFIES GRAMMAR: EXTREME SENTENCE LENGTH IN "HOOK"

Richard Allen (1950–   ) was born in Buffalo, New York. He studied at Arizona State University, where he received his degree in chemical engineering in 1972. In 1969, while he was a freshman, Allen won both first and fourth prizes for best freshman essay in all English classes. The first-prize essay is reprinted below.

Reprinted with permission of the author.

Like the short, choppy sentence, the excessively long sen- 1
tence is taboo in most grammar classes. The extremely long sentences
Walter Van Tilburg Clark uses in "Hook" might seem to be open to a
charge of ungrammaticality, but he has used the lengths of sentences rhetorically to achieve desired effect: emphasis on actions, climax of action,
and the poetic effect of action.

Clark uses the sentence length to emphasize action. For example, 2
when Hook battles with another hawk, Clark uses a long, zigzagging sentence which emphasizes the unorganized, flashing movements of the
birds:

> In the end, when Hook, having outmaneuvered his enemy and come above
> him, wholly in control, and going with the wind, tilted and plunged for the
> death rap, the other, in desperation, threw over on his back and struck up.
> (p. 309)

The sentence basically states, "... when Hook ... tilted and plunged for 3
the death rap, the other, ..., threw over on his back and struck up."
Clark has added participial phrases, such as "having outmaneuvered his
enemy and come above him," "wholly in control," and "and going with
the wind," to obtain the zigzagging effect of the birds fighting and darting
in air.

Immediately following this sentence, Clark, to emphasize the action 4
again, uses a short sentence. "Talons locked, beaks raking, they dived
earthward." This sentence begins specifically—"Talons locked, beaks raking,"—then ends in suspense. A similar example would be: "Engines ig-
nited, gears shifting, they raced down the dragway." Both sentences leave
the reader curiously asking "Who will win?"

The suspenseful sentence builds the reader up to a climax which 5
leaves him at a high degree of tension and hungering interest. Clark also
uses long climactic sentences which build the reader up, then bring him
down again. There are two good examples of this.

> On a hilltop projection of stone two miles inland, he struck her down, grip-
> ping her rustling body with his talons, beating her wings down with his
> wings, belting her head when she whimpered or thrashed, and at last clutch-
> ing her neck with his hook and, when her coy struggles had given way to
> stillness, succeeded. (p. 308)

In this one-sentence paragraph, Clark opens with a moderate state of ac- 6
tion—"On a hilltop projection of stone ..."—then builds to a climax—
"gripping her rustling body with his talons, beating her wings down with
his wings ..."—then back down to relief—"succeeded." He expresses this
action in the same procedure as the sexual act itself; it reaches a peak,
then recedes.

Another example of climactic action conveyed by the sentence struc- 7
ture is found after Hook is shot by the farmer.

> Wild with rage, he thrust up and clattered his beak, challenging, but when he
> had fallen over twice, he knew that the trailing wing would not carry, and
> then heard the boots of the hunter among the stones in the river bed and,
> seeing him loom at the edge of the bushes, crept back among the thickest
> brush and was still. (p. 310)

This sentence follows the same pattern of the previous example except that it begins near the climax and eases down slowly to the end—"and was still"; the sentence is actually anti-climactic.

Clark uses the long sentence again, but this time to achieve a poetic 8 effect. He relates this effect to the movement of the bird in flight.

> The third and consummating hunger did not awaken in Hook until the following spring, when the exultation of space had grown slow and steady in him, so that he swept freely with the wind over miles of coastal foothills, circling, and ever in sight of the sea, and used without struggle the warm currents lifting from the slopes, and no longer desired to scream at the range of his vision, but intently sailed above his shadow swiftly climbing to meet him on the hillsides, sinking away and rippling across the brush-grown canyons. (p. 307)

This long, one-sentence paragraph glides along like the flight of the bird, 9 Hook. Clark uses the long sentence here to describe the action of the gliding bird through a poetic stringing together of clauses which gives the reader a sense of floating in air. Here again, Clark has used the structure of his sentence to parallel, and therefore to convey, the action of the bird.

Devices typical of poetry, such as the mixing of the senses, allitera- 10 tion, and rhythm, are found in this paragraph. Clark mixes the senses— "scream at the range of his vision"—and on page 312 he mentions Hook's "choking thought." Alliteration, another device of poetry is found in this passage. The phrases "slow and steady," "shadow swiftly," and "sight of the sea" are found in the following sentence. These phrases also have a rhythm. The rhythm of these phrases is choppy as is the rhythm of this sentence: "Talons locked, beaks raking," which was discussed earlier. While many of the individual phrases have a staccato rhythm, the sentences, especially in this last paragraph, flow with lulling sentence structure.

Although Clark uses long sentences, he never becomes redundant. 11 He has mastered the long—as well as the short—sentence and has broken the taboo. In strict grammatical terms, extremely long sentences may be undesirable, but Clark has clearly demonstrated that rhetoric justifies grammatical liberties.

Study Questions

1. Which sentence is the *thesis statement?*
2. What three points does Allen choose to discuss? In what order does he discuss them?
3. How many paragraphs are devoted to each of the three points?
4. How does the conclusion draw us back to the introduction?

Rachel Carson
THE OBLIGATION TO ENDURE

Rachel Carson (1907–1964) was born in Springdale, Pennsylvania, and graduated from Pennsylvania College for Women and Johns Hopkins University. She was awarded honorary doctorates by Oberlin College, the Drexel Institute of Technology, and Smith College. She received the George Westinghouse AAAS Science Writing Award (1950), a Guggenheim fellowship (1951), the John Burroughs Medal (1952), and the Page One Award (1952), and was elected to the National Institute of Arts and Letters. Her books include *Under the Sea-Wind* (1941), *The Sea Around Us* (1951), *The Edge of the Sea* (1956), and *Silent Spring* (1962). The latter became one of the most controversial books of the 1960s.

The history of life on earth has been a history of interaction 1 between living things and their surroundings. To a large extent, the physical form and the habits of the earth's vegetation and its animal life have been molded by the environment. Considering the whole span of earthly time, the opposite effect, in which life actually modifies its surroundings, has been relatively slight. Only within the moment of time represented by the present century has one species — man — acquired significant power to alter the nature of his world.

During the past quarter century this power has not only increased to 2 one of disturbing magnitude but it has changed in character. The most alarming of all man's assaults upon the environment is the contamination of air, earth, rivers, and sea with dangerous and even lethal materials. This pollution is for the most part irrecoverable; the chain of evil it initiates not only in the world that must support life but in living tissues is for the most part irreversible. In this now universal contamination of the environment, chemicals are the sinister and little-recognized partners of radiation in changing the very nature of the world — the very nature of its life. Strontium 90, released through nuclear explosions into the air, comes to earth in rain or drifts down as fallout, lodges in soil, enters into the grass or corn or wheat grown there, and in time takes up its abode in the bones of a human being, there to remain until his death. Similarly, chemicals sprayed on croplands or forests or gardens lie long in soil, entering into living organisms, passing from one to another in a chain of poisoning and death. Or they pass mysteriously by underground streams until they emerge and, through the alchemy of air and sunlight, combine into new forms that kill vegetation, sicken cattle, and work unknown harm on those who drink from once pure wells. As Albert Schweitzer has said, "Man can hardly even recognize the devils of his own creation."

It took hundreds of millions of years to produce the life that now in- 3 habits the earth—eons of time in which that developing and evolving and diversifying life reached a state of adjustment and balance with its sur- roundings. The environment, rigorously shaping and directing the life it supported, contained elements that were hostile as well as supporting. Certain rocks gave out dangerous radiation; even within the light of the sun, from which all life draws its energy, there were short-wave radiations with power to injure. Given time—time not in years but in millennia— life adjusts, and a balance has been reached. For time is the essential in- gredient; but in the modern world there is no time.

The rapidity of change and the speed with which new situations are 4 created follow the impetuous and heedless pace of man rather than the deliberate pace of nature. Radiation is no longer merely the background radiation of rocks, the bombardment of cosmic rays, the ultraviolet of the sun that have existed before there was any life on earth; radiation is now the unnatural creation of man's tampering with the atom. The chemicals to which life is asked to make its adjustment are no longer merely the calcium and silica and copper and all the rest of the minerals washed out of the rocks and carried in rivers to the sea; they are the synthetic crea- tions of man's inventive mind, brewed in his laboratories, and having no counterparts in nature.

To adjust to these chemicals would require time on the scale that is 5 nature's; it would require not merely the years of a man's life but the life of generations. And even this, were it by some miracle possible, would be futile, for the new chemicals come from our laboratories in an endless stream; almost five hundred annually find their way into actual use in the United States alone. The figure is staggering and its implications are not easily grasped—500 new chemicals to which the bodies of men and ani- mals are required somehow to adapt each year, chemicals totally outside the limits of biologic experience.

Among them are many that are used in man's war against nature. 6 Since the mid-1940's over 200 basic chemicals have been created for use in killing insects, weeds, rodents, and other organisms described in the modern vernacular as "pests"; and they are sold under several thousand different brand names.

These sprays, dusts, and aerosols are now applied almost universally 7 to farms, gardens, forests, and homes—nonselective chemicals that have the power to kill every insect, the "good" and the "bad," to still the song of birds and the leaping of fish in the streams, to coat the leaves with a deadly film, and to linger on in soil—all this though the intended target may be only a few weeds or insects. Can anyone believe it is possible to lay down such a barrage of poisons on the surface of the earth without making it unfit for all life? They should not be called "insecticides," but "biocides."

The whole process of spraying seems caught up in an endless spiral. 8
Since DDT was released for civilian use, a process of escalation has been
going on in which ever more toxic materials must be found. This has
happened because insects, in a triumphant vindication of Darwin's principle of the survival of the fittest, have evolved super races immune to
the particular insecticide used, hence a deadlier one has always to be developed—and then a deadlier one than that. It has happened also because, for reasons to be described later, destructive insects often undergo
a "flareback," or resurgence, after spraying, in numbers greater than before. Thus the chemical war is never won, and all life is caught in its violent crossfire.

Along with the possibility of the extinction of mankind by nuclear 9
war, the central problem of our age has therefore become the contamination of man's total environment with such substances of incredible
potential for harm—substances that accumulate in the tissues of plants
and animals and even penetrate the germ cells to shatter or alter the very
material of heredity upon which the shape of the future depends.

Some would-be architects of our future look toward a time when it 10
will be possible to alter the human germ plasm by design. But we may
easily be doing so now by inadvertence, for many chemicals, like radiation, bring about gene mutations. It is ironic to think that man might determine his own future by something so seemingly trivial as the choice of
an insect spray.

All this has been risked—for what? Future historians may well be 11
amazed by our distorted sense of proportion. How could intelligent
beings seek to control a few unwanted species by a method that con-
taminated environment and brought the threat of disease and death even
to their own kind? Yet this is precisely what we have done. We have
done it, moreover, for reasons that collapse the moment we examine
them. We are told that the enormous and expanding use of pesticides is
necessary to maintain farm production. Yet is our real problem not one
of *overproduction?* Our farms, despite measures to remove acreages from
production and to pay farmers *not* to produce, have yielded such a staggering excess of crops that the American taxpayer in 1962 is paying out
more than one billion dollars a year as the total carrying cost of the sur-
plus-food storage program. And is the situation helped when one branch
of the Agriculture Department tries to reduce production while another
states, as it did in 1958, "It is believed generally that reduction to crop
acreages under provisions of the Soil Bank will stimulate interest in use
of chemicals to obtain maximum production on the land retained in
crops."

All this is not to say there is no insect problem and no need of con- 12
trol. I am saying, rather, that control must be geared to realities, not to
mythical situations, and that the methods employed must be such that
they do not destroy us along with the insects.

The problem whose attempted solution has brought such a train of 13
disaster in its wake is an accompaniment of our modern way of life. Long
before the age of man, insects inhabited the earth—a group of extraordinarily varied and adaptable beings. Over the course of time since man's

advent, a small percentage of the more than half a million species of insects have come into conflict with human welfare in two principal ways: as competitors for the food supply and as carriers of human disease.

Disease-carrying insects become important where human beings are 14 crowded together, especially under conditions where sanitation is poor, as in time of natural disaster or war or in situations of extreme poverty and deprivation. Then control of some sort becomes necessary. It is a sobering fact, however, as we shall presently see, that the method of massive chemical control has had only limited success, and also threatens to worsen the very conditions it is intended to curb.

Under primitive agricultural conditions the farmer had few insect 15 problems. These arose with the intensification of agriculture — the devotion of immense acreages to a single crop. Such a system set the stage for explosive increases in specific insect populations. Single-crop farming does not take advantage of the principles by which nature works; it is agriculture as an engineer might conceive it to be. Nature has introduced great variety into the landscape, but man has displayed a passion for simplifying it. Thus he undoes the built-in checks and balances by which nature holds the species within bounds. One important natural check is a limit on the amount of suitable habitat for each species. Obviously then, an insect that lives on wheat can build up its population to much higher levels on a farm devoted to wheat than on one in which wheat is intermingled with other crops to which the insect is not adapted.

The same thing happens in other situations. A generation or more 16 ago, the towns of large areas of the United States lined their streets with the noble elm tree. Now the beauty they hopefully created is threatened with complete destruction as disease sweeps through the elms, carried by a beetle that would have only limited chance to build up large populations and to spread from tree to tree if the elms were only occasional trees in a richly diversified planting.

Another factor in the modern insect problem is one that must be 17 viewed against a background of geologic and human history: the spreading of thousands of different kinds of organisms from their native homes to invade new territories. This worldwide migration has been studied and graphically described by the British ecologist Charles Elton in his recent book *The Ecology of Invasions*. During the Cretaceous Period, some hundred million years ago, flooding seas cut many land bridges between continents and living things found themselves confined in what Elton calls "colossal separate nature reserves." There, isolated from others of their kind, they developed many new species. When some of the land masses were joined again, about 15 million years ago, these species began to move out into new territories — a movement that is not only still in progress but is now receiving considerable assistance from man.

The importation of plants is the primary agent in the modern spread 18 of species, for animals have almost invariably gone along with the plants, quarantine being a comparatively recent and not completely effective innovation. The United States Office of Plant Introduction alone has introduced almost 200,000 species and varieties of plants from all over the world. Nearly half of the 180 or so major insect enemies of plants in the

United States are accidental imports from abroad, and most of them have come as hitchhikers on plants.

In new territory, out of reach of the restraining hand of the natural 19 enemies that kept down its numbers in its native land, an invading plant or animal is able to become enormously abundant. Thus it is no accident that our most troublesome insects are introduced species.

These invasions, both the naturally occurring and those dependent 20 on human assistance, are likely to continue indefinitely. Quarantine and massive chemical campaigns are only extremely expensive ways of buying time. We are faced, according to Dr. Elton, "with a life-and-death need not just to find new technological means of suppressing this plant or that animal"; instead we need the basic knowledge of animal populations and their relations to their surroundings that will "promote an even balance and damp down the explosive power of outbreaks and new invasions."

Much of the necessary knowledge is now available but we do not use 21 it. We train ecologists in our universities and even employ them in our governmental agencies but we seldom take their advice. We allow the chemical death rain to fall as though there were no alternative, whereas in fact there are many, and our ingenuity could soon discover many more if given opportunity.

Have we fallen into a mesmerized state that makes us accept as inev- 22 itable that which is inferior or detrimental, as though having lost the will or the vision to demand that which is good? Such thinking, in the words of the ecologist Paul Shepard, "idealizes life with only its head out of wa- ter, inches above the limits of toleration of the corruption of its own en- vironment ... Why should we tolerate a diet of weak poisons, a home in insipid surroundings, a circle of acquaintances who are not quite our ene- mies, the noise of motors with just enough relief to prevent insanity? Who would want to live in a world which is just not quite fatal?"

Yet such a world is pressed upon us. The crusade to create a chem- 23 ically sterile, insect-free world seems to have engendered a fanatic zeal on the part of many specialists and most of the so-called control agencies. On every hand there is evidence that those engaged in spraying opera- tions exercise a ruthless power. "The regulatory entomologists ... func- tion as prosecutor, judge and jury, tax assessor and collector and sheriff to enforce their own orders," said Connecticut entomologist Neely Turner. The most flagrant abuses go unchecked in both state and federal agencies.

It is not my contention that chemcial insecticides must never be 24 used. I do not contend that we have put poisonous and biologically po- tent chemicals indiscriminately into the hands of persons largely or wholly ignorant of their potentials for harm. We have subjected enormous numbers of people to contact with these poisons, without their consent and often without their knowledge. If the Bill of Rights contains no guarantee that a citizen shall be secure against lethal poisons distrib- uted either by private individuals or by public officials, it is surely only because our forefathers, despite their considerable wisdom and foresight, could conceive of no such problem.

I contend, furthermore, that we have allowed these chemicals to be 25 used with little or no advance investigation of their effect on soil, water, wildlife, and man himself. Future generations are unlikely to condone our lack of prudent concern for the integrity of the natural world that supports all life.

There is still very limited awareness of the nature of the threat. This 26 is an era of specialists, each of whom sees his own problem and is unaware of or intolerant of the larger frame into which it fits. It is also an era dominated by industry, in which the right to make a dollar at whatever cost is seldom challenged. When the public protests, confronted with some obvious evidence of damaging results of pesticide applications, it is fed little tranquilizing pills of half truth. We urgently need an end to these false assurances, to the sugar coating of unpalatable facts. It is the public that is being asked to assume the risk that the insect controllers calculate. The public must decide whether it wishes to continue on the present road, and it can do so only when in full possession of the facts. In the words of Jean Rostand, "the obligation to endure gives us the right to know."

Study Questions

1. What does Rachel Carson feel is the central problem of our age?
2. According to essay, how has the history of people's relationship to their environment changed in the twentieth century?
3. How has the chemical contamination of the environment upset the balance of nature?
4. In what way is experimentation with the atom "unnatural"?
5. How has Darwin's principle of the survival of the fittest escalated the production of toxic materials?

Loren C. Eiseley
USING A PLAGUE TO
FIGHT A PLAGUE

Loren C. Eiseley (1907–1977) was born in 1907 in Lincoln, Nebraska. He received his B.A. (1933) from the University of Nebraska
and his M.A. (1935) and Ph.D. (1937) from the University of Pennsylvania. He taught at the University of Kansas and Oberlin College
before returning, in 1947, to Pennsylvania, where he became University Professor in Anthropology and History of Science and head
of the Department of the History and Philosophy of Science. A
Guggenheim fellow, he published widely in both popular periodicals
and learned journals. *Darwin's Century* received the Phi Beta Kappa
science award in 1958, and *The Firmament of Time* (1960) received
the John Burroughs medal and the Lecomte de Nouy award. His
other books include *The Immense Journey* (1957), *Francis Bacon and
the Modern Dilemma* (1962), *Galapagos: The Flow of Wilderness* (1968),
The Invisible Pyramid (1972) and *All the Strange Hours* (1975).

A few days ago I stood amidst the marshes of a well-known   1
wildlife refuge. As I studied a group of herons through my glasses, there
floated by the margin of my vision the soapy, unsightly froth of a detergent discharged into the slough's backwaters from some source upstream.
Here nature, at first glance, seemed green and uncontaminated. As I left,
however, I could not help wondering how long it would be before seeping industrial wastes destroyed the water-life on which those birds sub-
sisted—how long it would be before poisonous and vacant mudflats had
replaced the chirping frogs and waving cattails I loved to visit. I thought
also of a sparkling stream in the Middle West in which, as a small boy, I
used to catch sunfish, but which today is a muddy, lifeless treacle filled
with oil from a nearby pumping station. No living thing now haunts its
polluted waters.

These two episodes out of my own experience are trifling, however,   2
compared with that virulent facet of man's activities treated in Rachel
Carson's latest book. It is a devastating, heavily documented, relentless
attack upon human carelessness, greed, and irresponsibility—an irresponsibility that has let loose upon man and the countryside a flood of
dangerous chemicals in a situation which, as Miss Carson states, is with-

out parallel in medical history. "No one," she adds, "yet knows what the ultimate consequences may be."

Silent Spring is her account of those floods of insecticides and well-in- 3 tentioned protective devices which have indiscriminately slaughtered our wildlife of both forest and stream. Such ill-considered activities break the necessary food chains of nature and destroy the livelihood of creatures not even directly affected by the pesticides. The water run-off from agricultural and forested areas carries to our major rivers and to the seas chemicals which may then impregnate the food we eat. We have no assurance that we are not introducing into nature heavy concentrates of non-natural substances whose effects are potentially as dangerous as those that came to light in the dramatic medical episode that shocked the public in recent weeks. I refer, of course, to the foetal monsters produced by the sleep drug Thalidomide. Imperfect though the present legal controls in the field of direct medical experiment may be, they are less inadequate than in the domain of agricultural chemistry, where aerial spraying is cascading a rain of poison over field and farmland.

D'Arcy Thompson, the great British biologist of the late nineteenth 4 century, commented astutely in 1897 that the increasing tempo of human cultural evolution produces a kind of evolution of chance itself—an increasing dissonance and complexity of change beyond what one finds in the world before man came. Though this evolution of chance arises within the human domain, it does not long remain confined to it. Instead, the erratic and growingly unpredictable fantasies created in the human mind invade nature itself. Tremendous agricultural productivity is correlated with the insatiable demands of ever-growing populations. Wastes in the air and wastes polluting the continental arteries increasingly disrupt the nature that we have taken for granted since the first simple hunters wandered out of the snowy winter of the Ice Age and learned to live in cities.

Man's sanitary engineering, in western civilization, never amounted 5 to much until the middle phase of the industrial revolution and the discovery of the relation of bacteria to disease. Now it is apparent that man must learn to handle more wisely the products of his own aspiring chemistry. He is faced with the prospect of learning to be a creative god in nature without, at the same time, destroying his surroundings and himself through thoughtless indifference to the old green world out of which he has so recently emerged and to which (though he forgets) he is as indissolubly bound in his own way as the herons that stalked before my field glasses.

Essentially there are two ways of approaching the control of noxious 6 insects: a natural and a chemical means. I am deliberately confining my remarks here, not to the effect of man's accidental industrial wastes upon his environment—a subject worthy of attention in itself—but to his deliberate and largely post-World War II use of peculiar carbon compounds in crop dusting and other forms of insect control. DDT is an excellent and spectacular example. With the passage of time the chemical industries have pressed more and more such substances upon the receptive public. Extensive research has been carried on in this field, frequently with results, at first glance, of an impressive character. That there may be other results, less favorable when viewed over a longer time span, is not always so well publicized.

The reason that Rachel Carson has chosen the more conservative bi- 7 ological approach to the problem of insect control lies in the following facts: Ill or uncontrolled spraying with deadly chemicals destroys beneficial as well as undesirable forms of life; furthermore, the poisonous residues may and do find their way into human food. Secondly, because insect generations are short and their numbers large, they rapidly become immune to the poisons that originally decimated them. By contrast, birds and the higher mammals, including man, cannot rapidly develop this selective immunity. They are eventually threatened not only by tougher and more formidable insect disease-carriers, but also by progressively dangerous chemicals devised against the mounting numbers of insects that refuse to succumb but whose natural enemies—the birds and fish—are being slaughtered in growing numbers by these same chemicals. The normal balance of life is thus increasingly disrupted. Man is whetting the cutting edge of natural selection, but its edge is turned against himself and his allies in the animal world.

In case after case, Miss Carson succeeds in documenting her thesis 8 with complete adequacy. It is not pleasant to learn of the casual spraying of the landscape with chemicals capable of mutagenic effects and regarded by some authorities as representing as great a menace as high levels of radiation. Nor is it reassuring to read that the hydrocarbons have an affinity for mammalian germ cells. At present there is no law on the statute books that requires manufacturers to demonstrate the genetic effects, as distinguished from the toxicity, of their concoctions. Nor is there any way of controlling what the average uninformed farmer may do with his insecticides. An equally ill-educated and impatient public wants its weeds, gnats, and mosquitoes eliminated in one fell blow. It is not sophisticated enough to trouble over the looming demise of our beautiful national bird, the bald eagle, nor to connect the return of many supposedly eliminated pests with the fact that the newer generation may be able to flourish in a sack of DDT and thus be twice as formidable.

The biological controls which Miss Carson favors, along with other 9 informed biologists, are not just more careful and discreet use of pesticides, but also such clever natural manipulations as the release of sterilized screw worm flies, causing a greater reduction in the population of this parasite than any insecticide would have achieved. Successful experiments such as this depend upon precise knowledge of the life history of an organism. They strike directly at the heart of the problem. They do not leave poisonous residues or resistant life-strains, nor do they result in the mass killing that frequently destroys valuable food chains on which even man is in the long run dependent.

All of these facts Rachel Carson has set forth sensibly in the quiet, 10 rational prose for which she is famous. If her present book does not possess the beauty of *The Sea Around Us,* it is because she has courageously chosen, at the height of her powers, to educate us upon a sad, an unpleasant, an unbeautiful topic, and one of our own making. *Silent Spring* should be read by every American who does not want it to be the epitaph of a world not very far beyond us in time.

Study Questions

1. What episodes from his own experience does Eiseley use to support Carson's thesis?
2. What two basic means of approaching the control of noxious insects are open to people?
3. According to Eiseley, what facts led Carson to choose the more conservative of these two approaches?

William J. Darby
SILENCE, MISS CARSON

William J. Darby (1913–   ) was born in Galloway, Arkansas. He received his B.S. (1936) and M.D. (1937) from the University of Arkansas and his M.S. (1941) and Ph.D. (1942) from the University of Michigan. He is now head of the Department of Biochemistry and director of the Division of Nutrition, School of Medicine, at Vanderbilt University. He has served with the National Research Council and the World Health Organization. Darby is coauthor of *Nutrition and Diet in Health and Disease* and codiscoverer of vitamin M and the activity of pteroylglutamic acid in sprue.

S*ilent Spring* starts with a bit of dramatic description of a situation which the author then acknowledges does not actually exist. It then orients the reader to its subject matter by stating that "only within ... the present century has man ... acquired significant power to alter the nature of his world." It identifies as irrecoverable and "for the most part irreversible" the effects of "this now universal contamination of the environment (in which) chemicals are the sinister and little recognized partners of radiation in changing the very nature of the world, the very nature of life itself." Man has, according to Miss Carson, now upset that ideal state of "adjustment and balance" of life on this planet through "synthetic creations of man's inventive mind, brewed in his laboratory, 1

A Review of *Silent Spring* by Rachel Carson. Reprinted from *Chemical and Engineering News,* Vol. 40, October 1, 1962, pp. 60–63. Copyright 1962 by The American Chemical Society and reprinted by permission.

and having no counterpart in nature." These products, the reader is told, are "staggering in number," have "power to kill," have "incredible potential for harm," represent a "train of disaster," result in a "chemical death rain," and are being used with "little or no advance investigation of their effect on soil, water, wildlife, and man himself." She further warns the reader that all of these sinister chemicals will not only extinguish plant life, wild life, aquatic life, and man, but they will produce cancer, leukemia, sterility, and cellular mutations.

There are 297 pages devoted to reiteration of these views. There then follows a 55-page "list of principal sources" designed to impress the reader with the extent of the support for Miss Carson's views. This list uses an extender and is artificially colored and flavored. Its apparent bulk is made one third greater through devoting a line of type to identify each page on which a source bears, and by repeating in full the title of each source in relation to recurrent pages. Its bulk will appeal to those readers who are as uncritical as the author, or to those who find the flavor of her product to their taste. These consumers will include the organic gardeners, the antifluoride leaguers, the worshipers of "natural foods," those who cling to the philosophy of a vital principle, and pseudo-scientists and faddists.

The flavor of this product is indicated in part by the source list. She refers frequently to testimony given at 1950, 1951, and 1952 Congressional hearings, seldom to later years, and to the opinion of Morton S. Siskind and W. C. Hueper.

The author ignores the sound appraisals of such responsible, broadly knowledgeable scientists as the President of the National Academy of Sciences, the members of the President's Scientific Advisory Committee, the Presidents of the Rockefeller Foundation and Nutrition Foundation, the several committees of the National Academy of Sciences-National Research Council (including the Food and Nutrition Board, the Agricultural Board, the Food Protection Committee) who have long given thoughtful study to these questions, and the special advisory committees appointed by the governors of California and Wisconsin. The latter committees were chaired by two distinguished scientist-presidents of universities, Dr. Emil Mrak and the late Dr. Conrad A. Elvehjem.

All of these groups of scientists have recognized the essentiality of use of agricultural chemicals to produce the food required by the expanding world population and to sustain an acceptable standard of living and health. They have recognized the safety of proper use of agricultural chemicals and, indeed, the benefits to the consumer which accrue from their proper use in food and agricultural production.

Miss Carson's book adds no new factual material not already known to such serious scientists as those concerned with these developments, nor does it include information essential for the reader to interpret the knowledge. It does confuse the information and so mix it with her opinions that the uninitiated reader is unable to sort fact from fancy. In view of the mature, responsible attention which this whole subject receives from able, qualified scientific groups such as those identified in the foregoing (and whom Miss Carson chooses to ignore); in view of her scientific qualifications in contrast to those of our distinguished scientific leaders and statesmen, this book should be ignored.

Logically, it should be possible to terminate this review here. Unfortunately, however, this book will have wide circulation on one of the standard subscription lists. It is doubtful that many readers can bear to wade through its high-pitched sequences of anxieties. It is likely to be perused uncritically, to be regarded by the layman as authoritative (which it is not), and to arouse in him manifestations of anxieties and psychoneuroses exhibited by some of the subjects cited by the author in the chapter "The Human Price." Indeed, the author's efforts at appraising psychologic evidence concerning the effects of substances reveal a remarkable lack of competence as a psychiatrist, even as great a lack in the area of toxicology or even knowledge of existing regulatory controls. The obvious effect of all of this on the reader will be to aggravate unjustifiably his own neurotic anxiety. 7

Her thesis is revealed by the dedicatory quotations: "Man has lost the capacity to foresee and to forestall. He will end by destroying the earth." (Albert Schweitzer) "Our approach to nature is to beat it into submission. We would stand a better chance of survival if we accommodated ourselves to this planet and viewed it appreciatively instead of skeptically and dictatorially." (E. B. White) 8

Such a passive attitude as the latter coupled with such pessimistic (and to this reviewer, unacceptable) philosophy as the former, means the end of all human progress, reversion to a passive social state devoid of technology, scientific medicine, agriculture, sanitation, or education. It means disease, epidemics, starvation, misery, and suffering incomparable and intolerable to modern man. Indeed, social, educational, and scientific development is prefaced on the conviction that man's lot will be and is being improved by greater understanding of and thereby increased ability to control or mold those forces responsible for man's suffering, misery, and deprivation. 9

The author's motivation is not quite so evident, but the emotional call to write the book is revealed by her acknowledgment that "In a letter written in January 1958, Olga Owens Huckins told me of her own bitter experience of a small world made lifeless, and so brought my attention sharply back to a problem which which I had long been concerned. I then realized *I must write this book*" (italics are the reviewer's). 10

So impelled, Miss Carson has effectively used several literary devices to present her thesis and make it appear to be a widely held scientific one. She "name-drops" by quoting or referring to renowned scientists out of context. A statement divorced from its original meaning is then approximated to an opinion of the author or else to a question posed by her with an implied answer. The reader is led to conclude thereby that the authority mentioned is in accord with the author's position. Nobel prize winners are recognized as especially useful names for such a purpose. 11

Another device used is that of confusion of the reader with (to him) unintelligible scientific jargon or irrelevant discussions of cellular processes. 12

Miss Carson's failure to distinguish between the occupational and 13
residue hazards is common to almost all popular writers on this subject.
The occupational hazard associated with the manufacture and application
of agricultural chemicals is similar to that of other work and can, should
be, and is being reduced. That accidents have occurred is well known,
but this is no more reason to ban useful chemicals than is the lamentable
occurrence of preventable automobile or airplane accidents reason to ban
these modern modes of transportation. Despite all of the implications of
harm from residues on foods, Miss Carson has not produced one single
example of injury resulting to man from these residues.

Miss Carson is infatuated with biologic control and the balance of na- 14
ture. Despite her statement that the really effective control of insects is
that applied by nature, one must observe that the very ineffectiveness of
such control is the raison de'etre of chemical pesticides.

She commits the scientifically indefensible fallacy of considering that 15
any substance which in any quantity is toxic must per se be a poison. By
such a definition almost everything—water, salt, sugar, amino acids, minerals, vitamins A or D, etc.—is a poison. She gives the reader a mistaken
concept of tolerances. Tolerances are not ill-defined levels of maximum
quantities which can be ingested without acute harm. They are minimum
amounts of a substance which should exist when the chemical has been
employed in good and proper beneficial practice. They are based on extensive use data and toxicologic testing in animals and frequently meta-
bolic studies in man. They include a very wide margin of safety, usually
being set at 100 times the *minimum* amount of the substance which induces any physiologic effect in the most sensitive of at least two species
of animals for lifetime or two- to four-year periods.

The benefit of use of chemicals, charges Miss Carson, is for the pro- 16
ducer. She ignores the requirement under the Miller bill that a chemical
must be *effective,* which means benefit to the consumer. She fails to recognize that "the consumer" includes the producer, farmer, wholesaler, re-
tailer, equipment manufacturer, their families, and even the scientists
who evaluate the chemicals. The toxicologists in industry, in the Food
and Drug Administration, in our universities and research institutes have,
as consumers, equal stake in protecting the nation's health as does Miss
Carson—and I believe, are better qualified to assume this protection.

Her ignorance or bias on some of the considerations throws doubt 17
on her competence to judge policy. For example, she indicates that it is
neither wise nor responsible to use pesticides in the control of in-
sectborne diseases. The July–August 1962 *World Health* (WHO publication) reports that a malaria eradication program in Mexico has since 1957
reduced the malaria area from 978,185 sq. km. with 18 million inhabitants to 224,500 sq. km. with 1.5 million inhabitants. "In most areas
the simple technique of indoor spraying of houses proved effective ...";
where bedbugs were resistant to DDT, an insecticide mixture was successfully used. "As a result of the campaign, the Mexican Government is
expanding its agricultural programme, distributing land, and undertaking
irrigation and hydroelectric schemes." It is most doubtful that Miss Carson really is ignorant of these and other facts which any objective ap-

praisal of this subject demands. Instead, it seems that a call to write a book has completely outweighed any semblance of scientific objectivity.

The public may be misled by this book. If it stimulates the public to 18 press for unwise and ill-conceived restrictions on the production, use, or development of new chemicals, it will be the consumer who suffers. If, on the other hand, it inspires some users to read and heed labels more carefully, it may aid in the large educational effort in which industry, government, colleges, and many other groups are engaged (despite Miss Carson's implication that they are not.)

The responsible scientist should read this book to understand the ig- 19 norance of those writing on the subject and the educational task which lies ahead.

Study Questions

1. What is the purpose of the numerous quotations in the first paragraph?
2. What objection does Darby raise to Carson's bibliography?
3. What significance does Darby find in Carson's reference to testimony given in the 1950–1952 Congressional hearings? Is this significance explicit or implicit?
4. What effect does Darby feel *Silent Spring* will have on the layman?
5. How does Darby explain Carson's having ignored the statistics he presents?

Virginia Woolf
THE DEATH OF THE MOTH

Virginia Woolf (1882–1941) is one of the most distinguished of twentieth-century novelists and critics. She was educated at home, and at a very early age began submitting articles to the *Times Literary Supplement*. Her reading included James Joyce, Marcel Proust, William James, Henri Bergson, and Sigmund Freud, and it is easy to trace their influence on her works. Her novels include *Jacob's Room* (1922), *Mrs. Dalloway* (1925), *To the Lighthouse* (1927), *Orlando* (1929), and *The Waves* (1931). Important critical works are *The Second Common Reader* (1933) and *The Death of the Moth and Other Essays* (1942). She and her husband Leonard were interested in fine printing and founded the Hogarth Press, which published the work of promising young authors. Ms. Woolf committed suicide at the age of 59.

Moths that fly by day are not properly to be called moths; they do not excite that pleasant sense of dark autumn nights and ivy-blossom which the commonest yellow-underwing asleep in the shadow of the curtain never fails to rouse in us. They are hybrid creatures, neither gay like butterflies nor sombre like their own species. Nevertheless the present specimen, with his narrow hay-coloured wings, fringed with a tassel of the same colour, seemed to be content with life. It was a pleasant morning, mid-September, mild, benignant, yet with a keener breath than that of the summer months. The plough was already scoring the field opposite the window, and where the share had been, the earth was pressed flat and gleamed with moisture. Such vigour came rolling in from the fields and the down beyond that it was difficult to keep the eyes strictly turned upon the book. The rooks too were keeping one of their annual festivities; soaring round the tree tops until it looked as if a vast net with thousands of black knots in it had been cast up into the air; which, after a few moments sank slowly down upon the trees until every twig seemed to have a knot at the end of it. Then, suddenly, the net would be thrown into the air again in a wider circle this time, with the utmost clamour and vociferation, as though to be thrown into the air and settle slowly down upon the tree tops were a tremendously exciting experience. 1

The same energy which inspired the rooks, the ploughmen, the horses, and even, it seemed, the lean bare-backed downs, sent the moth fluttering from side to side of his square of the window-pane. One could not help watching him. One was, indeed, conscious of a queer feeling of pity for him. The possibilities of pleasure seemed that morning so enormous and so various that to have only a moth's part in life, and a day moth's at that, appeared a hard fate, and his zest in enjoying his meagre opportunities to the full, pathetic. He flew vigorously to one corner of his compartment, and, after waiting there a second, flew across to the other. What remained for him but to fly to a third corner and then to a fourth? That was all he could do, in spite of the size of the downs, the width of the sky, the far-off smoke of houses, and the romantic voice, now and then, of a steamer out at sea. What he could do he did. Watching him, it seemed as if a fibre, very thin but pure, of the enormous energy of the world had been thrust into his frail and diminutive body. As often as he crossed the pane, I could fancy that a thread of vital light became visible. He was little or nothing but life. 2

Yet, because he was so small, and so simple a form of the energy that was rolling in at the open window and driving its way through so many narrow and intricate corridors in my own brain and in those of other human beings, there was something marvellous as well as pathetic about him. It was as if someone had taken a tiny bead of pure life and decking it as lightly as possible with down and feathers, had set it danc- 3 ing and zigzagging to show us the true nature of life. Thus displayed one could not get over the strangeness of it. One is apt to forget all about life, seeing it humped and bossed and garnished and cumbered so that it has to move with the greatest circumspection and dignity. Again, the thought of all that life might have been had he been born in any other shape caused one to view his simple activities with a kind of pity.

After a time, tired by his dancing apparently, he settled on the win- 4 dow ledge in the sun, and, the queer spectacle being at an end, I forgot about him. Then, looking up, my eye was caught by him. He was trying to resume his dancing, but seemed either so stiff or so awkward that he could only flutter to the bottom of the window-pane; and when he tried to fly across it he failed. Being intent on other matters I watched these futile attempts for a time without thinking, unconsciously waiting for him to resume his flight, as one waits for a machine, that has stopped momentarily, to start again without considering the reason of its failure. After perhaps a seventh attempt he slipped from the wooden ledge and fell, fluttering his wings, on to his back on the window sill. The helplessness of his attitude roused me. It flashed upon me that he was in difficulties; he could no longer raise himself; his legs struggled vainly. But, as I stretched out a pencil, meaning to help him to right himself, it came over me that the failure and awkwardness were the approach of death. I laid the pencil down again.

The legs agitated themselves once more. I looked as if for the enemy 5 against which he struggled. I looked out of doors. What had happened there? Presumably it was midday, and work in the fields had stopped. Stillness and quiet had replaced the previous animation. The birds had taken themselves off to feed in the brooks. The horses stood still. Yet the power was there all the same, massed outside indifferent, impersonal, not attending to anything in particular. Somehow it was opposed to the little hay-coloured moth. It was useless to try to do anything. One could only watch the extraordinary efforts made by those tiny legs against an oncoming doom which could, had it chosen, have submerged an entire city, not merely a city, but masses of human beings; nothing, I knew had any chance against death. Nevertheless after a pause of exhaustion the legs fluttered again. It was superb this last protest, and so frantic that he succeeded at last in righting himself. One's sympathies, of course, were all on the side of life. Also, when there was nobody to care or to know, this gigantic effort on the part of an insignificant little moth, against a power of such magnitude, to retain what no one else valued or desired to keep, moved one strangely. Again, somehow, one saw life, a pure bead. I lifted the pencil again, useless though I knew it to be. But even as I did so, the unmistakable tokens of death showed themselves. The body relaxed, and instantly grew stiff. The struggle was over. The insignificant little creature now knew death. As I looked at the dead moth, this minute wayside triumph of so great a force over so mean an antagonist filled me with wonder. Just as life had been strange a few minutes before, so death was now as strange. The moth having righted himself now lay almost decently and uncomplainingly composed. O yes, he seemed to say, death is stronger than I am.

Study Questions

1. What is the subject of this essay? Is it the death of a moth?
2. How does the description of the moth and its actions characterize Woolf for the reader?
3. How does the author use the outdoors in structuring her essay?
4. Cite specific examples that show how Woolf personifies the moth. Does the personification result in sentimentality?
5. Does the conclusion leave anything to be desired?

6 Language
"The Soul of Wit"

For this section we again followed the guidelines used for the earlier editions of *Strategies in Prose*. In general we selected essays that can supplement the rhetoric, handbook, or other such text used along with *Strategies in Prose*. We tried to select essays that will be more appealing to students than material on language found in rhetorics or handbooks.

We do not necessarily expect the essays to be assigned according to the order of their appearance in this book. Indeed, we do not expect that all the essays of any section will be assigned during the course of a single semester. But Mario Pei's "How Language — and Languages — Can Help You" is intended as an introduction to language study. If the Seymour essay, "Black English," is used, it could follow Pei's, for it expands some of the issues Pei raises.

Any contemporary consideration about language uses and abuses must include areas covered in Alleen Pace Nilsen's "Sexism in English: A Feminist View," Barbara Lawrence's "Four-Letter Words Can Hurt You," and Henryk Skolimowski's "The Semantic Environment in the Age of Advertising." Solidly documented with examples and illustrations, the Nilsen essay presents convincing evidence that our language is indeed a sexist institution. To counter this view, we have included Stefan Kanfer's "Sispeak: A Msguided Attempt to Change Herstory." This playful, satirical essay makes light of the feminists' attempts to purge the language of sexism.

The Skolimowski essay deals with an issue in language that has received special attention in recent years — the various ways our language is used to manipulate people, particularly by advertising copywriters. This essay presents many provocative arguments and examples that can stimulate theme topics and ideas for compositions.

In contrast to the tone and method of these essays, those by H. Allen Smith and Mark Twain give a humorous treatment to important aspects of language. In addition, they illustrate different rhetorical approaches that students may wish to imitate.

We have retained the Orwell essay, "Politics and the English Language," upon the recommendation of teachers who have used earlier editions of *Strategies in Prose*. Although it may prove to be a challenge to some students, it is a minor classic that is rich in information, presented in a lively and appealing manner. As a companion essay to Orwell's, Lawrence L. Langer's "The Human Use of Language" deals with the relationship between our feelings and what we are willing to reveal about ourselves when we write.

Mario Pei

HOW LANGUAGE – AND LANGUAGES – CAN HELP YOU

Mario Pei was born in Rome in 1901 and became a United States citizen in 1925. He graduated *magna cum laude* from City College of New York (1925) and received his Ph.D. (1932) from Columbia University. His teaching career at Columbia ended in 1970, after nearly thirty-five years. In those years he established himself as a scholar and perceptive critic of the Romance languages and literatures. His writings won him the recognition of numerous national leaders. Pei's most recent books include *Language Today* (1967), *Words in Sheep's Clothing* (1969), *Double Speak in America* (1973), and *The Story of Latin and the Romance Languages* (1976).

A well-known linguist advises you to "leave your language 1 alone"; that is, speak naturally, even if incorrectly, letting the chips fall where they may. Go ahead and use "ain't," "it's me," "who did you see?," "I laid on the bed," he advocates. Another distinguished authority in the field suggests that it would be a splendid thing if no more spelling were taught for half a century, and people were allowed to spell as they please; at the end of that period, he adds, the chances are we would have worked out a new system of spelling that would reflect the pronunciation.

Statements like these are spectacular, and they sound good on the 2 surface. They encourage the tendency, inborn in each of us, to follow the line of least resistance and avoid work and effort.

Also, they have in them a grain of sense. Consider, for example, the 3 different sorts of car driving you see on the road; some are glaringly bad and lead to crashes; but certainly, within the range of safety, there is room for various ways of holding the steering wheel, applying the brakes, making a turn. Not all good golf players hold their clubs in precisely the same fashion; one man who could never break ninety as long as he held his club in the way taught him by the pro found himself down in the low eighties as soon as he threw instruction overboard and handled the club in the way that was most natural for him. Some people pound the typewriter with two fingers of each hand and their eyes on the keyboard, and are almost as speedy and accurate as devotees of the touch system.

However, there are limits to the effectiveness of doing as you please. 4 This is particularly true in language. Even the man who wants you to "leave your language alone" admits that if you use "ain't" and "I done it" in the "best" circles, you won't get invited to tea again. As for the matter of spelling, we may get away with "thru" and "nite," but phonetic spellings like "natcherly," "watchagonnado," and "I should of done it" will mark you as an illiterate.

Rightly or wrongly, most people consider language as an index of 5 culture, breeding, upbringing, personality, sometimes even of intelligence, decency, and integrity. Under the circumstances, it is unwise, not to say harmful, to pay no heed to your language. The present status of the language being what it is, the use of wrong words and forms, or the inability to produce the right ones, may do as much damage to your chances of getting ahead (and along) as using a knife on your peas or slurping your soup.

Language is something more than a system of communications; it is 6 also a social convention which one must observe, under penalty of being misjudged. Ignorance or improper use of language can easily interfere with your success and advancement. It can take money out of your pocket.

Conversely, the proper use of the proper language in the environ- 7 ment for which it is designed can lead to success in both business and social relations. For this, there is a well-grounded psychological reason.

Language is a set of rules tacitly agreed to and accepted by common 8 consent of all the speakers. There is no intrinsic connection between the *object* hat" and the *word* "hat" save that the word has been set apart by the English-speaking community to serve as the *symbol* of the object. A French-speaking community will use not "hat" but *chapeau* to represent the object we call a hat. The validity of the language symbol for the object is subjective and unstable, in precisely the same way that a dollar bill, or a pound note, is a subjective and unstable token of purchasing power, and not at all identical with the things it can buy.

If you find yourself alone in a desert you will quickly realize that the 9 value of such dollar bills as you may have in your pocket shrinks to nil, and that a slab of bacon or a canteen of water is infinitely more valuable than a handful of hundred-dollar notes. You will also find that your language equipment is of no particular value, since there is no one to use it on.

But human beings normally do not live alone in deserts. They live in 10 communities of their fellowmen, and in such communities symbol values come into play. The dollar bill has no value in itself; it is only a piece of paper. But it is everywhere accepted as a *symbol* of purchasing power. In the same way, language becomes of value because it is accepted as the symbol of thought, the medium by which thought is transferred from one person to another.

It is at this point that the symbol comes in for close scrutiny. Why is 11 a forged dollar bill not accepted, while one produced by the government presses is? Intrinsically, the privately produced dollar note is just as valuable (or valueless) as the good note. But the community has decided that only such dollar bills as bear the authentic imprint of the U. S. government shall be valid as media of exchange and symbols of metal currency. This is because we know the government has the silver with which to redeem the paper note.

In language, the community has decided that certain words and 12 forms are valid as symbols of thought and shall be accepted by all members of the community, while others, for one reason or another (not necessarily a logical one), are not valid. Those not valid may serve the purpose of temporary exchange of meaning in a limited way, just as some forms of scrip served the purposes of money in small communities during the depression days, or in certain army units during the occupation of foreign lands. Their use, however, is limited, while the fully standard forms have universal currency throughout the entire speech community.

The type of language you ought to strive to write and speak should 13 therefore be the one that has the widest, not the narrowest, currency, that is universally accepted and understood wherever there are English speakers. You should not be content with a kind of language that is restricted to one locality, or one social class.

To discover what is universally current throughout the speech com- 14 munity calls for some effort. Through ignorance, you may sometimes delude yourself into believing that the local or class speech form you happen to be using is standard when as a matter of fact it is not. If you are wrong and don't know it, there is no way of correcting your error. But if you are wrong and are aware of the fact, you can do something about it.

The question is not so much one of striving to achieve "correctness" 15 in accordance with some arbitrary or antiquated model, but of striving to come as close as possible to the general usage of the community. To speak without gross and glaring localisms, and with a minimum of class features, slang, and jargon, is desirable. This can only be achieved by watching your language, not by "leaving it alone."

The person who speaks, easily and correctly, the standard speech of 16 the broad language community to which he belongs will normally find himself better off all around. He will be able to express his ideas and personality and get what he wants. He will be able to make friends and influence people. He will find that his opinions carry greater weight with the men and women he associates with. He will also find that he has greater understanding of others, their ideas, and their problems.

In addition to the comparison between authentic U.S. currency and 17 scrip or forged notes, another comparison is possible, between an authentic dollar bill and an authentic British pound note. Both are fully valid and fully accepted in their own areas. But the areas don't coincide. Dollar, pound, franc, mark, lira, ruble, yen are all legitimate forms of currency, but you cannot translate one into purchasing power in the area of another without going through the process of exchange.

Something quite similar happens in the case of foreign languages as 18 compared with your own native tongue. The other languages are valid media of thought transfer in their respective countries, just as yours is valid in your land. The process by which you get your linguistic money exchanged in the foreign area is to have translators and interpreters at your disposal to convey your thoughts to the local people and get theirs in return. But just as you may also provide yourself, before you set forth on your travels, with amounts of foreign money, you may, in like manner, provide yourself with greater or smaller amounts of foreign languages, which will save you the trouble of stopping at the local exchange office or securing the services of a translator or interpreter.

Materially speaking, a knowledge of foreign languages makes your 19 traveling easier and more comfortable and allows you to carry on your activities in the foreign country as naturally as you would in your own.

On another plane, a knowledge of foreign languages gives you a 20 keener insight into the world-wide human mind, permits you to compare ways of expression and modes of thought, gives you a greater understanding of other peoples, and makes for far more pleasant and friendly relations, and this is true whether you travel or not. A good deal of the antipathy and intolerance existing in the world today hinges upon lack of linguistic understanding.

It is therefore desirable to know, as well as possible, both your own 21 language and the languages of other groups. Language, once it is gained, can be put to work for you. It can help you in your business or occupation, in your social life, in your travels, in your enjoyment of the world in general. It expands your horizons, and makes accessible to you the treasuries of world thought, both in your own chosen line of endeavor and in that broad field of leisure which modern technology has put within reach of practically all men.

Study Questions

1. Is the thesis stated or implied? If stated, identify it; if implied, state it in your own words.
2. What is the function of the series of statements in the opening paragraph?
3. What is the purpose of examples in paragraph 3?
4. Identify the words or phrases that link paragraphs 1-2, 2-3, 3-4, 6-7, 9-10.
5. What is the function of paragraph 13?
6. Identify paragraphs that contain series of parallel sentences. What effect is achieved by these types of structures?

Henryk Skolimowski

THE SEMANTIC ENVIRONMENT IN THE AGE OF ADVERTISING

David Ogilvy is a very successful advertising man. In addition, 1
Mr. Ogilvy has turned out to be a successful writer. His book, *Confessions of an Advertising Man,* was a best-seller in 1965. His confessions are in fact intimate whisperings of one adman to another. These whisperings, however, turned out to be interesting enough to make his book one of the most readable and lucid stories of advertising ever written. What is so fascinating about this book is not the amount of linguistic contortions which he advocates, but the amount of truth which is expressed there incidentally. There is nothing more comforting than to find truth accidentally expressed by one's adversary. *Confessions of an Advertising Man* provides a wealth of such truths.

Mr. Ogilvy tells us that "the most powerful words you can use in a 2
headline are FREE and NEW. You can seldom use FREE," he continues, "but you can always use NEW — if you try hard enough." It is an empirical fact that these two words have a most powerful influence upon us. This fact has been established by scientific research. Whenever these words appear, they are used deliberately — in order to lull and seduce us.

The word FREE is especially seductive. Whether we are aware of this 3
or not, it has an almost hypnotic effect on us. Although we all know "nothing is for nothing," whenever the word FREE appears, it acts on us as

Reprinted from *Etc.,* Vol. 25, No. 1, by permission of the International Society for General Semantics.

the light of a candle acts on a moth. This is one of the mysteries of our language. And these mysteries are very skillfully exploited by advertising men.

Apart from the words FREE and NEW, other words and phrases "which 4 make wonders," as Mr. Ogilvy's research has established, are: "HOW TO, SUDDENLY, NOW, ANNOUNCING, INTRODUCING, IMPORTANT, DEVELOPMENT, AMAZ-ING, SENSATIONAL, REVOLUTIONARY, STARTLING, MIRACLE, OFFER, QUICK, EASY, WANTED, CHALLENGE, ADVICE TO, THE TRUTH ABOUT, COMPARE, BARGAIN, HURRY, LAST CHANCE." Should we not be grateful to Mr. Ogilvy for such a splen-did collection? Should we not learn these "miraculous" phrases by heart in order to know which particular ones drive us to the marketplace? To this collection I should like to add some of the phrases which I found: SIMPLE, SAVE, CONVENIENT, COMFORT, LUXURY, SPECIAL OFFER, DISTINCTIVE, DIFFER-ENT, RARE.

Having provided his collection, Ogilvy comments upon these words 5 that make wonders (and this comment is most revealing): "Don't turn up your nose at these cliches. They may be shopworn, but they work." Alas! They work on us. What can we do about their merciless grip? Nothing. Language and its workings cannot be controlled or altered through an act of our will. The cumulative process of the development of language used as the instrument of tyranny or as the bridge to God through prayers; as a recorder of everyday trivia or as a clarion trumpet announcing new epochs in human history; as an expression of private feelings of single in-dividuals or as a transmitter of slogans to the masses—this process has endowed some words with incredible subtleties and others with irresist-ible power. The only thing we can do about the influence of language on us is to become aware of it. This awareness may diminish the grip lan-guage has on us.

It is very gratifying to know that nowadays advertising is so punc- 6 tilious, so systematic, and so scientific in its approach to the customer. Mr. Ogilvy in *Confessions* relentlessly repeats that "research has shown" so and so, "research shows" this and that, "research suggests" that, "re-search has established" that, etc. This constant reference to research is not an advertising humbug. It is through systematic research that we are "hooked" more and more thoroughly. With perfect innocence Ogilvy in-forms us that "Another profitable gambit is to give the reader helpful ad-vice or service. It hooks about [was this a slip of the tongue, or inten-tional, plain description?] 75 per cent more readers than copy which deals entirely with the product."

Madison Avenue has, above all, established that through words we 7 may be compelled to perform certain acts—acts of buying. This con-clusion is not to be found in Ogilvy. Whether it is an historical accident or not, it is a rather striking fact that, independent of semanticists and logicians and linguistic philosophers, advertising men have made some important discoveries about language. And they have utilized these dis-coveries with amazing success. They are probably not aware of the theo-retical significance of their discoveries and are no doubt little interested in such matters.

J. L. Austin, one of the most prominent linguistic philosophers at Ox- 8 ford during the 1950's, developed a theory of what he called *performative utterances*. He observed that language is systematically employed not only for stating and describing but also for performing actions. Such utterances as "I warn you to..." or "I promise you x" are performances rather than descriptions. They function not only on a verbal level, but also as deeds, as concrete performances through words. The discovery and classification of performative utterances is an important extention of ordinary logic — that is, logic concerned with declarative utterances. On the other hand, it is an important finding of the hidden force of language in shaping our social and individual relationships.

Quite independently, advertising men have developed and successfully applied their own theory of performative utterances. They may be oblivious to the logical subtleties involved; however, they are not oblivious to the power of their medium — that is, the verbal utterances through which they induce our acts of buying. Again, there is very little we can do about it. This is the way language works. We can only recognize this fact. But once we recognize it, we acquire some immunity. 9

Now, we all know that advertising messages are conveyed in words. Usually, there are not only words, but pictures and images which suggest appropriate associations to the person reading the words. The images are projected to be psychologically appealing. Psychologically appealing images are those which appeal to our seven deadly sins: sexual urges, vanity, snobbery, gluttony, greed, etc. 10

Many analyses of advertising have shown the mechanism of psychological associations built into the ad message. In particular they showed that the level of most of these appeals is that of sheer brutes, of ultimate half-wits whose only desire is to satisfy their most rudimentary biological urges. However, not many analyses of advertising, if any at all, show how frail the link is between the picture set to evoke emotional reactions and the linguistic utterance which, in the final analysis, is the message of the ad. We must remember that it is the verbal message which ultimately draws us to the marketplace. The analysis of this verbal or linguistic level of the ad is our main concern here. 11

Language is, of course, basically a medium of communication. To be an adequate medium, language must be flexible. But to be flexible is one thing; to be entirely elastic and malleable is another. These other two characteristics, extreme elasticity and malleability, are required from the language which is set to infiltrate people's minds and contaminate their mental habits. It is in this latter capacity that admen want to employ language. And consequently, they do everything conceivable, and sometimes inconceivable, to make language infinitely flexible and as malleable as plasticene. 12

The point is very simple. If language is made a plasticene, the meaning of concepts is so stretched that words are deprived of their original sense and end up with whatever sense the wild imagination of the admen equips them. Since the language of ads often departs radically from ordinary language, advertisements could in one sense be regarded as pieces of poetry.[1] 13

[1] The idea that advertising is a kind of bad poetry was first forcibly and tellingly expressed by E. E. Cummings in his "Poem, or Beauty Hurts Mr. Vinal" (1926). See also "Poetry and Advertising," Chapter XV of Hayakawa's *Language in Thought and Action* (rev. ed., 1964).

A piece of poetry should have a nice ring to its words, pleasant or   14
extraordinary association of ideas, unusual combinations of meanings.
The factual content is not important. For communication, as I shall use
the term here, the factual content is most important. It is the content
that we wish to communicate, and this is conveyed in messages. Consequently, messages must contain factual information. If there is no factual information in the message, the message does not communicate anything. Usually the actual content of the message may be expressed in
many different ways. What is important is the content, not the manner of
expression. If the manner of expressing a message is more important
than its content, then the message does not serve the purpose of communication. It may serve many other purposes, but it does not serve the
purpose of conveying factual information.

And this is exactly the case with advertising. The advertising mes-   15
sages are pseudo-messages, not genuine messages. They do not contain
factual information. At any rate, this is not their main purpose. Their
main purpose is not to inform but to force us to buy. It is clear that if
the content of advertising were of any importance, then the same message worded differently would serve the same function; namely, of informing us. This is obviously not the case with advertising: the overwhelming majority of ads would have little effect, if any, if they were
phrased differently.

In art, our emotional involvement is the source of our delight. It is   16
the uniqueness of the form that inspires our thoughts and arouses our
emotions. The meaning and significance of the work of art hinge upon
the uniqueness of its form. Once the form is destroyed or altered, the
work of art does not exist any more. If the validity of advertisements depends on preserving their form intact, then they pretend to be pieces of
art, but not the carriers of factual information. The trouble is that they
do pretend to give factual and objective information—but in a rather peculiar way: in such a way that the "information" would force us to acquire the product which is the substance of the message.

Communication is for humans. It is the mark of a rational man to   17
grasp the content of a message irrespective of the form of its presentation—that is, irrespective of its linguistic expression. The nature of any
communication in which the actual information conveyed is less significant than the manner of its presentation is, to say the least, illogical. The
illogical man is what advertising is after. This is why advertising is so anti-
rational; this is why it aims at uprooting not only the rationality of man
but his common sense; this is why it indulges in exuberent but deplorable linguistic orgies.

Distortion of language, violation of logic, and corruption of values   18
are about the most common devices through which advertising operates.
This is particularly striking in endless perversions of the word FREE. Since
this word has such a powerful impact on us, there is no limit to its abuse.
In his novel *1984,* George Orwell showed that what is required for establishing a "perfect" dictatorship is perhaps no more than a systematic
reform of language. The condition is, however, that the reform must be

thorough and complete. "Doubletalk" as a possible reality has, since Orwell's novel, been viewed with horror, but not with incredulity. The question is whether doubletalk has not already become part of our reality, has not already been diffused in our blood stream through means different from those Orwell conceived of. Isn't it true that advertising has become a perfect Orwellian institution?

Nowadays there is in operation a doubletalk concept of freedom according to which protecting the public from fraud and deceit and warning people about dangers to their health is but "an erosion of freedom." This concept of freedom is, needless to say, advocated and defended by advertising agencies. In the opinion of admen, "freedom" for people means protecting people from their common sense and ability to think. For many admen "freedom" means freedom to advertise in whatsoever manner is profitable, freedom to force you to buy, freedom to penetrate your subconscious, freedom to dupe you, to hook you, to make a sucker of you, freedom to take away your freedom. Anything else is for them but an "erosion of freedom." Hail Mr. Orwell! Hail doubletalk! 19

Now to turn to some concrete illustrations: 20

> Mustang! A Car To Make Weak Men Strong,
> Strong Men Invincible

Do not say that we do not believe such obvious blusterings. We do. It seems that the art of magicians — according to which some incantations evoke events, bring rain, heal wounds; some amulets bring good luck, prevent bad luck or illness — has been re-established by contemporary advertising. Motor cars in particular are the amulets of the atomic age. They possess all the miraculous qualities you wish them to possess — from being a substitute for a sweetheart (or mistress, if you prefer) to being a soothing balm to a crushed ego. Dictionaries usually define an automobile as a self-propelled vehicle for the transportation of people or goods. The car industry and car dealers are of a quite different opinion. Perhaps lexicographers are outdated in their conception of "automobile."

Roughly speaking, motor cars are advertised to be amulets of two kinds. The first casts spells on us and makes us happy, or builds up our personality, or adds to our strength, or makes us invincible if we are already strong; the second casts spells on others and, while we drive this magic vehicle, makes other people see us as more important, more influential, more irresistible. As yet, there are no cars which, being driven by us, would bring punishment upon our enemies. Perhaps one day this will come to pass. The question is how many of us can really resist the incantations of car dealers and remain impervious to the "magical" qualities allegedly embodied in the modern automobile. How many of us can remain uninfluenced by the continuous flow of messages, in spite of our ability to see the nonsense of each one individually? 21

Our civilization has often been called the motor-car civilization. But in no less degree, it is the drug civilization; it is also the detergent civilization. Each of these elements is apparently essential to the well-being of our society. But it is by no means only detergents, cars, or drugs that 22 offer us full happiness "as a reasonable price." Nowadays, practically any product can give you happiness.

Happiness Is To Get (or Give) a Bulova

The only problem is to believe it. Whether Bulova is a yellow ca- 23 nary, a black watch, or a green giraffe, it unfortunately takes a bit more to achieve happiness than getting or giving a Bulova. But of course the counter-argument can go, "happiness" in this ad was not meant literally but only figuratively. Admen today are like poets; we must allow them poetic license. But must we? And how figuratively would they really like to be taken? It seems that they (and the producers of the products they advertise) would be very unhappy if we took all their messages figuratively. On the contrary, they want their messages to be taken as literally as possible. It is precisely their business to convince us about the "loveliness" of soaps, "happiness" in Bulovas, and "delights" of a cigarette puff. The poetic language they use is meant to break our resistance, to produce desirable associations which we usually associate with poetry.

The sad part of the story is that in the process of serving advertising, 24 poetry has gone down the drain. Poetic expressions are poetic so long as they are in the context of poetry; so long as they evoke unusual emotional reactions, serve as a substance of an esthetic experience — the experience of delight. In its exuberant development, advertising has debased almost the entire poetic vocabulary. And advertising seems to be responsible for a decline of the poetic taste and for a considerable indifference, if not hostility, of American youth toward poetry.

The nausea which one experiences on being bombarded by the 25 pseudo-poetry of advertising may recur when one approaches genuine poetry, unless one has developed love for poetry *before* becoming aware of advertising — which is impossible for young people nowadays. It is quite natural that such a reaction would develop. We are not likely to seek nausea deliberately, and so we would rather avoid whatever reminds us of it. It seems that if the process of debasing and abusing language by advertising is carried further, we may discover a new value in absolute simplicity of language. Perhaps one day, when the traditional poetry is completely ruined, we shall count as poetry some simple and concrete descriptions like this: "There is a table in the room. The table is brown. There are three chairs at the table. A man is sitting on one of the chairs."[2]

The main point is more significant. By applying highly charged emo- 26 tional terms like "lovely" to soaps, and "bold" and "proud" to automobiles, advertising pushes us to consider objects as if they were human beings. Through the language of advertising, we participate in the process of constant personification of objects which we should "love," be "enchanted by," be "delighted with," and "be happy with." Unconsciously we

---

[2] Perhaps some poets have discovered this principle already. Here is the complete text of "The Red Wheelbarrow" by William Carlos Williams: "so much depends/ upon/ a red wheel/ barrow/ glazed with rain/ water/ beside the white / chickens." (*Collected Poems 1921–1931*, Objectivist Press, 1934.)

have developed emotional attachments to objects surrounding us. We have become worshippers of objects. Advertising has been a powerful force in this process.

My thesis is that the semantic environment has a more profound in- 27 fluence on our behavior and our attitudes than we are aware. If this thesis is correct, it may throw some light on the phenomenon which we usually attribute to the population explosion and the mechanization of our lives; namely, the depersonalization of human relations. I should like to suggest that perhaps a transfer of attitudes through the change of the semantic environment has taken place. Previously, highly emotional expressions were applied to human beings. Nowadays, they are constantly and massively applied by the admen to objects. We have thus developed loving fondness for objects which we worship. Dehumanizing of human relations seems to be the other part of this process. It is quite natural that when we become more and more emotionally involved with objects, we tend to be less and less involved with people. As a consequence, attitudes traditionally reserved for objects are now displayed toward people. In love, in friendship, and in the multitude of other human relations, detachment, lack of interest, and coldness seem to prevail. Human beings are treated like objects.

To summarize, the success of advertising and our failure to defend 28 ourselves against it result mainly from our obliviousness to some of the functions of language. We think that language is a tool, an indifferent piece of gadgetry which simply serves the process of communication and that the only relation we have to language is that *we use language.* We do indeed use it. But this is only part of the story. The other part, which is usually overlooked, is that *language uses us* — by forming our personal and emotional habits, by forming our attitudes. Language is thus not only our servant; it is also our master. No one knows this better than the adman!

The relation between language and us is more complicated than we 29 usually are prepared to admit. To escape the tyranny of language, we have to recognize the double role of language in human relations, (1) as a carrier of messages we send, and (2) as a shaper of the content of human relations. We cannot reduce or nullify the influence of language on us by simply denying the existence of this influence. The only reasonable thing we can do is to recognize the force of language: its strength, the way it works, its theater of operations. By identifying the traps of language, by identifying the linguistic strategies of the admen and other propagandists, we shall be able to cope with the semantic environment much more effectively than we have done hitherto.

Study Questions

1. Describe the tone of this essay. What words, phrases, and sentences help establish the tone?
2. What is the author's overall rhetorical strategy?
3. Identify the paragraph that contains the thesis statement. Is the thesis implied earlier in the essay?

4. What types of sentences are used in the opening paragraph? How do they establish a pattern? If so, what is its effect?
5. In what ways and to what purpose does Skolimowski use comparison and contrast?
6. The opening paragraphs appear to introduce a review of a book. Where is it evident that this is not a book review?

H. Allen Smith
THE UGLIEST WORD

H. Allen Smith (1906–   ) was born in McLeansboro, Illinois, and educated in parochial schools. His writing career began at age 15 on a newspaper in Huntington, Indiana; in a few years he became a feature writer for United Press and soon established himself as a humorist of note. Smith's specialty has been writing about odd characters — Fred Allen called him the screwball's Boswell — and his humor is in the midwestern tradition of Twain, George Ade, et al. Among Smith's most recent works are *Son of Rhubarb* (1967), *The Great Chili Confrontation* (1969), *Low Man Rides Again* (1973), *Return of the Virginian* (1974), and *The Life and Legend of Gene Fowler* (1976).

Lullaby. Golden. Damask. Moonlight. Do these words seem aesthetically attractive to you? They have appeared with some regularity on lists of "the ten most beautiful words in our language." Along with *luminous, hush, anemone, mother,* and various others. These lists appear from time to time in the public prints, and there is almost always disagreement among the scholarly people who mine the dictionaries looking for lovely words. Sometimes these disagreements reach a point where ugly words are used. I can't recall ever having seen a list of the ten ugliest words in the language but I do remember that the late Ring Lardner, coming upon one of the beautiful word lists in a newspaper, remarked with chagrin and bitterness: "Why did they leave out *gangrene?*" 1

The people who assemble these lists actually can't make up their minds what they are after. Is a beautiful word beautiful because of its musical sound or because of the thing it describes? If *moonlight* was the name of the diamond-back rattlesnake, would *moonlight* be considered a romantic-sounding and pretty word? If there were no such word as *mother,* and your mother was your *sludge,* would *sludge* be poetically beau- 2 tiful? You ask my opinion and I'll tell you that *gangrene* is a downright lovely word, provided you keep your mind off gangrene. You want to hear a *real* ugly word? *Ugly.*

My own choice for the most beautiful word of them all would not 3 appeal to the generality of people; it is a word of glowing, glimmering loveliness and arouses intense feelings of well-being and even sensuality within me. The word is *End.* With a capital "E." As a professional writer of books and magazine articles, I almost swoon with gladness when, on the last page of the third draft of a long manuscript, I write: *The End.* I sit and stare at it, and the longer I do so, the more excruciatingly beautiful it becomes. *Lullaby* my ass! I have left instructions that *The End* be chiseled on my gravestone.

As for ugly words, almost every literate person has in his head an ag- 4 glomeration of them—words that can cause him to wince, and even shudder, such as *agglomeration.* I lay claim to several hundred of the uglies. *Mulcted* almost nauseates me (as I've indicated in an earlier essay in this book). I cringe in the face of *albeit, and/or, yelept, obsequies, whilom,* and *tinsmith.*

My own nomination for the meanest and low-downdest and ugliest 5 word of them all is *Oh.* Said twice, with maybe a hyphen, this way: *Oh-oh.* In its maximal ugliness, it is customarily spoken softly with inflections that would curl the toes of a South Georgia mule.

Something is wrong, let us say, with the engine of your car. You take 6 it to the garage. The mechanic lifts the hood and pokes around a bit and then you hear him murmur: "Oh-oh." The wretched creature says it in such a restrained dramatic manner that you know instantly that your whole motor has to be derricked out and thrown away and a new one put in.

Oh-oh almost always suggests tragedy, or impending tragedy. I re- 7 member standing with another man at a cocktail party when he, glancing across the crowded room, said, "Oh-oh." I followed his gaze. A prominent actor and an equally prominent newspaperman were squaring off, and blows began raining, and a nose was bloodied, and it took some doing to pry the two gentlemen apart.

Consider again our friends the dentists. Most of them have enough 8 gumption to conceal their opinions and judgments, but sometimes you'll run across one who forgets his chairside manner. He'll be inspecting a big molar in the back and suddenly he'll say, "Oh-oh." Or he'll come out of his darkroom carrying an X-ray taken a few minutes earlier, and he'll put it up against the light, and he'll look at it briefly, and then his head will give a jerk and he'll say, "Oh-oh." You know at once, without ESP, precisely what is meant. Out. All of them. From now on, plates. And you know what Aunt Gert says about plates. No apples. No corn on the cob. No a lot of things. You are a captive in the dentist's chair but you feel like busting out of the place and hiding in the woods.

Physicians as a general thing have schooled themselves carefully to 9 conceal any sinister condition they may find during an examination. Yet I have run across one offender in my checkered medical career. He was giving me the annual checkup. He took my blood pressure and tapped me for knee jerks and scratched me on the bottoms of my feet for God knows what and stethoscoped me front and back and had me blow into a machine to test my "vital capacity" and then he turned the electrocardiograph loose on me. As he studied the saw-toothed dossier on my heart, his brow crinkled and I heard him say quite softly but with an undercurrent of alarm, "Oh-oh." Everything inside me suddenly bunched together in one large knot.

"What is it?" I gulped. "Whad you find there?"   10

"Nothing really," he said. "Nothing important."   11

Nothing! Cancer of the heart is *nothing?* It had to be that at the very   12
least.

"I heard you say 'Oh-oh,'" I told him. "Come on. Give it to me. I'm   13
a man. I can take it. Let me have it straight."

"Okay," he said, and I steeled myself manfully for seven seconds and   14
then began to turn chicken. He resumed: "I said 'Oh-oh' because I just happened to think that I haven't made out my tax return yet, and the deadline is tomorrow."

I quit him the next day. Took my aches and agues elsewhere. I can't   15
use a doctor who is mooning over his income tax problems while he is looking at the record of my frightful heart disorders. I don't want a doctor *ever* to say "Oh-oh" in my presence, unless perhaps he has dropped his sphygmomanometer on the floor and busted it all to hell. Even in that contingency I think he should employ a more masculine and earthy expression. I surely would.

The saying of "Oh-oh" should be forbidden by federal statute. It is   16
the most frightening, nerve-shattering locution to come into general usage since Noah Webster quit slopping pigs on his father's farm in Connecticut. It is, in fact, so low-down mean in its usual implications that even the dictionaries won't let it in. I scorn it, and deride it, and let my mind dwell on its opposite — that most beautiful of words ...

Study Questions

1. What characterizes the tone of this essay? What does the diction have to do with the tone?
2. Why is the first-person point of view more effective than the third person in this type of essay?
3. How effective are the illustrations the author uses to support his nomination for the ugliest word?
4. What is gained by dramatizing the illustration in paragraphs 9–15?
5. Compare the structure of this essay with the structure of the Lawrence essay.

Barbara Lawrence
FOUR-LETTER WORDS CAN HURT YOU

Why should any words be called obscene? Don't they all de- 1
scribe natural human functions? Am I trying to tell them, my students
demand, that the "strong, earthy, gut-honest"—or, if they are fans of
Norman Mailer, the "rich, liberating, existential"—language they use to
describe sexual activity isn't preferable to "phony-sounding, middle-class
words like 'intercourse' and 'copulate'?" "Cop You Late!" they say with
fancy inflections and gagging grimaces. "Now, what is *that* supposed to
mean?"

Well, what is it supposed to mean? And why indeed should one 2
group of words describing human functions and human organs be acceptable in ordinary conversation and another, describing presumably the
same organs and functions, be tabooed—so much so, in fact, that some of
these words still cannot appear in print in many parts of the English-
speaking world?

The argument that these taboos exist only because of "sexual hang- 3
ups" (middle-class, middle-age, feminist), or even that they are a result of
class oppression (the contempt of the Norman conquerors for the language of their Anglo-Saxon serfs), ignores a much more likely explanation, it seems to me, and that is the sources and functions of the
words themselves.

The best known of the tabooed sexual verbs, for example, comes 4
from the German *ficken,* meaning "to strike"; combined, according to
Partridge's etymological dictionary *Origins,* with the Latin sexual verb *fu-*

tuere; associated in turn with the Latin *fustis,* "a staff or cudgel"; the Celtic *buc,* "a point, hence to pierce"; the Irish *bot,* "the male member"; the Latin *battuere,* "to beat"; the Gaelic *batair,* "a cudgeller"; the Early Irish *bualaim,* "I strike"; and so forth. It is one of what etymologists sometimes call "the sadistic group of words for the man's part in copulation."

The brutality of this word, then, and its equivalents ("screw," "bang," 5 etc.), is not an illusion of the middle class or a crotchet of Women's Liberation. In their origins and imagery these words carry undeniably painful, if not sadistic, implications, the object of which is almost always female. Consider, for example, what a "screw" actually does to the wood it penetrates; what a painful, even mutilating, activity this kind of analogy suggests. "Screw" is particularly interesting in this context, since the noun, according to Partridge, comes from words meaning "groove," "nut," "ditch," "breeding sow," "scrofula" and "swelling," while the verb, besides its explicit imagery, has antecedent associations to "write on," "scratch," "scarify," and so forth—a revealing fusion of a mechanical or painful action with an obviously denigrated object.

Not all obscene words, of course, are as implicitly sadistic or deni- 6 grating to women as these, but all that I know seem to serve a similar purpose: to reduce the human organism (especially the female organism) and human functions (especially sexual and procreative) to their least organic, most mechanical dimension; to substitute a trivializing or deforming resemblance for the complex human reality of what is being described.

Tabooed male descriptives, when they are not openly denigrating to 7 women, often serve to divorce a male organ or function from any significant interaction with the female. Take the word "testes," for example, suggesting "witnesses" (from the Latin *testis*) to the sexual and procreative strengths of the male organ; and the obscene counterpart of this word, which suggests little more than a mechanical shape. Or compare almost any of the "rich," "liberating" sexual verbs, so fashionable today among male writers, with that much-derided Latin word "copulate" ("to bind or join together") or even that Anglo-Saxon phrase (which seems to have had no trouble surviving the Norman Conquest) "make love."

How arrogantly self-involved the tabooed words seem in comparison 8 to either of the other terms, and how contemptuous of the female partner. Understandably so, of course, if she is only a "skirt," a "broad," a "chick," a "pussycat" or a "piece." If she is, in other words, no more than her skirt, or what her skirt conceals; no more than a breeder, or the broadest part of her; no more than a piece of a human being or a "piece of tail."

The most severely tabooed of all the female descriptives, in- 9 cidentally, are those like a "piece of tail," which suggests (either explicitly or through antecedents) that there is no significant difference between the female channel through which we are all conceived and born and the anal outlet common to both sexes—a distinction that pornographers have always enjoyed obscuring.

This effort to deny women their biological identity, their individ- 10 uality, their humanness, is such an important aspect of obscene language that one can only marvel at how seldom, in an era preoccupied with definitions of obscenity, this fact is brought to our attention. One problem, of course, is that many of the people in the best position to do this (critics, teachers, writers) are so reluctant today to admit that they are angered or shocked by obscenity. Bored, maybe, unimpressed, aesthetically displeased, but—no matter how brutal or denigrating the material— never angered, never shocked.

And yet how eloquently angered, how piously shocked many of 11 these same people become if denigrating language is used about any minority group other than women; if the obscenities are racial or ethnic, that is, rather than sexual. Words like "coon," "kike," "spic," "wop," after all, deform identity, deny individuality and humanness in almost exactly the same way that sexual vulgarisms and obscenities do.

No one that I know, least of all my students, would fail to question 12 the values of a society whose literature and entertainment rested heavily on racial or ethnic pejoratives. Are the values of a society whose literature and entertainment rest as heavily as ours on sexual pejoratives any less questionable?

Study Questions

1. Which paragraph contains the thesis sentence?
2. What effect is achieved by the first-person point of view?
3. How are questions in paragraphs 1 and 2 used to lead into paragraph 3?
4. What is the function of paragraph 4?
5. What effect is gained by the question that concludes the essay?
6. Identify the type of argument used to establish that words and phrases are taboo?

Alleen Pace Nilsen
SEXISM IN ENGLISH: A FEMINIST VIEW

Alleen Pace Nilsen (1936   ) was born in Arizona. She received
her B.A. from Brigham Young University (1958), her M.Ed. from the
American University (1961), and her Ph.D. from the University of
Iowa (1973). She has taught in American public schools and in the
American International School of Kabul, Afghanistan, as well as at
universities in New York, Michigan, Iowa, and Arizona. Ms. Nilsen
is a member of the NCTE Committee on the Image of Women in the
Council and the Profession; and since 1973 has been review editor
of "Books for Young Adults" in the *English Journal.* Her articles have
appeared in the *Journal of Reading, Elementary English, College English,*
and *Jack and Jill Magazine* among others. Published books are *Pronunciation Contrasts in English* (1971), *Semantic Theory: A Linguistic
Perspective* (1975), *Sexism in Language* (1977), and *Language Play: An
Introduction to Linguistics* (1978).

Does culture shape language? Or does language shape cul- 1
ture? This is as difficult a question as the old puzzler of which came first,
the chicken or the egg, because there's no clear separation between language and culture.

A well-accepted linguistic principle is that as culture changes so will 2
the language. The reverse of this—as a language changes so will the culture—is not so readily accepted. This is why some linguists smile (or
even scoff) at feminist attempts to replace *Mrs.* and *Miss* with *Ms.* and to
find replacements for those all-inclusive words which specify masculinity,
e.g., *chairman, mankind, brotherhood, freshman,* etc.

Perhaps they are amused for the same reason that it is the doctor at 3
a cocktail party who laughs the loudest at the joke about the man who
couldn't afford an operation so he offered the doctor a little something to
touch up the X-ray. A person working constantly with language is likely
to be more aware of how really deep-seated sexism is in our communication system.

Last winter I took a standard desk dictionary and gave it a place of 4
honor on my night table. Every night that I didn't have anything more interesting to do, I read myself to sleep making a card for each entry that
seemed to tell something about male and female. By spring I had a
rather dog-eared dictionary, but I also had a collection of note cards filling two shoe boxes. The cards tell some rather interesting things about
American English.

Alleen Pace Nilsen, "Sexism in English: A Feminist View," *Female Studies VI: Closer to
the Ground,* ed. by N. Hoffman, C. Secor, A. Tinsley. The Feminist Press, Box 334, Old
Westbury N.Y.: 1972, pp. 102–109.

First, in our culture it is a woman's body which is considered impor- 5
tant while it is a man's mind or his activities which are valued. A woman
is sexy. A man is successful.

I made a card for all the words which came into modern English 6
from somebody's name. I have a two-and-one-half inch stack of cards
which are men's names now used as everyday words. The women's stack
is less than a half inch high and most of them came from Greek mythology. Words coming from the names of famous American men include
*lynch, sousaphone, sideburns, Pullman, rickettsia, Schick test, Winchester rifle,
Franklin stove, Bartlett pear, teddy bear,* and *boysenberry.* The only really
common words coming from the names of American women are *bloomers*
(after Amelia Jenks Bloomer) and *Mae West jacket.* Both of these words
are related in some way to a woman's physical anatomy, while the male
words (except for *sideburns* after General Burnsides) have nothing to do
with the namesake's body.

This reminded me of an earlier observation that my husband and I 7
made about geographical names. A few years ago we became interested
in what we called "Topless Topography" when we learned that the Grand
Tetons used to be simply called *The Tetons* by French explorers and *The
Teats* by American frontiersmen. We wrote letters to several map makers
and found the following listings: *Nippletop* and *Little Nipple Top* near Mt.
Marcy in the Adirondacks, *Nipple Mountain* in Archuleta County, Colorado, *Nipple Peak* in Coke County, Texas, *Nipple Butte* in Pennington,
South Dakota, *Squaw Peak* in Placer County, California (and many other
places), *Maiden's Peak* and *Squaw Tit* (they're the same mountain) in the
Cascade Range in Oregon, *Jane Russell Peaks* near Stark, New Hampshire,
and *Mary's Nipple* near Salt Lake City, Utah.

We might compare these names to Jackson Hole, Wyoming, or Pikes 8
Peak, Colorado. I'm sure we would get all kinds of protests from the
Jackson and Pike descendants if we tried to say that these topographical
features were named because they in some way resembled the bodies of
Jackson and Pike, respectively.

This preoccupation with women's breasts is neither new nor strictly 9
American. I was amused to read the derivation of the word *Amazon.* According to Greek folk etymology, the *a* means "without" as in *atypical* or
amoral while *mazon* comes from *mazōs* meaning "breast." According to
the legend, these women cut off one breast so that they could better
shoot their bows. Perhaps the feeling was that the women had to trade in
part of their femininity in exchange for their active or masculine role.

There are certain pairs of words which illustrate the way in which 10
sexual connotations are given to feminine words while the masculine
words retain a serious, businesslike aura. For example, being a *callboy* is
perfectly respectable. It simply refers to a person who calls actors when
it is time for them to go on stage, but being a *call girl* is being a prostitute.

Also we might compare *sir* and *madam. Sir* is a term of respect while 11
madam has acquired the meaning of a brothel manager. The same thing
has happened to the formerly cognate terms, *master* and *mistress.* Because
of its acquired sexual connotations, *mistress* is now carefully avoided in

certain contexts. For example, the Boy Scouts have *scoutmasters* but certainly not *scoutmistresses*. And in a dog show the female owner of a dog is never referred to as the *dog's mistress*, but rather as the *dog's master*.

Master appears in such terms as *master plan, concert master, school-master, mixmaster, master charge, master craftsman*, etc. But *mistress* appears in a very few compounds. This is the way it is with dozens of words which have male and female counterparts. I found two hundred such terms, e.g., *usher--usherette, heir--heiress, hero--heroine*, etc. In nearly all cases it is the masculine word which is the base with a feminine suffix being added for the alternate version. The masculine words also travels into compounds while the feminine word is a dead end; e.g., from *king--queen* comes *kingdom* but not *queendom*, from *sportsman--sportslady* comes *sportsmanship* but not *sportsladyship*, etc. There is one—and only one—semantic area in which the masculine word is not the base or more powerful word. This is in the area dealing with sex and marriage. Here it is the feminine word which is dominant. *Prostitute* is the base word with *male prostitute* being the derived term. *Bride* appears in *bridal shower, bridal gown, bridal attendant, bridesmaid*, and even in *bridegroom*, while *groom* in the sense of *bridegroom* does not appear in any compounds, not even to name the groom's attendants or his prenuptial party. 12

At the end of a marriage, this same emphasis is on the female. If it ends in divorce, the woman gets the title of *divorcee* while the man is usually described with a statement, such as, "He's divorced." When the marriage ends in death, the woman is a *widow* and the *-er* suffix which seems to connote masculine (probably because it is an agentive or actor type suffix) is added to make *widower*. *Widower* doesn't appear in any compounds (except for *grass widower*, which is another companion term), but *widow* appears in several compounds and in addition has some acquired meanings, such as the extra hand dealt to the table in certain card games and an undesirable leftover line of type in printing. 13

If I were an anthropological linguist making observations about a strange and primitive tribe, I would duly note on my tape recorder that I had found linguistic evidence to show that in the area of sex and marriage the female appears to be more important than the male, but in all other areas of the culture, it seems that the reverse is true. 14

But since I am not an anthropological linguist, I will simply go on to my second observation, which is that women are expected to play a passive role while men play an active one. 15

One indication of women's passive role is the fact that they are often identified as something to eat. What's more passive than a plate of food? Last spring I saw an announcement advertising the Indiana University English Department picnic. It read "Good Food! Delicious Women!" The publicity committee was probably jumped on by local feminists, but it's nothing new to look on women as "delectable morsels." Even women compliment each other with "You look good enough to eat," or "You have a peaches and cream complexion." Modern slang constantly comes up with new terms, but some of the old standbys for women are: *cute tomato, dish, peach, sharp cookie, cheese cake, honey, sugar*, and *sweetie-pie*. A man may occasionally be addressed as *honey* or described as *a hunk of* 16 *meat,* but certainly men are not laid out on a buffet and labeled as women are.

Women's passivity is also shown in the comparisons made to plants. 17 For example, to *deflower* a woman is to take away her virginity. A girl can be described as a *clinging vine,* a *shrinking violet,* or a *wall flower.* On the other hand, men are too active to be thought of as plants. The only time we make the comparison is when insulting a man we say he is like a woman by calling him a *pansy.*

We also see the active-passive contrast in the animal terms used with 18 males and females. Men are referred to as *studs, bucks,* and *wolves,* and they go *tomcatting around.* These are all aggressive roles, but women have such pet names as *kitten, bunny, beaver, bird, chick, lamb,* and *fox.* The idea of being a pet seems much more closely related to females than to males. For instance, little girls grow up wearing *pigtails* and *ponytails* and they dress in *halters* and *dog collars.*

The active-passive contrast is also seen in the proper names given to 19 boy babies and girl babies. Girls are much more likely to be given names like *Ivy, Rose, Jewel, Pearl, Flora, Joy,* etc., while boys are given names describing active roles such as *Martin* (warlike), *Leo* (lion), *William* (protector), *Ernest* (resolute fighter), and so on.

Another way that women play a passive role is that they are defined 20 in relationship to someone else. This is what feminists are protesting when they ask to be identified as *Ms.* rather than as *Mrs.* or *Miss.* It is a constant source of irritation to women's organizations that when they turn in items to newspapers under their own names, that is, Susan Glascoe, Jeanette Jones, and so forth, the editors consistently rewrite the item so that the names read Mrs. John Glascoe, Mrs. Robert E. Jones.

In the dictionary I found what appears to be an attitude on the part 21 of editors that it is almost indecent to let a respectable women's name march unaccompanied across the pages of a dictionary. A woman's name must somehow be escorted by a male's name regardless of whether or not the male contributed to the woman's reason for being in the dictionary, or in his own right, was as famous as the woman. For example, Charlotte Brontë is identified as Mrs. Arthur B. Nicholls, Amelia Earhart is identified as Mrs. George Palmer Putnam, Helen Hayes is identified as Mrs. Charles MacArthur, Zona Gale is identified as Mrs. William Llwelyn Breese, and Jenny Lind is identified as Mme. Otto Goldschmidt.

Although most of the women are identified as Mrs. _____ or as the 22 wife of _____, other women are listed with brothers, fathers, or lovers. Cornelia Otis Skinner is identified as the daughter of Otis, Harriet Beecher Stowe is identified as the sister of Henry Ward Beecher, Edith Sitwell is identified as the sister of Osbert and Sacheverell, Nell Gwyn is identified as the mistress of Charles II, and Madame Pompadour is identified as the mistress of Louis XV.

The women who did get into the dictionary without the benefit of a 23 masculine escort are a group sort of on the fringes of respectability. They are the rebels and the crusaders: temperance leaders Frances Elizabeth Caroline Willard and Carry Nation, women's rights leaders Carrie Chapman Catt and Elizabeth Cady Stanton, birth control educator Margaret

Sanger, religious leader Mary Baker Eddy, and slaves Harriet Tubman and Phillis Wheatley.

I would estimate that far more than fifty percent of the women listed 24 in the dictionary were identified as someone's wife. But of all the men— and there are probably ten times as many men as women—only one was identified as "the husband of. . . ." This was the unusual case of Frederic Joliot who took the last name of Joliot-Curie and was identified as "husband of Irene." Apparently Irene, the daughter of Pierre and Marie Curie, did not want to give up her maiden name when she married and so the couple took the hyphenated last name.

There are several pairs of words which also illustrate the more pow- 25 erful role of the male and the relational role of the female. For example a *count* is a high political officer with a *countess* being simply the wife of a count. The same is true for a *duke* and a *duchess* and a *king* and a *queen*. The fact that a king is usually more powerful than a queen might be the reason that Queen Elizabeth's husband is given the title of *prince* rather than *king*. Since *king* is a stronger word than *queen*, it is reserved for a true heir to the throne because if it were given to someone coming into the royal family by marriage, then the subjects might forget where the true power lies. With the weaker word of *queen*, this would not be a problem; so a woman marrying a ruling monarch is given the title without question.

My third observation is that there are many positive connotations 26 connected with the concept of masculine, while there are either trivial or negative connotations connected with the corresponding feminine concept.

Conditioning toward the superiority of the masculine role starts very 27 early in life. Child psychologists point out that the only area in which a girl has more freedom than a boy is in experimenting with an appropriate sex role. She is much freer to be a *tomboy* than is her brother to be a *sissy*. The proper names given to children reflect this same attitude. It's perfectly all right for a girl to have a boy's name, but not the other way around. As girls are given more and more of the boys' names, parents shy away from using boy names that might be mistaken for girl names, so the number of available masculine names is constantly shrinking. Fifty years ago *Hazel, Beverley, Marion, Frances,* and *Shirley* were all perfectly acceptable boys' names. Today few parents give these names to baby boys and adult men who are stuck with them self-consciously go by their initials or by abbreviated forms such as *Haze* or *Shirl*. But parents of little girls keep crowding the masculine set and currently popular girls' names include *Jo, Kelly, Teri, Cris, Pat, Shawn, Toni,* and *Sam*.

When the mother of one of these little girls tells her to *be a lady*, she 28 means for her to sit with her knees together. But when the father of a little boy tells him to *be a man*, he means for him to be noble, strong, and virtuous. The whole concept of manliness has such positive connotations that it is a compliment to call a male a *he-man*, a *manly man*, or a *virile man* (*virile* comes from the Indo-European *vir*, meaning "man"). In each of these three terms, we are implying that someone is doubly good because he is doubly a man.

Compare *chef* with *cook, tailor* and *seamstress,* and *poet* with *poetess.* In 29
each case, the masculine form carries with it an added degree of excellence. In comparing the masculine *governor* with the feminine *governess*
and the masculine *major* with the feminine *majorette,* the added feature is
power.

The difference between positive male and negative female con- 30
notations can be seen in several pairs of words which differ denotatively
only in the matter of sex. For instance compare *bachelor* with the terms
spinster and *old maid. Bachelor* has such positive connotations that modern
girls have tried to borrow the feeling in the term *bachelor-girl. Bachelor*
appears in glamorous terms such as *bachelor pad, bachelor party,* and *bachelor button.* But *old maid* has such strong negative feelings that it has been
adopted into other areas, taking with it the feeling of undesirability. It
has the metaphorical meaning of shriveled and unwanted kernels of pop
corn, and it's the name of the last unwanted card in a popular game for
children.

Patron and *matron* (Middle English for *father* and *mother*) are another 31
set where women have tried to borrow the positive masculine connotations, this time through the word *patroness,* which literally means "female father." Such a peculiar term came about because of the high prestige attached to the word *patron* in such phrases as *"a patron of the arts"*
or *"a patron saint." Matron* is more apt to be used in talking about a
woman who is in charge of a jail or a public restroom.

Even *lord* and *lady* have different levels of connotation. *Our Lord* is 32
used as a title for deity, while the corresponding *Our Lady* is a relational
title for Mary, the moral mother of Jesus. *Landlord* has more dignity than
landlady probably because the landlord is more likely to be thought of as
the owner while the landlady is the person who collects the rent and en-
forces the rules. *Lady* is used in many insignificant places where the corresponding *lord* would never be used, for example, *ladies room, ladies sizes,
ladies aid society, ladybug,* etc.

This overuse of *lady* might be compared to the overuse of *queen* 33
which is rapidly losing its prestige as compared to *king.* Hundreds of
beauty queens are crowned each year and nearly every community in the
United States has its *Dairy Queen* or its *Freezer Queen,* etc. Male homosex-
uals have adopted the term to identify the "feminine" partner. And advertisers who are constantly on the lookout for euphemisms to make unpleasant sounding products salable have recently dealt what might be a
death blow to the prestige of the word *queen.* They have begun to use it
as an indication of size. For example, *queen-size* panty hose are panty hose
for fat women. The meaning comes through a comparison with *king-size,*
meaning big. However, there's a subtle difference in that our culture considers it desirable for males to be big because size is an indication of
power, but we prefer that females be small and petite. So using *king-size*
as a term to indicate bigness partially enhances the prestige of *king,* but
using *queen-size* to indicate bigness brings unpleasant associations to the
word *queen.*

Another set that might be compared are *brave* and *squaw.* The word 34
brave carries with it the connotations of youth, vigor, and courage, while

squaw implies almost opposite characteristics. With the set *wizard* and *witch,* the main difference is that *wizard* implies skill and wisdom combined with magic, while *witch* implies evil intentions combined with magic. Part of the unattractiveness of both *squaw* and *witch* is that they suggest old age, which in women is particularly undesirable. When I lived in Afghanistan (1967–69), I was horrified to hear a proverb stating that when you see an old man you should sit down and take a lesson, but when you see an old woman you should throw a stone. I was equally startled when I went to compare the connotations of our two phrases *grandfatherly advice* and *old wives' tales.* Certainly it isn't expressed with the same force as in the Afghan proverb, but the implication is similar.

In some of the animal terms used for women the extreme undesir- 35 ability of female old age is also seen. For instance consider the unattractiveness of *old nag* as compared to *filly,* of *old crow* or *old bat* as compared to *bird,* and of being *catty* as compared to being *kittenish.* The chicken metaphor tells the whole story of a girl's life. In her youth she is a *chick,* then she marries and begins feeling *cooped up,* so she goes to *hen parties* where she *cackles* with her friends. Then she has her *brood* and begins to *henpeck* her husband. Finally she turns into *an old biddy.*

Study Questions

1. What is the thesis of this essay, and what type of development is used to support it?
2. How does the author handle the transitions between the three major observations?
3. Compare and contrast the point of view used in this essay with that used in the Kanfer essay.
4. How does Nilsen establish her authority within the essay?
5. What is the difference between the humor in this essay and the humor in the Kanfer essay?

Stefan Kanfer

SISPEAK: A MSGUIDED ATTEMPT TO CHANGE HERSTORY

Stephen Kanfer has been on the staff of *Time* since 1967, as film critic, essayist, and book reviewer. He is now a Senior Editor and editor of the book review section. His essays have appeared in numerous other journals, including *Atlantic, Harper's, Esquire, The New York Times,* and the *New Yorker*. A guest lecturer at several universities, he was also writer-in-residence at the City University of New York. His *Journal of the Plague Year* was concerned with the political blacklisting of performers in the 50's and his novel *The Eighth Sin* was published in 1978.

As the chairperson of Senator McGovern's task force on the environment," begins Robert N. Rickles' letter to constituents. Chairperson? The title is no partisan issue: the G.O.P also had a chairperson in Miami Beach. Thus another label comes unglued. The man and his woman are Out: the neuter "person" is In — and only the chair is allowed to linger undisturbed. Chairperson is just the latest exchange in that great linguistic bazaar where new terms are traded for old. The elderly "Mrs." and the shy "Miss" now curtsy to the crisp, swinging "Ms." "Congressone" has been suggested in federal corridors to replace the Congressman-woman stigma. 1

Lexicographers Ms. Casey Miller and Ms. Kate Swift recently amplified the Women's Lib party line: men have traditionally used language to subjugate women. As they see it, William James' bitch-goddess Success and the National Weather Service's Hurricane Agnes are products of the same criminal mind, designed to foster the illusion of woman as Eve, forever volatile and treacherous. The authors therefore suggest the elimination of sexist terms. "Genkind," they think, would provide a great encompassing umbrella under which all humanity could huddle, regardless. Varda One, a radical philologist, asks for the obliteration of such repugnant pronouns as he and she, his and hers. In place she offers ve, vis and ver. "We don't go around addressing persons by their race, height or eye color," says One. "Why should we identify them by sex?" Unfortunately, such designations tend to remove rather than increase an individual's 2 sense of self. "Personalized" Christmas cards are about as personal as a paper cup.

Through the echoes of the new verbalism, one can sense the distress 3 of that crystal spirit, George Orwell. In *Nineteen Eighty-Four* he posited the principles of a new tongue. "In Newspeak," wrote Orwell, "words which had once borne a heretical meaning were sometimes retained for the sake of convenience, but only with the undesirable meanings purged out of them." "Goodsex" meant chastity: "crimethink" suggested equality. "The greatest difficulty facing the compilers of Newspeak," continued Orwell, "was not to invent new words, but, having invented them, to make sure what they meant: to make sure what ranges of words they canceled by their existence."

Certainly the compilers of the new Sispeak have no such totalitarian 4 purposes. Big Sister is not yet watching, and from the beginning the feminist wordsmiths have had to endure mockery and ridicule. Cartoonists and satirists have suggested that the ladies were Libbing under a Msapprehension. Their inventions were Msanthropic and Msguided attempts to change herstory. *The Godmother* was to be Mario Puzo's new Mafia novel: Womandarin Critic Susan Daughtertag was the new bottle for the old whine. Shedonism, girlcotting and countessdowns were to be anticipated in the liberated '70s. As for the enemy, he could expect to be confronted by female belligerents inviting him to put up his duchesses. He would find, in short, that his gander was cooked. All flagrantly gendered words would be swiftly unsexed. The ottoman would become the otto-it, the highboy would metamorphose into the high-thing, and ladyfingers would be served under the somewhat less appealing name of personfingers.

Yet beyond the hoots and herstrionics, the feminists seemed to have 5 reason on their side. Tradition does play favorites with gender. Man, master, father are the commonplaces of theological and political leadership. Who, for example, could imagine the Four Horsepersons of the Apocalypse or George Washington, first in the hearts of his countrypeople? Even the literature of equality favors the male: Robert Burns sang "A man's a man for a' that!" *"Mann ist Mann."* echoed Brecht. "Constant labor of one uniform kind," wrote Karl Marx, "destroys the intensity and flow of a man's animal spirits." The U.N. Charter speaks of the scourge of war, which, "has brought untold sorrow to mankind." It is pathetically easy to spy in this vocabulary a latent slavery, a cloaked prejudice aimed at further subjugating women in the name of language.

No wonder, then, that the movement has set out to change the dic- 6 tionary. With a touching, almost mystical trust in words, it seems to believe that definition is a matter of will. And indeed sometimes it is. The change from Negro to black has helped to remake a people's view of itself. But it is a lone example. Far more often, words have been corrupted by change. The counterculture's overuse of "love" has not resulted in a lessening of hostilities: "heavy" has become a lightweight adjective. The abuse of the word media has resulted in a breakdown of intelligence; invitations have even been sent out to "Dear media person." For the most part, the new lexicographers behave like Humpty Dumpty in *Through the*

Looking Glass: a word may mean whatever they want it to mean. Naturally, said Humpty, "when I make a word do a lot of work, I always pay it extra." One wonders what Women's Lib's new words will be paid. They are, after all, working overtime, and against immense cultural and sociological odds.

In the philosophy of semantics there is a standard rhetorical question: Is it progress if a cannibal eats with a knife and fork? Similarly, if society is sexist, is it altered when its language is revised? Or do its attitudes remain when its platitudes change? The prognosis is not good. Words, like all currency, need to be reinforced with values. Take away the Federal Reserve and its dollar bill is waste paper. Take away meaning and a word is only noise. Changing chairman to chairperson is mock doctrine and flaccid democracy, altering neither the audience nor, in fact, the office holder. Despite its suffix, chairman is no more sexist than the French designation of "boat" as masculine, or the English custom of referring to a ship with feminine pronouns. Chairman is a role, not a pejorative. Congressman is an office, not a chauvinist plot. Mankind is a term for all humanity, not some 49% of it. The feminist attack on social crimes may be as legitimate as it was inevitable. But the attack on words is only another social crime—one against the means and the hope of communication. 7

For *A Clockwork Orange,* Anthony Burgess created a wall-to-wall nightmare in which society dissolves into violence and repression. The condition is reflected in the breakdown of language into "nadsat," a jumble of portmanteau constructions ("He looked a malenky bit poogly when he viddied the four of us"). To Burgess, language is the breath of civilization. Cut it short and society suffocates. That is an insight worth pondering. For if the world is to resist the nadsat future, readers and writers of both sexes must resist onefully any meaningless neologisms. To do less is to encourage another manifestation of prejudice—against reason, meaning and eventually personkind itself. 8

Study Questions

1. Compare and contrast the tone of this essay with Nilsen's essay.
2. What is one of the author's indirect, but not so subtle, strategies in making his point?
3. Identify the types of arguments Kanfer uses to support his position.
4. What is the type of development used in paragraphs 5–7?
5. Why may the author choose to use the third-person point of view in this essay?

George Orwell
POLITICS AND THE ENGLISH LANGUAGE

George Orwell (1903–1950) was the pen name of Eric Blair, who was born in Bengal, India. He graduated from Eton, served with the Indian Imperial Police in Burma from 1922 to 1927, and then returned to England to begin his career as a writer. His works include *Burmese Days* (1934), *Homage to Catalonia* (1938), *Dickens, Dali, and Others* (1946), and *Shooting an Elephant* (1950). His fame, however, is primarily the result of *Animal Farm* (1945) and *1984* (1949), the former one of the most famous modern satires and the latter a classic novel of social protest. His *Collected Essays* were published in 1969.

Most people who bother with the matter at all would admit 1
that the English language is in a bad way, but it is generally assumed that we cannot by conscious action do anything about it. Our civilization is decadent and our language — so the argument runs — must inevitably share in the general collapse. It follows that any struggle against the abuse of language is a sentimental archaism, like preferring candles to electric light or hansom cabs to aeroplanes. Underneath this lies the half-conscious belief that language is a natural growth and not an instrument which we shape for our own purposes.

Now, it is clear that the decline of a language must ultimately have 2
political and economic causes: it is not due simply to the bad influence of this or that individual writer. But an effect can become a cause, reinforcing the original cause and producing the same effect in an intensified form, and so on indefinitely. A man may take a drink because he feels himself to be a failure, and then fail all the more completely because he drinks. It is rather the same thing that is happening to the English language. It becomes ugly and inaccurate because our thoughts are foolish, but the slovenliness of our language makes it easier for us to have foolish thoughts. The point is that the process is reversible. Modern English, especially written English, is full of bad habits which spread by imitation and which can be avoided if one is willing to take the necessary trouble. If one gets rid of these habits one can think more clearly, and to think clearly is a necessary first step towards political regeneration: so that the

From *Shooting an Elephant and Other Essays* by George Orwell, copyright, 1945, 1946, 1949, 1950, by Sonia Brownell Orwell. Reprinted by permission of Harcourt Brace Jovanovich, Inc.

fight against bad English is not frivolous and is not the exclusive concern of professional writers. I will come back to this presently, and I hope that by that time the meaning of what I have said here will have become clearer. Meanwhile, here are five specimens of the English language as it is now habitually written.

These five passages have not been picked out because they are espe- 3 cially bad—I could have quoted far worse if I had chosen—but because they illustrate various of the mental vices from which we now suffer. They are a little below the average, but are fairly representative samples. I number them so that I can refer back to them when necessary:

(1) *I am not, indeed sure whether it is not true to say that the Milton who* 4 *once seemed not unlike a seventeenth-century Shelley had not become, out of an experience ever more bitter in each year, more alien* [sic] *to the founder of Jesuit Jesect which nothing could induce him to tolerate.*

—*Harold Laski, Essay in* Freedom of Expression

(2) *Above all, we cannot play ducks and drakes with a native battery of* 5 *idioms which prescribes such egregious collocations of vocables as the Basic put up* with *for* tolerate *or* put at a loss *for* bewilder.

—*Lancelot Hogben,* Interglossa

(3) *On the one side we have the free personality: by definition it is not neu-* 6 *rotic, for it has neither conflict nor dream. Its desires, such as they are, are transparent, for they are just what institutional approval keeps in the forefront of consciousness; another institutional pattern would alter their number and intensity; there is little in them that is natural, irreducible, or culturally dangerous. But* on the other side, *the social bond itself is nothing but the mutual reflection of these self-secure integrities. Recall the definition of love. Is not this the very picture of a small academic? Where is there a place in this hall of mirrors for either personality or fraternity?*

—*Essay on psychology in* Politics *(New York)*

(4) *All the 'best people' from the gentlemen's clubs, and all the frantic fascist* 7 *captains, united in common hatred of Socialism and bestial horror of the rising tide of the mass revolutionary movement, have turned to acts of provocation, to foul incendiarism, to medieval legends of poisoned wells, to legalize their own destruction of proletarian organizations, and rouse the agitated petty-bourgeoisie to chauvinistic fervour on behalf of the fight against the revolutionary way out of the crisis."*

—*Communist pamphlet.*

(5) *If a new spirit is to be infused into this old country, there is one thorny* 8 *and contentious reform which must be tackled, and that is the humanization and galvanization of the B.B.C. Timidity here will bespeak cancer and atrophy of the soul. The heart of Britain may be sound and of strong beat, for instance, but the British lion's roar at present is like that of Bottom in Shakespeare's* Midsummer Night's Dream—*as gentle as any sucking dove. A virile new Britain cannot continue indefinitely to be traduced in the eyes or rather ears, of the world by the effete languors of Langham Place, brazenly masquerading as "standard English." When the Voice of Britain is heard at nine o'clock, better far and infinitely less ludicrous to hear aitches honestly dropped than the present priggish, inflated, inhibited, school-ma'amish arch braying of blameless bashful mewing maidens!*

—*Letter in* Tribune.

Each of these passages has faults of its own, but, quite apart from 9 avoidable ugliness, two qualities are common to all of them. The first is staleness of imagery: the other is lack of precision. The writer either has a meaning and cannot express it, or he inadvertently says something else, or he is almost indifferent as to whether his words mean anything or not. This mixture of vagueness and sheer incompetence is the most marked characteristic of modern English prose, and especially of any kind of political writing. As soon as certain topics are raised, the concrete melts into the abstract and no one seems able to think of turns of speech that are not hackneyed: prose consists less and less of *words* chosen for the sake of their meaning, and more and more of *phrases* tacked together like the sections of a prefabricated hen-house. I list below, with notes and examples, various of the tricks by means of which the work of prose-construction is habitually dodged:

Dying Metaphors

A newly invented metaphor assists thought by evoking a visual image, 10 while on the other hand a metaphor which is technically "dead" (e.g. *iron resolution*) has in effect reverted to being an ordinary word and can generally be used without loss of vividness. But in between these two classes there is a huge dump of worn-out metaphors which have lost all evocative power and are merely used because they save people the trouble of inventing phrases for themselves. Examples are: *Ring the changes on, take up the cudgels for, toe the line, ride roughshod over, stand shoulder to shoulder with, play into the hands of, no axe to grind, grist to the mill, fishing in troubled waters, on the order of the day, Achilles' heel, swan song, hotbed.* Many of these are used without knowledge of their meaning (what is a "rift," for instance?), and incompatible metaphors are frequently mixed, a sure sign that the writer is not interested in what he is saying. Some metaphors now current have been twisted out of their original meaning without those who use them even being aware of the fact. For example, *toe the line* is sometimes written *tow the line.* Another example is *the hammer and the anvil,* now always used with the implication that the anvil gets the worst of it. In real life it is always the anvil that breaks the hammer, never the other way about: a writer who stopped to think what he was saying would be aware of this, and would avoid perverting the original phrase.

Operators or Verbal False Limbs

These save the trouble of picking out appropriate verbs and nouns, and 11 at the same time pad each sentence with extra syllables which give it an appearance of symmetry. Characteristic phrases are: *render inoperative, militate against, make contact with, be subjected to, give rise to, give grounds for, have the effect of, play a leading part (role) in, make itself felt, take effect, exhibit a tendency to, serve the purpose of, etc., etc.* The keynote is the elimination of simple verbs. Instead of being a single word, such as *break, stop, spoil, mend, kill,* a verb becomes a *phrase,* made up of a noun or adjective tacked on to some general-purposes verb such as *prove, serve, form, play, render.* In addition, the passive voice is wherever possible used in preference to the active, and noun constructions are used instead of gerunds (*by examination of* instead of *by examining*). The range of verbs is further cut down by means of the *-ize* and *de-* formation, and the banal statements are given an appearance of profundity by means of the *not un-*formation. Simple conjunctions and prepositions are replaced by such phrases as *with respect to, having regard to, the fact that, by dint of, in view of, in the interests of, on the hypothesis that;* and the ends of sentences are saved from anticlimax by such resounding commonplaces as *greatly to be desired, cannot be left out of account, a development to be expected in the near future, deserving of serious consideration, brought to a satisfactory conclusion,* and so on and so forth.

Pretentious Diction

Words like *phenomenon, element, individual* (as noun), *objective, categorical,* 12 *effective, virtual, basic, primary, promote, constitute, exhibit, exploit, utilize, eliminate, liquidate,* are used to dress up simple statements and give an air of scientific impartiality to biased judgments. Adjectives like *epoch-making, epic, historic, unforgettable, triumphant, age-old, inevitable, inexorable, veritable,* are used to dignify the sordid processes of international politics, while writing that aims at glorifying war usually takes on an archaic colour, its characteristic words being: *realm, throne, chariot, mailed fist, trident, sword, shield, buckler, banner, jack-boot, clarion.* Foreign words and expressions such as *cul de sac, ancien regime, deus ex machina, mutatis mutandis, status quo, gleichshaltung, weltanschauung,* are used to give an air of culture and elegance. Except for the useful abbreviations *i.e., e.g.,* and *etc.,* there is no real need for any of the hundreds of foreign phrases now current in English. Bad writers, and especially scientific, political and sociological writers, are nearly always haunted by the notion that Latin or Greek words are grander than Saxon ones, and unnecessary words like *expedite, ameliorate, predict, extraneous, deracinated, clandestine, subaqueous* and hundreds of others constantly gain ground from their Anglo-Saxon opposite numbers.[1] The jargon peculiar to Marxist writing (*hyena, hangman, cannibal, petty bourgeois, these gentry, lacquey, flunkey, mad dog, White Guard,* etc.) consists largely of words and phrases translated from Russian, German or French; but the normal way of coining a new word is to use a Latin or Greek root with the appropriate affix and, where necessary, the -ize formation. It is often easier to make up words of this kind (*deregionalize, impermissible, extramarital, nonfragmentatory* and so forth)

---

[1] An interesting illustration of this is the way in which the English flower names which were in use till very recently are being ousted by Greek ones, *snapdragon* becoming *antirrkinum, forget-me-not* becoming *myosotis,* etc. It is hard to see any practical reason for this change of fashion: it is probably due to an instinctive turning-away from the more homely word and a vague feeling that the Greek word is scientific.

than to think up the English words that will cover one's meaning. The result, in general, is an increase in slovenliness and vagueness.

Meaningless Words

In certain kinds of writing, particularly in art criticism and literary criticism, it is normal to come across long passages which are almost completely lacking in meaning.[2] Words like *romantic, plastic, values, human, dead, sentimental, natural, vitality,* as used in art criticism, are strictly meaningless in the sense that they not only do not point to any discoverable object, but are hardly ever expected to do so by the reader. When one critic writes, "The outstanding feature of Mr. X's work is its living quality," while another writes, "The immediately striking thing about Mr. X's work is its peculiar deadness," the reader accepts this as a simple difference of opinion. If words like *black* and *white* were involved, instead of the jargon words *dead* and *living,* he would see at once that language was being used in an improper way. Many political words are similarly abused. The word *Fascism* has now no meaning except in so far as it signifies "something not desirable." The words *democracy, socialism, freedom, patriotic, realistic, justice,* have each of them several different meanings which cannot be reconciled with one another. In the case of a word like *democracy,* not only is there no agreed definition, but the attempt to make one is resisted from all sides. It is almost universally felt that when we call a country democratic we are praising it: consequently the defenders of every kind of regime claim that it is a democracy, and fear that they might have to stop using the word if it were tied down to any one meaning. Words of this kind are often used in a consciously dishonest way. That is, the person who uses them has his own private definition, but allows his hearer to think he means something quite different. Statements like *Marshal Petain was a true patriot, The Soviet Press is the freest in the world, The Catholic Church is opposed to persecution,* are almost always made with intent to deceive. Other words used in variable meanings, in most cases more or less dishonestly, are: *class, totalitarian, science, progressive, reactionary, burgeois, equality.* 13

Now that I have made this catalogue of swindles and perversions, let me give another example of the kind of writing that they lead to. This time it must of its nature be an imaginary one. I am going to translate a passage of good English into modern English of the worst sort. Here is a well-known verse from *Ecclesiastes:* 14

> I returned and saw under the sun, that the race is not to the swift, nor the battle to the strong, neither yet bread to the wise, nor yet riches to men of understanding, nor yet favour to men of skill; but time and chance happeneth to them all.

[2] Example: "Comfort's catholicity of perception and image, strangely Whitmanesque in range, almost the exact opposite in aesthetic compulsion, continues to evoke that trembling atmospheric accumulative hinting at a cruel, an inexorably serene timelessness... Wrey Gardiner scores by aiming at simple bull's-eyes with precision. Only they are not so simple, and through this contented sadness runs more than the surface bitter-sweet of resignation." (*Poetry Quarterly.*)

Here it is in modern English:

> Objective considerations of contemporary phenomena compels the con- 15
> clusion that success or failure in competitive activities exhibits no tendency
> to be commensurate with innate capacity, but that a considerable element of
> the unpredictable must invariably be taken into account.

This is a parody, but not a very gross one. Exhibit (3), above, for in- 16
stance, contains several patches of the same kind of English. It will be
seen that I have not made a full translation. The beginning and ending of
the sentence follow the original meaning fairly closely, but in the middle
the concrete illustrations — race, battle, bread — dissolve into the vague
phrase "success or failure in competitive activities." This had to be so, because no modern writer of the kind I am discussing — no one capable of
using phrases like "objective consideration of contemporary phenom-
ena" — would ever tabulate his thoughts in that precise and detailed way.
The whole tendency of modern prose is away from concreteness. Now
analyse these two sentences a little more closely. The first contains forty-
nine words but only sixty syllables, and all its words are those of everyday life. The second contains thirty-eight words of ninety syllables: eighteen of its words are from Latin roots, and one from Greek. The first sentence contains six vivid images, and only one phrase ("time and chance")
that could be called vague. The second contains not a single fresh, arresting phrase, and in spite of its ninety syllables it gives only a shortened
version of the meaning contained in the first. Yet without a doubt it is
the second kind of sentence that is gaining ground in modern English. I
do not want to exaggerate. This kind of writing is not yet universal, and
outcrops of simplicity will occur here and there in the worst-written
page. Still, if you or I were told to write a few lines on the uncertainty of
human fortunes, we should probably come much nearer to my imaginary
sentence than to the one from *Ecclesiastes.*

As I have tried to show, modern writing at its worst does not consist 17
in picking out words for the sake of their meaning and inventing images
in order to make the meaning clearer. It consists in gumming together
long strips of words which have already been set in order by someone
else, and making the results presentable by sheer humbug. The attraction
of this way of writing is that it is easy. It is easier — even quicker, once
you have the habit — to say *In my opinion it is a not unjustifiable assumption that* than to say *I think.* If you use ready-made phrases, you not only
don't have to hunt about for words; you also don't have to bother with
the rhythms of your sentences, since these phrases are generally so arranged as to be more or less euphonious. When you are composing in a
hurry — when you are dictating to a stenographer, for instance, or making
a public speech — it is natural to fall into a pretentious, Latinized style.
Tags like *a consideration which we should do well to bear in mind or a conclusion to which all of us would readily assent* will save many a sentence
from coming down with a bump. By using stale metaphors, similes and
idioms, you save much mental effort, at the cost of leaving your meaning
vague, not only for your reader but for yourself. This is the significance
of mixed metaphors. The sole aim of a metaphor is to call up a visual image. When these images clash — as in *The Fascist octopus has sung its swan*

song, the jackboot is thrown into the melting pot—it can be taken as certain that the writer is not seeing a mental image of the objects he is naming; in other words he is not really thinking. Look again at the examples I gave at the beginning of this essay. Professor Laski (1) uses five negatives in fifty-three words. One of these is superfluous, making nonsense of the whole passage, and in addition there is the slip *alien* for akin, making further nonsense, and several avoidable pieces of clumsiness which increase the general vagueness. Professor Hogben (2) plays ducks and drakes with a battery which is able to write prescriptions, and, while disapproving of the everyday phrase *put up with,* is unwilling to look *egregious* up in the dictionary and see what it means. (3), if one takes an uncharitable attitude towards it, is simply meaningless: probably one could work out its intended meaning by reading the whole of the article in which it occurs. In (4), the writer knows more or less what he wants to say, but an accumulation of stale phrases chokes him like tea leaves blocking a sink. In (5), words and meaning have almost parted company. People who write in this manner usually have a general emotional meaning—they dislike one thing and want to express solidarity with another—but they are not interested in the detail of what they are saying. A scrupulous writer, in every sentence that he writes, will ask himself at least four questions, thus: What am I trying to say? What words will express it? What image or idiom will make it clearer? Is this image fresh enough to have an effect? And he will probably ask himself two more: Could I put it more shortly? Have I said anything that is avoidably ugly? But you are not obliged to go to all this trouble. You can shirk it by simply throwing your mind open and letting the ready-made phrases come crowding in. They will construct your sentences for you—even think your thoughts for you, to a certain extent—and at need they will perform the important service of partially concealing your meaning even from yourself. It is at this point that the special connection between politics and the debasement of language becomes clear.

In our time it is broadly true that political writing is bad writing. 18 Where it is not true, it will generally be found that the writer is some kind of rebel, expressing his private opinions and not a "party line." Orthodoxy, of whatever colour, seems to demand a lifeless, imitative style. The political dialects to be found in pamphlets, leading articles, manifestos, White Papers and the speeches of under-secretaries do, of course, vary from party to party, but they are all alike in that one almost never finds in them a fresh, vivid, homemade turn of speech. When one watches some tried hack on the platform mechanically repeating the familiar phrases—*bestial atrocities, iron heel, bloodstained tyranny, free peoples of the world, stand shoulder to shoulder*—one often has a curious feeling that one is not watching a live human being but some kind of dummy: a feeling which suddenly becomes stronger at moments when the light catches the speaker's spectacles and turns them into blank discs which seem to have no eyes behind them. And this is not altogether fanciful. A speaker who uses that kind of phraseology has gone some distance towards turning himself into a machine. The appropriate noises are coming out of his larynx, but his brain is not involved as it would be if he were choosing his words for himself. If the speech he is making is one that he is accustomed to make over and over again, he may be almost unconscious of what he is saying, as one is when one utters the responses in church. And this reduced state of consciousness, if not indispensible, is at any rate favourable to political conformity.

In our time, political speech and writing are largely the defence of 19 the indefensible. Things like the continuance of British rule in India, the Russian purges and deportations, the dropping of the atom bombs on Japan, can indeed be defended, but only by arguments which are too brutal for most people to face, and which do not square with the professed aims of political parties. Thus political language has to consist largely of euphemism, question-begging and sheer cloudy vagueness. Defenceless villages are bombarded from the air, the inhabitants driven out into the countryside, the cattle machine-gunned, the huts set on fire with incendiary bullets: this is called *pacification*. Millions of peasants are robbed of their farms and sent trudging along the roads with no more than they can carry: this is called *transfer of population* or *rectification of frontiers*. People are imprisoned for years without trial, or shot in the back of the neck or sent to die of scurvy in Arctic lumber camps: this is called *elimination of unreliable elements*. Such phraseology is needed if one wants to name things without calling up mental pictures of them. Consider for instance some comfortable English professor defending Russian totalitarianism. He cannot say outright, "I believe in killing off your opponents when you can get good results by doing so." Probably, therefore, he will say something like this:

> While freely conceding that the Soviet regime exhibits certain features which the humanitarian may be inclined to deplore, we must, I think, agree that a certain curtailment of the right to political opposition is an unavoidable concomitant of transitional periods, and that the rigours which the Russian people have been called upon to undergo have been amply justified in the sphere of concrete achievement.

The inflated style is itself a kind of euphemism. A mass of Latin 20 words fall upon the facts like soft snow, blurring the outlines and covering up all the details. The great enemy of clear language is insincerity. When there is a gap between one's real and one's declared aims, one turns as it were instinctively to long words and exhausted idioms, like a cuttlefish fish squirting out ink. In our age there is no such thing as "keeping out of politics." All issues are political issues, and politics itself is a mass of lies, evasions, folly, hatred and schizophrenia. When the general atmosphere is bad, language must suffer. I should expect to find — this is a guess which I have not sufficient knowledge to verify — that the German, Russian and Italian languages have all deteriorated in the last ten or fifteen years, as a result of dictatorship.

But if thought corrupts language, language can also corrupt thought. 21 A bad usage can spread by tradition and imitation, even among people who should and do know better. The debased language that I have been discussing is in some ways very convenient. Phrases like *a not unjustifiable assumption, leaves much to be desired, would serve no good purpose, a con-*

sideration which we should do well to bear in mind, are a continuous temptation, a packet of aspirins always at one's elbow. Look back through this essay, and for certain you will find that I have again and again committed the very faults I am protesting against. By this morning's post I have received a pamphlet dealing with conditions in Germany. The author tells me that he "felt impelled" to write it. I open it at random, and here is almost the first sentence that I see: "(The Allies) have an opportunity not only of achieving a radical transformation of Germany's social and political structure in such a way as to avoid a nationalistic reaction in Germany itself, but at the same time of laying the foundations of a cooperative and unified Europe." You see, he "feels impelled" to write—feels, presumably, that he has something new to say—and yet his words, like cavalry horses answering the bugle, group themselves automatically into the familiar dreary pattern. This invasion of one's mind by ready-made phrases *(lay the foundations, achieve a radical transformation)* can only be prevented if one is constantly on guard against them, and every such phrase anaesthetizes a portion of one's brain.

I said earlier that the decadence of our language is probably curable.   22
Those who deny this would argue, if they produced an argument at all, that language merely reflects existing social conditions, and that we cannot influence its development by any direct tinkering with words and constructions. So far as the general tone or spirit of a language goes, this may be true, but it is not true in detail. Silly words and expressions have often disappeared, not through any evolutionary process but owing to the conscious action of a minority. Two recent examples were *explore every avenue* and *leave no stone unturned,* which were killed by the jeers of a few journalists. There is a long list of flyblown metaphors which could similarly be got rid of if enough people would interest themselves in the job; and it should also be possible to laugh the *not un-* formation out of existence,[3] to reduce the amount of Latin and Greek in the average sentence, to drive out foreign phrases and strayed scientific words, and, in general, to make pretentiousness unfashionable. But all these are minor points. The defence of the English language implies more than this, and perhaps it is best to start by saying what it does *not* imply.

To begin with it has nothing to do with archaism, with the salvaging   23
of obsolete words and turns of speech, or with the setting up of a "standard English" which must never be departed from. On the contrary, it is especially concerned with the scrapping of every word or idiom which has outworn its usefulness. It has nothing to do with correct grammar and syntax, which are of no importance so long as one makes one's meaning clear, or with the avoidance of Americanisms, or with having what is called a "good prose style." On the other hand it is not concerned with fake simplicity and the attempt to make written English colloquial. Nor does it even imply in every case preferring the Saxon word to the Latin one, though it does imply using the fewest and shortest words that will cover one's meaning. What is above all needed is to let

---

[3] One can cure oneself of the *not un-* formation by memorizing this sentence: *A not unblack dog was chasing a not unsmall rabbit across a not ungreen field.*

the meaning choose the word, and not the other way about. In prose, the worst thing one can do with words is to surrender to them. When you think of a concrete object, you think wordlessly, and then, if you want to describe the thing you have been visualizing you probably hunt about till you find the exact words that seem to fit. When you think of something abstract you are more inclined to use words from the start, and unless you make a conscious effort to prevent it, the existing dialect will come rushing in and do the job for you, at the expense of blurring or even changing your meaning. Probably it is better to put off using words as long as possible and get one's meaning as clear as one can through pictures or sensations. Afterwards one can choose — not simply *accept* — the phrases that will best cover the meaning, and then switch round and decide what impression one's words are likely to make on another person. This last effort of the mind cuts out all stale or mixed images, all prefabricated phrases, needless repetitions, and humbug and vagueness generally. But one can often be in doubt about the effect of a word or a phrase, and one needs rules that one can rely on when instinct fails. I think the following rules will cover most cases:

1. Never use a metaphor, simile or other figure of speech which you are used to seeing in print.
2. Never use a long word where a short one will do.
3. If it is possible to cut a word out, always cut it out.
4. Never use the passive where you can use the active.
5. Never use a foreign phrase, a scientific word or a jargon word if you can think of an everyday English equivalent.
6. Break any of these rules sooner than say anything outright barbarous.

These rules sound elementary, and so they are, but they demand 24 a deep change of attitude in anyone who has grown used to writing in the style now fashionable. One could keep all of them and still write bad English, but one could not write the kind of stuff that I quoted in those five specimens at the beginning of this article.

I have not here been considering the literary use of language, but 25 merely language as an instrument for expressing and not for concealing or preventing thought. Stuart Chase and others have come near to claiming that all abstract words are meaningless, and have used this as a pretext for advocating a kind of political quietism. Since you don't know what Fascism is, how can you struggle against Fascism? One need not swallow such absurdities as this, but one ought to recognize that the present political chaos is connected with the decay of language, and that one can probably bring about some improvement by starting at the verbal end. If you simplify your English, you are freed from the worst follies of orthodoxy. You cannot speak any of the necessary dialects, and when you make a stupid remark its stupidity will be obvious, even to yourself. Political language — and with variations this is true of all political parties, from Conservatives to Anarchists — is designed to make lies sound truthful and murder respectable, and to give an appearance of solidity to pure wind. One cannot change this all in a moment, but one can at least change one's own habits, and from time to time one can even, if one jeers loudly enough, send some worn-out and useless phrase — some *jackboot, Achilles' heel, hotbed, melted pot, acid test, veritable inferno* or other lump of verbal refuse — into the dustbin where it belongs.

Study Questions

1. What rhetorical methods does Orwell use to develop his thesis?
2. What types of development are used in paragraphs 16–18?
3. What are the most obvious differences in the diction of paragraphs 14–15?
4. What is the tone of the essay, and how does Orwell establish and maintain it?
5. What words and phrases link paragraphs 13–23?

Dorothy Z. Seymour
BLACK CHILDREN, BLACK SPEECH

Dorothy Z. Seymour is a freelance writer, editor, and consultant. Formerly a reading teacher and editorial specialist in linguistics, she has become widely known for her articles in education and linguistic journals, among them *The Elementary School Journal, The Instructor, The Reading Teacher,* and *Today's Education.* Her series for Wonder Books, among them *Ballerina Bess* and *Bill and the Fish,* have endeared her to many. Recent books are *The Crate Train* (1966) and *The Pine Park Team* (1974).

"Cmon, man, les git goin'!" called the boy to his companion. 1 "Dat bell ringin'. It say, 'Git in rat now!'" He dashed into the school yard.

"Aw, f'get you," replied the other. "Whe' Richuh? Whe' da' muvvuh? He be goin' to schoo'."

Reprinted from *Commonweal,* November 19, 1971, by permission of the Commonweal Publishing Co., Inc.

"He in de' now, man!" was the answer as they went through the 3
door.

In the classroom they made for their desks and opened their books. 4
The name of the story they tried to read was "Come." It went:

> Come, Bill, come.
> Come with me.
> Come and see this.
> See what is here.

The first boy poked the second. "Wha' da' wor'?"

"Da' wor' *is*, you dope."   5

"*Is?* Ain't no wor' *is*. You jivin' me? Wha' da' wor' mean?"   6

"Ah dunno. Jus' *is*."   7

To a speaker of Standard English, this exchange is only vaguely com- 8
prehensible. But it's normal speech for thousands of American children.
In addition it demonstrates one of our biggest educational problems: children whose speech style is so different from the writing style of their
books that they have difficulty learning to read. These children speak
Black English, a dialect characteristic of many inner-city Negroes. Their
books are, of course, written in Standard English. To complicate matters,
the speech they use is also socially stigmatized. Middle-class whites and
Negroes alike scorn it as low-class poor people's talk.

Teachers sometimes make the situation worse with their attitudes to- 9
ward Black English. Typically, they view the children's speech as "bad
English" characterized by "lazy pronunciation," "poor grammar," and
"short, jagged words." One result of this attitude is poor mental health
on the part of the pupils. A child is quick to grasp the feeling that while
school speech is "good," his own speech is "bad," and that by extension
he himself is somehow inadequate and without value. Some children react to this feeling by withdrawing; they stop talking entirely. Others develop the attitude of "F'get you, honky." In either case, the psychological
results are devastating and lead straight to the dropout route.

It is hard for most teachers and middle-class Negro parents to accept 10
the idea that Black English is not just "sloppy talk" but a dialect with a
form and structure of its own. Even some eminent black educators think
of it as "bad English grammar" with "slurred consonants" (Professor Nick
Aaron Ford of Morgan State College in Baltimore) and "ghettoese" (Dr.
Kenneth B. Clark, the prominent educational psychologist).

Parents of Negro school children generally agree. Two researchers at 11
Columbia University report that the adults they worked with in Harlem
almost unanimously preferred that their children be taught Standard
English in school.

But there is another point of view, one held in common by black 12
militants and some white liberals. They urge that middle-class Negroes
stop thinking of the inner-city dialect as something to be ashamed of and
repudiated. Black author Claude Brown, for example, pushes this view.

Some modern linguists take a similar stance. They begin with the 13
premise that no dialect is intrinsically "bad" or "good," and that a nonstandard speech style is not defective speech but different speech. More

important, they have been able to show that Black English is far from being a careless way of speaking the Standard; instead, it is a rather rigidly-constructed set of speech patterns, with the same sort of specialization in sounds, structure, and vocabulary as any other dialect.

The Sounds of Black English

Middle class listeners who hear black inner-city speakers say "dis" and "tin" for "this" and "thin" assume that the black speakers are just being careless. Not at all; these differences are characteristic aspects of the dialect. The original cause of such substitutions is generally a carryover from one's original language or that of his immigrant parents. The interference from that carryover probably caused the substitution of /J/ for the voiced *th* sound in *this,* and /t/ for the unvoiced *th* sound in *thin.* (Linguists represent language sounds by putting letters within slashes or brackets.) Most speakers of English don't realize that the two *th* sounds of English are lacking in many other languages and are difficult for most foreigners trying to learn English. Germans who study English, for example, are surprised and confused about these sounds because the only Germans who use them are the ones who lisp. These two sounds are almost nonexistent in the West African languages which most black immigrants brought with them to America.   14

Similar substitutions used in Black English are /f/, a sound similar to the unvoiced *th,* in medial word-position, as in *birfday* for *birthday,* and in final word-position, as in *roof* for *Ruth* as well as /v/ for the voiced *th* in medial position, as in *bruvver* for *brother.* These sound substitutions are also typical of Gullah, the language of black speakers in the Carolina Sea Islands. Some of them are also heard in Caribbean Creole.   15

Another characteristic of the sounds of Black English is the lack of /l/ at the end or words, sometimes replaced by the sound /w/. This makes word like *tool* sound like *too.* If /l/ occurs in the middle of a Standard English word, in Black English it may be omitted entirely: "I can hep you." This difference is probably caused by the instability and sometimes interchangeability of /l/ and /r/ in West African languages.   16

One difference that is startling to middle-class speakers is the fact that Black English words appear to leave off some consonant sounds at the end of words. Like Italian, Japanese and West African words, they are more likely to end in vowel sounds. Standard English *boot* is pronounced *boo* in Black English. *What* is *wha. Sure* is *sho. Your* is *yo.* This kind of difference can make for confusion in the classroom. Dr. Kenneth Goodman, a psycholinguist, tells of a black child whose white teacher asked him to use *so* in a sentence — not "sew a dress" but "the other *so.*" The sentence the child used was "I got a *so* on my leg."   17

A related feature of Black English is the tendency in many cases not to use sequences of more than one final consonant sound. For example, *just* is pronounced *jus', past* is *pass, mend* sounds like *men* and *hold* like *hole. Six* and *box* are pronounced *sick* and *bock.* Why should this be? Perhaps because West African languages, like Japanese, have almost no clus-   18 ters of consonants in their speech. The Japanese, when importing a foreign word, handle a similar problem by inserting vowel sounds between every consonant, making *baseball* sound like *besuboru*. West Africans probably made a simpler change, merely cutting a series of two consonant sounds down to one. Speakers of Gullah, one linguist found, have made the same kind of adaptation of Standard English.

Teachers of black children seldom understand the reason for these 19 differences in final sounds. They are apt to think that careless speech is the cause. Actually, black speakers aren't "leaving off" any sounds; how can you leave off something you never had in the first place?

Differences in vowel sounds are also characteristic of the non-stan- 20 dard language. Dr. Goodman reports that a black child asked his teacher how to spell rat. "R-a-t," she replied. But the boy responded "No ma'am, I don't mean rat mouse, I mean rat now." In Black English, *right* sounds like *rat*. A likely reason is that in West African languages, there are very few vowel sounds of the type heard in the word *right*. This type is common in English. It is called a glided or dipthogized vowel sound. A glided vowel sound is actually a close combination of two vowels; in the word *right* the two parts of the sound "eye" are actually "ah-ee." West African languages have no such long, two-part, changing vowel sounds; their vowels are generally shorter and more stable. This may be why in Black English, *time* sounds like *Tom*, *oil* like *all*, and *my* like *ma*.

Language Structure

Black English differs from Standard English not only in its sounds but 21 also in its structure. The way the words are put together does not always fit the description in English grammar books. The method of expressing time, or tense, for example, differs in significant ways.

The verb *to be* is an important one in Standard English. It's used as 22 an auxiliary verb to indicate different tenses. But Black English speakers use it quite differently. Sometimes an inner-city Negro says "He coming"; other times he says "He be coming." These two sentences mean different things. To understand why, let's look at the tenses of West African languages; they correspond with those of Black English.

Many West African languages have a tense which is called the habit- 23 ual. This tense is used to express action which is always occurring and it is formed with a verb that is translated as *be*. "He be coming" means something like "He's always coming," "He usually comes," or "He's been coming."

In Standard English there is no regular grammatical construction for 24 such a tense. Black English speakers, in order to form the habitual tense in English, use the word be as an auxiliary: *He be doing it. My Momma be working. He be running.* The habitual tense is not the same as the present tense, which is constructed in Black English without any form of the verb *to be: He do it. My Momma working. He running.* (This means the action is occurring right now.)

There are other tense differences between Black English and Stan- 25 dard English. For example, the non-standard speech does not use changes in grammar to indicate the past tense. A white person will ask, "What did your brother say?" and the black person will answer, "He say he coming." (The verb *say* is not changed to *said.*) "How did you get here?" "I walk." This style of talking about the past is paralleled in the Yoruba, Fante, Hausa, and Ewe languages of West Africa.

Expression of plurality is another difference. The way a black child 26 will talk of "them boy" or "two dog" makes some white listeners think Negroes don't know how to turn a singular word into a plural word. As a matter of act, it isn't necessary to use an *s* to express plurality. In Chinese and Japanese, singular and plural are not generally distinguished by such inflections; plurality is conveyed in other ways. For example, in Chinese it's correct to say "There are three book on the table." This sentence already has two signals of the plural, *three* and *are;* why require a third? This same logic is the basis of plurals in most West African languages, where nouns are often identical in the plural and the singular. For example, in Ibo, one correctly says *those man,* and in both Ewe and Yoruba one says *they house.* American speakers of Gullah retain this style; it is correct in Gullah to say *five dog.*

Gender is another aspect of language structure where differences can 27 be found. Speakers of Standard English are often confused to find that the nonstandard vernacular often uses just one gender of pronoun, the masculine, and refers to women as well as men as *he* or *him.* "He a nice girl," even "Him a nice girl" are common. This usage probably stems from West African origins, too, as does the use of multiple negatives, such as "Nobody don't know it."

Vocabulary is the third aspect of a person's native speech that could 28 affect his learning of a new language. The strikingly different vocabulary often used in Negro Nonstandard English is probably the most obvious aspect of it to a casual white observer. But its vocabulary differences don't obscure its meaning the way different sounds and different structure often do.

Recently there has been much interest in the African origins of 29 words like *goober* (peanut), *cooter* (turtle), and *tote* (carry), as well as others that are less certainly African, such as *to dig* (possibly from the Wolof *degan,* "to understand"). Such expressions seem colorful rather than low-class to many whites; they become assimilated faster than their black originators do. English professors now use *dig* in their scholarly articles, and current advertising has enthusiastically adopted *rap.*

Is it really possible for old differences in sound, structure, and vocab- 30 ulary to persist from the West African languages of slave days into present-day inner city Black English? Easily. Nothing else really explains such regularity of language habits, most of which persist among black people in various parts of the Western Hemisphere. For a long time scholars believed that certain speech forms used by Negroes were merely leftovers from archaic English preserved in the speech of early English settlers in America and copied by their slaves. But this theory has been greatly weakened, largely as the result of the work of a black linguist, Dr. Lorenzo Dow Turner of the University of Chicago. Dr. Turner studied the speech of Gullah Negroes in the Sea Islands off the Carolina coast and found so many traces of West African languages that he thoroughly discredited the archaic-English theory.

When anyone learns a new language, it's usual to try speaking the 31 new language with the sounds and structure of the old. If a person's first language does not happen to have a particular sound needed in the language he is learning, he will tend to substitute a similar or related sound from his native language and use it to speak the new one. When Frenchman Charles Boyer said "Zees ess my heart," and when Latin American Carmen Miranda sang "Souse American way," they were simply using sounds of their native languages in trying to pronounce sounds of English. West Africans must have done the same things when they first attempted English words. The tendency to retain the structure of the native language is a strong one, too. That's why a German learning English is likely to put his verb at the end: "May I a glass beer have?" The vocabulary of one's original language may also furnish some holdovers. Jewish immigrants did not stop using the word *bagel* when they came to America; nor did Germans stop saying *sauerkraut.*

Social and geographical isolation reinforces the tendencies to retain 32 old language habits. When one group is considered inferior, the other group avoids it. For many years it was illegal to give any sort of instruction to Negroes, and for slaves to try to speak like their masters would have been unthinkable. Conflict of value systems doubtless retards changes, too. As Frantz Fanon observed in *Black Skin, White Masks,* those who take on white speech habits are suspect in the ghetto, because others believe they are trying to "act white." Dr. Kenneth Johnson, a black linguist, put it this way: "As long as disadvantaged black children live in segregated communities and most of their relationships are confined to those within their own subculture, they will not replace their functional nonstandard dialect with the nonfunctional standard dialect."

Linguists have made it clear that language systems that are different 33 are not necessarily deficient. A judgment of deficiency can be made only in comparison with another language system. Let's turn the tables on Standard English for a moment and look at it from the West African point of view. From this angle, Standard English: (1) is lacking in certain language sounds, (2) has a couple of unnecessary language sounds for which others may serve as good substitutes, (3) doubles and drawls some of its vowel sounds in sequences that are unusual and difficult to imitate, (5) lacks a method of forming an important tense, (6) requires an unnecessary number of ways to indicate tense, plurality and gender, and (7) doesn't mark negatives sufficiently for the result to be a good strong negative statement.

Now whose language is deficient?   34

How would the adoption of this point of view help us? Say we ac- 35 cepted the evidence that Black English is not just a sloppy Standard but an organized language style which probably has developed many of its features on the basis of its West African heritage. What would we gain?

The psychological climate of the classroom might improve if teachers 36 understood why many black students speak as they do. But we still have not reached a solution of the main problem. Does the discovery that Black English has pattern and structure mean that it should not be tampered with? Should children who speak Black English be excused from learning the Standard in school? Should they perhaps be given books in Black English to learn from?

Any such accommodation would surely result in a hardening of the new separatism being urged by some black militants. It would probably be applauded by such people as Roy Innis, Director of C.O.R.E., who is currently recommending dual autonomous educational systems for white and black. And it might facilitate learning to read, since some experiments have indicated that materials written in Black English syntax aid problem readers from the inner city. 37

But determined resistance to the introduction of such printed materials into schools can be expected. To those who view inner-city speech as bad English, the appearance in print of sentences like "My mama, he work" can be as shocking and repellent as a four-letter word. Middle-class Negro parents would probably mobilize against the move. Any strategem that does not take into account such practicalities of the matter is probably doomed to failure. And besides, where would such a permissive policy on language get these children in the larger society, and in the long run? If they want to enter an integrated America they must be able to deal with it on its own terms. Even Professor Toni Cade of Rutgers, who doesn't want "ghetto accents" tampered with, advocates mastery of Standard English because, as she puts it, "if you want to get ahead in this country, you must master the language of the ruling class." This has always been true, wherever there has been a minority group. 38

The problem then appears to be one of giving these children the ability to speak (and read) Standard English without denigrating the vernacular and those who use it, or even affecting the ability to use it. The only way to do this is to officially espouse bi-dialectism. The result would be the ability to use either dialect equally well—as Dr. Martin Luther King did—depending on the time, place, and circumstances. Pupils would have to learn enough about Standard English to use it when necessary, and teachers would have to learn enough about the inner-city dialect to understand and accept it for what it is—not just a "careless" version of Standard English but a different form of English that's appropriate in certain times and places. 39

Can we accomplish this? If we can't, the result will be continued alienation of a large section of the population, continued dropout trouble with consequent loss of earning power and economic contribution to the nation, but most of all, loss of faith in America as a place where a minority people can at times continue to use those habits that remind them of their link with each other and with their past. 40

Study Questions

1. Compare and contrast the tone of this essay with the tone of the Nilsen essay.

2. How effective is the opening section (paragraphs 1–7) as an introduction?
3. What type of argument is used in paragraphs 32–33?
4. What types of examples and illustrations does Seymour use?
5. Is the thesis stated or implied?

Lawrence L. Langer
THE HUMAN USE OF LANGUAGE
Insensitive ears can't hear honest prose

Lawrence L. Langer (1929–   ) was born in New York City and educated at the City College of New York and Harvard University. He has taught at the University of Connecticut and Simmons College, and for a year was a Fulbright Lecturer in Austria. His earlier scholarly interest in the "moral and material imagination" of post-Civil War America has continued, but his more recent critical work has included studies of such contemporary authors as James Baldwin.

A friend of mine recently turned in a paper to a course on 1 behavior modification. She has tried to express in simple English some of her reservations about this increasingly popular approach to education. She received it back with the comment: "Please rewrite this in behavioral terms."

It is little wonder that human beings have so much trouble saying 2 what they feel, when they are told that there is a specialized vocabulary for saying what they think. The language of simplicity and spontaneity is forced to retreat behind the barricades of an official prose developed by a few experts who believe that jargon is the most precise means of communication. The results would be comic, if they were not so poisonous; unfortunately, there is an attitude toward the use of language that is impervious to human need and drives some people back into silence when they realize the folly of risking human words on insensitive ears.

The comedy is easy to come by. Glancing through my friend's text- 3 book on behavior modification, I happened on a chapter beginning with

Reprinted with permission of *The Chronicle of Higher Education* (Jan. 24, 1977). Copyright © 1977, by Editorial Projects for Education, Inc.

the following challenging statement: "Many of the problems encountered by teachers in the daily management of their classes could be resolved if...." Although I was a little wary of the phrase "daily management," I was encouraged to plunge ahead, because as an educator I have always been interested in ideas for improving learning. So I plunged. The entire sentence reads: "Many of the problems encountered by teachers in the daily management of their classes could be resolved if the emission of desirable student behaviors was increased."

Emission? At first I thought it was a misprint for "omission," but the 4 omission of desirable student behaviors (note the plural) hardly seemed an appropriate goal for educators. Then I considered the possibility of metaphor, both erotic and automotive, but these didn't seem to fit, either. A footnote clarified the matter: "'Emission' is a technical term used in behavioral analysis. The verb, 'to emit,' is used specifically with a certain category of behavior called 'operant behavior.' Operant behaviors are modified by their consequences. Operant behaviors correspond closely to the behavior colloquially referred to as voluntary." Voluntary? Is, jargon then an attack on freedom of the will?

Of course, this kind of abuse of language goes on all the time — 5 within the academic world, one regrets to say, as well as outside it. Why couldn't the author of this text simply say that we need to motivate students to learn willingly? The more I read such non-human prose, and try to avoid writing it myself, the more I am convinced that we must be in touch with ourselves before we can use words to touch others.

Using language meaningfully requires risk; the sentence I have just 6 quoted takes no risks at all. Much of the discourse that poses as communication in our society is really a decoy to divert our audience (and often ourselves) from that shadowy plateau where our real life hovers on the precipice of expression. How many people, for example, have the courage to walk up to someone they like and actually *say* to them: "I'm very fond of you, you know"?

Such honesty reflects the use of language as revelation, and that sort 7 of revelation, brimming with human possibilities, is risky precisely because it invites judgment and rebuff. Perhaps this is one reason why, especially in academe, we are confronted daily with no much neutral prose: Our students are not yet in touch with themselves; not especially encouraged by us, their instructors, to move in that direction; they are encouraged indeed to expect judgment and hence perhaps rebuff, too, in our evaluation of them. Thus they instinctively retreat behind the anonymity of abstract diction and technical jargon to protect themselves against us — but also, as I have suggested, against themselves.

This problem was crystallized for me recently by an encounter only 8 peripherally related to the issue. As part of my current research, I have been interviewing children of concentration-camp survivors. One girl I have been meeting with says that her mother does not like to talk about the experience, *except with other survivors.* Risk is diminished when we know in advance that our audience shares with us a sympathy for our theme. The nakedness of pain *and* the nakedness of love require gentle responses. So this survivor is reticent, except with fellow victims.

But one day a situation arose which tempted her to the human use 9
of language although she could not be sure, in advance, of the reception
her words would receive. We all recognize it. This particular woman, at
the age of 40, decided to return to school to get a college degree. Her
first assignment in freshman composition was to write a paper on something that was of great importance to her personally. The challenge was
immense; the risk was even greater. For the first time in 20 years, she resolved to confront a silence in her life that she obviously needed to
rouse to speech.

She was 14 when the Germans invaded Poland. When the roundup 10
of the Jews began a year later, some Christian friends sent their young
daughter to "call for her" one day, so that they might hide her. A half
hour later, the friends went themselves to pick up her parents, but during that interval, a truck had arrived, loaded aboard the Jewish mother
and father—and the daughter never saw them or heard from them again.
Their fate we can imagine. The girl herself was eventually arrested, survived several camps, and after the war came to America. She married,
had children of her own, and except for occasional reminiscences with
fellow survivors, managed to live adequately without diving into her
buried personal past. Until one day her instructor in English composition
touched a well-insulated nerve, and it began to throb with a painful impulse to express. I present verbatim the result of that impulse, a paper
called "People I Have Forgotten":

"Can you forget your own Father and Mother? If so—how or why? 11

"I thought I did. To mention their names, for me is a great emo- 12
tional struggle. The brutal force of this reality shakes my whole body and
mind, wrecking me into ugly splinters; each crying to be mended anew.
So the silence I maintain about their memory is only physical and valid
as such but not true. I could never forget my parents, nor do I want to
do it. True, I seldom talk about them with my husband or my children.
How they looked, who they were, why they perished during the war.
The love and sacrifices they have made for me during their lifetime,
never get told.

"The cultural heritage to which each generation is entitled to have 13
access to seems to be nonexistent [sic], since I dare not talk about anything relating to my past, my parents.

"This awful, awesome power of not-remembering, this heart-breaking 14
sensation of the conspiracy of silence is my dilemma.

"Often, I have tried to break through my imprisoning wall of irra- 15
tional silence, but failed: now I hope to be able to do it.

"Until now, I was not able to face up to the loss of my parents, much 16
less talk about them. The smallest reminder of them would set off a
chain reaction of results that I could anticipate but never direct. The destructive force of sadness, horror, fright would then become my master.
And it was this subconscious knowledge that kept me paralyzed with silence, not a conscious desire to forget my parents.

"My silent wall, my locked shell existed only of real necessity; I 17
needed time.

"I needed time to forget the tragic loss of my loved ones, time to 18 heal my emotional wound so that there shall come a time when I can again remember the people I have forgotten."

The essay is not a confrontation, only a prelude, yet it reveals quali- 19 ties which are necessary for the human use of language: In trying to reach her audience, the author must touch the deepest part of herself. She risks self-exposure — when we see the instructor's comment, we will realize how great was her risk — and she is prepared for judgment and perhaps even rebuff, although I doubt whether she was prepared for the form they took. This kind of prose, for all its hesitant phraseology, throws down a gauntlet to the reader, a challenge asking him to understand that life is pain as well as plenty, chaos as well as form. Its imagery of locked shells and imprisoning walls hints at a silent world of horror and sadness far less enchanting than the more familiar landscape of love where most of us dwell. Language is a two-edged tool, to pierce the wall which hides that world, or build high abstract barriers to protect us from its threats.

The instructor who graded the paper I have just read preferred walls 20 to honest words. At the bottom of the last page she scrawled a large "D-minus," emphatically surrounded by a circle. Her only comment was: "Your theme is not clear — you should have developed your 1st paragraph. You talk around your subject." At this moment, two realms collide: a universe of unarticulated feeling seeking expression (and the courage and encouragement to express) and a nature made so immune to feeling by heaven-knows-what that she hides behind the tired, tired language of the professional theme-corrector.

Suddenly we realize that reading as well as writing requires risks, and 21 that the metaphor of insulation, so central to the efforts of the Polish woman survivor to re-establish contact with her past, is a metaphor governing the response of readers, too. Some writing, like "the emission of desirable student behaviors," thickens the insulation that already separates the reader from the words that throw darts at his armor of indifference. But even when language unashamedly reveals the feeling that is hidden behind the words, it must contend with a different kind of barrier, the one behind which our instructor lies concealed, unwilling or unable to hear a human voice and return a human echo of her own.

Ironically, the victor in this melancholy failure at communication is 22 the villain of the piece, behavior modification. For the Polish survivor wrote her next theme on an innocuous topic, received a satisfactory grade, and never returned to the subject of her parents. The instructor, who had encountered a problem in the daily management of her class in the form of an essay which she could not respond to in a human way, altered the attitude of her student by responding in a non-human way, thus resolving her problem by increasing the emission of desirable student behavior. The student now knows how vital it is to develop her first paragraph, and how futile it is to reveal her first grief.

Even more, she has learned the danger of talking around her subject: 23 She not only refuses to talk *around* it now, she refuses to talk *about* it. Thus the human use of language leads back to silence — where perhaps it should have remained in the first place.

Study Questions

1. Is the thesis stated or implied? If it is stated, identify it; if it is implied, state it in your own words.
2. Why is the first-person point of view perhaps more appropriate in this essay than the third-person would be?
3. What is the purpose of presenting the English composition in paragraphs 11–18 verbatim, rather than summarizing it?
4. In what ways do the sentence structures in the quoted student composition differ from those written by Langer?
5. To what does the instructor object in his comment on the student essay in paragraph 20? Is this a valid objection?

Mark Twain
BUCK FANSHAW'S FUNERAL

Mark Twain, pen name for Samuel Langhorne Clemens (1835–1910), internationally known humorist and satirist, was born in Florida, Missouri, and spent his boyhood in Hannibal, Missouri. In his youth and early manhood he worked at a variety of occupations – journeyman printer, steamboat pilot, newspaper reporter, prospector, free-lance writer, and lecturer. His experiences gave him a lifetime of material for his writings. In his own time he enjoyed an international reputation as a wit and social commentator. In his later years he became bitterly cynical, but he is remembered by most Americans as the author of *Tom Sawyer* (1876) and *The Adventures of Huckleberry Finn* (1884).

Somebody has said that in order to know a community, one 1 must observe the style of its funerals and know what manner of men they bury with most ceremony. I cannot say which class we buried with most eclat in our "flush times," the distinguished public benefactor or the distinguished rough – possibly the two chief grades or grand divisions of society honored their illustrious dead about equally; and hence, no doubt, the philosopher I have quoted from would have needed to see

"Buck Fanshaw's Funeral," Chapter VI in *Roughing It* by Mark Twain. By permission of Harper & Row, Publishers, Inc.

two representative funerals in Virginia before forming his estimate of the people.

There was a grand time over Buck Fanshaw when he died. He was a representative citizen. He had "killed his man"—not in his own quarrel, it is true, but in defense of a stranger unfairly beset by numbers. He had kept a sumptuous saloon. He had been the proprietor of a dashing help-meet whom he could have discarded without the formality of a divorce. He had held a high position in the fire department and been a very Warwick in politics. When he died there was great lamentation throughout the town, but especially in the vast bottom-stratum of society.

On the inquest it was shown that Buck Fanshaw, in the delirium of a wasting typhoid fever, had taken arsenic, shot himself through the body, cut his throat, and jumped out of a four-story window and broken his neck—and after due deliberation, the jury, sad and tearful, but with intelligence unblinded by its sorrow, brought in a verdict of death "by the visitation of God." What could the world do without juries?

Prodigious preparations were made for the funeral. All the vehicles in town were hired, all the saloons put in mourning, all the municipal and fire-company flags hung at half-mast, and all the firemen ordered to muster in uniform and bring their machines duly draped in black. Now—let us remark in parentheses—as all the peoples of the earth had representative adverturers in the Silverland, and as each adventurer had brought the slang of his nation or his locality with him, the combination made the slang of Nevada the richest and the most infinitely varied and copious that had ever existed anywhere in the world, perhaps, except in the mines of California in the "early days." Slang was the language of Nevada. It was hard to preach a sermon without it, and be understood. Such phrases as "You bet!" "Oh, no, I reckon not!" "No Irish need apply," and a hundred others, became so common as to fall from the lips of a speaker unconsciously—and very often when they did not touch the subject under discussion and consequently failed to mean anything.

After Buck Fanshaw's inquest, a meeting of the short-haired brotherhood was held, for nothing can be done on the Pacific coast without a public meeting and an expression of sentiment. Regretful resolutions were passed and various committees appointed; among others, a committee of one was deputed to call on the minister, a fragile, gentle, spiritual new fledgling from an Eastern theological seminary, and as yet unacquainted with the ways of the mines. The committeeman, "Scotty" Briggs, made his visit; and in after days it was worth something to hear the minister tell about it. Scotty was a stalwart rough, whose customary suit, when on weighty official business, like committee work, was a fire-helmet, flaming red flannel shirt, patent-leather belt with spanner and revolver attached, coat hung over arm, and pants stuffed into boot-tops. He formed something of a contrast to the pale theological student. It is fair to say of Scotty, however, in passing, that he had a warm heart, and a strong love for his friends, and never entered into a quarrel when he could reasonably keep out of it. Indeed, it was commonly said that whenever one of Scotty's fights was investigated, it always turned out that it had originally been no affair of his, but that out of native good-heartedness he had dropped in of his own accord to help the man who was getting the worst of it. He and Buck Fanshaw were bosom friends, for years, and had often taken adventurous "pot-luck" together. On one occasion, they had thrown off their coats and taken the weaker side in a fight among strangers, and after gaining a hard-earned victory, turned and found that the men they were helping had deserted early, and not only that, but had stolen their coats and made off with them. But to return to Scotty's visit to the minister. He was on a sorrowful mission, now, and his face was the picture of woe. Being admitted to the presence he sat down before the clergyman, placed his fire-hat on an unfinished manuscript sermon under the minister's nose, took from it a red silk handkerchief, wiped his brow and heaved a sigh of dismal impressiveness, explanatory of his business. He choked, and even shed tears; but with an effort he mastered his voice and said in lugubrious tones:

"Are you the duck that runs the gospel-mill next door?" 6

"Am I the—pardon me, I believe I do not understand?" 7

With another sigh and a half sob, Scotty rejoined: 8

"Why you see we are in a bit of trouble, and the boys thought 9
maybe you would give us a lift, if we'd tackle you—that is, if I've got the rights of it and you are the head clerk of the doxology-works next door."

"I am the shepherd in charge of the flock whose fold is next door." 10

"The which?" 11

"The spiritual adviser of the little company of believers whose sanc- 12
tuary adjoins these premises."

Scotty scratched his head, reflected a moment, and then said: 13

"You ruther hold over me, pard. I reckon I can't call that hand. Ante 14
and pass the buck."

"How? I beg pardon. What did I understand you to say?" 15

"Well, you've ruther got the bulge on me. Or maybe we've both got 16
the bulge, somehow. You don't smoke me and I don't smoke you. You see, one of the boys has passed in his checks, and we want to give him a good send-off, and so the thing I'm on now is to roust out somebody to jerk a little chin-music for us and waltz him through handsome."

"My friend, I seem to grow more and more bewildered. Your obser- 17
vations are wholly incomprehensible to me. Cannot you simplify them in some way? At first I thought perhaps I understood you, but I grope now. Would it not expedite matters if you restricted yourself to categorical statements of fact unencumbered with obstructing accumulations of metaphor and allegory?"

Another pause, and more reflection. Then, said Scotty: 18

"I'll have to pass, I judge." 19

"How?" 20

"You've raised me out, pard." 21

"I still fail to catch your meaning." 22

"Why, that last lead of yourn is too many for me—that's the idea. I 23
can't neither trump nor follow suit."

The clergyman sank back in his chair perplexed. Scotty leaned his 24
head on his hand and gave himself up to thought. Presently his face came up, sorrowful but confident.

"I've got it now, so's you can savvy," he said. "What we want is a gos- 25
pel-sharp. See?"

"A what?"   26

"Gospel-sharp. Parson."   27

"Oh! Why did you not say so before? I am a clergyman—a parson."   28

"Now you talk! You see my blind and straddle it like a man. Put it 29
there!"—extending a brawny paw, which closed over the minister's small
hand and gave it a shake indicative of fraternal sympathy and fervent
gratification.

"Now we're all right, pard. Let's start fresh. Don't you mind my 30
snuffling a little—becuz we're in a power of trouble. You see, one of the
boys has gone up the flume—"

"Gone where?"   31

"Up the flume—throwed up the sponge, you understand."   32

"Thrown up the sponge?"   33

"Yes—kicked the bucket—"   34

"Ah—has departed to that mysterious country from whose bourne 35
no traveler returns."

"Return! I reckon not. Why, pard, he's *dead!*"   36

"Yes, I understand."   37

"Oh, you do? Well I thought maybe you might be getting tangled 38
some more. Yes, you see he's dead again—"

"*Again!* Why, has he ever been dead before?"   39

"Dead before? No! Do you reckon a man has got as many lives as a 40
cat? But you bet you he's awful dead now, poor old boy, and I wish I'd
never seen this day. I don't want no better friend than Buck Fanshaw. I
knowed him by the back; and when I know a man and like him, I freeze
to him—you hear *me.* Take him all round, pard, there never was a bullier
man in the mines. No man ever knowed Buck Fanshaw to go back on a
friend. But it's all up, you know, it's all up. It ain't no use. They've
scooped him."

"Scooped him?"   41

"Yes—death has. Well, well, well, we've got to give him up. Yes, in- 42
deed. It's a kind of a hard world, after all, *ain't* it? But pard, he was a
rustler! You ought to seen him get started once. He was a bully boy with
a glass eye! Just spit in his face and give him room according to his
strength, and it was just beautiful to see him peel and go in. He was the
worst son a thief that ever drawed breath. Pard, he was *on* it! He was on
it bigger than an Injun!"

"On it? On what?"   43

"On the shoot. On the shoulder. On the fight, you understand. *He* 44
didn't give a continental for *any*body. *Beg* your pardon, friend, for coming
so near saying a cuss-word—but you see I'm on an awful strain, in this
palaver, on account of having to cramp down and draw everything so
mild. But we've got to give him up. There ain't any getting around that. I
don't reckon. Now if we can get you to help plant him—"

"Preach the funeral discourse? Assist at the obsequies?"   45

"Obs'quies is good. Yes. That's it—that's our little game. We are go- 46
ing to get the thing up regardless, you know. He was always nifty him-

self, and so you bet you his funeral ain't going to be no slouch—solid-silver doorplate on his coffin, six plumes on the hearse, and a nigger on the box in a biled shirt and a plug hat—how's that for high? And we'll take care of *you,* pard. We'll fix you all right. There'll be a kerridge for you; and whatever you want, you just 'scape out and we'll 'tend to it. We've got a shebang fixed up for you to stand behind, in No. 1's house, and don't you be afraid. Just go in and toot your horn, if you don't sell a clam. Put Buck through as bully as you can, pard, for anybody that knowed him will tell you that he was one of the whitest men that was ever in the mines. You can't draw it too strong. He never could stand it to see things going wrong. He's done more to make this town quiet and peaceable than any man in it. I've seen him lick four Greasers in eleven minutes, myself. If a thing wanted regulating, *he* warn't a man to go browsing around after somebody to do it, but he would prance in and regulate it himself. He warn't a Catholic. Scasely. He was down on 'em. His word was, 'No Irish need apply!' But it didn't make no difference about that when it came down to what a man's rights was—and so, when some roughs jumped the Catholic boneyard and started in to stake out town lots in it he *went* for 'em! And he *cleaned* 'em, too! I was there, pard, and I seen it myself."

"That was very well indeed—at least the impluse was—whether the act was strictly defensible or not. Had the deceased any religious convictions? That is to say, did he feel a dependence upon, or acknowledge allegiance to a higher power?"

More reflection.

"I reckon you've stumped me again, pard. Could you say it over once more, and say it slow?"

"Well, to simplify it somewhat, was he, or rather had he ever been connected with any organization sequestered from secular concerns and devoted to self-sacrifice in the interests of morality?"

"All down but nine—set 'em up on the other alley, pard."

"What did I understand you to say?"

"Why, you're most too many for me, you know. When you get in with your left I hunt grass every time. Every time you draw, you fill; but I don't seem to have any luck. Let's have a new deal."

"How? Begin again?"

"That's it."

"Very well. Was he a good man, and—"

"There—I see that; don't put up another chip till I look at my hand. A good man, says you? Pard, it ain't no name for it. He was the best man that ever—pard, you would have doted on that man. He could lam any galoot of his inches in America. It was him that put down the riot last election before it got a start; and everybody said he was the only man that could have done it. He waltzed in with a spanner in one hand and a trumpet in the other, and sent fourteen men home on a shutter in less than three minutes. He had that riot all broke up and prevented nice before anybody every got a chance to strike a blow. He was always for peace, and he would *have* peace—he could not stand disturbances. Pard, he was a great loss to this town. It would please the boys if you could chip in something like that and do him justice. Here once when the Micks got to throwing stones through the Methodis' Sunday-school windows, Buck Fanshaw, all of his own notion, shut up his saloon and took a couple of six-shooters and mounted guard over the Sunday-school. Says he, 'No Irish need apply!' And they didn't. He was the bulliest man in the mountains, pard! He could run faster, jump higher, hit harder, and hold more tanglefoot whisky without spilling it than any man in seventeen counties. Put that in, pard—it'll please the boys more than anything you could say. And you can say, pard, that he never shook his mother."

"Never shook his mother?"   58

"That's it—any of the boys will tell you so."   59

"Well, but why *should* he shake her?"   60

"That's what *I* say—but some people does."   61

"Not people of any repute?"   62

"Well, some that averages pretty so-so."   63

In my opinion the man that would offer personal violence to his own   64
mother, ought to—"

"Cheese it, pard; you've banked your ball clean outside the string.   65
What I was drivin' at, was, that he never *throwed off* on his mother—don't you see? No indeedy. He give her a house to live in, and town lots, and plenty of money; and he looked after her and took care of her all the time; and when she was down with the smallpox I'm d—d if he didn't set up nights and nuss her himself! *Beg* your pardon for saying it, but it hopped out too quick for yours truly. You've treated me like a gentleman, pard, and I ain't the man to hurt your feelings intentional. I think you're white. I think you're a square man, pard. I like you, and I'll lick any man that don't. I'll lick him tell he can't tell himself from a last year's corpse! put it *there*!" [Another fraternal handshake—and exit.]

The obsequies were all that "the boys" could desire. Such a marvel   66
of funeral pomp had never been seen in Virginia. The plumed hearse, the dirge-breathing brass-bands, the close marts of business, the flags drooping at half-mast, the long, plodding procession of uniformed secret societies, military battalions and fire companies, draped engines, carriages of officials, and citizens in vehicles and on foot, attracted multitudes of spectators to the sidewalks, roofs, and windows; and for years afterward, the degree of grandeur attained by any civic display in Virginia was determined by comparison with Buck Fanshaw's funeral.

Scotty Briggs, as a pall-bearer and a mourner, occupied a prominent   67
place at the funeral, and when the sermon was finished and the last sentence of prayer for the dead man's soul ascended, he responded, in a low voice, but with feeling:

"AMEN. No Irish need apply."   68

As the bulk of the response was without apparent relevancy, it was   69
probably nothing more than a humble tribute to the memory of the friend that was gone; for, as Scotty had once said, it was "his word."

Scotty Briggs, in after days, achieved the distinction of becoming the   70
only convert to religion that was ever gathered from the Virginia roughs; and it transpired that the man who had it in him to espouse the quarrel

of the weak out of inborn nobility of spirit was no mean timber whereof to construct a Christian. The making him one did not warp his generosity or diminish his courage; on the contrary it gave intelligent direction to the one and a broader field to the other. If his Sunday-school class progressed faster than the other classes, was it matter for wonder? I think not. He talked to his pioneer small-fry in a language they understood! It was my large privilege, a month before he died, to hear him tell the beautiful story of Joseph and his brethren to his class "without looking at the book." I leave it to the reader to fancy what it was like, as it fell, riddled with slang, from the lips of that grave, earnest teacher, and was listened to by his little learners with a consuming interest that showed that they were as unconscious as he was that any violence was being done to the sacred proprieties!

Study Questions

1. Contrast the language of the narrator in paragraphs 1–5 and 61–64 with the language used by Scotty and by the minister.
2. How are Scotty and the minister characterized by their language?
3. What is the narrator's attitude toward Scotty? How does he express this attitude?
4. What type of paragraph development does Twain use in paragraph 5?
5. In addition to the situation between Scotty and the minister what are the other sources of humor in this essay?

7 The Media and the Arts
"The Winter of Our Discontent"

Cultural historians will no doubt remember the '70s as a decade when Americans spent an increasing number of hours and dollars on entertainment and leisure-time activities, and when the ideas and opinions of Americans were increasingly formed by images selected for them by the media. Although a cursory reading of *The New York Times* might indicate that the dance was the most popular of contemporary arts, statistics demonstrate the Americans took the greatest interest in sports, television, and film. A television showing of "Roots" attracted the largest viewing audience in history, while a television "party" to mark the conclusion of the successful Public Broadcasting series from England, "Upstairs, Downstairs," drew millions of dollars in financial pledges. On the big screen box-office records tumbled and tumbled again, as films like "The Exorcist," "Jaws," and "Star Wars" replaced such former box-office champions as "Gone with the Wind" and "The Sound of Music." It was an era of culture for the masses.

The first four selections in this section deal with the forms and content of popular music. Richard Goldstein's essay originally served as the introduction to an anthology of rock music lyrics; it is deservedly famous as a brief, informative history of contemporary rock as well as an analysis of why rock has appealed to so many. Ann Nietzke looks even more closely at country-and-western music and some of its most noted songsters and finds it sadly lacking in its attitudes toward women and man-woman relationships; she concludes that this music is an unfortunate reflection of equally unfortunate attitudes in American life. Eudora Welty uses another form of popular music — jazz — as the basis for her short story "Powerhouse"; a tour de force, it is one of those rare short stories where form and content are genuinely indistinguishable, where content is form. Finally, John Updike writes a tongue-in-cheek satire, a sci-fi narrative that both uses and parodies the form. "The Chaste Planet" sets up reverberations about American attitudes toward both music and sex.

Marya Mannes, Art Buchwald, and Jerzy Kosinski use different tones in their approaches to a single topic, television and its abuses. Television commercials and the image they present of women — and men — comes under Mannes' critical eye; she finds the commercials so unreal and yet so potentially divisive an element in American society that she calls television "the splitting image." Art Buchwald takes a more humorous approach, as he puts the production of the Declaration of Independence into the hands of television directors. His conclusions are not too different from Kosinski's. Though their methods and styles differ, they conclude that television reduces the world to the banal, the simple, and the trite. Implicit in the criticism is a call for radical surgery.

Deems Taylor, Joan Didion, and Daniel J. Boorstin next examine different types of culture heroes. In a now-famous essay Taylor asks to what extent we are willing to tolerate the excesses and eccentricities of genius. Joan Didion delves into the American fascination with Howard Hughes and his lifestyle; a man who was the subject of a major literary fraud and whose "will" offered almost limitless opportunities to defraud the estate, Howard Hughes seemed to dominate newspaper headlines of the '70s. Daniel J. Boorstin draws some more general conclusions in his study of celebrity and a specific hero, Charles A. Lindbergh.

Finally, acerbic John Simon puts his typewriter to a study of the film, an art form that he feels has moved from fake happy endings to fake unhappy endings. In this essay Simon is as much the sociologist as the film critic; he tries to determine whether or not the American cinema accurately reflects American society. In his discussion of many films that readers may not have seen, Simon shows the young writer how to handle unfamiliar material in such a way that it can be comprehended. In content his piece deals with the very essence of this section — the manipulation by the media of the American psyche; thus it provides a fitting conclusion to "The Winter of Our Discontent."

Richard Goldstein
THE POETRY OF ROCK

Richard Goldstein (1944-   ) was born in New York City. He received a B.A. from Hunter College (1965) and an M.S. from the Columbia University Graduate School of Journalism (1966). For a time he edited *US,* a paperback quarterly; but his columns continued to appear in such periodicals as *Vogue, New York,* and the *Village Voice.* Goldstein was a guest lecturer at Columbia University in 1969. His books include *One in Seven: Drugs on Campus* (1966), *The Poetry of Rock* (1969), and *Goldstein's Greatest Hits* (1969).

Ten years ago, a single, all-embracing criterion governed the 1
evaluation of a rock song. When matters of taste were at hand, you simply arched your back against the nearest lamppost, fixed the buckle of your garrison belt across your hip, and drawled with a hint of spittle between your teeth: "I like it. It's got a good beat. Y'can dance to it."

But those days of aesthetic simplicity have vanished with cinch belts 2
and saddle shoes. Today's rock partisan—plugged into a stereophonic nirvana—is more likely to arch his eyebrows than his pelvis. He may casually remark, with a gleam in his hookah, "I empathize with it. It has truth and beauty. Besides, my kids say it's psychedelic."

Rock 'n' roll has come a long way from its origins in the bargain 3
basement of American culture. Once a pariah of the musical world, it has evolved into a fullfledged art-form, perhaps the most preened and pampered of our time. Critics gush superlatives over the Beatles in little magazines. Bob Dylan addresses poets from the far side of Desolation Row, muttering nursery rhymes that fall like a well-oiled guillotine across their necks. Jazzmen do their thing in hippy beads. Serious composers marvel at the Beach Boys while filmmakers search for alienation behind the Doors.

Rock is de rigueur. Hip Broadway turns the Hadassah on, while psy- 4
chedelic swamis sell aspirin on tv. San Francisco is a teenybopper's holy land; London, a plastic Lourdes. Even Plato's Cave has become a discotheque. Amid its electronic shadows, longhaired princes tell it like it is. So shove over, Norman Mailer, Edward Albee, Allen Ginsberg, and Robert Lowell—make room for the Electric Prunes.

I've got no kick against modern jazz,
Unless they try to play it too darn fast;
And change the beauty of the melody,
Until they sound just like a symphony,
That's why I go for that rock 'n' roll music
Any old way you choose it;
It's got a back beat, you can't lose it,
Any old time you use it.
It's gotta be rock 'n' roll music
If you wanna dance with me.[1]

So wrote Chuck Berry, America's first rock poet, in 1957. When he burst upon the scene, with his hips as smooth as gears and his suit spangled with delight, pop music was sharply divided along racial lines, as it had been in America since before the invention of the phonograph. The black sound of the Fifties was Rhythm and Blues, a blunt, joyous party-jive with its language rooted in funky jazz. White America first received this message from black performers like Little Richard, Fats Domino, and Chuck Berry.

But Chuck Berry was special. He sang about an America of pure motion and energy. While the beats did battle with materialism in search of pure spirit, he spent his time behind the wheel of a new Ford, digging speed. Words and images spilled in staccato freeform across the body of his songs. He chose to work in bold clean shapes, rendered heroic by their sheer simplicity. In a Chuck Berry song, you couldn't tell the girls from the cars, and some of the best marriages ended up in traffic court. He could be as dazzling as a comet or as sentimental as a greeting card. But he was always wry, even in anger. His protest songs made you feel good instead of grim.

Only when he wrote about his music did Chuck Berry get serious. He virtually defined rock for the generation to come as the sound of an inner volcano, the hum of satisfied machinery, the triumph of the material not over, but in conjunction with, the soul.

Today, his lyrics have been largely ignored in the search for conscious poetry which dominates the rock scene. But behind the bouncing pop ball we seem so eager to follow lies a tradition rich in the kind of accidental art that Chuck Berry provided. No wonder auslanders like the Beatles began their careers in conscious imitation. In Chuck Berry's reckless comic energy they found a vision of America.

At its core, good rock has always provided that kind of mystical experience. But few adults tried to penetrate its gaudy cliches and rigid structure—until now. Today, it is possible to suggest without risking defenestration that some of the best poetry of our time may well be contained within those slurred couplets. But even its staunchest adult partisans seem to think that rock sprang fullblown from the electric loins of the Sixties. The Beatles get some credit for turning a primitive form into art; or, as one respected straight critic put it, for carrying pop music "be-

---

[1] *Rock n' Roll Music* by Chuck Berry. © 1957 Arc Music Corp. Used with permission of the publisher; all rights reserved.

yond patronization." But beneath its sequined surface rock has always contained a searing power to communicate where being young and yearning was at. Like blues, it became respectable only after its period of greatest vitality had passed.

Contemporary rock (sometimes known in post-graduate circles as the 10 "new music") is a mulatto. It was born of an unholy alliance between white Country music and Rhythm and Blues. Southerners like Buddy Holly, Jerry Lee Lewis, and Elvis Presley fused these styles into a hybrid sound called "rockabilly." They wrote brisk and brittle songs, laced with fiery verbal cadenzas and meant to be belted across, with a whole lotta shakin' goin' on. Elvis Presley earned his first million by paring lyrics down to a throbbing series of low moans and raunchy country hollers. He helped establish the tradition of sound-as-content, which has dominated rock since it moved north and captured the cities.

By the late Fifties, Presley's wail had become the cry of the city 11 streets. Every corner worth its traffic light had a resident group — and a surly lot they were. To uninitiated ears, theirs was punk-music: coarse, constrained, and claustrophobic. But, in fact, these superstars from the slums had democratized rock. Today's music is far too complex and the cost of instruments alone too staggering to permit mass participation. But in 1958, all the equipment a beginning group needed was a plastic pitchpipe, and all it had to master to start rocking was the five vowels.

The pop song had become a chant, carried by four or five voices in a 12 dissonant wail. Measured against the aesthetic standards of current rock, these nonsense syllables may seem ignoble. But the primary purpose of a lyric in 1957 was to convey mood, not meaning. The ideal scat song had to be simple enough for any voice to master, but intriguing enough to survive incessant repetition. Though they look absurd on paper (except, perhaps, as examples of concrete poetry), it is impossible to even read these lyrics without becoming immersed in their rhythmic pulse. That involvement was the experience these songs were intended to provide. Enshrined within the music of the late Fifties, like a sacred litany, they survive to this day, as do the unsteady bass and furious falsetto with which street singers assaulted a melody when their voices were the only instruments, and the only echo chamber within reach was under the neighborhood "el."

Without this heritage, rock is a bushel of pretty leaves pretending to 13 be a tree. The Beatles could not have written "She Loves You" or even "I Am the Walrus" without first experiencing "Get a Job." No young lyricist works in a stylistic vacuum. Even Leonard Cohen, a recognized Canadian poet who has recently turned to song-writing, says he prepared for his new role by listening to old Ray Charles records until they warped. It shows. Cohen's rock songs have the consistency of modern verse, but unlike linear poetry, they are wrapped tightly around a rhythmic spine.

It is impossible to speak of poetry in rock without mentioning the 14 pervasive influence of rhythm. Until recently, rigid conventions kept pop lyrics imprisoned within a metrical framework that poets had discarded

long ago. Even the most adventurous lyricists wrote even stanzas, made
frequent use of rhyme, and kept that mighty beat churning through their
words. Today, these rules are regarded as more of a legacy than an ulti-
matum. But most rock creators still rely heavily on basics. Even Dylan,
who comes closest to capturing the feel of modern verse in his songs,
usually caps his lines with rhyme.

One lesson we have learned from blues is that a familiar form can   15
produce both great art and drivel. The crucial factor is not the style, but
those who choose to work in it. Probably no one has had a greater influence on the texture of modern rock than Bob Dylan. He demolished
the narrow line and lean stanzas that once dominated pop, replacing
them with a more flexible organic structure. His rambling ballads killed
the three-minute song and helped establish the album as a basic tool for
communication in rock.

More important, he turned pop composers on to themselves. The in-   16
trospective music that followed has come to black fruition in groups like
the Doors. But it was Dylan's success which established beyond a doubt
that poetic imagery belonged in pop music. To claim that he is the major
poet of his generation is not to relegate written verse to the graveyard of
cultural irrelevance. Most young people are aware of linear poetry. But
they groove on Dylan, not because the rock medium has overwhelmed
his message for this generation, but because, in Dylan's songs, the two reinforce each other.

This, of course, is no accident. Dylan's intention is to reconcile po-   17
etry with song. Scattered throughout his liner notes are constant references to this aesthetic task. He juxtaposes symbols of high and low culture as though classicism were a haughty lady being raped by a bluesy
stud. If hearing "Desolation Row" is like discovering a plastic Parthenon
in a Times Square souvenir stand, that is exactly the effect Dylan means
his rock-apocalypse to convey.

Dylan's remarkable achievement has been to inject pop music with   18
poetic power by simply grafting his own sensibility onto what was already
implicit in rock. As weighty as his lyrics sometimes read, they never
sound artificial on record, because even their inconsistencies are intrinsic
to rock. For a poet who likes to speak in tongues, as Dylan often does,
pop music offers a fertile field for exploration. Rock composers have always employed symbols (cars, roses, blue suede shoes). Even in a classic
ballad like "To Know Him Is to Love Him," the cliches of teenage romance are used to express something much deeper. The lyric becomes a
chilling example of indirection when you realize that its author, Phil
Spector, took his title and refrain from the epitaph on his father's tombstone.

Such ambiguity has existed in rock since its earliest days, and for the   19
most elemental reason. To sell, a pop song had to be meaningful, but to
get on the radio, it had to sound harmless. Disc jockeys with a more
rigid sense of propriety than the most bluenosed censor actually helped
foster in young writers a profound awareness of slang and its implications. The ability of today's lyricist to say extraordinary things in ordinary

words has its roots in the enforced ambiguity of top-40 radio, where composers tried to express the forbidden in the context of the permissible.

Slang is to rock what classical allusions are to written poetry. It be- 20 gan as a simple code, freely adapted from blues or jazz, but it soon became a major mode of communicating attitudes. Rock writers expertly hid meaning behind stray vowels and half-muttered phrases, a practice which survives to this day on some Beatle records. The penalty for failure—when sensuality became too apparent or the code too explicit—was exclusion from the radio. Just last year, an innocent-sounding ballad called "That Acapulco Gold" was yanked off the air when disc jockeys realized that its title referred to a high quality of Mexican pot.

But slang still eludes the dubious ears of disc jockeys often enough 21 to provide a mass-snicker for the pop audiences. Today's rock poets deal with the drug experience in poeticized code, as jazzmen and blues singers before them did. It is enough for Grace Slick of the Jefferson Airplane to cry "Feed your head!" at the end of "White Rabbit" for teenagers to understand her suggestion. And John Phillips of the Mamas and the Papas has only to arch his brow over a lyric to make it seem ambiguous.

In a sense, this awareness of jargon is one sign of a repressed cul- 22 ture. But it has also provided teenagers everywhere with a solid sense of their own identity—something all good poetry is supposed to convey. So, it is almost sad to note that the golden age of rock slang is passing away. With the growth of liberal radio stations across the FM dial, lyricists are now becoming increasingly direct. Those many young savages from England, who could make even a virtuous love song sound like statutory rape, helped force this new frankness upon our virgin ears. With their long hair, tight pants, and eyes squinting like a dirty word, these angry musicians poured a defiant vitality into rock. Ten years ago, Chuck Berry had to content himself with indirect protest. You had to strain to catch the anger in those words, though it was present. But there's no doubt what Peter Townshend of the Who feels when he shouts:

> People try to put us down
> Just because we get around.
> Things they do look awful cold
> Hope I die before I get old.
> This is my generation, baby.
> Why don't you all f-f-f-fade away.[2]

With no further need for indirection in theme or language, rock 23 poets are beginning to regard ambiguity as an enchancement rather than a necessity. For all its frankness, liberated rock remains a devious music. Lyricists still bury meanings deep within their songs. An undertone of irony is still cultivated, and sometimes lyric and melody are pitted against each other in emotional counterpoint. The BeeGees, experts at mood

---

[2] *My Generation.* Words and music by Peter Townshend. © Copyright 1965 Fabulous Music Ltd., London, England. All publication rights controlled by Tro-Devon Music, Inc., New York, for the USA and Canada. Used by permission.

manipulation, often set singsong lyrics about love and devotion against tense, mournful melodies. In "Lady Jane," Mick Jagger of the Rolling Stones is a knight-errant with five days' growth of beard. He sings a chivalric ode against a tinkling dulcimer, but he keeps his voice thick, grainy, and unmistakably indelicate.

Even in their early days, the Beatles were far from tame. In the be- 24 ginning their lyrics seemed as straight-laced as the collarless suits they wore then. But there was always a smirk behind those innocent shouts of "Yeah! Yeah! Yeah!" When the creators of a recent television documentary about youth culture chose to score some war footage with a Beatle ballad called "We Can Work It Out," they discovered that this gentle love song actually contained an implicit anti-war message as well.

By 1965, the Beatles had begun to apply Dylan's freewheeling vi- 25 sion, and the result was a flowering of their own talent.

Though it doesn't look very liberated, "Norwegian Wood" is an im- 26 portant clue to the development of the Beatles' distinctive style. It begins easily enough, with a frank appraisal of the situation, and a concise glimpse of the hunter stalking his prey.

Using only the starkest of language, the Beatles create a tantalizing, 27 but stubbornly non-specific scene. What goes on? Why does the narrator inform us, in a wry undertone, that he "crawled off to sleep in the bath"? And this Norwegian Wood; could that be yet another word for pot?

This non-resolution was a strange twist for the lads who crooned, "I 28 wanna hold your hand." Future Beatle songs would become even less specific, their implications even more uncertain, and when John Lennon was the author, their language more ingenious. Lennon's power as a lyricist is greatest when he rips apart the actual texture of words and rearranges them into a sly puzzle, which is somehow as compelling as it is cryptic.

From the Beatles, and from Dylan, rock poetry radiates in every di- 29 rection. There is the pastel lyricism of Donovan, the literate narrative of Paul Simon, the gentle folkiness of John Sebastian, and the raunchy power of the San Francisco blues bands. There are dozens more—all young poets who call their lyrics "pop."

But do these lyrics really amount to art? Does Wordsworth speak to 30 Donovan from the great beyond? Is John Lennon's wordplay truly Joycean? Is Bob Dylan the Walt Whitman of the juke-box? In a sense, assertions like these are the worst enemy of liberated rock. They enslave it with an artificial heritage. The great vitality of the pop revolution has been its liberation from such encumbrances of form. Rock swings free, embracing chaos, and laughing at the notion that there could be anything more worth celebrating than the present.

Rock is, and always has been, the sacred squeal of now. It's got a 31 damned good beat. And you can dance to it.

Study Questions

1. How does Goldstein create variation within parallel structure in paragraph 3?

2. How is *defined* used in paragraph 6? In what sense is rock defined in that paragraph?
3. Comment on the metaphor and metaphorical language in paragraph 12.
4. Goldstein uses *slang* and *jargon* almost interchangeably. Look up these words, and *secret language* as well, in any good usage dictionary, and discuss Goldstein's comments on language in view of what you find.
5. How are the introduction and conclusion related?

Ann Nietzke
...DOIN' SOMEBODY WRONG

Ann Nietzke grew up in Alton, Illinois, and Columbus, Mississippi. She received an M.A. in English from Illinois State University, and has lived in Normal, Illinois, for the past eleven years. Her first article—a psychological-sociological analysis of Pepsi and Coke commercials—was published in the *Saturday Review* in 1972. Since 1973, she has been writing about the media for *Human Behavior,* where she is currently a contributing editor.

There was a time when country-and-western music was known 1 outside the rural South and Southwest only as hillbilly or redneck music, foot-stomping or, if you will, shit-kicking music. Now that its popularity has mushroomed nationwide (even New York has about 20 exclusively country stations), and the country-music business has become a giant industry, people are a little kinder in their references to the genre. In fact, there is a lot of talk now about country being *the* true American sound, and the Country Music Association (CMA) would have us believe it is "America's only native art form."

If that is true, it's ironic that country music has become more popu- 2 lar in the past decade or so precisely because it has become less "country," having been influenced—to the dismay of many older fans—by rock, pop, folk and whatever else has been in (or on) the air. Current pop-country stars such as Kris Kristofferson, Mac Davis, Glenn Campbell, John Denver, Anne Murray and Olivia Newton-John, for example, have quite a different sound from such current solid country stars as Merle Haggard, Johnny Cash, Freddy Hart and Loretta Lynn, just as these differ from the more traditional sounds of the late Hank Williams or Ernest Tubb, Mother Maybelle Carter or Kitty Wells.

Nowadays, many country singers dream of recording a "crossover" 3 single that will be a hit on both the country and pop charts, although at the same time they worry about becoming too "pop" and thus tarnishing their image with the hard-core country audience. This is a very legitimate concern because country audiences, more than any others (with the possible exception of political supporters and thus the parallel in Robert Altman's film *Nashville*), are vitally interested in the personal lives of the stars and seem to feel that the singers should be truly grateful to fans. They insist that singers who "make it big" appear to stay "country" and humble and poor at heart, in spite of the fact that many earn fantastic amounts of money, run big business enterprises and live in mansions.

The motto of the Illinois Country Opry, for example, is "Stay Coun- 4 try," but the difficulty in trying to stay country lies at least partly in figuring out what *country* means. Even a committee appointed by the CMA to work up a definition of a country song finally gave up. Kris "Me and Bobby McGee' Kristofferson says, "If it sounds country, man, it's country," but his own country credentials are highly suspect, his image being a little too hip and intellectual for many country fans (having been a former Rhodes scholar and English instructor at West Point). Tom T. Hall, composer of "Harper Valley PTA," insists that content is more important than sound in determining what's country — it's what *happens* in a country song that counts. In broader terms, the framework of country music has been described by Christopher Wren of the *New York Times* as rural southern in origin, conservative in politics, fundamentalist in religion, and blue-collar in economics. I myself think the CMA is right on target when it states that "country music is no longer strictly rural, as the name implies, but has become the folk music of the working classes."

If you really want to know what country music is, though, you have 5 to find out for yourself by listening to it. Set you radio dial at your country station for a few days and, if you feel any affinity for what you hear there, stop by your local discount drugstore, where you will probably find at least a few not-so-current albums by top country stars for as little as two or three dollars. Then, with the money you've "saved" on the records, buy yourself a 12-pack of beer so you'll have something to cry in while you listen to them, for you will probably discover, just as I did, that the world of country music is essentially a world of "heartaches by the number, troubles by the score."

My own interest in country was first aroused early this year when I 6 read of the controversy stirred up by Loretta Lynn's single called "The Pill" in which a wife is telling her husband, all in chicken-farm metaphors, that she's tired of his screwing around with other hens while she stays at home constantly pregnant and that, in fact, now that she has the Pill, she's going out to have some fun of her own unless he wants to "make a deal" and start behaving himself ("There's gonna be some changes made right here on nursery hill/You've set this chicken your last time 'cause now I've got the Pill").

I found Lynn's manifesto of liberation so funny and touching that I 7 became an instant fan. How could any feminist, whatever medical reservations she might have about the Pill, resist loving such lines as "I'm tearin' down your brooder house" or "This chicken's done tore up her nest" or, finally, "This incubator's overused because you kept it filled/But feelin' good comes easy now since I got the Pill"? The very sentiments that made the song irrestible to me, however, made it very resistible to many country dejays across the nation, and the record was banned by so many stations that sales were actually boosted by the controversy—all of which shook up the Nashville establishment, since Loretta Lynn is probably the current queen of the country music and has won just about every award in the business.

You might think that the song would be banned because of its 8 "earthiness" and, indeed, some dejays did use that as an excuse. But the truth is that a lot of country music is earthy—more sexually explicit than rock, I think, if only because in country the words are so simple and direct and clearly sung that you understand immediately just what's being said. Stations that refused to air "The Pill" had no qualms about playing Conway Twitty's "You've Never Been This Far Before," during the course of which somebody's virginity is lost ("I don't know what I'm saying as my fingers touch forbidden places"). And 17-year-old Little Tanya Tucker gets away with "Would You Lay with Me in a Field of Stone?" in which she asks, "Should my lips grow dry would you wet them. dear/In the midnight hour, if my lips were dry?" So it could hardly have been sex per se that folks found to be offensive in "The Pill."

Out of curiosity, I called my local country station request line and 9 asked for the song. I was told that the entire staff had decided not to air it because it was too "commercial." This seemed a bit farfetched to me, since the station repeatedly plays such songs as Ray Steven's faddish and corny "The Streak" and an incredibly, *literally* commercial number called "Red Necks, White Socks and Blue Ribbon Beer." It began to seem that Lynn's own outspoken estimate of the situation at the radio stations was indisputably true: "If all the disc jockeys were women there wouldn't be no confusion. The song's not dirty—it's threatening because it says what's good for the gander is good for the goose."

After listening to more and more country music, I began to realize 10 that a great portion of the heartache and trouble in the songs stems from disastrous relationships of one kind or another between men and women from the disastrous ways in which men and women see themselves and each other. I think one reason the world of country music is often such a sad one—despite all its humor, corn and high spirit—is that it is so often a world of diminished personhood and, although the world at large is sad for the same reason, I think the working-class lifestyle and mentality, as depicted in most country music, accentuates it.

To begin with, the only really acceptable role for decent woman 11 seems to be that of housewife and mother. The indecent women who work are all waitresses, barmaids or prostitutes who travel from "Barrooms to Bedrooms," as David Wills sings it, and are in many songs referred to collectively as "honky-tonk angels." The men, decent and indecent work hard and play hard, travel or wander, drink a lot and sometimes end up in prison, while the women stay home and take care of the kids. To the tune of Roger Miller's big hit "King of the Road," Jody Miller sings "Queen of the House," in which she describes the life of the hardworking housewife and mother who rules a domain of children, dirty floors and bathtub rings — the regalia that yet ennoble her.

This image is reinforced by the lives of the women country stars as   12 described in various country music publications and in their album notes. No matter that these women had to be extremely strong and determined in order to make successful careers for themselves, or that they may spend as many as 250 nights a year in a bus, traveling to reach their fans all over the United States. What matters, so far as their public images go, is how devoted they are as wives and mothers. This description of Dottie West is typical in tone and content of much of the publicity I've seen on Lynn Anderson, Tammy Wynette, Jeanne Pruett, Brend Lee, Loretta Lynn and others: "To her mother, she's the oldest of 10 children; to her husband, the greatest wife in the world; to her four lovely children, she's a devoted mother; and to her friends, an excellent cook." Even Canadian pop-country star Anne Murray has said she'll quit the business at 30 to get married and have children because she believes that "career and marriage don't mix."

One star who managed literally to mix her career with marriage is   13 Tammy Wynette, formerly a cosmetologist named Wynette Pugh who, after she started singing, married her childhood idol and one of the kings of country music — George Jones. Both made something of a career out of the marriage itself as they performed together, even including a reenactment of their wedding ceremony as a climax to their act. Their recent divorce or "D-I-V-O-R-C-E," as Tammy would sing it) is her third and proves that she is unable to live out the philosophy that underlies so many of her songs, a philosophy epitomized in "Stand By Your Man," the largest-selling single ever recorded by a woman in the history of country music, that bad times are often the lot of a woman, particularly when her man is out enjoying himself or doing things she finds incomprehensible. But if you love him, ladies, you're supposed to "be proud of him" and give him "all the love you can" for, above everything else it's important to "stand by your man."

Nowhere in country, I think, does the relationship between diminished personhood and sadness become more apparent than in the work   14 of Tammy Wynette, for her voice conveys a little teardrop in every syllable, and most of the syllables add up to portrayals of women who feel "I am nothing, my man is everything." So Tammy is full of advice on how to hold your man. "There's no secret, just some little things to do," she says and recommends that you start his day out right with a loving smile, support him, understand him and let him know that you think he's "better than the rest." A woman is supposed to maintain this attitude no matter how badly the man treats her. "Sometimes," Tammy sings, "I lay in bed and cry, cry, cry," but she insists, "for better or worse, I took him 'til the day I die."

Women who treat men similarly, however, women who do any "slip- 15 pin' around," may very well get shot as punishment (Johnny Cash's "Kate" and Claude King's "Laura"), because men view women as their sexual property. Surely this is partly because the men work so hard to pay for everything else that they must feel they are paying for as well for their women, who wait passively at home. Tex Ritter sings, for example, "I've had enough of your two-timing/You've had enough of my bank-roll," and Bobby Bare complains of "Alimony, same old blues in it/I'm payin' for it while someone else is usin' it." For whatever reasons, a woman who cheats, even if she isn't killed for it, is very rarely forgiven in country. Over and over and over again men are driven to the bottle by their unfaithful women ("My heart is breaking like the tiny bubbles/She's actin' single, I'm drinkin' doubles").

The Good Woman — Bad Woman split is, in fact, a major theme in 16 the music, because the married men are constantly tempted by "honky-tonk angels" of various types who, I gather, are generally better lays than their wives ("She's the one I love," Mel Street tells one, "but you make me feel more like a man"). While many do give in to temptation, they of-ten suffer from the conflict within themselves: "Lord, I'm only human, and I can feel the glow," Jim Mundy sings. "My body's saying yes but my heart is saying no."

The happiest songs narrated by married men, therefore, are those in 17 which the conflict is resolved for them by a wife who can be sexy at the appropriate times. The best known example of these is probably Charlie Rich's "Behind Closed Doors," in which his woman is always a "lady" un-til he gets her behind closed doors where no one sees what goes on, where she lets her hair hang down and makes him glad he's a man. Jerry Wallace brags of a similar ideal setup in "I've Got So Many Wives At Home," for his wife, too, is both lady and satisfying lover, and "If I need a devil, as all men sometimes do/You got just enough to make me love the devil out of you."

It is taken for granted by both men and women in country music 18 that men have to be "the way they are," while women have to be what their men want them to be. In "I Can't Be Myself," Merle Haggard im-plies he'll be leaving a woman who wants him to change. George Jones demands, "Take Me As I Am," and Billy Edd Wheeler says straight out, "If you're expectin' me to change my old ways for the new/Baby, don't hold your breath until I do." Dottie West, however, is pictured on one of her album covers as a paper doll about to be cut out by a huge pair of scissors held by a big male hand ("Take your scissors and take your time/And cut along the dotted line"). She begs her man to keep his scis-sors handy and trim her edges now and then, and "Fit me in with all your plans/For I want to be what I'm cut out to be."

It would appear from such examples that the men have a good deal 19 of ego strength and personal pride, but a close look at many lyrics by both male and female singers reveals to what a great extent men rely on their women for emotional support and for a sense of "manhood"

("Whenever I'm down you come around/And you make me feel like a man"). The male counterpart of Tammy Wynette's "Stand By Your Man" is not "Stand By Your Woman" but rather "Only A Woman Like You (Can Make A Man of Me)," a woman capable of turning even small dreams into "the greatest thing."

Whatever power women do have in the world of country music 20 stems, I think, from this twisted emotional setup, and I find a subtle but definite thread of contempt for men running through a number of female songs. Tammy Wynette advises, "If you love him, be proud of him/'Cause after all he's *just a man*," and elsewhere admits that she's "quit lookin' for a perfect man/'Cause their ain't any more of them." Obviously, if men need women to make men of them, then without women they are nothing but little boys ("I'd love to just deceive 'em, playin' with 'em like a toy/Then leave 'em like a little boy"). So, although "It's A Man's World," as Diana Trask sings, "He's got an awful lot of little boy in him/He wants to have his way." And little boys, of course, have to be mothered ("Baby me, baby, as only you can do").

One reason men need so much emotional support is that they are 21 not supposed to do anything so "unmanly" as to feel or express deep emotion themselves. Although men in country do a whole lot of crying, mostly boozy crying, they are nearly always ashamed of it and a little surprised at their own capacity for hurt. Johnny Cash sings of a man "six-foot-six" who weighed 235 lb. but who cried "like a whipped pup" and was "brought down to his knees" by "A Thing Called Love." It is implied that this is a very strange occurrence. The idea is stated as bluntly as possible by Waylon Jennings, when he warns his woman, "Don't mistake my tenderness for any sign of weakness in your man." All of this places the burden of emotion squarely on the women. "I will feel your loneliness and I will feel your pain," Jeannie C. Riley promises, and Jerry Wallace loves his woman, he tells her, because "If I hurt, it makes you cry."

The price men pay, however, for the questionable benefit of keeping 22 women at home to be mothers and emotional buffers for themselves is a great one, for in order to maintain some kind of balance, this arrangement also requires men to be daddies to their little girl—women, who can't take care of themselves financially or any other way. Dottie West sings an incredible song called "Everything's A Wreck (Since You're Gone)," in which a home turns into a disaster area when the man of the house leaves. The wife can't start the mower or unstop the sink or change a fuse or paint a room or even call a TV repairman so she can watch "Edge of Night." (My gut reaction was, "Christ, no wonder he left her—she's an idiot.")

In song after song by such singers as Charlie Rich and Charley Pride, 23 men express anxieties about whether they are materially successful enough to keep their women happy ("I don't know how to tell her I didn't get that raise in pay today/I know how much she wanted that dress in Baker's window"). The men age fast and wear themselves down trying to pay for the fancy clothes and new cars and houses they are convinced their wives want. George Jones thinks of giving up since he can't get ahead: "I work hard and I work overtime/And I'm still deep in dept."

Even if a man gets rich, however, there is no guarantee he can keep 24
his woman, for he also has the pressure of responsibility to satisfy her
sexuality. Tammy Wynette sings of having "satin sheets to lie on" and a
"big long Cadillac" and "tailor-mades upon her back," yet she is going to
leave her rich man for another because he doesn't "keep her satisfied."
For their part, the women have to learn all the tricks of catching and
holding a man, because the Other Woman, portrayed in country music as
Enemy Number One, is always out there waiting to steal him away
("She's a whole lot better lookin' than me and you/And she can do
things to a man you never dreamed a woman can do").

In short, both men and women in country music have a hard life, 25
made worse by the limited ways in which they see themselves and each
other. For comfort they retreat into their respective fantasy worlds. The
women "watch their stories on TV every day/And eat at McDonald's
once a week to get away," and read movie magazines ("They say to have
her hair done Liz flies all the way to France/And Jackie's seen in a discotheque doin' a brand new dance"). The men romanticize themselves as
"lovable losers, no-account boozers and honky-tonk heroes," studs who
value their "Low Down Freedom," who can love women and leave 'em
and be happy on the road as wandering gypsies. The prison records and
down-and-out images of such singers as Merle Haggard and Johnny Pay-
check and Johnny Cash (before he got on the religion bandwagon) appeal
to these fantasies.

The central male image in country, alas, is probably still the cowboy. 26
"It ain't easy bein' a cowboy in this day and time," say the album notes of
Waylon Jennings's *Honky-Tonk Heroes*. But Jennings ("tough and mean
and wild") manages to be one, and "the cowboy will live on just as long
as there is the sound of music." The authentic cowboys of the country-
music world, though, are the truck drivers, who represent a perfect fusion of the cowboy myth and working-class reality.

There are scores and scores of trucking songs and, in many of them, 27
it becomes obvious that the truckers are cowboys, trucks are their horses,
highways are the plains, truck stops are saloons and waitresses are saloon
girls. In song after song, the monotony and sheer hard work of being a
trucker are romanticized into something noble and exciting through stories of how trucks serve the nation, of how drivers help and rescue fellow travelers, of how they speed and manage to outsmart Smokey the
Bear (state police) with their CB radios and especially of how every waitress in every truck stop finds every driver absolutely irresistible. Although often the men remain loyal to their wives at home and don't take
advantage of this, they do seem to think about it quite a bit ("I could
have a lot of women, but I'm not that kind of a guy"). Narrating as a trucker's wife, Tammy Wynette sings, "Last night he called from Dallas/He
was havin' a beer at the Crystal Palace/And he said, honey, you won't be
alone for long." He's calling to tell her he's going to bring his "big ol' engine" home to her, even though there are "a million chicks" out there
who want to make love with him. And Tammy, as always, is patiently
waiting, waiting, waiting at home for her man in order to give him "everything he needs."

And so my journey through the world of men and women in country 28
music, inspired by Loretta Lynn's "The Pill," was entertaining and funny
and touching, but for a feminist it was pleasurable only in a masochistic
sort of way. Only the work of Lynn herself provided me with any comfort or any hope that things might someday be different. In an interview
I found Lynn, who was the model for Barbara Jean in Altman's *Nashville*,
to be a charming combination of fragility and spunk (in the movie,
Ronee Blakely conveyed the fragility and left out the spunk). She has unquestionably "paid her dues" as a woman, having married at 13, totally ignorant of sex, and having had four babies by age 17, plus twins several
years later ("If I'd known about the Pill back then, I'd've popped 'em like
popcorn"). By age 28 she was a grandmother. Nearly illiterate, she
worked for years as a domestic to help pay the rent, as she puts it, and
admits, "I had very few things bought from a store that wasn't from the
Salvation Army 'til way after I started singin'."

Now Lynn is a millionaire, albeit a very hard-working one, and she fi- 29
nally is beginning to feel strong eough to defy her manager-husband
("one of these kind that when he hollers he thinks you should jump").
One of her most remarkable songs, called "Two Mules Pull This Wagon,"
is about equality, of sorts, in marriage. A working-class wife and mother
tells her husband in no uncertain terms that she is sick of his not appreciating the fact that she works as hard at home as he does on his job: "I
wash and iron and cook and sew and find time for your naggin'/But you
seem to forget, big boy, that two mules pull this wagon."

Lynn sings many different kinds of songs, from gospel to auto- 30
biographical stories of being a coal miner's daughter in Butcher Hollow,
Kentucky, but my favorites, naturally, are her high-spirited declarations
of "what's good for the gander is good for the goose." A major theme in
her work is that women should be as free as men are sexually — she told
me that women should be able to do whatever men do outside of marriage, "because, as far as the Bible is concerned, it's just as wrong for one
as it is for the other." In a great many of her songs, such as "The Pill,"
she threatens to seek pleasure for herself if her man doesn't quit "step-
pin' out" on her ("Better listen to what I say now/'Cause there's gonna
come a day now/You'll have a hanky-panky woman on your hands").

If her man does come home for his sex, though, Lynn wants him so- 31
ber. Her "Don't Come Home Adrinkin' [With Lovin' on Your Mind]" is
a courageous if humorous statement of sexual self-respect bound to
touch the heart of any woman who's ever been to bed with a drunken
man. You may recall the besotted porter in *Macbeth* describing how
drink "provokes and unprovokes" lechery — "it provokes the desire, but it
takes away the performance." In "Your Squaw Is on the Warpath," Loretta Lynn expresses in this way: "That firewater that you've been drinkin'/Makes you feel bigger, but chief, you're shrinkin'." Interestingly,
"Don't Come Home Adrinkin'" is one of Lynn's songs that Tammy Wynette has also recorded, although in "Stand By Your Man" she seems to
imply that a woman should be passive and always ready to give her man
"something warm to come to."

But whatever else Loretta Lynn might be in her music, she is seldom 32 passive. While other women, as in all country music, are depicted only as devils and manstealers in her songs, she at least has the spunk to fight for her man instead of suffering quietly. "You ain't woman enough to take my man," she tells one rival and threatens another. "You better close your face and stay out of my way/If you don't want to go to Fist City." In "Rated X," though, she sings sympathetically of the plight of the divorced woman ("The women all look at you like you're bad/And the men all hope you are") and advises her to go ahead and live her life and "let 'em talk."

However bright a ray of hope Loretta Lynn may symbolize for 33 women (and therefore men) through country music, though, the final stanza of her song called "One's on the Way" unfortunately tells it like it is for now, that while cosmopolitan women fight for equal rights, while glossy magazines promote the latest decor and while birth control may revolutionize the world of tomorrow, still, today, in Topeka, where "the flies are abuzzin'," a woman's life revolves around her chores and her children, and the child that's on the way.

Obviously the state of relationships between men and women in the 34 world of country music, as in the world at large, is pretty depressing. "Hey, won't you play another somebody done somebody wrong song," sings B. J. Thomas, and indeed there are so many such songs because men and women, through the diminishing, rigid ways in which they see themselves and each other, are constantly "doing each other wrong" in quiet, terrible fashion. And that, my friends, is the *real* tearjerker.

Study Questions

1. In which paragraph does Nietzke get to the heart of her essay? Are the paragraphs that precede it necessary?
2. Comment on the use of quotation marks in this essay.
3. To what extent does Nietzke utilize various *rhetorical modes* in developing her thesis?
4. For whom is this essay written? What do the content and style tell you about its potential audience?

Eudora Welty
POWERHOUSE

Eudora Welty (1909–   ) was born in Jackson, Mississippi, where she now lives. She attended Mississippi State College for Women, the University of Wisconsin, and Columbia. Her first short stories were published in the 1930s in the *Southern Review;* her considerable skill resulted in Katherine Anne Porter's writing the introduction to *A Curtain of Green* (1941). Miss Welty's other books include *The Robber Bridegroom* (1942), *Delta Wedding* (1946), *The Ponder Heart* (1954), *Losing Battles* (1970), and *The Optimist's Daughter* (1972). She is a member of the National Institute of Arts and Letters and an honorary consultant in American letters of the Library of Congress.

Powerhouse is playing! He's here on tour, from the city — Pow- 1
erhouse and His Keyboard — Powerhouse and His Tasmanians — all the things he calls himself! There's no one in the world like him. You can't tell what he is. He looks Asiatic, monkey, Babylonian, Peruvian, fanatic, devil. He has pale gray eyes, heavy lids, maybe horny like a lizard's, but big glowing eyes when they're open. He has feet size twelve, stomping both together on either side of the pedals. He's not coal black — beverage-colored; looks like a preacher when his mouth is shut, but then it opens — vast and obscene. And his mouth is going every minute, like a monkey's when it looks for fleas. Improvising, coming upon a very light and childish melody, *smooch —* he loves it with his mouth. Is it possible that he could be this! When you have him there performing for you, that's what you feel. You know people on a stage — and people of a darker race — so likely to be marvelous, frightening.

This is a white dance. Powerhouse is not a show-off like the Harlem 2
boys — not drunk, not crazy, I think. He's in a trance; he's a person of joy, a fanatic. He listens as much as he performs — a look of hideous, powerful rapture on his face. Big arched eyebrows that never stop traveling. When he plays, he beats down piano and seat and wears them away. He is in motion every moment — what could be more obscene? There he is with his great head, big fat stomach, little round piston legs, and long yellow-sectioned strong fingers, at rest about the size of bananas. Of course you know how he sounds — you've heard him on records; but still you need to see him. He's going all the time, like skating around the skating rink or rowing a boat. It makes everybody crowd around, here in

this shadowless steel-trussed hall with the rose-like posters of Nelson Eddy and the testimonial for the mind-reading horse in handwriting magnified five hundred times.

Powerhouse is so monstrous he sends everybody into oblivion. 3 When any group, any performers, come to town, don't people always come out and hover near, leaning inward about them, to learn what it is? What is it? Listen. Remember how it was with the acrobats. Watch them carefully; hear the least word, especially what they say to one another, in another language; don't let them escape you — it's the only time for hallucination, the last time. They can't stay. They'll be somewhere else this time tomorrow.

Powerhouse has as much as possible done by signals. Everybody, 4 laughing as if to hide a weakness, will sooner or later hand him up a written request. Powerhouse reads each one, studying with a secret face: that is the face which looks like a mask, anybody's; there is a moment when he makes a decision. Then a light slides under his eyelids and he says, "Ninety-two!" or some combination of figures — never a name. Before a number the band is all frantic, misbehaving, pushing, like children in a schoolroom, and he is the teacher getting silence. His hands over the keys, he says sternly, "You-all ready? You-all ready to do some serious walking?" — waits — then, STAMP. Quiet. STAMP, for the second time. This is absolute. Then a set of rhythmic kicks against the floor to communicate the tempo. Then, "Oh Lord," say the distended eyes from beyond the boundary of the trumpets; "Hello and good-bye" — and they are all down the first note like a waterfall.

This note marks the end of any known discipline. Powerhouse seems 5 to abandon them all; he himself seems lost — down in the song — yelling up like somebody in a whirlpool — not guiding them, hailing them only. But he knows, really. He cries out, but he must know exactly. "Mercy! ... What I say! ... Yeah!" and then drifting, listening, — "Where that skinbeater?" (wanting drums), — and starting up and pouring it out in the greatest delight and brutality. On the sweet pieces, such a leer for everybody! He looks down so benevolently upon all the faces and whispers the lyrics, and if you could hear him at this moment on "Marie, the Dawn Is Breaking"! He's going up the keyboard with a few fingers in some very derogatory triplet routine; he gets higher and higher, and then he looks over the end of the piano, as if over a cliff. But not in a show-off way: the song makes him do it.

He loves the way they all play, too — all those next to him. The far 6 section of the band is all studious — wearing glasses, every one; they don't count. Only those playing around Powerhouse are the real ones. He has a bass fiddler from Vicksburg, black as pitch, named Valentine, who plays with his eyes shut and talking to himself, very young. Powerhouse has to keep encouraging him: "Go on, go on, give it up, bring it on out there!" When you heard him like that on records, did you know he was really pleading?

He calls Valentine out to take a solo. 7

"What you going to play?" Powerhouse looks out kindly from be- 8 hind the piano; he opens his mouth and shows his tongue, listening.

Valentine looks down, drawing against his instrument, and says with- 9
out a lip movement, "Honeysuckle Rose."

He has a clarinet player named Little Brother, and loves to listen to 10
anything he does. He'll smile and say, "Beautiful!" Little Brother takes a
step forward when he plays and stands at the very front, with the whites
of his eyes like fishes swimming. Once when he played a low note Powerhouse muttered in dirty praise, "He went clear downstairs to get that
one!"

After a long time, he holds up the number of fingers to tell the band 11
how many choruses still to go — usually five. He keeps his directions
down to signals.

It's a bad night outside. It's a white dance, and nobody dances, ex- 12
cept a few straggling jitterbugs and two elderly couples; everybody just
stands around the band and watches Powerhouse. Sometimes they steal
glances at one another. Of course, you know how it is with *them* — they
would play the same way, giving all they've got, for an audience of one.
. . . When somebody, no matter who, gives everything, it makes people
feel ashamed for him.

II

Late at night, they play the one waltz they will ever consent to play. By 13
request, "Pagan Love Song." Powerhouse's head rolls and sinks like a
weight between his waving shoulders. He groans and his fingers drag into
the keys heavily, holding on to the notes, retrieving. It is a sad song.

"You know what happened to me?" says Powerhouse.   14

Valentine hums a response, dreaming at the bass.   15

"I got a telegram my wife is dead," says Powerhouse, with wandering 16
fingers.

"Uh-huh?"   17

His mouth gathers and forms a barbarous O, while his fingers walk 18
up straight, unwillingly, three octaves.

"Gipsy? Why, how come her to die? Didn't you just phone her up in 19
the night last night long distance?"

"Telegram say — here the words: 'Your wife is dead.'" He puts four- 20
four over the three-four.

"Not but four words?" This is the drummer, an unpopular boy 21
named Scoot, a disbelieving maniac.

Powerhouse is shaking his vast cheeks. "What the hell was she trying 22
to do? What was she up to?

"What name has it got signed, if you got a telegram?" Scott is spit- 23
ting away with those wire brushes.

Little Brother, the clarinet player, who cannot now speak, glares and 24
tilts back.

"Uranus Knockwood is the name signed." Powerhouse lifts his eyes 25
open. "Ever heard of him?" A bubble shoots out on his lip, like a plate
on a counter.

Valentine is beating slowly on with his palm and scratching the 26

strings with his long blue nails. He is fond of a waltz; Powerhouse inter-
rupts him.

"I don't know him. Don't know who he is." Valentine shakes his 27
head with the closed eyes, like an old mop.

"Say it again." 28

"Uranus Knockwood." 29

"That ain't Lenox Avenue." 30

"It ain't Broadway." 31

"Ain't ever seen it wrote out in any print, even for horse-racing." 32

"Hell, that's on a star, boy, ain't it?" Crash of the cymbals. 33

"What the hell was she up to?" Powerhouse shudders. "Tell me, tell 34
me, tell me." He makes triplets, and begins a new chorus. He holds three
fingers up.

"You say you got a telegram." This is Valentine, patient and sleepy, 35
beginning again.

Powerhouse is elaborate. "Yas, the time I go out — go way downstairs 36
along a long *corridor* to where they put us. Coming back, steps out and
hands me a telegram: 'Your wife is dead.' "

"Gipsy?" The drummer is like a spider over his drums. 37

"Aaaaaa!" shouts Powerhouse, flinging out both powerful arms for 38
three whole beats to flex his muscles, then kneading a dough of bass
notes. His eyes glitter. He plays the piano like a drum sometimes — why
not?

"Gipsy? Such a dancer?" 39

"Why you don't hear it straight from your agent? Why it ain't come 40
from headquarters? What you been doing, getting telegrams in the *corridor,* signed nobody?"

They all laugh. End of that chorus. 41

"What time is it?" Powerhouse calls. "What the hell place is that? 42
Where is my watch and chain?"

"I hang it on you," whimpers Valentine. "It still there." 43

There it rides on Powerhouse's great stomach, down where he can 44
never see it.

"Sure did hear some clock striking twelve while ago. Must be *mid-* 45
night."

"It going to be intermission," Powerhouse declares, lifting up his fin- 46
ger with the signet ring.

He draws the chorus to an end. He pulls a big Northern hotel towel 47
out of the deep pocket in his vast, special-cut tux pants and pushes his
forehead into it.

"If she went and killed herself!" he says with a hidden face. "If she 48
up and jumped out that window!" He gets to his feet, turning vaguely,
wearing the towel on his head.

"Ha, ha!" 49

"Sheik, sheik!" 50

"She wouldn't do that." Little Brother sets down his clarinet like a 51
precious vase, and speaks. He still looks like an East Indian queen, implacable, divine, and full of snakes. "You ain't going to expect people doing
what they say over long distance."

"Come on!" roars Powerhouse. He is already at the back door; he 52
has pulled it wide open, and with a wild, gathered-up face is smelling the
terrible night.

III

Powerhouse, Valentine, Scoot, and Little Brother step outside into the 53
drenching rain.

"Well, they emptying buckets," says Powerhouse in a mollified voice. 54
On the street he holds his hands out and turns up the blanched palms
like sieves.

A hundred dark, ragged, silent, delighted Negroes have come around 55
from under the eaves of the hall, and follow wherever they go.

"Watch out, Little Brother, don't shrink," says Powerhouse. "You 56
just the right size now—clarinet don't suck you in. You got a dry throat,
Little Brother, you in the desert?" He reaches into the pocket and pulls
out a paper of mints. "Now hold 'em in your mouth—don't chew 'em. I
don't carry around nothing without limit."

"Go in that joint and have beer," says Scoot, and walks ahead.   57

"Beer? Beer? You know what beer is? What do they say is beer? 58
What's beer? Where I been?"

"Down yonder where it say World Cafe, that do?" They are across 59
the tracks now.

Valentine patters over and holds open a screen door warped like a 60
seashell, bitter in the wet, and they walk in, stained darker with the rain
and leaving footprints. Inside, sheltered dry smells stand like screens
around a table covered with a red-checkered cloth, in the centre of which
flies hang onto an obelisk-shaped ketchup bottle. The midnight walls are
checkered again with admonishing. "Not Responsible" signs and black-
figured smoky calendars. It is a waiting, silent, limp room. There is a
burnt-out-looking nickeldeon, and right beside it a long-necked wall instrument labeled "Business Phone, Don't Keep Talking." Circled phone
numbers are written up everywhere. There is a worn-out peacock feather
hanging by a thread to an old, thin, pink, exposed light bulb, where it
slowly turns around and around, whoever breathes.

A waitress watches.   61

"Come here, living statue, and get all this big order of beer we fixing 62
to give."

"Never seen you before anywhere." The waitress moves and comes 63
forward and slowly shows little gold leaves and tendrils over her teeth.
She shoves up her shoulders and breasts. "How I going to know who
you might be—robbers? Coming in out of the black night right at midnight, setting down so big at my table!"

"Boogers" says Powerhouse, his eyes opening lazily as in a cave.   64

The girl screams delicately with pleasure. Oh Lord, she likes talk and 65
scares.

"Where you going to find enough beer to put out on this-here 66
table?"

She runs to the kitchen with bent elbows and sliding steps.   67

"Here's a million nickels," says Powerhouse, pulling his hand out of 68
his pocket and sprinkling coins out, all but the last one, which he makes
vanish like a magician.

Valentine and Scott take the money over to the nickelodeon, which 69
is beginning to look as battered as a slot machine, and read all the names
of the records out loud.

"Whose 'Tuxedo Junction'?" asks Powerhouse.   70

"You know whose."   71

"Nickelodeon, I request you please to play 'Empty Bed Blues' and 72
let Bessie Smith sing."

Silence: they hold it, like a measure.   73

"Bring me all those nickels on back here," says Powerhouse. "*Look* at 74
that! What you tell me the name of this place?"

"White dance, week night, raining—Alligator, Mississippi—long ways 75
from home."

"Uh-huh."   76

"Sent for You Yesterday and Here You Come Today" plays.   77

The waitress, setting the tray of beer down on a back table, comes 78
up taut and apprehensive as a hen. "Says in the kitchen, back there putting their eyes to little hole peeping out, that you is Mr. Powerhouse.... They knows from a picture they seen."

"They seeing right tonight—that is him," says Little Brother.   79

"You him?"   80

"That is him in the flesh," says Scoot.   81

"Does you wish to touch him?" asks Valentine. "Because he don't 82
bite."

"You passing through?"   83

"Now you got everything right."   84

She waits like a drop, hands languishing together in front.   85

"Babe, ain't you going to bring the beer?"   86

She brings it, and goes behind the cash register and smiles, turning 87
different ways. The little fillet of gold in her mouth is gleaming.

"The Mississippi River's here," she says once.   88

Now all the watching Negroes press in gently and bright-eyed 89
through the door, as many as can get in. One is a little boy in a straw
sombrero which has been coated with aluminum paint all over. Powerhouse, Valentine, Scoot, and Little Brother drink beer, and their eyelids come together like curtains. The wall and the rain and the humble
beautiful waitress waiting on them and the other Negroes watching en-
close them.

"Listen!" whispers Powerhouse, looking into the ketchup bottle and 90
very slowly spreading his performer's hands over the damp wrinkling
cloth with the red squares. "How it is. My wife gets missing me. Gipsy.
She goes to the window. She looks out and sees you know what. Street.
Sign saying 'Hotel.' People walking. Somebody looks up. Old man. She
looks down, out the window. Well?... *Ssst! Plooey* What she do? Jump
out and bust her brains all over the world."

He opens his eyes.   91

"That's it," agrees Valentine. "You gets a telegram." 92

"Sure she misses you," Little Brother adds. 93

"Now, it's nighttime." How softly he tells them! "Sure. It's the night- 94
time. She say, 'What do I hear? Footsteps walking up the hall? That
him?' Footsteps go on off. It's not me. I'm in Alligator, Mississippi; she's
crazy. Shaking all over. Listens till her ears and all grow out like old
music-box horns, but still she can't hear a thing. She says, 'All right! I'll
jump out the window then.' Got on her nightgown. I know that nightgown, and she thinking there. Says, 'Ho hum, all right,' and jumps out
the window. Is she mad at me! Is she crazy! She don't leave *nothing* behind her!"

"Ya! Ha!" 95

"Brains and insides everywhere — Lord, Lord." 96

All the watching Negroes stir in their delight, and to their higher 97
delight he says affectionately, "Listen! Rats in here."

"That must be the way, Boss." 98

"Only, naw, Powerhouse, that ain't true. That sound too *bad*." 99

"Does? I even know who finds her," cries Powerhouse. "That no- 100
good pussy-footed crooning creeper, that creeper that follow around after
me, coming up like weeks behind me, following around after me everything I do and messing around on the trail I leave. Bets my numbers,
sings my songs, gets close to my agent like a betsy-bug — when I going
out he just coming in. I got him now! I got him spotted!"

"Know who he is?" 101

"Why, it that old Uranus Knockwood!" 102

"Ya! Ha!" 103

"Yeah, and he coming now, he going to find Gipsy. There he is, com- 104
ing around that corner, and Gipsy kadoodling down — oh-oh! Watch out!
Sssst-flooey! See, there she is in her little old nightgown, and her insides
and brains all scattered round."

A sigh fills the room. 105

"Hush about her brains. Hush about her insides." 106

"Ya! Ha! You talking about her brains and insides — old Uranus 107
Knockwood," says Powerhouse, "look down and say, 'Lord!' He say,
'Look here what I'm walking in!'"

They all burst into halloos of laughter. Powerhouse's face looks like 108
a big hot iron stove.

"Why, he picks her up and carries her off!" he says. 109

"Ya! Ha!" 110

"Carries her *back* around the corner ..." 111

"Oh, Powerhouse!" 112

"You know him." 113

"Uranus Knockwood!" 114

"Yeahhh!" 115

He take our wives when we gone!" 116

"He come in when we goes out!" 117

"Uh-huh!" 118

"He go out when we comes in!" 119

"Yeahhh!" 120

"He standing behind the door!"   121
"Old Uranus Knockwood!"   122
"You know him."   123
"Middle-size man."   124
"Wears a hat."   125
"That's him."   126
Everybody in the room moans with reassurance. The little boy in the   127
fine silver hat opens a paper and divides out a jelly roll among his follow-
ers.

And out of the breathless ring somebody moves forward like a slave,   128
leading a great logy Negro with bursting eyes, and says, "This-here is
Sugar-Stick Thompson, that dove down to the bottom of July Creek and
pulled up all those drownded white people fall out of a boat. Last summer—pulled up fourteen."

"Hello," says Powerhouse, turning and looking around at them all   129
with his great daring face until they nearly suffocate.

Sugar-Stick, their instrument cannot speak; he can only look back at   130
the others.

"Can't even swim. Done it by holding his breath," says the fellow   131
with the hero.

Powerhouse looks at him seekingly.   132
"I his half-brother," the fellow puts in.   133
They step back.   134
"Gipsy say," Powerhouse rumbles gently again, looking at *them,*   135
" 'What is the use? I'm gonna jump out so far—so far—Ssst—' "
"Don't, Boss, don't do it again," says Little Brother.   136
"It's awful," says the waitress. "I hates that Mr. Knockwoods. All that   137
the truth?"

"Want to see the telegram I got from him?" Powerhouse's hand goes   138
to the vast pocket.

"Now wait, now wait, Boss." They all watch him.   139
"It must be the real truth," says the waitress, sucking in her lower   140
lip, her liminous eyes turning sadly, seeking the windows.

"No, Babe, it ain't the truth." His eyebrow fly up and he begins to   141
whisper to her out of his vast oven mouth. His hand stays in his pocket.
"Truth is something worse—I ain't said what, yet. It's something hasn't
come to me, but I ain't saying it won't. And when it does, then want me
to tell you?" He sniffs all at once, his eyes come open and turn up, almost too far. He is dreamily smiling.

"Don't Boss. Don't, Powerhouse!"   142
"Yeahhh!"   143
"Oh!" The waitress screams.   144
"Go on, git out of here!" bellows Powerhouse, taking his hand out of   145
his pocket and clapping after her red dress.

The ring of watchers breaks and falls away.   146
"*Look* at that! Intermission is up," says Powerhouse.   147
He folds money under a glass, and after they go out Valentine leans   148
back in and drops a nickel in the nickelodeon behind them, and it lights

up and begins to play, and the feather dangles still. That was going to be
a Hawaiian piece.

"Take a telegram!" Powerhous shouts suddenly up into the rain. 149
"Take a answer. — Now what was that name?

They get a little tired.   150

"Uranus Knockwood."   151

"You ought to know."   152

"Yas? Spell it to me."   153

They spell it all the ways it could be spelled. It puts them in a won- 154
derful humor.

"Here's the answer. Here it is right here. 'What in the hell you talk- 155
ing about? Don't make any difference: I gotcha.' Name signed: Powerhouse."

"That going reach him, Powerhouse?" Valentine speaks in a maternal 156
voice.

"Yas, yas."   157

All hushing, following him up the dark street at a distance, like old 158
rained-on black ghosts, the Negroes are afraid they will die laughing.

Powerhouse throws back his vast head into the steaming rain, and a 159
look of hopeful desire seems to blow somehow like a vapor from his
own dilated nostrils over his face and bring a mist to his eyes.

"Reach him and come out the other side."   160

"That's it, Powerhouse, that's it. You got him now."   161

Powerhouse lets out a long sigh.   162

"But ain't you going back there to call up Gipsy long distance, the 163
way you did last night in that other place? I seen a telephone. ... Just to
see if she there at home?"

There is a measure of silence. That is one crazy drummer that's go- 164
ing to get his neck broken some day.

"No," growls Powerhouse. "No! How many thousand times tonight I 165
got to say *No?*"

He holds up his arm in the rain, like someone swearing.   166

"You sure-enough unroll your voice some night, it about reach up 167
yonder to her," says Little Brother, dismayed.

They go on up the street, shaking the rain off and on them like 168
birds.

IV

Back in the dance hall they play "San" (99). The jitterbugs stiffen and 169
start up like windmills stationed over the floor, and in their orbits (one
circle, another, a long stretch and zigzag) dance the elderly couples with
old smoothness, undisturbed and stately.

When Powerhouse first came back from intermission (probably full 170
of beer, everyone said) he got the band tuned up again and not by striking the piano keys for the pitch: he just opened his mouth and gave falsetto howls — in A, D, and so on. They tuned by him. Then he took hold

of the piano, like seeing it for the first time, and tested it for strength, hit it down in the bass, played an octave with his elbow, and opened it and examined its interior, and leaned on it with all his might. He played it for a few minutes with terrific force and got it under his power — then struck into something fragile and smiled. You couldn't remember any of the things he said — just inspired remarks that came out of his mouth like smoke.

They've requested "Somebody Loves Me," and he's already done   171
twelve or fourteen choruses, piling them up nobody knows how, and it will be a wonder if he ever gets through. Now and then he calls and shouts, "Somebody loves me! Somebody loves me — I wonder who!" His mouth gets to be nothing but a volcano when he gets to the end.

"Somebody loves me — I wonder who!   172

"Maybe — " He uses all his right hand on a trill.   173

"Maybe — " He pulls back his spread fingers and looks out upon the   174
place where he is. A vast, impersonal, and yet furious grimace transfigures his wet face.

" — Maybe it's you!"   175

Study Questions

1. Why does Welty use the *present tense?* How would *past tense* change the effect of her story?
2. The author is careful to tell the reader what songs Powerhouse and his combo play. Is there any significance in these particular songs insofar as they contribute to the development of the plot?
3. Is Uranus Knockwood real? Did Gipsy really die? Are the members of the combo merely improvising on a theme provided by Powerhouse?
4. What is humorous about, "Brains and insides everywhere — Lord, Lord" (paragraph 96)?
5. What is the reason for Powerhouse's "furious grimace"? What is the effect of the words *vast, impersonal.* and *transfigures* (paragraph 174)?
6. How accurate is Welty's use of black dialogue?

John Updike
THE CHASTE PLANET

John Updike (1932–   ) was born in Shillington, Pennsylvania, attended Harvard University, where he was an editor of the *Lampoon,*
and graduated *summa cum laude.* Later he attended the Ruskin School
of Drawing and Fine Art at Oxford. While still in his twenties, he
was an established figure in contemporary American letters. He has
been a recipient of the O. Henry Prize Story Award as well as a
Guggenheim fellowship, the Rosenthal Award of the National Institute of Arts and Letters, of which he is a member, and the National
Book Award. In the 1950s he was on the staff of the *New Yorker* as a
reporter for the "Talk of the Town" column. He also contributed
parodies, humorous essays, and witty verse to this magazine. Updike
has published verse, *Telephone Poles and Other Poems* (1963), and is
well-known for his short stories, many of which have appeared in collections such as *The Same Door* (1959) and *Pigeon Feathers* (1962).
However, his fame largely rests on his best-selling novels: *The Poor-
house Fair* (1959), *Rabbit Run* (1960), *The Centaur* (1963), *Of the
Farm* (1965), *Couples* (1968), *Bech: A Book* (1970), *Rabbit Redux*
(1971), *A Month of Sundays* (1975), and *Marry Me* (1976).

In 1999, space explorers discovered that within the warm, tur-   1
bulent, semi-liquid immensity of Jupiter a perfectly pleasant little planet
twirled, with argon skies and sparkling seas of molten beryllium. The
earthlings who first arrived on the shores of this new world were
shocked by the unabashed nakedness of the inhabitants. Not only were
the inhabitants naked—their bodies cylindrical, slightly curved, and longi-
tudinally ridged, like white pickles, with six toothpick-thin limbs stuck in
for purposes of locomotion, and a kind of tasselled seventh concentrating
the neural functions—but there appeared to be no sexual differentiation
among them. Indeed, there was none. Reproduction took place by an ab-
sentee process known as "budding," and the inhabitants of Minerva (so
the planet was dubbed, by a classics-minded official of the Sino-American
Space Agency) thought nothing of it. Evidently, wherever a mathematical
sufficiency of overlapping footsteps (or jabs, for their locomotion left
marks rather like those of ski poles in crusty snow) impressed the porous
soil of intermingled nickel and asbestos, a new pickleoid form slowly
sprouted, or "budded." Devoid both of parentage and of progenitive de-

sires, this new creature, when the three Minervan years (five of our weeks) of its maturation period brought it to full size (approximately eighteen of our inches), eagerly shook the nickel from its roots and assumed its place in the fruitful routines of agriculture, industry, trade, and government that on Minerva, as on Earth, superficially dominated life.

The erotic interests of the explorers and, as argon-breathing apparatus became perfected, of the ambassadors and investigators and mercantile colonists from our own planet occasioned amazement and misunderstanding among the Minervans. The early attempts at rape were scarcely more of a success than the later attempts, by some of the new world's economically marginal natives, to prostitute themselves. The lack of satisfactory contact, however, did not prevent the expatriate earthlings from falling in love with the Minervans, producing the usual debris of sonnets, sleepless nights, exhaustive letters, jealous fits, and supercharged dreams. The little pickle-shaped people, though no Pocahontas or Fayaway emerged among them to assuage the aliens' wonderful heat, were fascinated: How could the brief, mechanical event described (not so unlike, the scientists among them observed, the accidental preparation of their own ground for "budding") generate such giant expenditures of neural energy? "We live for love," they were assured. "Our spaceships, our skyscrapers, our stock markets are but deflections of this basic drive. Our clothes, our meals, our arts, our modes of transportation, even our wars, are made to serve the cause of love. An earthling infant takes in love with his first suck, and his dying gasp is clouded by this passion. All else is sham, disguise, and make-work." 2

The human colonies came to include females. This subspecies was softer and more bulbous, its aggressions more intricate and its aura more complacent; the Minervans never overcame their distaste for women, who seemed boneless and odorous and parasitic after the splendid first impression made by the early space explorers carapaced in flashing sheets of aluminum foil. These females even more strongly paid homage to the power of love: "For one true moment of it, a life is well lost. Give us love, or give us death. Our dying is but a fleck within the continuous, overarching supremacy of *eros*. Love moves the stars, which you cannot see. It moves the birds, which you do not have, to song." The Minervans were dumbfounded; they could imagine no force, no presence beneath their swirling, argon-bright skies, more absolute than death—for which the word in their language was the same as for "silence." 3

Then the human females, disagreeably and characteristically, would turn the tables of curiosity. "And you?" they would ask their little naked auditors. "What is it that makes *you* tick? Tell us. There must be something hidden, or else Freud was a local oracle. Tell us, what do you dream of, when your six eyes shut?" And a blue-green blush would steal over the warty, ridged, colorless epiderms of the Minervans, and they would titter and rustle like a patch of artichokes, and on their slender stiff limbs scamper away, and not emerge from their elaborate burrows, until the concealment of night—night, to earthling senses, as rapid and recurrent as the blinking of an eyelid. 4

The first clue arose from the sonnets the lovelorn spacemen used to 5 recite. Though the words, however translated, came out as nonsense, the recitation itself held the Minervans' interest, and seemed to excite them with its rhythms. Students of the pioneer journals also noted that, by more than one account, before prostitution was abandoned as unfeasible the would-be courtesans offered from out of the depths of themselves a shy, strangulated crooning, a sort of pitch-speech analogous to Chinese. Then robot televiewers were sufficiently miniaturized to maneuver through the Minervans' elaborate burrows. Among the dim, shaky images beamed back from underground (the static from the nickel was terrific) were some of rods arranged roughly in sequence of size, and of other rods, possibly hollow, flared at one end or laterally punctured. The televiewer had stumbled, it turned out, upon an unguarded brothel; the objects were, of course, crude Minervan equivalents of xylophones, trumpets, and flutes. The ultimate reaches of many private burrows contained similar objects, discreetly tucked where the newly budded would not find them, as well as proto-harps, quasi-violins, and certain constructions percussive in purpose. When the crawling televiewers were fitted with audio components, the domestic tunnels, and even some chambers of the commercial complexes, were revealed as teeming with a constant, furtive music — a concept for which the only Minervan word seemed to be the same as their word for "life."

Concurrent with these discoveries, a team of SASA alienists had persuaded a number of Minervans to submit to psychoanalysis. The pattern of dreamwork, with its load symbolization of ladders, valves, sine curves, and hollow, polished forms, as well as the subjects' tendency under drugs to deform their speech with melodious slippage, and the critical case of one Minervan (nicknamed by the psychiatric staff Dora) who suffered from the obsessive malady known as "humming," pointed to the same conclusion as the televiewers' visual evidence: the Minervans on their sexless, muffled planet lived for music, of which they had only the most primitive inkling. 6

In the exploitative rush that followed this insight, tons of nickel were traded for a song. Spies were enlisted in the Earth's service for the bribe of a plastic harmonica; entire cabinets and corporation boards were corrupted by the promise of a glimpse of a clarinet-fingering diagram, or by the playing of an old 78-r.p.m. "Muskrat Ramble." At the first public broadcast of a symphony, Brahms' Fourth in E Minor, the audience of Minervans went into convulsions of ecstasy as the strings yielded the theme to the oboe, and would doubtless have perished *en masse* had not the sound engineer mercifully lifted the needle and switched to the Fred Waring arrangement of "American Patrol." Even so, many Minervans, in that epoch of violated innocence, died of musical overdose, and many more wrote confessional articles, formed liberational political parties, and engaged, with sometimes disappointing results, in group listening. 7

What music meant to the Minervans, it was beyond the ken of earthlings to understand. That repetitive mix of thuds, squeaks, and tintinnabulations, an art so mechanical that Mozart could scribble off some of the best between billiard shots, seemed perhaps to them a vibration implying all vibrations, a resolution of the most inward, existential an- 8 tagonisms, a synthesizing interface—it has been suggested—between the nonconductivity of their asbestos earth and the high conductivity of their argon sky. They remained about the Minervans' musicality, even after it had been thoroughly exploited and rapaciously enlarged, something fastidious, balanced, and wary. A confused ancient myth gave music the resonance of the forbidden. In their Heaven, a place described as mercifully dark, music occurred without instruments, as it were inaudibly. An elderly Minervan, wishing to memorialize his life, would remember it almost exclusively in terms of music he had heard, or had made.

When the first Minervans were rocketed to Earth (an odyssey deserv-   9 ing its own epic: the outward flight through the thousands of miles of soupy hydrogen that comprised Jupiter's thick skull; the breakthrough into space and first sight of the stars, the black universe; the backward glance at the gaseous stripes and raging red spot dwindling behind them; the parabolic fall through the solar system, wherein the Minervans, dazzled by its brightness, mistook Venus for their destination, their invaders' home, instead of the watery brown sphere that expanded beneath them), the visitors were shocked by the ubiquitous public presence of music. Leaking from restaurant walls, beamed into airplanes as they landed and automobiles as they crashed, climbing from steeples, thundering from parade sounds, tingling through apartment walls, carried through the streets in small black boxes, violating even the peace of the desert and the forest, where drive-ins featured blue musical comedies, music at first overwhelmed, then delighted, then disgusted, and finally bored them. They removed the ear stopples that had initially guarded them from too keen a dose of pleasure; surfeit muffled them; they ceased to hear. The Minervans had discovered impotence.

Study Questions

1. Is this a short story or an essay? How do you know?
2. What is the target of the satire?
3. The first paragraph includes frequent *alliteration.* Can you determine when Updike deliberately uses alliterative words for their aural values?
4. Why does Updike use parentheses where he does? Does he use them with increasing or decreasing frequency as he advances his case?
5. Does the last sentence come as a surprise? Why or why not?

Marya Mannes

TELEVISION: THE SPLITTING IMAGE

Marya Mannes (1904–   ), magazine writer, editor, television personality, and lecturer, was born in New York City. She has received awards from, among others, the Federation of Jewish Women's Organizations and Theta Sigma Phi. Mannes had her own television program, "I Speak For Myself," in New York in the late 1950s, and since that time has been a frequent guest on other television programs. She has been feature editor of *Vogue* and *Glamor,* and writes for such magazines as *Esquire, Harper's* and *Book Week.* Her published works include a novel, *Message from a Stranger* (1948); a book of verse, *Subverse;* and several collections of essays, the latest being *Last Rights* (1974).

A bride who looks scarcely fourteen whispers, "Oh, Mom, 1 I'm so *happy!*" while a doting family adjust her gown and veil and a male voice croons softly, "A woman is a harder thing to be than a man. She has more feelings to feel." The mitigation of these excesses, it appears, is a feminine deodorant called Secret, which allows our bride to approach the altar with security as well as emotion.

Eddie Albert, a successful actor turned pitchman, bestows his atten- 2 tion on a lady with two suitcases, which prompt him to ask her whether she has been on a journey. "No," she says, or words to that effect, as she opens the suitcases. "My two boys bring back their soiled clothes every weekend from college for me to wash." And she goes into the familiar litany of grease, chocolate, mud, coffee, and fruit-juice stains, which presumably record the life of the average American male from two to fifty. Mr. Albert compliments her on this happy device to bring her boys home every week and hands her a box of Biz, because "Biz *is* better."

Two women with stony faces meet cart to cart in a supermarket as 3 one takes a jar of peanut butter off a shelf. When the other asks her in a voice of nitric acid why she takes that brand, the first snaps, "Because I'm choosy for my family!" The two then break into delighted smiles as Number Two makes Number One taste Jiffy for "mothers who are choosy."

If you have not come across these dramatic interludes, it is because 4 you are not home during the day and do not watch daytime television. It also means that your intestinal tract is spared from severe assaults, your credibility unstrained. Or, for that matter, you may look at commercials like these every day and manage either to ignore them or find nothing—given the fact of advertising—wrong with them. In that case, you are either so brainwashed or so innocent that you remain unaware of what this daily infusion may have done and is doing to an entire people as the long-accepted adjunct of free enterprise and support of "free" television.

"Given the fact" and "long-accepted" are the key words here. Only 5 socialists, communists, idealists (or the BBC) fail to realize that a mass television system cannot exist without the support of sponsors, that the massive cost of maintaining it as a free service cannot be met without the massive income from selling products. You have only to read of the unending struggle to provide financial support for public, noncommercial television for further evidence.

Besides, aren't commercials in the public interest? Don't they help 6 you choose what to buy? Don't they provide needed breaks from programing? Aren't many of them brilliantly done, and some of them funny? And now, with the new sexual freedom, all those gorgeous chicks with their shining hair and gleaming smiles? And if you didn't have commercials taking up a good part of each hour, how on earth would you find enough program material to fill the endless space/time void?

Tick off the yesses and what have you left? You have, I venture to 7 submit, these intangible but possibly high costs: the diminution of human worth, the infusion and hardening of social attitudes no longer valid or desirable, pervasive discontent, and psychic fragmentation.

Should anyone wonder why deception is not an included detriment, I 8 suggest that our public is so conditioned to promotion as a way of life, whether in art or politics or products, that elements of exaggeration or distortion are taken for granted. Nobody really believes that a certain shampoo will get a certain swain, or that an unclogged sinus can make a man a swinger. People are merely prepared to hope it will.

But the diminution of human worth is much more subtle and just as 9 pervasive. In the guise of what they consider comedy, the producers of television commercials have created a loathsome gallery of men and women patterned, presumably, on Mr. and Mrs. America. Women liberationists have a major target in the commercial image of woman flashed hourly and daily to the vast majority. There are, indeed, only four kinds of females in this relentless sales procession: the gorgeous teen-age swinger with bouncing locks; the young mother teaching her baby girl the right soap for skin care; the middle-aged housewife with a voice like a power saw; and the old lady with dentures and irregularity. All these women, to be sure, exist. But between the swinging sex object and the constipated granny there are millions of females never shown in commercials. These are—married or single—intelligent, sensitive women who bring charm to their homes, who work at jobs as well as lend grace to their marriage, who support themselves, who have talents or hobbies or commitments, or who are skilled at their professions.

To my knowledge, as a frequent if reluctant observer, I know of only 10 one woman on a commercial who has a job; a comic plumber using Comet. Funny, heh? Think of a dame with a plunger.

With this one representative of our labor force, which is well over 11 thirty million women, we are left with nothing but the full-time housewife in all her whining glory: obsessed with whiter wash, moister cakes, shinier floors, cleaner children, softer diapers, and greaseless fried chicken. In the rare instances when these ladies are not in the kitchen, at the washing machine, or waiting on hubby, they are buying beauty shops (fantasy, see?) to take home so that their hair will have more body. Or out at the supermarket being choosy.

If they were attractive in their obsessions, they might be bearable. 12 But they are not. They are pushy, loud-mouthed, stupid, and—of all things now—bereft of sexuality. Presumably, the argument in the tenets of advertising is that once a woman marries she changes overnight from plaything to floor-waxer.

To be fair, men make an equivalent transition in commercials. The 13 swinging male with the mod hair and the beautiful chick turns inevitably into the paunchy slob who chokes on his wife's cake. You will notice, however, that the voice urging the viewer to buy the product is nearly always male: gentle, wise, helpful, seductive. And the visible presence telling the housewife how to get shinier floors and whiter wash and lovelier hair is almost invariably a man: the Svengali in modern dress, the Trilby (if only she were!), his willing object.

Woman, in short, is consumer first and human being fourth. A wife 14 and mother who stays home all day buys a lot more than a woman who lives alone or who—married or single—has a job. The young girl hell-bent on marriage is the next most susceptible consumer. It is entirely understandable, then, that the potential buyers of detergents, foods, polishes, toothpastes, pills, and housewares are the housewives, and that the sex object spends most of *her* money on cosmetics, hair lotions, soaps, mouthwashes, and soft drinks.

Here we come, of course, to the youngest class of consumers, the 15 swinging teen-agers so beloved by advertisers keen on telling them (and us) that they've "got a lot to live, and Pepsi's got a lot to give." This affords a chance to show a squirming, leaping, jiggling group of beautiful kids having a very loud high on rock and—of all things—soda pop. One of commercial TV's most dubious achievements, in fact, is the reinforcement of the self-adulation characteristic of the young as a group.

As for the aging female citizen, the less shown of her the better. She 16 is useful for ailments, but since she buys very little of anything, not having a husband or any children to feed or house to keep, nor—of course—sex appeal to burnish, society and commercials have little place for her. The same is true, to be sure, of older men, who are handy for Bosses with Bad Breath or Doctors with Remedies. Yet, on the whole, men hold up better than women at any age—in life or on television. Lines on their faces are marks of distinction, while on women they are signatures of decay.

There is no question, in any case, that television commercials (and 17 many of the entertainment programs, notably the soap serials that are part of the selling package) reinforce, like an insistent drill, the assumption that a woman's only valid function is that of wife, mother, and servant of men: the inevitable sequel to her earlier function as sex object and swinger.

At a time when more and more women are at long last learning to 18 reject these assumptions as archaic and demeaning, and to grow into individual human beings with a wide option of lives to live, the sellers of the nation are bent upon reinforcing the ancient pattern. They know only too well that by beaming their message to the Consumer Queen they can justify her existence as the housebound Mrs. America: dumber than dumb, whiter than white.

The conditioning starts very early: with the girl child who wants the 19 skin Ivory soap has reputedly given her mother, with the nine-year-old who brings back a cake of Camay instead of the male deodorant her father wanted. (When she confesses that she bought it so she could be "feminine," her father hugs her, and, with the voice of a child-molester, whispers, "My little girl is growing up on me, huh.") And then, before long, comes the teen-aged bride who "has feelings to feel."

It is the little boys who dream of wings, in an airplane commercial; 20 who grow up (with fewer cavities) into the doers. Their little sisters turn into *Cosmopolitan* girls, who in turn become housewives furious that their neighbors' wash is cleaner than theirs.

There is good reason to suspect that this manic obsession with clean- 21 liness, fostered, quite naturally, by the giant soap and detergent interests, may bear some responsibility for the cultivated sloppiness of so many of the young in their clothing as well as in their chosen hideouts. The compulsive housewife who spends more time washing and vacuuming and polishing her possessions than communicating to, or stimulating her children creates a kind of sterility that the young would instinctively reject. The impeccably tidy home, the impeccably tidy lawn are—in a very real sense—unnatural and confining.

Yet the commercials confront us with broods of happy children, 22 some of whom—believe it or not—notice the new fresh smell their clean, white sweatshirts, exhale thanks to Mom's new "softener."

Some major advertisers, for that matter, can even cast a benign eye 23 on the population explosion. In another Biz commercial, the genial Eddie Albert surveys with surprise a long row of dirty clothes heaped before him by a young matron. She answers his natural query by telling him gaily they are the products of her brood of eleven "with one more to come!" she adds as the twelfth turns up. "That's great!" says Mr. Albert, curdling the soul of Planned Parenthood and the future of this planet.

Who are, one cannot help but ask, the writers who manage to com- 24 bine the sales of products with the selling-out of human dreams and dignity? Who people this cosmos of commercials with dolts and fools and shrews and narcissists? Who know so much about quirks and mannerisms and ailments and so little about life? So much about presumed wants and so little about crying needs?

Can women advertisers so demean their own sex? Or are there no 25
women in positions of decision high enough to see that their real selves
stand up?

Do they not know, these extremely clever creators of commercials, 26
what they could do for their audience even while they exploit and entertain them? How they could raise the levels of manners and attitudes
while they sell their wares? Or do they really share the worm's-eye view
of mass communication that sees, and addresses, only the lowest common
denominator?

It can be argued that commercials are taken too seriously, that their 27
function is merely to amuse, engage, and sell, and that they do this
brilliantly. If that were all to this wheedling of millions, well and good.
But it is not. There are two more fallouts from this chronic sales explosion that cannot be measured but that at least can be expected. One
has to do with the continual celebration of youth at the expense of maturity. In commercials only the young have access to beauty, sex, and joy
in life. What do older women feel, day after day, when love is the exclusive possession of a teenage girl with a bobbing mantle of hair? What
older man would not covet her in restless impotence?

The constant reminder of what is inaccessible must inevitably pro- 28
duce a subterranean but real discontent, just as the continual sight of
things and places beyond reach has eaten deeply into the ghetto soul. If
we are constantly presented with what we are not or cannot have, the
dislocation deepens, contentment vanishes, and frustration reigns. Even
for the substantially secure, there is always a better thing, a better way, to
buy. That none of these things makes a better life may be consciously acknowledged, but still the desire lodges in the spirit, nagging and pulling.

This kind of fragmentation works in potent ways above and beyond 29
the mere fact of program interruption, which is much of the time more
of a blessing than a curse, especially in those rare instances when the
commercial is deft and funny: the soft and subtle sell. Its overall curse,
due to the large number of commercials in each hour, is that it reduces
the attention span of a people already so conditioned to constant change
and distraction that they cannot tolerate continuity in print or on the air.

Specifically, commercial interruption is most damaging during that 10 30
percent of programing (a charitable estimate) most important to the mind
and spirit of a people: news and public affairs, and drama.

To many (and among these are network news producers), com- 31
mercials have no place or business during the vital process of informing
the public. There is something obscene about a newscaster pausing to introduce a deodorant or shampoo commercial between an airplane crash
and a body count. It is more than an interruption; it tends to reduce
news to a form of running entertainment, to smudge the edges of reality
by treating death or disaster or diplomacy on the same level as household appliances or a new gasoline.

The answer to this would presumably be to lump the commercials 32
before and after the news or public affairs broadcasts—an answer unpalatable, needless to say, to the sponsors who support them.

The same is doubly true of that most unprofitable sector of televi- 33 sion, the original play. Essential to any creative composition, whether drama, music, or dance, are mood and continuity, both inseparable from form and meaning. They are shattered by the periodic intrusion of commercials, which have become intolerable to the serious artists who have deserted commercial television in droves because the system allows them no real freedom or autonomy. The selling comes first, the creation must accommodate itself. It is the rare and admirable sponsor who restricts or fashions his commercials so as to provide a minimum of intrusion or damaging inappropriateness.

If all these assumptions and imponderables are true, as many suspect, 34 what is the answer or alleviation?

One is in the course of difficult emergence: the establishment of a 35 public television system sufficiently funded so that it can give a maximum number of people an alternate diet of pleasure, enlightenment, and stimulation free from commercial fragmentation. So far, for lack of funds to buy talent and equipment, this effort has been in terms of public attention a distinctly minor operation.

Even if public television should, hopefully, greatly increase its scope 36 and impact, it cannot in the nature of things and through long public conditioning equal the impact and reach the size of audience now tuned to commercial television.

Enormous amounts of time, money, and talent go into commercials. 37 Technically they are often brilliant and innovative, the product not only of the new skills and devices but of imaginative minds. A few of them are both funny and endearing. Who, for instance, will forget the miserable young man with the appalling cold, or the kids taught to use—as an initiation into manhood—a fork instead of a spoon with a certain spaghetti? Among the enlightened sponsors, moreover, are some who manage to combine an image of their corporation and their products with accuracy and restraint.

What has to happen to mass medium advertisers as a whole, and es- 38 pecially on TV, is a totally new approach to their function not only as sellers but as social influencers. They have the same obligation as the broadcast medium itself: not only to entertain but to reflect, not only to reflect but to enlarge public consciousness and human stature.

This may be a tall order, but it is a vital one at a time when Ameri- 39 cans have ceased to know who they are and where they are going, and when all the multiple forces acting upon them are daily diminishing their sense of their own value and purpose in life, when social upheaval and social fragmentation have destroyed old patterns, and when survival depends on new ones.

If we continue to see ourselves as the advertisers see us, we have no 40 place to go. Nor, I might add, has commercial broadcasting itself.

Study Questions

1. Explain the use of *splitting*.
2. What is the tone of this essay? How is it established?

3. How and why does Mannes use rhetorical questions?
4. Is there evidence that this article was based on research, or does it represent educated opinion?

Art Buchwald
LET'S SEE WHO SALUTES

Art Buchwald (1925–   ) was born in Mt. Vernon, New York, and attended the University of Southern California for three years. His sydicated column appears daily in hundreds of newspapers and has made him one of the most respected American humorists. His recent books include *And Then I Told the President* (1965), *The Establishment Is Alive and Well in Washington* (1969), *I Never Danced at the White House* (1973), and *I Am Not a Crook* (1974).

Have you ever wondered what would have happened if the 1 people who are in charge of television today were passing on the draft of the Declaration of Independence?

The scene is Philadelphia at WJULY TV. Several men are sitting 2 around holding copies of the Declaration.

Thomas Jefferson comes in nervously.   3

"Tommy," says the producer, "it's just great. I would say it was a 4 masterpiece."

"We love it, Tommy boy," the advertising agency man says. "It sings. 5 Lots of drama, and it holds your interest. There are a few things that have to be changed, but otherwise it stays intact."

"What's wrong with it?" Mr. Jefferson asks.   6

There's a pause. Everyone looks at the man from the network.   7

"Well, frankly, Tommy, it smacks of being a little anti-British. I 8 mean, we've got quite a few British listeners and something like this might bring in a lot of mail."

"Now don't get sore, Tommy boy," the agency man says. "You're the 9 best declaration of independence writer in the business. That's why we hired you. But our sponsor the Boston Tea Company is interested in selling tea, not independence. Mr. Cornwallis, the sponsor's representative, is here, and I think he has a few thoughts on the matter. Go ahead, Corney. Let's hear what you think."

From *Don't Forget to Write*, published by World Publishing Company, 1970. Reprinted with permission.

Mr. Cornwallis stands up. "Mr. Jefferson, all of us in this room want   10
this to be a whale of a document. I think we'll agree on that."

Everyone in the room nods his head.   11

"At the same time we feel—I think I can speak for everybody—that   12
we don't want to go over the heads of the mass of people who we hope
will buy our product. You use words like despotism, annihilation, migration, and tenure. Those are all egghead words and don't mean a damn
thing to the public. Now I like your stuff about 'Life, Liberty, and the
pursuit of Happiness.' They all tie in great with tea, particularly pursuit
of happiness, but it's the feeling of all of us that you're really getting into
controversial water when you start attacking the King of Britain."

Mr. Jefferson says, "But every word of it is true. I've got documen-   13
tary proof."

"Let me take a crack at it, Corney," the agency man says. "Look,   14
Tommy boy, it isn't a question of whether it's true or not. All of us here
know what a louse George can be. But I don't think the people want to
be reminded of it all the time. They have enough worries. They want escape. This thing has to be upbeat. If you remind people of all those taxes
George has laid on us, they're not going to go out and buy tea. They're
not going to go out and buy anything."

"Frankly," says the network man, "I have some strong objections on   15
different grounds. I know you didn't mean it this way, but the script
strikes me as pretty left-wing. I may have read the last paragraph wrong,
but it seems to me that you're calling for the overthrow of the present
government by force. The network could never allow anything like that."

"I'm sure Tommy didn't mean anything like that," the producer says.   16
"Tommy's just a strong writer. Maybe he got a little carried away with
himself. Suppose Tommy took out all references to the British and the
King. Suppose we said in a special preamble this Declaration of Independence had nothing to do with persons living or dead, and the whole thing
is fictitious. Wouldn't that solve it?"

Mr. Jefferson says, "Gentlemen, I was told to write a Declaration of   17
Independence. I discussed it with many people before I did the actual
writing. I've worked hard on this declaration—harder than I've worked
on anything in my life. You either take it or leave it as it is."

"We're sorry you feel that way about it, Tommy," the agency man   18
says. "We owe a responsibility to the sponsor. He's paying for it. We're
not in the business of offending people, British people or any other kind
of people. The truth is, the British are the biggest tea drinkers of anyone
in the colonies. We're not going to antagonize them with a document
like this. Isn't that so, Mr. Cornwallis?"

"Check—unless Mr. Jefferson changes it the way we want him to."   19

Mr. Jefferson grabs the Declaration and says, "Not for all the tea in   20
China," and exits.

The producer shakes his head. "I don't know, fellows. Maybe we've   21
made a mistake. We could at least have run it up a flagpole to see who
saluted."

"As far as I'm concerned," Mr. Cornwallis said, "the subject is closed.   22
Let's talk about an hour Western on the French and Indian War."

Study Questions

1. The real point of this essay is not directly stated in the opening question. What is the author trying to demonstrate?
2. What specific aspects of commercial television come under Buchwald's gun?
3. How does the language within the dialogue help characterize the speakers and reinforce the satire?
4. What is the effect of the nicknames for men like Jefferson and Cornwallis?
5. Does this essay require any other sort of conclusion?

Jerzy Kosinski
TV AS BABYSITTER

Jerzy Kosinski (1933–   ) was born in Poland and became a United States citizen in 1965. After earning graduate degrees in political science and history from the University of Lodz, he did postgraduate work at Columbia University. He has taught English at Wesleyan, Princeton, and Yale, and has been awarded both Ford and Guggenheim fellowships. His works have earned a National Book Award and an award from the American Academy of Arts and Letters. Kosinski published two books under the pseudonym of Joseph Novak; then under his real name he published, among others, *The Painted Bird* (1965), *Steps* (1968), *The Devil Tree* (1973), and *Cockpit* (1975.

With the advent of television, for the first time in history, all 1 aspects of animal and human life and death, of societal and individual behavior have been condensed on the average to a 19 inch diagonal screen and a 30 minute time slot. Television, a unique medium, claiming to be neither a reality nor art, has become reality for many of us, particularly for our children who are growing up in front of it.

Imagine a child watching this little world within which Presidents 2 and commoners walk; mice and lions, kissing lovers and dying soldiers, skyscrapers and dog houses, flowers and detergents, all are reduced to the same size, mixed together, given the same rank, and set in the same

Reprinted by permission of the author and the National Broadcasting Company, Inc. Broadcast on NBC's Comment Series on September 3, 1973.

screen to be looked at. The child watches this crowded world as he or she pleases, while eating, yawning, playing. What is the outlook of such a child? What does it expect of the world? What can it expect?

It expects all things to be as equal as on television: neither bad nor good, neither pleasant nor painful, neither real nor unreal, merely more or less interesting, merely in better or worse color. It is a world without rank. To such a child, the world is to be looked upon; it is there to entertain its viewer. If it doesn't one alters it by switching the channel.

In the little world of television, all is solved within its magic 30 minutes. In spite of the commercials, the wounded hero either rises or quickly dies, lovers marry or divorce, villains kill or are killed, addicts are cured, justice usually wins, and war ends. All problems are solved again this week, as they were last, and will be next week. Life on TV must be visual. This means single-faceted, revealed in a simple speech and through the obvious gesture. No matter how deep the mystery, the TV camera penetrates it.

Parents leave their children in front of the TV as baby-sitter, because many feel it is infinitely safer to watch the Sesame world of television than to walk in the world outside of their home. But is it?

Unlike television, the child grows older. One day it walks out of the TV room. Against his expectations, he's finally put in a classroom full of other children. A child who has been trained to control the little world, by changing the channels when he didn't like it, and was accustomed to maintaining the same distance between himself and the world televised for his amusement, is naturally threatened by the presence of people he cannot control. Others push him around, make faces at him, encroach. There is nothing he can do to stop them. He begins to feel that this real world unjustly limits him; it offers no channels to turn to.

In this unpredictable world of real life, there are no neatly ordered thirty-minute private slots. Here, in life, the child brought up only as a viewer must feel persecuted. Ironically, our industrial state offers few things that can be resolved in thirty minutes. But the teenager keeps expecting it; when it is not, he grows impatient, then adamant, disillusioned, oscillating between the revolutionary scream, "Now," and a political cool "So what?" He is easily depressed and beaten down. In this world of hierarchy and brutish competition, he is challenged and outranked by others. Soon he believes he is defective; instead of coming of age, he's coming apart. This breeding of weak and vulnerable beings knows few exceptions. The kids of the upper classes counteract TV by being involved with real events — real horses, real forests, real mountains — all things they have seen, touched, experienced. They have been given an opportunity to exist outside the television room. However, many middle class children, and almost all from poor families are at the mercy of five or six hours of television a day.

My own attitude toward television is neutral. The medium is here to stay. The danger is in the use we make of it. I'm involved with TV the way I am with the motor car. The motor car has been for us for over 50 years, but it is only recently that we learned its exhaust pollutes our very environment.

In today's atomized, disjointed technological society, with so little at- 9
tention paid to the individual, men need more than ever the inner
strength to carry them through the daily pressures. This strength should
come from early exposure to life at its most real—its sudden pleasures,
joys and abandonment; but also its violence, its lack of justice, its pain,
illness, and death. There is subtlety to man's fate which lies beyond the
thirteen channels.

Study Questions

1. How many meanings of *aspect* are applicable to its use in
   the first sentence?
2. How do the questions in the second paragraph serve to organize this essay?
3. Does Kosinski exaggerate? Note, for example, paragraph 6.
4. What is the thesis here? Is it stated in either of the last
   two paragraphs?
5. Does this article seem dated, in view of what the author
   asks of television in the last paragraph? Does TV now provide us with the sort of violence he requests?

Deems Taylor
THE MONSTER

Deems Taylor (1885–1966) was born in New York City and received an A.B. from New York University in 1906. His professional career began as a member of the editorial staff for various encyclopedias, house organs, and newspapers. For two years he was the associate editor for *Collier's Weekly*. His expertise in music resulted in his becoming intermission commentator for the New York Philharmonic Symphony broadcasts from 1936 to 1943. His own compositions include "Portrait of a Lady," "The King's Henchman," and "Christmas Overture." Among his books are *Of Men and Music* (1937), *The Well-Tempered Listener* (1940), *A Pictorial History of the Movies* (1943), *Music to My Ears* (1949), *Some Enchanted Evenings* (1953) and *The One-Track Mind* (1953).

He was an undersized little man, with a head too big for his 1
body — a sickly little man. His nerves were bad. He had skin trouble. It was agony for him to wear anything next to his skin coarser than silk. And he had delusions of grandeur.

He was a monster of conceit. Never for one minute did he look at 2
the world or at people, except in relation to himself. He was not only the most important person in the world, to himself; in his own eyes he was the only person who existed. He believed himself to be one of the greatest dramatists in the world, one of the greatest thinkers, and one of the greatest composers. To hear him talk he was Shakespeare, and Beethoven, and Plato, rolled into one. And you would have had no difficulty in hearing him talk. He was one of the most exhausting conversationalists that ever lived. An evening with him was an evening spent in listening to a monologue. Sometimes he was brilliant; sometimes he was maddeningly tiresome. But whether he was being brilliant or dull, he had one sole topic of conversation: himself. What *he* thought and what *he* did.

He had a mania for being in the right. The slightest hint of dis- 3
agreement, from anyone, on the most trivial point, was enough to set him off on a harangue that might last for hours, in which he proved himself right in so many ways, and with such exhausting volubility, that in the end his hearer, stunned and deafened, would agree with him, for the sake of peace.

It never occurred to him that he and his doing were not of the most 4
intense and fascinating interest to anyone with whom he came in contact.

He had theories about almost any subject under the sun, including vege-
tarianism, the drama, politics, and music; and in support of these theories
he wrote pamphlets, letters, books...thousands upon thousands of
words, hundreds and hundreds of pages. He not only wrote these things,
and published them—usually at somebody else's expense—but he would
sit and read them aloud, for hours, to his friends and his family.

He wrote operas; and no sooner did he have the synopsis of a story, 5
but he would invite—or rather summon—a crowd of his friends to his
house and read it aloud to them. Not for criticism. For applause. When
the complete poem was written, the friends had to come again, and hear
that read aloud. Then he would publish the poem, sometimes years before the music that went with it was written. He played the piano like a
composer, in the worst sense of what that implies, and he would sit down
at the piano before parties that included some of the finest pianists of his
time, and play for them, by the hour, his own music, needless to say. He
had a composer's voice. And he would invite eminent vocalists to his
house, and sing them his operas, taking all the parts.

He had the emotional stability of a six-year-old child. When he felt 6
out of sort, he would rave and stamp, or sink into suicidal gloom and talk
darkly of going to the East to end his days as a Buddhist monk. Ten
minutes later, when something pleased him, he would rush out of doors
and run around the garden, or jump up and down on the sofa, or stand
on his head. He could be grief-stricken over the death of a pet dog, and
he could be callous and heartless to a degree that would have made a Roman emperor shudder.

He was almost innocent of any sense of responsibility. Not only did 7
he seem incapable of supporting himself, but it never occurred to him
that he was under any obligation to do so. He was convinced that the
world owed him a living. In support of this belief, he borrowed money
from everybody who was good for a loan—men, women, friends, or
strangers. He wrote begging letters by the score, sometimes groveling
without shame, at others loftily offering his intended benefactor the privilege of contributing to his support, and being mortally offended if the recipient declined the honor. I have found no record of his ever paying or
repaying money to anyone who did not have a legal claim upon it.

What money he could lay his hands on he spent like an Indian rajah. 8
The mere prospect of a performance of one of his operas was enough to
set him running up bills amounting to ten times the amount of his prospective royalties. On an income that would reduce a more scrupulous
man to doing his own laundry, he would keep two servants. Without
enough money in his pocket to pay his rent, he would have the walls and
ceiling of his study lined with pink silk. No one will ever know—certainly he never knew—how much money he owed. We do know that his
greatest benefactor gave him 6,000 dollars to pay the most pressing of
his debts in one city, and a year later had to give him 16,000 dollars to
enable him to live in another city without being thrown into jail for debt.

He was equally unscrupulous in other ways. An endless procession 9
of women marches through his life. His first wife spent twenty years enduring and forgiving his infidelities. His second wife had been the wife of

his most devoted friend and admirer, from whom he stole her. And even while he was trying to persuade her to leave her first husband he was writing to a friend to inquire whether he could suggest some wealthy woman — *any* wealthy woman — whom he could marry for her money.

He was completely selfish in his other personal relationships. His lik- 10 ing for his friends was measured solely by the completeness of their devotion to him, or by their usefulness to him, whether financial or artistic. The minute they failed him — even by so much as refusing a dinner invitation — or began to lessen in usefulness, he cast them off without a second thought. At the end of his life he had exactly one friend left whom he had known even in middle age.

He had a genius for making enemies. He would insult a man who 11 disagreed with him about the weather. He would pull endless wires in order to meet some man who admired his work, and was able and anxious to be of use to him — and would proceed to make a mortal enemy of him with some idiotic and wholly uncalled-for exhibition of arrogance and bad manners. A character in one of his operas was a caricature of one of the most powerful music critics of his day. Not content with burlesquing him, he invited the critic to his house and read him the libretto aloud in front of his friends.

The name of this monster was Richard Wagner. Everything that I 12 have said about him you can find on record — in newspapers, in police reports, in the testimony of people who knew him, in his own letters, between the lines of his autobiography. And the curious thing about this record is that it doesn't matter in the least.

Because this undersized, sickly, disagreeable, fascinating little man 13 was right all the time. The joke was on us. He *was* one of the world's great dramatists; he *was* a great thinker; he *was* one of the most stupendous musical geniuses that, up to now, the world has ever seen. The world did owe him a living. People couldn't know those things at the time, I suppose; and yet to us, who know his music, it does seem as though they should have known. What if he did talk about himself all the time? If he talked about himself for twenty-four hours every day for the span of his life he would not have uttered half the number of words that other men have spoken and written about him since his death.

When you consider what he wrote — thirteen operas and music dra- 14 mas, eleven of them still holding the stage, eight of them unquestionably worth ranking among the world's great musico-dramatic masterpieces — when you listen to what he wrote, the debts and heartaches that people had to endure from him don't seem much of a price. Eduard Hanslick, the critic whom he caricatured in *Die Meistersinger* and who hated him ever after, now lives only because he was caricatured in *Die Meistersinger.* The women whose hearts he broke are long since dead: and the man who could never love anyone but himself has made them deathless atonement, I think, with *Tristan und Isolde.* Think of the luxury with which for a time, at least, fate rewarded Napoleon, the man who ruined France and looted Europe; and then perhaps you will agree that a few thousand dollars' worth of debts were not too heavy a price to pay for the *Ring* trilogy.

What if he was faithless to his friends and to his wives? He had one 15
mistress to whom he was faithful to the day of his death: music. Not for
a single moment did he ever compromise with what he believed, with
what he dreamed. There is not a line of his music that could have been
conceived by a little mind. Even when he is dull, or downright bad, he is
dull in the grand manner. There is a greatness about his worst mistakes.
Listening to his music, one does not forgive him for what he may or may
not have been. It is not a matter of forgiveness. It is a matter of being
dumb with wonder that his poor brain and body didn't burst under the
torment of the demon of creative energy that lived inside him, struggling,
clawing, scratching to be released; tearing, shrieking at him to write the
music that was in him. The miracle is that what he did in the little space
of seventy years could have been done at all, even by a great genius. Is it
any wonder that he had no time to be a man?

Study Questions

1. Why is the identification of the subject withheld until paragraph 12?
2. What is the point of this essay?
3. Does Taylor provide us with any clues to the sources for the information presented here?
4. Are the topic sentences explicit or implicit within paragraphs?
5. What is the effect of so many sentences begun with *he, his, it?*

Joan Didion
7000 ROMAINE, LOS ANGELES

Joan Didion (1934–   ) was born in Sacramento, California. She received a B.A. from the University of California in 1956. Her published books include *Run River* (1963), *Slouching Towards Bethelehem* (1968), *Play It as It Lays* (1970), and *A Book of Common Prayer* (1976). *Play It as It Lays* was filmed with Tony Perkins and Tuesday Weld starring. Didion has coauthored a number of screenplays, among them the Streisand version of *A Star Is Born*. Her work has appeared regularly in periodicals, among them *Vogue, Saturday Evening Post, National Review, Holiday, Harper's Bazaar,* and *Esquire.* Honors and awards include *Vogue's* Prix de Paris (1956) and the Bread Loaf Fellowship in Fiction (1965).

Seven thousand Romaine Street is in that part of Los Angeles 1
familiar to admirers of Raymond Chandler and Dashiell Hammett: the
underside of Hollywood, south of Sunset Boulevard, a middle-class slum
of "model studios" and warehouses and two-family bungalows. Because
Paramount and Columbia and Desilu and the Samuel Goldwyn studios
are nearby, many of the people who live around here have some tenuous
connection with the motion-picture industry. They once processed fan
photographs, say, or knew Jean Harlow's manicurist. 7000 Romaine looks
itself like a faded movie exterior, a pastel building with chipped *art moderne* detailing, the windows now either boarded or paned with chicken-
wire glass and, at the entrance, among the dusty oleander, a rubber mat
that reads WELCOME.

Actually no one is welcome, for 7000 Romaine belongs to Howard 2
Hughes, and the door is locked. That the Hughes "communications center" should lie here in the dull sunlight of Hammett-Chandler country is
one of those circumstances that satisfy one's suspicion that life is indeed
a scenario, for the Hughes empire has been in our time the only industrial complex in the world—involving, over the years, machinery manufacture, foreign oil-tool subsidiaries, a brewery, two airlines, immense
real-estate holdings, a major motion-picture studio, and an electronics and
missile operation—run by a man whose *modus operandi* most closely resembles that of a character in *The Big Sleep.*

As it happens, I live not far from 7000 Romaine, and I make a point 3

First appeared in the *Saturday Evening Post* under the title, "The Howard Hughes Underground." Reprinted with permission.

of driving past it every now and then, I suppose in the same spirit that Arthurian scholars visit the Cornish coast. I am interested in the folklore of Howard Hughes, in the way people react to him, in the terms they use when they talk about him. Let me give you an example. A few weeks ago I lunched with an old friend at the Beverly Hills Hotel. One of the other guests was a well-married woman in her thirties who had once been a Hughes contract starlet, and another was a costume designer who had worked on a lot of Hughes pictures and who still receives a weekly salary from 7000 Romaine, on the understanding that he work for no one else. He has done nothing but cash that weekly check for some years now. They sat there in the sun, the one-time starlet and the sometime costume designer for a man whose public appearances are now somewhat less frequent than those of The Shadow, and they talked about him. They wondered how he was and why he was devoting 1967 to buying up Las Vegas.

"You can't tell me it's like they say, that he bought the Desert Inn 4 just because the high rollers were coming in and they wouldn't let him keep the penthouse," the ex-starlet mused, fingering a diamond as big as the Ritz. "It must be part of some larger mission."

The phrase was exactly right. Anyone who skims the financial press 5 knows that Hughes never has business "transactions," or "negotiations"; he has "missions". His central mission, as *Fortune* once put it in a series of love letters, has always been "to preserve his power as the proprietor of the largest pool of industrial wealth still under the absolute control of a single individual." Nor does Hughes have business "associates"; he has only "adversaries." When the adversaries "appear to be" threatening his absolute control, Hughes "might or might not" take action. It is such phrases as "appear to be" and "might or might not," peculiar to business reportage involving Hughes, that suggested the special mood of a Hughes mission. And here is what the action might or might not be: Hughes might warn, at the critical moment, "You're holding a gun to my head." If there is one thing Hughes dislikes, it is a gun to his head (generally this means a request for an appearance, or a discussion of policy), and at least one president of T.W.A., a company which, as Hughes ran it, bore an operational similarity only to the government of Honduras, departed on this note.

The stories are endless, infinitely familiar, traded by the faithful like 6 baseball cards, fondled until they fray around the edges and blur into the apocryphal. There is the one about the barber, Eddie Alexander, who was paid handsomely to remain on "day and night standby" in case Hughes wanted a haircut. "Just checking, Eddie," Hughes once said when he called Alexander at two in the morning. "Just wanted to see if you were standing by." There was the time Convair wanted to sell Hughes 340 transports and Hughes insisted that, to insure "secrecy," the mission be discussed only between midnight and dawn, by flashlight, in the Palm Springs Municipal Dump. There was the evening when both Hughes and Greg Bautzer, then his lawyer, went incommunicado while, in the conference room of the Chemical Bank in New York, the money men waited to lend T.W.A. $165 million. There they were, $165 million in hand, the men from two of the country's biggest insurance companies and nine of its most powerful banks, all waiting, and it was 7 p.m. of the last day the deal could be made and the bankers found themselves talking by phone not to Hughes, not even to Bautzer, but to Bautzer's wife, the movie star Dana Wynter. "I hope he takes it in pennies," a Wall Street broker said when Hughes, six years later, sold T.W.A. for $546 million, "and drops it on his toes."

Then there are the more recent stories. Howard Hughes is en route 7 to Boston aboard the Super Chief with the Bel Air Patrol riding shotgun. Howard Hughes is in Peter Bent Brigham Hospital. Howard Hughes commandeers the fifth floor of the Boston Ritz. Howard Hughes is or is not buying 37 1/2 percent of Columbia Pictures through the Swiss Banque de Paris. Howard Hughes is ill. Howard Hughes is dead. No, Howard Hughes is in Las Vegas. Howard Hughes pays $13 million for the Desert Inn. $15 million for the Sands. Gives the State of Nevada $6 million for a medical school. Negotiates for ranches, Alamo Airways, the North Las Vegas Air Terminal, more ranches, the rest of the Strip. By July of 1967 Howard Hughes is the largest single landholder in Clark County, Nevada. "Howard likes Las Vegas," an acquaintance of Hughes's once explained, "because he likes to be able to find a restaurant open in case he wants a sandwich."

Why do we like those stories so? Why do we tell them over and 8 over? Why have we made a folk hero of a man who is the antithesis of all our official heroes, a haunted millionaire out of the West, trailing a legend of desperation and power and white sneakers? But then we have always done that. Our favorite people and our favorite stories become so not by any inherent virtue, but because they illustrate something deep in the grain, something unadmitted. Shoeless Joe Jackson, Warren Gamaliel Harding, the *Titanic: how the mighty are fallen.* Charles Lindbergh, Scott and Zelda Fitzgerald, Marilyn Monroe: *the beautiful and damned.* And Howard Hughes. That we have made a hero of Howard Hughes tells us something interesting about ourselves, something only dimly remembered, tells us that the secret point of money and power in America is neither the things that money can buy nor power for power's sake (Americans are uneasy with their possessions, guilty about power, all of which is difficult for Europeans to perceive because they are themselves so truly materialistic, so versed in the uses of power), but absolute personal freedom, mobility, privacy. It is the instinct which drove America to the Pacific, all through the nineteenth century, the desire to be able to find a restaurant open in case you want a sandwich, to be a free agent, live by one's own rules.

Of course we do not admit that. The instinct is socially suicidal, and 9 because we recognize that this is so we have developed workable ways of saying one thing and believing quite another. A long time ago, Lionel Trilling pointed out what he called "the fatal separation" between "the ideas of our educated liberal class and the deep places of the imagination." "I mean only," he wrote, "that our educated class has a ready if mild suspiciousness of the profit motive, a belief in progress, science, social legislation, planning and international cooperation. . . . Those beliefs do great credit to those who hold them. Yet it is a comment, if not on our beliefs then on our way of holding them, that not a single first-rate writer has emerged to deal with these ideas, and the emotions that are consonant with them, in a great literary way." Officially we admire men who exemplify those ideas. We admire the Adlai Stevenson character, the rational man, the enlightened man, the man not dependent upon the potentially psychopathic mode of action. Among rich men, we officially admire Paul Mellon, a socially responsible inheritor in the European mold. There has always been that divergence between our official and our unofficial heroes. It is impossible to think of Howard Hughes without seeing the apparently bottomless gulf between what we say we want and what we do want, between what we officially admire and secretly desire, between, in the largest sense, the people we marry and the people we love. In a nation which increasingly appears to prize social virtues, Howard Hughes remains not merely antisocial but grandly, brilliantly, surpassingly, asocial. He is the last private man, the dream we no longer admit.

Study Questions

1. Which words in the first paragraph reinforce the description of "that part of Los Angeles" as the underside or a slum?
2. Analyze the simile in paragraph 6, and comment on its appropriateness.
3. Suggest some of the sources from which Didion picked up "stories" about Hughes.
4. Show how the reader is moved from point to point so that the conclusion seems valid.
5. What do you learn about the author herself in this essay?

Daniel J. Boorstin
FROM HERO TO CELEBRITY

Daniel J. Boorstin (1914–   ) was born in Atlanta, Georgia. He graduated *summa cum laude* from Harvard in 1934 and became a Rhodes Scholar. He did postgraduate work in law at the Inner Temple in London and was awarded the Litt.D. by Cambridge University in 1967. He has taught at Swarthmore College, the University of Chicago, and the University of Rome, among others. His books include *The Mysterious Science of the Law* (1941), *The National Experience* (1965), *The Democratic Experience* (1973), and *Democracy and Its Discontents* (1974). He is currently the Librarian of Congress.

Our age has produced a new kind of eminence. This is as 1 characteristic of our culture and our century as was the divinity of Greek gods in the sixth century B.C. or the chivalry of knights and courtly lovers in the middle ages. It has not yet driven heroism, sainthood, or martyrdom completely out of our consciousness. But with every decade it overshadows them more. All older forms of greatness now survive only in the shadow of this new form. This new kind of eminence is "celebrity."

The word "celebrity" (from the Latin *celebritas* for "multitude" or 2 "fame" and *celeber* meaning "frequented," "populous," or "famous") originally meant not a person but a condition—as the Oxford English Dictionary says, "the condition of being much talked about; famousness, notoriety." In this sense its use dates from at least the early seventeenth century. Even then it had a weaker meaning than "fame" or "renown." Matthew Arnold, for example, remarked in the nineteenth century that while the philosopher Spinoza's followers had "celebrity," Spinoza himself had "fame."

For us, however, "celebrity" means primarily a person—"a person of 3 celebrity." This usage of the word significantly dates from the early years of the Graphic Revolution, the first example being about 1850. Emerson spoke of "the celebrities of wealth and fashion" (1848). Now American dictionaries define a celebrity as "a famous or well-publicized person."

The celebrity in the distinctive modern sense could not have existed 4 in any earlier age, or in America before the Graphic Revolution. *The celebrity is a person who is known for his well-knownness.*

His qualities—or rather his lack of qualities—illustrate our peculiar 5 problems. He is neither good nor bad, great nor petty. He is the human pseudo-event. He has been fabricated on purpose to satisfy our exaggerated expectations of human greatness. He is morally neutral. The product of no conspiracy, of no group promoting vice or emptiness, he is made by honest, industrious men of high professional ethics doing their job, "informing" and educating us. He is made by all of us who willingly read about him, who like to see him on television, who buy recordings of his voice, and talk about him to our friends. His relation to morality and even to reality is highly ambiguous. He is like the woman *in* an Elinor Glyn novel who describes another by saying, "She is like a figure in an Elinor Glyn novel."

The massive *Celebrity Register* (1959), compiled by Earl Blackwell and 6 Cleveland Amory, now gives us a well-documented definition of the word, illustrated by over 2,200 biographies. "We think we have a better yardstick than the *Social Register,* or *Who's Who,* or any such book," they explain. "Our point is that it is impossible to be accurate in listing a man's social standing—even if anyone cared; and it's impossible to list accurately the success or value of men; but you *can* judge a man as a celebrity—all you have to do is weigh his press clippings." The *Celebrity Register's* alphabetical order shows Mortimer Adler followed by Polly Adler, the Dalai Lama listed beside TV comedienne Dagmar, Dwight Eisenhower preceding Anita Ekberg, ex-president Herbert Hoover following ex-torch singer Libby Holman, Pope John XXIII coming after Mr. John the hat designer, and Bertrand Russell followed by Jane Russell. They are all celebrities. The well-knownness which they have in common overshadows everything else.

The advertising world has proved the market appeal of celebrities. In 7 trade jargon celebrities are "big names." Endorsement advertising not only uses celebrities; it helps make them. Anything that makes a well-known name still better known automatically raises its status as a celebrity. The old practice, well established before the nineteenth century, of declaring the prestige of a product by the phrase "By Appointment to His Majesty" was, of course, a kind of use of the testimonial endorsement. But the King was in fact a great person, one of illustrious lineage and with impressive actual and symbolic powers. The King was not a venal endorser, and he was likely to use only superior products. He was not a mere celebrity. For the test of celebrity is nothing more than well-knownness.

Studies of biographies in popular magazines suggest that editors, and 8 supposedly also readers, of such magazines not long ago shifted their attention away from the old-fashioned hero. From the person known for some serious achievement, they have turned their biographical interests to the new-fashioned celebrity. Of the subjects of biographical articles appearing in the *Saturday Evening Post* and the now-defunct *Collier's* in five sample years between 1901 and 1914, 74 per cent came from politics, business, and the professions. But after about 1922 well over half of them came from the world of entertainment. Even among the entertainers an ever decreasing proportion has come from the serious arts—literature, fine arts, music, dance and theater. An ever increasing proportion (in recent years nearly all) comes from the fields of light entertainment, sports, and the night club circuit. In the earlier period, say before World War I, the larger group includes figures like the President of the United States, a Senator, a State Governor, the Secretary of the Treasury, the banker J. P. Morgan, the railroad magnate James J. Hill, a pioneer in aviation, the inventor of the torpedo, a Negro educator, an immigrant scientist, an opera singer, a famous poet, and a popular fiction writer. By the 1940's the larger groups included figures like the boxer Jack Johnson, Clark Gable, Bobby Jones, the movie actresses Brenda Joyce and Brenda Marshall, William Powell, and the woman matador Conchita Cintron, the night club entertainer Adelaide Moffett, and the gorilla Toto. Some analysts say the shift is primarily the sign of a new focus of popular attention away from production and toward consumption. But this is oversubtle.

A simpler explanation is that the machinery of information has 9 brought into being a new substitute for the hero, whos is the celebrity, and whose main characteristic is his well-knownness. In the democracy of pseudo-events, anyone can become a celebrity, if only he can get into the news and stay there. Figures from the world of entertainment and sports are most apt to be well known. If they are successful enough, they actually overshadow the real figures they portray. George Arliss overshadowed Disraeli, Vivian Leigh overshadowed Scarlett O'Hara, Fess Parker overshadowed Davy Crockett. Since their stock in trade is their well-knownness, they are most apt to have energetic press agents keeping them in the public eye.

It is hardly surprising then that magazine and newspaper readers no 10 longer find the lives of their heroes instructive. Popular biographies can offer very little in the way of solid information. For the subjects are themselves mere figments of the media. If their lives are empty of drama or achievement, it is only as we might have expected, for they are not known for drama or achievement. They are celebrities. Their chief claim to fame is their fame itself. They are notorious for their notoriety. If this is puzzling or fantastic, if it is mere tautology, it is no more puzzling or fantastic or tautologous than much of the rest of our experience. Our experience tends more and more to become tautology — needless repetition of the same in different words and images. Perhaps what ails us is not so much a vice as a "nothingness." The vacuum of our experience is actually made emptier by our anxious straining with mechanical devices to fill it artificially. What is remarkable is not only that we manage to fill experience with so much emptiness, but that we manage to give the emptiness such appealing variety.

We can hear ourselves straining. "He's the greatest!" Our descrip- 11 tions of celebrities overflow with superlatives. In popular magazine biographies we learn that a Dr. Brinkley is the "best-advertised doctor in the United States"; an actor is the "luckiest man in the movies today"; a Ringling is "not only the greatest, but the first real showman in the Ringling family"; a general is "one of the best mathematicians this side of Einstein"; a columnist has "one of the strangest of courtships"; a statesman has "the world's most exciting job"; a sportsman is "the loudest and by all odds the most abusive"; a newsman is "one of the most consistently resentful men in the country"; a certain ex-King's mistress is "one of the unhappiest women that ever lived." But, despite the "supercolossal" on the label, the contents are very ordinary. The lives of celebrities which we like to read, as Leo Lowenthal remarks, are a mere catalogue of "hardships" and "breaks." These men and women are "the proved specimens of the average."

No longer external sources which fill us with purpose, these new- 12
model "heroes" are receptacles into which we pour our own purposelessness. They are nothing but ourselves seen in a magnifying mirror. Therefore the lives of entertainer-celebrities cannot extend our horizon. Celebrities populate our horizon with men and women we already know. Or, as an advertisement for the *Celebrity Register* cogently puts it, celebrities are "the 'names' who, once made by news, now make news by themselves." Celebrity is made by simple familiarity, induced and re-enforced by public means. The celebrity therefore is the perfect embodiment of tautology: the most familiar is the most familiar.

II

The hero was distinguished by his achievement; the celebrity by his im- 13
age or trademark. The hero created himself; the celebrity is created by the media. The hero was a big man; the celebrity is a big name.

Formerly, a public man needed a *private* secretary for a barrier be- 14
tween himself and the public. Nowadays he has a *press* secretary, to keep him properly in the public eye. Before the Graphic Revolution (and still in countries which have not undergone that revolution) it was a mark of solid distinction in a man or a family to keep out of the news. A lady of aristocratic pretensions was supposed to get her name in the papers only three times: when she was born, when she married, and when she died. Now the families who are Society are by definition those always appearing in the papers. The man of truly heroic stature was once supposed to be marked by scorn for publicity. He quietly relied on the power of his character or his achievement.

In the South, where the media developed more slowly than else- 15
where in the country, where cities appeared later, and where life was dominated by rural ways, the celebrity grew more slowly. The old-fashioned hero was romanticized. In this as in many other ways, the Confederate General Robert E. Lee was one of the last surviving American models of the older type. Among his many admirable qualities, Southern compatriots admired none more than his retirement from public view. He had the reputation for never having given a newspaper interview. He steadfastly refused to write his memoirs. "I should be trading on the blood of my men," he said. General George C. Marshall (1880–1959) is a more recent and more anachronistic example. He, too, shunned publicity and refused to write his memoirs, even while other generals were serializing theirs in the newspapers. But by his time, few people any longer

considered this reticence a virtue. His old-fashioned unwillingness to enter the publicity arena finally left him a victim of the slanders of Senator Joseph McCarthy and others.

The hero was born of time: his gestation required at least a genera-   16
tion. As the saying went, he had "stood the test of time." A maker of tradition, he was himself made by tradition. He grew over the generations as people found new virtues in him and attributed to him new exploits. Receding into the misty past he became more, and not less, heroic. It was not necessary that his face or figure have a sharp, well-delineated outline, nor that his life be footnoted. Of course there could not have been any photographs of him, and often there was not even a likeness. Men of the last century were more heroic than those of today; men of antiquity were still more heroic; and those prehistory became demigods. The hero was always somehow ranked among the ancients.

The celebrity, on the contrary, is always a contemporary. The hero is   17
made by folklore, sacred texts, and history books, but the celebrity is the creature of gossip, of public opinion, of magazines, newspapers, and the ephemeral images of movie and television screen. The passage of time, which creates and establishes the hero, destroys the celebrity. One is made, the other unmade, by repetition. The celebrity is born in the daily papers and never loses the mark of his fleeting origin.

The very agency which first makes the celebrity in the long run inev-   18
itably destroys him. He will be destroyed, as he was made, by publicity. The newspapers make him, and they unmake him — not by murder but by suffocation or starvation. No one is more forgotten than the last generation's celebrity. This fact explains the newspaper feature "Whatever Became Of . . .?" which amuses us by accounts of the present obscurity of former celebrities. One can always get a laugh by referring knowingly to the once-household names which have lost their celebrity in the last few decades: Mae Bush, William S. Hart, Clara Bow. A woman reveals her age by the celebrities she knows.

There is not even any tragedy in the celebrity's fall, for he is a man   19
returned to his proper anonymous station. The tragic hero, in Aristotle's familiar definition, was a man fallen from great estate, a great man with a tragic flaw. He had somehow become the victim of his own greatness. Yesterday's celebrity, however, is a commonplace man who has been fitted back into his proper commonplaceness not by any fault of his own, but by time itself.

The dead hero becomes immortal. He becomes more vital with the   20
passage of time. The celebrity even in his lifetime becomes passé: he passes out of the picture. The white glare of publicity, which first gave him his specious brilliance, soon melts him away. This was so even when the only vehicles of publicity were the magazine and the newspaper. Still more now with our vivid round-the-clock media, with radio and television. Now when it is possible, by bringing their voices and images daily into the living rooms, to make celebrities more quickly than ever before, they die more quickly than ever. This has been widely recognized by entertainment celebrities and politicians. President Franklin Delano Roosevelt was careful to space out his fireside chats so the citizenry would not

tire of him. Some comedians (for example, Jackie Gleason in the mid-1950's) have found that when they have weekly programs they reap quick and remunerative notoriety, but that they soon wear out their images. To extend their celebrity-lives, they offer their images more sparingly — once a month or once every two months instead of once a week.

There is a subtler difference between the personality of the hero and that of the celebrity. The figures in each of the two classes become assimilated to one another, but in two rather different ways. Heroes standing for greatness in the traditional mold tend to become colorless and cliche. The greatest heroes have the least distinctiveness of face or figure. We may show our reverence for them, as we do for God, by giving them beards. Yet we find it hard to imagine that Moses or Jesus could have had other special facial characteristics. The hero while being this idealized and generalized loses his individuality. The fact that George Washington is not a vivid personality actually helps him serve as the heroic Father of Our Country. Perhaps Emerson meant just this when he said that finally every great hero becomes a great bore. To be a great hero is actually to become lifeless; to become a face on a coin or a postage stamp. It is to become a Gilbert Stuart's Washington. Contemporaries, however, and the celebrities made of them, suffer from idiosyncrasy. They are too vivid, too individual to be polished into a symmetrical Greek statue. The Graphic Revolution, with its klieg lights on face and figure, makes the images of different men more distinctive. This itself disqualifies them from becoming heroes or demigods.   21

While heroes are assimilated to one another by the great simple virtues of their character, celebrities are diffentiated mainly by trivia of personality. To be known for your personality actually proves you a celebrity. Thus a synonym for "a celebrity" is "a personality." Entertainers, then, are best qualified to become celebrities because they are skilled in the marginal differentiation of their personalities. They succeed by skillfully distinguishing themselves from others essentially like them. They do this by minutiae of grimace, gesture, language, and voice. We identify Jimmy ("Schnozzola") Durante by his nose, Bob Hope by his fixed smile, Jack Benny by his stinginess, Jack Paar by his rudeness, Jackie Gleason by his waddle, Imogene Coca by her bangs.   22

With the mushroom-fertility of all pseudo-events, celebrities tend to breed more celebrities. They help make and celebrate and publicize one another. Being known primarily for their well-knownness, celebrities intensify their celebrity images simply by becoming widely known for relations among themselves. By a kind of symbiosis, celebrities live off one another. One becomes better known by being the habitual butt of another's jokes, by being another's paramour or ex-wife, by being the subject of another's gossip, or even by being ignored by another celebrity. Elizabeth Taylor's celebrity appeal has consisted less perhaps in her own talents as an actress than in her connections with other celebrities — Nick Hilton, Mike Todd, and Eddie Fisher. Arthur Miller, the playwright, became a "real" celebrity by his marriage to Marilyn Monroe. When we talk or read or write about celebrities, our emphasis on their marital relations and sexual habits, on their tastes in smoking, drinking, dress, sports   23 cars, and interior decoration is our desperate effort to distinguish among the indistinguishable. How can those commonplace people like us (who, by the grace of the media, happened to become celebrities) be made to seem more interesting or bolder than we are?

III

As other pseudo-events in our day tend to overshadow spontaneous   24 events, so celebrities (who are human pseudo-events) tend to overshadow heroes. They are more up-to-date, more nationally advertised, and more apt to have press agents. And there are far more of them. Celebrities die quickly but they are still more quickly replaced. Every year we experience a larger number than the year before.

Just as real events tend to be cast in the mold of pseudo-events, so in   25 our society heroes survive by acquiring the qualities of celebrities. The best-publicized seems the most authentic experience. If someone does a heroic deed in our time, all the machinery of public information — press, pulpit, radio, and television — soon transform him into a celebrity. If they cannot succeed in this, the would-be hero disappears from public view.

A dramatic, a tragic, example is the career of Charles A. Lingbergh.   26 He performed single-handed one of the heroic deeds of this century. His deed was heroic in the best epic mold. But he became degraded into a celebrity. He then ceased to symbolize the virtues to which his heroic deed gave him a proper claim. He became filled with emptiness; then he disappeared from view. How did this happen?

On May 21, 1927, Charles A. Lindbergh made the first nonstop solo   27 flight from Roosevelt Field, New York, to Le Bourget Air Field, Paris, in a monoplane, "The Spirit of St. Louis." This was plainly a heroic deed in the classic sense; it was a deed of valor — alone against the elements. In a dreary, unheroic decade Lindbergh's flight was a lightning flash of individual courage. Except for the fact of his flight, Lindbergh was a commonplace person. Twenty-five years old at the time, he had been born in Detroit and raised in Minnesota. He was not a great inventor or a leader of men. He was not extraordinarily intelligent, eloquent, or ingenious. Like many another young man in those years, he had a fanatical love of flying. The air was his element. There he showed superlative skill and extraordinary courage — even to foolhardiness.

He was an authentic hero. Yet this was not enough. Or perhaps it   28 was too much. For he was destined to be made into a mere celebrity; and he was to be the American celebrity par excellence. His rise and fall as a hero, his tribulations, his transformation, and his rise and decline as a celebrity are beautifully told in Kenneth S. Davis' biography.

Lindbergh himself had not failed to predict that his exploit would   29 put him in the news. Before leaving New York he had sold to *The New York Times* the exclusive story of his flight. A supposedly naive and diffident boy, on his arrival in Paris he was confronted by a crowd of newspaper reporters at a press conference in Ambassador Myron T. Herrick's residence. But he would not give out any statement until he had clearance from the *Times* representative. He had actually subscribed to a newspaper clipping service, the clippings to be sent to his mother, who was then teaching school in Minnesota. With uncanny foresight, however, he had limited his subscriptions to clippings to the value of $50. (This did not prevent the company, doubtless seeking publicity as well as money, from suing him for not paying them for clippings beyond the specified amount.) Otherwise he might have had to spend the rest of his life earning the money to pay for clippings about himself.

Lindbergh's newspaper success was unprecedented. The morning af- 30 ter his flight *The New York Times,* a model of journalistic sobriety, gave him the whole of its first five pages, except for a few ads on page five. Other papers gave as much or more. Radio commentators talked of him by the hour. But there was not much hard news available. The flight was a relatively simple operation, lasting only thirty-three and a half hours. Lindbergh had told reporters in Paris just about all there was to tell. During his twenty-five years he had led a relatively uneventful life. He had few quirks of face, of figure, or of personality; little was known about his character. Some young women called him "tall and handsome," but his physical averageness was striking. He was the boy next door. To tell about this young man on the day after his flight, the nation's newspapers used 25,000 tons of newsprint more than usual. In many places sales were two to five times normal, and might have been higher if the presses could have turned out more papers.

When Lindbergh returned to New York on June 13, 1927, *The New* 31 *York Times* gave its first sixteen pages the next morning almost exclusively to news about him. At the testimonial dinner in Lindbergh's honor at the Hotel Commodore (reputed to be the largest for an individual "in modern history") Charles Evans Hughes, former Secretary of State, and about to become Chief Justice of the United States, delivered an extravagant eulogy. With unwitting precision he characterized the American hero-turned-celebrity: "We measure heroes as we do ships, by their displacement. Colonel Lindbergh has displaced everything."

Lindbergh was by now the biggest human pseudo-event of modern 32 times. His achievement, actually because it had been accomplished so neatly and with such spectacular simplicity, offered little spontaneous news. The biggest news about Lindbergh was that he was such big news. Pseudo-events multiplied in more than the usual geometric progression, for Lindbergh's well-knownness was so sudden and so overwhelming. It was easy to make stories about what a big celebrity he was; how this youth, unknown a few days before, was now a household word; how he was received by Presidents and Kings and Bishops. There was little else one could say about him. Lindbergh's singularly impressive heroic deed was soon far overshadowed by his even more impressive publicity. If well-knownness made a celebrity, here was the greatest. Of course it was remarkable to fly the ocean by oneself, but far more remarkable thus to dominate the news. His stature as hero was nothing compared with his stature as celebrity. All the more because it had happened, literally, overnight.

A large proportion of the news soon consisted of stories of how 33

Lindbergh reacted to the "news" and to the publicity about himself. People focused their admiration on how admirably Lindbergh responded to publicity, how gracefully he accepted his role of celebrity. "Quickie" biographies appeared. These were little more than digests of newspaper accounts of the publicity jags during Lindbergh's ceremonial visits to the capitals of Europe and the United States. This was the celebrity after-life of the heroic Lindbergh. This was the tautology of celebrity.

During the next few years Lindbergh stayed in the public eye and re- 34 mained a celebrity primarily because of two events. One was his marriage on May 27, 1929, to the cultivated and pretty Anne Morrow, daughter of Dwight Morrow, a Morgan partner, then Ambassador to Mexico. Now it was "The Lone Eagle and His Mate." As a newlywed he was more than ever attractive raw material for news. The maudlin pseudo-events of romance were added to all the rest. His newsworthiness was revived. There was no escape. Undaunted newsmen, thwarted in efforts to secure interviews and lacking solid facts, now made columns of copy from Lindbergh's efforts to keep out of the news! Some newspapermen, lacking other material for speculation, cynically suggested that Lindbergh's attempts to dodge reporters were motivated by a devious plan to increase his news-interest. When Lindbergh said he would co-operate with sober, respectable papers, but not with others, those left out pyramided his rebuffs into more news than his own statements would have made.

The second event which kept Lindbergh alive as a celebrity was the 35 kidnaping of his infant son. This occurred at his new country house at Hopewell, New Jersey, on the night of March 1, 1932. For almost five years "Lindbergh" had been an empty receptacle into which news makers had poured their concoctions — saccharine, maudlin, legendary, slanderous, adulatory, or only fantastic. Now, when all other news-making possibilities seemed exhausted, his family was physically consumed. There was a good story in it. Here was "blood sacrifice," as Kenneth S. Davis calls it, to the gods of publicity. Since the case was never fully solved, despite the execution of the supposed kidnaper, no one can know whether the child would have been returned unharmed if the press and the public had behaved differently. But the press (with the collaboration of the bungling police) who had unwittingly destroyed real clues, then garnered and publicized innumerable false clues, and did nothing solid to help. They exploited Lindbergh's personal catastrophe with more than their usual energy.

In its way the kidnaping of Lindbergh's son was as spectacular as 36 Lindbergh's transatlantic flight. In neither case was there much hard news, but this did not prevent the filling of newspaper columns. City editors now gave orders for no space limit on the kidnaping story. "I can't think of any story that would compare with it," observed the general news manager of the United Press, "unless America should enter a war." Hearst's INS photo service assigned its whole staff. They chartered two ambulances which, with sirens screaming, shuttled between Hopewell and New York City carrying photographic equipment out to the Lindbergh estate, and on the way back to the city served as mobile darkrooms in which pictures were developed and printed for delivery on arrival. For on-the-spot reporting at Hopewell, INS had an additional five men with three automobiles. United Press had six men and three cars; the Associated Press had four men, two women, and four cars. By midnight of March 1 the New York *Daily News* had nine reporters at Hopewell, and three more arrived the next day; the New York *American* had a dozen (including William Randolph Hearst, Jr., the paper's president); the New York *Herald Tribune,* four; the New York *World-Telegram, The New York Times,* and the Philadelphia *Ledger,* each about ten. This was only a beginning.

The next day the press agreed to Lindbergh's request to stay off the 37 Hopewell grounds in order to encourage the kidnaper to return the child. The torrent of news did stop. Within twenty-four hours INS sent over its wires 50,000 words (enough to fill a small volume) about the crime, 30,000 words the following day, and for some time thereafter 10,000 or more words a day. The Associated Press and United Press served their subscribers just as well. Many papers gave the story the whole of the front page, plus inside carry-overs, for a full week. There were virtually no new facts available. Still the news poured forth—pseudo-events by the score—clues, rumors, local color features, and what the trade calls "think" pieces.

Soon there was almost nothing more to be done journalistically with 38 the crime itself. There was little more to be reported, invented, or conjectured. Interest then focused on a number of sub-dramas created largely by newsmen themselves. These were stories about how the original event was being reported, about the mix-up among the different police that had entered the case, and about who would or should be Lindbergh's spokesman to the press world and his go-between with the kidnaper. Much news interest still centered on what a big story all the news added up to, and on how Mr. and Mrs. Lindbergh reacted to the publicity.

At this point the prohibition era crime celebrities came into the picture. "Salvy" Spitale and Irving Bitz, New York speakeasy owners, briefly held the spotlight. They had been suggested by Morris Rosner, who, because he had underworld connections, soon became a kind of personal secretary to the Lindberghs. Spitale and Bitz earned headlines for their effort to make contact with the kidnapers, then suspected to be either the notorious Purple Gang of Detroit or Al Capone's mob in Chicago. The two go-betweens became big names, until Spitale bowed out, appropriately enough, at a press conference. There he explained: "If it was someone I knew, I'll be God-damned if I wouldn't name him. I been in touch all around, and I come to the conclusion that this one was pulled by an independent." Al Capone himself, more a celebrity than ever, since he was about to begin a Federal prison term for income-tax evasion, increased his own newsworthiness by trying to lend a hand. In an interview with the "serious" columnist Arthur Brisbane of the Hearst papers, Capone offered $10,000 for information leading to the recovery of the child unharmed and to the capture of the kidnapers. It was even hinted that to free Capone might help recover the child.

The case itself produced a spate of new celebrities, whose signifi- 40 cance no one quite understood but whose newsworthiness itself made them important. These included Colonel H. Norman Schwarzkopf, commander of the New Jersey State Police; Harry Wolf, Chief of Police in Hopewell; Betty Gow, the baby's nurse; Colonel Breckenridge, Lindbergh's personal counsel; Dr. J. F. ("Jafsie") Condon, a retired Bronx schoolteacher who was a volunteer go-between (he offered to add to the ransom money his own $1,000 life savings "so a loving mother may again have her child and Colonel Lindbergh may know that the American people are grateful for the honor bestowed on them by his pluck and daring"); John Hughes Curtis, a half-demented Norfolk, Virginia, boatbuilder, who pretended to reach the kidnapers; Gaston B. Means (author of *The Strange Death of President Harding*), later convicted of swindling Mrs. Evalyn Walsh McLean out of $104,000 by posing as a negotiator with the kidnapers; Violet Sharpe, a waitress in the Morrow home, who married the Morrow butler and who had had a date with a young man not her husband on the night of the kidnaping (she committed suicide on threat of being questioned by the police); and countless others.

Only a few years later the spotlight was turned off Lindbergh as sud- 41 denly as it had been turned on him. *The New York Times Index*—a thick volume published yearly which lists all references to a given subject in the pages of the newspaper during the previous twelve months—records this fact with statistical precision. Each volume of the index for the years 1927 to 1940 contains several columns of fine print merely itemizing the different news stories which referred to Lindbergh. The 1941 volume shows over three columns of such listings. Then suddenly the news stream dries up, first to a mere trickle, then to nothing at all. The total listings for all seventeen years from 1942 through 1958 amount to less than two columns—only about half that found in the single year 1941. In 1951 and 1958 there was not even a single mention of Lindbergh. In 1957 when the movie *The Spirit of St. Louis,* starring James Stewart, was released, it did poorly at the box office. A poll of the preview audiences showed that few viewers under forty years of age knew about Lindbergh.

A *New Yorker* cartoon gave the gist of the matter. A father and his 42 young son are leaving a movie house where they have just seen *The Spirit of St. Louis.* "If everyone thought what he did was so marvelous," the boy asks his father, "how come he never got famous?"

The hero thus died a celebrity's sudden death. In his fourteen years 43 he had already long outlasted the celebrity's usual life span. An incidental explanation of this quick demise of Charles A. Lindbergh was his response to the pressure to be "all-around." Democratic faith was not satisfied that its hero be only a dauntless flier. He had to become a scientist, an outspoken citizen, and a leader of men. His celebrity status unfortunately had persuaded him to become a public spokesman. When Lindbergh gave in to these temptations, he offended. But his offenses (unlike those, for example, of Al Capone and his henchmen, who used to be applauded when they took their seats in a ball park) were not in themselves dramatic or newsworthy enough to create a new notoriety. His pronouncements were dull, petulant, and vicious. He acquired a reputation as a pro-Nazi and a crude racist; he accepted a decoration from Hitler. Very soon the celebrity was being uncelebrated. The "Lindbergh Beacon" atop a Chicago skyscraper was renamed the "Palmolive Beacon," and high in the Colorado Rockies "Lindbergh Peak" was rechristened the noncommittal, "Lone Eagle Peak."

Study Questions

1. What basic method or rhetorical mode is used to organize this essay?
2. The first three paragraphs deal specifically with definition. In what sense is the whole essay an extended attempt to define *celebrity?*
3. How does parallel structure aid Boorstin in his comparison of heroes and celebrities?
4. Lindbergh is the only figure treated at length. Why? How does he suit Boorstin's needs in developing his case?
5. Does the conclusion imply more than its actually states?

John Simon

FROM FAKE HAPPY ENDINGS TO FAKE UNHAPPY ENDINGS

John Simon (1925–   ) was born in Yugoslavia in 1925. He attended Harvard University, where he received an A.B. (1946), A.M. (1948), and Ph.D. (1959). Although he has taught English and humanities at such schools as M.I.T., Bard College, and the University of Washington, professionally he is best known as a critic of film and theater. He has regularly contributed to the *Hudson Review, New Leader, Commonweal, Esquire,* and currently *New York.* Simon has received both Fulbright and Rockefeller grants. Among his books are *Acid Test* (1963), *Private Screenings* (1967), *Movies into Film* (1971), *Ingmar Bergman Directs* (1972), and *Uneasy Stages* and *Singularities* (both 1976).

Does the American cinema reflect accurately the society in 1 which we live? To answer this question for our day requires a brief retrospect. From the advent of the talkies (which, to my way of thinking, marked the beginning of film as a potentially mature art form) to somewhere in the sixties — it is hard to pinpoint the exact moment, if indeed there was one — the American cinema was a vast wish-fulfillment industry, the expression of collective self-delusion, self-gratification and self-censorship, and had, with very few exceptions, little or nothing to do with truth or art.

In a recent article, Arthur Miller quoted a useful statement about 2 America in the eighteen-forties from Alexis de Tocqueville: "The majority lives in the perpetual utterance of self-applause, and there are certain truths that the Americans can learn only from strangers or from experience." What prevailed in American films of the thirties, forties, and fifties was, above all else, the happy ending. So much so that several European languages coined a neologism, "happyend" — pronounced in these languages as *heppiend.* It meant a joyous resolution of complicated intrigues and overwhelming problems, allowing the hero and heroine to fall in the last shot, against all probability, into each other's arms and live, by implication, happily ever after.

What, more precisely, did this "happyend" mean, and how wide- 3 spread was it? There were, of course, movies that ostensibly ended sadly, with the death of the hero or heroine (significantly, much more seldom both). But even these were disguised *heppiends.* If the hero died, it was defending his country, or rescuing a child or dog from a fire—in the fulfillment of a heroic mission, or as expiation for previously committed sins. If the hero was a gangster, his death was both mandatory and expiatory, but, at the same time, brave and bought with the blood of numerous lawmen, so that whatever the dark, ambiguous satisfactions the film aroused in the audience's unconscious, the ostensible effect was still that of a happy ending. And if the heroine died, this usually meant that she, too, was paying some "debt to society," or gaining release from some intolerable sickness or marital impasse, or accomplishing something noble, with the implicit understanding that her guy would, after a suitable period of mourning, find solace in the embraces of some less complicated, more grass-roots American girl who, as often as not, was seen lurking about the film's periphery.

By far the most common, however, was the happyend pure and simple: 4 wedding bells, going off together, or just going into a clinch, with the final title, "The End," really meaning The Beginning of everything eternally blissful. It is hard to say which spectators were more benighted: those who believed that this is the way life is or could be, and therefore loved the picture; or those who knew better, but loved the picture anyway. Now it might be supposed that the representation of American life preceding the last shot, or last reel, was more or less accurate, and that only the ending was a compromise with convention. In some rare cases, this was indeed so; more often, however, the preceding events and characterizations were equally hoked up.   •

Yet before we go on, we must answer the question: What's wrong 5 with such a happy ending? Don't people fall in love, get married, and, in some cases, remain that way? Of course they do, but the emphasis in these films was nevertheless false. For the Hollywood *heppiend* always implied that once The Problem is licked—the war is over, the families are reconciled, the misunderstanding is cleared up, there is more money somehow—and licked it always was, the closing kiss ushered in a sempiternally sunny future. There was a way of ending European movies with men and women coming, or going on, together—take Fellini's "The White Sheik," Vigo's "L'Atalante," Bergman's "The Naked Night" (or, to descend a few notches, "The Baker's Wife," "Hobson's Choice," "Two Cents' Worth of Hope")—which would yet preclude the feeling of a cellophane-wrapped Ever After.

If we look back now at the major Hollywood movies in which harsh 6 truths might have been given believable utterance, we find almost invariably that some sort of fudging or a variant of the happy ending disqualifies the entire film in which it occurs. Typical is Billy Wilder's "The Lost Weekend," with its totally unconvincing last-reel regeneration of the alcoholic hero, and the prospect of bliss with his patient fiancee. Even more revealing, perhaps, is another Wilder film, "Ace in the Hole," where the hero-villain's improbable death at the last minute leaves us with a taste of quasi-divine retribution, rather than general greed and corruption, in our mouths. Still more typical is Kubrick's "Paths of Glory," where a bitter view of mankind (mind you, as a safeguard, the scene is France, and the time, World War I) is glossed over by a last sequence reeking with redemptive fellow feeling. Even when a milieu is truly sordid, as in Hawk's "The Big Sleep," the sordidness is nevertheless glamorous, and the film's outcome happy. When a film was both vaguely realistic and less than sunny in its ending, there was always some way of sugar-coating the pill: The characters, after all, were or became criminals ("Dead End," "The Asphalt Jungle"), the deaths were a kind of *Liebestod* ("Duel in the Sun," "We Were Strangers" and, even in its more naturalistic way, "You Only Live Once"), or the whole thing was, under a mildly realistic veneer, just a tear-jerker, like all the so-called women's films.

The nearest thing to frankness about the way we lived was to be 7 found in certain comedies. So, for instance, in Hawks's "His Girl Friday" and Joseph Mankiewicz's "All About Eve," both of which substitute for the happy ending, not exactly an unhappy one, but an ominous note; yet the warning is lost for all but the most discerning viewers in clouds of merriment or a haze of enviable opulence. Even the one unquestionably great film that came out of Hollywood in the period under discussion, Welles's "Citizen Kane," has its version of a bittersweetly gratifying ending: the revelation that Rosebud was the name of Kane's childhood sled — that, in other words, the tough, mean old man recalled on his deathbed his former innocence. And Chaplin's main social-protest film, "Modern Times," ends with hero and heroine walking contentedly into the promise of a sunrise. Later, in his very overrated film "Monsieur Verdoux," Chaplin did have the murderer-hero die, a victim of social hypocrisy. But the feebleness of the film — particularly in its sentimental and pretentious homilies — militates against its efficacy.

What it all means is that America was the home of a profound, un- 8 shakable optimism, a country whose worst problems were the Depression and World War II, the former not lasting all that long, and the latter ending in victory without enemy action reaching American families and soil. This optimism combined with puritanism to create a Production Code that kept even moderately seamy or slightly erotic aspects of daily life nicely out of the pictures, and enforced a kind of official innocence and hopefulness that most Americans managed to harbor despite such slight setbacks as an occasional Teapot Dome scandal or Sacco-Vanzetti affair. Officially, then, there was no anti-Semitism, no black ghetto or discrimination against Negroes (the best American antilynching film, "Fury," was made by a German, Fritz Lang, concerned a white victim, and ended happily), and if dire poverty did exist in such a film as "The Grapes of Wrath," John Ford and Nunnally Johnson, the director and scenarist, nevertheless substituted a fairly positive ending for Steinbeck's apocalyptic and catastrophic one.

If it was not exactly a "perpetual utterance of self-applause," in 9 Tocqueville's phrase, it was yet a representation, by and large, not of American society, but of that society as it wanted to see itself, or as the studio bosses wanted to see it. But these moguls were men of the people, and their vision was geared to the box office and derived from the popular novel's infantile insistence on chastity of action and utterance, fascination with wickedness (but with the wicked always punished in the end, while virtue triumphs) and a naive faith in one's country and those who run it under God.

This was the view of America and of life that was first dented by the 10 films of the sixties, and that the films of the seventies have made great gashes in. What happened was, in Tocquevillian terms, learning from "strangers"—the great, exemplary films of Europe and, later, Japan; and from "experience"—the unholy trio of Vietnam, Watergate and Nixon: three scourges almost mighty enough to educate America out of its false security and genuine naiveté. And there was more: racial unrest and black militancy, the series of political assassinations, and the new economic and foreign-policy crises. Just as the dollar no longer bought everything throughout the world at bargain-basement prices, so a rumble from the Pentagon or White House no longer made foreign governments bow low or fall. And when American intervention had its way—as in certain Latin countries—large segments of our population greeted this not with cheers but with catcalls.

So, like other nations before it, America came of age through suffer- 11 ing, through grim rites of passage. The movies, inevitably, began to echo the change. Being, in the main, a popular rather than an elite art form, film does not lead and shape public opinion the way great writers and thinkers have led and influenced (usually post-humously) their readers. Yet, as a popular genre, film cannot afford to lose touch with the hopes and fears, the needs and awareness of its clientele. If the country has had a rude awakening, rude awakenings of one kind or another are what the movies will purvey.

But there's the catch: of one kind or another. The trouble with rude 12 awakenings in a popular medium is that they are apt to be more rude than awakening, or, in other words, excessively, indiscriminately, crudely rude. They end up peddling impacts rather than ideas, effects rather than causes of even truthful observations. The most obvious examples of this are the black-exploitation, political-paranoia and disaster films. Yes, there is a black revolution of sorts going on; so the black-exploitation film panders to the militants and their white partisans by showing black superman outwitting and beating the daylights out of white-power figures, right and left. Yes, there has been a string of political assassinations of a horrible and perhaps not wholly solved sort; so we have films like "Executive Action" and "The Parallax View," with conspiracies turning up under every bed, crawling out from behind the doors of every seemingly respectable business enterprise. And a film like "The Conversation" suggests that the country has been transformed into two camps, the buggers and the bugged, with the additional horror that the worm, or bug, turns, and that the spied-upon may be the sinister manipulators of the duped spies.

And yes, we have now had our share of great military, political and 13 social disasters. But there have been few if any story films about Vietnam, for example, the earliest of these debacles, and the black problem has more often than not been treated with ludicrous oversimplification. Even the few available documentaries on these subjects have done very poorly or had difficulties in getting released at all. What we do get, however, are disaster films like "The Poseidon Adventure," "Airport 75," "Juggernaut," "Earthquake" and "The Towering Inferno." Here we have the climate of calamity without any troublesome consequences: This may be harrowing, but it is not the sort of thing that might involve the whole nation, let alone, God forbid, us. But in the unlikely event that it should befall us, we need only comport ourselves like Paul Newman and Steve McQueen, and all will end well — at least for us.

More interesting (sociologically — we are not dealing with art here) than any of these are the neo-Fascist films, a bloody wave of which has lately been washing over our screens. Certainly, there has always been much violence in American movies, but of a simplistic, fairy-tale sort: There were the good guys — cowboys, cops, the U.S. Cavalry, G.I.'s, G-men, T-men, etc. — in short, Us; and the bad guys — Indians, gangsters, Krauts, Japs, Commies foreign and domestic — in short, Them. When, in the first part of the movie, some of Us got it, it may have been grim but, thanks to the Production Code, not excessively gory. And when, toward the end, all of Them got it from Us, it was brutal but just, and quietly cleansing and uplifting.

The good old days? Not at all: lying, dishonest, dumb old days, simple-minded and stultifying and bourgeois-reactionary, enshrining, among other things, racism, xenophobia and smugly imbecile belief in American superiority and infallibility. But today's permissive equivalent is uglier and gorier, with only one dubious gain: There is now a good dose of self-hatred mixed in with the "righteous" violence. In today's movies, Americans have become as beastly as the rest, or even beastlier, yesterday's Us having become today's Them, and vice versa. This might, in its equally simplistic way, have some transitional value as a corrective, but, in the long run, as we shall see, it is just as sterile as what went before. In any case, the old cinematic dishonesty has not died out, either; it is alive and well at its new address: television.

In these movies of the new violence — just as in the movies of the new sexuality — sheer quantity, however spectacular, is not the most significant feature. True, the enormous intensification of violence may dull one's sensitivity to the meaning of cruelty and pain; but it is also possible that to people capable of some kind of thought, saturation with violence may eventually bring about boredom and revulsion. What is much more interesting is the neo-Fascism behind many of these films, for example (to take only a handful of the best known ones) "Dirty Harry," the "Billy Jack" films, "Walking Tall," the Sam Peckinpah films culminating in "Bring Me the Head of Alfredo Garcia," and Death Wish." The Fascism here consists of the notion that order comes only through strength, superior armed strength, and that only when the right-minded individual virtuously kills off a number of vicious opponents does social, political and even sexual sanity reassert itself.

In the more ingenious and insidious films — like "Dirty Harry," "Death Wish" and "Straw Dogs" — the idea is that the powers of law enforcement are corrupted by wishy-washy liberalism and misguided humanitarianism, and only when the hero realizes that creeps are creeps and fit only for instant extermination by himself does goodness come into its own. This is a kind of Fascism from above, from a relatively sophisticated source, which exploits the frustrated, exacerbated temper of the times by peddling the concept that leniency and scruples are the problem and Every Man His Own Gunman the solution.

Meanwhile, the more primitive, populist films display a Fascism from below. Here the enemy is direct and obvious corruption in high places, the System, Them, and the Fascist-hero is not the member of a privileged class (city planner in "Death Wish," professor of mathematics in "Straw Dogs") but some plain and simple fellow who is elected sheriff ("Walking Tall") or mysterious, half-Indian outcast ("Billy Jack"), who helps the underdogs everywhere. In either type of neo-Fascist film, the hero must fight more or less single-handedly, because even among Us most people are corrupt, except perhaps Indians, school children and an occasional golden-hearted whore. In the rare case that such a hero is finally defeated ("Alfredo Garcia"), he at least drags half the assembled powers of darkness down with him.

The image of the person who gets it in the end has changed, too. There was considerable sympathy for the Cagney-Bogart gangster—though nothing so subtle as the portrayal of the psychopath and other criminals in "M," a European film by Fritz Lang. In "Dirty Harry," the villain is simply a vicious pervert, a mad dog; in "Death Wish," the villains are muggers who will kill and rape as well, but have no further dimensions whatsoever; in the "Billy Jack" films, the heavy is the Establishment, a tentacular, many-headed monster with, however, less than one brain.

The effect of these neo-Fascist films is to elicit a curious, unholy participation from the audience. When the heroes of films like "The French Connection," "Straw Dogs," "Death Wish," "Freebie and the Bean" kill or manhandle their victims, a great glee overcomes the spectators (just as in the black-exploitation films when "whitey" gets his): They laugh, cheer, applaud, sometimes even give standing ovations. Somehow the implication is that, in an indiscriminately vicious world, the only release and relief come from beating up or killing, from taking the law into one's own hands and becoming Superman, Superblack, Super-whatever. In the old days, it was the victory of the forces of right over those of wrong, even if right was represented mainly by a solitary hero; now, however, it is I (or my alter ego) against everyone else—Them, Us, the whole kit and kaboodle. It is impotence suddenly becoming potent through bloodletting: Every mugger killed by Charles Bronson is to the depressed audience an orgasm, a social orgasm rather than a sexual one, and made all the sweeter by restoring potency to the impotent.

But the powerless can also be indulged in their impotence, and there is also a cinema of unbeatable darkness, of masochism rather than sadism. It peddles simplistic defeatism just as the old movies peddled idiotic optimism. In film after film—"The French Connection," "McCabe and Mrs. Miller," "The Godfather I and II," "Serpico," "The Last Detail," "Chinatown," even in such a mere gambling film as "California Split," the point is that nobody wins: In the end, one way or the other, there are only losers. The first step in this transvaluation was the series of films about good Germans, good Japanese, good drug addicts and pushers. Then came the good Mafia, and the good promiscuous sexualists; and, conversely, films about the imbecile or murderous Allies in World War II.

Once the old bad values had been suitably confused and undermined, 22 we were at last ready for the new bad value: total, bleak despair. Consider now the new commonplace: the deliberately contrived, universal unhappy ending of films like "Easy Rider," "The Last Detail," "Serpico," "Godfather II," even "Dirty Harry," whose conquering cop-hero ends by disgustedly throwing away his badge, and "Chinatown," where the gun that would mete out justice barely wounds the archfiend at point-blank range, whereas the gun that brings death and heartbreak to the good, or better, people scores a deadly bull's-eye under the most prohibitively difficult shooting conditions. Such sophisticated, manipulative unhappy endings are no better than the infantile "happyends" of yesteryear: they are wish-fulfillment fantasies of self-justification for the demoralized and powerless of today, replacing the triumphant wish-fulfillment fantasies of the barbarians of yesterday basking in false security.

It is worth looking more closely at some of the sophisticated new 23 films, the sophistication of most of which is only celluloid-deep. Take the matter of the new sexual freedom. The movies are now allowed to show sexual activity in some detail, as well as abundantly suggest, if not actually record, acts rightly or wrongly considered perversions. But what attitudes accompany these revelations? Sniggering or moralizing. In "Lenny," for instance, we see Mrs. Bruce in bed with another woman, first watched and then joined by Lenny Bruce. But, from beginning to end, this mini-orgy is played lugubriously, the principal participants not only not enjoying themselves, but also either visibly suffering or audibly complaining, and the aftermath is all anger and bitterness. In such a spirit, no one would have entered into this sexual bout, or persisted in it for more than 30 seconds. But the price of including it in a major, commercial movie is the sermonizing commentary that accompanies and follows it.

Similarly, in a film like "Shampoo," though there is a great deal of glib 24 sexuality, the protagonist, soon after affirming his enjoyment of the swinging life, is shown miserably losing the one woman he really wanted. Yet preachment is not the only payment to puritanism for the new permissiveness; derision, as I suggested, is the other. Thus, all the sexual acts in "Shampoo" end in the comic humiliation of one or the other partner, and sometimes both. Even in a film as seemingly impudent in its iconoclasm as "M*A*S*H*," the big sex scenes are always coupled with some form of embarrassment, usually by someone being caught and exposed *in flagrante.* The *locus classicus* here is the scene in "Loving," in which the act of adultery is watched on closed-circuit television by all the guests at the party, including the errant protagonist's wife. Clearly, the motto "Crime does not pay" has been adapted to read, "Promiscuity [or sex] does not pay," except for the film makers who cash in on it.

What about political and social honesty in the new film? One ten- 25 dency is to minimize unsavory truths by keeping them offscreen or otherwise slurring them over. Thus, for example, Sydney Pollack made an honest and powerful film in "They Shoot Horses, Don't They?" but the society that was being anatomized was America during the Depression. The poverty and hunger that reduced people to nonstop jumping jacks in a dance marathon did not exist in 1969 — or so those who permitted the film to be made must have figured. But when the same director came up with "The Way We Were," dealing with McCarthyism among other things, we did not see any of the Congressional witch-hunts, only one rather limply staged public demonstration against presumed left-wing Hollywoodites returning from a Senate hearing. This matter is, apparently, still too sensitive to go into; indeed, one of the political scenes that can be found in the published book version was cut from the film as released.

Corruption of a quasi-political sort was to be seen in "Downhill 26 Racer," which suggested that everything was not milk and ozone in the world of Olympic skiing, even on our own U.S. team, but this story of what makes Sammy schuss, though fairly hard-hitting, hardly hit what one might consider very important targets. More directly concerned with politics was "The Candidate," a decent enough film showing the questionable and self-soiling ways in which even an honest man gets elected Senator (and, by implication, anything else), but the political corruption depicted was kid stuff compared with Watergate on your home screen fairly soon thereafter. It is perhaps not coincidental that Robert Redford was involved in the last three films mentioned, as he will be in a forthcoming movie about Watergate (though not about what it was or meant, but only about how the scandal was unearthed). This would seem to mean that political film-making in America depends largely on the willingness of a star to get involved in it. Certainly we owe, on the other side of the fence, "The Green Berets" to John Wayne's extreme rightism.

Typically, the most important political issue of the past 10 years was 27 our involvement in Vietnam. Yet there were, as I have already mentioned, no story films about that war, although a few very bad or juvenile movies made more or less explicit references to it, rather in the same spirit in which a gratuitous nude scene is dragged into an otherwise undistinguished and unsalable movie. This contrasts significantly with World War II, which was an inexhaustible cinematic subject, both during and after the fighting, but there, of course, we were on the side of the angels. Yet the public is obviously just as guilty as Hollywood: When a fine film about Vietnam, Raoul Coutard's "Hoa-Binh," came to us from abroad, it could make no headway with American audiences.

Taking an essentially neutral position — i.e., showing both humanity 28 and inhumanity among North and South Vietnamese alike, and not throwing obvious stones at the Americans either — "Hoa Binh" contented itself with focusing on the sufferings of children, perhaps greater in this than in any other war. Considered too tame by the doves, too incendiary by the hawks, and too depressing by the great, gray, neutral mass, it undeservedly incurred almost universal displeasure.

There was, in all these years, only one worthy American story film 29 that squarely confronted the major political issues of the times, and was critical of the way the country is run. (I discount a movie like "Advise and Consent," which is pure hokum, or Gore Vidal's "The Best Man," which, though a film *a clef*, presents minor political skulduggeries too patly and cutely, at too many removes from reality.) That worthy film was Haskell Wexler's "Medium Cool," produced by Paramount.

The film showed America's political and social troubles in the sum- 30 mer of 1968 as background for a tragic romance between a newsreel cameraman and a young schoolteacher from Appalachia, caught up along with the woman's young son in the riots and racial tensions surrounding Chicago's stormy Democratic Presidential convention. Paramount fought Wexler all the way, demanding innumerable cuts. The director capitulated on a few points, but stoutly held out on many others. The film, a very respectable though by no means flawless achievement, did well enough with the critics but fairly poorly with the public, an X rating doing much to prevent it from reaching a mass audience. Yet what is really interesting is the opprobrium it earned for Wexler, one of Hollywood's previously most highly regarded cinematographers. So reactionary is the film capital of America that when Wexler did photograph one film subsequently ("American Graffiti"), he could be given only ancillary credit as a "visual consultant" for his contribution.

That leaves the area of social commentary, which might tell us truth- 31 fully how we live, or suggest ways in which we ought, or ought not to, do it. This category contains the largest number of disappointments, ranging from the insufferable cuteness of "Harry and Tonto" to the prettifications of "Lenny," the latter made all the more culpable by posturing as documentary truth. A social phenomenon like the student rebellion of the late sixties begot a minor cinematic genre, but the pictures in it— "The Strawberry Statement," "The Magic Garden of Stanley Sweetheart," "Getting Straight," "The Revolutionary," "R.P.M." (screenplay by Erich Segal)—were all edulcorations, trivializations or sensationalizations of their subject. In the case of "The Activist," even though the film-makers went to the lengths of hiring two college-student lovers to play themselves and something very close to their actual experiences on the screen, the result was nevertheless indistinguishable from the standard formula picture.

But, surely, the new young directors, who have come up the hard, in- 32 dependent way (whatever that is), or were sponsored by the American Film Institute, might be assumed to "tell it like it is." Let us take two archetypal movies by this type of film-maker, Bob Rafelson's "Five Easy Pieces" and Martin Scorsese's "Mean Streets." In the former, we never really understand what ails the hero. He is a malcontent among the working class, into which he escaped from his bourgeois-artistic background, so he returns to the lovely Oregon setting where his family lead comparatively graceful, music-making lives, and once again cannot stand it there. In the end, he hitchhikes toward Alaska without so much as an overcoat. We never find out anything about his motivation, which would be all right if we could become deeply interested in his daily doings, but we can't: His only intense stirring is toward running off with his brother's fiancee, which she understandably turns down. So off he goes to the frozen north, presumably symbolic of death. The character seems much too aberrant — and unexplainably so — to be representative of anything but dementia.

In "Mean Streets," which is a mess even technically, the alternatives 33 seem to be growing up overtly criminal and absurd or growing up covertly criminal and dreary. The basic friendship between the two youths coming of age in Little Italy is never made believable, nor are other relationships examined with convincing insight. Instead, we get mostly disjointed, flashy anecdotes of minor violence, a soundtrack full of gratuitous period pop songs, and some of the fuzziest photography this side of home movies.

The only serious and persuasive attempt by a film to comment on 34 American society in the last few years was Terrence Malick's "Badlands," a free retelling of the Starkwether-Fugate case. A young psychopath and his 15-year-old girl friend, after killing the girl's dour father, embark on something that is part murderous crime spree, part Thoreauvian idyll — a bloody pastorale. There is a stronge sense of lost contact with reality: affectlessness based on mental disorder in the boy, boredom and childish fantasies in the girl. What Malick conveys magisterially is the way in which middle-class proprieties can coexist with murderousness in the hero, sentimentality with amorality in the heroine. How pathetic and even sympathetic the monstrous occasionally is! Though society is not directly indicted, the film is rich in suggestive overtones vibrating in its striking images, revealing disconnected scraps of lopsided dialogue, brilliantly selected background music, and general emotional restraint, forcing us to think about causes as well as shudder at effects. Despite generally favorable notices, the film was a box-office flop.

People who see great promise in new modes of movie financing 35 might consider the case of "Badlands": Made with the writer-director's own money, as well as that of his friends, and with support from A.F.I., it was shot slowly, carefully, exactly as Malick wanted it to be. Good reviews at the New York Film Festival persuaded Warner Brothers to buy, but not necessarily to promote and distribute it wisely and widely. It ended up making no money whatever. (A similar story, dealt with blatantly and factitiously, made "The Sugarland Express" rather more successful.)

Meanwhile, muddled or mendacious films that merely pretend to 36 make social comments — like "Alice Doesn't Live Here Anymore" or "A Woman Under the Influence" — are packing them in. Why? The one plays into the hands of the Women's Liberation movement while peddling underneath the same old Hollywood clichés; the other purports to show how the working class lives while giving us a schematic, simplistic and ultimately quite incoherent view based on foolish actors' improvisations rather than recognizable verities. But both films have their "happyends" and so bring us back to where we began.

Let us ask ourselves again: Does the American film reflect accurately 37 the society in which we live? The answer seems to be no, if you mean honestly coming to grips with the difficulties we face, the insufficiencies of the society that we have fashioned and that, in turn, molds us. But the answer is yes, if you mean the wish fulfillments and immature excesses, the crude farce and vulgar melodrama, the fake unhappy endings that have partly supplanted the still thriving fake happy ones. Yes, if you mean a still basically infantile movie-making that mirrors a still fundamentally childish society.

Study Questions

1. Does the title of essay imply an answer to its introductory question? Is the answer ultimately equivocal?
2. John Simon is considered the most crotchety of American film critics. Does this aspect of his personality come through in this essay?
3. To what extent must you have seen the films alluded to in order to appreciate the argument? Does the author simply name films or does he discuss them?
4. Simon calls "Badlands" a serious and persuasive attempt to comment on American society. How does what he says about "Badlands" inform us about both the film and society? Is Simon here a film critic or a social critic?
5. What distinguishes Simon's film criticism from other film critics you have read?

8 Writing About Literature

"Imagination all Compact"

In all the earlier editions of *Strategies in Prose* this section on Nathaniel Hawthorne's "Young Goodman Brown" was included in the section on The Individual. In the fourth edition we have set it apart in a section of its own. The comments we have received through the years have convinced us that the selections are the right ones to help the instructor deal with the problem of writing about literature. Students are able to deal with Hawthorne's story; and, because Cochran and Connolly continued their debate through a series of articles, the issues and methods of dealing with them became very clear. Thus, this group of essays on "Young Goodman Brown" has come through intact. It *has* stood the test of time.

The critical discussion of "Young Goodman Brown"—by offering a variety of opinions on a single story—can be used as either a mini-research unit or as the lesson in writing about literature. Richard Allen's student commentary has proven to be of particular interest to struggling freshmen who too often feel their efforts at composition are futile.

Nathaniel Hawthorne
YOUNG GOODMAN BROWN

Nathaniel Hawthorne (1804–1864) was born in Salem, Massachusetts. Among his ancestors was the Judge Hathorne who presided over the Salem witch trials. He graduated from Bowdoin College, where his fellow students included Henry Wadsworth Longfellow and Franklin Pierce. His first novel, *Fanshawe,* was published in 1828. This was followed by *Twice-Told Tales* (1837), *Mosses from an Old Manse* (1846), *The Scarlet Letter* (1850), *The House of the Seven Gables* (1851), *The Blithedale Romance and A Wonder Book* (1852), *Tanglewood Tales* (1853), and *The Marble Faun* (1860). Hawthorne worked at both the Boston and Salem Custom Houses and, after the publication of his campaign biography, *The Life of Franklin Pierce* (1852), was named consul to Liverpool.

Young Goodman Brown came forth at sunset into the street 1 at Salem village; but put his head back, after crossing the threshold, to exchange a parting kiss with his young wife. And Faith, as the wife was aptly named, thrust her own pretty head into the street, letting the wind play with the pink ribbons of her cap while she called to Goodman Brown.

"Dearest heart," whispered she, softly and rather sadly, when her lips 2 were close to his ear, "prithee put off your journey until sunrise and sleep in your own bed tonight. A lone woman is troubled with such dreams and such thoughts that she's afeard of herself sometimes. Pray tarry with me this night, dear husband, of all nights in the year."

"My love and my Faith," replied young Goodman Brown, "of all 3 nights in the year, this one night must I tarry away from thee. My journey, as thou callest it, forth and back again, must needs be done 'twixt now and sunrise. What, my sweet, pretty wife, dost thou doubt me already, and we but three months married?"

"Then God bless you!" said Faith, with the pink ribbons; "and may 4 you find all well when you come back."

"Amen!" cried Goodman Brown. "Say thy prayers, dear Faith, and go 5 to bed at dusk, and no harm will come to thee."

So they parted; and the young man pursued his way until, being 6 about to turn the corner by the meeting-house, he looked back and saw

First published 1835.

the head of Faith still peeping after him with a melancholy air, in spite of her pink ribbons.

"Poor little Faith!" thought he, for his heart smote him. "What a 7 wretch am I to leave her on such an errand! She talks of dreams, too. Methought as she spoke there was trouble in her face, as if a dream had warned her what work is to be done tonight. But no, no; 't would kill her to think it. Well, she's a blessed angel on earth; and after this one night I'll cling to her skirts and follow her to heaven."

With this excellent resolve for the future, Goodman Brown felt him- 8 self justified in making more haste on his present evil purpose. He had taken a dreary road, darkened by all the gloomiest trees of the forest, which barely stood aside to let the narrow path creep through, and closed immediately behind. It was all as lonely as could be; and there is this peculiarity in such a solitude, that the traveller knows not who may be concealed by the innumerable trunks and the thick boughs overhead; so that with lonely footsteps he may yet be passing through an unseen multitude.

"There may be a devilish Indian behind every tree," said Goodman 9 Brown to himself; and he glanced fearfully behind him as he added, "What if the devil himself should be at my very elbow!"

His head being turned back, he passed a crook of the road, and, 10 looking forward again, beheld the figure of a man, in grave and decent attire, seated at the foot of an old tree. He arose at Goodman Brown's approach and walked onward side by side with him.

"You are late, Goodman Brown," said he. "The clock of the Old 11 South was striking as I came through Boston, and that is full fifteen minutes agone."

"Faith kept me back a while," replied the young man, with a tremor 12 in his voice, caused by the sudden appearance of his companion, though not wholly unexpected.

It was now deep dusk in the forest, and deepest in that part of it 13 where these two were journeying. As nearly as could be discerned, the second traveller was about fifty years old, apparently in the same rank of life as Goodman Brown, and bearing a considerable resemblance to him, though perhaps more in expression than features. Still they might have been taken for father and son. And yet, though the elder person was as simply clad as the younger, and as simple in manner too, he had an indescribable air of one who knew the world, and who would not have felt abashed at the governor's dinner table or in King William's court, were it possible that his affairs should call him thither. But the only thing about him that could be fixed upon as remarkable was his staff, which bore the likeness of a great black snake, so curiously wrought that it might almost be seen to twist and wriggle itself like a living serpent. This, of course, must have been an ocular deception, assisted by the uncertain light.

"Come, Goodman Brown," cried his fellow-traveller, "this is a dull 14 pace for the beginning of a journey. Take my staff, if you are so soon weary."

"Friend," said the other, exchanging his slow pace for a full stop, "hav- 15 ing kept covenant by meeting thee here, it is my purpose now to return whence I came. I have scruples touching the matter thou wot'st of."

"Sayest thou so?" replied he of the serpent, smiling apart. "Let us 16 walk on, nevertheless, reasoning as we go; and I convince thee not thou shalt turn back. We are but a little way in the forest yet."

"Too far! too far!" exclaimed the goodman, unconsciously resuming 17 his walk. "My father never went into the woods on such an errand, nor his father before him. We have been a race of honest men and good Christians since the days of the martyrs; and shall I be the first of the name of Brown that ever took his path and kept—"

"Such company, thou wouldst say," observed the elder person, inter- 18 preting his pause. "Well, said, Goodman Brown! I have been as well acquainted with your family as with ever a one among the Puritans; and that's no trifle to say. I helped your grandfather, the constable, when he lashed the Quaker woman so smartly through the streets of Salem; and it was I that brought your father a pitch-pine knot, kindled at my own hearth, to set fire to an Indian village, in King Philip's war. They were my good friends, both; and many a pleasant walk have we had along this path, and returned merrily after midnight. I would fain be friends with you for their sake."

"If it be as thou sayest," replied Goodman Brown, "I marvel they 19 never spoke of these matters; or, verily, I marvel not, seeing that the least rumor of the sort would have driven them from New England. We are a people of prayer, and good works to boot, and abide no such wickedness."

"Wickedness or not," said the traveller with the twisted staff, "I have 20 a very general acquaintance here in New England. The deacons of many a church have drunk the communion wine with me; the selectmen of divers towns make me their chairman; and a majority of the Great and General Court are firm supporters of my interest. The governor and I, too—But these are state secrets."

"Can this be so?" cried Goodman Brown, with a stare of amazement 21 at his undisturbed companion. "Howbeit, I have nothing to do with the governor and council; they have their own ways, and are no rule for a simple husbandman like me. But, were I to go on with thee, how should I meet the eye of that good old man, our minister, at Salem village? Oh, his voice would make me tremble both Sabbath day and lecture day."

Thus far the elder traveller had listened with due gravity; but now 22 burst into a fit of irrepressible mirth, shaking himself so violently that his snakelike staff actually seemed to wriggle in sympathy.

"Ha! ha! ha!" shouted he again and again; then composing himself, 23 "Well, go on, Goodman Brown, go on; but, prithee, don't kill me with laughing."

"Well, then, to end the matter at once," said Goodman Brown, con- 24 siderably nettled, "there is my wife, Faith. It would break her dear little heart; and I'd rather break my own."

"Nay, if that be the case," answered the other, "e'en go thy ways, 25 Goodman Brown. I would not for twenty old women like the one hobbling before us that Faith should come to any harm."

As he spoke he pointed his staff at a female figure on the path, in 26
whom Goodman Brown recognized a very pious and exemplary dame,
who had taught him his catechism in youth, and was still his moral and
spiritual advisor, jointly with the minister and Deacon Gookin.

"A marvel, truly, that Goody Cloyse should be so far in the wilder- 27
ness at nightfall," said he. "But with your leave, friend, I shall take a cut
through the woods until we have left this Christian woman behind. Being
a stranger to you, she might ask whom I was consorting with and whither
I was going."

"Be it so," said his fellow-traveller. "Betake you to the woods, and 28
let me keep the path."

Accordingly the young man turned aside, but took care to watch his 29
companion, who advanced softly along the road until he had come within
a staff's length of the old dame. She, meanwhile, was making the best of
her way, with singular speed for so aged a woman, and mumbling some
indistinct words—a prayer, doubtless—as she went. The traveller put
forth his staff and touched her withered neck with what seemed the serpent's tail.

"The devil!" screamed the pious old lady.   30

"Then Goody Cloyse knows her old friend?" observed the traveller, 31
confronting her and leaning on his writhing stick.

"Ah, forsooth, and is it your worship indeed?" cried the good dame. 32
"Yea, truly is it, and in the very image of my old gossip, Goodman
Brown, the grandfather of the silly fellow that now is. But—would your
worship believe it?—my broomstick hath strangely disappeared, stolen, as
I suspect, by that unhanged witch, Goody Cory, and that, too, when I was
all anointed with the juice of smallage, and cinquefoil, and wolf's bane—"

"Mingled with fine wheat and the fat of a new-born babe," said the 33
shape of old Goodman Brown.

"Ah, your worship knows the recipe," cried the old lady, cackling 34
aloud. "So, as I was saying, being all ready for the meeting, and no horse
to ride on, I made up my mind to foot it; for they tell me there is a nice
young man to be taken into communion tonight. But now your good
worship will lend me your arm, and we shall be there in a twinkling."

"That can hardly be," answered her friend. "I may not spare you my 35
arm, Goody Cloyse; but here is my staff, if you will."

So saying, he threw it down at her feet, where, perhaps, it assumed 36
life, being one of the rods which its owner had formerly lent to the
Egyptian magi. Of this fact, however, Goodman Brown could not take
cognizance. He had cast up his eyes in astonishment, and, looking down
again, beheld neither Goody Cloyse nor the serpentine staff, but his fellow-traveller alone, who waited for him as calmly as if nothing had happened.

"That old woman taught me my catechism," said the young man; and 37
there was a world of meaning in this simple comment.

They continued to walk onward, while the elder traveller exhorted 38
his companion to make good speed and persevere in the path, discoursing so aptly that his arguments seemed rather to spring up in the
bosom of his auditor than to be suggested by himself. As they went, he

plucked a branch of maple to serve for a walking stick, and began to strip it of the twigs and little boughs, which were wet with evening dew. The moment his fingers touched them they became strangely withered and dried up as with a week's sunshine. Thus the pair proceeded, at a good free pace, until suddenly, in a gloomy hollow of the road, Goodman Brown sat himself down on the stump of a tree and refused to go any farther.

"Friend," said he, stubbornly, "my mind is made up. Not another 39 step will I budge on this errand. What if a wretched old woman do choose to go to the devil when I thought she was going to heaven: is that any reason why I should quit my dear Faith and go after her?"

"You will think better of this by and by," said his acquaintance, com- 40 posedly. "Sit here and rest yourself a while; and when you feel like moving again, there is my staff to help you along."

Without more words, he threw his companion the maple stick, and 41 was as speedily out of sight as if he had vanished into the deepening gloom. The young man sat a few moments by the roadside, applauding himself greatly, and thinking with how clear a conscience he should meet the minister in his morning walk, nor shrink from the eye of good old Deacon Gookin. And what calm sleep would be his that very night, which was to have been spent so wickedly, but so purely and sweetly now, in the arms of Faith! Amidst these pleasant and praiseworthy meditations, Goodman Brown heard the tramp of horses along the road, and deemed it advisable to conceal himself within the verge of the forest, conscious of the guilty purpose that had brought him thither, though now so happily turned from it.

On came the hoof tramps and voices of the riders, two grave old 42 voices, conversing soberly as they drew near. These mingled sounds appeared to pass along the road, within a few yards of the young man's hiding-place; but, owing doubtless to the depth of the gloom at that particular spot, neither the travellers nor their steeds were visible. Though their figures brushed the small boughs by the wayside, it could not be seen that they intercepted, even for a moment, the faint gleam from the strip of bright sky athwart which they must have passed. Goodman Brown alternately crouched and stood on tiptoe, pulling aside the branches and thrusting forth his head as far as he durst without discerning so much as a shadow. It vexed him the more, because he could have sworn, were such a thing possible, that he recognized the voices of the minister and Deacon Gookin, jogging along quietly, as they were wont to do, when bound to some ordination or ecclesiastical council. While yet within hearing, one of the riders stopped to pluck a switch.

"Of the two, reverend sir," said the voice like the deacon's, "I had 43 rather miss an ordination dinner than tonight's meeting. They tell me that some of our community are to be here from Falmouth and beyond, and others from Connecticut and Rhode Island, besides several of the Indian powwows, who, after their fashion, know almost as much deviltry as the best of us. Moreover, there is a goodly young woman to be taken into communion."

"Mighty well, Deacon Gookin!" replied the solemn old tones of the 44 minister. "Spur up, or we shall be late. Nothing can be done, you know, until I get on the ground."

The hoofs clattered again; and the voices, talking so strangely in the 45 empty air, passed on through the forest, where no church had ever been gathered or solitary Christian prayed. Whither, then, could these holy men be journeying so deep into the heathen wilderness? Young Goodman Brown caught hold of a tree for support, being ready to sink down on the ground, faint and overburdened with the heavy sickness of his heart. He looked up to the sky, doubting whether there really was a heaven above him. Yet there was the blue arch, and the stars brightening in it.

"With heaven above and Faith below, I will yet stand firm against the 46 devil!" cried Goodman Brown.

While he still gazed upward into the deep arch of the firmament and 47 had lifted his hands to pray, a cloud, though no wind was stirring, hurried across the zenith and hid the brightening stars. The blue sky was still visible, except directly overhead, where this black mass of cloud was sweeping swiftly northward. Aloft in the air, as if from the depths of the cloud, came a confused and doubtful sound of voices. Once the listener fancied that he could distinguish the accents of towns-people of his own, men and women, both pious and ungodly, many of whom he had met at the communion table, and had seen others rioting at the tavern. The next moment, so indistinct were the sounds, he doubted whether he had heard aught but the murmur of the old forest, whispering without a wind. Then came a stronger swell of those familiar tones, heard daily in the sunshine at Salem village, but never until now from a cloud of night. There was one voice of a young woman, uttering lamentations, yet with an uncertain sorrow, and entreating for some favor, which, perhaps, it would grieve her to obtain; and all the unseen multitude, both saints and sinners, seemed to encourage her onward.

"Faith!" shouted Goodman Brown, in a voice of agony and desper- 48 ation; and the echoes of the forest mocked him, crying, "Faith! Faith!" as if bewildered wretches were seeking her all through the wilderness.

The cry of grief, rage, and terror was yet piercing the night, when 49 the unhappy husband held his breath for a response. There was a scream, drowned immediately in a louder murmer of voices, fading into far-off laughter, as the dark cloud swept away, leaving the clear and silent sky above Goodman Brown. But something fluttered lightly down through the air and caught on the branch of a tree. The young man seized it, and beheld a pink ribbon.

"My Faith is gone!" cried he, after one stupefied moment. "There is 50 no good on earth; and sin is but a name. Come, devil; for to thee is the world given."

And, maddened with despair, so that he laughed loud and long, did 51 Goodman Brown grasp his staff and set forth again, at such a rate that he seemed to fly along the forest path rather than to walk or run. The road grew wilder and drearier and more faintly traced, and vanished at length, leaving him in the heart of the dark wilderness, still rushing onward with the instinct that guides mortal man to evil. The whole forest was peopled with frightful sounds—the creaking of the trees, the howling of wild beasts, and the yell of Indians; while sometimes the wind tolled like a distant church bell, and sometimes gave a broad roar around the traveller, as if all Nature were laughing him to scorn. But he was himself the chief horror of the scene, and shrank not from its other horrors.

"Ha! ha! ha!" roared Goodman Brown when the wind laughed at 52 him. "Let us hear which will laugh loudest. Think not to frighten me with your deviltry. Come witch, come wizard, come Indian powwow, come devil himself, and here comes Goodman Brown. You may as well fear him as he fear you."

In truth, all through the haunted forest there could be nothing more 53 frightful than the figure of Goodman Brown. On he flew among the black pines, brandishing his staff with frenzied gestures, now giving vent to an inspiration of horrid blasphemy, and now shouting forth such laughter as set all the echoes of the forest laughing like demons around him. The fiend in his own shape is less hideous than when he rages in the breast of man. Thus sped the demoniac on his course, until, quivering among the trees, he saw a red light before him, as when the felled trunks and branches of a clearing have been set on fire, and throw up their lurid blaze against the sky, at the hour of midnight. He paused, in a lull of the tempest that had driven him onward, and heard the swell of what seemed a hymn, rolling solemnly from a distance with the weight of many voices. He knew the tune; it was a familiar one in the choir of the village meetinghouse. The verse died heavily away, and was lengthered by a chorus, not of human voices, but of all the sounds of the benighted wilderness pealing in awful harmony together. Goodman Brown cried out, and his cry was lost to his own ear by its unison with the cry of the desert.

In the interval of silence he stole forward until the light glared full 54 upon his eyes. At one extremity of an open space, hemmed in by the dark wall of the forest, arose a rock, bearing some rude, natural resemblance either to an altar or a pulpit, and surrounded by four blazing pines, their tops aflame, their stems untouched, like candles at an evening meeting. The mass of foliage that had overgrown the summit of the rock was all on fire, blazing high into the night and fitfully illuminating the whole field. Each pendent twig and leafy festoon was in a blaze. As the red light arose and fell, a numerous congregation alternately shone forth, then disappeared in shadow, and again grew, as it were, out of the darkness, peopling the heart of the solitary woods at once.

"A grave and dark-clad company," quoth Goodman Brown.   55

In truth they were such. Among them, quivering to and fro between 56 gloom and splendor, appeared faces that would be seen next day at the council board of the province, and others which, Sabbath after Sabbath, looked devoutly heavenward, and benignantly over the crowded pews, from the holiest pulpits in the land. Some affirm that the lady of the governor was there. At least there were high dames well known to her, and wives of honored husband, and widows, a great multitude, and ancient maidens, all of excellent repute, and fair young girls, who trembled lest their mothers should espy them. Either the sudden gleams of light flashing over the obscure field bedazzled Goodman Brown, or he recognized a score of the church members of Salem village famous for their especial sanctity. Good old Deacon Gookin had arrived, and waited at the skirts of that venerable saint, his revered pastor. But, irreverently consorting with these grave, reputable, and pious people, these elders of the church, these chaste dames and dewy virgins, there were men of dissolute lives and women of spotted fame, wretches given over to all mean and filthy vice, and suspected even of horrid crimes. It was strange to see that the good shrank not from the wicked, nor were the sinners abashed by the saints. Scattered also among their palefaced enemies were the Indian priests, or powwows, who had often scared their native forest with more hideous incantations than any known to English witchcraft.

"But where is Faith?" thought Goodman Brown; and, as hope came 57 into his heart, he trembled.

Another verse of the hymn arose, a slow and mournful strain, such as 58 the pious love, but joined to words which expressed all that our nature can conceive of sin, and darkly hinted at far more. Unfathomable to mere mortals is the lore of fiends. Verse after verse was sung; and still the chorus of the desert swelled between like the deepest tone of a mighty organ; and with the final peal of that dreadful anthem there came a sound, as if the roaring wind, the rushing streams, the howling beasts, and every other voice of the unconcerted wilderness were mingling and according with the voice of guilty man in homage to the prince of all. The four blazing pines threw up a loftier flame, and obscurely discovered shapes and visages of horror on the smoke wreaths above the impious assembly. At the same moment the fire on the rock shot redly forth and formed a glowing arch above its base, where now appeared a figure. With reverence be it spoken, the figure bore no slight similitude, both in garb and manner, to some grave divine of the New England churches.

"Bring forth the converts!" cried a voice that echoed through the 59 field and rolled into the forest.

At the word, Goodman Brown stepped forth from the shadow of the 60 trees and approached the congregation, with whom he felt a loathful brotherhood by the sympathy of all that was wicked in his heart. He could have well-nigh sworn that the shape of his own dead father beckoned him to advance, looking downward from a smoke wreath, while a woman, with dim features of despair, threw out her hand to warn him back. Was it his mother? But he had no power to retreat one step, nor to resist, even in thought, when the minister and good old Deacon Gookin seized his arms and led him to the blazing rock. Thither came also the slender form of a veiled female, led between Goody Cloyse, this pious teacher of the catechism, and Martha Carrier, who had received the devil's promise to be queen of hell. A rampant hag was she. And there stood the proselytes beneath the canopy of fire.

"Welcome, my children," said the dark figure, "to the communion of 61 your race. Ye have found thus young your nature and your destiny. My children, look behind you!"

They turned; and flashing forth, as it were, in a sheet of flame, the 62 fiend worshippers were seen; the smile of welcome gleamed darkly on every visage.

"There," resumed the sable form, "are all whom ye have reverenced 63
from youth. Ye deemed them holier than yourselves, and shrank from
your own sin, contrasting it with their lives of righteousness and pray-
erful aspirations heavenward. Yet here are they all in my worshipping assembly. This night it shall be granted you to know their secret deeds:
how hoary-bearded elders of the church have whispered wanton words to
the young maids of their households; how many a woman, eager for widows' weeds, has given her husband a drink at bedtime and let him sleep
his last sleep in her bosom; how beardless youths have made haste to in-
herit their fathers' wealth; and how fair damsels—blush not, sweet ones—
have dug little graves in the garden, and bidden me, the sole guest to an
infant's funeral. By the sympathy of your human hearts for sin ye shall
scent out all places—whether in church, bedchamber, street, field, or forest—where crime has been committed, and shall exult to behold the
whole earth one stain of guilt, one mighty blood spot. Far more than this.
It shall be yours to penetrate, in every bosom, the deep mystery of sin,
the fountain of all wicked arts, and which inexhaustibly supplies more
evil impulses than human power—than my power at its utmost—can
make manifest in deeds. And now, my children, look upon each other."

They did so; and, by the blaze of the hell-kindled torches, the 64
wretched man beheld his Faith, and the wife her husband, trembling before than unhallowed altar.

"Lo, there ye stand, my children," said the figure, in a deep and sol- 65
emn tone, almost sad with its despairing awfulness, as if his once angelic
nature could yet mourn for our miserable race. "Depending upon one another's hearts, ye had still hoped that virtue were not all a dream. Now
are ye undeceived. Evil is the nature of mankind. Evil must be your only
happiness. Welcome again, my children, to the communion of your race."

"Welcome," repeated the fiend worshippers, in one cry of despair 66
and triumph.

And there they stood, the only pair, as it seemed, who were yet hesi- 67
tating on the verge of wickedness in this dark world. A basin was hol-
lowed, naturally, in the rock. Did it contain water, reddened by the lurid
light? or was it blood? or, perchance, a liquid flame? Herein did the
shape of evil dip his hand and prepare to lay the mark of baptism upon
their foreheads, that they might be partakers of the mystery of sin, more
conscious of the secret guilt of others, both in deed and thought, than
they could now be of their own. The husband cast one look at his pale
wife, and Faith at him. What polluted wretches would the next glance
show them to each other, shuddering alike at what they disclosed and
what they saw!

"Faith! Faith!" cried the husband, "look up to heaven, and resist the 68
wicked one."

Whether Faith obeyed he knew not. Hardly had he spoken when he 69
found himself amid calm night and solitude, listening to a roar of the
wind which died heavily away through the forest. He staggered against
the rock, and felt it chill and damp; while a hanging twig, that had been
all on fire, besprinkled his cheek with the coldest dew.

The next morning young Goodman Brown came slowly into the 70
street of Salem village, staring around him like a bewildered man. The
good old minister was taking a walk along the graveyard to get an appetite for breakfast and meditate his sermon, and bestowed a blessing, as he
passed, on Goodman Brown. He shrank from the venerable saint as if to
avoid an anathema. Old Deacon Gookin was at domestic worship, and
the holy words of his prayer were heard through the open window.
"What God doth the wizard pray to?" quoth Goodman Brown. Goody
Cloyse, that excellent old Christian, stood in the early sunshine at her
own lattice, catechizing a little girl who had brought her a pint of morning's milk. Goodman Brown snatched away the child as from the grasp of
the fiend himself. Turning the corner by the meeting-house, he spied the
head of Faith, with the pink ribbons, gazing anxiously forth, and bursting
into such joy at sight of him that she skipped along the street and almost
kissed her husband before the whole village. But Goodman Brown
looked sternly and sadly into her face, and passed on without a greeting.

Had Goodman Brown fallen asleep in the forest and only dreamed a 71
wild dream of a witch-meeting?

Be it so if you will; but, alas! it was a dream of evil omen for young 72
Goodman Brown. A stern, a sad, a darkly meditative, a distrustful, if not
a desperate man did he become from the night of that fearful dream. On
the Sabbath day, when the congregation were singing a holy psalm, he
could not listen because an anthem of sin rushed loudly upon his ear and
drowned all the blessed strain. When the minister spoke from the pulpit
with power and fervid eloquence, and, with his hand on the open Bible,
of the sacred truths of our religion, and of saint-like lives and triumphant
deaths, and of future bliss or misery unutterable, then did Goodman
Brown turn pale, dreading lest the roof should thunder down upon the
gray blasphemer and his hearers. Often, waking suddenly at midnight, he
shrank from the bosom of Faith; and at morning or eventide, when the
family knelt down at prayer, he scowled and muttered to himself, and
gazed sternly at his wife, and turned away. And when he had lived long,
and was borne to his grave a hoary corpse, followed by Faith, an aged
woman, and children and grandchildren, a goodly procession, besides
neighbors not a few, they carved no hopeful verse upon his tombstone,
for his dying hour was gloom.

Study Questions

1. What is an *allegory?* A *parable?* Is "Young Goodman
   Brown" allegory or parable?
2. Why does Hawthorne repeatedly focus attention on Faith's
   pink ribbons?
3. What is the significance of Young Goodman Brown's "excellent resolve for the future" (paragraph 7)?
4. Does Young Goodman Brown actually see the minister

and Deacon Gookin riding through the forest? How does he identify them?

5. In what instances are reality and appearance called into question?

6. Why does the narrator call Young Goodman Brown the "chief horror of the scene" (paragraph 51)?

Thomas E. Connolly
HAWTHORNE'S "YOUNG GOODMAN BROWN": AN ATTACK ON PURITANIC CALVINISM

Thomas E. Connolly (1918–   ) was born in New York City. He received a B.S. (1939) from Fordham University and an M.A. (1947) and Ph.D. (1951) from the University of Chicago. He has taught at the University of Idaho and Creighton University, and is currently Professor of English at the State University of New York at Buffalo. Connolly has received recognition for his book-length studies of James Joyce, Algernon Charles Swinburne, and Nathaniel Hawthorne.

It is surprising, in a way, to discover how few of the many 1 critics who have discussed "Young Goodman Brown" agree on any aspect of the work except that it is an excellent short story. D. M. McKeithan says that its theme is "sin and its blighting effects."[1] Richard H. Fogle observes, "Hawthorne the artist refuses to limit himself to a single and doctrinaire conclusion, proceeding instead by indirection,"[2] implying, presumably, that it is inartistic to say something which can be clearly understood by the readers. Gordon and Tate assert, "Hawthorne is dealing with his favorite theme: the unhappiness which the human

Reprinted from *American Literature*, 28 (November 1956), 370–375, by permission of Thomas E. Connolly and the Duke University Press.

[1] D. M. McKeithan, "Hawthorne's 'Young Goodman Brown': An Interpretation," *Modern Language Notes*, 67 (February 1952), 94.

[2] Richard H. Fogle, "Ambiguity and Clarity in Hawthorne's 'Young Goodman Brown,'" *New England Quarterly*, 18 (December 1945), 453.

heart suffers as a result of its innate depravity."[3] Austin Warren says, "His point is the devastating effect of moral scepticism."[4] Almost all critics agree, however, that Young Goodman Brown lost his faith. Their conclusions are based, perhaps, upon the statement, "My Faith is gone!" made by Brown when he recognizes his wife's voice and ribbon. I should like to examine the story once more to show that Young Goodman Brown did not lose his faith at all. In fact, not only did he retain his faith, but during his horrible experience he actually discovered the full and frightening significance of his faith.

Mrs. Leavis comes closest to the truth in her discussion of this story 2 in the *Sewanee Review* in which she says: "Hawthorne has imaginatively recreated for the reader that Calvinist sense of sin, that theory which did in actuality shape the early social and spiritual history of New England."[5] But Mrs. Leavis seems to miss the critical implications of the story, for she goes on to say: "But in Hawthorne, by a wonderful feat of transmutation, it has no religious significance, it is a psychological state that is explored. Young Goodman Brown's Faith is not faith in Christ but faith in human beings, and losing it he is doomed to isolation forever."[6] Those who persist in reading this story as a study of the effects of sin on Brown come roughly to his conclusion: "Goodman Brown became evil as a result of sin and thought he saw evil *where none existed*."[7] Hawthorne's message is far more depressing and horrifying than this. The story is obviously an individual tragedy, and those who treat it as such are right, of course; but, far beyond the personal plane, it has universal implications.

Young Goodman Brown, as a staunch Calvinist, is seen at the begin- 3 ning of this allegory to be quite confident that he is going to heaven. The errand on which he is going is presented mysteriously and is usually interpreted to be a deliberate quest of sin. This may or may not be true; what is important is that he is going out to meet the devil by prearrangement. We are told by the narrator that his purpose in going is evil. When the devil meets him, he refers to the "beginning of a journey." Brown admits that he "kept covenant" by meeting the devil and hints at the evil purpose of the meeting.

Though his family has been Christian for generations, the point is 4 made early in the story that Young Goodman Brown has been married to his Faith for only three months. Either the allegory breaks down at this point or the marriage to Faith must be looked upon as the moment of conversion to grace in which he became fairly sure of his election to heaven. That Goodman Brown is convinced he is of the elect is made clear at the beginning: "... and after this one night I'll cling to her skirts and follow her to heaven." In other words, at the start of his adventure, Young Goodman Brown is certain that his faith will help man get to heaven. It is in this concept that his disillusionment will come. The irony

---

[3] Caroline Gordon and Allen Tate (eds.), *The House of Fiction* (New York, 1950), p. 38.

[4] Austin Warren, *Nathaniel Hawthorne* (New York, 1934), p. 362.

[5] Q. D. Leavis, "Hawthorne as Poet," *Sewanee Review*, 59 (Spring 1951), 197–198.

[6] *Ibid.*

[7] McKeithan, *op. cit.,* p. 95. Italics mine.

of this illusion is brought out when he explains to the devil the reason for his tardiness: "Faith kept me back awhile." That is what he thinks! By the time he gets to the meeting place he finds that his Faith is already there. Goodman Brown's disillusionment in his belief begins quickly after meeting the devil. He has asserted proudly that his ancestors "have been a race of honest men and good Christians since the days of the martyrs," and the devil turns his own words on him smartly:

> Well said, Goodman Brown! I have been as well acquainted with your family as with ever a one among the Puritans; and that's no trifle to say. I helped your grandfather, the constable, when he lashed the Quaker woman so smartly through the streets of Salem; and it was I that brought your father a pitch-pine knot, kindled at my own hearth, to set fire to an Indian village, in King Philip's war. They were my good friends, both; and many a pleasant walk have we had along this path, and returned merrily after midnight. I would fain be friends with you for their sake.

Goodman Brown manages to shrug off this identification of his parental and grandparental Puritanism with the devil, but the reader should not overlook the sharp tone of criticism in Hawthorne's presentation of this speech.

When the devil presents his next argument, Brown is a little more 5 shaken. The devil has shown him that Goody Cloyse is of his company and Brown responds: "What if a wretched old woman do choose to go to the devil when I thought she was going to heaven: is that any reason why I should quit my dear Faith and go after her?" He still believes at this point that his faith will lead him to heaven. The devil's reply, "You will think better of this by and by," is enigmatic when taken by itself, but a little earlier the narrator had made a comment which throws a great deal of light on this remark by the devil. When he recognized Goody Cloyse, Brown said, "That old woman taught me my catechism," and the narrator added, "and there was a world of meaning in this simple comment." The reader at this point should be fairly well aware of Hawthorne's criticism of Calvinism. The only way there can be a "world of meaning" in Brown's statement is that her catechism teaches the way to the devil and not the way to heaven.

From this point on Brown is rapidly convinced that his original conception about his faith is wrong. Deacon Gookin and the "good old minister," in league with Satan, finally lead the way to his recognition that his faith is diabolic rather than divine. Hawthorne points up this fact by a bit of allegorical symbolism. Immediately after he recognizes the voices of the deacon and the minister, we are told by the narrator that "Young Goodman Brown caught hold of a tree for support, being ready to sink down on the ground, faint and overburdened with the heavy sickness of his heart. He looked up to the sky, doubting whether there really was a heaven above him. Yet there was a blue arch, and the stars brightened in it." Here the doubt has begun to gnaw, but the stars are symbols of the faint hope which he is still able to cherish, and he is able to say: "With heaven above and Faith below, I will yet stand firm against the devil." But immediately a symbolic cloud hides the symbolic stars: "While he still gazed upward into the deep arch of the firmament and had lifted his hands to pray, a cloud, though no wind was stirring, hurried across the zenith and hid the brightening stars." And it is out of his black cloud of doubt that the voice of his faith reaches him and the pink ribbon of his Faith falls.[8] It might be worthwhile to discuss Faith's pink ribbons here, for Hawthorne certainly took great pains to call them to our attention. The ribbons seem to be symbolic of his initial illusion about the true significance of his faith, his belief that his faith will lead him to heaven. The pink ribbons on a Puritan lady's cap, signs of youth, joy, and happiness, are actually entirely out of keeping with the severity of the rest of her dress which, if not somber black, is at least gray. When the ribbon falls from his cloud of doubt, Goodman Brown cries in agony, "My Faith is gone!" and it is gone in the sense that it now means not what it once meant. He is quick to apply the logical, ultimate conclusion of Goody Cloyse's catechizing: "Come devil; for to thee is this world given."

Lest the reader miss the ultimate implication of the doctrine of pre- 7 destination, Hawthorne has the devil preach a sermon at his communion service: "Welcome, my children ... to the communion of your race. Ye have found thus young your nature and your destiny." Calvinsim teaches that man is innately depraved and that he can do nothing to merit salvation. He is saved only by the whim of God who selects some, through no deserts of their own, for heaven while the great mass of mankind is destined for hell. The devil concludes his sermon: "Evil is the nature of mankind. Evil must be your only happiness. Welcome again, my children, to the communion of your race." It is not at all insignificant that the word *race* is used several times in this passage, for it was used earlier by Goodman Brown when he said, "We have been a race of honest men and good Christians...." After this sermon by the devil, Young Goodman Brown makes one last effort to retain the illusion that faith will lead him to heaven; he calls out: "Faith! Faith! ... look up to heaven, and resist the wicked one." But we are fairly sure that he is unsuccessful, for we are immediately told: "Whether Faith obeyed he knew not."

Young Goodman Brown did not lose his faith (we are even told that 8 his Faith survived him); he learned its full and terrible significance. This story is Hawthorne's criticism of the teachings of Puritanic-Calvinism. His implication is that the doctrine of the elect and damned is not a faith which carries man heavenward on its skirts, as Brown once believed, but, instead, condemns him to hell—bad and good alike indiscriminately—and for all intents and purposes so few escape as to make one man's chance of salvation almost disappear. It is this awakening to the full meaning of his faith which causes Young Goodman Brown to look upon his minister as a blasphemer when he teaches "the sacred truths of our religion, and of saint-like lives and triumphant deaths, and of future bliss or misery unutterable," for he has learned that according to the truths of his faith

---

[8] F. O. Matthiessen made entirely too much of the wrong thing of this ribbon. Had Young Goodman Brown returned to Salem Village clutching the ribbon, there might be some point in what Mathiessen says (*American Renaissance,* New York, 1941, pp. 282–284). As it is, the ribbon presents no more of a problem than do the burning trees turned suddenly cold again.

there is probably nothing but "misery unutterable" in store for him and all his congregation; it is this awakening which causes him to turn away from prayer; it is this awakening which makes appropriate the fact that "they carved no hopeful verse upon his tombstone."

Though much is made of the influence of Puritanism on the writings 9 of Hawthorne, he must also be seen to be a critic of the teachings of Puritanism. Between the position of Vernon L. Parrington,[9] who saw Hawthorne as retaining "much of the older Calvinistic view of life and human destiny," and that of Regis Michaud,[10] who saw him as "an anti-puritan and prophet heralding the Freudian gospel," lies the truth about Hawthorne.

Study Questions

1. Connolly quotes Richard H. Fogle and then interprets Fogle's statement. Is the interpretation of Fogle a just one?
2. What is the *thesis* of this essay? Is this stated explicitly or implicitly?
3. Connolly feels that the narrator's comment on Young Goodman Brown's remark about Goody Cloyse reveals Hawthorne's criticism of Calvinism. Can you interpret Brown's remark in another way? The narrator's comment?
4. What does Connolly think Faith's ribbons symbolize?
5. Does the last paragraph suggest that his purpose was two-fold: to interpret Hawthorne's story for the reader, and to interpret Hawthorne *himself* for the reader? Is the last paragraph gratuitous?

---

[9] *Main Currents in American Thought* (New York, 1927), II, 443.
[10] "How Nathaniel Hawthorne Exorcised Hester Prynne," *The American Novel Today* (Boston, 1928), pp. 25–46.

Robert W. Cochran

HAWTHORNE'S CHOICE: THE VEIL OR THE JAUNDICED EYE

Robert W. Cochran (1926–   ) was born in Williamsport, Pennsylvania. He received his B.A. (1948) from Indian University and his M.A. (1949) and Ph.D. (1957) from the University of Michigan. Cochran's critical articles have appeared in *College English* and *Explicator*. He is Professor of English at the University of Vermont.

In his stories "Young Goodman Brown" and "The Minister's 1 Black Veil," Hawthorne presents the opposite extremes of reaction to mankind within a single alternative view of man's nature. Both young Goodman Brown and the Reverend Mr. Hooper view men as sinners. Yet Brown ends his life in darkness, disillusionment, and despair; whereas Mr. Hooper achieves a steady acceptance of life through relative enlightenment, a total recognition of sin and sorrow, and a firm belief in a traditional afterlife.

Such an interpretation of "The Minister's Black Veil," is at sharp 2 variance with the consensus view that Hooper, like Brown, lives out his days and enters the grave the victim of a dark obsession. In his admirably balanced reading of "The Minister's Black Veil," R. H. Fogle interprets the tale as mirroring the ambiguity of life in a parallel ambiguity of meaning.[1] But the veil can be more definitely identified, without the oversimplification of which Mr. Hooper's parishoners are guilty and without arriving at what Fogle terms "a single dogmatic conclusion."

The Reverend Mr. Hooper is regularly said to indulge in a special 3 form of self-pity, masochistic at base: Hooper is characterized by Fogle as having an "infatuated love of mystification." The best that may be said of Hooper, in keeping with the generally accepted interpretation of his actions, is to be found in a question Fogle raises:

> ... is it possible that we can go further afield and determine that the message of the veil *is* representative and universal: that the failure to recognize it is simply the last and most chilling proof of man's imprisonment within himself?

Reprinted from College English, 23 (February 1962), 342–346, by permission of Robert W. Cochran and the National Council of Teachers of English.

[1]R. H. Fogle, "'An Ambiguity of Sin or Sorrow,'" *The New England Quarterly,* 21 (September 1948), 342–349.

Considering the implications of his question with respect to Hawthorne's problem of achieving artistic unity, Fogle concludes:

> ... in order to present forcibly the tragic isolation of one man, Hawthorne is obligated to consider society as a solid group arrayed against his hero, ignoring for the time being the fact that this hero is Everyman.

But, to pursue the direction of Fogle's question yet a step further, Hawthorne's hero is not Everyman: Hooper's experience is not typical, for that which he glimpses is the outer limit of earthly wisdom. The vision he gains is granted to few, though the perception is of a truth which is at the very heart of the nature of all mortal existence.

Ironically, from this new point of view Rev. Hooper achieves a far 4
more penetrating equivalent of that "steady view of life, the *aurea mediocritas*" which Fogle assigns only to Hooper's sweetheart, Elizabeth, and which Fogle believes to be Hawthorne's conception of the "highest good."

II

By considering the two stories and their protagonists together, it is possible 5
to reject not only Fogle's interpretation of "The Minister's Black Veil," but Thomas E. Connolly's interpretation of "Young Goodman Brown" as well. "Young Goodman Brown" is not, as Connolly says it is, a specific attack on Puritanic Calvinism.[2] In Hawthorne's tales and romances, the Puritan New England setting in time and place is illustrative, not restrictive. The diametrically opposed perspectives on man to which the main characters of these two stories come represent a universal difference in approach to the reading of the human condition.

Just as surely as Aylmer, Dr. Rappaccini, or Ethan Brand, Young 6
Goodman Brown is guilty of the Unpardonable Sin of Pride. In fact, Young Goodman Brown's mistake is essentially the same as that which Hawthorne laments in Aylmer, in the concluding sentence of "The Birthmark." In his impatience with human imperfection, Brown loses his Faith in mankind; the milk of human kindness dries up within him. Connolly's argument that "Young Goodman Brown did not lose his faith (we are even told that his Faith survived him)" is certainly based on a too strictly theological interpretation. Hawthorne explicitly states that Faith survives Brown to symbolize the very general religious belief that Faith is always available to the man capable of embracing her. This belief in the availability of Faith to the human heart which remains open to invite her in is familiar to any reader who knows conventional Christianity: invitations to Christ to "enter in" are central to traditional Christian worship.

That Hawthorne uses the term "Goodman" in Brown's name to in- 7
dicate that Brown is a member of the race which includes Goody Cloyse, Deacon Gookin, and his own father and grandfather is generally recog-

---

[2.] Thomas E. Connolly, "Hawthorne's 'Young Goodman Brown': An Attack on Puritanic Calvinism," *American Literature*, 28 (November 1956), 370–375.

nized (one could go much farther in citing evidence from the story suggesting a breadth of applicability, to include all strata and all generations
of Salem society and, by extension, of all human society). But the deeper
irony—that Brown is but a youth—is curiously overlooked. That Brown
is young suggests that his journey into the forest is not simply pre-
meditated and prearranged, but that it is inevitable. Brown's is therefore
a typical human journey—out of innocence and into experience. To borrow from William Blake, Brown is pictured in this story at the moment
when he leaves the realm of pink ribbons and the gentle lamb to enter
into the disquieting and mysterious realm where the tiger burns bright in
the forests of the night.

To this extent, Young Goodman Brown is representative of all man- 8
kind; we all have a rendezvous with the Devil. Only for form which the
Prince of Darkness takes varies in individual cases. Brown's journey is inevitable, but the results of his journey are not. That Brown is young is
significant; that he is called "Goodman" is ironic but primarily tragic, in
the sense that it helps the reader to identify with Brown not only the
other characters in the story, but himself as well. But that Brown is "but
three months married" to Faith is especially meaningful. Brown is representative of all who are innocent and undeveloped. Had he been wed to
his Faith longer, had he put his Faith and himself to the test by degrees,
he might have won through in his struggle with despair. But he did not
because he could not. If the reader condemns Brown, he, like Brown, has
become self-righteous. Or, if the reader believes, conversely, that Young
Goodman Brown is representative of all mankind and that there is no escape from despair once evil is encountered, he, like Brown, delivers himself into the hands of the Devil, in the terms of the story.

III

The Reverend Mr. Hooper does not make Brown's mistake. He does not 9
view his fellow creatures with a jaundiced eye. Father Hooper sees the
same truth about human nature that Young Goodman Brown sees, but
he does not fall prey to Evil by obsessively viewing man as hopelessly
sinful and disqualified from Salvation.

Unlike Goodman Brown, Father Hooper profits from his vision: he 10
becomes more understanding of human frailty than he was before he
learned his lesson and donned the veil. This increased compassion and
pity is the product of Mr. Hooper's sharpened awareness that the black
veil figuratively covers all faces, including even the Earth's face. Thus
Hooper's isolation is different from other men's only in degree—in intensity—and not in kind.

Hawthorne called "The Minister's Black Veil" a "parable," and one 11
purpose of a parable is to clarify. The parable of the veil clarifies not simply by mirroring the ambiguity of life in a parallel ambiguity of meaning
which Fogle has so ably demonstrated, but also by identifying the source
of life's ambiguity. In the story, the veil is frequently identified as an emblem of mortality, of human imperfection. It is therefore comparable to

the small hand on Georgiana's cheek in "The Birthmark"; for it is similarly a mark visited by Nature on all human beings, although seldom in so concrete a form.

After he has put on the veil, Father Hooper becomes a man apart, in [12] that for him the secret of sin lies in its mysterious depths and not in a sense of particular shame or guilt. He is awed by Sin, rather than fearful of any single manifestation or consequence of sin. One important result of his vision of the truth about the human condition is of course his heightened sense of isolation. Even Elizabeth, the women he truly loves, is cut off from him. But no two humans can be completely wed, as Hooper is made to realize very sharply when he sees his own reflection in a mirror, just after he has officiated at the wedding ceremony. His spiritual chill upon glimpsing the outside of the veil, presumably coupled with a keen sense that no earthly marriage can be the wedding of two isolated spirits—the perfect union which romantic young couples dimly hope for—indicates the price Reverend Hooper must pay for his vision.

Still, that vision even as it isolates and chills also provides Reverend [13] Hooper with the ultimate in earthly wisdom; for, having recognized the fearful truth of human isolation, Hooper does not withdraw from the human race. The reality of man's innate depravity blinds Goodman Brown to man's innate goodness. Hooper, on the other hand, sees man's mixed nature precisely because he faces at every moment that same reality embodied in the veil.

As Fogle observes, "In one respect, however, the veil makes Mr. [14] Hooper a more efficient clergyman, for 'it enabled him to sympathize with all dark affections.'" From the moment of his vision of the truth, Mr. Hooper becomes a more effective instrument of God, if indeed he does not become the very voice of God:

> Mr. Hooper had the reputation of a good preacher, but not an energetic one: he strove to win his people heavenward by mild, persuasive influences, rather than to drive them thither by the thunders of the Word. The sermon which he now delivered was marked by the same characteristics of style and manner as the general series of his pulpit oratory. But there was something, either in the sentiment of the discourse itself, or in the imagination of the auditors, which made it greatly the most powerful effort that they had ever heard from their pastor's lips. It was tinged, rather more darkly than usual, with the gentle gloom of Mr. Hooper's temperament.
>
> The subject had reference to secret sin, and those sad mysteries which we hide from our nearest and dearest, and would fain conceal from our own consciousness, even forgetting that the Omniscient can detect them. A subtle power was breathed into his words. Each member of the congregation, the most innocent girl, and the man of hardened breast, felt as if the preacher had crept upon them, behind his awful veil, and discovered their hoarded iniquity of deed or thought. Many spread their clasped hands on their bosoms. There was nothing terrible in what Mr. Hooper said, at least, no violence; and yet, with every tremor of his melancholy voice, the hearers quaked. An unsought pathos came hand in hand with awe. So sensible were the audience of some unwonted attribute in their minister, that they longed for a breath of wind to blow aside the veil, almost believing that a stranger's visage would be discovered, though the form, gesture, and voice were those of Mr. Hooper.

Furthermore, from this point in the story forward, those who will 15
not—indeed, cannot bring themselves to—admit their sins, even to themselves, shun Hooper's presence or defensively "throw themselves in his
way." But those who recognize their own sins call for the one minister
who has "qualified" himself by previous words and actions, and Mr.
Hooper does not fail them. At the same time that the veil isolates Father
Hooper from meaningful human relationships, then, it increases his com-
municative power as a minister. Paradoxically, Mr. Hooper is not so isolated or so misunderstood as the villagers' oversimplified interpretations
of why he wears the veil would lead us to suppose.

The Reverend Mr. Hooper has been permitted to cross over beyond 16
the veil of mystery to achieve the ultimate in human knowledge. By reason of his intellect and his years of dedication to God and devotion to
duty, he has been vouchsafed a unique comprehension of what morality
means. The danger to Hooper, as any careful reader of Hawthorne will
know, is that, being only in part spirit and in part frail flesh, he may exult
in his superior knowledge and fall victim to the sin of Pride. That he
does not become self-righteous or contemptuous in his dealings with his
fellows is, of course, painstakingly established by Hawthorne.

The veil, then, serves two large functions: First, it captures the imagi- 17
nation of men, not merely during Mr. Hooper's lifetime, but also after
his physical death:

> Still veiled, they laid him in his coffin, and a veiled corpse they bore him to
> the grave. The grass of many years has sprung up and withered on that
> grave, the burial stone is moss-grown, and good Mr. Hooper's face is dust;
> but awful is still the thought that it mouldered beneath the Black Veil!

And equally important, the veil is a constant reminder to Hooper of his
fellowship with man and of his obligation to God. Hooper's sorrow is his
steady and painful awareness that all men are sinners and that all men,
himself most particularly, are isolated in this life. Hooper's reward is his
conviction that "'.... hereafter there shall be no veil over my face, no
darkness between our souls! It is but a mortal veil—it is not for eternity!'" For all the horror he feels whenever he sees his reflection in a
mirror or a fountain, Mr. Hooper's sad smiles and his "gentle, but in-
conquerable obstinacy" whenever he is begged to remove the veil show
the minister to be a man of comparative serenity and of great steadfast-
ness. Hooper's refusal to remove the veil demonstrates that he is wed to
it in his life. The veil represents harsh reality, and Hooper understands
that so long as he exists in the mortal condition, his spirit is bound to the
veil.

Thus, "The Minister's Black Veil" is central to Hawthorne's view of 18
life: in life there is little cause for joy and much cause for gloom; yet wisdom lies not in submitting to despair but in developing a quiet, hopeful
patience—in the promise of a traditional Christian afterlife.

How different in effect is Mr. Hooper's comprehension that all men 19
are sinners from Young Goodman Brown's destructive discovery. After
his physical death, Mr. Hooper achieves even earthly immortality, in that
he inspires feelings of awe in those who survive him. It is not too much
to suggest that in contrast Young Goodman Brown, on whose tombstone

"no hopeful verse" was carved, lies in an absolutely desolate grave, like Hooper's untended in fact, but unlike Hooper's in that it is not kept green in memory.

Unquestionably, Hawthorne himself felt the pull toward Young 20 Goodman Brown's view of man. His publication of "The Minister's Black Veil" and other parables of life may be interpreted as Hawthorne's public displaying of a black veil over his own face. Hawthorne's works are, therefore, both a measure of his own need for a reminder that he was a member of the human race and a signal of his success in avoiding the Unpardonable Sin.

Study Questions

1. What is meant in paragraph 5 by the statement that Hawthorne's Puritan New England setting is "illustrative, not restrictive"?
2. Why does Cochran feel that Young Goodman Brown's youth is significant (paragraph 8)?
3. Does Cochran's discussion of "The Minister's Black Veil" lend credence to his interpretation of "Young Goodman Brown"?
4. What does paragraph 20 say about Hawthorne's view of life?
5. In what way do Cochran and Connolly reach similar conclusions in their interpretation of the story?

Thomas E. Connolly

HOW YOUNG GOODMAN BROWN BECAME OLD BADMAN BROWN

Thomas E. Connolly (1918-   ) was born in New York City. He received a B.S. (1939) from Fordham University and an M.A. (1947) and Ph.D. (1951) from the University of Chicago. He has taught at the University of Idaho and Creighton University, and is currently Professor of English at the State University of New York at Buffalo. Connolly has received recognition for his book-length studies of James Joyce, Algernon Charles Swinburne, and Nathaniel Hawthorne.

Mr. Cochran's thought-provoking essay on Hawthorne's two 1 short stories, "Hawthorne's Choice: Veil or Jaundiced Eye" (*CE* February 1962), prompted me to review my own thoughts on "Young Goodman Brown" (*AL,* November 1956). Unfortunately, I was not moved to renounce my position, but, like a hardened sinner confirmed in my sin, I reject the new way to light and cling to the old habits. Mr. Cochran unconsciously contributed to the hardening of my heart by a few comments. First, he referred to my theological interpretation as being "too theological." This is very much like saying, "His artistic interpretation is too artistic"; or "His political interpretation is too political." Second, the placement of the adverb *explicitly* in this sentence in his article confirmed me in my Calvinistic awareness of sin in this world: "Hawthorne explictly states that Faith survives Brown to symbolize the very general religious belief that Faith is always available to the man capable of embracing her." The casual reader might feel from this sentence that it was Hawthorne who had made that symbolic interpretation. I went back to the short story and could find Hawthorne saying nothing of the kind.

Third, Mr. Cochran emphasizes that the protagonist Brown is young. 2 I answer that he is young at the beginning of the story but old at the end.

I went back, as I say, and reconsidered my theological interpretation 3 of the story and decided to cling to it, but, as a concession to Mr. Cochran, I decided to broaden the base of it and so parallel the theological (spiritual) with a sexual (naturalistic) interpretation. With all this concen-

Reprinted from *College English,* 24 (November 1962), 153, by permission of Thomas E. Connolly and the National Council of Teachers of English.

tration on sin, I asked myself, just what sin did Young Goodman Brown contemplate (not, I suggest, commit)? The only sin that begs for recognition is that of sexual infidelity. But the sting in the newly married Young Goodman Brown's temptation to have one last fling is that he realizes (from Faith's warning to him as he marches off to his tryst in the forest) that marital infidelity is a game at which two can play. The first note is struck by Faith as she begs her husband, ". . . prithee, put off your journey until sunrise and sleep in your own bed tonight. . . ." His reply is significant: "What, my sweet, pretty wife, dost thou doubt me already, and we but three months married?" Faith immediately responds with a grim warning: "Then God bless you! and may you find all well when you come back."

As he goes off to the tryst, Brown's conscience gives him a slight 4 marital and theological twinge: "Well, she's a blessed angel on earth; and after this one night I'll cling to her skirts and follow her to heaven." The disillusionment comes as he realizes that, while he is on his way to his sin, his wife may very well be on her way to hers: "Moreover, there is a goodly young woman to be taken into communion."

Finally, turning back from what he thought would be a theologically 5 (he is of the Elect and therefore not vulnerable) and maritally (he is married to a blessed angel) safe last fling, Young Goodman Brown is shocked to discover that his faith-Faith is not what he thought it-her to be (a doctrine that smugly places him in the Elect whatever he does, or a wife that is beyond the temptations of the flesh) and spends his life alternating from attraction to and revulsion from faith-Faith: often, awakening at midnight, he shrank from the bosom of Faith," and "Children and grandchildren, a goodly procession," followed him to his grave.

Robert W. Cochran
REPLY

Robert W. Cochran (1926–   ) was born in Williamsport, Pennsylvania. He received his B.A. (1948) from Indiana University and his M.A. (1949) and Ph.D. (1957) from the University of Michigan. Cochran's critical articles have appeared in *College English* and *Explicator*. He is Professor of English at the University of Vermont.

First, any theological interpretation which is strictly theological, restrictively theological is "too" theological. I am not immediately suspicious of art or artistic interpretation; but with politics as with theology, I consider any unreconstructed political position "too political." 1

Second, the statement is explicit, the symbolism implicit. 2

Third, Mr. Connolly's casual reader might suppose from one of Mr. Connolly's sentences that Hawthorne refers to Brown as "old" and not as "young," as "Badman" and not as "Goodman" toward the end of the story. On the contrary, Hawthorn writes "young Goodman Brown" and "Goodman Brown" even in his final paragraph. 3

Fourth, I caution Mr. Connolly not to harden in his "broadened" interpretation, based as it is on an attempt to identify the sin which Young Goodman Brown contemplated. I remind Mr. Connolly of Edgar Allan Poe's similarly oversimplified interpretation of why Reverend Hooper donned the black veil. 4

In conclusion, I feel that Brown's belief that his Faith was "a blessed angel on earth" is not only hopelessly naive, but hopelessly demanding. The wife Faith cannot be angelic, for she is "on earth." But Brown makes impossible demands on his wife and on all the other townspeople as well. Thus he remains young and foolish to his death. A "good man" he has never been; and an intimate, meaningful relationship in his "own bed" and in "the bosom of Faith," he had never had, his "goodly procession" of children and grandchildren notwithstanding. (The purpose of reference to succeeding as well as preceding generations is to place Brown in the human continuum.) 5

Reprinted from *College English*, 24 (November 1962), 153–154, by permission of Robert W. Cochran and the National Council of Teachers of English.

Study Questions

"How Young Goodman Brown Became Old Badman Brown" and
"Reply"

1. How does Connolly answer Cochran's criticism that his interpretation of "Young Goodman Brown" is "too theological"?
2. Is Connolly's point about the adverb *explicitly* well taken?
3. Does Connolly's decision "to broaden the base" of his argument make that argument more convincing?
4. Comment on the difference of opinion between Connolly and Cochran on the words *young* and *Goodman.*
5. How significant is the seemingly parenthetical last sentence of this reply?

Richard Allen
GOODMAN BROWN THE EXTREMIST

Richard Allen (1950–   ) was born in Buffalo, New York in 1950. He studied at Arizona State University where he received his degree in Chemical Engineering in 1972. In 1969, while he was a freshman, Allen won both first and fourth prizes for best freshman essay in all English classes. The first-prize essay is reprinted below.

Once some friends spread Limburger cheese on a man's nose 1 while he was sleeping. After he awoke, the man thought that everything smelled bad everywhere he went. His mistake was that he didn't realize that the smell was coming from the cheese on his very nose. This is the case with Goodman Brown in Nathaniel Hawthorne's short story "Young Goodman Brown." At the beginning of the story, Brown could see only the good in people; he was naive. But at the end of the story, after Brown had witnessed the Witches' Sabbath—or thought he had—Brown could see only the evil in people; he became cynical. Brown doesn't have cheese on his nose, but he is unaware at the beginning of the story, as at the end, that man is both good and evil.

Brown is naive at the story's outset. When he suspects that Faith, his 2

Reprinted by permission of the author.

wife, might know or have dreamed of his errand with the devil, he states: " 'But no, no: 't would kill her to think it. Well, she's a blessed angel on earth; and after this one night I'll cling to her skirts and follow her to heaven.' " This passage exemplifies Brown's bad judgment and unsophisticated attitude. Brown feels that he can sin this one night, then "cling to her skirts and follow her to heaven." Like a child who puts all his "faith" in mother, Brown gives to Faith the responsibility of getting to heaven and taking him with her. When the devil tells Brown of his acquaintances with his ancestors, all of whom were good "people of prayer," Brown replied, " 'I marvel they never spoke of these matters ...' " This is naivete at its worst!

Brown is naive, but he isn't innocent as Robert W. Cochran suggests 3 in his essay "Hawthorne's Choice: The Veil or the Jaundiced Eye." Cochran states:

> Brown is pictured in this story at the moment when he leaves the realm of pink ribbons and the gentle lamb to enter into the disquieting and mysterious realm where the tiger burns bright in the forests of the night.

Cochran suggests here that Brown is innocent, but Brown had prearranged his meeting with the devil. How innocent can one be if he deliberately makes plans with the devil? Cochran misses Hawthorne's point; Brown is naive — and is ignorant of the fact that he is — but not innocent.

But his naivete gradually decreases after he meets the devil and 4 when Brown sees Faith in the forest, immediately instead of seeing the good in people, he sees only the evil:

> "My Faith is gone!" cried he, after one stupefied moment. "There is no good on earth; and sin is but a name. Come devil; for to thee is this world given."

Thus, the cheese is spread. From this point on, Brown sees only evil and learns more of wickedness. Though one of the main Calvinistic doctrines states that man is by nature evil, this is only a catechism lesson Goody Cloyse probably taught him. He is like a young schoolboy who, leaving the classroom to go out in the world, becomes disillusioned because what he had learned in the classroom was in fact reality.

Though he becomes disillusioned with his Puritan faith, he does not 5 lose faith in it. The faith that he does lose in his faith in man. Brown becomes cynical because he feels that the townspeople have lost their faith (Puritanic), because he believes that they are hypocrites who go through the ritual of their religion during the day but go to the forest at night. But doesn't the fact that Brown was in the forest make him a hypocrite also? Brown can scowl and mutter and avoid all his "anathemas" and accuse the townspeople of hypocrisy, but Brown is just as vulnerable to the charge as they; he was in the forest on the same errand — sin.

Sin, Hawthorne seems to imply, is universal; evil flourishes as well in 6 "King William's court" as it does in the forest with a "simple husbandman."

> ... [the devil] had an indescribable air of one who knew the world, and who would not have felt abashed at the governor's dinner table or in King William's court, were it possible that his affairs should call him thither.

The devil, referred to as the "shape of evil," represents the evil in this world. Hawthorne also refers to an "instinct that guides mortal man to evil." The word "instinct" again suggests that man has evil tendencies. But Hawthorne does not make the mistake that Brown does by labeling man as completely evil. When the devil tells Brown of how he helped his forefathers, Brown mentions that they were "people of prayer" and many of the people in the forest are referred to as "grave, reputable, and pious people." It is good to repent of one's sins, and a church is as good a place as any. The more sinful a person, the more repentance is needed. Though the townspeople seem to go deliberately into the forest every night, it doesn't necessarily follow that they are hypocrites. Hawthorne seems to equate the day and night with good and evil; man is some good and evil. Hawthorne does not equate them in the sense that man is half good and half evil, but uses chiaroscuro to symbolize good and evil by use of light and darkness. The sinner should attend church, and he is not hypocritical in doing so. Goodman Brown's mistake is the same as that of the man with the cheese on his nose; he feels that everyone is to blame but him. Brown is an extremist—an extremity being caused by his cynicism; there is no in-between. Brown feels that a man is either good or evil, neglecting the fact that he could be only partly right.

Study Questions

1. How does the limburger cheese *analogy* unify this essay?
2. Often, a *metaphor* or *simile* makes sense in and of itself but, in a specific context, seems strained: the material that the metaphor draws from is too far removed from the subject matter of the context; the comparison is too farfetched. Are Allen's comparisons appropriate?
3. Does Allen do justice to Cochran's argument? What does he mean by the distinction between *naive* and *innocent?*
4. Allen distinguishes Hawthorne's views on good and evil from those of Young Goodman Brown. On what evidence does he base his conclusions about Hawthorne?

INDEX TO AUTHORS AND TITLES

0176